HUDSON TAYLOR

&

CHINA'S OPEN CENTURY

PEACE: HUDSON TAYLOR IN 1904
at his wife's graveside, Vevey, Switzerland

HUDSON TAYLOR

&

CHINA'S OPEN CENTURY

Book Seven: It is not Death to Die!

By the same author:

Hudson Taylor and China's Open Century
Book 1: Barbarians at the Gates
Book 2: Over the Treaty Wall
Book 3: If I had a Thousand Lives
Book 4: Survivors' Pact
Book 5: Refiner's Fire
Book 6: Assault on the Nine

Strong Tower: (the Nosu of Guizhou) CIM 1947
Strong Man's Prey: (the Nosu of the Daliangshan) CIM 1953
Time for Action: IVP 1965 (Inter-Varsity Press)

HUDSON TAYLOR

&

CHINA'S OPEN CENTURY

BOOK SEVEN
It is not Death to Die!

A J Broomhall

Hodder & Stoughton

and
THE OVERSEAS MISSIONARY FELLOWSHIP

British Library Cataloguing in Publication Data

Broomhall, A J
    Hudson Taylor & China's open century.
    Bk. 7: It is not Death to Die!
    1. China. Christian missions. Taylor, Hudson, 1832–1905
    I. Title
    266′.0092′4

    ISBN 0 340 50270 3

FOREWORD TO THE SERIES

China appears to be re-opening its doors to the Western world. The future of Christianity in that vast country is known only to God. It is, however, important that we in the West should be alert to the present situation, and be enabled to see it in the perspective of the long history of missionary enterprise there. It is one of the merits of these seven remarkable volumes that they provide us with just such a perspective.

These books are much more than just the story of the life and work of Hudson Taylor told in great detail. If they were that alone, they would be a worthwhile enterprise, for, as the *Preface* reminds us, he has been called by no less a Church historian than Professor K S Latourette 'one of the greatest missionaries of all time'. He was a man of total devotion to Christ and to the missionary cause, a man of ecumenical spirit, a man of originality in initiating new attitudes to mission, a doctor, a translator, an evangelist, an heroic figure of the Church.

The historian – whether his interests be primarily military, missionary, or social – will find much to interest him here. The heinous opium traffic which led to two wars with China is described. The relationship of 'the man in the field' to the society which sent him is set before us in all its complexity and (often) painfulness. And the story of Biblical translation and dissemination will be full of interest to those experts who work under the banner of the United Bible Societies and to that great fellowship of men and women who support them across the length and breadth of the world.

Dr Broomhall is to be congratulated on writing a major work which, while being of interest *primarily* to students of mission, deserves a far wider readership. We owe our thanks to Messrs Hodder and Stoughton for their boldness in printing so large a series of volumes in days when all publishers have financial problems. I believe that author and publisher will be rewarded, for we have here a fascinating galaxy of men and women who faced the challenge of the evangelisation of China with daring and devotion, and none more so than the central figure of that galaxy, Hudson Taylor himself. The secret of his perseverance, of his achievement, and of his significance in missionary history is to be found in some words which he wrote to his favourite sister, Amelia:

'If I had a thousand pounds, China should have it. If I had a thousand lives, China should have them. No! not *China*, but *Christ*. Can we do too much for Him?'

Sissinghurst, Kent   Donald Coggan

AFTERWORD TO THE SERIES

When the first of these volumes appeared, I had the privilege of writing a 'Foreword to the Series'. That was in 1981. Now, eight years later, I am honoured to write a Postlude.

For twelve years Dr Broomhall has been beavering away at the archives. The result is seven volumes, of which this is the last – some three thousand pages of research.

Who would have guessed, even when he began his research, that when he ended it the Amity Press would have been set up in Nanjing, equipped to provide Bibles and New Testaments in Chinese for the People's Republic of China? Who would have dreamed that 'by 1986 China' would have 'become the fastest-expanding nation for church growth ever'? (David B Barrett, *Annual Statistical Table on Global Mission: 1987*).

Hudson Taylor might have dared so to guess and so to dream, for he was a man of faith, and 'faith laughs at the impossible and cries, "It shall be done"'.

It is well that the Church should have these volumes available – to remind it of the centrality of its missionary outreach and the faithfulness of its God. If its sometimes deaf ears are opened by the reading of this extraordinary story, the author will be rewarded – his labour will not have been in vain.

Winchester   Donald Coggan

PREFACE

(See also the General Preface in Book One)

The exclamation 'It is not death to die!' came from an eye-witness at the bedside of a dying Chinese. Briefly regaining consciousness, this Christian seemed to have 'been to the very door of heaven'. 'Inexpressibly *happy*,' she said. 'I have seen the Lord! I have seen heaven! . . . I wish you could come . . . There is *nothing* to fear.' Whether seen in reality or not is immaterial; the truth was the same. Death was a gateway, a transition in the eternal life already being enjoyed (Book 6, p. 295).

In this last volume, thousands of Christians suffer and die at the murderous hands of the so-called 'Boxers'. Scores of missionaries and their children are among them, some already known to us from the preceding books. The CIM loses more than any other mission. But Bunyan's imagery was true in the experience of the victims. The last river was deep and cold, but those crossing it knew that death was only physical. The welcome beyond already looked glorious. The Empress Dowager's great gamble failed, as more recent attempts to stifle the gospel have also failed. The living proof of martyr seed being sown in China's good soil is the still-expanding Church today. Imprisonment and death go so far but seldom far enough to stop its progress. As for Hudson Taylor, his passing marked a triumph of its own, at Changsha, capital of Hunan, the last province to allow the gospel to take root.

Assault on the Nine showed how obedience to God's direction, and determination 'not to try but to do it', brought success within ten or fifteen years. The deep corners of the Chinese empire were penetrated and partly 'occupied' for Christ by the planting of his Church. Christian literature was widely distributed, sooner or later to germinate in men's minds. Not all the individuals introduced to the reader can be followed through the story. In the late nineteenth century, rank and family, sport and education brought the spotlight to bear on the Cambridge Seven. So what became of them and of others who showed great promise needs to be included. And a few more must be singled out from the hundreds, even thousands, who joined them. When Hudson Taylor died many believed his mission would disintegrate like 'a rope of sand'. But his work was *God's*, so it lived on and flourished, and 'he being dead still speaks'.

Inseparable from all the excitement and activity is the dark skein of Satanic attacks on the Mission; on its weaker members, its most valued ones and its leaders. Good men and women faltered and failed, fell ill and died, or were murdered in their prime. Time and again Hudson Taylor recognised in his writings the essentially spiritual battle and the devilish enemy they faced. 'Your enemy the devil' was the apostle Peter's phrase (1 Pet. 5:8). 'For we are not unaware of his schemes,' St Paul agreed (2 Cor. 2:1), and, 'The weapons we fight with are not the weapons of the world' (2 Cor. 10:4). 'Let Satan rage – God reigns,' Hudson Taylor repeated defiantly as the survival of the Mission was threatened by purely internal discord and disruption. How close he came to that disaster this book reveals. Beaten down, almost to surrender, it was not how he felt but how he acted that speaks most loudly.

Earlier biographies had to respect the feelings of people still alive. More than fifty years later the facts can be told, as a lesson on how 'your enemy the devil . . . like a roaring lion' looks for victims to attack and new 'devices' to employ. Failing on the spiritual front in Hudson Taylor's day, Satan turned to physical annihilation and failed again. Mass expulsions in our own day proved to be the best thing that could happen to the Chinese Church. How Hudson Taylor handled strong challenges not only to his leadership but to the founding principles of the CIM deserves attention – how he made his point without being dictatorial or alienating the colleagues whose convictions differed from his own.

Book Six ended with his return to Britain to face his critics, to justify the Mission's manual of instructions called the Book of Arrangements which was to become such 'dynamite'; and in the face of distrust and impasse to find and send to China 'The Hundred' reinforcements needed. Book Seven is also the story of reconciliation and unthinkable expansion, ending the solely British phase of the CIM, and making it international and seven times the size it was, 188 on May 26, 1886; 265 in December 1887; and 1,368 in 1934.

Tempted as we always are to include more narrative of a personal nature, of striking conversions and the testimony of new Christians, each has to be judged by the yardstick of relevance to the life and influence of Hudson Taylor, and to the broad history of the Church in China. To discerning readers, among them many familiar with China and the Chinese, the 'mass of detail' in these 'dull annals' is an ant-hill of industry, alive with significance.

AJB

Note. During the years since this series began, the Western world has become accustomed to 'Peking' being spelt 'Beijing' – a truer indication of how it has always been pronounced. In this book, therefore, we adopt this *pinyin* form, with some concession to historical convention where to change would appear anachronistic, as in 'the Peking siege'.

Parentheses within quotations are used as follows: round brackets ( ) indicate original source material, including abbreviations and Romanisation of Chinese words; square brackets [ ] indicate my own added comment or parentheses other than from original sources.

ACKNOWLEDGMENTS

My special thanks to Donald Coggan for his kind benediction on my swansong.

I admire the patience of Hodder's David Wavre with my slow progress and his generosity in allowing so many pages; of my wide family in enduring a decade of my preoccupation with work, of my wife in typing thousands of pages of notes and draft manuscripts in her spare time,

of Molly Robertson in so cheerfully turning seven much-edited typescripts into immaculate copy;

of Val Connolly in transforming a long succession of rough maps and engravings into their attractive final form;

and of my faithful critics and advisers, Jane Lenon and Howard Peskett in particular, for keeping going to the last gasp.

Mrs W P K Findlay gave me valuable insights into her great-uncle Dr A W Douthwaite's notable life in China. To thank her by establishing that he was probably the first Protestant missionary to work in Korea and survive, gives me great pleasure.

I am indebted, too, to Dr Charles A Curwen of the School of Oriental and African Studies, and to Mr P D Coates, HBM consular service (retired), for help in tracing 'General' Mesny.

Frequent enquiries, 'When is the next book due?' have put me in debt to kind readers worldwide. The knowledge that some are in East Asia (not content to wait for the translation now being made) has spurred me on. Much more source material than for the earlier books, and limited time, if not space, have forced me to be more selective. I am sorry we have come to the end.

AJB

KEY TO ABBREVIATIONS

American Board (ABCFM)	= American Board of Commissioners for Foreign Missions
APM	= American Presbyterian Mission
Bible Societies	= American Bible Society; British and Foreign Bible Society (B&FBS); National Bible Society of Scotland (NBSS)
BMS	= Baptist Missionary Society
C&MA	= Christian and Missionary Alliance
CCC	= China Christian Council; Chinese Christian Church
CCP	= Chinese Communist Party
CEZMS	= Church of England Zenana Missionary Society
CICCU	= Cambridge Inter-Collegiate Christian Union
CIM	= China Inland Mission
CLS	= Christian Literature Society
CMS	= Church Missionary Society
DEH	= Dixon Edward Hoste
FHT	= Frederick Howard Taylor
HTCOC	= Hudson Taylor and China's Open Century
IVF, IVCF	= Inter-Varsity (Christian) Fellowship
JET	= Jane Elizabeth (Jenny) Taylor
JHT	= James Hudson Taylor
JWS	= John Whiteford Stevenson
KMT	= Kuo Min Tang (Guomindang); Nationalist Party
LMS	= London Missionary Society
MGT	= Mary Geraldine (Howard) Taylor, née Guinness
MMA	= Medical Missionary Association
MRCS	= Member of the Royal College of Surgeons
OMFA	= Overseas Missionary Fellowship Archives
P&O	= Peninsular and Oriental Steam Navigation Company
PDRC	= People's Democratic Republic of China
PLA	= People's Liberation Army
RAB	= Religious Affairs Bureau

RTS	= Religious Tract Society
SCM	= Student Christian Movement
SDK	= Society for the Diffusion of Religious and General Knowledge
SPCK	= Society for Promoting Christian Knowledge
SPG	= Society for the Propagation of the Gospel in Foreign Parts
SVM	= Student Volunteer Movement
SVMU	= Student Volunteer Missionary Union
TEAM	= The Evangelical Alliance Mission (ex-Scandinavian Alliance)
The Mission	= China Inland Mission
TSPM	= Three Self Patriotic Movement
UFWD	= United Front Work Department (of the CCP)
WMMS	= Wesleyan Methodist Missionary Society
YMCA	= Young Men's Christian Association
YWCA	= Young Women's Christian Association

GLOSSARY OF CHINESE TERMS

bao	= protect
baojia	= government by graded responsibility, each to the next
bianzi	= hair queue ('pigtail')
cangue, kang	= large wooden yoke worn by petty criminals as punishment (originally from Portuguese)
chinshi	= Doctor, of the arts, literature, by examination in Beijing
Dadaohui	= Great Sword Society, revolutionary secret sect
daotai	= Intendant of Circuit over 2 or 3 prefectures; Prefect
fengshui	= 'wind and water', harmony of nature governing decisions
fu, zhou	= prefectures, cities
gengzi nian	= year of the geng symbol in the cycle of sixty years
Golaohui	= Society of Elder Brothers, revolutionary secret sect
Hanlin	= Academy, Library, academician, by examination in Beijing
ketou	= ninefold bow and prostrations
laobeixing	= 'old hundred names', proletariat
likin	= Chinese tax on goods in transit between provinces
manzi	= barbarians, wild men
pinyin	= romanised Chinese syllables
Qingming	= Springtime feast of the tombs
Qüren	= Master, of arts, literature, by provincial examination
sha	= kill
wenli	= literary Chinese, in varying grades
wenshu	= official document or pass
xian	= county town, district magistrate
Xiucai	= Bachelor of arts, literature, by provincial examination
yamen	= official residence of any mandarin
Yihochuan	= the association of secret societies to

                    'overthrow the dynasty and exterminate foreigners', later to 'uphold the dynasty . . .'; meaning 'Association for Justice and Harmony' or 'Fist of Patriotic Union', hence 'Boxers'

Zongli Yamen   = Chinese Ministry of Foreign Affairs

BOOK SEVEN: IT IS NOT DEATH TO DIE!

CONTENTS

PART 3 'THE SLEEP AND THE
AWAKENING' 1895–1905

PART 4 THE BOXER MADNESS 1898–1900

MAPS AND DIAGRAMS

ILLUSTRATIONS

PART 1

'YOUR ENEMY THE DEVIL'

1886–90

Your enemy the devil prowls around like a roaring lion looking for someone to devour.

1 Peter. 5:8 NIV

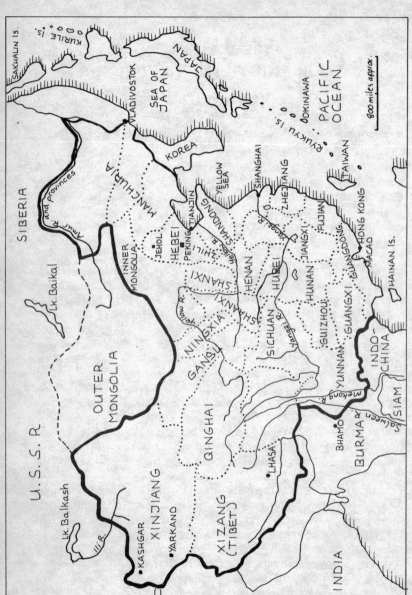

GREATER CHINA: PROVINCES AND MAIN FEATURES

THE ACCUSER

A mission in decline?   *1886–87*

The 'bombshell' scattering the pioneers to China's farthest points had succeeded. The 'shock troops' had dug in, consolidating local churches to be 'the nucleus of expansion'. But 'trouble ahead' loomed ominously at the heart of the empire and the Mission.

The nearer he came to Britain the more apprehensive Hudson Taylor felt. Throughout the past year, 1886, the strain on his relationship with his London colleagues had increased (Book 6). Ever since William Berger had resigned in March 1872, none of the arrangements for replacing him as the Mission's administrator in Britain had worked smoothly. The honorary director, secretaries and treasurer had found the demands upon their time too many. Communication between London and China had been inadequate, not from neglect but by preoccupation. At heart they were with him, but in practice fell far short. The steps he had taken before returning to China in early 1885 had been enough to ensure a regular flow of information and funds as recruits and donations reached London. But inexperience, a mounting workload and personal shortcomings had together left him too often in the dark. Again and again his ingenuity had been strained to the limit to allocate such irregular transmissions of money as were forwarded to him. To arrive and take a hand in these matters would bring him personal relief and lift the burden from the shoulders of his deputy in China, John Stevenson. 'The Lord will provide' involved being 'diligent in business'.

More distressing was the disapproval by the council in London of his own handling of affairs in China. Restraining strong-willed men in unwise actions, and weaker men from abandoning their principles under influences to compromise or to enter salaried employment, had been difficult enough. When 'London' listened to their complaints and sided with them, his leadership had been undermined. The 'father of lies' had maligned him personally, and self-defence against false accusation is under a handicap from the start.

On arrival in China the year before, Hudson Taylor had been greeted with the news that George Stott and Jackson, whose homes had been burned down during the Sino-French hostilities in the south, had claimed and received greater reparations that the consul considered right. Arising from this, their relationship with their colleagues and with Hudson Taylor and John Stevenson had become strained. No one was willing to work with them.

When the bookshelf fell on Hudson Taylor's head at Jinhua (HTCOC Book 6, p 395), his business with the even-tempered Robert Grierson had been to ask him to put himself under Stott's heavy hand knowing full well what to expect. For Stott, the Scottish dominie, ruled his little kingdom with a rod of iron. Grace (Ciggie), his doughty wife, knew how to get on with him. Remarkably, the Chinese Christians in gratitude for the gospel accepted his powerful paternalistic regimen and thrived. At a time of tension the Church paradoxically grew and spread. (Today's strong Church at Wenzhou dates from those beginnings.) He resented Hudson Taylor's 'interference' and complained to 'London', threatening to resign. He was 'impossible'. There was nothing for it but to let him go and, at last, Josiah Jackson too – in some ways also a successful missionary but a thorn in the side for twenty years.

After Hudson Taylor had written many letters and made several journeys to Wenzhou and Ningbo, E C Lord offered to be a go-between and found a formula which George Stott and his directors would accept. But Stott was taken very ill, went home, and for the sake of auld lang syne ended his last extremely painful days at Cannes through the kindness of the Bergers. 'We witnessed the King of Terrors doing his worst,' an old friend wrote. He (Stott) was fighting for breath and 'strong pains were tearing at the vitals . . . But not for one moment did he falter, saying "It is only the poor body that is suffering, the soul is happy" . . . How truly death is a vanquished enemy.'[1]

George King, honoured for his early pioneering in Shaanxi, and twice bereaved, had once again lost his foothold in Xi'an. He was tired and depressed. He sent in his resignation and if he had had the funds would have gone home. Hudson Taylor talked him out of wild ideas and recognised the low Mission income at this time as truly 'providential' in restraining him. Griffith John wrote to Hudson Taylor agreeing that King was a sick man, needing not discipline but the warm, brotherly yet firm letters he was receiving from his leader.[2]

At a time when instability in several young missionaries was causing serious administrative problems, Hudson Taylor wrote giving Stevenson some advice from his own experience of deploying personnel. Solitary ones are 'apt to run dry spiritually if left too long alone'. Christian fellowship is health-giving. Rather than put two good workers together – a 'loss of strength' to the work – put each one with a weaker one whom he or she could lead and train. 'When a dear brother is too wise to take other counsel and too unwise to do without it, what can you do but regret the pain he causes to himself and the hindrance his non-success makes to the efforts of others?' One or two restless members of the Cambridge Seven might find their feet in a demanding situation on the Tibetan or Mongolian borders. 'I think you will in that way prevent their unsettledness from damaging others.' To one vacillating colleague he wrote, 'Pray about this and do what you think right,' expressing his firm belief that God who said 'I will guide you . . .' and had given sound faculties of wisdom and judgment to his people, would direct them through those abilities, if genuinely submitted to him. And to another, the advice to 'spend the night praying about it, and in the morning tell me your decision.'[3]

Annie Taylor he saw as strong, determined, an individualist, so bad at harmonious relationships with colleagues that she would have to be returned to Britain or stretched to her own limits. She was another who no one wanted to have with them. She was sent to the Gansu-Tibetan border (Qinghai) and in due course almost single-handed came closer to Lhasa than any expedition, secular or religious, with their accoutrements, had yet succeeded (p 166).

Others were so congenial or conciliatory that they needed to be protected from harmful influences they might not recognise. Schofield's successor Dr Edwards and even Archibald Orr Ewing were such delightful gentlemen that Hudson Taylor feared for them. 'Orr Ewing is too good and unsuspicious a man to be wisely left in contact with' Timothy Richard, when he returned to Shanxi. The Chefoo community of teachers and convalescing missionaries were a different kettle of fish, bickering 'like children' needing parental intervention, he confided to Jennie. The squabbling between some missionaries could make him feel 'frantic'. At the same time he could truthfully say that there had never been so much love in the CIM, the good compensating for the deplorable. As for the ineptitude of others – two men who wrote proposing marriage to unsuspecting women, in the same letter asked the recipient, if she declined his offer, to be go-between in approaching one of two or three others!

Disgruntled, unsettled and 'touchy' (JHT's word), members of the Mission could be tolerated as natural variations from the contented, hard-working majority – the loving happy family who increasingly looked up to their fifty-four-year-old leader as a father. But 'W is *such* a nuisance', another inveterate slanderer and fabricator of lies, 'I don't know what to do to get rid of him.' Another, a veteran, 'with all his faults is one of our best workers'. One or two who took their complaints to other societies created a more painful problem. The first he knew of it in two exceptional instances was finding the name of the missionary in another mission's list of members. The courtesies were almost always observed between administrators, and most knew from experience that turncoats tended to bring trouble with them. How far he had been from reality when he wrote to Jennie in April 1885, 'Soon I hope all the greatest difficulties will be past, and the way open for quietly and harmoniously organising the Mission'! That sound, efficient reorganisation itself became the reef on which the CIM nearly perished.

Physically remote from Hudson Taylor, the London Council had been undergoing a gradual change in its viewpoint, unknown to him. The basic principle on which the CIM had been founded, that its leadership and control must be in China, had paled in the light of contemporary practice by other missions, merchant houses and the government. All paid the piper and called the tune from the homeland in Europe or America. Complaints to the London Council against the directors in China were taken as valid, without proper verification. In China the facts were known and understood. Men at a distance with no personal knowledge of China or of the circumstances could not adjudicate. Yet it was right that the London staff and council should be intimately concerned for the men and women they had prepared and sent to China. Correspondence on these issues had worsened rather than resolved the differences between London and Hudson Taylor. Only his return to Britain held any hope of agreement.

When he broke his journey to visit William Berger at Cannes he found little to reassure him. Cannes was full of visitors escaping the British winter, and social obligations prevented unhurried consultation about the things most on the two men's minds. William Berger approved of the call for 'the Hundred'. The success of 'the Eighteen' in 'the Nine' provinces had won him over. But he had blunt things to say about the practical Book of Arrangements (Book 6, pp 420–3) and repeated them in a letter after his guest had gone. It was as Hudson Taylor feared. The controversy had spread beyond the staff and council to referees and supporters. The dissident missionaries' side of the story had been given a sympathetic hearing, by the Home Director, Theodore Howard, the General Secretary, Benjamin Broomhall, and the lawyer, William Sharp, in particular.

Benjamin's propensity had for long been to champion the underdog.[4] In December 1886 he had cabled the good news of a doctor, two schoolmasters and two potential headmistresses sailing for Chefoo, and wrote, 'As to the hundred desired we shall rejoice if a hundred of the right type are forthcoming', but in the mail Hudson Taylor received at Marseilles or Cannes were ominous signs of deep trouble in store for him. 'Joe' Coulthard, addressing Hudson Taylor as 'my dear Papa' on the strength of his engagement to Maria, warned of serious discontent in 'some parts'. A small China Council, it was being said, 'much younger in every way than those who have been over twenty years in the Mission', had laid down arbitrary rules for over two hundred others. In fact its part had been advisory, and the decisions were the General Director's, but after cosy personal relationships since *Lammermuir* days, any reorganisation was understandably distasteful to a few of that vintage.[5]

For London to question the composition and actions of the China Council they had supported Hudson Taylor in setting up was far more serious. Law had replaced the grace and love demonstrated by Hudson Taylor, they contended. 'Now the Mission is growing so large we don't want it to be a big machine, but what it has been in the past – a family, only a larger one.' These words could have been written by Hudson Taylor himself or by any one of the China Council (or for that matter any of the hundreds, indeed thousands, who have been in the Mission up to the present day, for a family it still is). But protests against change were as predictable as teething troubles from the rapid influx of novices.

Benjamin's letter harked back to April 1886 when Hudson Taylor had responded in 'strong words' to London's intervention in George Stott's quarrel with his leaders.[6] They must have an early conversation, he said, and come to an understanding if they were to work harmoniously as both desired. 'I do not think our separation would be for the good of the work.' Far from it. Confidence in the Mission would be shaken. But was feeling as strong as that? In John Stevenson's view, Benjamin was the best asset the CIM had after

Hudson Taylor himself. As the chief executive in Britain, since 1877 when there were fifty-two CIM missionaries in all, he had played the major part in sending out most of the two hundred or so since added. All the dealings between their supporting churches and the Mission had been with the Secretary, whom they had come to value. Discord between Hudson Taylor and the London Council, especially his boyhood friend and brother-in-law at the heart of the Mission, could be most damaging. Separation could be lethal. The issue had become constitutional. The London Council as a whole in objecting to the revision of the Principles and Practice (P and P) and the introduction of 'rule' in the Book of Arrangements were claiming a say in both.

This was how things stood when he and Jennie met in Paris and crossed the Channel together, comparing notes on their agonising two-year separation from each other. To their delight his welcome home was as warm as ever. No one was in a hurry to air grievances.

CHAPTER ONE

THE YEAR OF THE HUNDRED
1887

'Expansiveness'   *February–August 1887*

The boldness of the call for a hundred new members within a year had fired the imagination of the Christian public. Hudson Taylor's home-coming to share in their selection and despatch to China smacked of the spirit they associated with the Eighteen in 1875 and the Cambridge Seven in 1885. The characteristic, very human slump in interest a few months after the Seven left Britain, had been offset by continuing enthusiasm in the universities and colleges. The potential was still there, and the evangelical churches welcomed the return of a focal point in Hudson Taylor and his dynamism.

As soon as his Shanghai cable of December 29, 'Coming', arrived, Benjamin had publicised the fact, and invitations for Hudson Taylor to speak at conferences and preach at churches began to pour in. Only the first week after his arrival seems to have been kept free for him to find his feet. On February 25, after personal conversations with Theodore Howard and Benjamin, he could tell John Stevenson, 'The Lord *reigns* – let us grasp that great truth – a gospel indeed! . . . Our action (in China) has not met with unmixed approval, but when all is better understood I hope it will' be satisfactorily resolved, and four days later they were in the thick of a 'United Conference of Foreign Missions' at Leicester. With Benjamin as chairman, Hudson Taylor spoke twice on March 1, in the evening on 'The Baptism of the Spirit and the World for Christ'. From then onwards the succession of meetings around the British Isles arranged by Benjamin was 'intense', such as Hudson Taylor enjoyed.

More requests for him were coming in than could be met. 'Enough work for two months had to be crowded into one.'[1] After conducting William Cooper's wedding and then a big meeting in the Mildmay Conference Hall on March 3, and another at the Eccleston Hall, he went up to Glasgow. Sixty candidates, more women than men, were waiting in Scotland to be interviewed. He saw forty at Glasgow, approved of thirty and received a promise of £2,500 towards their passages. One young man he told to go and meet the party about to sail to China as the best way to crystallise his thinking. And he wrote to Jennie, 'I told him you would give him a bed or sofa till Mrs B has room for him . . . We shall not get the 100 if we do not strain our resources somewhat.' Amelia, still with five children under twenty, the youngest aged twelve, had her house constantly filled with people coming and going.

At Edinburgh where there were twenty more applicants, Jennie wrote, 'even his head has begun to swim'. Audiences of 1,600 or 1,700 in the United Presbyterian Synod Hall and more than 2,500 in St Cuthbert's Church heard him, supported by George Clarke, the lumberjack pioneer of Dali and the Mongolian border, on leave and a good speaker. One hundred and twenty stood to declare themselves at God's disposal, to go anywhere or to stay. But at Glasgow the meeting of the anti-opium society he took part in was a fiasco, with 'more speakers than hearers'. This cause was at its lowest ebb.

Month after month this travelling and speaking went on and during the whole year he wrote or dictated on average thirteen or fourteen letters each day. He believed in giving himself to the hilt and resting when he could keep going no longer. By March 17 he had not yet had a free half-hour with some of his own children. Howard, his second son, had become a Member of the Royal College of Surgeons on January 20, and went on to achieve a first-class degree and graduate honours. Charles Edward, the fourth son, was preparing to enter Cambridge University with Benjamin's son, Marshall. And Hudson Taylor had been free for only one session of the council, on March 23, between meetings in Scotland, London and Scotland again.

Objections to the revision of the Principles and Practice had been voiced at that session, and Hudson Taylor had replied, but with so much urgent business affecting the Hundred, the subject had not been pursued. Enough had been said to betray the strength of feeling that existed. William Sharp apologised afterwards for having 'spoken more with salt than with grace', 'a thorn in your side', and offered to resign as Hudson Taylor had evidently not agreed with his (Sharp's) convinced opinion. The incessant travelling to meetings and selection of the Hundred with all that both involved went ahead while under the surface he was conscious of the existence of the Mission's being threatened.[2] Beyond the inner circle, however, an explosive force seemed to characterise this extraordinary society, abroad as much as in Britain.

Whatever the pace at home, events in China and John Stevenson's success as deputy director stayed at the front of Hudson Taylor's thinking. His long business letters could not but give Stevenson the sense of companionship in his duties. As far as he was able at a distance, Hudson Taylor commented on the matters reported or referred to him, and took up issues Stevenson might not be alive to.[3] His constant reference to the Word of God for assurance and guidance matched his deputy's own attitude to his responsibilities. Feasting 'in the presence of my enemies' (Ps. 23:5) was Hudson Taylor's continuing theme. Let Satan rage and scheme; 'God reigns' and fills our cup till it runs over. 'I have unbroken rest in (that) assurance.' Move Orr Ewing away from Shanxi for the present; keep engaged couples' eyes on the sound reasons for delaying marriage until acclimatised, speaking Chinese and being able to do useful work; do not hesitate to pass the onus of decision on to me if faced with determined insistence; encourage the missionary whose son has been committed to prison for embezzlement.

Pastor Hsi was in the wrong to treat Stanley Smith as he did, but had apologised; consider visiting Shanxi again – 'No part of the work is more important. If the Seven should go wrong or things go wrong between them and others, the result might be very serious and they are very young men and liable to young men's mistakes.' Studd needs careful handling. As an independent associate, not a member of the CIM, he was going his own way and failing to keep in touch, which associates all agreed to do.[4] 'I think (Beauchamp) chafes a little at the thought of being a layman under Cassels.' 'Pigott has mortally offended Hsi and cannot return to Shanxi; could he develop the part of Zhili between Baoding and the mountain route to Taiyuan? I am so thankful . . . that as far as you know the spirit of unity and harmony is growing everywhere.' Go ahead with getting Chinese clothes made for the hundred soon to be on their way. The women at Shashi are incomparably superior to the men as evangelists: 'Cannot you . . . get possession of that useful (Buddhist) machine that grinds men into women and vice versa? It would add wonderfully to your efficiency as Director.' On and on in letter after letter, showing a detailed grasp of affairs and a light touch, even to details of buildings being erected at Yangzhou and Anqing. Physically he might be ageing, but mentally and spiritually he was as strong as ever.

From Aberdeen on April 13 he wrote at length to *The Christian* in support of some correspondents who had advocated the very principles he and John Nevius were emphasising.[5]

If the young Church in other lands was to stand on its own feet, foreign funds should not be used to support or employ them directly, the effect of doing so was too often to diminish their influence. A man preaching the gospel in his own spare time impressed his hearers and was benefited himself. But the fact that he received money from foreigners created prejudice against him and what he said. It induced inferior men to attempt hypocritically to be taken on. Independent, voluntary preachers and church workers welcomed teaching and advice, and were respected wherever they went. The apostle Paul's example at Ephesus should be followed, remembering the Lord's words, 'I will build my church' (Matt. 16:18). God's strategy, to build, would be fulfilled through his tactics, the gospel to all the world. Teach constantly, to consolidate the ground gained.[6]

The Jubilee of Queen Victoria was being celebrated and in a climate of rejoicing Hudson Taylor could say in his 21st *Lammermuir* anniversary letter, 'The prospects (in China) were never so bright as today.' Enthusiastic audiences heard him speak confidently at the annual meetings, of the Hundred being given (not only 'forthcoming') during the year.

> If . . . my brother-in-law . . . had sent me out a printed list of one hundred accepted candidates, it would not have added to our confidence one whit . . . We began the matter aright – with God – and we are quite sure we shall end aright . . . Whether God (send) more than the literal hundred, or whether by stirring up other branches of the Church to send many hundreds – which I would greatly prefer – or whether by awakening a missionary interest all over the Church, and blessing the whole world through it, I do not know . . . but sure I am that God will do it handsomely.[7]

In his words we again recognise a note of pure prophecy, as if he had known that before the year was out the great snowball would start rolling which made the CIM international, the Student Volunteer Missionary Union (SVMU) the force it became, and a host of other societies come into existence.

Funds were coming in dramatically to send and support the Hundred of whom fifty had already been accepted and thirty had reached China. As always at annual meetings, receipts and estimates were reported without hesitation or elaboration. A visiting speaker said he was impressed by 'the expansiveness of the China Inland Mission', so involved with God that there seemed to be no limit to the number who could be sent to China, and provided for.

As far back as April 1886 Hudson Taylor's vision of expansion and extension of the Mission had included the provision of business premises and residences in the major ports, at Tianjin, Wuchang or Hankou and the Yangzi ports of call, including the language schools. As John Stevenson remembered it in later years, Hudson Taylor had been slow to adopt the concept of central headquarters in Shanghai. But his memory was at fault, for while Stevenson was travelling, Hudson Taylor had bought the large site on Wusong Road and was working steadily towards developing it, with a residence capable of taking seventy in transit, offices, a small hospital and a shipping and supplies warehouse.

From Aberdeen on April 14, 1887, he telegraphed the £1,500 to Stevenson for raising the site above Shanghai's seasonal flood level, in spite of the immediate need of funds for Yangzhou, Anqing, London and the Hundred. He was ahead in his thinking and leadership. Archibald Orr Ewing's £2,500 were received on August 5, and preparations in Shanghai continued, but architectural planning of the actual buildings had to wait (while the raised earth settled) until Hudson Taylor returned to China in 1888; then construction began in 1889. What John Stevenson remembered was Hudson Taylor's urging that while he was away, Stevenson should make Zhenjiang his base – close to the language school at Yangzhou and away from the cloying influences of Shanghai on Lewis, his secretary, and the many impressionable young missionaries passing through the port; for the accommodation at Yuan Ming Yuan Road was inadequate.[8]

As the numbers of men and women asking in Britain to be included in the Hundred increased, it became clear that a second hundred would be given. They could not sail within the year 1887, but accommodation in Pyrland Road would continue to be taxed to the limit for months to come. To meet this situation the Pigotts authorised the transfer of their legacy from Shanghai to London, requiring only that the deeds of property purchased in the name of the CIM 'you will hold to my order as an equitable security for the money'.[9] Negotiations for Inglesby House, a gentleman's residence overlooking Newington Green, ended in July with the acceptance of the Mission's offer of £2,800 for the house and grounds, and the pressure was relieved. After general use for a time, Inglesby House became the men candidates' training home.[10]

At the same time another experiment began. Several members of the CIM had taken medical courses under Mission sponsorship and from having four doctors in China in 1886 the number was seven in 1887. Then a house was leased in Cambridge for seven years as lodgings for candidates whom further education would make more useful. By the time of the annual meetings in 1888 more than 600 men and women had offered to go to China, and even with Inglesby House much more space was needed:

> more office room, more storage rooms, more packing rooms, more bedrooms . . . and classrooms [to allow candidates to meet and mix with experienced missionaries coming and going]. The new missionary goes not from lodgings but from a home. The older missionary returning for rest and change . . . feels he is not calling at an office, but coming to a home.

So plans for building a headquarters residence and office block on the Newington Green site had to begin. 'Expansiveness' entailed far more than people and money.[11]

The travellers   1886–89

The merry-go-round in Britain could not obscure the advancing process of expansion in China, too. While the rush to be in the Hundred was astounding those who witnessed its progress, a new aspect of the unconventional CIM was taking shape. Not content with reaching the far boundaries of the vast region that had challenged them so recently – the nine unevangelised provinces – some pioneers had raised their sights to the outlying dependencies. Strong, silent, glamorous Tibet beckoned some. Sullen, rebellious, Muslim Turkestan and the nomad millions of Mongols stretching from Manchuria to historic Sungaria of the Golden Hordes (HTCOC Book 1) challenged others.

On the international scene the constant manoeuvring of Russia on her eastern and southern borders threatened her neighbours. But with the British empire having extended farther still, China was not so much Russia's competitor or antagonist as Britain, and both had their eyes on Tibet. Both, therefore, kept watchful representatives in Kashgar, gleaning information on the other's movements.

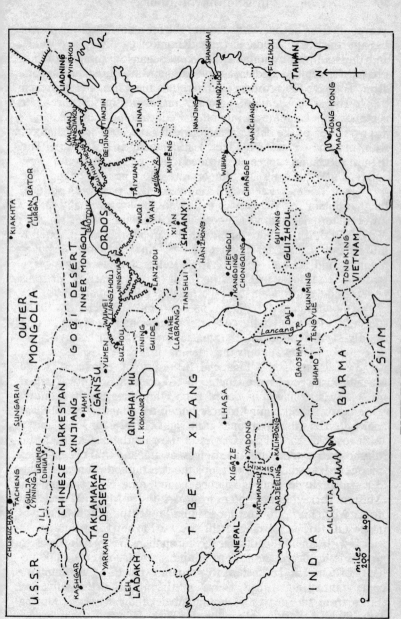

EXTREMITIES OF THE EMPIRE

Travellers from both, and from other European countries, explored the approaches to Tibet, the vast deserts of the 'Xinjiang' to be, and the southern mountains. Lhasa was the lodestone; to reach Lhasa, the symbolic goal of explorers, and of Christian missionaries. To leave the Word of God in the monasteries, and to preach the gospel at the heart of Lamaism inspired some, as the sheer romance and danger drew others.

Two-thirds of the Tibetan tableland lie at 15,000 feet or more, with some passes at 20,000 feet. Lhasa stands at 12,000 feet. The highest mountain ranges on earth wall in Tibet on the south, west and north. Water boils at a temperature tolerable to the hand. The borders of Tibet have always been ill-defined, varying with political fluctuations or the vicissitudes of armed power, especially on the lower eastern flank where Chinese and tribal claims were strongest. 'True Tibet', if its ethnographic extent can be so labelled, extends into the politically determined regions of Qinghai, Gansu, Sichuan, Yunnan and Ladakh. Sir Charles Bell's 'Greater Tibet' is a reasonable term for it. Until the tenth century, warring Tibetans penetrated western China, the Turfan oases and Samarkand.

The Government of India was naturally most concerned with the southern border and in the convention with China signed at Peking on July 24, 1886, following the annexation of Upper Burma, Britain agreed 'not to press unduly the opening of Tibet'.[12] Consequently, the expedition of the Financial Secretary of Bengal, Colman Macaulay, agreed by the Chefoo Convention in 1876, was called off. He was to have proceeded from Darjeeling up the Chumbi Valley through Sikkim with three hundred Indian troops, but was confronted by Tibetan troops within sight of Darjeeling.

Meanwhile, in China, George Parker and his Chinese wife Minnie had established themselves at Lanzhou, the capital of Gansu, but outside the city. It took the determined young individualist Annie Royle Taylor to secure the first foothold inside the city and from there to lay her plans for taking the gospel to Tibet.[13] On January 27, 1887, Hudson Taylor told Stevenson that the Parkers proposed moving 500 miles farther west to Suzhou (now Jiuquan) in March with a minimum of baggage. From there George alone was to go 600 miles even deeper into Xinjiang to Urumqi (Dihua), the heart of Chinese Turkestan, to prepare a place for his family to come in the spring of 1888. They would be more than thirty-five day stages from the nearest other member of the Mission. During 1888–89 he was to travel among the Turki Uigurs south of Aksu, almost to Kashgar (map 2, p 45), and northwards among the Mongols beyond Lake Barkul. On this venture he would come close to the Russian border.

By April Hudson Taylor was co-ordinating a new turn of events. But it must be kept secret, he warned Stevenson, lest the authorities raise objections. An enterprising clergyman, the Rev. Dr Henry Lansdell, DD, FRGS, one-time vicar of St Stephen's, Eltham, in south-east London, who had already been to Bokhara and Samarkand, was planning another expedition and wanted the CIM's co-operation. He proposed to go to Yarkand investigating routes into Tibet, and then if possible to go in and find southern routes out to India. Parker would be glad to join him, Hudson Taylor said. How about Cameron? The American Bible Society was to supply a consignment of selected Christian books in appropriate languages, which Stevenson was to freight to Lanzhou. Before long he could expect Dr Lansdell to be in touch with him at Shanghai. After getting travel passes from the Zongli Yamen, Lansdell would meet Parker and others up-country.

On June 17 Hudson Taylor wrote again. The philanthropist Robert Arthington (almost a millionaire who 'lived like the poorest of the poor' that he might promote the propagation of the gospel worldwide) had sent £200 for the CIM to take the gospel to Turkestan and Mongolia.[14] Parker's and Lansdell's journey came into this category. Hudson Taylor and another donor had each added £100, but Lansdell's own efforts to raise £600 more for the three-year enterprise were meeting with little success. The American Bible Society gave him a glowing testimony and voted $500 a year for three years to be applied by Dr Gulick, their Shanghai agent, 'for the exploration of Central Asia and Tibet, with a view of promoting the circulation of the Scriptures in that part of the world'.[15]

At this point the Episcopal Church of America offered Dr Lansdell a bishopric, which he declined. But in October when he visited Hudson Taylor he still lacked the essential funds. They left it that he would cable Stevenson to make definite arrangements with Parker or to release him from any obligation.[16]

At last, on Christmas Eve 1887, Hudson Taylor wrote that he was meeting Henry Lansdell again. 'Tibet seems retiring further and further in the distance, but all else seems promising.' The American Bible Society were contributing £1,000, and George Parker went ahead with his brave venture to take the Word of God into

Turkestan. At the May meetings in 1889 Parker's successful arrival at Gulja (Kuldja, the Chinese Yining) on the Sino-Russian (Alma Ata) border beyond Urumqi was reported (map 2 p 45) – two decades before George Hunter in 1908 and three and a half decades before Eva and Francesca French and Mildred Cable ('The Trio') in 1923 followed in his footsteps. The epic journeys by Colonel Mark Bell VC and Lieutenant (at the time) Francis Edward Young-husband took place in 1887. Sven Hedin, Sir Aurel Stein and others followed in the late nineteenth and early twentieth centuries with Sir Eric Teichmann among contemporaries of the Trio.[17]

Dr Lansdell's story diverged after that from the CIM's. In the winter of 1888–89 he proposed to Archbishop Benson of Canterbury that as an Anglican lama he should carry a message from the Grand Lama of the West to the Grand Lama of the East. The archbishop responded dispassionately with the note, 'This is to certify that the Reverend Henry Lansdell, Doctor of Divinity and Fellow of the Royal Geographical Society' was undertaking a journey with 'no political, military or commercial objects' and asked for special facilities for him to visit Lhasa. Not to be outdone, and with far better understanding of the Asian mind, Lansdell mounted the document, signature and seal on yellow silk, rolled up as a scroll within a satin-lined red morocco case and cylinder of tin. But reaching Leh, the Ladakhi capital, in November 1888, he could find no one prepared to risk almost certain death simply for carrying the scroll to the Dalai Lama. At Kalimpong and Kathmandu he was similarly frustrated, so he went on to Peking. A Christian gentleman, lacking the wisdom of a serpent, he frankly stated his intentions. On March 21, 1888, two thousand British Indian troops had clashed with nine hundred Tibetans on Sikkim territory. The British minister in Peking warned him, 'It would be out of the question to ask the Chinese for a passport to Tibet.' His attempt would worsen Anglo-Tibetan relations. Patriotically, Lansdell withdrew, and with inadequate funds seems to have ended his attempts.

The man who was eventually to enter Lhasa, but at the head of the British-Indian troops in 1904–05, was, in 1887, Lieutenant Younghusband.[18] Leaving Peking on April 4 and Kalgan on the 10th, he passed through the Great Wall and reached Guihuacheng (Hohhot) on the 17th, to traverse China from east to west by a route never in recent centuries taken by a European. In his book, *The Heart of a Continent*, he told appreciatively of his welcome by George and Agnes Clarke at Guihuacheng.

I met with that warm reception which is characteristic of missionaries . . . The zeal and energy which this mission shows is marvellous . . . There is an excellent rule that, for a year or two after coming to China, the recruits need not belong permanently to the Mission; but if they find that they are not suited for the work, can return to England. The wisdom of this rule anyone can readily understand.

George Clarke was indefatigable in his search for a camel-owner willing to go with so small a party as Younghusband's instead of waiting for the next monthly trade caravan, and succeeded. A contract to reach Hami in sixty days was drawn up and they parted. In his assessments towards the end of his great travelogue, Younghusband wrote,

My sympathies are entirely with the missionaries, and having seen the noble men I have met with in the far interior of China [Catholic and Protestant] and realised the sacrifices they have made, I say that the hearts of all . . . Christian nations ought to go out to encouraging and helping them.

Little effect may have been produced in so short a time as a couple of centuries upon . . . the most stationary and unimpressionable race in the world. But that was to be expected. In the first two centuries after Christ only the most infinitesimal effect had been produced upon Europe . . .

As Lieutenant-Colonel Sir Francis Younghusband (President of the Royal Geographical Society, 1919–22), he was to support and to honour the intrepid 'Trio' forty years later.[19]

George Parker confined his attention to the great north-west, and later in life to the Muslims of Henan. But Annie Taylor and Cecil Polhill-Turner, whose first aim was to take the gospel to Tibetans and only to Lhasa if the way should open, in 1887 chose the two frontier cities of Taozhou and Xining as their respective springboards.

Touch and go   *March–November 1887*

After the 'more salt than grace' meeting of the London Council in March, Hudson Taylor was touring Scotland until mid-April and northern England until the end of the month. On his return to London the change of atmosphere could not but strike him. After the warmth of affection he had been receiving, even courtesy from friends was chilling. In his absence the Council had considered resigning over 'the P and P and little book' of arrangements. The influence of two or three had swayed the less discerning members. When grasping the nettle could have been disastrous he evaded it carefully. A busy month of May culminated in the annual meetings, and he could only say to John Stevenson, 'Things may go awkwardly . . . and the project of the 100 be brought to grief . . . (Yet) never was God's help more manifest or more marvellous than this year, and all will yet be well.' In William Sharp he had a restive lawyer, prone to taking independent action when what was wanted was professional advice; or to jump to conclusions, as over the current issue of the P and P and Book of Arrangements.[20]

To hear of 'the spirit of unity and harmony growing everywhere' in the Mission in China brought immense relief, for 'all Satan's strength is set on breaking it up' in Britain. 'Divide and conquer.' Nothing was more necessary to such a mission as unity and harmony. Fortunately in July the Council was pressed for time, meeting three times a week to interview and decide about candidates, while Hudson Taylor was here, there and everywhere from the south coast to the far north. Briefly back in London to meet the Council on July 19 he wearily confessed to Stevenson that he was not only 'utterly used up' and 'tempted to wish that my turn had come, but He giveth power to the faint'. Subversion was always more sapping to the spirit than overt opposition. Off again on the 22nd to Keswick, Ireland, Wales and the south-west, he gasped, 'Well, praise the Lord. He helps me through day by day and fills one's heart with blessing and one's mouth with praise.'

Great changes had taken place at the Keswick Convention. Instead of missionary interests being excluded or a tent being grudgingly made available for a missionary meeting without the presence of any Convention speaker as in the previous years, the Church's obedience in spreading the gospel to the wide world had been recognised as fundamental to consecration and spiritual health. Listed for the first time with Evan Hopkins, F B Meyer and Handley Moule (newly convinced by the 'Keswick message') was Hudson Taylor. His presence there had two incidental by-products. Lord and Lady Tankerville, seeing his weariness, offered him and his family the use of a cottage and a servant near Chillingham Castle, their home.[21] And Graham Wilmot Brooke, 'a young man of extraordinary capacity and great spiritual fervour', who had been trying since contacts with General Gordon in 1881 'to reach the heart of Mohammedan Africa', probably consulted Hudson Taylor at Keswick, for he sailed again for Africa as leader of a small team, gratefully armed with a copy of the Book of Arrangements, about which they had corresponded.[22]

A short holiday at Hastings and Hudson Taylor was off to Belfast, while normally calm, efficient Jennie, getting worried, had to content herself with writing, 'My own treasure . . . You are nice. I am so glad to have had you yesterday.' A few days earlier she had written, 'Do, as a duty, get all the rest you can . . . Do rest before it is too late. It will not pay to kill yourself, even to get the 100.' And again, 'Darling, my heart trembles for you. I wish you had declined speaking this evening when you had three engagements for tomorrow.' He took to telling her in his frequent notes, barely legible from the vibration of the trains, how much rest he was getting day by day, and good advice on the editing and lay-out of *China's Millions*. But it was that spirit of his which resulted in half of one of his audiences flocking to the station to see him on his way. The occasional critic might speak of his talent for 'making friends and influencing people' as a 'propagandist flair', but those who knew him saw it in the light of a man 'filled with the Spirit' and unable to contain the exuberance of concern for God's glory and China's salvation. A committee of clergymen and aldermen at Bolton, announcing his meetings by handbill said,

> This mission was founded by the simple but courageous faith of the Rev. Hudson Taylor, whose whole life has been a living exhibition of the wonderful works of the Lord. This visit is not for the purpose of soliciting funds, nor in the sole interests of the China Inland Mission . . .[23]

By then his policy of meeting members of the London Council individually was beginning to pay dividends. William Sharp was friendly, and on August 5 it was possible to write, 'Things have nearly come round, as to our Home Council, and with a little patience all will be well. God has worked for us, or all would have been broken up . . .' And on the 19th, 'If I were to doubt, you would not have the 100 missionaries, and the glory of God and good of China demand that we make this our first work this year.' It was still touch and go, with personal relationships cordial again, but the flashpoint of opinion still critical. Benjamin was in Wales and Somerset arranging more and more meetings, farewells to the

Hundred as well as for Hudson Taylor. William Berger expressed his warmth in a long public letter of support and by sending £500 from time to time, but again added his own protests about the Arrangements.[24]

By September the Mission's membership list had reached 235, including five Bible Christian Mission associates. And by mid-October eighty-nine had been accepted and were preparing to go. Many more were 'under consideration', a euphemism for all the correspondence and arrangements for bringing them to London, housing and interviewing them, and trying them out in mission halls and 'open-air' evangelism. One of Grattan Guinness's tutors, a Mr Barfield, joined the staff to train them, as a step towards a CIM training institute.[25]

The London staff were all exhausted, Hudson Taylor told John Stevenson (in the same letter as he suggested that Bhamo would have to be handed over to another mission if two good men could not be found to go there) that 'our excitable brethren in Shansi' must be handled carefully;[26] and that if Baller and Landale handled the mature language students at Anqing too autocratically they must be diverted to the academic work that suited them better. Then on November 1 the Council accepted the three missionaries who brought the total within the year so far to 102, with as many more in the pipeline. What was God doing to the CIM?

Frost's 'bog of blasted hopes'   *October–December 1887*

If the London staff and Hudson Taylor were working themselves to the bone, they were seeing the outcome of it. Sunday, October 30, saw him addressing four services at Liverpool and walking seven miles between them. Yet the next day the 'Great Social Gathering' in Lincoln at which he was the attraction began at 7.30 pm. Every day of the week had its quota, in Doncaster, at Wakefield, and at Leeds by the invitation of a committee comprising Anglican, Congregational, Wesleyan, Baptist, Primitive Methodist and Quaker 'Friends'. His themes attracted all kinds and he needed little time for preparation for (as he explained to curious enquirers) he spoke from his heart, drawing upon his early morning feasting on God's Word: 'Our Lord's delight in the consecration of His people'; 'The evangelisation of the world'; or simply commenting phrase by phrase through a passage of Scripture. A meeting at St Stephen's parish church in Leeds led to its vicar, the Rev. E O Williams, MA, of Trinity College, Oxford, offering to join William Cassels in Sichuan. He and his family sailed on December 13, 1888.

Audiences might be drawn by the hyperbole of organisers, as in Dublin where he was billed as 'MD, FRS', but the stocky little man with his low fatherly voice might as well have been standing among them as on a platform, and once heard he needed no more advertisement. It was at Glasgow (in Scotland!) that he had the temerity on December 11 to speak on the 23rd Psalm and the Song of Songs to packed congregations in the United Presbyterian Church and the Town Hall with more turned away. In the words of the Provost, John Colville, whose guest Hudson Taylor was that weekend: the congregation listened 'with ears and eyes and mouths'.[27] And in the evening 'after a wonderful exposition of Zephaniah 3 . . . (We never heard it on this wise)', Hudson Taylor's new personal secretary, S F Whitehouse, wrote, 'Mr T . . . hadn't finished till close on 9.00, but you could have heard any ordinary clock tick most of the time . . . Not a few of us were moved to tears . . .'

Hudson himself told Jennie, 'Hundreds are daily finding blessing through our meetings. We are not separated for nothing.' At Doncaster, with John N Forman, a young graduate of Princeton University, he had written, 'Yesterday I caught myself thinking: By this time next week I shall be on my way home. I shall be with my Jennie! You see what it is to have too little to think of!' But he would only be passing through London. At Limerick, after Dublin with Forman, Pigott and J J Luce, he was in bed with a bad cold, leaving Forman to go ahead to Belfast. When he wrote to Stevenson he was feeling irritable, saying, 'The dentists are a bore', after crossing out 'a nuisance', and struggled on page after page of sheer administrative business.

> Nothing is clearer to me than that obtaining a hundred this year we have obtained a second hundred; to send them out and sustain them will require another £10,000 additional income, and in times like these it is a tremendous rise from a little over £20,000 to £40,000. [With accuracy impossible, to multiply by fifty may roughly suggest the 1989 equivalent.] One is so glad that God has Himself asked us the question – 'Is anything too hard for the Lord?' But . . . if we get less prayerful about funds, we shall soon get *sorely tried* about funds.
>
> Every day I feel more and more thankful to God for giving you to us and for giving you such general acceptance. No human prescience or wisdom is sufficient for your position, but so long as you continue to seek His guidance in every matter and in the midst of the pressure

of work take time to be holy and take time to pray for the workers, the LORD will continue to use and own and bless you.

'A second hundred'? He could not have endured the knowledge of what would in fact happen.

The Glasgow Foreign Mission Students Union (General Secretary, John Torrance) made him their Honorary President. It had been the same in Belfast on December 5 where he shared meetings with John Forman. After the 'galleries, aisles and pulpit stairs were packed', crowds could not get in. 'Some twenty students . . . fine young fellows' came on Forman's advice to talk with Hudson Taylor. Forman had come to Britain from the States as one of the early leaders of the new Student Volunteer Movement (SVM). It had originated in 1886 during D L Moody's conference for students at Mount Hermon, Massachusetts. Robert P Wilder, the son of a retired missionary to India, had enrolled one hundred kindred spirits to form the SVM. They adopted the watchword, 'The evangelization of the world in this generation', a strong echo of Wilder's father and the General Missionary Conference of 1877 in Shanghai.[28] As Bishop Stephen Neill said in his *History of Christian Missions* (p 394) after stressing what it did *not* mean, for its critics had set up their own misconceptions as men of straw and proceeded to denounce them:

> The slogan was based on an unexceptionable theological principle – that each generation of Christians bears responsibility for the contemporary generation of non-Christians in the world, and that it is the business of each such generation of Christians to see to it, as far as lies within its power, that the gospel is clearly preached to every single non-Christian in the same generation.

The SVM burgeoned rapidly, thousands signing the pledge, 'It is my purpose, if God permit, to become a foreign missionary.' Robert Wilder was travelling in 1887 through the colleges and universities of North America recruiting volunteers, while John Forman was in Britain. John R Mott, one of the founder members, became the chairman of SVM in 1888, and Robert E Speer the travelling secretary. Speer attributed his awakening to responsibility for taking the gospel to the world, to reading the CIM's *The Evangelization of the World*.[29]

While John Forman was travelling with Hudson Taylor to

Oxford, Cambridge, Dublin and other major cities, urging upon university students the message of the SVM, another young American, Henry Weston Frost, was making his first approach to the CIM. In his college room as an undergraduate at Princeton, the son of an admiral had been casually showing Frost an old revolver his father had carried in the Civil War, assuming it to be unloaded. It had gone off, narrowly missing Henry Frost's head. 'Too moved for words', neither had spoken, but to Frost 'came the conviction that his life had been saved for a purpose'.[30]

Then one day when he was twenty-seven and married, he heard Jonathan Goforth declaiming the need of the unevangelised world for a Saviour, and on leaving the meeting was arrested by the attractive appearance of a book on display, larger and more decorative than most. He bought it, *A Missionary Band*, the first edition of *The Evangelization of the World*, and read about the Seven and the Mission to China. Kynaston Studd told him more. But in 1886 he attended a conference at Niagara-on-the-Lake and heard Dr A T Pierson's arraignment of the disobedience of the Church in relation to Christ's command 'Go – into all the world – and preach the gospel' (Mark 16:15). And at last, in 1887, Frost wrote to consult the CIM in London and even filled in an application form. His health was not good, and his wife was caring for an invalid father, so they were advised 'to wait upon God for further guidance'. But 'China's claim' weighed on him and he began to think, if he and his wife could not go themselves, could the CIM not open a branch in America to send young North Americans as it was sending young Britons to China? After profound thought and prayer he decided he would go and make this proposition in person to Hudson Taylor.

He sailed from New York on November 12 and on arriving in Glasgow met John Forman. 'I found that he too had been praying for something of the same kind for a long time, and that Mr Wilder, his companion [in the States], has also had the matter laid on his heart.' But he reached London to find Hudson Taylor away on his travels. Frost was taken into Amelia's family home and then moved into lodgings to wait for Hudson Taylor. The comings and goings of the Hundred, the 'simplicity, earnestness, comprehensiveness and spirituality (of the daily prayer meeting) beyond anything I had ever known' impressed him. But with the warmth of Hudson Taylor's welcoming letter and then on December 27 with his handshake and first remarks in his 'low, kindly voice',

> I had, then and there, what amounted to a revelation – first of a man
> and then of his God . . . From that moment my heart was fully
> his . . . and also in a new and deeper sense, his Lord's. [And
> afterwards] Mr Taylor had seemed to encourage the hope that the
> Mission would be extended to America.[31]

By the evening when they met beside a glowing coal fire in the
office, Hudson Taylor had learned from Benjamin how strongly he
opposed the 'transfer of a British organisation to American soil'.
American missions would not welcome it, Benjamin thought, and
too much would be involved when the CIM was already doubling its
size. So Hudson told Frost frankly that 'he could not see the leading
of the Lord'. Frost could not know that deep rifts were already
threatening the structure, even the existence of the Mission. It was
the wrong moment to introduce a revolutionary new development
without unity of mind in the administration. A purely American
society on the lines of the CIM might be the better way.

Frost was shattered, tempted to despair, in 'a veritable bog of
blasted hopes'. He returned to America three days later, after
seeing the last of the Hundred sail away, asking himself how he
could ever again be sure of the guidance of God. In due time he
realised that he need not have been so shaken. Everything was
under God's control. What Hudson Taylor did promise when they
said goodbye was that he would be willing to speak at Niagara-on-
the-Lake and Moody's Northfield Conference on his way back to
China, if invited by the conveners.

If 'the leading of the Lord' was not clearly discernible in December 1887, it was steadily unfolding. Other signposts were in sight.
While Henry Frost was waiting in London for Hudson Taylor to
return, a tall young Swedish pastor, Josef F Holmgren, was writing,
on December 10, from Stockholm. So his letter was before Hudson
Taylor at the same time as Henry Frost's proposition. He was not
unknown to the CIM. In the first week of September 1883, in the
office of *The Christian* in Paternoster Row under the shadow of St
Paul's Cathedral, Hudson Taylor had been 'kind and courteous' to
the muscular young stranger from Örebro, and they met once or
twice more at Mildmay.[32]

A year later Holmgren subscribed to *China's Millions* and
launched his own Swedish magazine on missions in all lands. By
May 1887 he had translated parts of *China's Spiritual Need and
Claims* and formed a committee in Stockholm, where by then he
was pastor of a leading church, to assist an outstanding young

gentleman, Erik Folke, who had gone independently to China and was in touch with John Stevenson. Folke had proposed joining the CIM under Hudson Taylor's leadership, financially supported from Sweden. Now Josef Holmgren was suggesting that they form 'the Swedish branch of the China Inland Mission'. Would Hudson Taylor come over to discuss it? 'I could arrange meetings for you in the chief towns of Sweden and the people would flock to hear you by thousands. (A week in Stockholm and three weeks for other cities would be needed.) If you can't come, please write an appeal to the Swedish people.'

With Henry Frost's proposal of a North American branch of the Mission running into rough water, Hudson Taylor replied to Holmgren also offering alternative ways of co-operating. Swedish missionaries could become full members of the CIM (through London as Dr Stewart of Philadelphia had done) or associates (as several individuals and the Bible Christians were doing). Folke chose the system of association and his committee agreed, as the Swedish churches would find it more attractive and the name Swedish Mission in China had already been adopted. In China individual associates were all but members of the CIM, adhering to its principles and practice, while in their homelands the organisations were independent of each other.[33]

If Hudson Taylor had not already caught sight of the Delectable Mountains of a new international wave of response to the Great Commission, he must have glimpsed its possibility and been open to it in his first interview with Henry Frost. It mattered little to him whether more and more men and women went to China in the CIM or in association with it or with other societies, so long as they preached the same gospel with the same love for the Chinese. So if Benjamin's answer to Frost's proposition was the right one, the result would be just as satisfactory. He valued Benjamin's judgment and could understand his reluctance to expand the Mission yet further into uncharted channels at such a time. Insularity was a pardonable outcome of having no experience of foreign travel.

In his own field of public relations Benjamin inspired confidence. When the father of the girl betrothed to Herbert Norris (the Chefoo schoolmaster who sailed in 1884, ahead of the Cambridge Seven) refused to permit her to go to China, Hudson Taylor told Stevenson, 'I do not know any man in the world who is more likely to help . . . than my good brother-in-law.' When there was a move to change the name of *China's Millions*, Benjamin's insight and

diplomacy saved the day for Jennie's inspiration. The overtones
of the title, encapsulating Hudson Taylor's supreme message in
China's Spiritual Need and Claims – its hold upon people's minds –
were established assets not to be thrown away.[34] His success as the
executive secretary had been due more to his flair and drive than to
system and efficiency. He was genial but masterly, usually getting
from his colleagues what was needed. So when he differed in
opinion from Hudson Taylor both needed great grace.

The year of the Hundred with its excessive pressures had shown
that changes were needed, not only in premises. The staff could not
cope with a second Hundred unless reinforced with competent men.
The right ones were at that moment learning in the hard school,
China. But after the Second World Missionary Conference in
London, 1888,[35] the greatest achievement of Benjamin's life was
to germinate and thrive in parallel with his commitment to the
Mission – he was to play the major role for the CIM in ending the
scandal of Britain's opium production and trade.

Prospects 'never so bright'   1887

To John Stevenson, at the helm after Hudson Taylor had gone
home in January 1887, everything seemed promising.[36] The
Hundred would soon be coming in successive waves to fill the new
language schools and go on into the provinces. The men and women
of the big influx of 1885, led by the Cambridge Seven, were progressing well enough to make their mark wherever they went – T E S
Botham constantly on the road in Shaanxi, Thomas James with
Dorward and Dick on the Hunan border, Grierson at Wenzhou.
The veteran Edward Pearse was travelling extensively and
continuously in Sinchuan and Shaanxi, and occupied the city of
Chenggu in the Hanzhong plain (map 9, p 234). But yet again the
anti-foreign Hunanese in Xi'an drove out the latest arrival, Charles
F Hogg.

In Shanxi Stanley Smith had left Hongtong to pioneer Lu'an and
Jincheng (Tsechow), and over the border in Henan. Charlie and
Priscilla Studd had joined him. Together they alarmed Hudson
Taylor by adopting Salvation Army methods, marching through the
streets with drums and gongs before preaching the gospel. 'A
reckless SA band might easily drive us all out of any province in
China . . . (and) Stanley Smith will not bear too much stimulus with
safety.' As for the independent 'associate', 'C T', 'we must do all we

CHINA PROPER AND SOME MAIN CITIES

can to knit him more closely to us *for his own sake*. We can do better without him than he can without us.'[37] The personal charisma that had given these two men the leading role in Britain needed the stability of Cassels and Hoste to make them successful in China. Marked progress in George Clarke's Guihuacheng district on the Mongolian border kept pace with the expanding church under Pastor Hsi in the south, though not as spectacularly.

'The formidable men' of Henan resisted the gospel still, but at Zhoujiakou, J J Coulthard baptised nine, to form the first Protestant church in the province. Maria Taylor, at Dagutang in March, held an audience of women for half an hour, listening with 'quite breathless attention'. Later she moved to Guiqi among the woman pioneers of the Guangxin River, more good preparation for Henan after her marriage in 1888 to 'Joe' Coulthard.[38]

Annie Royle Taylor launched out from Lanzhou in July to live among Tibetans at Taozhou and master their language. Before the year was out her Tibetan serving man, Pontso, a native of Lhasa, was a true believer. Her sights then were on going with him to his home. He stayed with her for nearly twenty years. Cecil Polhill made Xining (now in Qinghai) his base for learning Tibetan.[39]

Yunnan was still excited by the French war in the south and Britain's annexation of Upper Burma, but the diplomatic settlement of July 1886 had opened the way for F A Steven to cross the border into Bhamo on his second attempt. Stevenson even wrote hopefully of a 'highway' being opened between Bhamo and Dali (by which he meant a mule trail). In Guizhou the unrest continued. George Andrew and Thomas Windsor were unable to obtain passes to travel outside Guiyang. But while Adam Dorward was away in Britain, Henry Dick made his daring visit to Changsha. Even if no foothold could be gained, the populace would slowly become more accustomed to having foreigners coming and going.

Any rejoicings in the sailings from Britain of party after party of the Hundred were tempered with sadness, especially for Hudson Taylor, when in September the news came from Ningbo that Dr E C Lord and his wife had died of cholera on September 17 and 15. Commissioned as US Consul in Ningbo, by Abraham Lincoln himself, Edward Lord had combined consular and missionary service for nineteen years with marked respect by the mandarins. Two of his household staff had been with him for thirty-two years, as well as his cook for nineteen and his 'outside man' for seventeen – a tribute to his personality. He had been in Ningbo himself since 1847, a veteran before Hudson Taylor arrived as a youth. The CIM in Zhejiang had always had free access to his home and advice, and the Church at large would miss his strong influence. The year also saw the death of Alexander Wylie, the apostle of Christian literature in China; of Dr Douthwaite's wife in Chefoo; of John Challice, the treasurer in London; and of George Stott. The fleeting brevity of life on earth was seldom far from Hudson Taylor's thoughts. A work to be done must be done 'now'.[40]

Since the arrival of the *Lammermuir* party in China in 1866, the Protestant missionary community in China had increased by 500, apart from wives. The CIM had spread into fourteen provinces previously unoccupied by any Protestant mission and had put down roots in sixty-four base cities and as many additional advanced posts, with 110 chapels, 666 organised churches, twelve ordained and forty-nine lay preachers and others making a total of 132 Chinese colleagues. The Mission had seven working doctors, three hospitals and sixteen opium-refuges, apart from Pastor Hsi's. Douthwaite and Cameron ran the Chefoo hospital until Cameron returned to Chongqing; Edwards and Stewart carried on the work Schofield had begun in Taiyuan; Pruen and Herbert Parry in Chengdu won a welcome where preachers had been unable to stay. Pruen then moved to Guiyang to ease the pressure on Andrew and Windsor. Henry Soltau had resigned, but Frank Trench and Horace Randle were nearing graduation at Edinburgh.

F W Baller completed his *Mandarin Primer* and sent a consignment home to Britain in the care of J E Cardwell. But Cardwell suffered shipwreck, escaping only with his life. In China the *Primer* earned high praise among the Sinologues, including Griffith John, the leading missionary author in Chinese. John's dream of the LMS opening work in Sichuan at last came true with the despatch of Wallace Wilson and an evangelist from Hankou to Chongqing.[41]

Twenty-two years after the little *Lammermuir* party battled through typhoons to attempt 'the impossible', the arrival of the Hundred in one year brought the strength of the CIM to 225 in May and 265 at the end of 1887. When the *Chinese Recorder* tabulated the statistics of Protestant missions in China for December 1887, the American Presbyterian Mission (North) had ninety-eight, two other missions seventy, one sixty-six, one fifty-three and thirty-two other societies each had fewer than fifty, making a total of 1,040, including wives. The CIM's annual income had increased from under £3,000 in 1866 (£2,971.19s 9d, May–May) to £33,000 in 1887

(UK £29,961.10s 3d; China £3,756.1s 0d; total £33,717.11s 3d), an increase of £10,000 over the previous year.

In retrospect even the periods of scarcity had been sheer asset, for the lesson they clearly taught was that less was needed than had been thought necessary. The great gap between the foreigners' standard of living and the Chinese Christians' had been narrowed; adaptation had been accelerated; and undreamed-of expansion on a more cost-effective budget had become possible. The Lord's provision for his own work could literally be 'taken for granted' in response to trust and obedience, but the true indicator of success lay in the three thousand and more baptisms through the CIM and the churches these Christians formed.

If at the beginning of the year the prospects had been 'never so bright', even by mid-October John Stevenson felt justified in claiming, 'the work is advancing *all along the line*'.[42]

CHAPTER TWO

TO BECOME INTERNATIONAL?
1888

After the Hundred c *1888*

Among the scores of men and women offering to follow the Hundred to China or enquiring about the CIM were many most attractive candidates. In 1888 fifty-three were sent out, and forty-one the following year. On February 6, 1888, the council interviewed a superlative young Cambridge 'first' named G L Pilkington. Because there was 'a kind of feeling . . . at Cambridge', to quote Eugene Stock, 'that the CMS was stiff, inelastic, old-fashioned, lacking in spiritual fervour . . . Pilkington offered himself to the China Inland Mission'.[1] But, without explanation in the council's minutes, he was deferred. His father was urging him to wait two years before taking action, and at the end of that time he offered to go to Africa in the CMS. The Master of Pembroke saw in him 'a Hannington or a Gordon'. Eugene Stock typically wrote in his *History of the CMS*, 'It was like Hudson Taylor's unfailing generosity to say – to a CMS Secretary [Stock himself?] "The Lord give you many more such men."' Pilkington and Wilmot Brooke (p 50) were accepted by the CMS at the same committee meeting, on December 3, 1889, and the Exeter Hall was filled to overflowing on January 20 for a great valedictory meeting addressed by the African Bishop Crowther, with Dr A T Pierson taking part. China, Africa – it was all one 'harvest field'. 'Mackay of Uganda' was lying ill at the time, and died within three weeks. The CIM mourned with the CMS.

In the first CIM party to sail, on January 26, was Geraldine (Grattan) Guinness, followed later by Edith, the third of Benjamin's and Amelia's family to go; by H N Lachlan MA, a barrister who quickly made his mark; by E O Williams of Leeds, the vicar, and his family; by the Barclay sisters Priscilla and Florence; and, among more than can be named, by E J Cooper, the architect's assistant who became the gifted architect-builder of the CIM. For accepting Florence Barclay 'an inexperienced child' on his own responsibility, and at short notice (except that he had known her family for years and Florence herself as she grew up) Hudson Taylor was rebuked by William Sharp of the Council.[2] She had become a professing Christian only a few weeks previously! He had no qualms; she did well as a missionary and married Montagu Beauchamp.

The incessant round of meetings continued to keep Hudson Taylor stretched to his limit, in the north and west country, until he exchanged them for a similar treadmill in Cannes, with scarcely a moment his own – in Alsace-Lorraine, Mentone, San Remo, Geneva, Lausanne, Vevey, Montreux and Neuchatel, from March 9 to April 7. If suggestions of North American and Scandinavian extensions of the Mission had occupied his thoughts, no hint of Switzerland's following suit appears in his correspondence at this time. That came later.

The annual meetings in May were the highlight, before he fulfilled his promise to Henry Frost by sailing to North America in June. His report on the year 1887, published in the *Millions*, began on the note, 'What a FATHER we have to depend on!' He had sent more than the Hundred prayed for, and not only the extra £10,000 needed but an increase of income from £22,000 to more than £33,700.[3] Not only so; instead of an overwhelming flood of small donations involving many letters of thanks, God had moved major donors to send eleven gifts ranging from £500 to £2,500 to a total of £10,000. And CIM members had reached 294, with 132 Chinese colleagues. All but one of the unevangelised interior provinces now had resident missionaries, only Hunan still defying all attempts. Since 1866 over four thousand Chinese had 'been brought to Christ', and 551 tested believers had been added to the Church by baptism during 1887 – all so different from the ones and twos of the Mission's early years. Sixty-six organised churches, eighteen schools and three hospitals indicated progress in consolidation of the extensive pioneering, while the teaching of Christians and in-action training of Chinese companions continued all the time.

When 'China's Sorrow', the Huang He (literally, Yellow River), had overflowed and washed away its banks again, the Mission had sent relief (through Dorward and others) and would continue to do so as famine followed the devastation. Dorward, after his long relief operation, returned to Shashi and quietly occupied the little town of Shishou a few miles from the Hunan border. From Shishou, inconspicuously reached by river, Hunan was to be penetrated from time to time.

The CMS had an unusual member in J Heywood Horsburgh. While William Cassels's conviction deepened that Anglican Church principles and government were compatible with the CIM, Horsburgh's contentment in eastern China diminished.[4] He visited Sichuan in May 1888 with Arthur Polhill-Turner and conceived a plan to bring in a team of CMS missionaries dedicated to living and working 'on lines of unusual simplicity', even by CIM standards. His graphic letters to Britain created a stir upon which he built with 'persuasive earnestness' when he returned home in 1890.

The Committee of the CMS sanctioned his scheme and he set about recruiting his party. To meet resistance to his appeal he wrote a booklet, *Do Not Say*, of which Eugene Stock wrote that it 'has perhaps been used of God to touch more hearts and to send more men and women into the Mission Field . . . than any modern publication'. That the CMS should sponsor independent action like that of Wilmot Brooke in Africa, Barclay Buxton in Japan and Heywood Horsburgh in China dispelled the undeserved reputation for fustiness it had acquired. Horsburgh wrote, 'Risks, sacrifices, the stretching of nerves, muscles, faith all to the very limit, are the stuff of conquest . . . Is the Christian warfare the only one in which it is wrong to run any risk?'[5]

In Shanxi, Pastor Hsi had weathered the storm of Fan's attack on the opium refuges (HTCOC Book 6, p 410), and his mind was expanding in the warmth of John Stevenson's and Orr Ewing's encouragement to extend his opium refuges not only in his own but in neighbouring provinces also. He could never forget that he had been an addict, burning away his health and wealth in that sickly-sweet smoke. The shame and suffering, the enslavement of his nation, of his emperor and imperial court, viceroys, governors and magistrates, fired his determination to do all he could to free all who would accept his help, and to complete their liberation by binding them to Christ.[6] But while Western nations forced opium incessantly upon China there was nothing he could do to stop the flood. Missions protested while merchants made much of their opportunities and governments supported them by imposing favourable trade agreements. But missions and even the anti-opium societies were half-hearted after decades of failure to stem the tide. In June 1888 the CIM was to supply the missing impetus in a way that Hudson Taylor himself took time to recognise.

An opium war declared   *1888*

Those of us who have lived under the curse of opium know the
enormity of its evil. To see, too late, the wreck of skin and bones
who was once a mandarin, scholar or merchant was to know the long
story of debt, of decimation of heirlooms and household effects, and
the break-up of family and hopes. Dirt, disease and despair turned
the cultured townsman and contented village elder into a scheming
rogue and common thief. To walk or ride mile after mile through
territory given over to the opium poppy where good crops once
thrived; to see the magistrate with his armed escort collecting his
dues – for turning a blind eye; to meet bowls of black opium syrup
on market stalls as both a commodity and currency in place of legal
tender; to watch a mother feed opium to a child to keep it quiet; to
hear children crying not only for the food their parents could no
longer afford, but crying for opium; to know that men were selling
their wives and daughters to buy more of the drug; to find one
person teaching another to smoke it, simply to pass the time of day;
to march the would-be opium suicide up and down, hour after hour,
administering emetics and stimulants, and slapping his face, anything to keep him going while his overdose wore off – was all reality,
yet no more than a microcosm of the vast scale on which this curse
existed. Some, forced by pain to find relief in opium for lack of other
treatment, had become dependent on it, but welcomed cure. True
medicinal opium formed a minute fraction of the ship-loads being
imported.

Missionaries could not travel without being guided, rowed, carried and accommodated by opium addicts, or robbed by opium
fiends. To fall asleep after a long, hard day's travel, to the tune of
the animals munching and the opium pipes sizzling in the close
atmosphere of hay and sweat and sickly opium fumes, was the
up-country traveller's common experience.

Every CIM missionary in this history was familiar with it and
powerless to do much to help. Palliatives were futile. Treatment
refuges (the best way of all) succeeded only when the patient was
determined to be freed, or received new life through faith in Jesus
Christ. Prevention would only be possible when the Chinese government made opium unobtainable. And that could only happen
when foreign nations stopped the iniquitous traffic in opium from
abroad – when Britain ceased to base the revenue of her Indian
empire on its production and sale to China.[7]

From its inception, *China's Millions* had highlighted the opium

THE OPIUM-SMOKER
a woodcut from a Chinese equivalent of 'A Rake's Progress'

scandal, with frequent articles and letters from CIM missionaries and staff.[8] Readers had a clear impression of social and personal conditions in a China plagued by opium. Chinese woodcuts reminiscent of William Hogarth's 'Rake's Progress' accompanied a long series of articles in 1878–79 by S Mander on the history and effects of the traffic. Editorials by Hudson Taylor and Benjamin, and articles from other periodicals, reported what was being done, or said at anti-opium conferences. An appeal by the Society of Friends against the opium trade, and a report of the Anti-Opium Conference at Mildmay in April 1881 were given space, with Lord Shaftesbury's denunciation of this 'greatest of modern abominations'. In April 1882 Hudson Taylor wrote strongly in condemnation of Britain's guilt and responsibility.

> Nothing is more clear than that the Chinese had both the *right, the power, and the will to stamp out the use of opium in China* at the time when they first came into collision with the power of England. We are fully convinced that but for England they would then have accomplished this; and hence we feel that *England is morally responsible* for every ounce of opium now produced in China, as well as for that imported from abroad . . . She wishes to make the importation of Indian opium unprofitable, for England's *profession* of Christian principles she too fully believes to be hollow and insincere . . .

After a united meeting of the societies on March 15, 1882, on 'The Truth about Opium-Smoking', Hodder and Stoughton published Benjamin Broomhall's booklet of the same title, amplifying the Exeter Hall addresses and exposing the lies of the pro-opium lobby.[9] And in 1883 *China's Millions* ran an illustrated series by Julius Jeffrey FRS, on the production of opium in India – 'all going to debauch the Chinese'.

The *Chinese Recorder* spoke up strongly, and Sir Robert Hart's data cited from the Chinese Imperial Maritime Customs substantiated the contentions.[10] The total export trade of China in 1879 had been $100 million, but the opium imported from abroad totalled 100,000 chests of 1,000 million Chinese pounds weight (13⅓ million British pounds or 6 million kg). An equal amount of opium was by then being grown in China. The cost to Chinese consumers of 12 million kg weight of the drug was £25 million, but the value of wages in China was only one half of the value in Britain. So British people should regard this cost to Chinese consumers as £50 million, with opium imports exceeding China's total export trade of one hundred million dollars by twenty million dollars – as he expressed it.

A mandarin fellow-passenger told Hudson Taylor with conviction that Britain's plot was clearly to seize China by means of opium. Sir Robert's statement, with a sigh, that in his region of north China alone, of five viceroys three were opium smokers, indicated the extent to which the alleged plot was succeeding. And Benjamin's daughter, Gertrude, witnessed this penetration when a viceroy's daughter came to stay with her in Taiyuan to overcome her addiction. She became an active Christian.

In 1884 the *Church Missionary Intelligencer* published a Paper by Dr R N Cust, an Indian Civil Service official who from being a supporter of missions became a notorious critic of them. His arguments represented the attitude of the opposition:

> The missionary should not meddle in politics, or in culture of the soil, or in commerce . . . Nor should he be tempted . . . to try his prentice-hand at ruling men . . . (He is) in a false position when he attempts to hold the reins of Civil Government . . . When he goes out of his way to deal with such tangled questions as a gigantic commerce betwixt two such great nations as India and China, he fails in his object, being unable to measure the surrounding forces . . . Let him leave Caesar's business to Caesar, and keep his mind on the affairs of God.[11]

Dr Cust was answered as he deserved by the CMS and others, but he had demonstrated the probability that the British government in India would not change its ways without strong coercion from outside. The immense task of turning the British Indian economy away from opium and on to other sources of revenue could only be decided and enforced by the national will in Parliament at Westminster. The whole issue of the degradation of China, the imposition of the hated drug upon China, the opium economy of India and its perpetuation by successive governments in Whitehall was too vast to be undermined by spasmodic criticism or protest at any level. Sustained pressure to mould the minds of the nation had become imperative. Moral indignation must drive members of Parliament to support strong measures calling upon the government of the day to find those substitute sources of revenue for India. Only long sustained pressure would ensure measure after measure reaching the statute-book until all opium production and trade under British patronage came to an end.

But it would be a long haul first to change the ingrained attitudes of thousands who thought as R N Cust did. They were to be found even in the councils and committees of missionary societies, and to be met in specious statements such as Sir George Birdwood's that 'opium was not only innocuous but positively beneficial to the Chinese'.[12] The third International Missionary Conference held at the Exeter Hall in London, June 9–20, 1888, under the presidency of the Earl of Aberdeen, not only provided a glaring demonstration of this truth that national indignation must be aroused, but inadvertently launched the movement which did as much as any to win success in the end.

'National Righteousness' at stake[13]   *1888*

Two men approached the International Missionary Conference of 1888 with determination not to let the occasion pass without strong action being taken to end the opium scandal fully and finally. Such meetings of minds and organisations could only be arranged at intervals of ten or twenty years. Their potential was unique. If they spoke with one voice even governments would listen.

Dr James Laidlaw Maxwell, the English Presbyterian pioneer and first Protestant missionary to Taiwan, had figured prominently as an eye-witness speaker in the anti-opium cause. Benjamin Broomhall, on the executive committee of the Society for the Suppression of the Opium Trade and as secretary to the China Inland Mission, using *China's Millions* to make his voice heard, shared James Maxwell's indignation and resolve. In 1881 he had been nominated to join a deputation to Mr Gladstone, and reporting on the agreement protecting opium he declared, 'We ought never to cease our protest until the Indian Government ceases to manufacture or to encourage the manufacture of opium for sale in China.'[14] His biographer son wrote,

> The sufferings of humanity (and) his strong sense of justice made him the passionate denouncer of the iniquitous opium traffic and the fearless advocate of national righteousness . . . (Parliamentary) blue books and papers (were) accumulated for his anti-opium crusade . . . He trembled lest the judgments of God might fall upon his beloved country because of the wrong she had done to China.

These two men on the executive committee of the international conference urged their fellow-conveners from several leading societies to allocate time for debating this major obstacle to the gospel among a quarter of the world's population. But the abundance of subjects claiming the attention of the conference blinded the committee's eyes to the value of the potent instrument in their hands.

> They were told that the subject did not properly belong to a Mission-
> ary Conference, that it touched on politics, that there were different
> opinions on the evil of the opium habit, that the raising of such a
> question would cause trouble . . .[15]

So thorny a subject might antagonise the government and endanger harmony among missions! For decades the same cavils had
paralysed all attempts to coerce governments into halting the traffic.
W A P Martin had written a book in 1856 describing the effects of
opium abuse and of current trade and legislation. For his pains his
colleagues had reported him to his mission board for wasting his
time. He had replied,

> The missionaries are the only ones to speak out – the merchants are
> involved and the officials are fearful. [And again] If the early
> missionaries had done more in pointing out the enormity of the
> opium evil, a curse might have been averted from China and a
> mountainous obstacle out of the way of Christian missions.[16]

Thirty years had passed and the enormity of the crime had
correspondingly increased. When the majority on the executive
committee decided that no action should be taken, Maxwell and
Benjamin appealed to the General Committee. The appeal was
upheld, even though to provide for it the conference had to be
extended by an additional day.

Delegates numbering 1,579 assembled from fifty-seven American societies, eighteen Continental societies and fifty-three British
societies (eleven from the colonies). The Third Lambeth Conference of Anglican bishops (worldwide) was to take place three weeks
later, but only one English bishop took part in this International
Missionary Conference and few clergymen. The Christian public
also appeared to think it was not for them. Exeter Hall could have
held many more. Good addresses by outstanding men followed one
on the heels of another, the American delegates of whom A T
Pierson was one, were 'quite in the front for ability, culture and
eloquence'. Hudson Taylor found accommodation in the Strand
near by, and as one among many speakers waited his turn. Eugene
Stock was there, conscious of 'a sense, not exactly of failure, but of
incompleteness, in the minds of many . . .'

Maxwell and Benjamin saw it in stronger terms. As it transpired, their session was to be the grand finale of the conference. But instead of having the whole time with an incisive single topic, three were to be run together – Opium in China, Drink in Africa, and Licensed Vice in India. Undeterred, they made capital out of this triad of targets. Sir Stevenson Arthur Blackwood, KCB, presiding, delivered a powerful opening speech that called for both protest and action. Each subject was then taken up separately, adding to instead of detracting from the others, with a resolution on each being moved by the main speaker. In an address full of proof and testimony to the evils of opium-smoking and Britain's culpability for imposing the scourge upon China, Hudson Taylor moved:

> That this Conference, representing most of the Protestant Mission-ary Societies of the Christian World desires to put on record its sense of the incalculable evils, physical, moral and social, which continue to be wrought in China through the opium trade – a trade which has strongly prejudiced the people of China against all Missionary efforts.
>
> That it deeply deplores the position occupied by Great Britain, through its Indian administration, in the manufacture of the drug and in the promotion of a trade which is one huge ministry to vice.
>
> That it recognises clearly that nothing short of the entire suppres-sion of the trade, so far as in the power of the Government to suppress it, can meet the claims of the case.
>
> And that it now makes its earnest appeal to the Christians of Great Britain and Ireland to plead earnestly with God, and to give them-selves no rest, until this great evil is entirely removed. And, further, that copies of this resolution be forwarded to the Prime Minister and the Secretary of State for India.[17]

This was the first step, Hudson Taylor continued – not primarily to catch the ear of the government, but of Christians; to mobilise Christians to ceaseless involvement 'until this great evil is entirely removed'. Christians were influential in Victorian Britain. Direct political activism was to follow.

> It is with sin that we have to wage war, it is against sin that we have to protest . . . The power of Satan must be seen behind the actions of government and individuals . . . But the Son of God was manifested to destroy the devil and his work.

This was part of the spiritual objective of missions. While the result of eighty years of Protestant evangelism in China was a Church of 32,000 communicant members, eighty years of opium traffic had enslaved 150 millions of opium addicts and their families.

He had often borne eyewitness testimony to the evils of opium, so on this occasion he would call others as witnesses. Griffith John of the LMS had declared at the Shanghai Conference from personal observation, 'Opium is a curse – a curse physically, a curse morally, and a curse socially to the Chinese.' Alexander Wylie of the Bible Society had added, 'It bids fair to accomplish the utter destruction, morally and physically, of that great Empire.' 'This death-dealing poison' manufactured and supplied by Britain, in the words of the Earl of Shaftesbury 'the greatest of modern abominations since the slave trade', 'will bring upon this country . . . one of the fiercest judgments that we have ever known.'

Dr Maxwell reinforced Hudson Taylor's plea, saying,

> There is the British House of Commons to be reached; and before that there is the conscience of England to be reached; and still before that, and most important of all, there is the heart of the Christian Church in England to be touched . . . Of late years there has crept over Christians in this country a very strange and terrible apathy in dealing with this opium trade . . . We have not got this matter inside our hearts as a burden upon our souls (of our great guilt) before God . . . I am sometimes amazed at myself, at the want of feeling concerning the terribleness of this evil among the Chinese . . . In this hall tonight there is a constituency large enough, if set on fire by the Spirit of God on this subject, to begin to move England from end to end.

Among the 'specially animated debates' of the conference, the one on the opium resolution was outstanding. Dr Cust 'faced an almost unanimously hostile audience'.[18] The resolution was 'unanimously adopted by the meeting' and they moved on to the other two subjects. But the conference committee had the final word. They declared themselves reluctant to recognise the resolution as representative of the conference as a whole. No appeal against this judgment was possible.

James Maxwell and Benjamin Broomhall were indignant. It was as they had feared. The resolution would languish as so many others on the same subject had, year after year, decade after decade. They felt driven to independent action. They would undertake themselves to carry the message to the nation through an alliance of Christians 'for the severance of the connection of the British Empire with the opium traffic'.

Hudson Taylor sailed from Liverpool three days later, with a daunting programme of engagements ahead of him in the States and

Canada. On the same day, June 23, Jennie wrote to him, saying that Benjamin was 'full of a Christian Union against opium and a paper to be called *National Righteousness*'. Like the Society for the Suppression of the Opium Trade, which they intended to complement not to rival, their motto was to be 'Righteousness exalteth a nation, but sin *is* a reproach to any people' (Prov. 14:34 AV). 'Union' was a current term. Trade Unions were in the news. 'Christians United' might today carry the same thrust. Forty years had passed since Charles Gutzlaff's Christian Union in Hong Kong. This title, 'The Christian Union', spoke for itself. With a minimum of entangling, time-consuming organisation, and not even a 'constitution' to be debated and defined, Christians would work together and pray together until its purpose was achieved. 'Benjamin B' with his already wide contacts through Britain would be the publicist, and edit the periodical, *National Righteousness*, in his own time. James Maxwell, as secretary, would handle the resulting correspondence, although founder and director since 1878 of the Medical Missionary Association (of London).[19]

Sir Stevenson Arthur Blackwood agreed to be president, with J Bevan Braithwaite, as chairman and James E Mathieson of Mildmay completing the committee. An annual subscription of one shilling was to cover costs, including *National Righteousness*, post free. 'As the Opium Question must ultimately be settled in the House of Commons it is intended to form Committees in the principal towns of the kingdom' to arrange public meetings and 'prepare for speedy and decisive action' – political pressure groups. Inside the cover of Volume 1, Number 1, was the statement: 'The Christian Union was formed on Tuesday, June 26, 1888. Already the membership exceeds sixteen hundred.'[20]

> The clergy of the Church of England, and the ministers of nearly every section of the Christian Church, in their great assemblies, by formal resolution, denounced the traffic; but *still the dreadful trade has gone on unchecked, unhindered, and even increasing*, till the net revenue which was for twenty years ending 1863–4, £77,660,127, in the next twenty years ending 1884–5, rose to £135,857,583 . . . How is it that the people of England, who willingly gave twenty millions sterling to free the slave, have so contentedly acquiesced in a traffic compared with which, we have been repeatedly told, the slave trade itself was merciful? . . . From the year 1844 to 1884 we poured into China a quantity of opium so enormous that the profit its manufacture brought to our Indian Government was no less than two hundred

and thirteen millions sterling . . . Are we for the sake of revenue to go on in this work of iniquity?

A major achievement by the CIM for China was to be accomplished outside China.

> It was Mr Broomhall's keen perception of the secret of the weakness of the anti-opium movement *in the ignorance and apathy of the Churches*, that lay behind this new effort [Dr Maxwell wrote]. There could be no hope of victory until the Churches had been thoroughly aroused . . . (He) had a peculiar gift for incisive and tactful names, and . . . *National Righteousness* as it began its course among the thousands and ten thousands of clergy and ministers and influential Christian laymen . . . was nothing less than a summons to the Christian mind of the country.

So Benjamin added this work to the already oppressive burden of selecting and sending 'the second hundred' to China. And to organising the CIM's endless succession of farewell, annual and deputation meetings he added more to awaken the conscience of Britain through the Church. Yet none of these provided enough expression of his most effective gift, which Maxwell again described.

> He loved to bring men together in large social conferences. His breakfast gatherings, first in the Exeter Hall and later in the Hotel Cecil and other places, were a real strength to the movement. They brought together leading men in the Churches and members of Parliament and influential laymen, over this one subject. They might be expensive, but Mr Broomhall was so trusted by wealthy Christian men who were themselves interested in the anti-opium crusade that whenever he judged that the right time had come for such a social conference, the funds were always ready.
>
> Nor did he neglect the House of Commons. He steadily strove to bring the influence of *National Righteousness* to bear on its members. The magazine was always so strikingly got up, its point so clear, its information so trustworthy, and the urgency of its morals so definite . . . the cumulative effect of its messages had, there is no room to doubt, a powerful effect in moulding legislative opinion.

Benjamin was to continue this campaign until it succeeded – when he was on his death-bed in 1911, twenty-three years later. Inescapably he earned from the apathetic the label of 'extreme and rabid'. Although his policy was to avoid 'red rag' publicity, he expressed it as, 'We must be as pungent as we can.' 'We have no need to go cap in hand humbly to Ministers . . . or any other official. We must demand, and press our demand.' So persuasion on a large scale was to be sustained interminably. 'Even a quarter of a million copies of Dr (Handley) Moule's speech is little more than a drop in the bucket to arouse England . . . I propose to circulate a quarter of a million . . . and 20,000 of Holcombe's book.' His tremendous energy and ability to work until midnight and later, day after day, were matched by as great a gift. 'In the goodness of God I have been saved through many years from yielding to discouragement for five minutes, and yet there are times when one feels weary . . .'

Hudson Taylor himself had attacked the opium scandal without remission for years already and continued to do so, but always as a complement of his great obsession, the gospel to the whole of China as soon as possible. His surviving documents contain few references to this side of Benjamin's work, but he played his part. Opium refuges could only save the scores, body and soul, while hundreds more became addicted. Benjamin had seen through to the heart of the evil. Prevention must overtake cure. Far from being a distraction from the main task, the eradication of this blot on the face of Christianity in China was a major prerequisite to the acceptance of the gospel. Hudson Taylor agreed. But to some extent Benjamin's commitment to the crusade undermined their mutual confidence and contributed to disharmony between them on matters of Mission policy. At the same time developments arising from Hudson Taylor's whirlwind preaching tour in the States and Canada looked in London even more like a red herring – the avoidable distraction of establishing the CIM in North America.

A journey in the dark   *June–October 1888*

Henry Frost's visit to Britain, the 'veritable bog of blasted hopes', within a few weeks showed firm ground for optimism. Unknown to any of those involved, that visit had already marked an epoch in the life of Hudson Taylor and the history of the CIM. At home again Frost looked for invitations to bring Hudson Taylor to the States. Dr W J Erdman, convener of the 'Believers Bible Study Conference' at Niagara-on-the-Lake, near to the Falls, responded at once and wrote to Hudson Taylor. Dr A T Pierson, the great expositor, and editor of *The Missionary Review of the World*, wrote to him (before the international conference), 'No man on earth whom I have not seen in the flesh has so much of my heart's best love as you.

I am in profound sympathy with your aims, methods, mission and spirit.' Would he come at least for a short visit? But D L Moody who already knew Hudson Taylor (HTCOC Book 6, p 328) failed to reply to Frost's suggestion that he should invite him to his summer conference for students at Northfield, Mount Hermon. For before Henry Frost's letter reached him he had already asked his brother-in-law, Fleming H Revell (son of the ship-owner of the same name), on a visit to Britain, to deliver an invitation to him.[21] Frost had done his part and a welcome was clear. Hudson Taylor could only fulfil his promise.

Reginald Radcliffe, the fiery evangelist with whom Hudson Taylor had had so much to do in 1884 and whose stentorian voice had taken up the cause of the evangelisation of the world, had been invited, too. They met at Liverpool and sailed on Saturday, June 23, by the ss *Etruria*. Hudson Taylor, his personal secretary S F Whitehouse, Howard Taylor (free for a few weeks before taking up appointments as house-surgeon and house-physician at the London Hospital) travelled 'semi-steerage' by 'intermediate class', and Mr and Mrs Radcliffe less austerely; but the ship's captain asked Hudson Taylor to conduct the Sunday service in the first-class saloon. Neither could know what lay ahead.

THE 1888 VISIT TO THE USA AND CANADA

Annie Macpherson had written from Canada, where large numbers of her East End orphans had settled, 'I believe there are more brave and well-educated men waiting for your loved China in the Canadian colleges than in any other part of the globe.' But, Hudson Taylor was to write, 'Mr Radcliffe had remarked to me, and I to him, more than once as we were crossing the ocean together, that we felt we did not know what God was taking us to America for, though we felt that we were following His leading.'

An expansive movement among students had begun in North America as in Britain, interweaving British and American strands to direct tens of thousands of men and women into the service of God overseas and at home.[22]

In the States and Canada the American Inter-Collegiate YMCA was gaining strength in the 1870s and two members, Luther Wishard and Charles K Ober, saw in D L Moody's Northfield conferences the right medium for rapid growth.

Northfield in Massachusetts on the Connecticut River that separates Vermont from New Hampshire, was Moody's lifetime home, his birthplace and retreat between strenuous campaigns and missions. In the rolling countryside along the river he created school campuses, one for girls and in 1881 at beautiful Mount Hermon one for boys. A training school for young Christians also grew up at Mount Hermon. During vacations he used them for conferences. The first Northfield Convocation (variously called Bible Conference or Christian Workers' Conference) in 1880 for anyone 'hungering for intimate fellowship with God and power to do His work', drew three hundred.[23]

Moody's second mission to Britain, 1881–84 (HTCOC Book 6, pp 328–35), directly resulted in a conquest at Cambridge, the conversion of the Studds' father and some of the Cambridge Seven, and the surrender of others' lives to the service of Christ. Moody returned to his responsibilities at Northfield and Chicago, while the student world in Britain caught fire from the Seven. The fire then leapt the Atlantic to America. When J E Kynaston Studd (President of the CICCU in 1882, 'and in later years twice Lord Mayor of London') went over in place of Stanley Smith, the third Northfield Conference, of August 1885, was ripe for A T Pierson's bombshell. Moody had allotted August 11 to 'prayer for worldwide missions'. A thousand Christians heard Pierson call at this 'hour for advance' for an appeal to the entire Church to unite in planning a worldwide campaign to take the gospel to every living soul in the shortest possible time. Kynaston Studd was one of the signatories to the appeal, and Moody called for a vote of acclamation to ratify it. The ecumenical International Missionary Conference of June 1887 in London had been the outcome.

Luther Wishard was there at Northfield, and Studd toured the colleges with him. At Cornell, John R Mott, a law student, was converted through 'JEK'. Big things were happening. Moody was still chary of close dealings with students, but Wishard knew his honest, bluff directness of speech and athletic friendliness counted for more than an academic education. 'He brought religion out of the clouds.' So Luther Wishard prevailed on him to invite not only YMCA leaders for a summer camp in 1886 but two hundred and fifty students, for 'Bible' morning and evening, with hours of baseball and swimming every afternoon.

Robert P Wilder was among them, another of the great names of the student contribution to world mission. In 1883 Robert Wilder and four other students, in binding themselves together as the Princeton Foreign Missionary Society, had signed a declaration: 'We are willing and desirous, God permitting, to become Foreign Missionaries.' He and his sister Grace covenanted together to pray for a thousand volunteers from North American universities, and at Northfield brought together the twenty-three who were already committed, to pray for more. While swimming in the Connecticut River he urged Mott to become a missionary. He prevailed on Moody to give A T Pierson the session in which he spoke on 'the evangelisation of the world in this generation', the theme that had its germ in the 1877 Shanghai Conference (HTCOC Book 6, p 113) and anticipated the Student Volunteer Missionary Union's great watchword. Three weeks later he asked Moody to allow nine students from overseas and a North American Indian to address the conference. That so-called 'meeting of the Ten Missions' made history. In the shade of the Mount Hermon trees, the natural trysting place with God, student upon student made his covenant, and one hundred signed a declaration of willingness to go 'into all the world'.

The Student Volunteer Movement (SVM) had been born. From it came the Student Volunteer Missionary Union (SVMU) in 1896 when the same watchword was adopted. Charles Ober recorded the part the CIM played in its inception: 'The story . . . of the Cambridge band, particularly the account of the visit of a deputation of these students to other British universities, with their missionary message, made a profound impression on us. *Here really was the germ thought of the Student Volunteer Movement.*'[24]

Robert Wilder and John Forman toured the universities, and in 1887 Forman crossed over to the British Isles (p 54) and found himself welcomed to visit the universities with Hudson Taylor. The Northfield Conferences had become annual events, the students' conference preceding the general conference for the Christian public. Every year several hundreds signed the Volunteers' declaration and within the fifty years 1889–1939 'more than 25,000 university graduates – the great majority being North American – (entered) that service.'[25] But the upheaval of the First World War contributed to changes in the nature of the SVM and its product the Student Christian Movement (SCM), while the Inter-Varsity (Christian) Fellowship (IVF in UK, IVCF in North America) with Robert Wilder's strong encouragement perpetuated the original aims and principles.

By 1888 the Northfield Conferences and many like them in other parts of North America were drawing Christians in their thousands 'to wait upon God and learn from Him'. Bible teachers from Britain and the continent of Europe were in demand, as were North Americans in the British Isles. Reginald Radcliffe's prophetic cry at Perth in 1877 (HTCOC Book 6, p 113) was seen to be less immoderate than some had thought: 'Let us pray God to gift 2,500 women at a stroke and 2,500 men at a stroke, and . . . to scatter them to the ends of the earth.' North America was more ready for his and Hudson Taylor's visit than they realised. As for the CIM, it was about to 'leap over (yet another) wall'.

'A very serious matter'[26]   *July 1888*

Henry Frost was on the wharf at New York when the *Etruria* tied up on July 1. He took them to his father's affluent home at 80 Madison Avenue. Descended from a family which had endowed the foundation of St John's College, Cambridge, and then helped to found Harvard University, the Frosts had thrived in the New World. Henry's father was a civil engineer and became a railroad owner-manager. He had a country home at Attica, near Buffalo in New York State, where he and Henry had installed the town's gas and water supplies. And he gave Henry and his wife another fine house near by.

The five raw British guests were given a royal welcome at

Madison Avenue and had their first lesson in adaptation to America. As the English custom was, on retiring to bed all put their footwear outside the bedroom door to be cleaned by the household servants. Henry and his father discovered and worked on them late at night. But Hudson Taylor found out what had happened, bought polish and brushes, and tongue in cheek daily cleaned the Radcliffes' shoes while they were with him.

They travelled the next day to Moody's Mount Hermon campus at Northfield Mass., to join the hundreds of students from ninety different colleges in their conference. D L Moody himself met them 'in the middle of the night' and took them to his home. From then, July 2, for two weeks they were at the disposal of the students, with an interval of two days, July 10–12, to address the Bridgeton, New Jersey, conference. George Studd was there, with ten or twelve British and Continental students. Moody's notice of the 'College students' summer school and encampment for Bible Study' had read, 'Special attention will be given to athletics and to systematic recreation . . . Delegates should come fully equipped for bathing, tennis, baseball, football, hill climbing and other outdoor exercise. They should also bring their own reference Bibles and a good supply of notebooks.'

'Mr Radcliffe thundered forth impassioned utterances of missionary obligation,' Henry Frost recalled, 'and after them earthquakes; as Mr Taylor spoke there was the still, small voice . . . the voice that was longest remembered.' They wanted more and asked for extra sessions taken from recreation time. It was not, however, 'the words only . . . it was the life of the man'. John Forman years later told Robert Wilder, 'One of the greatest blessings of my life came to me through, not from, the Rev. J Hudson Taylor.' Wilder knew exactly what he meant, for 'that was how we all felt'. Writing of return visits to Madison Avenue and to the Frosts' country homes at Attica, Henry said, 'His Bible readings at morning prayers upon the *Song of Solomon* were thrilling and transforming . . . they left us, not only at the feet of the Lord, but also at his.'[27] At Northfield 'he not only made the needs of the mission field very real, he showed us the possibilities of the Christian life . . . His sympathy and naturalness attracted men to him.'

Howard Taylor also made a strong impression when he testified that he was preparing to go to China. And the death of a student by drowning concentrated the minds of others. Two weeks later Hudson Taylor received a letter saying, 'I am one of the Student

Volunteers for Foreign Missions . . . Can you kindly tell me . . . the possibility of a student from America obtaining an appointment in your Mission . . . ?' It was signed by Samuel M Zwemer, future apostle to the Muslims of the Middle East.[28] By then Hudson Taylor had received one of the great revelations of his life.

From Northfield he and the Radcliffes, Howard Taylor, George Studd and Robert Wilder, strongly drawn to them, went on to 'a little gathering of perhaps 400' at Niagara-on-the-Lake, a quiet town on the southern shore of Lake Ontario, twenty miles from the twin cities of Niagara Falls. The abundance of ministers of various denominations in both Canada and the States led Howard to write of 'Collegians at Northfield and parsons at Niagara'. There Hudson Taylor received two unexpected letters.

One, from Bridgeton, where he had spent only one day on a flying visit, was a copy of a letter addressed to fellow-missionaries, saying that 'the Union', a new interdenominational approach to the conference there, had 'put Foreign Missions on a new footing'. 'People who have never believed in Foreign Missions are declaring their interest; people who had spoken against the coming of the Union express great satisfaction with it; some say that it has been the greatest religious event that Bridgeton has ever known . . . the sales of Hudson Taylor's books also were phenomenal for this community.'

The other came from Clifton Springs, also dated July 18, and signed by twenty-one church leaders, including William Dean, DD, the veteran of fifty years in Bangkok and China. 'To the Rev. J Hudson Taylor; the Hon. Reginald Radcliffe and Mr (George) Studd' inviting them to fit Clifton Springs into their itinerary. This too was to make history.

At Niagara, Hudson Taylor spoke at only two meetings, 'on the subject of Missions', but characteristically made little mention of the CIM or even of China, in view of the general nature of the conference. 'He had only one theme, it appeared, that of the beauty and glory of Christ. Once he spoke on the spiritual meaning of the Song of Solomon and once on the words . . . "Have faith in God" or . . . "Hold fast God's faithfulness". It is not so much *great faith* that we need, as faith in a *great God*.' Henry Frost, himself an organising secretary of the conference, learned afterwards that a young woman had come dreading the thought of being told about China and would have backed out if her train ticket had not been bought. 'Instead of hearing much about China,' he wrote, 'she heard a great deal about the Lord Jesus, and it ended in her offering for China . . . There is no difficulty about getting blessing when souls deal directly with the great Blesser.'[29]

But D L Moody had prevailed upon Hudson Taylor to give him a long weekend, July 21–24, at his and other churches in Chicago, and he left Niagara with Howard on July 20. The year before Moody founded his Bible Institute in 1889, Reginald Radcliffe and Robert Wilder stayed at Northfield, and the Friday evening session was given to them. 'And how they did speak!' Henry Frost recorded. 'Mr Radcliffe's utterance was a polemic and Robert Wilder's a plea', for worldwide evangelism. Neither was speaking for the CIM, but an extraordinary response gradually developed in the conference. Wilder used as an illustration the case of 'a lady he knew who worked twenty-four hours a day'. 'She herself worked twelve hours, and then had a representative in India who worked the other twelve while she slept.'

Someone then asked Reginald Radcliffe, 'How much it would take to support a missionary for a year in connection with the China Inland Mission?' and he, 'British to the end', replied '"Fifty pounds", leaving it to the American to multiply the amount by five.'

The conference committee had decided that the annual collection should be given to the CIM, 'with the suggestion that it should be used for North American workers in connection with the Mission'. But Dr Stewart in Shanxi was the only one, and he was self-supporting. Henry Frost as a conference secretary in touch with Hudson Taylor found to his surprise that more than $500 had been contributed. But the next morning 'a spirit of enthusiasm' came over the large meeting, and Dr W J Erdman, the chairman, allowed all the informality the audience wanted. One person and then another stood up to say he intended 'to work twenty-four hours a day for missions'. A group of ten young women called Henry Frost outside to ask whether they could combine by giving twenty-five dollars each. Their offer stirred the audience and 'other contributions were set on foot'. Then someone suggested that another 'offering' be taken up. 'There are big hearts and heavy purses in America,' Mrs Radcliffe wrote to Jennie, 'but like the old country, men are bound by preconceived notions . . .'

Unintentionally, by the nature of the CIM and his own personality, Hudson Taylor was breaking through those prejudices and moving those big hearts. When Henry Frost in his hotel room added up 'the spoils', as he put it, he had enough given or pledged for eight non-existent missionaries and 'I suddenly found myself an informal treasurer of the China Inland Mission. After all it looked very much as if the leading I had followed in going to England was no *ignis fatuus.*' Mr Radcliffe had underestimated the costs, if travel and housing were included, but the response was clear enough. Frost was elated.[30]

Hudson Taylor 'was an unusual man . . . He did unusual things; and . . . he did them in an unusual way.' He had reached Attica from Chicago after twenty-one hours in the train. ('It is a country of magnificent distances, 3,500 miles across. Chicago is 1,000 from New York.') Yet he was on the station platform when Frost's train from Niagara pulled in at midnight. As soon as they reached his bedroom in the Frost parents' house Henry could keep the news to himself no longer. 'Mr Taylor usually had a responsive face . . . But this time his face fell . . . For once I was deeply disappointed in him.' He said, 'I think we had better pray.' They knelt beside his bed and he 'began to ask God what it all meant'. They stood up again and he asked gravely, Was the money to be used for North Americans? Yes, that was requested. '"This is serious," was all he said, more to himself than to me.' He 'had had an immediate perception of the meaning of what had taken place . . . Previously, he had refused to extend the Mission to North America. Was God forcing him to reverse that decision?' Incidental donations handed to him since his arrival in America he had been transmitting to London. But this was another matter.

'He said afterwards, "To have had missionaries and no money would not have caused me any anxiety; but to have money and no missionaries was a very serious matter."' If he appealed for North Americans, 'which so far he had carefully refrained from doing . . . the Mission would be established on this side of the ocean . . . His only concern at any time was to discover the Lord's will.' They parted at about one o'clock, and Hudson Taylor wrote to Jennie calculating more realistically than Reginald Radcliffe had done, 'The means for a year's support of 5 or 6 new missionaries is given or promised, and great issues are likely to result from our visit.' He was weighing the alternatives: to return the donations given by a conference (now scattered) for a specific purpose, or to acknowledge the inescapable and apply them as requested. He was coming round to seeing the unfolding events as the hand of God.[31]

A North American 'Lammermuir *party'*   *August–October 1888*

Not far from New York was the seaside resort of Ocean Grove, NJ, an Episcopal Church 'camp meeting' where conventions were conducted all through the summer. Chalets and tents housed 20,000 –30,000 at the height of the season. From July 28 to August 1 Hudson Taylor gave daily addresses – 'last night three or four thousand people, perhaps more,' and 'Howard spoke last night on the beach. I suppose there were 10,000 people present.' 'I think we must have an American branch of the Mission,' he wrote from there to John Stevenson. 'Do not be surprised if I should bring reinforcements with me.' The way the funds had come in surely indicated that actual men and women would soon materialise. It looked as if 'God was really working' to send Americans and Canadians to China. But he knew of no one to entrust with their selection or preparation. Even Henry Frost he had known very briefly so far. He must handle it himself. 'I never felt more timid about anything in my life', even 'frightened', he was to comment a year later. But after consulting Moody and other mature Christians his uncertainty vanished.[32]

Then on to Northfield again for Moody's third general conference, August 1–9, where Hudson Taylor grasped the nettle. Leaving arrangements for managing affairs in North America to be settled later, and believing that God would provide for all whom God took to China, he appealed for men and women to go. 'It is trying to live in a crowd,' he groaned to Jennie, 'I am so sought after that I can scarcely cross the hall without being stopped.' Three of Moody's Northfield students approached him, from churches as far afield as Pittsfield, Mass., near the east coast; Detroit, Michigan, between Chicago and Toronto; and St Paul, Minnesota, three hundred miles north-west of Chicago. And Samuel Zwemer's letter (p 82) of August 2 came from Chicago.

As Hudson Taylor's meetings progressed through August and September, Canadians also applied to him until he had assessed and accepted seventeen or eighteen out of forty-two who offered themselves. He decided to take six of the mature men and eight women with him to China in October, and to Henry Frost's alarm told him 'he would have to do the best (he) could with the rest'. But Hudson Taylor's own difficulties increased, in that he had more money than he could use.

D L Moody undertook to provide the outfit and passage money of the first, Edith Lucas, who offered to go at short notice, and her

church at St Paul promised her support. 'A relative of the late Sir
Moses Montefiore and the Rothschilds' and well educated, she had
been cast off by her family when she became a Christian, and was
working for Moody as a trained nurse. The second had been at
Northfield for four years; her father said he had savings enough to
support her for one year if not longer, and would not hear of others
paying for his daughter while he had the means. The third, Susie
Parker, was given permission by her parents to go, in her father's
words, 'I have nothing too precious for my Lord Jesus.'[33]

Henry Frost had to stay at home with his own father, who had
been taken ill, but donations kept coming to him. When eight
volunteers had been accepted, the original Niagara conference fund
was still untouched. Enough for fifteen was received. Cautiously
Frost asked Hudson Taylor again, 'Will it not be well to establish a
branch here? I have much to say to you . . .' He would need help
and advice, and knew good men whom he believed would be willing
to join him. But while Hudson Taylor could write, 'I feel sure that
the Lord has sent me here . . . We shall get a few missionaries at
once I hope,' he also went on (to Jennie), 'Others will go to England
and come out in the usual way [meaning first generation immigrants
whose parents were in Britain. Edith Lucas's mother was in London
and Jeanie Munro's in Scotland] and I hope the day will come when
BB will come over and form a branch of our work here. It might
soon become a very important part of the mission.' Whether he had
in mind at this moment a branch under the only existing 'Home
Council', the one in Britain, or a branch of the Mission in general,
with a second Home Council, is not clear.

A letter came from William Berger at this stage with another gift
of £500. Someone had written to ask him, was it true that the CIM
had come to an end; that Mr Taylor had gone to America? So ready
were they to believe the worst! Far from it. The 'flea in a blanket'
was on a bigger hop than that. What struck John Stevenson when
Hudson Taylor reached Shanghai in October was that his ideas had
taken wings. The influence of Northfield and American big-thinking
and doing had expanded Hudson Taylor's concept of what the
Mission could become.[34]

After the Northfield conference things began to move more
rapidly. Besides his prearranged speaking engagements he now had
to visit the new missionaries' home churches. At Clifton Springs the
welcome by William Dean and his fellow-ministers (p 82) could not
have been warmer. In place after place he was melted by 'such a

wealth of love'. 'It is not uniformity that we want but really manifested heart unity,' he wrote. From August 14 to 29 he was at ten towns and cities in Canada. Howard Taylor was usually with him (until he left Detroit for England on the 29th, addressing meetings on the way). But Reginald Radcliffe and George Studd came and went, sometimes together, sometimes apart, to meet the demand for meetings. Toronto, Ottawa, as guests of Lady Cavan and her son, and then Montreal for August 17 to 20. Then Hamilton, between Toronto and Niagara, a fertile fiasco of mismanagement by a 'muddly' organiser, but 'a hard, full Sunday, business and three meetings on Monday – direct to station and travel all night and day till 2 pm – meeting here at 3–5 and another 8–9. Conversation and supper and business to 11.30. Neuralgia and a letter to BB begun.'[35]

Interviewing five or six candidates took the whole of the next morning, a wonder in itself. The secretary of the Hamilton YMCA told him that the Hamilton Christian Associations were praying that seven of their number would go to China. Four young women and two from Hamilton sailed with Hudson Taylor in October, and Rough, the secretary, himself went via Europe. 'Some dozen of our circle ultimately landed in China.' A local newspaper was impressed but baffled, saying, 'The venerable gentleman concluded a long, most interesting address, by informing the audience that the members of the China Inland Mission depended upon chance providences for a scanty subsistence.' Back at Toronto he preached four times on Sunday, 26th, and was in Chicago, 500 miles away, with Radcliffe and George Studd by the 30th. The demands on his stamina were unrelenting. Reading the mail accumulated there took until 2 a.m., but answering it adequately proved impossible. 'Such a nice long one from BB. I wish I could repay it.' But there were more candidates to be seen, and on Sunday, September 2, he walked sixteen miles and preached twice.

In the auditorium of the YMCA Hudson Taylor finished speaking and, sensing the mood of the audience, D L Moody called for the ushers to take up a collection. Hudson Taylor intervened, but the opportunity was too good for Moody to let slip. Might he explain, Hudson Taylor asked? He thanked Moody and the meeting for their generous impulse. But the CIM never took collections lest money be diverted from the older missions. If anyone after supporting their own boards wished to help the CIM they could always write. When the Moody Bible Institute was inaugurated a year later, a Christian merchant revealed that he left Hudson Taylor's meeting glad that the $50 note he was going to donate still lay safely in his wallet. But his conscience troubled him until the next morning he sent a cheque for $500.[36]

In a sleeping-car on the way to Minneapolis and St Paul, four or five hundred miles beyond Chicago, Hudson Taylor wrote, 'I think I shall get 8 or 10 associates [that is, fully supported and independent but working by CIM practices and under CIM direction]. How often I have wished for BB to give counsel about some of the candidates. I believe had he been here we might have had double the number and full support for them.' If Hudson Taylor underestimated his own judgment and influence, it was because 'the people have need to be understood, more than the Canadians, who are more like ourselves'. But he was undeterred. The British 'Bible Christians' in associate relationship with the CIM were on a different footing. They belonged to the Bible Christian Mission, as Erik Folke represented the Swedish Mission in China. There was no such organisation in North America, and none of these men and women was financially independent.

After St Paul they made a great detour south to Kansas city and St Louis, before returning by other places to the Frosts' Attica home. The scale of development of the CIM was clearly in his mind. By then the Mission had 216 members in China, with fifty more from Britain 'this season', and a growing number winding up their personal affairs and outfitting in North America. In comparison, he showed Jennie in a letter from the train near Kansas city, American missionaries in China currently totalled 234 while British and Continental numbered 235. The CIM would reach 300 before long.[37] (Map 4 p 77.)

The party to travel with him to China were already assembling at Attica. The Frosts (Henry, his wife and parents) put their homes at their disposal and set no limit. They could overflow if necessary into lodgings and hotels. More farewell meetings for the travellers and their families and churches were to be held at Lockport, Hamilton, Guelph, Toronto and Montreal, where they would board the transcontinental train to Vancouver.

Accepting the substance of two accounts which diverge in detail, we have an example of the composure that Hudson Taylor's American friends remembered long afterwards. A Mr Joshua S Helmer of Lockport had undertaken the arrangements for the party to board the Toronto train early one morning. But a delay in the carriage(s) coming to take them to the station left too little time for all handling of the baggage to be finished before the train moved off. To Mr Helmer's great distress 'the whole company' were left standing on the platform. He turned to make abject apologies to Hudson Taylor, for no later train would get them to their destination for their farewell meeting. Instead he found him 'as calm and possessed as if the train were still waiting', and saying that the Lord could still get them there if it was his will. While they were still speaking, an unscheduled excursion train drew in: It connected with another and they arrived on time.

In the other account Hudson Taylor (with no companions mentioned) was alleged to say, 'My Father manages the trains and I'll be there.' He took a train in the opposite direction although the possible connection involved catching a train which normally left the junction ten minutes before he could arrive – and caught it. But hearsay notoriously gathers myth.[38]

The last days, in Canada[39]   *September–October 1888*

The climax was in sight. Large-hearted America had swept them on from one great welcome to another. The crescendo continued. Remarkable meetings, 'which I have certainly never seen exceeded anywhere' followed closely on each other at Hamilton, Guelph and Toronto when the six men and eight women forgathered with Hudson Taylor and his secretary, Whitehouse. On Sunday, September 23, Hudson Taylor spoke in 'three or four of the principal churches' and Reginald Radcliffe elsewhere, before the final meeting in the new YMCA hall. All the approaches were so packed that the speakers could not reach the doors. A circuitous route brought them somehow to the platform. Standing people packed all aisles after the seats were filled. And when a second hall was full 'vast numbers were unable even to enter the building'. The meeting lasted from 8.00 until almost 11.00 pm with 'no slackening of the pressure', 'close attention' and 'deep emotion'; 'meetings such as no one present would ever forget', the papers reported.

Each of the fourteen (all but two from Ontario) told how God had led them to 'give themselves for China'. Monday and Tuesday they spent with their families and friends, making final preparations, while Hudson Taylor discussed arrangements with Frost and others before leaving for Montreal, to rejoin them at North Bay on the transcontinental railroad. After a communion service in Knox Church, at 9 p.m. on Tuesday night, the fourteen went to the Union

THE FIRST NORTH AMERICAN PARTY
with the Radcliffes and Hudson Taylor; Henry Frost behind
Mrs Radcliffe

Station, where a crowd of between five hundred and a thousand congregated to see them off. The station 'trembled with farewell songs', and when they had steamed out the YMCA men walked four abreast and singing through the main streets back to the Association hall.[40]

In his factual account of those days, Henry Frost went on to tell of how Hudson Taylor and he spent that Monday afternoon. Alfred Sandham, of the Christian Institute, Toronto, had agreed to interview and assess a continuing stream of Canadian volunteers, while Henry Frost was to deal with Americans – twenty-eight and almost daily increasing. (As Benjamin could not come to take over, Hudson Taylor felt duty-bound to make provision of some sort.) The three of them were together in the Institute building, working out how to proceed after Hudson Taylor had gone. He explained that permanent arrangements would follow consultation with the China and London Councils, but a tentative auxiliary council was desirable, for Sandham and Frost to consult. They were of one mind, and soon agreed that Dr H M Parsons of Knox Church, William Gooderham with 'philanthropic' connections, and J D Nasmith, a business man, should be approached. As they talked there was a knock at the door and Dr Parsons came in. He consented to act with Frost and Sandham and the conversation continued until interrupted by another knock. J D Nasmith appeared, and Hudson Taylor was able personally to invite him to join the others. At this Dr Parsons began to talk about prophecy. But when William Gooderham arrived as unexpectedly,

> his presence was almost like an apparition . . . it was so startling . . .
> It seemed to border on the miraculous (for) not one of the three knew
> that Mr Taylor was in the Institute, that all were seeking Mr Sandham
> and that two of the three had not been in the building for several
> months past. Thus gathered together by the Spirit of the Lord, we
> had – on Monday, September 24th, 1888, what was practically the
> first Council meeting of the Mission held in North America.[41]

Eight others were added soon afterwards.

In the train to Montreal Henry Frost read a Knox College magazine article, 'Hudson Taylor in Toronto' – 'a diatribe' which made him hot with indignation. Lest Hudson Taylor see it, he slipped it under a pile of papers beside him. But Hudson Taylor had been told about it. He asked for it and read it 'from start to finish'.

> Hudson Taylor is rather disappointing. I . . . had in my mind an
> idea of what (great missionaries) should look like . . . He being
> professedly one of the greatest missionaries of modern times must be

such as they. But he is not . . . A stranger would never notice him on the street . . . except, perhaps, to say that he is a good-natured-looking little Englishman. Nor is his voice in the least degree majestic . . . He displays little oratorical power . . . He elicits little applause . . . launches no thunderbolts . . . Even our own Goforth used to plead more eloquently for China's millions, and apparently with more effect . . . It is quite possible that were Mr Taylor, under another name, to preach as a candidate in our Ontario vacancies there are those who would begrudge him his probationer's pay.

For some moments Hudson Taylor sat lost in thought. Then he smiled at Henry Frost and said, 'That is a very just criticism, for it is all true. I have often thought that God made me little in order that He might show what a great God He is.' They turned into their sleeping berths, but Frost

lay there in the darkness, the train rushing along at the rate of forty miles an hour . . . thinking, thinking . . . about the saint in the berth beneath me . . . It is not hard for a little man to try to be great; but it is very hard for a great man to try to be little. Mr Taylor, however . . . had entered into that humility which is alone found in the spirit of the lowly Nazarene.[42]

They parted at Montreal station, and Frost returned to Attica, dreading the task he had taken up, until welcomed home by 'someone therein who thinks – however great the hallucination – that you are something'. He had said to Hudson Taylor, 'But I don't know anything about dealing with candidates,' and the reply 'distressingly simple, characteristic of the man, but not exactly practical' had been, 'Quite true, but the Lord will help you.' That was before the episode at the Institute taught him new values. When Henry Frost went ahead trusting the Lord to direct him, he quickly knew the advice was 'exactly practical'.

Hudson Taylor and his party boarded SS *Batavia* at Vancouver and sailed on October 5 straight into rough seas. Most were prostrated, but not the 'good sailor', Hudson Taylor himself. In the three busy months since July 1 when he landed at New York, he had received 824 letters and dealt with most of them. Knowing too well that China would confront him with stresses of its own, he used the voyage to finish his correspondence and accounts and to update *China's Spiritual Need and Claims*. The respite ended at Yokohama, where the mail awaiting him contained the first blow in an onslaught unrelenting until he sailed again for Britain six months later. But he seems to have been oblivious of the worst dangers ahead.[43]

CHAPTER THREE

A NATION OF FAMILIES
1888–91

Six nightmare months   *November 1888–April 1889*

Trouble at the Chefoo schools through loss of staff and indiscipline among the teenage boys had ended with a new headmaster's arrival in 1884. Everyone liked Herbert L Norris, and standards quickly rose under his direction. Results in the examinations were recognised in universities at home. Frank McCarthy, John's son, joined him, a future headmaster in the making. All was going well until early September 1888 when a 'miserable-looking dog entered the boys' schoolroom, and rushed in turn at several of the boys'. They dodged it by leaping on to their desks and it ran next to a bedroom where others were preparing for bed. Herbert Norris heard the commotion, pursued and cornered it. 'It flew at him and bit his finger', but lest it harm the boys he delayed getting the wound cauterised until the dog had been killed. On September 24 Norris fell ill, and died of hydrophobia three days later. The mail at Yokohama gave Hudson Taylor the news.[1]

But that was not all. Adam Dorward was dead. Adam Dorward of all people – 'the apostle of Hunan' – such an exceptional man in personality, achievement and sheer saintliness, and one of the new China Council. A year before, in October 1887, he had cut short his home leave to take relief funds to the flood and famine areas of north Henan. Then back to Shashi, his springboard for Hunan. Of his Chinese companions and himself, he had said, '(Again and again) we have come to a city, by foot or native boat, and have entered it not knowing whether we should leave it alive or not.' From Changde, deep in Hunan, he had written in August, 'I feel as if I would be willing to do almost anything that would be honouring to God, and undergo any hardship, if only I could get footing in Changde, and see men and women turning to God.'

The same mail as brought to his mother the news of his death brought also a long letter from Adam: Thomas James in their advanced post at Shishou was expecting a riot. The town was placarded with incitements to destroy the mission house. And in

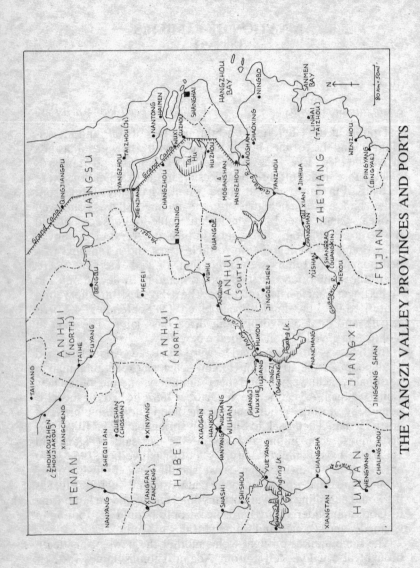

THE YANGZI VALLEY PROVINCES AND PORTS

Shashi cholera was rampant. Men were falling down and dying in the streets. Would Dorward come and help to quell the disturbance? But Adam told her, 'You need not be in any way anxious on my account. I am just as much in the Lord's keeping here as I would be if I were at home . . . (He) can easily command that no evil befall me . . . But if the Lord should will otherwise *still all will be well* . . . Praise God that I am again honoured to go to the front of the battle! . . . May our confidence be in God alone.'

Hardly had he reached Shishou than he fell ill with dysentery. A very sick man was no use so, lest he add to Thomas James's difficulties, Dorward returned home. Three times James faced death from spears and from being drowned by the mob, and escaped only when a tropical deluge scattered them. But Dorward, all alone, suffered a perforated intestine and was dying of peritonitis when another colleague found him. They buried him at Yichang, the consul, customs officials and merchants honouring him at the graveside.[2]

That two such outstanding men should be taken was a counterblow from Satan, but allowed by God 'lest we get puffed up', Hudson Taylor wrote to Jennie. 'I feel almost overwhelmed . . . feel like a "weaned child" – I want to be alone with God. May He . . . make us all holy – more fit for His service, *here or there*.' 'The Lord reigneth! . . . He can make *no* mistakes.' But there was no privacy on board ship, and he had sixty other letters to answer and the ship's services to take.

John Stevenson met them at Shanghai on October 30 and the two directors paced the wharf together with immediate problems to be solved. Unexpected arrivals from the interior, sick missionaries and others in transit, left little room in the Yuan Ming Yuan buildings for the large party. They went straight to the shipping office and booked passages on the Yangzi river steamer for the next evening. Quick transformations into Chinese clothes, and they were all away again. At Zhenjiang Hudson Taylor handed the women over to John McCarthy's care, and went on upstream to Anqing with the men, returning with Arthur Eason ill with typhoid.

From November 10 to 14 he buried himself in conference 'far into the night' with Stevenson and McCarthy at Yangzhou, not neglecting to give long, highly practical Bible discourses and talks about the Principles and Practice (the P and P) to the language students preparing to go up-country. As arrangements stood, business and transit quarters in Shanghai, Broumton's finance department at

Wuchang, and the directors' offices at Zhenjiang were a good working system not to be jettisoned lightly. The objections to centralisation in Shanghai still held. Not for nothing had Shanghai earned its reputation as a sink of iniquity. And social distractions even in the large inter-mission community could consume precious time and blunt the edge of concentration on the job to be done.

Hudson Taylor was loth to yield to the advantages of closer teamwork in a compact headquarters. But these crises of inadequate accommodation were becoming more frequent; the Wusong Road site was paid for and ready, and the cost of the first two big buildings had been promised by Archibald Orr Ewing. Continuing expansion of the Mission must be expected. The American potential promised that. 'I saw how Northfield had impressed him,' John Stevenson recalled. 'He was in an impressionable state of mind, open to new developments, and was *looking forward* . . . Everything seemed possible.' If he had known more he would have said 'Niagara' instead of Northfield, for there the matter had been taken out of Hudson Taylor's hands. 'This work really originated at the Niagara Believers' Meetings,' he had said in his article for *The Christian* and A T Pierson's *Missionary Review*.[3]

The choice was made. While John Stevenson carried on the routine administration, Hudson Taylor would take over the problem cases, the discouraged and disgruntled people and those who wished to resign and go home, good men like Henry Dick and Charles Hogg among them. And he with the businessman David Cranston's help (HTCOC Book 5, p 389) would plan the new premises before calling in the architects and engineers. As it turned out, a flood of tribulations descended upon him, and creative planning became the relaxation that he needed. He designed two large buildings which by their very appearance and convenience gave future missionaries a sense of friendliness and home while providing all the facilities required (p 134).

All kinds of trouble came his way. Another missionary died of typhus at Jinhua. The consuls declined to accept as valid Stanley Smith's marriage in Shanxi to Sophie Reuter, a Norwegian citizen, and they had to come to Shanghai and repeat the ceremony. 'Anti-CIM' feeling had developed among CIM missionaries in Chefoo through one or two influential malcontents. Far worse, hardly had John Stevenson's daughter Mary arrived at Shanghai to help her father than she went out of her mind. 'Our house has been a hospital. It is now a lunatic asylum, too.' Then word came that

William Cooper, the member of the China Council whom Hudson Taylor valued more highly than all, had become desperately ill on the way out from Britain and might not live beyond Hong Kong. He recovered. But for weeks on end Hudson Taylor had Mary and other patients to care for while overburdened with office work. In the room next to his, Mary raved and tore her clothes and sheets in ribbons, anything she could lay hands on, taking several people to hold her in her most maniacal moments.[4]

Hudson Taylor took another house[5] and moved in with his patients, to spare the Mission home. But how could he work or sleep with Mary the other side of a thin wall? 'While the spiritual tone of the Mission is much higher than ever before – the trials and conflicts are very great,' he told Jennie. 'The constant tension of sorrow and trial are enough to break one's heart. But I *know* the Lord's ways are *all* right and I would not have them otherwise. "Even so, Father," if our hearts do break or minds give way.' He faced it as an onslaught from the devil.

A few days later it was even worse. One mental case was being sent home. Another far up the Han River was reported by telegram to be 'demented'. But Mary might die. Stevenson was looking ten years older. Then lovely, beautiful Maggie McKee of the Hundred, 'one of our brightest and most promising flowers,' was smothered with 'black smallpox' and dead in six days. 'I do not know,' said John Stevenson, 'what we would have done without Mr Taylor, but oh! the look on his face at that time.'[6]

A missionary couple had brought a nursemaid from England with them, dismissed her and left her in Shanghai to be sent home. But she too fell ill with typhoid. They never forgave Hudson Taylor for rebuking them.

Henan was in the forefront of the news.[7] After reaching twenty-one and marrying 'Joe' Coulthard, Maria had gone with him to Zhoujiakou, the first woman missionary in the province. Simply by visiting one home after another she had personally explained the essentials of the gospel to 1,500 women. In November Herbert Taylor took his wife and child and Geraldine Guinness, a beginner, to Sheqidian. The river level being too low for boats, they had to endure hard, primitive overland travel all the way. But the Huang He (Yellow River) floods and resulting famine in the north still called for funds, and missionaries to distribute them. The need in other provinces was even greater, and funds donated for the CIM to use were shared with the Baptists and Presbyterians in Shandong

where a million and a half were homeless and starving. Not until
May 1889 were the breaks in the Yellow River banks closed, sixteen
months after they were breached.[8]

The 'Canadian men' gave unmixed comfort to the hard-pressed
directors. 'I wish we had a hundred such men.' The more they
understood the Mission's principles the more they approved. Conferring with Stevenson, McCarthy and Marcus Wood (in charge of
the Anqing training school, newly appointed a superintendent and a
member of the China Council), they said they wanted to become full
members, not only associates. Hudson Taylor saw no reason for
excluding them. During 1888 five men of the CIM had died, two had
resigned, and three might have to leave, but twelve new men had
come to China. The Canadians were pure gain. They, not mission
politics, settled the issue. North Americans were as much the CIM
as anyone. He designated them to difficult Henan.

The women's special sphere on the Guangxin River (HTCOC
Book 6, p 394) was the natural place for the girls of the party when
their time came. Meanwhile, less than twenty miles from their
Yangzhou training-school, a riot broke out at Zhenjiang. Miss C L
Williams[9] reported to Hudson Taylor, 'We stayed in the house until
the flag was taken and the consul's house burning, and then we were
taken . . . to the steamer . . . until the morning.' (They returned to
feed the schoolchildren, but then had to withdraw again.) 'The mob
was very great and they threw large stones and pieces of rock at us.'
When the mob began setting fire to the mission house, Chinese
soldiers drove them away. 'And after Chinese, American and
British gunboats anchored offshore . . . we soon had everything in
order again.'

Only his letters to Jennie once more revealed how painfully he
was feeling their separation from each other. Far from it becoming
easier with time, he confessed, 'I feel sometimes, dearie, as if the
charm and even power of life were taken out of me by these long
absences from you . . . Hope deferred makes the heart sick . . . but
I cannot shake it off.' 'Longing removes the power of thought.' 'The
cross does not get more comfortable, does it?'[10] He had good reason
for wanting to be able to talk with her as he could with no one else,
not even John Stevenson, about new trouble with the London
Council and Benjamin. Jennie as co-editor of *China's Millions*, was
relieving him of almost all but editorials and annual reports. Correspondence went to and fro about an article by Montagu Beauchamp
to which some readers had objected.[11] Taking a month or six weeks

in each direction, it demonstrated the difficulty of co-ordinating the overseas and home sides of the Mission. But it exacerbated the feeling stirred up when Hudson Taylor formed the 'tentative auxiliary council' in Toronto without consulting London. He had kept them informed, but had not sought their approval. What *was* the status of the London Council?

No crisis after all   1888–89

Rough water is found where strong currents meet. For the time being the contention over the Book of Arrangements and 'P and P' had been set aside. But when Hudson Taylor left even a tentative auxiliary council in Toronto without formally consulting London, he met strong resistance. Dixon Hoste in later years made the comment,

> It would have been little short of a miracle if the brethren at home had *not* raised difficulties and objections. It was a *new* thing (the ugly duckling!) – would excite suspicion, objections . . . It is the fate of all inventors, every man who is leading ahead. People don't understand what he is after; don't grasp his thought.[12]

Not one other missionary society was international. Even the denominational missions and Bible societies were nationally distinct and independent. Hudson Taylor was making a new contribution to the high politics of missions as he had by initiating the principle of control over the field of action by men on the field.

> (Both were) experimental, bound to be opposed by men of more ordinary lines of thought . . . All tradition was against it . . . For the particular job in hand, the men in China were the experts.

So when London heard of a North American council they reacted adversely. 'The question will be,' wrote Theodore Howard, 'whether it should be a Branch of the Home work . . . or work independently under the same lines and in fellowship and sympathy, but not under the same direction as the CIM.' Either subsidiary to the London Council or quite separate? But a sibling 'Home' department in the same family, autonomous in relation to London but equal in status under the General Director, seems not to have occurred to 'London'.

At first Benjamin was pleased with Hudson's letters and his

discovery of such fine material ready to proceed at once to China. Then doubts appeared. 'Anything of the nature of an American branch' could bring 'disappointment if not utter failure', simply through inherent national differences of outlook and method. By the end of October, with all the labour of running 'about seventy meetings', including some in parts of Britain where China and the CIM were previously unknown, it looked foolhardy to Benjamin to take incalculable risks by expanding across the Atlantic. So he advised, first exploit the half-tapped reservoir, 'the richest mine' of Britain!

A month later Jennie wrote, 'Benj. and the Council are very dissatisfied . . . It would be far wiser to get them (the North Americans) to run a mission and help all we can. I hope it will be so for I think he is right.' By then the strain of having too much to do and too many callers who stayed too long was making Benjamin impatient; and in a Shanghai under deep snow the stresses and broken nights were having the same effect on Hudson. Where in writing to anyone else they would have been more careful, between old friends hurried notes and ill-considered wording left wrong impressions. Benjamin voiced his concern to Henry Frost. He would rather retire than take part in a false move. And soon afterwards he wrote to Hudson, 'I am deeply distressed', and 'the interests of the CIM will be imperilled', it would be 'suicidal' to go international. Hudson replied, 'Without a visit to America you cannot fully understand.' He must meet the same people. But rather than have a hand in what he saw with such misgivings, a replica of the British arrangements over in America, Benjamin wrote 'If you are resolved upon it I shall not offer opposition . . . I do not desire contention – I would rather retire altogether.'[13]

By February the new famine in China was adding a hundred letters a day to the burden on the CIM in London. Reports in the papers were conflicting with the facts observed by missionaries, and Benjamin was having to tread carefully. He declined an invitation to join the Lord Mayor's Famine Committee after Hudson told Jennie 'the money from the Lord Mayor's Fund is most of it going into the hands of the (mandarins) . . . The (Shanghai Famine Relief) Committee dare not publish here some of the bogus reports got up for the occasion.'

With no time in which to think dispassionately, 'this American question' loomed all the larger as a potential threat to the Mission. Strong supporters and members of the council were warning against it, he wrote, naming James Mathieson of Mildmay, George Williams of the YMCA and Robert Scott of *The Christian*, a major donor. Another said Hudson Taylor had been 'carried away by (his) reception in America'. So he, Benjamin, wished to dissociate himself from this 'peril to the work'. And then, ominously because ambiguously, 'I must ask you to accept my resignation if you have resolved to carry out this American plan.' Henry Frost understood him to mean, 'I shall have to resign if it comes to that', as Benjamin intended to convey, but Hudson Taylor in the Shanghai nightmare read it as a firm declaration of intent.

In August John Stevenson had written to Benjamin, 'It is often a wonder to me to see the unity and harmony that exists in the CIM', that strong differences of opinion could be held without hostility. Harmony and unity were coming under greater strain at the heart of the Mission. Looking back on these days, John Stevenson said, 'There had been so much success and such rapid extension. We were going forward with full sail set before a favourable wind and ballast was needed, but we did not realise it . . .'

Hudson Taylor's difficulty lay in his sincere submission of everything to God, and conviction that God would 'direct his steps'. This was how God had dealt with him for nearly forty years. 'I know God guided in the formation of the [Toronto] council' sounded arrogant to some who did not know him well. But to Stevenson his was 'a life that stands looking into, looking behind . . . Of course he was liable to the weaknesses of human nature. But I have watched it very closely under all conditions.' Hudson Taylor felt he had no choice. 'To hesitate would be disobedience in me,' he confessed to Jennie. 'I am not praying now that he (BB) may stay, but that he may "be filled with the knowledge of God's will" and that (our) love may be deepened . . .' And then the disclosure of how far his thoughts had progressed: 'This Canadian Council is His will – and others like it He will give us unless I am greatly mistaken.' So it turned out. The first approaches from Australia came during 1889 and from Germany in 1890 and 1891.

In March 1889 the future was still veiled. Plainly he must get home to London, clear up the confusion, and be ready to appoint someone to succeed Benjamin if he could not be persuaded to stay. He himself felt it deeply and saw it all as a spiritual battle, a diabolical counter-attack. 'Satan is simply raging – he sees his kingdom attacked all over the land – and the conflict is awful.'[14]

Mary Stevenson was quieter when he wrote to ask Jennie to meet him in Paris as usual. But he was keyed up, under strain, hurrying through his letters before catching the midnight river steamer to Hankou, to go over the accounts with Broumton. Henry Frost had kept some prospective missionaries back from sailing, while the standing of the 'auxiliary' was under debate, and two men had turned to other missions. Were North Americans to be referred to London, he asked Hudson Taylor? What should he do?

> If you have any godly men fit for the work, *don't keep them back;* [Hudson Taylor replied] and if you have any suitable women and a suitable escort . . . *don't keep them back*. The Lord Himself, whose they are will care for them. The support of our missionaries is not dependent upon the existence of the China Inland Mission, but on the Word of the living God. [And on March 14, with plans to leave by German mail steamer in April] I am more than ever convinced that it is the will of God that our International Auxiliary (in North America) should exist and flourish . . .[15]

China and the work of God came first. Administrative niceties were subsidiary. But Hudson Taylor was already talking of an international CIM. 'These brave words were followed by a braver action,' Frost wrote. Hudson Taylor characteristically went to meet his opponents in person. And 'without further reference to the London Secretary or Council' Henry Frost sent off two more young women of whom Hudson Taylor had approved. Then he wrote, and his 'full explanations' to Benjamin 'were received in a most gracious spirit'.

Perhaps the gap was narrower than they thought. But the word was getting around that all was not well, and Hudson Taylor was alarmed. A frank explanation struck him as the best way to account for his abrupt return to Europe, and he hastily wrote a 'strictly private' letter to all members of the Mission. All too soon he was to regret it. Stress carries a red flag. Too often it leads to false moves.

The opening words betrayed his ruffled spirit. 'My dear Friends, A serious complication, involving very grave issues requires my immediate return to England.' After referring to events leading up to the time of writing, March 25, he described with undisguised feeling the steps leading to Benjamin's 'intention if (an auxiliary) were formed, of resigning his position as Secretary'. In normal circumstances he chose his words carefully. In this letter he laid bare the reasons why he himself was 'greatly distressed', going into far greater detail than the young majority of the Mission needed to know. He was writing, he said, to correct misunderstandings, and emphasised that the China Council agreed, the 'Toronto auxiliary' should be retained. It was so unlike him. It must have been plain to the discerning reader that this injudicious letter was written under exceptional strain.[16] So although it brought him candid rebukes from his friends, the warmth of their welcome surprised him when he got back to England.

He completed his work on the accounts and remittances with Broumton, spent a few days at Anqing in conference with William Cooper at the training school, returned to Shanghai for three days with the China Council, completed his work with David Cranston on the Wusong Road building plans and contracts[17] and sailed as planned, on April 12. Even on the steam launch going out to the liner he was dictating final messages. On board he wrote to John Stevenson whom he had just left. It would be good to appoint a peripatetic midwife for the confinements due in the north-west.

> Deal with and through our superintendents so as to make and keep them loyal and satisfied . . . And yet it will not do to lose the advantage of direct communication with the missionaries ourselves . . . Make (the superintendents) feel *you* are carrying out *their* views and wishes . . . We need *each* brother to recognise a *helper* in the one immediately over him, not a *master*, and all to feel they have this in you and me. [And, nearing Aden] Pray much for me: it is so solemn to feel one may go to war against the enemies of the Lord as Samson did, *unconscious* that the Lord has left one, to win defeat and captivity and blindness. May the Lord keep me and keep you very near to Himself.[18]

Did he fear that he had acted without the Lord's approval?

Theodore Howard wrote to greet him at Marseilles, opening his heart, like the true friend he was,

> Your letter (to the Mission) . . . came on me like a thunder clap. (The American issue had never been discussed at a Council meeting. And he himself could form no opinion without the relevant facts, though he considered Benjamin's arguments 'very weighty'.) He (Mr B) did not think of taking any action . . . during your absence . . . (or) contemplate retirement (before) the matter had been fully gone into. (How could Hudson Taylor treat it as a fait accompli and 'publish it abroad' without first doing all in his power to avert 'a most fatal and disastrous mistake'!) I have no doubt that some modus vivendi *can* be found . . . It is quite as certain . . . that God has given

you a most invaluable helper in Mr B . . . as it is that He has given you an auxiliary council in America . . . God only knows the whole-hearted devotion of Mr B to the work; wise, loving, careful, he binds it together, and keeps it together in such a way as no other man could do it. (He was 'over-pressed', and 'somewhat hasty' in expressing his views, but) you cannot, you must not think of losing (him) . . . the best helper God has given you. (Everyone shared this opinion, he went on. As for North America, Theodore Howard could not understand why the North American Council should not be independent of the CIM but affiliated like the Bible Christians. But) I shrink from the thought of setting up my judgment against that of a man of God at whose feet I willingly sit, and reverence almost with awe, but I would be unfaithful to my deepest convictions had I written otherwise.[19]

William Sharp wrote in similar vein. Both Hudson Taylor and Mr B had been too precipitate. 'Things have been written on both sides that should not have been written or even said, and we must all forget them, and unitedly press forward . . .'

After a night at William Berger's hospitable home at Cannes, Hudson Taylor went on to meet Jennie in Paris. But more plain speaking followed him from his faithful old friend. Hudson Taylor's attitude towards divine guidance was questionable and dangerous, he suggested 'a spirit of infatuation, claiming for yourself, shall I say it, divine and infallible guidance in the matter of the auxiliary'. As for personal relationships, William Berger continued, 'It takes two to make a quarrel . . . You are to all intents married to Mr B and cannot be divorced.' So he must not think of separating, but must find that modus vivendi.

Richard Hill went further. If Mr B was to be lost, he himself would resign as well. Charles Fishe was brief and to the point, 'No one will *hear* of BB going – Some modus vivendi *must be found*. It would be disaster for the Mission. It is *details* that need adjusting.'

'I reached England on May 21st (my birthday) and found the stone already rolled away,' Hudson Taylor reported to John Stevenson. Strong currents were as nothing where Christian love existed. Two evenings with Benjamin and the next day with the London Council giving an account of his tour in the States and Canada, and the clouds dispersed. At last they understood. Discussion of permanent arrangements was deferred until after the annual meeting. On June 18 it all ended amicably with the London Council accepting lock, stock and barrel Hudson Taylor's outline of the arrangements and status of the North American Council. Its duties were to be the same as the London Council's. It was to deal directly with the directors in China, not through London. Its funds would be distinct and its missionaries on the same footing as those from Britain. And they would be directed in China, not from America. What was left of the 'mare's nest'?

Benjamin had accepted the majority view. By common consent the modus vivendi was to be as Hudson Taylor had intended . . . He told John Stevenson, 'The Council have been very cordial . . . and I do not think BB will think again of leaving us.' 'Better arrangements have been introduced in the offices,' relieving the pressure on BB. And better still, on July 4, he could say of the disagreements over the P and P, 'All now cordially accepted' and being referred to the China Council for approval. A delightful letter was to be carried by Hudson Taylor 'from the London Council to the American Council . . . I do not think things have been so cordial for years.'[20]

Sound lessons had been learned – the inherent dangers in correspondence; the value of face to face courtesy and prayer together; the dangers of physical and mental exhaustion when matters of moment were under debate; and the truth that 'reckless words pierce like a sword' but 'love covers a multitude of sins'. If only that had been the end of disharmony. But 'the accuser of the brethren' (Rev. 12:10) had more mischief in mind.

The emperor takes over   *1889–92*

Thinking Chinese never forgot that the Manchus were aliens. Ci Xi was Empress Dowager of the Da Qing, of the Manchu dynasty rather than of the Chinese people. Ceaseless domestic intrigues and jockeying for influence among the imperial families and 'bannermen' were internal, and alien to Han Chinese, a nation apart. Secret societies dreamed of a Chinese dynasty restored, while Chinese serving in the highest ranks of government consciously waited for the dynasty to crumble. Some, such as Li Hongzhang, were faithful to the ruling power. In 1884 Ci Xi's edict about the critical state of affairs had admitted, 'There is chaos in the Government and a feeling of insecurity among the people.' As the last decade of the nineteenth century was reached, many saw the end approaching. Ill-omens multiplied. The rumblings of deep unrest began to break the surface, recognisably disguised as anti-foreign action, but designed to shake the dragon throne. It lacked only a clear

大清國當今聖母陛下慈禧端佑康頤昭豫莊誠壽恭欽獻崇熙皇太后

CI XI, EMPRESS DOWAGER, IN 1903

demonstration of the rulers' weakness to hasten the inexorable slide towards dissolution.

Ci Xi and her chosen courtiers clung tenaciously to the ancient ways, while the enlightened watched Japan's metamorphosis into a modern state with a new constitution, a constitutional monarchy, a Chamber of Peers and elected Diet (and religious liberty at last), and sought ways of emulating her. The Guang Xü emperor had come of age in 1887 but Ci Xi had not relinquished her command. Delicate as a child, nervous and retiring, with an air of great gentleness and intelligence, but always taught to regard Ci Xi's word as law, the emperor waited until he was 19 before assuming power, declaring the regency (of 1881–89) ended. Ci Xi had hated him with 'a terrible, relentless hatred' since he spurned the bride she had foisted upon him. She retired to the Palace of Tranquil Old Age, fully intending to wield power as before. He could play the emperor in minor matters while still in duty bound to *ketou* to her as the most senior in the dynastic hierarchy.

She rebuilt the Summer Palace, burned out by the French and Lord Elgin's troops in 1860, using funds from the imperial treasury allocated to the navy Li Hongzhang had been commissioned to build up. No empress in the history of China was so pampered and luxuriously served by her attendant eunuchs. Li Lianying, her chief

THE GUANG XÜ EMPEROR BEFORE THE COUP

eunuch, said of her when her prayers to the Buddha appeared to end a great drought, 'It is as though she were Buddha herself.' The court were amused and quickly the habit spread through China of good-humouredly referring to her as 'Old Buddha'.[21]

Guang Xü had listened to people of liberal views, and knew that modernisation was China's only hope. The great famine had shown the urgent need of rapid means of bulk transport. A demonstration railway line from the Dagu forts to Tianjin had been followed by Zhang Zhitong's proposal, endorsed by Li Hongzhang, that Peking and Hankou be linked by a strategic direct line. Guang Xü gave them his support, and appointed Zhang Zhitong viceroy of Hubei, Hunan and Anhui. He held this vital post for eighteen years, 1889–1907, the key to the opening of Hunan to foreigners, and to the safety of the Yangzi valley in the terrors of 1900. Zhang, the beneficent governor of Shanxi in the great 1877–79 famine (HTCOC Book 6, pp 165–87), had taken up Timothy Richard's far-seeing advice. On August 27, 1889, the emperor signed an edict:

> The Sovereign is of the opinion that to make a country powerful railways are essential, but recognising that at the outset the people will have doubts and suspicions, orders the governors and viceroys of Zhili, Henan and Hubei to issue explanatory proclamations, exhorting and commanding them to throw no impediments in the way. It is the Imperial desire that all shall work together to make this great work a success.[22]

Guang Xü's reforms had begun, but even Li Hongzhang had qualms. He had employed foreign civil engineers to close the Yellow River dikes, and had become financially involved in the railway projects. When the Tianjin railway was declared open a palace gate had been burned down. What if a new Yellow River flood or a fire in the palace took place? Instead, the Temple of Heaven, jewel of Peking, went up in flames. The circular pavilion in three tiers, roofed with azure tiles of the finest porcelain clay, under which the dragon throne itself was placed when the emperor worshipped Heaven, had 'illuminated the whole sky' in its agony.[23] A shudder ran throughout China. The omen was conclusive. The emperor was doomed. But a great deal was to happen and Guang Xü was to live another nineteen years before Ci Xi's final act of premeditated evil fulfilled the prediction. For a while he had the cultured friendship and instruction of Zeng Guofan's remarkable son, 'Marquis Zeng', Chinese minister to France, Russia and then the Court of St James, before becoming a member of the Zongli Yamen, the Peking Foreign Office.

Viceroy Zhang Zhitong opened an imperial iron foundry at Hanyang (across the Han River from Hankou), as Li had opened his shipyard, naval college, engineering works in Shanghai and Tianjin, and cotton mills. The old issue of *fengshui* (Glossary, p 19; HTCOC Book 4, Appendix 8) again proved amenable to the profit motive. And the emperor went so far as to declare himself friendly towards foreigners, and ready to receive foreign envoys in audience. 'The modern movement' in China had begun. He kept his word on March 5, 1891.

Whether or not there were direct links or causes, May and June of the same year were to see anti-foreign riots in several places in Jiangsu and along the Yangzi Valley, and at Nanjing, Wuhu, Wuxüe and Hanyang, and at Yichang in September 1891 and November 1892. On June 5, 1981, a Wesleyan missionary named Argent and a customs officer, Green, were murdered apparently without reason. J K Fairbank explained: 'There is evidence that the Yangtze Valley riots of 1891 were fomented in part by disgruntled secret society members whose aim was not to do injury to Christians, but to bring down the dynasty by forcing it into conflict with the Western powers.'[24]

At the same time vigilant Chinese were all too aware of the circle of steel and fire surrounding their country and pressing ever closer – France and Britain in the south, Japan in the east and Russia in the north and west. The Trans-Caspian railway to Bokhara and Samarkand facilitated fresh encroachments on Chinese Turkestan; and the Trans-Siberian railway was under construction, with a southward line through Alma Ata, a blatant strategic threat to China, however necessary to Russia's southern states. A resurgence of vile accusations from Hunan moved the emperor to prohibit all anti-foreign publications, by an edict on May 21, 1892. Significantly, Hudson Taylor with his ear to the ground, in constantly close relations with Chinese, referred from time to time to the 'eve of revolution', the possible imminence of an outright rebellion.

Henry W Frost: man of faith　　　　　　　　*July–December 1889*

With the London Council apparently satisfied, and a genial letter of greeting to the North American Council in Hudson Taylor's pocket, the time had come to put matters over there on to a secure footing. Throughout June he had had a ceaseless succession of business and speaking engagements, and a good friend in Liverpool, Stephen Menzies, undertook to book his Atlantic passage for him. When Cunard told Menzies that intermediate-class cabins could not be reserved, he returned Hudson Taylor's cheque, claiming the privilege of himself meeting the cost of 'cabin-class' accommodation. So instead of tight-packed austerity between decks Hudson Taylor found himself travelling first class (July 6–14) and arrived rested and ready for thirty-four days of non-stop work, his prime purpose being to meet the provisional council and work out permanent arrangements for Canada and the States. He also addressed forty meetings in eighteen different places, most of them those he had been to in 1888. Travelling the long distances between cities afforded time for correspondence.[25]

The timing of his visit coincided roughly with that of the year before. From New York, met by Henry Frost's father, he travelled to Attica for three days' consultation with Henry. Then together to the conference at Niagara-on-the-Lake where the members of the provisional council assembled to meet him. The most urgent matter was quickly resolved. A joint council for Canada and the United States was formally instituted, and the decision taken to base the Mission in Toronto.[26] A full-time secretary-treasurer was needed to handle the growing business affairs of the Mission in North America, and Henry Weston Frost's suitability for the post no one doubted. But it would mean his leaving Attica with his wife and three children, and moving to Toronto, in rented quarters with no fixed salary. Nor would they have a buoyant organisation behind them. In effect, in North America they themselves would to a large extent be the China Inland Mission, looking to God alone for the funds and wisdom, judgment in selecting and training candidates, and ability to submit the right matters to the council for advice. Until then, 'First in business life and then [after becoming an evangelist] through my father, all our wants had been supplied.' Now Hudson Taylor could only give him $250 towards the expense of moving to Toronto, and the few small sums he had in hand. Otherwise he would have 'only the Lord' to look to, for his father and brother had fallen upon hard times – bought out of their railroad business by an unscrupulous take-over. The means of livelihood could no longer come from them. And most North American missionaries were individually supported by their churches. No comforting 'general fund' could be drawn upon, least of all from London. Henry Frost and his wife faced a supreme test of faith.[27]

A scrap of reminiscence remains to throw light on the days at Niagara. Captain the Hon R Moreton, who had followed William Pennefather at the Mildmay Conference Centre, was presiding at a conference session addressed by Hudson Taylor on Solomon and the Queen of Sheba. Dr A T Pierson, the expositor, sitting beside Moreton, slapped him on the knee as Hudson Taylor finished, and said, 'Did you ever hear anything so profound? Wonderful!' A week later at Clifton Springs the audience contained leaders of several denominational missions, when he spoke on the same subject. It gave them the opportunity to ask him in depth about the CIM and his principles. Their missions were sending abroad few unordained men, except medicals, and most of what they knew about the CIM was hearsay. 'Dr Clark of the American Board, Dr Ellinwood of the American Presbyterian Mission, Dr Reed of the American Episcopal Mission (and others) were all there.' 'They all expressed themselves as greatly relieved of misapprehensions and left I believe in real sympathy – an object worth the whole journey.'[28]

In August, Hudson Taylor and Frost met members of the council in long morning and afternoon business sessions at Toronto. Frost then returned home to Attica while Hudson Taylor spent a long weekend at Moody's Northfield conference, and met Susie Parker's parents again (p 86), none of them yet knowing that she had died of 'malignant fever' (or 'typhoid') at Guiqi in Jiangxi. The news was on its way. When it reached them her father said, 'It is still true. Nothing is too precious for my Lord Jesus' – even if their one remaining child were to take Susie's place. The good work must go on. Moody offered his 'Northfield Hotel' during the winter as a training home for CIM candidates with a month of teaching on the Bible to be given by himself and Dr Pierson.

In Attica Henry Frost and his wife were contemplating another revolution in their way of life. One day a heavy plaster ceiling in their home had fallen, harming no one but revealing the danger if other ceilings were as insecure. They had replaced them all, adding to the attractions of their home. Faced with leaving it, they happened to be praying in separate rooms when the words of Haggai 1:4 came to her with startling relevance, 'Is it a time for you, O ye, to dwell in your ceiled houses, and this house lies waste?' She took her Bible and laid it open on Henry's lap. 'From that moment . . . there was never a doubt in her heart or in mine . . .' For the sake of God's spiritual house in China they made the decision to leave Attica and take what God might give them in Toronto, as soon as Hudson Taylor had gone back to Britain.

During the month together Hudson Taylor and Frost had interviewed and accepted five men for China, and received donations for the Mission amounting to about $4,700, the Niagara conference contributing even more generously than in the previous year. A gift of $1,000 to Hudson Taylor personally he also handed over to Henry.[29] William Gooderham made available the top storey of his Christian Institute in Toronto for offices, and 30 Shuter Street was rented as a home for the Frosts and candidates coming for interviews or preparing to leave for China. So began the saga described in the Howard Taylors' biography of Henry Frost, and in David Michell's new history of the Mission in North America.

Fifty million families?   *September–October 1889*

The imperial edict on railways was promulgated on August 27 (three days after Hudson Taylor landed again at Liverpool). The news of it and the razing of the Temple of Heaven was common property in September. The events of this autumn and winter and Hudson Taylor's vision for the future were therefore against the backdrop of new liberal trends in China, and of the ominous warnings of trouble to come. The whole scale of his thinking had undergone a change.

Writing to Jennie as he left England on July 6 he had said,

> Darling, I do want our whole life to be an ascending plane – not resting in anything we have learned or felt or attained, but a pressing on and up . . .
> What would a Sovereign think of a proposal to add one hundred soldiers in the course of a year to his army of invasion in a country like China? We must get on to a higher plane of thought altogether, and of prayer, if we are to . . . deal in any sensible way with the world's crying need.[30]

God save us from pettiness when vision is needed. 'Expect great things from God. Attempt great things for God' were Carey's words in 1792, a century before. Bolder thinking was needed. He felt 'in his bones' the stirrings of new developments. His immediate concern was to have the right men and women for each and every department of the Mission in the homelands and China. An uphill struggle against incompetence, wrong attitudes and unspiritual mediocrity could end with really good people – Stevensons, Henry Frosts, Dorwards, Coopers – in positions of influence and action.

'An enduement of power' in place of shallow consecration would be effective against 'the one, united, combined front of the flesh, the world and the devil.' Even the rapid growth of the CIM had come to seem paltry against the immensity of China and her spiritual need, and of the world. The last thing he wanted was a great unwieldy, bureaucratic CIM. But if all the societies increased their numbers and dedication, their common goal would be attainable. The untapped potential in America had fired his imagination again. After his return home his thoughts continued on this trend.

In 1888 Howard Taylor had relieved his father of the tiring and time-consuming petty affairs of travelling – packing, searching timetables, buying tickets, finding the way, or food and drink. They had grown together as never before, to Hudson Taylor's deep joy. Howard had just ended his year of medical and surgical appointments, and was taking three months to travel and work with his father before tackling the highest postgraduate examinations. So they gave September and October to England and Scotland, and November to Scandinavia.[31]

During his absence from the country, Hudson Taylor had heard from the ageing William Berger of his intention to give £4,000 to set up a superannuation fund 'for decayed, aged and retired CIM missionaries, and to give us £3,000, life interest to us, and then to our children equally divided'.[32] His old friend was thinking constantly of how to help the Mission before his own life ended. Nor could he forget the hardships and long separations suffered by the Taylor children. He wrote from experience of successful management of his manufacturing firm suggesting principles and practical details which could be applied to the CIM: sufficient office space, sufficient staff and well-defined division of labour; reward according to responsibility and capability; 9.30 am to 5.30 pm with an hour off at midday as the extreme demand on his employees; overtime compensated by early release on another day; everything 'to secure a real interest and pleasure in work'; heads of department not doing what a junior could do; promotion whenever possible, to encourage all to do their best, the right complement of the CIM's austerity and self-denial.

Then he went on: Hudson Taylor should provide for the CIM to continue if he himself should 'be taken'. It was time for the Mission to be incorporated by deed poll, with clearly stated procedures for appointing his successor if one had not by then been chosen. Aware that disharmony had arisen largely through overwork in China and London, Hudson Taylor was open to advice, and found to his delight that Benjamin and the London Council were 'equally prepared to go any length with me in reorganisation'. The only difficulty lay in finding the right people.

His letters to John Stevenson reflected the issues each was facing. Cecil Polhill-Turner must be given his head soon or he would be lost altogether. He was champing at the bit to get closer to Tibet. Annie Taylor had been home on leave and was in India for six or twelve months to find a way to Lhasa, starting from Darjeeling. A rash of threatened resignations and misdemeanours led him to advise, 'Go and talk with them if you can. If not, send for them to come and talk with you. Let them *see* that you do not lack sympathy, that you are with them in their troubles.' 'It is a far greater triumph for Christ to put a man right than to get rid of him.' Rather than accept resignations easily, persuade them to wait until Hudson Taylor returned. 'Though we cannot scold people right, we may often love them into right.'[33] Recognise spiritual warfare and win a way through by spiritual means. Time and again the myth of Hudson Taylor being authoritarian is shown as in this context to be hollow. Their use of a popular code for long-distance cables ('Unicode') appears increasingly: '*amabilis*': 'assistance is urgently required' was often used.

He formed a 'Ladies Council' which met for the first time on September 23, 1889, to help with the assessment of women for China. Recognising the close involvement of the wives of council members, the first to be appointed were Mrs Theodore Howard, Mrs Sharp, Jennie and Amelia.[34] Henrietta Soltau was asked to serve as secretary for women candidates, and then to run a women's training home. While he was in Glasgow, September 21–30, he formed an auxiliary council for Scotland under Provost John Colville, to handle all Scottish candidates. This was the occasion of the well-known story of J Elder Cumming's train journey with Hudson Taylor.

> I ventured to say that he must often have felt the wonderful honour that God had put upon him as the founder of the Mission . . . He turned to me, and with a voice trembling with suppressed feeling said he sometimes thought that God must have looked . . . to find

someone weak enough to do such a work, so that none of the glory could go to the man himself . . .

In (another) long railway journey he was very silent, but at the close he said to a companion . . . that he was constantly occupied and had no time to rest. His companion said, 'Come now, you have had two or three hours now without anything to do.' . . . 'I do not know what you call rest [Hudson Taylor answered] . . . Since I entered this carriage I have prayed by name for every missionary in the CIM' . . . some hundreds.[35]

He and his son Howard were back for a London Council meeting on October 2, to discuss the duration of a term of service overseas before home leave would be justified. Acknowledging exceptional circumstances of ill-health and obligations to parents, Hudson Taylor considered ten years a reasonable span for the physically fit. 'While the rule is ten years for those in good health, not a few have returned within six or eight years, and some earlier.' Reason not rigidity governed the issue. To a mother he explained, 'If each missionary came home at the end of ten years and spent one year in England . . . more than one-fifth of the whole sum available for the support of missionaries would be spent on furlough and the passages to and fro. In point of fact the actual expense is much greater . . . and donors might with reason complain . . . were it increased.'[36]

On Sunday, October 6, they were in Hastings, spending Jennie's forty-sixth birthday with her father Joseph (Wm) Faulding. Hudson Taylor was mulling over the subject for his editorial in the December issue of *China's Millions* – that 'higher plane' of thought than even one hundred new missionaries a year for China's multiplying millions. A nagging question troubled him. The Lord's 'Great Commission' and last command, 'Go into all the world, and preach the gospel to every creature' was plain enough, but 'What did our Lord *really mean* by His command . . . ?' The CIM had enlarged from 91 members in 1880 to over 300, reaching an ever-increasing number of cities with a corresponding increase in the number of believing Chinese. But of China's 250 millions (at the most conservative estimate since recent holocausts), how many had heard 'the gospel' even once, or ever would?

In 1877 the General Missionary Conference in Shanghai had called for 'the Christian Church to evangelise China in the present generation', even in the present century. Half the time had gone and not one hundredth of the population had been given the gospel. In A T Pierson's words, Christ's command had 'laid the responsibility on the Church of each successive generation to give the gospel to each individual living in its own period'; Not to Christianise the nation or to convert everyone, but 'to give them the gospel', the gospel that the apostles preached, 'that Christ died for our sins according to the Scriptures, that he was buried, that he was raised on the third day' and that 'By this gospel you are saved . . .' (I Cor. 15:1–4). Not 'another gospel' of 'social uplift', or adapted Confucian precepts, but 'Christ and him crucified'. Jesus said it, so he meant it. It could be done. But *how*? Hudson Taylor asked himself. 'Baptise and teach' were another matter, the next phase. Then why did Jesus not say *how* every man, woman and child was to be told the gospel?

At last he understood. There was no mystery. Difficulty lay only in regarding his words as unreasonable. They were not. 'There is no impossibility in our Lord's command.' Obey! Do it! Stop thinking, 'We will not have this man to *reign* over us.' Do what he said. It was mathematically practicable.

Consider, as an oversimplified example to illustrate the fact, that the average family in China, a nation of families, numbered five. Then the nation would consist of roughly fifty million families. And 'a large proportion of Chinese live in courts or quadrangles containing from four to ten families each'. A thousand evangelists on a thousand working days (call it three years) could each day visit and present the gospel in ten or twenty such homes or to their equivalents on the streets and market-places. How much more in five, or ten years. It was already being done on a small scale. So in the decade remaining of the nineteenth century, and allowing for other demands on time, missionaries and Chinese Christians together could at least give the whole nation an opportunity to hear the gospel put simply but intelligibly to them.

But was there the will to do what could be done, allowing for the fact that many existing missionaries were committed to established institutions and could not be released? To supplement those familiar with China and the language who could concentrate on evangelism, it would not be too much for Europe to send five hundred more – only one hundred from each main denomination with their thousands of ordained men and more thousands of lay men and women. They would soon be replaced. Scandinavia and the continent had made a beginning. Britain had risen to the challenge several times already and would do so again. North America was already responding with thousands of college students pledging themselves to be missionaries 'if God opened the way'. This was realism, not a pipe dream.

What then should be done? 1. Christ's answer was firstly, pray that he would send them out; 2. 'united, simultaneous action by the whole body' of Christians would bring the fullest results; 3. intelligent co-operation, comity, in deploying across the whole of China would avoid any region's being neglected and duplication in others, already a serious problem; 4. 'Christly giving' by churches and individuals in support of their missions, in the sense of Christ's example, emptying himself, working and suffering to achieve what he came to earth to do; 5. immediate action: pray for '1000 evangelists for China' without loss of time.

This article 'Every Creature' and two more in succeeding issues of the *Millions* he published in booklet form, *To Every Creature*, to be distributed far beyond the 20,000 circulation of *China's Millions*. It quickly sold out and was reprinted. Churches and societies of all kinds would read this opening salvo of what developed into a continuous campaign. Objections were raised, of course, and in reply he cited example after example of conversions through one hearing or reading of the gospel, sometimes from posters left on village walls. But that was not the point. He proposed seed sowing. Reaping would follow. 'Some thirty, some a hundred fold' depended on where the seed fell. 'If one offer of the gospel is insufficient, what shall we think of *none*?' But responsible evangelism was what he had in mind, the preachers spending time in a locality, available to build on impressions made, and if possible returning time and again. A valuable by-product of itineration was thorough knowledge of the country, with a view to the best choice of where eventually to base more settled work.[37]

As one of the senior veterans in China, Hudson Taylor had been invited to give the keynote address at the Third General Missionary Conference at Shanghai in May. He knew now what he would say. J K Fairbank wrote of 'Taylor's organisation taking the lead' in the missionary cause from early on, even before the Chefoo Convention of 1876. It had fallen to their lot again.

The first associate missions   *1887–1915*

A spate of new missionary societies springing up in Europe around this time owed their origins in part to Hudson Taylor's personal influence and in part to his articles and booklet, *To Every*

Creature. The Swedish American, Fredrik Franson, who played so big a part, did so by taking up and pressing home this message among Scandinavians especially. A call from the Shanghai conference of missionary societies in 1890 served to add impetus to what had already begun.

Louise Desgraz of the *Lammermuir* party, a Swiss, was the first full member of the CIM from Continental Europe; and the first individual associate was Erik Folke of the Swedish Mission in China. But the first associate mission, the Bible Christian Mission, who paved the way in 1884, created such a good impression that Hudson Taylor had no qualms about co-operating with any other society which could accept the CIM's Principles and Practice as the basis for association, and himself as their director in China. The Church Army enquired about associate status, but went no further. And the Quaker 'Friends' sent their first missionary to China in 1883 under the CIM's wing in Sichuan, but without formal connections. Each associate mission sprang from spiritual movements of the kind familiar to Hudson Taylor, being concerned to foster a closer personal relationship between each individual Christian and the Lord, 'the deepening of spiritual life'.

The Bible Christian Mission had strong roots. In 1815 the Anglican curate of Shebbear in North Devon brought together Christians, regardless of denomination, to learn from the Bible how to please God. But those who formed the Bible Christian Society in a Shebbear kitchen were predominantly Wesleyan Methodists.[38] In May 1884 some of them attended an undenominational conference for the enrichment of spiritual life at Newport, Isle of Wight. As it happened, most of the speakers and participants were Anglicans, but Hudson Taylor 'was given two sessions to speak on China's millions'. 'With a map before him on a scale that almost extended to the width of the wall . . . he passed from province to province of the Empire with the facility of long familiarity, and with a wealth of graphic detail such as no other European living could probably have given.'

The Bible Christians had begun in 1821 to send missionaries to Canada, Australia and New Zealand. What they heard and learned by questioning Hudson Taylor convinced them that they could send and support men in China also. When he and 'Benjamin B' attended their annual conference at Hoxton (near Pyrland Road), on August 4, 1884, he 'fanned the missionary enthusiasm of the Conference to white heat'. They agreed with Hudson Taylor that 'the apostolic plan was not to raise ways and means, but to go, and do the work'. Two young ministers, Samuel Thomas Thorne and Thomas Grills Vanstone, were 'set apart' for Yunnan province on Hudson Taylor's recommendation. There were Methodists of the CIM already at Chongqing, Guiyang and Kunming. But the whole north-eastern region of Yunnan between Guizhou and the upper reaches of the Yangzi River (the River of Gold) had no one, from Kunming through Dongchuan and Zhaotong as far as the Sichuan border near Yibin.

As well as Chinese, hundreds of thousands of aboriginal tribesmen, Miao (Hmong) and Nosu, peopled the hills. No one had yet taken the gospel to them. Across the provincial border with Guizhou they extended in millions to where the CIM were preaching to them in the region of Guiyang and Anshun. And across the River of Gold, the Jinjiang, at least a million more 'wild, independent, Nosu' inhabited the Daliangshan, 'the Great Cold Mountains' of Colborne Baber's and George Nicoll's epic travels in 1877.[39]

The Bideford conference 'subscribed £700 in a few minutes' to send Thorne and Vanstone off on November 4, 1884, with John Stevenson, Hope Gill and others of the CIM. 'And I shall be the next', a Shebbear man in London, Samuel Pollard, wrote to his parents. Francis John Dymond then offered to go with him, and in 1886 they were commissioned together – two of the most outstanding missionaries to China. They sailed with three of the CIM Hundred on January 27, 1887, and were taught Chinese under Frederick Baller at the Anqing language school. Baller was impressed. He watched them closely and declared them 'good pioneers'.

A model relationship existed between the Bible Christian Mission and the CIM. Vanstone and Thorne, Pollard and Dymond fitted in ideally. Sam Pollard had 'the heart of a troubadour and carolled gaily as he walked the highway of life . . . buoyant, full of initiative and enterprise'. Dymond and Pollard 'incited and braced each other, faced death together, nursed each other through sickness, and one [eventually] buried the other'. They were wrecked on the way up the Yangzi gorges. 'He who has seen the corpses floating down the swift current, and watched brave men struggle for their lives . . . and then go under, knows . . . More than once that all-devouring Tiger River has almost captured me.' They were posted to Zhaotong but alternated with Thorne and Vanstone at

Kunming as part of the CIM team, working the cities between. 'What a lot of light these people received (from Confucius); but what little influence it has had on their hearts,' Pollard wrote.

Dymond went down with smallpox, nursed by Pollard. When death seemed close they took the Lord's Supper together, but Pollard wept and Dymond finished saying the words for him. Far from friends, not knowing how to arrange for a grave, Pollard faced a nightmare experience. But Dymond recovered, married one of the first women pioneers to Yunnan, and became the father-in-law of J O Fraser, apostle of the ethnic Lisu. Again and again Thorne and Vanstone and other Bible Christians as they joined the first four, fell ill with malaria. John Carter died of dysentery in 1890; Thorne of malaria in 1891. Pollard went to help and himself contracted malaria, running a high fever on his way to marry Emily Hainge, another of the CIM Hundred. On their return from Sichuan (December 4, 1891) they made Zhaotong their base. The sight of 'the Mountains of the Manzi' (the Wild Men) made him long 'to spend a month among them'. Twelve years later, in November 1903, a Nosu chief took him in, but only for a week or ten days.[40] Instead the subjugated Nosu and Miao of the Yunnan-Guizhou border hills captured his affections. From July 1904 a 'mass movement' with its centre at 'Stone Gateway' (Shimenkan) occupied all his energies, and (Frank) Dymond buried him there in 1915.

Dymond wrote to Hudson Taylor on September 5, 1890, 'You have so won our hearts that I think we feel more CIM than anything else.' He proposed to make his base at one city after another, itinerating for one or two months at a stretch and returning to base for two weeks – precisely what Hudson Taylor was advocating and admired in Benjamin Ririe at Jiading in West Sichuan, and Botham on the Shaanxi plains. To his regret, the Bible Christian Mission's leaders later changed their policy and withdrew from association with the CIM, but the model of marriage between two missions set a pattern for future developments.

By then Scandinavian, German and other associate missions were finding their feet in several provinces. Associate members of the CIM were as much part of the CIM as were the full members. Their superintendents became members of the China Council. Their contribution to the life of the CIM made it what it became. Twentieth-century members saw almost no distinction, feeling as much one with the multinational associates as with the full members from the same European and North American countries. The difference lay only in the 'sending societies' they belonged to. But at this level it was Hudson Taylor and John Stevenson who suffered the vicissitudes of a growing variety of associate missions.

The European associate missions · *1889–99*

In the eventful years that lay ahead, and the Boxer nightmare especially, the Continental arm of the CIM was to play a major part. An all-too-short outline of its origins must replace the full chapter it deserves, but later pages will put flesh on these bare bones.

Two years passed after Hudson Taylor's consultations with Josef Holmgren of Örebro and Stockholm about the Swedish Mission in China (pp 56, 57). Erik Folke of Uppsala University made a good beginning at the Anqing language school and then in Shanxi, and three others joined him in the far south-western Yüncheng region of the province. In Sweden the committee wanted closer ties with Hudson Taylor and the CIM, and invited him to Stockholm. So on November 1, 1889, he and his son Howard crossed the North Sea to 'Gothenburg' and a welcome in Sweden that outshone all he had ever experienced. They addressed two thousand people at a meeting the same day, with Josef Holmgren as their interpreter, and found wherever they went throughout the month that audiences numbering 'two to five thousand daily' were to be expected. They spoke at Helsingborg, Copenhagen and Malmö at the southern tip of Sweden before separating. While Howard went to Lund and spoke five times at Linköping, Hudson Taylor went via Tranas and Norrköping to rejoin him at Linköping.

Howard had crowned his postgraduate studies with three high honours and the launching on October 15, 1889, at a Missionary Convention with C H Spurgeon in the chair, of the 'Students Foreign Missionary Union'. More than 1,500 students attended, and 152 signed the pledge, 'It is my earnest hope, if God permit, to engage in foreign missionary work.' The first name in the book of members reads, 'Taylor, F Howard, MD, MRCP, FRCS (England), the London Hospital.'[41]

Then father and son together worked through ten more towns including Jonköping on the way to Stockholm. At fifty-seven Hudson Taylor no longer enjoyed the vigour he had once had, and soon felt weary, but everywhere the enthusiasm bore him along. His insistence on not being lionised, on travelling third class and carrying his own suitcase, left a deeper impression 'than his faith in God'.[42]

An audience of 3,500 in Stockholm and a private 'Bible reading' (on 1 Kings 10) with Queen Sophia and four of her ladies-in-waiting at the palace[43] were the highlights of three days in conference with the committee of the Swedish Mission in China. Working point by point through the Principles and Practice of the CIM, discussing their meaning and implications – not least the wisdom of delaying marriage for two years of adaptation to China – an historic decision was reached. Instead of Folke and his companions being individually associate members of the CIM in China, the Swedish Mission itself was to be an Associate Mission in alliance with the CIM as a whole. Within the next five years one hundred Swedish men and women offered and twenty-one were judged suitable to go in this mission alone.

After the friendly informality of the hour with the queen came

FREDRIK FRANSON, SWEDISH EVANGELIST AND
FOUNDER OF MISSIONS
(by courtesy of TEAM)

another drawing-room meeting 'with the nurses (all titled ladies) at the Queen's Hospital'. Father and son could hardly tear themselves away to catch the train to Uppsala for a weekend of appointments, before going on to 'Christiania' (as Oslo was still called) for the rest of the week. Even before reaching Norway Hudson Taylor estimated that in twenty-four towns and cities they had addressed fifty thousand 'probably over 60,000'. Only three meetings, including the queen's, had been in English.

In 1879 Reginald Radcliffe had awakened Norwegian interest in foreign missions. A leading businessman, named Rasmussen, and his family at Kristiansand on the southern tip of Norway came to be closely linked with the CIM.[44] Four years later, in 1883, the Swedish evangelist, Fredrik Franson (1852–1908), when travelling widely in Europe addressed meetings in the Rasmussen home. Two or three of the daughters eventually became missionaries in China, but their governess, Sophie Reuter (who married Stanley Smith), and a housemaid, Anna Jakobsen, whom we shall meet as a Hunan pioneer, went to England in 1884 and sailed on November 18, 1885, as full members of the CIM. Two years later a committee was formed to help Norwegian missionaries already in China and to send others. The chairman and treasurer of this Norwegian Mission in China[45] was Captain Hans Guldberg, a riding-master.

From Christiania, Hudson Taylor and Howard went south to Kristiansand for five meetings arranged by the Rasmussens, but formal association of the Norwegian Mission (as such) with the CIM appears to have followed some years later. In effect, although not in name, these Scandinavian missions became 'branches' of the CIM. Their members shared all the facilities and benefits of full members. In contrast, the British, North American and later the Australasian councils were established in consultation with Hudson Taylor as integral parts of the CIM.

Fredrik Franson had studied D L Moody's methods since 1875 and spent six years in evangelism in the States, but with a growing concern for the wider world he had then returned to Europe, 'more to harvest than to sow. Tens of thousands in Sweden heard him preach and thousands came to personal faith in Christ.' After four years in Scandinavia he moved on to Germany, Switzerland, France and Italy.

At Barmen he found Christians whose hearts were already 'aflame' with concern for China, and his own 'burning message on China's need' so fanned the flames that a Deutsche-China-Allianz

Mission was proposed. When the December issue of *China's Millions* arrived, and Hudson Taylor's booklet, *To Every Creature*, calling for a thousand new missionaries (evidence that they were subscribers?), they wrote to the London Council asking whether the German China Alliance could enter into the same relationship with the CIM as the Swedish and Norwegian Missions in China had established.[46] Fredrik Franson and his Swedish fellow-evangelist Emmanuel Olsson, who hoped to be one of the thousand, went over to England to discuss plans with the London Council on June 2, 1890, and were promised all possible help. A third associate mission of the CIM was the outcome, and its first three missionaries, led by Olsson, of the Swedish Holiness Union, set foot in China on December 3, 1890.

They joined the CIM team at Baotou on the Mongolian Yellow River border of Shanxi (now deep in Inner Mongolia). When Hudson Taylor visited Sweden again in 1896, the Swedish Holiness Union accepted responsibility for the region between the two arms of the Great Wall.[47] The snowball was gathering snow, and China receiving a succession of fine evangelists.

Thoroughly international   *1890–1951*

Once the willingness of the CIM to foster like-minded but inexperienced missions became known, leaders in other European countries approached Hudson Taylor. Fredrik Franson returned to the States on September 7, 1890, and announced a brief course of teaching on evangelism at Brooklyn in mid-October. In it he commended Hudson Taylor's concept of a thousand evangelists for China, and of the fifty attending the course about twenty volunteered to go at short notice, as members of an 'expedition' to leave at the end of January 1891. More eleven-day courses followed at Chicago, Minneapolis and Omaha, and he published an article on November 25 setting out his ideas for an Alliance Mission of Scandinavians from America. The title, *China's Millions*, and the aim, 'to concentrate on the evangelisation of China within three years', under Hudson Taylor's leadership while responsible to the church sending them, were loosely based on Hudson Taylor's original article.

Thirty-five were chosen to leave on January 17 as the first expedition, and fifteen more to follow on the 29th. Further courses followed during 1891, and twelve more men and women went to

China on February 14, 1892. Other expeditions went to Japan, the Himalayas, South Africa and elsewhere, all under what Franson named The Scandinavian Alliance Mission – afterwards known as The Evangelical Alliance Mission (TEAM), an associate mission of the CIM until 1951 when China closed its gates to foreigners again.[48]

When Franson arrived at New York in September 1890 he met A B Simpson, who had started an International Alliance Mission in 1881. (It became the Christian and Missionary Alliance – C & MA – in 1897.) Franson offered to find two hundred recruits for this society, and returned to Scandinavia for the purpose. By the spring of 1893, forty-five had arrived in China in two parties (unconnected with the CIM). Sixteen more members of the International Missionary Alliance joined them in 1894, and eventually extended their field from Kalgan to Ningxia. The area was vast, but the overlapping of new societies without comity agreements or experienced missionaries to guide them led inevitably to difficulties, exacerbated by the failure of funds to reach some of the late arrivals. With hard-earned experience, however, a strong and effective mission developed.

Seven other European associate missions come into the picture here, for their roots can be traced to this period, although some matured later. (Appendix 5.) In 1891 a German pastor, H Koerper, read Hudson Taylor's *Retrospect*, and spoke on his life and work at a Student Volunteer Conference at Frankfurt in 1892. This led to Hudson Taylor himself being invited to the 1893 conference and another at Blankenburg (the German 'Keswick') in 1896. As a result on June 27, 1896, some of these German friends were present at the CIM Saturday prayer-meeting in London when Hudson Taylor arrived unannounced from China and quietly took a seat at the back. The emotional welcome he was given when his presence became known so confirmed the visitors in their impressions of the CIM that the Liebenzell Mission was constituted in 1897 as 'an integral part' or 'branch' of the CIM. It became an associate mission in 1906, when members were also sent to the Caroline Islands of the Pacific.[49]

The grand old man, C F Spittler, who had supplied the impetus in the founding of the Basel Missionary Society (circa 1815), also established the Pilgrim Mission in 1840 at St Chrischona outside Basel.[50] By 1915 it had about eighty of its own evangelists and had provided about nine hundred missionaries worldwide. The first formal link with the CIM was in 1895, when a Pilgrim missionary went to China as the first full member. Two years later (February 1897) Hudson Taylor was travelling from Cannes to Hamburg via Nice and Basel when, through not knowing that his connection at Basel was from a different station, he missed his train and found he had six hours to spare. He went up to St Chrischona on its hilltop and made himself known. The 'poverty and simplicity' observed on principle by St Chrischona and the CIM became a natural bond to strengthen ties between the two societies.[51]

One by one these associate missions multiplied until the inescapable transmutation of the CIM into an international society was seen to have come only just in time. The experience of a mature organisation was essential to the reception and initiation of the scores of raw evangelists, the thousand, so soon to arrive in China. The 'incurable idiot' of just twenty years before (HTCOC 5, p 198) had made his point.

PART 2

THE ADVERSARY

1889–95

CHAPTER FOUR

THE ULTIMATE AUTHORITY?
1889–90

Turbulence in China *1889–90*

The steady advance of missions in China often fortified Hudson Taylor when events close at hand were unsettling. He basked in the knowledge that whatever the risks and setbacks, the grousing or failure of the very few, the main body of missionaries battled on steadily. As father of the mission family it was for him to step in where necessary. Some excelled, showing initiative, courage and qualities of leadership and faithfulness to God and the Mission. Ones and twos failed to learn enough Chinese, or in a strange and often trying environment showed traits of personality unrecognised at home, and had to be sent back. Most disappointing were those who 'did run well' and out of pride or under harmful influences became hostile or power-seekers. A few lone wolves worked well without colleagues, but in company left a trail of injured feelings. The correspondence between the directors and superintendents all too often carried 'ballast' of this kind.

It belongs to a true picture of the Mission, as does an insight from one of Hudson Taylor's letters to his wife. On September 1, 1885, when it was still exhaustingly hot at 90°F after a long summer, he told her about one of the usually most saintly older men: 'Harsh, rude, censorious, (he) has nearly lost all the influence for good he had at first.' Hudson Taylor recognised that all too easily he himself could go the same way. The extreme heat was soul-searing, he said, like being parted from her. The 'ballast' was offset by more examples of staunch devotion to the work in hand.

While Hudson Taylor was in Scandinavia, George and Minnie Parker were nearing the end of their year-long journey of evangelism and Bible selling from Lanzhou to Gulja (Kuldja) on the Russian border. They arrived in Britain on March 11, 1890, six days before Hudson Taylor left for China, but sixteen years before the second George Hunter followed in their footsteps to Urumqi, twenty-four years before Percy Mather and thirty-three years before Eva and Francesca French and Mildred Cable (p 48).[1]

'Minnie' Parker (Shao Mianzi, the Yangzhou schoolgirl) spoke in excellent English at the London annual meetings in May 1890.

Two travelling CIM evangelists, T H King and Lund, were ejected from Henan. 'Henan is Henan still' their leader commented, not surprised. In Shaanxi, Thomas Botham continued his itinerant life, on and on, round and round, to city, town and village one after another, unable to rent premises to which he could bring a wife. His fiancée, Ellen Barclay, waited at Tianshui, across the Gansu border, until at last an innkeeper offered Botham three small rooms. He told her, 'The place won't do for you,' but she chose to join him whether on the road or in a shanty. So they married in 1889 and together continued his travelling life. Models of faithful perseverance, they demonstrated the soundness of Hudson Taylor's contention that China's families could be given the gospel systematically by persistence in going to them.[2]

Annie Taylor, the lone wolf, was a true missionary. Unlike Cecil Polhill and his wife (no less first-rate), choosing to win Tibetans for Christ and see them take the gospel to Lhasa, she looked for ways to reach the heart of Tibet in that forbidden city. After reconnoitring in the Qinghai region from her base at Luqü (Taozhou) in Gansu, she returned briefly to Britain and prospected Darjeeling as an approach to Tibet and Lhasa through Sikkim. The British threat meant strong Tibetan forces barring the way, so she went back to Gansu and laid new plans.[3]

But all was not plain sailing throughout China. As long as the anti-foreign, anti-Christian viceroy remained in Sichuan it was unsafe to travel about. The British consul asked missionaries to restrict their movements as much as possible. George Nicoll was an exception. He could go out to the 'Lolos' (as the Nosu were derisively called) on the wild fringes of the Daliangshan. (HTCOC Book 6, Index.) Hunan, far from relaxing its xenophobia, was republishing its scurrilous anti-Christian pamphlets (p 109), and Thomas James was in two minds about holding on year after year as Adam Dorward had done. He wanted to marry Fanny (Stroud) Riley in Sichuan (HTCOC Book 6, p 420). The city of Luzhou (Luhsien) had suffered a devastating fire with over a thousand lives lost. Should they or should they not look for a foothold there? He consulted Hudson Taylor. Leave Hunan (Shashi and Shishou) with no one to take his place, and start again in riot-prone Sichuan? He must decide for himself, he was told; settle it with God. James vacillated, wanted more advice. Then it was that Hudson Taylor advised:

Spend a night in prayer, responsive to God's will, and in the morning do what you believe to be right.[4]

In Shanxi, always turbulent, new problems called for John Stevenson's intervention. But he was on sensitive ground. Stanley Smith was doing excellent work, training five evangelists by teaching and fieldwork with them, but he and Charlie Studd, two volatile men, as feared were not being good for each other. Call Stanley away for a time, Hudson Taylor suggested. Let him teach and inspire language students at Anqing. Worse still, the Shanxi superintendent, Benjamin Bagnall, and Pastor Hsi had clashed, and afterwards Hsi had been attacked by his Chinese opponents. 'I wish Bagnall could see,' Hudson Taylor wrote, with deep knowledge of Chinese thinking, 'that this attack upon Mr Hsi is to no small extent a backhanded attack upon him (Bagnall).' No course was open but to commission Bagnall to open up a new area, as superintendent of the Shunde-Huolu area in Zhili, and to give T W Pigott the oversight of part of Shanxi.[5]

'We have had official commendation in government bluebooks for settling our difficulties without (appealing to) consular officials,' Hudson Taylor wrote to Stevenson. 'Do all you can to keep aggrieved men like Lund from trying to redress their wrongs in the old controversial ways. Go if you can, but if not, send for dissatisfied men to *talk* with you. Show sympathy and bring them round as friends. And (with the old 'Shanxi spirit' stirring again) try to get things settled before the Shanghai conferences in May or "no small trouble" could erupt during them.'

Discord at the top   1889–90

A completely new threat to harmony had raised its head. The strong-willed senior missionary who had dismissed his family servant and expected the Mission to send her home to Britain, began lobbying for appointments in the CIM to be 'elective'. This challenge to the Principles and Practice was contrary to the very genius of the CIM, Hudson Taylor immediately saw. In fact no missonary society chose its leaders in that way. The family of the CIM had been built up from the beginning on the principle of co-operation with its founder. Were self-opinionated men to stand like politicians for election by colleagues who scarcely knew them? Another senior refused to recognise the China Council unless he himself had a place on it. A deplorable new spirit had arisen.

But worse was to come. Although, or because, he was responsible to John Stevenson as Hudson Taylor's deputy, the campaigner for elections wrote to the London Council objecting to changes in the 'P and P' and to the restrictions in the 'Book of Arrangements' which affected him. Bringing a servant to China was one. Instead of referring him back to John Stevenson or consulting Hudson Taylor, Theodore Howard and some Council members took up his complaints by challenging the China Council's action. From this small beginning the status of councils, not least of the London Council, became a major issue. The seeds of a constitutional controversy had been sown, and not until five years later was peace fully restored. When it was, genuine misunderstandings were again seen to lie behind strong differences of opinion. But the damage had been done.[6]

The controversy held many lessons for the Mission, and its relevance today justifies its inclusion in this record. Most remarkable, perhaps, was the maintenance of personal friendships and affection when strong words and even rudeness threatened them.

One clause in the handbook touched off a debate on the right of Hudson Taylor and the administration in China to reject probationers or dismiss serious offenders without the approval of the men who sent them. In effect, it raised the question: Was London to have the last word? The Principles and Practice and Book of Arrangements themselves then became the chief bone of contention. The London Council believed they were witnessing an authoritarian departure from the comfortable family relationship between Hudson Taylor and the missionaries that had satisfied all for twenty-five years. The fact that the Mission had quadrupled in size seemed to be forgotten. The sustained pressure on Hudson Taylor to delegate his duties was lost sight of. These new challenges to his leadership emphasised the need for agreement on the essential principles, and after that the logical next step must be a handbook applying the principles to practical situations – a 'book of arrangements'. Most front-line missionaries had welcomed it, but the well-meaning men in London were too far from the scene to understand.

The rumble of distant thunder reverberates through letters of this period – references to the Book of Arrangements as 'a law of the Medes and Persians'; to another 'crisis' of Hudson Taylor's making; to some fearing a 'smash up' with 'deplorable injury to the work and sad humiliation' for him if he did not retract his new regulations – 'too much management – too much policy'.

After returning to London, Hudson Taylor had told John Stevenson he did not think the 'crisis' as great as some feared. 'I was surprised and very thankful at the real earnest desire manifested (by the Council) to leave my conviction of the proper lines for the Mission uninterfered with.' 'But Satan is certainly very busy.' Each daring advance seemed to be met by Satanic disruption. A tragic sequence of illnesses and deaths once again darkened the year, but what he feared more, as the General Missionary Conference at Shanghai approached, was the disgrace of disagreements between major societies and individual missionaries being thrashed out in public. Instead of doing good, such a conference could do inestimable harm. Crises in China and Britain at the same time might be more than he and the CIM could weather.

Intending to leave for Shanghai by the next mail steamer after his son, Howard, sailed with the Ballers, Hudson Taylor had to change his plan. William Berger's advice about a Deed of Incorporation of the Mission to provide for the General Director's death had been followed, but the deed had not been completed; reorganisation of the London offices had been delayed by Charles Fishe having pneumonia; and John Stevenson's two sons in Scotland had become dangerously ill. Hudson Taylor himself kept in touch with the surgeons, went up to Edinburgh to make arrangements personally, and kept their father informed. But the delay resulted in tentative acceptance in London of a clarified P and P. Finally, on March 6, he cabled in economy code to Shanghai. 'Sons better. Sailing 23rd.'

Hudson Taylor had been described as having 'a big head on broad shoulders' and, not surprisingly, during these painful days a candidate who was to be interviewed by him had gained the impression that he was very stern (see cover portrait). But as so many testified, 'he had not spoken to me more than a dozen words before all my previous ideas of him were turned upside-down, and I felt I could do anything for him.' That he had a big head in more senses than one, and a big heart, all but a few in the Mission would have agreed. But he needed a broad back while the discord among his leading colleagues lasted.[7]

For the time being he was free to return to China. On March 17, 1890, he agonisingly tore himself away from Jennie again and from the family, was seen off at the station by Benjamin, spent three days in Cannes in conference with William Berger, and on the 23rd joined his ship at Marseilles.

Wusong Road and the General Conference   *March–May 1890*

Travel by coal-burning steamer had few of the pleasures of the sea which Hudson Taylor had so much enjoyed. Smelly, smutty, crowded and crude third-class accommodation had to be endured. Noisy, rough fellow-passengers, loud-mouthed and drunken, had led him to comment, 'P & O is no line for our sisters to travel by – or for luggage,' often damaged. The French mail was no better and his only English-speaking fellow-passenger a Scottish manual labourer. But years of the rough and tumble of life had taught him how to make his own cocoon of silence. He prepared his keynote address for the General Missionary Conference, and read the newly published *Life of Bishop Hannington*, the martyr of Uganda. 'Our travelling is child's play compared with his.' Sitting in the half-shade of an umbrella on the seashore at Colombo, streaming with perspiration, he thanked Jennie for her prayers for him.

> Spiritual blessing . . . is the one thing I want and need and must have. Given this and I have no fears; without it nothing else will (avail) . . .

WUSONG ROAD, SHANGHAI
one of the three CIM buildings

> May God forgive all that is wrong in me and in our mission . . .
> Unwillingness to be separated from you . . . has brought me under a
> cloud . . . but I have left you unwillingly, instead of joyfully . . . I do
> *want* to be whole-hearted in God's service. [And on July 12] My
> solitary life must continue as far as I can see *indefinitely!* . . .
> However heart-breaking it may be. We are His, His *slaves*.[8]

When he had sailed away from Shanghai just a year before (April 12, 1889) the plans and contract were complete for the new Mission headquarters on the Wusong Road site. On February 18, 1890, the first occupants had moved in. So when Hudson Taylor landed on April 27 it was to Wusong Road that he was taken. Everything was as he and David Cranston had designed it, down to the details of doors and windows, stair-treads and risers. On two sides of a large grassy quadrangle with a Chinese pavilion or summer-house in the centre, the gift of the building contractor, stood the Mission Home and the office block, with a meeting hall seating two hundred. Not only made-to-measure, the Home in particular had a charm that made it pleasant to live in, a resounding success.

With a series of conferences due to begin on May 1, about sixty CIM missionaries had arrived already. They thronged to greet him. The inscription at the entrance read, 'To the glory of God and the furtherance of His Kingdom in China.' 'I feel glad,' Hudson Taylor commented, 'that the CIM was not even mentioned . . .'

Instead of finding John Stevenson in good health with a strong hold on the administration, he found him hoping to hand over his responsibilities. While Hudson Taylor's horizon had broadened markedly during his year away, Stevenson still thought in the old terms of himself as a deputy rather than as the China Director. They agreed that he would continue routine administration while Hudson Taylor took over liaison with other missions, and the major problems, the threatened resignations and dissidents. In a few days' time he would be able to put his concept of a thousand more missionaries to the appraisal of the assembled societies.[9]

A new factor had arisen since he left home. His international commitments were about to embrace the Australasian colonies. Letters to him and to the London Council told of several potential members of the Mission waiting at Melbourne to be interviewed. Would he sanction the formation of a provisional council, and come himself to confer with them? Two days after he himself reached Shanghai, a young ordained Anglican arrived from Australia at his own expense, and asked to be admitted. This was the spirit Hudson Taylor liked – conviction followed by action. C H Parsons had brought a letter of commendation from his vicar, H B Macartney, the potential chairman of an Australian council. Without delay Hudson Taylor welcomed Charles Parsons into the CIM and cabled to Melbourne, 'Sanction committee'.[10]

On April 30 the new meeting hall at Wusong Road was inaugurated, with a full house of two hundred including his good friends of many years, William Muirhead, Joseph Edkins, Alexander Williamson, John Nevius and others. On that day the CIM had 382 members in China at 89 stations, a far cry from the much criticised *Lammermuir* party of 1866. The visionary enlargement of the Mission's Shanghai premises had come only just in time. Every corner was filled. Some old-timers like Charles Judd, from his quiet city of Ninghai in Shandong, were amazed. What had happened to Hudson Taylor, the exponent and protagonist of simplicity and the Chinese way of life? Immediately they saw that simplicity and adequacy were compatible. 'The sanest man I ever knew,' was one man's description of his leader.

The Wusong Road premises were to be stretched to their limit time and again in the coming months, and in the years ahead. The last decade of the century had begun on a prophetic note. The next was to begin with this haven crammed with refugees from the Boxer holocaust. Each decade was to see it filled to capacity in emergencies. There were 'only thirty-one bedrooms available for those not on the permanent staff; but to the missionary accustomed to Chinese inns, a bed on the floor – and he generally carries his own bedding – in the hall, office or attics, is gratefully welcomed when others cannot be had.' At the time of the revolution which ended the Manchu dynasty, 1,333 passed through the Home between September 1911 and October 1912.[11]

No danger existed of the 'Shanxi spirit' sweeping the General Missionary Conference of May 7–20, but a strong possibility of disharmony drove Hudson Taylor to call for six days of 'consecration' and waiting on God, from May 1–6, before the conference began. As many from other societies joined with the CIM, meetings in the new hall saw 180 to 240 daily taking part. Many were to recognise the success of a resolution in Parliament on May 3, a step towards ending the opium traffic, as being linked with this week of prayer for China.[12] On the last day Archibald Orr Ewing and Mary Scott (Robert Scott's daughter) were married at the cathedral. And the next day Howard Taylor and Geraldine Guinness became engaged.

The major conference began with a short session of prayer followed by Hudson Taylor's hour-long keynote address. None doubted the nature of what he would have to say, but the mood of the 430 delegates (226 men and 204 women) gave him wings. Almost exactly one-third of the entire Protestant missionary staff in China were present.[13] The simplicity of his subject and presentation, the feeding of the four thousand, and its application as a parable to the theme of 'the gospel to every creature' may have misled some who looked for an academic or philosophical address. But if they were disappointed, its clarity captivated the rest – a multitude to feed, a few to feed them, systematic co-operation, a lesson in comity, and the staff of life reached all.

Then his application to China: 'It would only want twenty-five (evangelists) to be associated with each society, to give us 1,000 additional workers.' A thousand more and every Chinese family could, as he showed mathematically, be given the chance of an intelligent hearing of the gospel before the turn of the century. No quibbling about calculations (mere visual aids) interrupted the discussion. His points went home – obedience required; obedience possible; obedience imperative – so that the resolution based upon his exposition became one of the historic features of the conference. 'The 1,000 idea is spreading,' he wrote home to Jennie.

To anticipate the conclusions of the conference, three appeals to the worldwide Church resulted from the twelve days of deliberation: 1. to send out as many hundreds of messengers of the gospel as could be secured; 2. that the best kinds of laymen and women including educationists and medical personnel should supplement the ordained ones – a revolutionary step for some societies; and 3. an appeal for '1,000 men within 5 years of this time.'

From England Hudson Taylor had written to John Stevenson, 'I do not propose making any definite attempt on account of the CIM before the conferences . . . If *all* (missions) will take it up so much the better. If not, we shall see if *any* will, or whether we must do it alone.' A thousand more in the CIM? It came to that. But the conference had risen to the occasion. Now it remained to see what mission boards and committees would do.[14]

The Third General Missionary Conference,
Shanghai[15]   *May 7–20, 1890*

Two inter-mission conferences had previously been held, in
August 1843 in Hong Kong, and in 1877 at Shanghai. (HTCOC
Book 1, p 279; Book 6 pp 108–15.) At that time, 1877, the total
number of Protestant missionaries in China was fewer than those
who met together in 1890. Only two Chinese delegates were included. The English language was used, and the role of Chinese
Church leaders had not yet progressed to one of influence on the
policy of missions.[16] The third conference (in the Lyceum Theatre)
was more wide-ranging and ambitious. Its official report ran to
eighty pages of close print. But, as the election of John Nevius and
David Hill as chairmen indicated, a wish prevailed for a high
spiritual tone throughout. They managed to preserve it.

As a practical business forum it worked methodically through a
long agenda of semi-technical subjects covering all aspects of
missionary work – social, Biblical, evangelistic, educational, medical, and related political and cultural topics, some highly debatable.
Y K Yen, a Chinese minister of the Protestant Episcopal Church,
urged missionaries to 'adopt a Chinese mode of life', and that 'none
should be brought out who were overbearing in manner'. Hudson
Taylor had been asked for a second paper on 'The Missionary', the
physical, mental and spiritual qualifications he and she should have.
Others spoke on the 'Evils of the Use of Opium' and 'The Value of
Opium Refuges', self-support of the Churches, and the role of
women. One decision taken by the conference was greeted with the
doxology ('three notes too high'): instead of having several versions
of the Bible in circulation, agreement was reached that 'a version of
the Scriptures uniform for all China' should be prepared, to be
supplemented by three levels of *Wenli*, and regional dialect versions. That this was 'the crowning work of the conference' reflects
the disorder that previously existed.

The resolution to appeal for a thousand men in five years,
prepared by an elected committee, was also carried unanimously. A
memorial to the emperor at first favoured by the conference was
finally discarded for fear of its motives being misconstrued and
resulting in the persecution of Chinese Christians. David Hill
advocated the far-reaching enlistment of unordained men and
women, stressing that the evangelisation of the world is the work of
the whole Church, not of a separated order among Christians. In

this he complemented Hudson Taylor's own proposition to the conference, and a committee was appointed to frame an appeal to the worldwide Church. It called for 'a largely increased force' of both ordained and unordained men. When asked if the work in China could not be done by Chinese Christians, Hudson Taylor gave it as his opinion that the ideal could not yet be realised. Were not all missions already encouraging Chinese of the right type to be evangelists? The report of a committee on Unity and Division in the Field (Comity) presented through Hudson Taylor as its spokesman, was also received with 'splendid warmth of unanimity'.

But on the subject of 'ancestral worship', strong divergence of views became apparent. The minority school of thought represented by Timothy Richard, W A P Martin, Gilbert Reid and a few others, had been vocal for twenty years. This was their prime opportunity. The grey area of uncertainty about what was purely cultural, to be preserved and emulated, and what was part of pagan religious practice contradictory to Christian truth, needed to be discussed and clarified. The differences of opinion lay in the interpretation of common Chinese beliefs and observances. If Christians were to reject the idolatrous and to worship the true God alone, the distinction needed to be drawn between veneration, in the sense of deep respect to the point of awe and reverence, on the one hand, and outright worship, whether as adoration of the divine or appeasement of menacing spirits, on the other hand. The main difficulty lay in great variations among the Chinese themselves. The mandarin might hold an intellectual, agnostic or sceptical view of temple worship and ancestor worship in the home. Or he might in every way be like the common man, devoid of philosophical reservations, fearing and worshipping the spirits of the unseen world. Ancestor worship is, in fact, by common agreement, the basic religion of the Chinese.

So intricate a subject cannot be adequately treated in a biography with the limitations of this one, but because unfactual statements about the Shanghai conferences of 1877 and 1890 have recently been made, we must briefly consider what 'ancestor' and 'ancestral' worship involved.[17] Following two papers on the topic, 'How far should Christians be required to abandon native customs?' by the American Episcopal, F Ohlinger, and the American Presbyterian, H V Noyes, one from W A P Martin (who had arrived in China in 1850) was read by his supporter, Gilbert Reid. His title, 'The Worship of Ancestors – a plea for toleration', summarised his case much as he aired it in 1877 (see HTCOC Book 6, pp 283–8, and note his train of thought). If this great obstacle to the conversion of the nation were to be removed, he argued, it must either be swept away wholesale, which was unthinkable, or be met by adaptations, as stepping-stones towards a satisfying conclusion. The effect of strengthening family bonds and moral restraints was to be admired in the rites. The cohesive social and ethical values of the ancient customs could not be destroyed without disastrous effects. Therefore the physical practices must be examined.

Martin admitted that the system of ancestral rites was tainted by 'a large admixture of superstition and idolatry' through 'invocations and offerings which implied that the deceased were tutelary deities'.[18] He agreed that 'anything that can fairly be construed as idolatry', the offerings and invocations, could not be countenanced. But, he claimed, these were accretions which could be eliminated. The rites could be made compatible with Christianity. The 'announcements' to ancestors could be so worded as to express affection without petition. Martin then ventured on to more dangerous ground. Bowing and kneeling, even the *ketou* were marks of respect and not idolatrous in some contexts, even if they were in others. Nor were salutations addressed to the departed, as much a Western custom as Chinese.

Here eyebrows were raised in the conference. Glaring differences lay between the Chinese *status quo*, idolatrous worship addressed to the dead, and poetic expression in the West. Martin's concern to honour the best in Chinese tradition and to bridge the chasm between the Chinese and Christian positions, appeared to blind him to reality. The sympathy of the conference was forfeited. If he had incorporated into his address the emphases of the debate after the turn of the twentieth century, namely to discover Christian ways of showing respect for ancestors, without any vestige of worship or appeasement, a strongly positive note might have forestalled the controversy that erupted.

The next paper by a Dr Gilbert on 'The Attitude of Christianity towards Ancestral Worship' 'was greeted with great applause', showing the conservative mood of the conference. The scholar E Faber DD of the Rhenish Mission (in China since 1865), chairman of the executive committee on the *Wenli* version of the Bible, and other committees, then summarised the main features of 'Ancestral Worship' to demonstrate its complete incompatibility with Christian truth, and William Muirhead (1847) protested that 'toleration of ancestral worship would be most injurious to the Christian Church'. Matthew Yates (1847) said that 'toleration of idolatry is treason to Christianity'. That a label of chief opponent to Martin has been attached to Hudson Taylor is clearly undeserved.

Some told of Chinese who said that relaxation to allow of worshipping their ancestors would see many, including mandarins, 'entering the Church'. What kind of 'Christians' they would be was another matter. But in Dr Martin's defence Timothy Richard (1869) reminded the conference that he was not asking for toleration of what was idolatrous. He had distinctly said that whatever was idolatrous 'cannot for a moment be entertained'. What Martin wanted was 'toleration of such rites in ancestral reverence as are not idolatrous'. For example, Richard suggested, the spring festival of *qing ming* 'so nearly coincided in time with Easter, that it afforded a very suitable opportunity to dwell on immortality and the resurrection of the dead'.

At least a positive note had been sounded, but it offered a substitute and did not exemplify 'toleration of such rites in ancestral reverence'. Gilbert Reid then defended Martin by saying that he was seeking a *via media* for 'those who adhere to reverence but not to idolatry'. 'Make the worship of Christ the foundation, and the Chinese would not worship ancestors as they worship God'. Put in these terms the problem looked more like one of lucid communication than of conflicting opinions. But was this in fact Martin's 'plea', or wishful thinking? Or was it juggling with words to dress up 'the Worship of Ancestors – a plea for toleration'? Would the introduction of Christ into Chinese ancestral rites displace the misdirected worship of ancestors or legitimise the worship of both together? Few agreed that a solution lay in this direction.

The allotted time was up and Hudson Taylor (1854) who so far had listened without taking part, wanted the time extended. Frank Whitehouse, Hudson Taylor's personal secretary, in his own report of the conference, *Items of Interest*, wrote that Hudson Taylor, to make his point, had suggested that 'a rising vote of dissent' *should be put* to the conference. But an aroused audience had reacted spontaneously, pre-empting a formal motion, 'and there was something like a scene'. The official report reads, however, 'Without making a motion to that effect (he) asked those who dissented from the conclusion of Dr Martin's paper to rise. Most of the audience then rose, upon which one of the preceding speakers [Timothy Richard or Gilbert Reid] protested that this was not a fair way to treat such a subject.' It was agreed to return to the discussion in the evening. The action most in keeping with Hudson Taylor's personality would then have been to make an apology if he had acted unconstitutionally or unfairly. That he did not do so, but allowed Whitehouse's factual statement, supports the contention that he was misunderstood and chose not to justify himself.

When the subject was reopened in the evening the interlude had given time for reflection. Y K Yen, the Christian minister, rose to explain 'the notions underlying the use of ancestral tablets. He said he would not have in his house even a picture of his parents.' Non-Christians would assume that they were worshipped. When resolution and counter-resolution were proposed, the veteran Alexander Williamson (1855) warned that any hasty declaration by the conference could be misconstrued and rouse the angry opposition of all classes of Chinese. Any negative crusade against ancestor worship would be a disastrous mistake. The conference agreed. J L Gibson (1874), the Shantou (Swatow) Presbyterian, then stressed the fact that *fear*, not veneration or worship, was 'the real essence' of the rite. The gospel of deliverance from the power and bondage of demons was 'a great gift' which Chinese would learn to recognise.

Still the delegates had not had enough. The next morning C W Mateer (1863), the American Presbyterian of Shandong, proposed a resolution of dissent from his fellow-Presbyterian W A P Martin's conclusions, and Hudson Taylor supported it with an amendment to end the debate, the resolution was 'carried by a large majority', 'almost unanimously', 'Affirming the belief of the conference "that idolatry is an essential constituent of ancestor worship" and dissenting from the view that missionaries "should refrain from any interference with the native mode of honouring ancestors"'.[19]

Most missionaries could give examples of how Chinese when they put their faith in Christ Jesus knew 'instinctively', by the prompting of the Holy Spirit, that ancestor *worship* would have no place in their lives. Many destroyed the tablets and paraphernalia of worship. Some openly burned them with the family idols.[20]

The unresolved problem remained. How could Christians honour their ancestors in a Chinese way (for the Chinese certainly excelled in remembering and celebrating their debt to their forebears), keeping permanent records and yet avoiding all appearance of idolatry? But apart from the brief disturbance in the 1890 conference until time was allowed for talking the matter through, a spirit of harmony prevailed. Significantly, *Christian Alternatives to*

Ancestor Practices, in referring to J L Nevius's influence in Korea, says: 'The clear-cut break of the Korean Church from ancestor worship had become one of the important factors for the rapid growth of the Korean Church.' After the Boxer Rising a new debate developed in the *Chinese Recorder*, in which W A P Martin repeated his old contentions, and replies concentrated on finding Christian substitutes for ancestor worship. And late in the twentieth century the debate has been revived.[21]

Growing pains   May 1890

At the height of the general conference a photograph of the delegates was to be taken. All who could forgathered at the photographer's where a bamboo scaffolding with 'cat-walks' had been erected. To discerning men it looked precarious, but Chinese scaffolding traditionally served its purpose well. Rank upon rank, 'about 300', missionary men and women found a place on it. Hudson Taylor climbed to perch 'eighteen or twenty feet' from the ground and at one end of the back row. Suddenly the whole structure began to sag and disintegrate. People, planks and bamboo poles fell on top of those below. 'With some 200 ladies falling, there was not a shriek.' An uncanny silence followed as those pinned down waited for those above them in the heap to climb off first. William Rudland saw Hudson Taylor high up on the one corner that remained intact. He helped him down and (in the heat of May) worked to free others until he himself fainted. A Dr Wright, who also helped, said, 'Hudson Taylor . . . was as calm as if he were waiting for a wedding.' Mrs Jenkins of Shaoxing had a collar-bone and two ribs fractured. Not one other person suffered more than cuts and bruises. The photograph was taken four days later.[22]

But 'all the starch seems gone and I feel weak and weary,' Hudson Taylor told Jennie, in the same breath as, 'There is a great spirit of love and unanimity.' Annie Dunn, another recently arrived language student, was dying of 'black smallpox', her fiancé at her bedside in Zhenjiang. Vaccination was still an unperfected technique.[23] One of the Canadians of the first party had 'galloping consumption' and died on May 23, two days after another of the same group died on returning to the States. Arthur Polhill had typhoid, far away in Sichuan. An accumulation of anxieties again left Hudson Taylor drained of strength.

On May 16 the CIM was at home to the whole missionary

community with a buffet reception on the lawns and broad-walks surrounding the pavilion at Wusong Road. The tall office block, with its spiral, iron, external staircase, and the inviting Mission Home were open for inspection. Photographs of the reception and of the wrecked scaffolding were reproduced in *China's Millions*, 1890 – the first to replace engravings. Hudson Taylor was too unwell to join the guests. But they 'accorded (him) generous recognition as a leading influence among missions in China', and the necessity of having such extensive premises reflected the degree to which the Mission had progressed.[24]

On his fifty-eighth birthday, May 21, the eighty-three members of the Mission still in Shanghai presented him with an illuminated address and $480 for his personal use. He felt he should not accept it – unless it could be used for travelling 'in the Colonies'. The address read, 'We desire (to express) our unshaken conviction that those principles on which you were led . . . to found this Mission, and on which it has grown to its present extent and usefulness, are of God.' He was to leave in July with Montagu Beauchamp as his companion. Montagu had handed him a note the previous day expressing gratitude for his influence and enclosing £100. Before they left, H N Lachlan also sent a gift of fifty-two taels towards his expenses, and Orr Ewing £1,000 for the Mission. Criticism of the Principles and Practice and 'Arrangements' had become public knowledge, and his loyal friends wished to demonstrate their support.

Sunday, May 25, they kept as a day of fasting and prayer for the CIM conference beginning the next day. Outstanding among speakers in the 'consecration' meetings before the General Conference and again on this day was Dixon Hoste. His words were taken down in shorthand.

> We must get to know God *in secret* – alone in the desert. (Like Joseph in the dungeon and David as a shepherd and a hunted man, we must expect testing and trial as a matter between God and each of us individually.) It does seem to me that true spirituality lies in this – utter dependence on God for everything . . . We shall dread to . . . do anything in our own wisdom . . . If a man can only get down before God and get His plan of work for him, individually, that is what will make him irresistible. It does not matter whether (he) is a strong man or a weak one . . .

Hoste was exceptional and Hudson Taylor had his eye on him. He had written giving Hoste advice he could not accept, but afterwards received this letter: 'More than a year ago you wrote . . . As you know, I replied that I did not see my way to doing so . . . I felt free to keep my own opinions. I wish to say that experience has since then caused me to change my views . . . I thank you for your advice and your constant forbearance.' A man with this personality, honesty, humility, saintliness and strength would with experience one day prove his worth. Regular reports of his work with Pastor Hsi already showed his wisdom.

The informal CIM conference was incidental to the General Conference and not representative of the Mission, so decisions were not taken. But frank discussion of the Principles and Arrangements threw strong light on some weaknesses in administration, especially in Britain. Consultation before the appointment of superintendents was a good thing, but 'democratic election' and committee rule failed to win support. Hudson Taylor himself was convinced that the Biblical pattern was Godly leadership, and progress was too often hampered by committees.[25] He prized initiative and evidence of considerate leadership. As for itinerant evangelism of the kind necessary to take the gospel to 'every creature', Hudson Taylor said,

> This work will not be done without crucifixion – without consecration that is prepared at any cost to carry out the Master's commands . . . *Given that*, I believe it will be done. (But only) the operation of the Holy Ghost (would make it produce results). A man's conversion is, I believe, a regenerative change produced by (Him) – it is *not* an influence produced by man on the mind of his fellow-man . . . If the Lord sends Paul to plant, He will certainly send Apollos to water.

The greatest practical obstacle to the CIM welcoming a large share of the thousand evangelists was paradoxically its need of administrative staff in China and Britain, of businessmen and doctors. The sheer labour of getting large numbers equipped and transported to their spheres of work had demonstrated the short-comings of unskilled staff.[26] A thoroughly efficient machine had become his own administrative priority. He could see some young men showing promise of this nature – Graham Brown, Marcus Wood, Hayward, Hardman and Amelia's son, Hudson, among them. Not yet free to come to China was another of Orr Ewing's friends, Walter B Sloan, a Keswick Convention figure who would be one of God's best gifts to the Mission.

As soon as the conference ended, the China Council met for six hours daily, straining to eliminate features of the Book of Arrangements which could give offence, while retaining essentials. In this they met resistance from one of their own number, the proponent of elections to whom Hudson Taylor had given a district to superintend. No regulations had been introduced that were not a definition of essentials to harmony in the Mission, yet this superintendent now wished for autonomy in his own region. And more: 'If he should retire from the Mission at any time he wished to take the work with him. The Council could not entertain that thought for a moment.' Not only so, but he intended to recruit his own colleagues, independently of the Mission. As he could not have his own way, he chose to resign. (C T Studd followed his example soon afterwards.) The China Council then completed its work with agreement to make separate administrative offices of shipping and postal services at Shanghai, so heavy had each become.[27]

From mid-June until mid-July Hudson Taylor visited the Yangzi River stations and Yantai again, designating language school students to their inland appointments, 'trouble-shooting' and discussing finance with Broumton at Wuchang. One of the bitterest tribulations was Mary Stevenson's relapse into 'mania' again. Her brothers in Scotland had recovered, but the strain of work and sorrow were telling on their father. With his staff in Shanghai reorganised and strengthened, however, he agreed to carry on.

At midnight on Saturday, July 19, Hudson Taylor, Montagu Beauchamp and Frank Whitehouse, the secretary, embarked for Hong Kong to await their ship to Australia.

The second 'branch' – Australia   *July–December 1890*

The hidden history of God at work in the world admits of a clearing of the mist from time to time. The evangelist whose text, 'My son, give me thine heart' (Prov. 23:26), first stirred the twelve-year-old Hudson Taylor to respond to God, was Henry Reed.[28] In later years he moved to Australia and made his home at Mount Pleasant, near Launceston, Tasmania. From time to time after Hudson Taylor thanked him for his influence, they kept in touch, and after her husband died Mrs Reed sent donations to the Mission. It is probable that when George Nicoll spent four years in Australia to recover his health, 1885–89, he had close links with the family. The eldest daughter, Mary (Maggie to the inner circle), was in England when she offered in 1887 to be one of the Hundred. She sailed to

China as a self-supporting associate on January 26, 1888, with Grattan Guinness's daughter, Geraldine, but ill-health forced her out in 1889 – out of China, but not of the Mission. She became an indefatigable ambassador to the Australian churches. Incidentally, Geraldine's brother, Harry, newly qualified as a doctor, escorted his younger brother and sister (Whitfield and Lucy) to stay with Mrs Reed in Tasmania, fell in love with Maggie's sister, Annie, and took her home to England – the mother-to-be of future members of the CIM and other notables.[29] So their connection with the CIM was strong over many years. Moreover, George Soltau was their minister at Launceston.

In Melbourne four ministers had begun in 1889 to pray together for China, knowing nothing of Mary Reed having joined the CIM, until she was invalided home. H B Macartney and his curate, C H Parsons, were Anglicans, W Lockhart Morton, a Presbyterian, Alfred Bird, a Baptist. Correspondence with Hudson Taylor through his friend Philip Kitchen led to Charles Parsons arriving at Shanghai in April 1890 and their consulting together about developments in Australia. Mary Reed was also writing of other potential missionaries and asking if they could not proceed to China as associates rather than go through the formalities in England. But H B Macartney proposed a council of the CIM, and Mary wrote at length to Hudson Taylor about it and her own activities.[30]

Strong prejudice against the Chinese, stemming from their immigration in large numbers, bringing opium, had diminished as Australians were given unbiased information about China. Soon there were crowded meetings. After Charles Parsons left for China, Mary Reed was all the more in demand as a speaker. Then Hudson Taylor was invited to come. George Soltau, one-time member of the London Council, had written to Theodore Howard proposing an Australasian Council, and in April a London minute noted that this was beyond London's brief. It was for Hudson Taylor to decide. The cable he sent on May 21, 'Sanction committee', raises a question, however, for he used words carefully. It would have been most like him to authorise a committee to assess the waiting candidates, but to delay the formation of a council at Melbourne until he had met and consulted with Macartney and his friends in person. Perhaps an intermediate letter had not reached them. They took the cable at full value and called a meeting for the very next day, May 22, at which an Australasian Council was constituted with Macartney as chairman, Alfred Bird as hon. secretary and Philip Kitchen, treasurer. With a flying start the applications of eight candidates were considered. Within five years fifty, and in a decade a total of 101, missionaries had sailed from Australia and New Zealand.

Before he became Archbishop of Sydney, Marcus Loane, already a member of the Sydney Council for ten years, wrote *The Story of the China Inland Mission in Australia and New Zealand, 1890–1964*, to commemorate the centenary of the Mission and the sailing of the *Lammermuir*. It frees this present account to draw on other sources. Taking nothing for granted, Hudson Taylor and his companions (still in Chinese clothes) went to a Chinese hotel in Hong Kong until John Burdon, his companion on the Chongming Island adventure (HTCOC Book 2, pp 252–60), insisted that he always make his, the bishop's, residence his home when passing through.

Hudson Taylor had reached the dregs of endurance of seemingly interminable separations from Jennie and the children. In his polyglot Bible, Jacob's prayer is marked (Genesis 32:11 undated) 'Deliver me, I pray . . . lest he will come and smite me, and the mother with the children.' It would seem that Hudson Taylor had Satan's assaults in mind. His son, Charles Edward, a Cambridge undergraduate, was 'far from God' and having a bad influence at home.[31] Millie Duncan, their adopted daughter, was engaged and going to Canada and then India. Ernest and Amy were fifteen and fourteen. They needed Jennie. But so did he. 'Ask for me more *patience* and more joy in the *will of God*, in respect of our separation. Sometimes I feel as if I *cannot* bear it, and this is not right, is it? And people say, "Oh you are so much accustomed to it, it is nothing to you!" . . . Do you think you *could* rightly join me on my return to China, darling?'

He was needed in London, too. The Council were challenging him again on their rights. But he feared lest John Stevenson break down completely, and must relieve him. Did that mean another year apart from Jennie? 'God has given us a costly sacrifice to offer to Him, an alabaster box to break at His feet.' If it was right he was willing; but like Lewis, his previous secretary, Whitehouse's shortcomings were making Hudson wish he could always count on Jennie's efficiency and discretion instead. Then, two days later, Yes, it was right. Make preparations, hand over *China's Millions* to Charles Fishe. 'I think that we must not separate as we have done,' again and again over twenty years. Yet on September 9, this solution created a new fear: 'It would be altogether heartbreaking if any harm came to our dear children through my selfishness in taking

you away. To die, alone, would be better than that! God guides.'
God did, and all was well.[32]

The ship to Australia had only first-class and steerage decks, so
steerage it had to be, with rough Portuguese sailors as companions.
But also a good friend in the cabin steward he had had on the voyage
from Vancouver in 1888. They passed close to Mindoro, Mindanao
and Celebes, and berthed at primitive Port Darwin on August 12,
still in cool Chinese clothes, keeping their Western suits uncrum-
pled for Australia. Wrecks on previously uncharted reefs were
etched into their memories of this voyage. Typically they found
the Methodist manse and spent Sunday ashore, preaching and
addressing an ad hoc meeting. But the young minister, F E Finch,
warned them not to be too hopeful of finding missionary recruits in
Australia, nor money. Trade was bad and the Chinese despised, he
said.

Back at the ship they found their cabin empty. They had been
moved up to the first class as the captain's guests. The steerage
accommodation was all needed for Chinese labourers coming
aboard, he explained. 'We saw no sign of any Chinese,' Beauchamp
wrote. Then Thursday Island where 'Monty' went ashore to post
letters and recognised the broad back of Professor Drummond of
Edinburgh, of all people, on his way to China. Of course he must be
the guest of the CIM at Wusong Road.[33]

Australia was gripped by strikes, enough to disrupt their planned
travels, but August 26–September 1 at Sydney gave scope for meetings, the students glad to hear one of the Cambridge Seven.[34]
Then on by ship to Melbourne and the first session with the new
council on September 3. Interviewing candidates, addressing
crowded meetings – shaking the hand of John G Paton, apostle of
the cannibal islands – their days were full. Hudson Taylor's thought-
fulness for others, not least the domestic servants, impressed his
host, H B Macartney. In Tasmania from September 15–24 it was the
same. 'Money poured in,' a ballroom reception was held at Government House, and men and women offered to go to China. Mary
Reed became a full member of the Mission, and her mother handed
Hudson Taylor a gift to pay Jennie's fare to China and to America if
they should want to go there. George Soltau and his wife delighted
in seeing him again. 'The joy it was to me to hear again the familiar
much-loved voice.' And to be shown how to recognise the right type
of candidate . . . 'How quietly he led us on to see the needs so that
we suggested the rules that must be made and the provisions by the

THE FIRST AUSTRALASIAN PARTY
Montagu Beauchamp behind and to Hudson Taylor's right

Council.' They collected as many Chinese as they could to hear him. George Soltau was walking arm in arm with him in Launceston when Hudson Taylor stopped, turned to him and said, 'There should be only one circumstance in our lives and that circumstance is God' – a memorable two weeks.[35]

Back to Ballarat, Adelaide, 'the city of churches', for twelve days, with meetings daily and Bible-expositions four days running, 'His Honour the Chief Justice' as chairman on another occasion. Then Melbourne again, and the pace maintained. Three thousand young people in the Academy of Music; forty ministers from 10 am to 5 pm; fifty-eight more candidates to interview; they were well into October and 'very busy', with Hudson Taylor troubled by neuralgia. This was when he suggested to the council that they pray for a hundred missionaries in ten years, one tenth of a thousand.

New Zealand wanted him to come, and Sir William Fox, 'long interested in the CIM', invited him to be his guest. But he had to be back at Shanghai to tackle the London Council's problems before the year ended; and a party of four men and eight women (including Mary Reed) was ready to travel with him. He could give them daily training and a start on learning Chinese.[36] Three thousand came to farewell them at Melbourne Town Hall on October 27, and on the 31st they left for Sydney. The formal photograph shows strong, intelligent young men and women and in the back row the magnificent figure of the eminent oarsman, Montagu Beauchamp. Jennie and a party of new missionaries had left Britain the day before.

On November 1 John Southey, an English clergyman of Ipswich, near Brisbane, wrote to say that after an illness he had come to Australia in 1880 on his doctor's advice. Riding ten or twelve miles between each of three services every Sunday, he had remained in good health. But he was thirty-four with a wife and three children. Might he go to China? Hudson Taylor, Montagu Beauchamp and the Australian twelve sailed from Sydney on November 10, leaving Whitehouse to help the council at Melbourne to cope with a flood of sixty candidates. The coal strike forced the ship to coal at Newcastle, and gave time for a visit to Ipswich, rejoining the ship at Brisbane. Hudson Taylor's train was due between four and five am. He wired ahead to Southey, who afterwards wrote, 'In the dim light I saw a little gentleman alighting . . . I (had) expected a man of striking bearing . . . On reaching home I mentioned my disappointment to my wife, but after a (while with him she) said to me, "Look at the light in his face" . . . The first sense of disappointment gave place to deep reverence and love . . . We could not help noticing the utter lack of self-assertion about him.'

After meetings at Brisbane from November 13–20 they at last sailed away from Australia on the 20th. By then the party had the measure of the CIM and their director and were calling him their 'dear Father'. On December 3 they reached Darwin. Hudson Taylor took his companions to near the manse and went on alone. When the door was opened he said to Fitch, 'How many cups have you?' 'Why?' Fitch asked. 'And to (his) amazement we filed in thirteen strong.'[37] Again they sailed through the Tores Strait, where Hudson Taylor collected plants on an uninhabited island. He cared for them on board ship and planted them at Wusong Road. Then through the Philippines, close to Panay and Mindoro, and reached Hong Kong on the 13th.

Jennie and her party had arrived and gone on. If she had stayed, her note explained, his duty to his Australia party would have meant the two of them having little time together. She knew him too well. But the next ship to Shanghai had only first-class accommodation. He waited until the 18th to bring his companions with him. Some scraps of paper tell more about him and his influence on them than the contents at first suggest – letters of thanks to the captains of both Australian ships, and from the party for so much kindness on board. He told Maria in a letter how restful the voyage had been and how well he was. But the mail waiting for him at Hong Kong had its bitter vein, from William Sharp about the London Council, and from the Shanghai veteran claiming a seat on the China Council. When others advised a firm rebuff, Hudson Taylor said, 'He is an old man now. Be kind to him,' and kind they were. Over tea with the council men he was benign – his wife had driven him to write![38]

At last on December 21 they reached Shanghai and Wusong Road. Reunited, until her death in his old age, Hudson and Jennie never had to part again.

CHAPTER FIVE

'SATAN'S BEWILDERING ATTACK'
1890–94

We are not unaware of his schemes (2 Cor. 2:11 NIV).

Franson's flood
1890–93

Erik Folke of Uppsala University had arrived in China at his own expense in March 1887. Because he had gone there, his friend Josef Holmgren and two others had formed the committee to support him, which naturally came to be called 'The Swedish Mission in China', as there was no other. Folke consulted John Stevenson at Shanghai and their friendly relationship from the first was reflected in the agreements reached between his friends in Sweden and Hudson Taylor. Folke adopted Puzhou and the south-western tip of Shanxi as his sphere, surveyed by Turner and James in 1876 (HTCOC Book 6, pp 84–6 map p 85), and found a foothold at Yüncheng. Before long his industry and gifts as a pioneer and leader of men led to his extending his territory to include thirty-eight counties in Shanxi, Shaanxi and Henan. After twenty-five years his mission had developed twelve central bases for fifty-four missionaries, a thousand Christians and a training school for evangelists. All was in such close association with the CIM in China as to be virtually part of it, working on the same lines.[1]

While Hudson Taylor was preparing for his Australia journey, Fredrik Franson had met the London Council (June 2, 1890) and been assured of help for the Barmen mission, the 'German China Alliance', before going back to America, to inspire the Scandinavian churches with his message of 'the gospel to every creature' and his axiom 'from each church a missionary'. Within three and a half months the first thirty-five volunteers had their support guaranteed by the churches who sent them, and Franson was given $5,000 in addition for general expenses. The first to arrive at Shanghai from the Swedish churches in the States, on October 28, 1890, was followed by a married couple. Then, two months after the Australians reached Shanghai with Hudson Taylor, the incredible happened. Word had come that Fredrik Franson was sending a party of twenty-five Swedes and Norwegians, towards the Thousand, but no more was known. On the morning of February 17, 1891, two blond young men were seen approaching the Mission Home and said they were the vanguard.[2] 'How many are you?' asked Stevenson, wondering how to accommodate them, for the house was full and several parties from other countries were expected. 'Thirty-five,' they answered, 'and ten more next week.' Never before in the history of Protestant missions in China had so many come at one time. All were taken in.

The letter they brought from Fredrik Franson was as cheerful as it was unbusinesslike, a true reflection of the man himself, and as much a surprise as the advent of so many unannounced. 'The intention of this Mission is to be associated with the China Inland Mission, just as Mr Folke (of the Swedish Mission in China) and Mr Olsson (with the German China Alliance) are . . . Hoping you will extend the same fraternal feelings of sympathy to our present party'![3] Hudson Taylor had 'a very warm view of (Franson); a most remarkable man of God, worthy of the utmost honour,'[4] and of the seventeen men and eighteen women of good quality, trained as evangelists, and ready to take conditions as they found them. The house was filled with music, singing to their guitars, and as the language schools were already full (with sixty at Yangzhou), the Swedes had to stay in Shanghai. On the day of their arrival they were set to work learning Chinese and improving their English, until arrangements could be made to distribute them up-country.

From October 19 to December 25, 1890, nine parties had reached Shanghai from Europe, Canada and Australia, numbering fifty-three in all. From January 1 to April 12, 1891, seven parties from Europe, the United States, Canada and Australia were received (including John Southey, his family and seven women) adding seventy-eight more novices. In a period of little over three weeks sixty-six had arrived: Franson's thirty-five on February 17, nine from England on February 21, four from Canada with Henry Frost on February 26, and fifteen instead of ten in Franson's second batch on March 10. Without the new premises the Mission could not have coped. In six months, before a year had elapsed since the General Conference's appeal, 131 men and women (members and associates) were added to the CIM. The stalwart lady-in-charge of the Home was the Scottish landowner, Miss Williamson, thoroughly competent and in command of the seventy-five new arrivals she had at one point in her care. A rising bell sounded at six am followed by breakfast at 7.30 and prayers at table. After the midday meal at 12.30 they sang a hymn and prayed for China. Tea at 3.30 pm made a break in language study and family prayers again followed the evening meal at 7.00 pm. They revelled in it.

Franson's men and women told Geraldine Guinness (in Shanghai to write the first volume of her *Story of the CIM*) that they had come 'with no certainty as to where or how they might be received' in China. Twenty-six men were sent under escort to Shanxi to be divided up between a dozen locations, and seven to Qü Xian in Zhejiang; and eighteen women to Dagutang on the Poyang Lake, followed by eight more of the second party. A field in Shaanxi and Gansu was allotted to them in 1894 and the Zhejiang seven joined the rest after Hudson Taylor had made another of his epic journeys.[5] A B Simpson's International Alliance Mission (p 125) had by then sent the forty-five Scandinavians recruited for him by Franson after despatching his own fifty to China. They also arrived in two parties on February 15 and 23, 1893.

The godly Fredrik Franson little knew what difficulties he created for the young men and women he despatched to the unknown, or for the already hard pressed veterans who received and supervised them in China, but these scores of zealous pioneers gave many years of good work. When Hudson Taylor drew A B Simpson's attention to the problems which Franson's flood created, he intervened. A thousand new missionaries in five years could readily be received, taught to speak Chinese and set to work in an orderly way, each mission taking its share of responsibility with due regard for the existing circumstances.

It happened that John Stevenson was taking his 'poor, afflicted Mary' home to Scotland, sailing on March 7 (the day Stanley Smith's wife died); that James Broumton had typhoid and his wife a life-threatening liver abscess; and that Hudson Taylor with his own work to do was the only one available with the necessary experience to take over the administration from Stevenson, and the financial responsibilities of Broumton when funds were uncomfortably low. Yet the overcrowding and coming and going made any work well-nigh impossible at times – all at a period of renewed attack on his own and his colleagues' integrity.[6]

The 'father of lies' and 'accuser of our brethren'   *1890–94*

Frequent references to Satan in the correspondence at this time show how convinced the writers were that the CIM was under his concerted attack. Every major advance seemed to be answered by major onslaughts, often taking the form of false accusations. Dr A P Happer, the veteran (1884) American Presbyterian of Canton, twice wrote to Hudson Taylor for the facts, that he might refute rumours in circulation.[7] One of his letters arrived while the China Council was in session, so Hudson Taylor consulted the leading men of the Mission. His reply was a window on otherwise seldom mentioned subjects, for 'when gossip has distorted facts, and misunderstanding and misrepresentation have gone on indefinitely, the mischief done is often past recall'.

> You mention 'the matter of written instructions to (our) missionaries . . . not to associate with other missionaries'. Such instructions *have never been given* . . . None of (the Council) has ever given, or seen, or heard of, such instructions.

Dr Happer had been told that members of the CIM were prevailed upon to become Baptists. 'The statements you have heard of proselytism are entirely false and ungrounded.' The only possible source might be in the fact that the Mission Secretary in London often gave a book of Spurgeon's sermons to missionaries leaving for China. But he himself was both Methodist and Anglican in sympathy! Many joined the CIM because in it they would be free to immerse. A recent example was an Anglican clergyman from Australia. 'Though a Baptist myself,' Hudson Taylor continued, 'as the head of a pan-denominational mission I have for twenty years refused (to give) instruction on this point . . . We have six organised Presbyterian churches (in North Anhui and Zhejiang) . . . four Episcopal stations (in Sichuan), four Methodist stations (in Yunnan).'[8]

The safety of women up-country caused him no anxiety:

> They feel as much at home as they would in England, and are quite as safe – I think more safe – from annoyance and insults. The (Chinese) pastor or evangelist and his wife take great care of them . . . My own daughter before her marriage was three months (without a foreign companion), as happy as the day was long, and too busy to be lonely. I have never heard of any insult even, much less assault, on any lady worker inland; more care is needed in a place like Shanghai or

Hankou . . . The ladies 'walk with God', and the beauty of holiness
. . . gives them a dignity before which lewdness cannot live . . . They
are really *entrusted* to the care of our Lord Himself . . . and He is
faithful to the trust.

Far more painful were letters from a member of the London
Council. On the strength of hearsay and without verification, an
honoured veteran was being accused and condemned at a distance
for alleged indiscretions with young women of the Yangzhou
language school.[9] Hudson Taylor knew the circumstances too well
to allow of a moment's doubt about his good friend. Since he had
arrived twenty-five years before, he had been all that had been
hoped of him. Full enquiry showed there was no substance to the
rumours. Colleagues had only good to say of him. Anything ill-
judged in what gave rise to complaint was outweighed by the
indiscretion of someone writing to a member of the London Council
instead of to the directors in China, and of 'London' in minuting
their discussion and conclusions.

Far worse, it precipitated another constitutional crisis. The
London Council began to take a strong hand in 'Field' affairs. One
member wrote saying it was 'time to consider whether someone
indiscreet was *wise enough* and had the *gravity enough* for the post
of superintendent.' He should be removed from the China Council.
The Home Director had also acquired the wholly false impression of
his personality, 'that (he) "loves power and the exercise of it"'. But,
Hudson Taylor replied, 'Few men care less about it than he does.'
Because false impressions developed all too easily in correspondence, he went on, 'Is it possible for you to come out and look into
things with me?' It was not.[10] His reminder that the directors in
China were in a better position to know and act in such a matter was
curtly answered by William Sharp with, 'Your letter manifests such
marked absence of trust . . . in your Home Council', whereas the
trouble lay in 'your wrong ideas – and your China Council's'. And
this was followed by the misconception, 'Your chief contention for
several years past has been that we as a Council should be entirely
cut off from the missionaries once they have sailed for China.' Far
from it. Missionaries and directors in China were troubled that so
few friendly letters came from London.

For the London Council to intervene in administrative and
disciplinary action from a distance was a very different matter.
These bones of contention were evidence of underlying attitudes

and more misconceptions. The status of the London Council and a supposed threat to it from the new China Council quickly emerged as the main issue. Confidence in Hudson Taylor could not be extended to 'a few of the brethren' comprising the China Council. 'You have a Council here (in London) *nominally* to advise you', but it should be recognised as having administrative power. 'It would appear . . . that your view of unity or unanimity is accordance by all concerned in your own view.' So he, Sharp, 'could wish you were led to leave the Mission to get on by itself while you took up more largely the expounding of Scripture and stirring up of the Churches'!

Instead of Hudson Taylor, let London run the Mission? The Principles and Practice appeared to have been forgotten, and the role of other councils overlooked. How would the Mission recover from such a rift, in such a spirit? Never before had such propositions been advanced, or Hudson Taylor's leadership been challenged. From its inception the London Council had been advisory, and Hudson Taylor had taken pains to explain and give reasons when his judgment differed from theirs. But the Principles pre-dated the Council, and he must maintain them, whoever might object. All members had agreed with the P and P in joining the Mission. The full manuscript sources show adamant insistence by London in exercising power which it had never had nor wanted until 1891 – 'the fact constantly affirmed by Mr Howard, Mr Hill and others [until now] that the London Council never had and were never supposed or intended to have any authority over the work in China, and by the fact that when appealed to, the Council always repudiated such appeals as being out of their province.'[11]

Strong-willed men confronted each other, but the crux was not whose will would prevail but which view was right? As for the allegations, Hudson Taylor protested to Theodore Howard, 'He thought (the Council) would wish to reconsider their action in the matter, with further information already sent to England: "I trust you will be led to cancel the minute."' They did.[12] The slandered veteran agreed to pioneer Guangxi, if moving away for a time would clear the air. But 'that sorrowful persecution of a beloved servant of God' continued until Henry Frost invited him to help him in North America 'for six months or a year'. He went, in December 1891. Then other pretexts for raising the status of the London Council were found. The 'accuser of the brethren' had had a heyday.

'Not against flesh and blood' *1891–94*

Following the General Conference in Shanghai, criticisms appeared in the *Chinese Recorder* under the heading 'Chinese Dress in the Shanghai Conference'. The writer quoted rumours 'that one half of those who enter China under its (the CIM's) auspices, return within two years, either to their homeland on earth or to the home above', and, 'That the average term of service for the whole body is only three and a half years.' Hudson Taylor wrote at once to give the facts. 'I find that 539 persons have been connected with the China Inland Mission . . . during the last 26 years.' Instead of 'one half' (270) only forty-four left China within two years – twenty-one by death, five by illness, four resigned, five were asked to withdraw, and nine for marriage or family claims. Of 373 full members, not probationers, twenty died after an average of eight and a half years' service; twelve were invalided home after six and a half years on average, twenty-one retired, nine were asked to leave, eighteen left to marry or for family claims and four were transferred to the home staff. These eighty-six served for six years one month on average, not three and a half. Not included in those categories were 287 full members, about to complete an average of seven years' service – the inevitable result of the recent rapid increase in numbers. The first fifty members of the CIM completed seventeen years on average, and of them sixteen averaged twenty-four and three-fourths years. 'We are led to conclude that our Mission is, by God's blessing, one of the healthiest in China.'[13]

In July 1891 the *North China Daily News* published a letter from an Yichang resident accusing CIM women and men of travelling 'huddled together' in the same boat without chaperones and 'promiscuously travelling in company overland', 'apeing Chinese dress and manners' as a disguise, but ignorantly breaking their customs. Hudson Taylor wrote on his copy, *'Untrue.* Their man-servant was a quiet disciple, and the boat-woman who acted as their servant, there is some hope was converted and helped them to preach.' From the Chinese point of view they were fully chaperoned. The Chongqing correspondent of the *Daily News* 'spoke up warmly' on the 20th, saying he had known every party of missionaries making the journey up the gorges for the past eight years (so was he a customs officer?) and had 'never known of anything improper in their travelling arrangements'. The only exception to single women travelling in the care of a missionary couple had been the one instance – wrongly criticised because no male missionary was with them. Dr James Cameron joined in. As women on their own, the travellers had had less trouble than experienced men often met with from unfriendly people.[14]

'The accuser' had not finished. His next barb was from the China secretary of another mission in August 1891 to James Meadows, the senior CIM superintendent in Zhejiang. Apparently overlooking Hudson Taylor's rebuttal in the *Chinese Recorder*, this writer questioned 'the very great loss of missionaries . . . year by year' in the CIM – 'a grave defect in the management of the Mission'. Hudson Taylor replied that the single women who had 'disappeared' from the Mission's lists were those who had married. Excluding associates for whose selection and medical condition the CIM was not responsible (although Dr Howard Taylor and others were constantly on call for anyone in need), the losses in the first two years compared favourably with other missions. Those with conscientious objections to vaccination came to China at great risk to themselves and affected the calculation. (But because of the danger to others who had to nurse smallpox cases, no more unvaccinated people were sent by the CIM from about this time.)[15]

An unusually tragic sequence of harrowing deaths had recently wracked the emotions of mission leaders, friends and families. Soon after the General Conference the veteran Presbyterian, Alexander Williamson, died suddenly. In November 1890 James Meadows' wife, Elizabeth (Rose), succumbed when nine foreigners and eight Chinese were ill with influenza in the same house. Travelling back to Sichuan from the coast, Arthur Polhill and his wife found too late that a Chinese passenger on the same boat had 'typhus'. Arthur himself contracted it and nearly died. And on March 7, 1891, Stanley Smith's wife of three years (Sophie Reuter, of Kristiansand) died of typhus (or typhoid). In September Miss E Tanner, a new missionary, fell off the Ningbo city wall, sustained a compound fracture and osteomyelitis, and later died after amputation. Returning from Yantai with George Andrew and his son, Hudson Taylor's ship barely survived a typhoon which smashed to wreckage another ship accompanying them. On October 3, Thomas Thorne of the Bible Christians died of typhus. 'Black smallpox' took its toll of some, dysentery of others. Most missions shared the suffering. For Hudson Taylor, Frederick Gough's death in Ningbo and C H Spurgeon's in London, on February 5, 1892, removed two more strong human props.[16]

The CIM had become several times larger than any other society in China and correspondingly conspicuous. Misconceptions were understandable. If the CIM was named more often than other missions, surely its care of its personnel must be at fault. After deaths at Yangzhou from smallpox and malignant malaria, even the Zhenjiang (Chinkiang) acting consul complained of neglect. How strange, Hudson Taylor commented to him, for 'all Chinkiang' had depended on CIM doctors. Dr Cox had his hospital there, close to Yangzhou, and Howard Taylor, MD, FRCS, 'paid special attention' to the language schools. 'The . . . statistics of our Mission as a whole are more favourable than those of the whole body of Protestant missionaries.' So often criticism was voiced before the facts were ascertained. But still the deaths followed one upon another.

None of these events surprised those who saw the missionary adventure as a conflict 'not against flesh and blood but against principalities, against powers, against the rulers of the darkness of this world, against spiritual wickedness in high places,' from which the people of God were not immune. In his New Year editorial for January 1892 Hudson Taylor remarked that 'almost every little church, and almost every station has had its trials' as sickness, death, disharmony, flood, drought, persecution with violence, slanderous handbills and low funds tested the Church and mission.[17] But it was not one-sided. Baptisms were being reported from the worst affected places, and the gospel was being taken to the remotest regions – even to the gates of Lhasa.

The glamour of Tibet   *1816–94*

Ever since an Englishman named Manning met the Dalai Lama in Lhasa in 1816, the magnetism of this city of his Bodala (Potala) palace has drawn others. In the secular dress of lamas the Abbé Huc and Joseph Gabet travelled in 1846 with a Tibetan dignitary and his two thousand-strong escort, and were well received by the Dalai Lama and Tibetan regent.[18] Asked as Christian lamas to write something in their own language, Huc wrote, 'What does it profit a man if he conquers the whole world but loses his own soul?' Translated into Tibetan, these words of Christ impressed his hosts. Huc and Gabet would gladly have lived out their lives in Lhasa, but the unfriendly Chinese resident or ambassador had them expelled.

Nearly every subsequent traveller in Tibet has seen Lhasa as the goal. For some the lure has been geographical discovery; for others adventure and personal achievement; for some political influence or escape; and for the missionaries, carrying the gospel to 'all the world'. Repeated attempts by the Société des Missions Étrangères de Paris to cross the border were thwarted, until a firm foothold on the threshold at Batang and unlimited patience became their policy. We saw how Henry Lansdell with his message from the Archbishop of Canterbury in November 1888 (p 48) failed to penetrate beyond Leh in Ladakh. The American William Woodville Rockhill was trying at the time to find companions for an attempt on Lhasa, with no greater success.

A comparison of dates showed the CIM pioneers in the perspective of efforts to cross Tibet and to reach Lhasa. They took their time. Annie Royle Taylor (p 130) arrived in China in early November 1884. After language study and an introduction to conditions inland, she went to Gansu and rented a house in Lanzhou before any foreign man was tolerated in the city. But Tibet was her goal, she insisted, not China. Because she was an individualist and needed scope, she was given a free rein and learned lessons the painful way. But nothing could stop her.

By the summer of 1888 she had done her prospecting and found a springboard at Taozhou (now Luqü) on the Gansu-Qinghai border of ethnological 'Greater Tibet'. There she learned Tibetan, made contacts and prepared to take the big plunge. She returned to Britain in 1889 and on the way back to China spent six months at Darjeeling investigating the possibility of entering Tibet through Sikkim. In June 1890 Hudson Taylor wrote of 'dear Annie Taylor (having) a very hard time of it', but she persevered and set out from Taozhou on September 2, 1892, for Lhasa. In Peter Hopkirk's Trespassers on the Roof of the World[19] is this tribute to Annie Taylor: 'Unshakable courage and absolute faith shine forth from every page of her battered journal.'

Cecil Polhill-Turner[20] continued his language study in Chengdu with Samuel Clarke's help, and then joined the Laughtons at Xining, a hundred miles west of Lanzhou and inside the Eastern Tibetan region of Ando, included in Qinghai on modern maps. A life in and out of the saddle suited the one-time dragoon. He married Eleanor Marsden in 1888 – another of the strong 1884 additions to the CIM – and together they learned Tibetan from an old man who had travelled with Huc and Gabet. For a time they lived at 'Tankar', the last Chinese town before Lake Kokonor, and found the monks of the great Kumbum monastery friendly. Better still, the abbot Pancheda of Maying monastery, four days' travel from Xining, listened earnestly to the gospel, showed that he understood its implications and was 'convinced but not converted'. He also taught Cecil Polhill more Tibetan. They then took a house at 'Wachia' right among Tibetans sixty miles south of Xining, and succeeded in planting a church at Guide, fifteen miles nearer to Xining. But they had no thought of settling down.

During this period, in 1890–91 a Frenchman, Bonvalot, and Prince Henry of Orleans penetrated Tibet from the north, but were turned away from Lhasa when only ninety-five miles remained to be covered. They were permitted to travel eastwards to leave Tibet at Batang. Two Britons, Captain (later Major-General Sir) Hamilton Bower and Surgeon-Captain W G Thorold, entered western Tibet on July 3, 1891, only to be thwarted like everyone else. They regained Chinese territory in January 1892. But all bare statements convey nothing of the privations and dangers to life involved in every journey on 'the Roof of the World'.

In 1891 the Polhills handed over the Xining region to H French Ridley of the CIM, soon to make history in the Muslim rebellion, and joining a caravan of seventy Muslim merchants travelled to the important Labrang monastery (at Xiahe on present-day maps p 234). Labrang with its four or five thousand monks ruled over 108 similar monasteries. From there they returned to Gansu, to find Annie Taylor living in the main Chinese inn at Taozhou, before her attempt on Lhasa. In the Taozhou-Choni region the Polhills worked for a month, everywhere well received, before returning to Lanzhou and beginning another chapter of their lives. A B Simpson's C&MA Scandinavians then began in 1892 to take responsibility for the nucleus of Christian Chinese and Tibetans in the Taozhou-Choni area.

Already a distinct pattern is recognisable in the approach by the CIM to Tibet. Lhasa remained Annie Taylor's goal, but steady evangelism and thorough adaptation to the people and their ways was allowed to take even years before the big venture. The aim was to reach people, not places; the hearts of Tibetans wherever they might be. The heart of Lamaism might be Annie Taylor's ambitious goal, but Cecil Polhill's sense of commission was to preach Christ to Tibetans and have them carry the truth to others, eventually to Lhasa itself.

To digress for a moment, the complete freedom they had to

develop their work in their own way, with Hudson Taylor's strong support and no interference, was also recognisable in Thomas Botham's incessant itineration on the Shaanxi plains and Benjamin Ririe's in West Sichuan, just as Dixon Hoste's choice of playing second string to Hsi Shengmo had his blessing. Dr Arthur Douthwaite, building up a strong hospital practice at Yantai, also appreciated this policy, as did Dr William Wilson at Hanzhong.

> There is as much liberty in the CIM as any man could reasonably desire [Douthwaite wrote to his father-in-law, one of the Groves family of Bristol (HTCOC Books 1–4, Personalia)]. After he has given proof of ability to learn the language and has had five years experience under his seniors, he may choose his own sphere of permanent work and carry on that work in his own way as the Lord may lead him.[21]

In November 1891 Cecil Polhill left his wife and boys at Tianshui and after visiting his brother, Arthur, at Bazhou and Cassels at Langzhong, reconnoitred the mountainous region of Sichuan, south of Gansu and bordering the Tibetan marches with their semi-Tibetan and fully Tibetan ethnic divisions.[22] Montagu Beauchamp accompanied Cecil for part of the way, and a Christian ex-soldier, Wang Cuan-yi (Wang Ts'uan-i), volunteered to join him, unpaid.[23]

They found the people of the remote frontier post, Songpan, to be friendly and pleased to meet a Westerner speaking Chinese and Tibetan. So while Wang stayed, Polhill rode across wild country with a government courier and the obligatory escort of soldiers as protection against robbers, making for Tianshui. At a monastery on his route the abbot assembled all his monks to hear the gospel and exhorted them to ponder what they heard and to do what their consciences might dictate. Cecil Polhill declined the escort of armed monks offered by the abbot, but welcomed the companionship of unarmed monks. They overtook a party of merchants who had been attacked, and one killed, on the day Polhill would have gone that way had the abbot not been so hospitable.

In March 1892 he set out again with his wife and sons, overland by pack train from Tianshui to Guangyuan in twelve days by safer roads, and from there westwards to Songpan in twenty-two days. Home was a room with two Chinese beds, two chairs and a small table, beside a yard often filled with yak. The Tibetans treated Cecil as one of their own monks, and for two and a half months all went well. Then drought drove the Chinese to pin the blame on someone.[24]

On July 29, 1892, he, his wife, Wang the soldier and another Christian named Zhang were bound, beaten by the mob, stripped to the waist (Eleanor included) and led out of the walled town to cries of 'Throw them in the river!' 'Stone them!' 'Tie them up in the sun till rain falls!' No Tibetan or Muslim joined in. A military official rescued them and took them to the magistrate's *yamen*. But the mob had to be placated. For several hours the victims were left with arms tightly bound. Then Wang and Zhang were asked if they were willing to be flogged in lieu of the foreigners. They agreed, were beaten with sticks until raw and put in *cangues* (*see* HTCOC 2, p 369). The Polhills were then freed and the two men shared a room with them until at last they were all allowed to leave and travel painfully to the plains.

On August 13 they found some missionaries on holiday at a hill temple, and at last had their injuries treated and wholesome food to restore them to strength. They then travelled through Guanxian to Chengdu, at the height of plague. Hundreds of coffins were piled up waiting for burial. After eight years in China, home leave followed, and Cecil Polhill urged that the CIM should expand to the extremities of China. Songpan was reoccupied by young men of the CIM and Heywood Horsburgh's CMS team.

The heroes of the Songpan riot had been Wang and Zhang, showing courage 'beyond the call of duty'. Zhang afterwards said, 'I couldn't help smiling . . . when we were being marched through the town with wrists tied – smiling that we were in a very small way like our Master, Jesus Christ.' But not only he. In 1923 a mature Christian gentleman told a missionary that he had witnessed the events at Songpan and decided he must become a Christian. Wang and Zhang returned to East Sichuan and were known as exemplary evangelists in the Langzhong (Paoning) church.[25]

Before the Polhills left for home in November 1892, Annie Taylor was ready to cross Tibet to Lhasa, one thousand miles 'as the crow flies', with Pontso, the Tibetan she had won for Christ. In addition to two men to manage her sixteen saddle and pack horses, for her tents and provisions she took on a Chinese, who used the Tibetan name Noga, and his Tibetan wife. Annie herself dressed and lived as a Tibetan, shaving her head like a Tibetan nun or 'Annia'.[26]

They left Taozhou, near Kumbum, on September 2, 1892, and

four months later, January 3, 1893, were closer to Lhasa than any foreigner since Huc and Gabet in 1846, only three marches away. By then bandits had harassed them, killed most of their animals and taken a tent and their changes of clothing. One man had died and the other forsook them. Noga turned on her, demanding money with threats to denounce her to the Lhasa authorities. Yet she kept a daily diary, never complained in it, and gamely made a Christmas pudding with the currants and black sugar, flour and suet she had brought with her. At that high altitude the centre remained un-cooked. But Noga rode ahead and betrayed her. She was arrested. For bringing an alien with him Pontso was in danger of execution – and she of death if they forced her to travel out alone. A battle of wits with the help of God seemed her only hope. High spirited, she demanded justice, argued that in their reduced condition they could not travel further than Lhasa. And when they insisted that she return to China, she argued until she was on friendly terms with them and had an escort, horses, clothing, bedding and food provided.

On January 22, 1893, they left Lhasa territory, on a journey through Batang even more harrowing than the first when she was her own master. Kangding was reached on April 12, and they passed through Chongqing on May 6, to arrive at Shanghai on May 20. The *North China Daily News* carried some of the facts, but another report had them choicely garbled to complete a journey from Darjeeling to Chongqing via Tibet. After all that, Pontso deserved the voyage via Canada to reach Britain on July 1.[27] (He looked as intelligent and at home in Western dress in London and Keswick group photographs as in his homeland.)

Annie Taylor's story was far from over. Within eight months she had floated the Tibetan Pioneer Mission with a London committee led by William Sharp, and left again for Kalimpong with a party of fourteen missionaries. They sailed on February 23, 1894, and on March 1 the Anglo-Chinese Convention on Burma and Tibet settled the confrontation. The way was open for them to approach Tibet through Sikkim. But before the end of the year they were in serious trouble (p 237). –

A former French naval officer, Jules Dutreuil de Rhins, who was exploring the Karakoram and Kunlun mountain ranges, started for Lhasa on September 3, 1893. After four months he was only six days' march from Lhasa when he and his party were halted. They refused to be forced back and argued for fifty days before accepting the inevitable. At last on January 20, 1894, they too began the long trek out, only to lose de Rhins who died on the way. Sven Anders Hedin's remarkable travels also began in 1893 when this Swedish geographer of twenty-eight penetrated Chinese Turkestan from Tashkent and Bokhara, to enter north-western Tibet, two years before his Taklamakan desert journey.

The last five years of the century had no less dramatic a saga in store.

'The eve of rebellion?'   *1891–94*

If 1891 began with a flourish as floods of American-Scandinavians and Europeans arrived in China, the year continued packed with excitement of a different kind. The *Chinese Recorder*, mirror of the general community of Protestant missions, took note that the CIM had blossomed suddenly into international colours. Fifteen nationalities could be named, including Dutch, Finnish, German, Norwegian, Russian, Swedish and Swiss newcomers. As soon as they and others from the Australian colonies, Canada and the States could be dispersed from Shanghai they were sent on.

In April, twenty-nine of the thirty-one North Americans of Henry Frost's branch of the CIM met with Hudson Taylor and Frost (April 14–21) and unanimously voted in favour of becoming full members of the Mission. They wished their own funds from home to be merged with the general fund. They would sink or swim with the rest.[28] They then scattered to their stations and Henry Frost toured their districts with the bereaved Stanley Smith as escort, beginning with Zhejiang and the Guangxin River region of Jiangxi. Hudson Taylor himself started up the Yangzi River to visit the language schools at Yangzhou, Anqing and Dagutang.

While he was at Yangzhou on May 6 the Catholic 'foundling hospital' was again the focus of a riot. Crowds collected threatening violence, but 'the magistrate acted promptly and with 400 soldiers dispersed the mob'. At Anqing the main Catholic orphanage building was burned to the ground and as much property destroyed as possible. The CIM premises were untouched. Foul accusations of what was being done with children were in circulation again, originating in Hunan as usual.[29] Hudson Taylor paid a courtesy call on the Yangzhou magistrate and after four days went on up the Yangzi to the seat of trouble at Anqing. Returning on the 12th his boat stood offshore at Wuhu for twelve hours, while the RC cathedral was burned down, waiting to evacuate foreign refugees from the riot.

On June 5 a Methodist missionary named Argent (p 109) was on the wharf at Wuxüe (Wusueh, now Guangji, map p 94) in Hubei when a rumour spread that children were being taken downstream for immoral purposes. A mob attacked and killed him and a customs officer, Green, who went to his help. The authorities protected the two men's wives until a ship took them to safety. Some missionary refugees who reached Shanghai from Nanjing and Suzhou were welcomed at Wusong Road. But by the 8th Shanghai itself was in danger from the high feeling in the Chinese city. All missionary women and children were taken into the Settlement; troops protected the Jesuit headquarters at Siccawei (HTCOC Book 1, p 63); and Chinese guards were posted around the Wusong Road property. The night of Saturday, June 13, was 'crisis night', when an attack on the Settlement was expected. Tension reached its peak when a screaming child could not be quietened. It was impossible to know what this wave of rioting through the Yangzi valley would lead to. They could but wait and see. 'A good spirit' prevailed among the refugees at Wusong Road, and Hudson Taylor glazed the verandah of his room as a conservatory for the tropical plants he had collected in the Torres Strait. The climbers were beginning to clothe the pillars of the building itself.

Word then came from Jiujiang that the consul was advising the removal of the CIM women from Dagutang on the Poyang Lake. 'I wired back asking them to stop where they were, until Mr McCarthy should arrive. He left immediately for Jiujiang.' But on receiving the consul's letter the women had felt bound to leave Dagutang at once, reaching Jiujiang safely by boat. No riot developed, but the soldiers sent to guard their premises broke in and helped themselves. 'Even the foreigners (at Jiujiang) cannot scrape together enough reason for being scared just now,' McCarthy reported. 'They were beginning in the city, but it was all over in five minutes. The officials are all on the alert. We praised the Lord, (but) even the Lord's servants get into the current of unbelief.' He calmly took the women back to Dagutang.[30]

Hudson Taylor wrote to warn Theodore Howard that while organised riots were indeed taking place, alarming newspaper reports should be read with reserve. Missionaries' relatives who enquired anxiously could be reassured. The riots were against Catholic property, not lives. 'Many attribute these riots to the

(Golaohui) and say the object of this secret society is to involve China in war with foreign powers with a view to overthrowing the present dynasty.' Others blamed disbanded soldiery whose pensions had been cut off. War would get them reinstated. In the *Cambridge History of China*, John King Fairbank stated,

> There is evidence that the Yangtze Valley riots of 1891 were fomented in part by disgruntled secret society members whose aim was not to do injury to Christians, but to bring down the dynasty by forcing it into conflict with the Western powers . . . Conversely, the authorities themselves, in some instances, intentionally associated themselves with extreme anti-foreign stands . . . because this was the only way to prevent popular anti-foreign feeling from being turned against them.[31]

What mattered to Hudson Taylor was that the CIM should set an example of calmness from 'trust in the Living God, who is able to protect . . . and will do so unless for His own wise purposes He sees His own glory will be more advanced by their suffering.' At McCarthy's suggestion he wrote a general letter to all the Mission on *The Attitude of Missionaries in Times of Danger*. Often in the past he had spoken and written on this subject, but the majority of those he was now responsible for were young and inexperienced.

First of all, he pointed out, the Biblical injunction 'not to speak evil of dignitaries' applied to Chinese officials. Second, national pride had no place in the matter; missionaries were not representatives of foreign powers, but in China solely to preach Christ. Third, there were three good reasons for not leaving their posts from fear, but only if forced out: they were under God's protection; they were given an opportunity to set an example, encouraging the Christians to be brave; and the influence of their calmness would be great. 'A holy joy in God is far better protection than a revolver,' he assured them. He could have gone on to cite instance after instance in the twenty-five years of the Mission's history. Expounding Acts 9 one day in June at Shanghai, he said, 'The Lord did not say to Saul, "How hard for those you are persecuting," but "How hard it is for *you* . . ."' How easy it would be for God to change the aspect of affairs (for us).' We must pray for those who persecute us.[32]

Charles Fishe, following Jennie Taylor as sub-editor of *China's Millions* in London, took the same line in his editorial. The policy of the *Millions* was to exclude political matter, and not to follow the

press, but to wait for facts and opinions from Hudson Taylor. Even
The Times had exaggerated the news by giving space to rumours.
Anyway, 'the wave of outrage . . . has probably spent its force.'
Canton, historically notorious for its xenophobic outbreaks, had
remained quiet, a sign that the Yangzi Valley riots were local in
significance. A report which reached Hudson Taylor that the Shashi
house had been burned down proved untrue. The 'looting' by
soldiers at Dagutang turned out to be no more than a raid on the
pantry. An imperial proclamation had quieted the people to the
extent that they were prepared for missionaries to rent premises
again. And the official *Peking Gazette* reminded the nation of the
famine relief done by missionaries with 'a cheerful readiness to do
good', so that they 'deserve high commendation'.

Even so, disturbances continued, though not on the scale of June
1891.[33] Petite Kate Mackintosh, writing from Yüshan at the head of
the Guangxin River where six Swedish girls were learning Chinese,
showed the right spirit: 'A good deal of rumour (has been circulating) since the riots, but we go on quietly as usual.' Most who lived
far from any human protection other than the *yamen* might afford
shared her faith. (She married H N Lachlan, the barrister, later in
the year.)

Hangzhou was threatened; the Catholics at Chongqing had some
trouble; Yichang and Shashi simmered in the summer heat, and
when the riot erupted in September all foreign property in Yichang
was destroyed. At Wenzhou people screamed and hid when a
foreign warship without warning turned on its apocalyptic search-
lights, a new and terrifying phenomenon. The atmosphere was
tense.[34] Hudson Taylor was badly needed in London, but the
possibility that China was 'on the eve of rebellion', and an urgent
need for him to visit some places in the interior made it impossible to
go home. Torrential rains in October damped the ardour of rioters,
and 1892 ended with relatively little disturbance.

An order on March 25 for the arrest of Zhou Han, the Hunanese
author of scurrilous pamphlets and posters, may have had some
effect. One edition of 'Death to the devil's religion', the most
notorious pamphlet, of eight hundred thousand copies, had been
distributed without charge.[35] At Chenggu in Shaanxi accusations
that the missionaries were poisoning wells provoked a riot. The
premises were wrecked and plundered, but all except one Chinese
Christian escaped injury by hiding in a neighbour's house. The
magistrates did not deny the rumours, but announced that Henan

men were the culprits, so peace returned. The Songpan riot appeared to have been genuinely due to superstition. It showed no evidence of outside instigation having used the drought as a pretext. Another major riot at Yichang on November 26 ushered in more violence in 1893. And at Jiangjin between Chongqing and Luzhou, two CIM women and one of the associate Friends' Mission had to escape over the roof to a neighbour's house when their own was broken into.[36]

Then on July 1, 1893, at Songbu near Macheng, sixty miles north-east of Hankou, the two Swedish missionaries were killed in the street. Strong suspicions of official instigation were strengthened by the refusal of any compensation. Their death seemed to the Shanghai Missionary Association, a forum of different societies, to be a knell, the withdrawal of God's protection. They issued an appeal for fasting and prayer. 'Something of a crisis seems approaching . . . signs of the times . . . to be up and calling upon our God to stay the hands of His and our enemies.'[37] Chinese and foreigners felt tension in the air, an intangible feeling of threat on the political, international and missionary fronts. J A Wylie, a Presbyterian, was murdered by Manchu soldiers in Manchuria in 1894, and in June of that year events began to move inexorably towards the fateful Sino-Japanese war. With a Mission membership of 560 (apart from home-staffs) in his care, and hundreds of Chinese, Hudson Taylor was bearing heavy responsibility. But far outweighing the physical dangers was a resurgence of the spiritual conflict, 'Satan's bewildering attack', in the guise of yet more conflict of opinion between the London Council and the General Director.

Heading for the rocks: a reminder   *1886–93*

Violence and even massacre have strengthened rather than weakened the China Inland Mission on many occasions in the century and a quarter of its existence. Tightening its belt at times of low income has done it good, focusing its attention on the One who provides because it is his own work. What shook the Mission to its foundations in the last decade of the nineteenth century was the controversy over the Principles and Practice. The seven-year challenge to parts of the P and P and to Hudson Taylor's leadership coincided not only with attack from other quarters but, as we have seen, with several major developments – the numerical and territorial expansion, extension to America, Europe and Australasia, and the essential reorganisation in China. Yet, as he pointed out, the lessons learned did more to shape and settle the Mission than any points at issue did to weaken it – a fact to bear in mind as the story unfolds. An outline of what transpired is essential to this history.

From November 1886 tension persisted between him and London until July 1893. We remember that when the far-seeing action of the first China Council at Anqing in October 1886 came to the knowledge of the London Council they were up in arms. Led by Hudson Taylor, the China Council had called for the Hundred reinforcements and submitted for comment their draft revision of the Principles and Practice and the highly practical little Book of Arrangements (HTCOC Book 6 pp 420–3). It is difficult to see why the Home Director and London Council forgot that before he returned to China Hudson Taylor had gone through the P and P with them and this revision was only the expression of what had been agreed. And the reorganisation of the Mission to cater for its expanding membership and ever more complicated make-up had been with London's encouragement and even insistence. What appeared to gall them was that they had been left out of the implementation. In fact they had not.

The Mission from its inception had by definition existed specifically 'to assist' Hudson Taylor in his work of evangelising China. Even his co-founder William Berger had regarded it as Hudson Taylor's mission and him as the undisputed leader. This fact of history was fundamental to an understanding of the ethos of the CIM. When the sheer volume of administrative work (let alone his medical care of all and sundry) outstripped his time and strength, he had repeatedly been pressed to delegate duties to others. Eventually suitable colleagues had emerged to share responsibility and he had gradually installed Stevenson as his deputy director, Broumton as treasurer in China, and provincial superintendents to care for and guide the multiplying missionaries in their regions. That they should meet as a China Council to consult together, unify their policies and actions in the 'field', and speak with one voice, was the logical outcome.

Two understandable but discordant reactions touched off the resistance to this progress that came close to wrecking the Mission. In China some senior members who had enjoyed years of the free and easy family relationship in the early mission resented having others, even younger men, set over them. Deplorably, in Britain also the China Council was seen as a rival and, as argument developed, it became clear that the London Council saw itself as the chief council of the CIM and other councils as subordinate.

Few of these attitudes were apparent at first. Hudson Taylor was nonplussed. Urged to delegate he found his delegation of duties met with the cry, 'We want to deal with you personally.' Told to organise, and carrying out what London had agreed was necessary, he saw the London Council claiming rights and authority it had disclaimed in the past. The voluminous correspondence and recollections show beyond question, far from an authoritarian Hudson Taylor forcing his 'dictates' on 'nonentities', an embattled leader was having to defend the basic principles on which he had founded the Mission, and was being prevailed upon to withdraw concessions which he himself had introduced. We see how he was driven into the position of 'final headship', with all councils of the Mission having equal status as advisers to a director or chairman whose responsibility it was to make the decision.

Objections to a North American branch of the Mission claimed priority over affairs in China during 1888–89, but strong criticism by the London Council of the Principles and Practice soon overshadowed that issue. With every courtesy they told Hudson Taylor, '. . . The Council wish you to be assured that there is no desire to interfere with the conduct of the work in China. They have never done so; on the contrary they have on various occasions of difficulty given you moral support.'[38] This endorsed what Theodore Howard had written (p 159), denying the notion that members could appeal to London against the directors in China. Yet when complaints came from China, the council had taken them up instead of referring them back.

Objections to the Book of Arrangements as 'a law of the Medes and Persians' (p 132) were made in a different spirit. It was only a manual to guide missionaries in the field, with a few rulings on unacceptable practices. The conference of CIM missionaries in May 1890 had found little in the documents to question. A field handbook was welcomed as useful. Yet in the light of London's comments Hudson Taylor and the China Council again reviewed both the P and P and the Arrangements. Another proof-edition with wide margins was printed and circulated for yet more comment and correspondence, to be revised again after eight months or a year. Three and a half years had already passed since these papers had first been drafted. It was high time for them to be made official. The Principles and Practice concerned the whole Mission, including Home departments, but practical 'Arrangements' for China were outside the London Council's sphere. Even so, courtesy copies again went to them and London returned month after month to discussing them, finding objections where those in China could see none. On January 6, 1891, they adopted a new tone. The Council minutes referred to their discussion as being 'final'. Attitudes were hardening. But a redeeming feature was that the sections of the Arrangements with which they had no quarrel were already in use.

In the autumn of 1891 feelings ran high in London on their demands for the last word in some field matters. 'The supreme question is that of final headship,' Hudson Taylor wrote to Stevenson, 'but great gentleness and patience will be needed to make the reasonableness of this clear to all, and it is equally clear to me that it can only be vested in China.'[39] London had little idea of how much they would become involved if their demand was conceded, or how impossible it would be to debate personnel problems by long-distance correspondence. How could the administration in China proceed, if London's views on any issue differed from the China directors'? Was the London Council to become the final court of appeal against the decisions of the directors in China, even of the General Director when he was there? Hudson Taylor could see no solution other than the status quo – the foundation principle of running field affairs on the field – and the China Council agreed with him. Still London saw the China Council as a departure from the principle of government in China by Hudson Taylor himself.

John Stevenson was still in Britain when Hudson Taylor wrote desperately from Shanghai on July 31, 1891.

> While I let you know in confidence that my mind is made up, I do not wish to bring pressure on the Home Council . . . Do your best to get them *individually* to see (that they cannot take power by force), but do not put our refusal of it in the form of an ultimatum. Should I and certain other members of the (China) Council conclude on retiring, we will endeavour to do so in such a form as shall do least harm to a work dear to us all. Those of us who retire may form another mission for the purpose of preaching the gospel . . . But surely God will avert the danger as He has so many others.
>
> [And on August 28 to Theodore Howard, swayed by persuasive arguments:]
>
> You very clearly stated the position in your draft of your letter . . .

of February 6, 1890: 'We were never supposed or intended to have and never have had any authority over the work in China; we never interfered . . . we have been a Council of advice and consultation, not for government, as regards the China work . . . Nor would it ever have been admitted that we were in any sense a Council to which missionaries in China could appeal from any decision of the China Directors or China Council.'

. . . Do not I beseech you for Christ's sake rend the Mission asunder by claiming what you yourself have repeatedly affirmed was never intended and would never be agreed to.[40]

The new international nature of the Mission confirmed and reinforced the wisdom of the original principle. The work in China being done by so diverse a team from different nations, different denominations, different social and educational backgrounds, must be unified *in China*. London's arm could only reach British members. Together Hudson Taylor and the China Council set out in detail their 'Reasons' (as the document came to be called) for insisting on jurisdiction over affairs in China being exercised solely in China.

To fuse the whole into one united body of workers is a matter of the utmost moment. Everything tending to keep up a feeling of distinctness and separation is to be avoided . . . Either we must be equally free to deal with them all, or if necessary to decline to deal further with any one of them, or the harmony, the unity, and the welfare of the work will be sacrificed. 'No man can serve two masters.' The introduction of the proposed principle [of London having the last word] would in practice not only lead many to become disaffected, but to feel and say, 'We come from such and such a body; we owe allegiance to them, not to you.' . . . A task already sufficiently difficult would be made ten times more so.[41]

Well might he have added that a right of appeal to London against the word of the General Director would be fatal to the Mission's existence.

This internal crisis reached its height when the 'eve of rebellion' unrest in China was at its worst and the wave of criticisms in the press increased the strain on Hudson Taylor. In London, however, the Council were busy drafting and adopting a letter on 'the Council's relation to missionaries in the field', which ended as an ultimatum such as Hudson Taylor had never before seen and never used.[42]

Impossible ultimatum   *1890–92*

The letter which Theodore Howard, as Home Director, signed on October 22, 1891, 'on behalf of the Home Council', was intended to establish the relationship of the London Council to the administration in China. In challenging the existence and powers of the China Council they argued that for the London Council to adopt Hudson Taylor's view 'would be a serious departure from the lines of the Mission hitherto prevailing'. The Christian public would trust Hudson Taylor's judgment in administrative matters, but not the China Council's. His devolution of any administrative powers to it was unacceptable. The decision on dismissals must be entirely his own. It was a vote of no confidence in the China Council – and in John Stevenson, although no one had objected when he was made Hudson Taylor's deputy in China. The 1886 revision of the P and P, they protested, had been the work of 'the small section (of the Mission) engaged in the actual revision'. That they were Hudson Taylor's chosen provincial leaders made no difference. Then followed an ambiguity rather than a concession – the London Council must at least have 'the right to make representations to the China Council'. It continued:

> This letter intimates as kindly but as firmly as possible the final (and I may say unanimous) decision of the Council in this matter, and we await your agreement, by wire or otherwise, before proceeding with the revision of the Book of Arrangements.[43]

This letter reached Shanghai on November 30. Archibald Orr Ewing and Walter B Sloan had arrived on the 4th, with Orr Ewing unsettled by close friendship with the Council in London, his wife being the treasurer Robert Scott's daughter. When Hudson Taylor talked it all out with him as a member of the China Council, Orr Ewing saw the impossibility of conceding London's demands. That same day, December 4, Hudson Taylor wrote his 'eve of rebellion' letter to Stevenson, about the political state of China, and the next day replied to the London Council – the persuasive letter of a friend, with no hint of defiance or coercion, or of claiming God as his ally against his opponents, as had been suggested.

Shanghai
December 5, 1891

To the Members of the London Council
Dear and valued Friends,
    I am in receipt of Mr Howard's letter on behalf of the Home

Council dated October 22nd and adopted by yourselves. I am greatly distressed and perplexed by it. I feel you do not apprehend the situation nor at all understand the gravity of the position you seek to establish; for I know your love for me personally and your desire to help me, and I know also your deep and abiding interest in this work of God on behalf of which you have spent so much time and thought. I feel that we have reached perhaps the gravest crisis that the Mission has yet passed through, and am very glad that our annual day of united fasting and prayer is so near at hand and will precede the next meeting of our Council here, when your letter must be considered. I have not at present any light modifying the conclusions we have already communicated to you. I dare not for peace's sake be untrue to my convictions, for if we forfeit the favour of GOD we have nothing to stand upon. You have not funds to support 500 missionaries; you cannot protect them against an insurrection or in riot; you cannot come out here and administer the affairs of the Mission; we must walk before God. I am sure you are agreed with me in this. For the present the only thing I can see is quietly to wait upon God. The wire we have just received of £170 to £270 of general funds [a drop in the bucket] is an instance of how vain it would be to trust in British resources instead of in the living God; but while we walk with Him we can rest in his faithfulness.

Yours gratefully and affectionately in Christ
J H Taylor[44]

On December 14 Hudson Taylor wrote at length to John Stevenson as his spokesman in London. It had at last dawned on him that the London Council had from the beginning taken the offending P and P and Book of Arrangements as faits accomplis imposed upcn them, whereas both had been (and still were) 'proposed, not promulgated'. He took them up point by point to clarify the facts, becoming clouded by months of discussion, and again urged Stevenson to arrange to meet the Council members one by one for calm conversations. But, as Jennie's diary reveals, he himself was prostrate from the accumulation of strains upon him. In a letter to Mrs Howard she said the strain was too much for him. She feared for his life.

Meanwhile, in the crowded Wusong Road premises a series of public meetings was being held, with Geraldine Guinness a leading speaker, 'filled with the Spirit'. Night after night people were being converted. When HMS *Caroline* arrived at Shanghai there were no professing Christians on board. By January 6, after services at Wusong Road and on the ship, an officer and twenty men were claiming to have been converted and eager to learn more. At the same time 'the enemy' seemed to be out to 'harass and distress' missionaries on all fronts, Hudson Taylor told Theodore Howard. 'When any member of the Mission may double or quadruple his income' by transferring to another society or going into business, it was not surprising that some were tempted, especially if it meant that they need no longer wait two years before getting married. Others succumbed, disheartened, and returned home.

The toll of illnesses continued unabated. One whole family died of 'high fever'. Benjamin and Amelia in London were going through severe 'testing' at this very time through three of their family in China contracting nearly fatal typhoid or typhus – Edith, Hudson, and Marshall after he nursed Hudson. But almost daily conversions continued into March through Geraldine's and others' preaching.[45] Jennie Taylor herself was riding the waves with her spirit strong. 'Now is the time to ask great things for China' from the Lord God 'who rideth on the heavens for *thy* help,' she told Mariamne Murray, still in charge at Yangzhou.

In February John Stevenson left Britain for Shanghai and arrived on March 14. He found Hudson Taylor almost worn out with work which it was impossible to delegate. In mid-April he was prostrate again, giddy and helpless, preparing to face the music in London, but appalled by the prospect, so imminent did complete shipwreck of the Mission appear to be. The China Council in session addressed a letter to him identifying themselves with his view of the crisis, particularly as it concerned 'exclusion from the Mission' and dismissals.[46]

> We value exceedingly the services rendered . . . by the Home Councils, and especially . . . for so many years by members of the London Council. But we fully agree with you . . . It is manifestly impossible for those in the Home lands to know as fully as can be known here the character and influence, the competence or incompetence, of our fellow-workers . . . [Ten signatures were appended.]

Loyal support encouraged him, yet while Hudson Taylor's spirit remained unbowed, stresses of this kind continued to undermine his physical endurance. He knew full well that his long-standing friends on the London Council were under forceful persuasion by the lawyer's scrutinising mind and the secretary's strong will, for reams of argument came in the mail to him also. Even Theodore Howard as director was too kindly a man to stand up to the pressure. So once again the best hope of a settlement was to go home and talk it out, however difficult it might be. It was like mounting the tumbril. He and Jennie sailed on May 10 to Canada, for he had learned to value Henry Frost's wise opinions.

This crucial period had begun with London's intervention in support of individuals at odds with the administration in China (p 33), and objections to the Book of Arrangements. Both were 'field' not 'home' matters. But when individual candidates sent to China by the London Council were sent home at the end of their probationary two years, only for strong reasons of unsuitability, London claimed the right not only of a voice, but the deciding voice in the action. One or two cases of disciplinary dismissal after all possible had been attempted to avert it were also challenged by the 'Home' council. With the basic principle of management under attack, great courage and wisdom were needed.

'Unanimity of decision'   *1892–93*

An ill-ventilated cabin, 'gastritis' and neuralgia this time made the voyage an ordeal for Hudson Taylor, normally a good sailor. They had to break the journey across Canada at several points in an attempt to regain strength before meeting the North American Council. The 'esteem and love' in which he was held in Canada and the States made a few addresses and attendance at the Niagara conference inescapable, but Henry Frost persuaded him to stay for a complete rest before crossing to Britain. They cabled to Benjamin, who replied reassuringly, 'run no risks'. So it was July 26 and the summer recess before they reached Liverpool.

The Keswick Convention had started and interest in missions had grown since he had first shown the inseparability of 'sanctification' and 'obedience to the Great Commission'. He took the chair and addressed an anti-opium meeting on August 1. They were in Keswick when word came that Mrs Robert Howard, Theodore's mother and Hudson Taylor's dear friend since 1850, had died. He and Benjamin were asked to conduct the funeral, so he travelled overnight and met the Council members 'at the grave' on August 2. Instead of tension, the mood was 'chastened'. At night at William Sharp's home, and conversations with Theodore Howard, Benjamin and Robert Scott individually raised his hopes.[47] Staying with the Grattan Guinnesses at Cliff House, he wrote, 'Eyes are upon us just now, and there are those who think that as the Council have been appointed by me, they are really nonentities and just carry out my or our plans and are not allowed to use their own discretion . . . We must be careful that this contention is not a true one.' A Council meeting on September 6, 1892 – 'a prayerful, happy one', at which he was 'cordially welcomed' – avoided thorny subjects, keeping them for the following week. Then, on the 13th from 2.30–9.00 pm they grasped the nettle. The meeting was 'harmonious throughout, and light seems to have been given as to how to meet *the* difficulty.'[48]

So far, so good. Hudson Taylor explained to John Stevenson, 'the Council do not now wish to claim the power to adjudicate in dismissals or even to veto, but that in ordinary cases of inefficiency where there is no urgency they might have the statement of the case with a view to either concurrence or suggestion . . . they will then accept our conclusion . . . it being fully understood that there is no appeal from one Council to another.' The formal Minute stated that the council 'had no desire to be a Court of Appeal', but was given the right to have its representations carefully considered by the China Council. The thunder-clouds had vanished in an anticlimax. All seemed settled.

Another letter to Stevenson, packed with business detail, showed in October how firmly Hudson Taylor still had his finger on the Mission's pulse. He pointed out that estimates for building the new Chefoo boys' school were unreasonably lavish, and commented knowledgeably about one problem after another. 'Hitherto the Chinese government have known that we have never published anything against them,' was his observation on protests about the Songpan riots. But a passing reference to the London Council hinted at more trouble ahead: 'There is a nice spirit shown in our meetings; *the* point that was the difficulty seemed almost settled when a larger one cropped up involving . . . the reconstruction of the Home work' – 'what I considered necessary to restore confidence.' As he had not yet discussed reorganisation with Benjamin, the secretary, he deferred making it a matter of debate. But Theodore Howard later explained to him that deep feelings were involved. They were still very far from a peaceful solution of problems in London. There was even more talk of the issues thought to be settled, and of an impending 'break-up'. Benjamin might resign. It would have wide repercussions.[49]

This possibility gave Hudson Taylor an inspiration. If they lost

'BB', would not Walter Sloan be the ideal successor? Or better still the ideal colleague to halve Benjamin's load, freeing him for his major role, and his anti-opium campaign. 'It would infuse new life . . . and restore and increase confidence.' But how was Benjamin to be offered this idea? Discussion in Council of the need of reorganisation was producing heated exchanges. 'Everyone is very tired and the strain is great.' Hudson Taylor was in Scotland for meetings when 'a trying letter (came) from Mr Howard showing they think my objections to Mr Broomhall's ways are bad temper; they had decided not to meet again until we are reconciled.

'I wrote to Mr Howard explaining (our) difficulties were not anything personal but official, and that if we in China had difficulties we met them with a day of fasting and prayer.' The suggestion was welcomed and the Ladies' Council joined the London Council 'for prayer *only* . . . a very good meeting'.

Part of the problem was Benjamin's increasing deafness, so Hudson Taylor set out his proposition in writing: 'The work is increasing and likely to increase; an infusion of vigorous young life is essential to continuous success . . . Would a partnership in the work be desirable or practicable, do you think?'[50] To Jennie's relief Benjamin was 'in a good spirit', for 'Mr T will not be able to bear the strain much longer', but in keeping John Stevenson informed, Hudson Taylor wrote again in November, 'Matters here are approaching a crisis.' A cable calling for Walter Sloan was more likely than not. As an economy the code words 'VIOLA RUSTICE' would mean 'Sloan marry at once and come as soon as practicable'. If Benjamin decided to resign, the unpredictable effect could be catastrophic, others retiring with him and confidence in the Mission plummeting. Then a timely new factor appeared. Henry Frost and two of his council were coming over for consultations with Hudson Taylor about administrative changes in America. If they were to spend a few days at Pyrland Road, it would give the London staff and Council an opportunity to see what 'men of rare qualifications' they were, and Frost's wisdom could be drawn upon.[51]

So it proved. Henry Frost, Joshua S Helmer and J D Nasmith arrived on January 4, 1893, and on the 17th met the London Council. As Henry Frost had expected, his companions impressed and delighted the Council, who confided frankly in the visitors. Even the old wounds about the North American Council were reopened. Frost played a major role in finding a way out of the quagmire, and, where Hudson Taylor and the London Council were 'so weary of strife, jealousy (and) division', Frost's fresh mind saw light. Bold changes in organisation would benefit everyone. Hudson Taylor even wrote to Stevenson of 'the Mission-to-be', a phoenix from the ashes. He waited until Walter Sloan was suggested by William Sharp, as the right man to work with Benjamin, and the Council acclaimed the inspiration. W B Sloan's business ability and exceptional personality as a Christian made him no ordinary colleague.

On January 20 Hudson Taylor was still uncertain of what the outcome in the Council would be, but wrote to prepare Sloan for the cable as soon as everything was settled. Someone was needed 'to pull things together', with a place on the Council. Would Sloan take over management of all the routine office work in London, 'as head and not hands' of all departments, superintending other members of staff and missionaries on furlough in Britain, and handling all correspondence 'except such as Mr B (as senior secretary) selected to deal with himself'? Benjamin would advise and help to maintain continuity, and concentrate on his forte, public relations.[52]

The CMS were also going through a long-drawn-out period of 'Controversies Within and Attacks from Without' – as Eugene Stock called his chapter 87 (1882–95), for 'the adversary' was a lion at large. And a serious clash between the CIM and CMS in Zhejiang on details of comity was occupying the attention of both societies' leaders. An unwise CIM missionary had complained to the consul about a Church Mission evangelist poaching converts with the archdeacon's encouragement! Pettiness as disgraceful as it was ludicrous? 'Salisbury Square' could no more intervene in the bishop's affairs in China than Benjamin could in John Stevenson's.

After the letter went off to Walter Sloan, events moved fast. On the 25th Hudson Taylor sent the cable and Sloan replied that he and his fiancée, a sister of Graham Brown, had felt it coming and were glad to comply. By February 17 difficulties were 'melting away' and there was 'a general feeling of relief and thankfulness'. (The same letter to Stevenson said that a 'Keswick missionary', Amy Wilson-Carmichael, had not been accepted as a candidate, on grounds of health and temperament, but was to sail with a CIM party to join Barclay Buxton in Japan. The same Amy Carmichael was to become the 'Amma' of Dohnovur, a lifelong friend of the CIM.)

By February 27 Hudson Taylor could see that unimportant concessions would secure agreement on the fundamental prin-ciples, and on March 3 he outlined to John Stevenson the decisions reached. He was redrafting parts of the Principles and Practice to incorporate them, and after approval by the London Council the way should be clear for making it final. After four more years of disagreement, Theodore Howard, William Sharp and 'Benjamin B', the most vocal objectors, had come to realise how great a gap existed between their understanding of conditions in China and the considerable expertise of the field leaders. Then they accepted the wisdom of the ultimate control being in the hands of those on the spot, and the status of the London Council as being advisory to the Directors and representative of the Mission to the public at home.

'It brings to an end difficulties that are tearing the Mission to pieces,' Hudson Taylor continued; 'it settles the question of where the seat of power is, and with the consent of the London Council dismisses all question of their being a seat of power; it does not interfere with any working arrangements.' Once again peace reigned. All councils were to meet and act as before, but only to advise directors and not to be executive. In this he was conceding a major preference; preparing for his own death or retirement he had intended councils to have executive functions as an extension of his own management of affairs, until London took the bit between its teeth. In future the directors with authority would be responsible for decisions and action. Paradoxically, what had been challenged as autocratic was to become permanent by the insistence of the London Council itself.

> One sees more and more that we must get the officers from God and leave them to do their work unfettered . . . The first thing is to get love and confidence fully re-established . . . It seems to me that practically this solution leaves the working of the Mission just where it was.[53]

For nearly a hundred years more, that solution has worked admirably.

As for the Book of Arrangements 'which frightens a great many people', its abandonment as a handbook was 'the only price of peace'. It would be broken up and used in separate sections for the guidance of each grade of missionary – hints for candidates, instructions for newly arrived missionaries, and so on. 'We are gaining what I felt was so essential – non-interference with the China administration.' Already it had led to the resignation of nearly thirty missionaries, unsettled by the controversy.

Henry Frost had been the catalyst of success. Years later he explained to Dixon Hoste,

> I found that the London Director and Council were strongly tending to the thought that they had and should have a pre-eminent place, as related to all the other Directors and Councils of the Mission . . . (As) it had a definite bearing upon our work in North America . . . I could not pass over the subject . . . for manifestly, if the London Director and Council were supreme, then they were over us and we were under them, an arrangement to which we were not willing to agree. After much consultation, Mr Taylor took the position that all Assistant Directors and Councils, as related to the General Director, were and should be wholly and unconditionally on a par . . . The 'seat of authority' is in the person of the General Director. If he is in China it is there; but if he is in some other country, it is there. In other words, the seat of authority is no more connected with the China Council than with any other Council.[54]

Dixon Hoste's forthright comment on the whole sad upheaval was, 'Any idiot can wreck a train,' but it took consummate skill to steer a way through years of disputation and ultimata with the survival of the Mission at stake. In November 1892 when civil rebellion threatened in China and the London crisis was at its 'gravest', Hudson Taylor's editorial for the coming January 1893 issue of *China's Millions* reflected the depths of distress he could envisage. 'When the Apostle was nearing shipwreck his heart relied on the truth . . . "Whose I am and whom I serve."' When all else fails, 'THOU REMAINEST'.

By the end of February 'cordial understanding' had been restored and an administrative principle of 'unanimity' had been recognised: the Deed of Constitution had stated it in March 1890, surprisingly, but in faith as, 'It is intended that as a rule the principle of unanimity shall continue to prevail in the management of the Mission,' and the China Council in July 1891 had declared their contentment with nothing less than 'unanimity' between themselves and London in reaching conclusions.[55] But how could men with conflicting opinions attain unanimity? The answer lay in respect for each other's views, and willingness to accept them under the influence of the Holy Spirit. Therefore any impasse was an indication for 'waiting upon God'. Doing so led to a more satisfactory conclusion than by a majority decision against a reluctant minority. Even 'my opinion is unchanged, but I accept the preference of the majority'

THE NEWINGTON GREEN OFFICES AND HOME OF
THE CIM
occupied in 1895

was a genuine form of unanimity, 'of decision', though not of
opinion.

The deliberations in London had demonstrated again the godliness and practicability of this concept of 'unanimity of decision'. But
that willingness in the presence of God often brought unanimity of
conviction also. With the painful differences settled, the Council
moved on to deciding which architectural plans to adopt for the
Newington Green headquarters building. Completed plans for
offices, meeting hall, thirty bedrooms and public rooms were before
the Council on May 2, 1893. Robert Scott and Benjamin, who
preferred an alternative design, agreed that work should start on
that chosen by the rest. Scott gave £500 and offered £2,000 on loan
towards it. He had intended them for the scheme he favoured. The
loan was declined, but an offer of £3,000 by a Miss Josephine Smith
was accepted on the assurance that it was already left to the CIM
in her will. Work therefore began on the first 120 feet of the
foundations, the final forty feet of the building to be added later.[56]

Walter Sloan and his bride arrived on March 25 and on the 28th he advised at a Council meeting that the creation of small provincial or regional councils in China would be regretted. For members to advise and not be decisive, might make difficulties for the missionaries and their superintendents. So here, too, Hudson Taylor accepted the choice of leadership by chosen individuals rather than by committees. (That he imposed it on the Mission is another myth.)

The completed revision of the P and P was sent to Shanghai on May 16 and accepted by the China Council on July 7. W B Sloan was installed as Secretary, and Benjamin as General Secretary gave the annual report at the May meetings. With demands on his time reduced, he had more to devote to the abolition of the opium trade, from then on his major preoccupation. In June Hudson Taylor announced the appointment of Henry Frost as Home Director in North America, and by November was anticipating 'a forward movement' – Advance. A new era had begun.[57]

CHAPTER SIX

'GOD REIGNS'
1890–95

'Successful crime': the opium trade   1888–94

'This is the triumph of successful crime,' said an American diplomat to the Bishop of Victoria, Hong Kong in 1858 when the Treaty of Tientsin ended the first phase of the second opium war. 'We force them by treaty to take it from us,' Sir Rutherford Alcock admitted. 'The Chinese had both the *right, the power and the will, to stamp out the use of Opium in China* at the time when they first came into collision with the power of England,' Hudson Taylor wrote. 'England is morally responsible for every ounce of opium now produced in China, as well as that imported from abroad.'[1]

The launch of the activist Christian Union and its magazine *National Righteousness* in 1888 saw the propaganda against the opium trade multiplied from then on. Information about the trade and evidence of its evils were presented, with calls for the conscience of Britain to awaken. The government must be shamed into finding alternative revenue for India.

On May 3, 1889, the first resolution for the extinction of the trade was presented to Parliament and the names of those members who voted for it were listed in *National Righteousness*. A British-Indian newspaper sensed danger and estimated that if only one hundred or so votes for each parliamentary candidate in an election were swayed by the issue, the effect would be significant. Sixty thousand copies of the magazine reviewing the history of the opium wars, with photographs of Chinese killed in the fighting, and in January 1891 a letter bearing the facsimile signatures of leading Christians of fifteen denominations in the country was sent to 45,000 ministers. Another letter went to each member of both Houses of Parliament, with a statement about the opium trade.

A few weeks later a National Christian Anti-opium Convention was held, March 9–11, fully reported in *National Righteousness*. Highly respected witnesses from China spoke in session after session. Two Members of Parliament told of what was being done. A new resolution was to be presented in the Commons on April 10,

1891.[2] A Committee of Urgency was set up. And one incisive resolution after another was unanimously adopted, including Benjamin's that the Guang Xü Emperor should be assured that action for the abolition of the traffic was being pursued by Christians in England. Li Hongzhang had more than once requested this.[3]

Publicity of one kind and another in time would move the most reluctant government in Whitehall. Sessions of two or two and a half hours for prayer alone, with no one called upon to take part, saw 'no awkward pauses (as) prayer flowed solemnly on'. 'The remarkable success of the Convention, the place Sir Joseph Pease obtained (in Parliament) for his resolution, the startling outburst of public feeling throughout the country, and the great moral victory in the House of Commons' were answers to prayer, Benjamin's editorial claimed. The resolution, carried by 160 votes to 130, had declared the opium trade to be 'morally indefensible'.

> The moral effect of this vote was unspeakably great; it startled both the British Government and the Government of India, and at once lifted the question from despised fanaticism to the level of the foremost questions of the day.[4]

It was followed by a memorial to Lord Salisbury, Prime Minister, signed by 1,500 Wesleyan ministers and 271,680 church members urging the abolition of the growth and manufacture of opium in India.[5] And another signed by more than five thousand medical men in the United Kingdom declared that in India, as in Britain, opium should be classed as a poison and its manufacture and sale be prohibited except for medicinal purposes.

China's Millions joined in the action. George Andrew wrote about the prevalence of suicide by opium overdosage, and Minnie Parker (Shao Mianzi) told how her affluent family had been reduced to penury by the curse of opium. News of Pastor Hsi's refuges was given from time to time. And a report of the annual meeting of the CIM in May 1891 included a resolution that the people of Britain should 'bear some (fiscal) sacrifice in order to secure the immediate cessation of our Indian opium trade', unanimously adopted. In the March 1892 issue came a call to daily prayer for no less than,

> (i) The total and immediate prohibition of the growth and manufacture of Opium in our Indian Empire, except for medicinal purposes.
> (ii) The sale of Opium in India under such restrictions as shall ensure for the people of India safeguards against its improper use, similar to those provided for the protection of the people of Great Britain.

The alarm of the pro-opium lobby was heard in solemn claims that opium was no more harmful than the mildest tobacco and had no social ill-effects. Evidence to the contrary was already well publicised. And the press resorted to familiar kinds of criticism. 'The injurious results of the traffic are declared by the all-competent authorities to be grossly exaggerated, *if they are not purely imaginary*'. ('Only an opium smoker could have said that,' a Chinese commented on hearing such a remark.)

'The 160 geese who formed the majority (in Parliament)' – 'this scratch majority represents (those) still outside the walls of lunatic asylums'. 'It seems probable that the cackling of geese will destroy the British Empire.' 'The House of Commons has been caught sleeping', by 'fussy sentimentalists', 'intolerant faddists' and 'fanatics'. And the *Hong Kong Telegraph* declared that missions (to Chinese the 'tools of foreign imperialism') were to the imperialists 'the curse of foreign enterprise' (meaning the opium trade), but 'played out' and doomed to failure.[6]

As a general election approached in 1892, politicians began to adopt cautious attitudes to the subject. In a speech at Penicuik, near Edinburgh (where there was strong feeling on the opium issue), Mr Gladstone himself referred to

> bloodshed and shame in our former history . . . The evil may be put down at last, but think of the human misery and sin that have been engendered in the interval caused by delay . . . Subject to the obligations of good faith, I shall . . . forward any measure within the bounds of reason for (bringing the trade), if it can be done, altogether to an end.

As the incoming Prime Minister at the age of eighty-one he included in his cabinet seven ministers who had voted in favour of the anti-opium resolution, among them the two future premiers H H Asquith and Henry Campbell-Bannerman. 'What will Mr Gladstone do?' Benjamin asked in a heavy caption. The prospects looked promising.

Another Anti-Opium Convention was convened on October 6, at which Hudson Taylor, Marcus Wood and Geraldine Guinness made major speeches. And on December 17 Benjamin addressed a letter to Mr Gladstone enclosing a copy of *National Righteousness* which reported the Penicuik speech and the convention. 'You may now do a work for which millions will remember your name with gratitude.' The Prime Minister's reply showed how the politician's mind worked. He would 'always act in the spirit of his words (at Penicuik)', but would have to 'consult the Department more immediately concerned'. 'Mr Gladstone's letter is not satisfactory,' Benjamin's next editorial ran, in the February 1893 issue. 'He does not need to be told what are the prerogatives of a Prime Minister of England; nor is he the man to accept meekly the dictum of a Department . . .' The Penicuik speech had been specious electioneering. A leading article in the *Daily News* declared,

> The conscience of the British people will one day be fully roused on this point. The traffic will go, and, in half a dozen years after it has gone, we shall be wondering why it was ever regarded as the mainstay of Indian finance.

A government blue book on opium in India and Burma was presented to Parliament on February 9, 1892 and *National Righteousness* quoted eight testimonies by ranking officials to the 'unmitigated evil', 'an absolute poison', 'a vice which we have introduced'. 'It could have been called, "The Strong Condemnation of the Opium Traffic by the Indian Government."' Yet it had no noticeable effect. 'Officials are blinded, the nation is not,' Mrs Grattan Guinness declared. When the Decennial Missionary Conference at Bombay of seven hundred missionaries from 36 societies withdrew a resolution against regulated vice, already adopted by an overwhelming majority, and refused resolutions against the abuse of alcohol and opium, the April 1893 *National Righteousness* devoted every line of the issue to the scandal, and a protest meeting took place in London.[7]

June 30 was named for a new resolution on opium to be presented to Parliament. The motion took the wording of the successful April 10, 1891, resolution as its premise, and urged action without further delay. But an amendment independently introduced to specify action, called for a Royal Commission on ways and means of implementing it. Poor politics, this false step gave Gladstone a way out. What could have been 'the death blow of the Opium trade' supported by the strong body of anti-opium opinion among government ministers, became by Gladstone's own intervention a delaying tactic and a denial of the 'morally indefensible' nature of the trade. In a subtle amendment he advocated a Royal Commission on the whole complex subject. This time, while 105 members voted against

Gladstone and for action to end the trade, 184 supported the aged Prime Minister. 'We forget our conscience. We barter our souls under a narcotic deadlier than the poppy,' a London evening paper protested. After this fiasco the 1894 annual meeting of the CIM gave the opium question a leading place with an address by Yen Yung-king, the Chinese Christian minister (pp 138, 142).[8]

The terms of the Royal Commission focused attention on opium consumption in India (never a major factor) rather than the effects of the trade with China. But the tendentious and specious proceedings and report of the Royal Commission scandalised the Christian public who knew the facts. Eugene Stock indignantly recorded what happened. The Commissioners examined witnesses in Britain and India, but not one member of the Commission went to China.

> Some grave complaints were made of the manner in which the Indian evidence was collected. (Only four of forty-four missionaries consulted in India) were in the smallest degree favourable to the use of opium; yet three of this four were quoted in the Report, and not one of the forty-one. (Only documentary evidence from China was considered, and only five and a half pages out of ninety-seven dealt with China at all.) There was a similar selection in the Report of one side of this evidence. A weighty memorial signed by seventeen missionaries of over twenty-five years' standing (including Burdon, Moule, Muirhead, Griffith John, Mackenzie and Hudson Taylor) was entirely ignored; and while it was acknowledged that 'by the majority of the missionaries of every community in China the use of opium is strongly condemned', the only quotations were from three who claimed to 'take a less decided view'. (The Report is therefore) utterly inadequate and misleading.[9]

Arnold Foster, whom we met as an organiser of relief in the great famine of 1877–79 (HTCOC Book 6, Chapter 5) published *An Examination and an Appeal* in the format of a Parliamentary blue book with a preface signed by the Archbishop of Canterbury and 144 other distinguished men. The Society for the Suppression of the Opium Trade, the Christian Union and *National Righteousness* continued their campaign. But Gladstone's Royal Commission had set back their hopes of final success by a full decade. Wilberforce had freed the slaves in British colonial territories. But sixty years later Parliament remained deaf to demands that Britain's part in the greater evil of enslavement to opium, affecting millions, should be brought to an end.

A sharp drop in income was the natural result of whispers about the CIM circulating in Britain. For some years the Mission had been riding the crests, but no longer: £29,961 in the year of The Hundred; £32,924 in 1888; £48,662 in 1889 and £29,932 in 1890 had dropped in the next two years to £26,188 and £24,496 before recovering to £32,178 in 1893. But in North America and China receipts had risen in the two lean years, so that progress was 'restrained, not hindered'. The Hundred had brought the Mission to 225 strong by the end of 1887, and all who had stayed the pace had five years or more of the language and experience – enough to make them mature 'senior missionaries'. Between then and May 1893 more than three hundred had been added, beyond those lost by death or retirement. The troughs and setbacks, riots and fatal illnesses had been localised, while the main body of the Mission and of missionaries in general had steadily progressed.[10] The LMS in spite of a £14,000 deficit in 1890, had risen enthusiastically to the appeal for one thousand missionaries to China, and called for one hundred to add to the Society's world total of two hundred.

In spite of anti-foreign excitement, seven new CIM work centres had been established, and 637 baptisms in 107 organised churches had increased the number of Chinese communicants to 3,637. The year 1893 saw 821 more baptisms take place in 134 churches, but baptism candidates and enquirers 'numbered thousands'. 'Despise not the day of small things!' Hudson Taylor's report in May 1894 took particular delight in noting that the indigenous Hangzhou church under his old friend Wang Lae-djün, and the circuit of churches which he supervised within a radius of a hundred miles, was not only independent of foreign funds and supervision, but had made a gift of $1,000 to Hudson Taylor. The gross income of the Mission had exceeded the previous year's by £6,000.

During his year and a half in Britain (July 26, 1892 to February 14, 1894), Hudson Taylor again travelled widely, in Scotland, Ireland and much of England. He owed it to the growing army of supporters to whom he personified the Mission. Confidence was quickly restored. But the impression gained from reading his voluminous correspondence is of the effect of the ceaseless battering he had endured for several years. The warm, relaxed, affectionate letters characteristic of him had become terse and to the point. He admitted to being no longer confident of remembering conversations accurately and had to keep more detailed memoranda. He felt older than his true age of sixty and could not stand the pace without sometimes having to sit while he addressed a meeting. Yet he drove himself on, until Jennie pleaded with him not to kill himself by overdoing it. She kept the news of James Cameron's death from cholera from him until he returned home from Ireland and had rested. But he rebuked her for her anxiety about him, 'so unlike you'.[11] His long and frequent letters to John Stevenson showed no sign of any diminished grasp of administrative detail. He was a man for detail to the end. (At the worst periods of the constitutional crisis, he still tended the plants he had gathered in the Rocky Mountains on the way from China.) James Williamson (of the *Lammermuir*), speaking in 1895 of working with Hudson Taylor on the China Council, said,

> I was remarkably struck . . . that (his) mental power and grasp . . . his ability to take in all the details of the work . . . and his Christ-like personal sympathy with every worker in all their varied circumstances . . . remained as strong as ever.

In April 1893, after welcoming Walter Sloan from China, Hudson Taylor visited the associate mission centres of Barmen, Cassel and Frankfurt with his daughter Amy. An award she had won by a Paper on political economy covered her costs. And at this time also, Millie Duncan, the orphaned daughter of Duncan, pioneer of Nanjing, whom the Taylors had adopted, came of age, married and went to India. In August he returned with Jennie to Frankfurt, Heidelberg and Barmen, consolidating the Mission's bonds with the associate missions (August 9–21). His concerns had become more far-flung than ever before. The Australasian council minuted the need of a representative in New Zealand, and he was planning to go there as soon as possible to make arrangements.

Two hundred children of the CIM needed to be provided with schooling at Chefoo, and the sons and daughters of merchants, consuls and customs officials and of other missions swelled the number. The rapid growth of the mission also meant expanding the Chefoo sanatorium for convalescents. A good site was bought for a new school and playing-fields for one hundred boys, and Hudson Taylor was considering a proposal for financing its erection. His Liverpool friend, Menzies, offered to raise the funds through a limited liability company of a few friends, and to build the school for the CIM to rent very cheaply. After going into all that was involved, Hudson Taylor declined the generous offer. If for any reason the premises were to pass into other hands, the CIM could have a large body of close neighbours on its own territory, but not of its own choice. Influences on the children took priority over money. The outbreak of the Sino-Japanese war kept matters in abeyance, but when peace was restored Archibald Orr Ewing one day quietly offered to bear the whole cost of £5,000 in three instalments, as he had also donated a third building at Wusong Road.[12]

The Rijnhardt hornets' nest   1893–94

Problems seldom came singly. In 1893 a new disciplinary crisis startled John Stevenson and soon involved Hudson Taylor. Some Americans had begun to arrive in Shanghai, hoping to join the CIM without first approaching the North American 'Home' Council. Among them was a Dutchman named Petrus Rijnhardt (variously referred to in correspondence and tales of his exploits as Peter Reynhart or by similar names). His bizarre story was to involve the CIM for several years. He created a good impression, so Stevenson consulted Toronto. As a pastor in Canada gave him a good testimonial, the North American Council recommended that he be admitted on probation.[13] Rijnhardt went to language school and on to Lanzhou in Gansu. There he became engaged to Annie Slater of Carlisle, who with her friend Rose Basnett was a colleague of the Laughtons at Wuwei (Liangzhou), far off on the Great Silk Road towards Turkestan.

Meanwhile enquiries had been made in Holland where Rijnhardt had been a Salvation Army officer. From the information supplied there could be no doubt that he was a consummate impostor. Rijnhardt was called to the coast, faced with the evidence and dismissed. Annie and her friend could not believe what they were told. In great distress they resigned and followed him to the States. But by then his record of a dissolute life in Canada had also been exposed. In 1894 he married an American doctor with private means and they went to the Gansu–Qinghai border independently.

Meanwhile, during 1891–92 Robert P Wilder followed in John Forman's footsteps, touring the British universities and reaping hundreds of student volunteers for service overseas. The Students' Foreign Missionary Union, started by Howard Taylor, had suffered from poor leadership since he went abroad, but now it merged with

Wilder's Student Volunteer Missionary Union and the watchword 'The evangelisation of the world in this generation' was adopted – again showing strong roots in China.[14] On November 22, 1893, John R Mott wrote inviting Hudson Taylor to speak at the second International Student Convention at Detroit, Michigan, February 28–March 4, 1894, an opportunity for the starting of a great advance movement for missions.

> Our chief and only burden is that it may be a markedly spiritual Convention . . . and we have faith to believe that you would be a great channel of spiritual blessing to this Continent and through it to the world . . . You will have an opportunity to touch the leading representatives of every missionary agency of Canada and the United States . . .
> We also very much want Miss Geraldine Guinness to be present. She has a wonderful hold on the students of America through her writings . . .

This fitted in well with plans to return to China via North America. Once again Hudson Taylor paid a farewell visit to William Berger at Cannes (each time it could be the last in their long friendship) and was back in London for the Mission's farewell meetings. The Exeter Hall was still crowded at 11.40 pm. Mrs Grattan Guinness's life was 'hanging in the balance', but Geraldine was preparing to travel with the Taylors to the States and China. She had been working on her *Story of the China Inland Mission* since early 1891, postponing her marriage. At last the second volume was finished and Howard was to be in Shanghai for their wedding when she arrived.

They joined their ship at Liverpool on February 14, and there Hudson Taylor signed the 'China Inland Mission Declaration of Trust', the completed legal document describing the structure of the Mission with its 'councils of advice' and 'arrangements for the control and management of the present and future properties and funds of the Mission'. He as General Director and the Home Director in the United Kingdom were 'advised and assisted in the work of the Mission in the United Kingdom by a body known as the 'London Council'. Provision for his death and the procedures to be followed were clearly laid down. They sailed that day and reached New York on February 23, to be received by A B Simpson, and to meet a group of his International Alliance Mission students about to sail for Hong Kong to evangelise Guangxi.[15]

'Six of the principal addresses' at the student convention had been allocated to Hudson Taylor, and the students benefited by 'as much blessing as they were prepared to receive'. After CIM meetings at Toronto and an interview with Rijnhardt, Hudson Taylor went to Iowa to meet Rijnhardt's pastor, and on to Omaha to confront Rijnhardt in person again. Defiant and threatening, he vowed to wreck the CIM. Annie Slater had been saved from a shameless scoundrel. But the story had a sequel.

The Taylors and Geraldine travelled on, via Chicago for meetings, to San Francisco, and sailed for Shanghai, arriving (he for the ninth time) on April 17 'for a brief visit'. It lasted two years. He found the China Council in session facing a new upheaval. The Scandinavians of Fredrik Franson's and A B Simpson's Alliance Missions were in difficulties and the consul for Scandinavian affairs had called for urgently needed advice and persuasion.[16]

John Nevius strikes gold   1890–93

John and Helen Nevius had arrived in China in mid-February 1854, two weeks before Hudson Taylor. Their unbroken friendship through forty years had seen Helen recover from tuberculosis (HTCOC Book 3, pp 370, 412–3), but Maria Taylor die. In Shandong from 1861 John had worked out his 'methods' for planting Chinese churches untrammelled by foreign domination or sapped by dependence on foreign funds. Loyal to his Presbyterian colleagues, and in due time moderator of the northern synod, he had suffered from inability to convince the body of them that his methods held the key to success. He and Hudson Taylor had often compared notes on the subject. John Wesley had worked on similar principles, based on his own itineration. Nevius patiently worked on, making Yantai his base and travelling out to teach and advise the scattered congregations. (The bone-shaking torture of riding crude wheelbarrows led him to modify one with springs, and to sell one to Hudson Taylor.) Arising from discussions with intellectual friends, consuls, merchants and missionaries, who met from time to time to sharpen each other's wits, he also made a study of demon possession and wrote the tome *Demon Possession in China*.[17]

In 1890 his opportunity came. Presbyterian missionaries in Korea where the church was in its infancy invited him to come and expound his principles. His greatest success sprang from that brief visit to Seoul, for the missionaries and Christians adopted what

MANCHURIA, KOREA AND SHANDONG

came to be called the 'Nevius plan'. The Korean church attributes its dramatic growth largely to his influence, and China's 'Three Self' concept for the Church owes its origin in part to the papers Nevius published.

The first principle was that the Bible should be taught systematically and thoroughly to all Christians, with periods of intensive study each year. Going away to distant institutions should be exceptional. Second, while each one continued in his or her own way of life and occupation, providing his own livelihood, he should witness actively for Christ in his own area – 'self-propagation'. Third, each group of believers should choose its own leaders. Only if they as a congregation could afford to support a full-time evangelist or pastor would chosen individuals stop earning their own living. The methods, buildings and equipment used would also be governed by what the church could afford – 'self-government' and 'self-support'. Fourth, a thoroughly Korean form of church activity, architecture and worship should be preserved. This high aim succumbed all too soon to foreign influence, due also to the highly

independent nature of the Korean personality but a truly
indigenous Church developed. The first baptisms in 1886 resulted
by 1894 in a church of 236 communicant members, and of thirty
thousand by 1910, in spite of the Sino-Japanese war and of Japanese
domination and suspicion. Today the Protestant Church in South
Korea alone numbers over two million in a population of more than
thirty million.[18]

But on October 19, 1893, John Nevius was preparing his mule
litter for another tour of the Yantai circuit of country churches,
when Dr Arthur Douthwaite rode across from his Chefoo hospital
to see him. Nevius had been suffering from a 'weak heart' and
his wife was anxious about him. One of his mules attacked
Douthwaite's horse, giving Douthwaite a kick which reduced him to
crutches for several days. But Nevius pelted the mule with stones,
drove it off and helped Douthwaite indoors. They were sitting
together when suddenly John Nevius slumped forward and died in
spite of all the doctor did for him.[19]

'Forward' – too fast   1890–94

Although Hudson Taylor declared after the General Conference
appeal for one thousand men in five years, that the CIM would take
no special measures to increase its numbers, by March 1893 they
were coming too fast. In his enthusiasm Fredrik Franson was
sending them as soon as they responded to his fluent appeals. But
without enough preparations for receiving them in China. Those
who came in the CIM's associate missions were treated as new
members of the CIM. Others unconnected with the CIM no less
needed help as they went straight out to the provinces. They had no
language, experience or organisation to introduce them to a totally
new life, so they were welcomed by the missionaries already
established in Shanxi, on the Mongolian border, and in Shaanxi.
Associates generally adhered to the CIM Principles and Practice.
Others did as they judged best, unaware of how strange their
foreignness was to the Chinese. And some had beliefs and practices
different enough from the CIM's to make co-operation difficult.

Emmanuel Olsson of the Swedish Holiness Union and his wife
had agreed to act as leaders of those sent by A B Simpson's
International Alliance Mission (Christian and Missionary Alliance
from 1897), but were inundated. The first group arrived on February 15, 1893, and sixteen more followed a week later. When

arrangements for the transmission of their funds broke down, they were dependent on the help of other missions and their consul. Hudson Taylor had seen trouble coming and advised Stevenson to steer clear of 'a full share of blame with very small power to help', but it was a matter of friends in need. For one thing, the CIM had decided not to accept anyone who refused on 'faith healing' principles or other grounds to be vaccinated, because of the danger to those who nursed them when they caught smallpox. Within five months of landing in China, five of the Scandinavian women had the disease.

But more serious factors made close co-operation difficult. In K S Latourette's words, 'As a rule the Alliance representatives had only a scanty education and attempted, with but imperfect adaptation to the Chinese environment, to reproduce the revivalism to which they usually owed their own religious experience. (But they) lived courageous and self-denying lives.' When the British ambassador, N O'Conor, asked the foreign minister, Lord Rosebery, to alert the Swedish government to the dangers arising from the young Scandinavians' unwise actions, calling them CIM missionaries, it was time to act positively.[20]

'Forward' and 'forward movement' were catch-phrases of the day in military and journalistic jargon. They found a place in Christian language not at first as a title but as a trend. While constitutional crises racked the Mission, any organised advance was unlikely, but on November 10, 1893, Hudson Taylor told John Stevenson, 'I propose organising a thorough campaign for the Mission such as has not yet been attempted.' They might be ready for it by May 1894. Some missions were responding well to the 1890 appeal for one thousand men, but women were outnumbering the men in volunteering. A month later, Hudson Taylor wrote, 'We are being encouraged as to our forward movement.' A gift or promise of £1,600 towards advance had been received, 'receipts in 1893 exceeded those in 1892 by £7,500', and without special effort sixty-three new missionaries were sent from Britain. '(God) always prospers us when we go *forward*, does He not?' 'Several good men' were accepted in Britain during December, and Australia had 'five young men ready to sail', but low income was making the Melbourne council hesitate to send them. 'Send them as soon as you have the passage money available,' Hudson Taylor advised. 'If they are good men it would not be a great matter if for a time we had to help them' with funds from Britain and the States. This practice of pooling funds pleased everyone, and came into general use.[21]

On arrival at Shanghai Hudson Taylor found John Stevenson utterly swamped with work and worn out although he had the very capable William Cooper and George Andrew to assist him. Stevenson was capable of more than most men, but although Hudson Taylor exhorted him to treat Cooper as a 'junior partner', he found it difficult to delegate to others. Cooper needed specific responsibilities of his own. And the whole mission needed to know what was happening. Hudson Taylor sent out a general letter saying that eight or nine years before, when the CIM had grown to two hundred strong, 'increasing dissatisfaction was felt because I was unable single-handed to meet the requirements of the work,' so John Stevenson had been appointed Deputy Director and the council of superintendents had been created. However, by the year 1893 that two hundred had become six hundred, three times as many, so William Cooper, as Assistant Deputy Director (in line to wear Stevenson's mantle), would handle all administrative correspondence except what was addressed to Stevenson or Hudson Taylor and marked 'Private'. In addition, after seventeen years on the London staff, Charles Fishe was moving to Shanghai again. Stevenson, Cooper, Fishe and Broumton, the treasurer, were to be a Standing Council of Advice when the rest of the China Council scattered to the provinces. With hindsight and the accumulated documents, the evidence seems clear that at thirty-four, with twelve years' experience in China, the physically powerful but gentle William Cooper had won Hudson Taylor's profound confidence and was being groomed for leadership at the highest levels.[22] Anxiety over John Stevenson's state of health may have been a factor, for Jennie wrote, 'Your life and health are very precious.'

While most of the Mission were hard at work, progressing steadily, pockets of restlessness convinced Hudson Taylor that only a personal visit to Shaanxi and Shanxi would restore order. Dangerous individualism was threatening not only the Scandinavians but the future of the whole Mission. The Minister, O'Conor, appeared to be associating the CIM with whatever irregularities were being reported to him. And the CIM missionaries in Shanxi were themselves at sixes and sevens, with Stanley Smith and C T Studd deep in their own difficulties. When Lord Rosebery, Foreign Minister, wrote 'kindly and courteously' but firmly, Hudson Taylor informed Stevenson,

Remembering that we have now a Roman Catholic ambassador at Peking is very important, the main point being that the Foreign Office will sustain any consul in refusing passports to British missionaries if they are convinced that the (Chinese) authority cannot restrain the people from rioting. Now, nothing is easier for the (mandarins) than to pretend that they cannot restrain the people whom they have incited to riot, and many of our consuls . . . may be very easily convinced of the impossibility of restraining a riotous population.

Missionaries should be reminded of the last article of the P and P enjoining them to avoid dealings with the magistrates and consuls.[23]

Soon after reaching China, Hudson Taylor had received a friendly letter from the consul for Sweden and Norway asking for advice. A German newspaper at Shanghai had reported that 'twenty unmarried unprotected females' of Scandinavian missions were in danger in the far north of Shanxi without male missionaries to help them. 'Can the Chinese fathom their good intentions – without the current of suspicion running in another direction' – of loose morals, he asked? 'Do you consider a female more protected in China generally than a man?' 'The [Swedish] Foreign Office have had their attention called to the matter.' Hudson Taylor wrote to reassure him and offered to intervene, but had his misgivings. A women's language school near Shanghai was a very different matter from congregating young women together at Guihuacheng near the Mongolian border.

Unfortunately the worst possible time of year was approaching. At the height of summer a long overland journey to Shanxi invited the dangers of heat stroke, dysentery, typhoid, malaria, and quick tempers in places where the populace were unfriendly. But the journey was unavoidable. Hudson Taylor and Jennie decided they must go, fully aware that it might cost them their lives. 'If the Lord has further work for us to do He will bring us safely through, and I think He will do so, but should it prove otherwise "we ought to lay down our lives for the brethren."'[24] Howard and Geraldine were married at the cathedral on April 24 and after they had left on a canal-boat honeymoon to Hangzhou, his parents prepared for their own journey.

Meanwhile a conference of twenty-one Scandinavians had been held at Qüwu in south Shanxi. All were connected in some way with Fredrik Franson, though in different missions. They were novices of less than five years in China and unrepresentative of many more

F HOWARD TAYLOR AND M GERALDINE TAYLOR,
NÉE GUINNESS

who were not present. But this had not deterred them from passing resolutions of intention to move en bloc into Shaanxi, where the Scandinavian Alliance Mission from America and the original CIM pioneers were already deployed. They did not realise that by an influx of so many of them the resistant province would become dangerously overloaded with foreigners.

On hearing of their decision, Hudson Taylor addressed a pointed general letter to the Scandinavian and China Alliance missionaries (p 614) and others acting with them, whether CIM associates or not, reminding them that they had been received and sent on their way by the CIM, who felt entitled to show concern for them. 'We cannot consider these resolutions as binding on those of your Mission who were not present; and even with regard to those who were there, it is probable that the full bearing of the steps they are proposing is scarcely realised by them.' He went on to show that from lack of experience and advice some had fallen into grave mistakes from which those accepting guidance had been saved.

The Swedish government were considering recalling all its nationals to the coast and cancelling their passports. They and other European governments were 'making very minute enquiries and watching our proceedings very jealously'. To renounce consular control and help could land them in serious difficulties, financially and otherwise. And to cut themselves off from the CIM could be no less hazardous. The CIM were glad to help, whether they were associates or not, 'but anything like a rush into a large number of unoccupied centres (in Shaanxi) might be attended not only with riot and danger (murder) to the missionaries concerned, but also to those who are now safely and usefully settled in centres already open.' Footholds in Henan and Shaanxi had been gained only after years of perseverance and hardship. Thomas Botham had even written of danger from too many foreigners being already in Shaanxi, where he had been 'fleeing in circles' for years.

> We hope never to see a very large staff of foreign workers on the (Xi'an) plain. I think there may be too many missionaries in a place. I should not like to see foreign pastors of all the Chinese churches any more than I should like to see Russian pastors of all English churches.[25]

Botham and his colleague, Bland, would give seasoned advice on opening new work where they judged it to be safe.

Association 'cannot be one-sided'. Accepting help should be answered by consultation and co-operation. 'We must insist, that in all future arrangements Lady Associates be located with or near to married missionaries, or in suitable stations occupied by ladies only' – 'not with single men.' He then outlined the arrangements adopted by the CIM to restrain irresponsible moving around or leaving a place of work without approval by provincial leaders. So urgent was this matter that he was cancelling engagements in America and Britain and starting at once for Xi'an and then Shanxi in spite of the risks to health and life itself. 'I affectionately urge on all . . . to make no change and to begin no new movements until we can meet.' Scandinavian Alliance missionaries in Zhejiang and Jiangxi were also asked 'whether it is their purpose to maintain their connection with the China Inland Mission or to retire from it in the event of any . . . concluding to form a separate mission.'

It looked as if wholesale recruitment had got out of hand. The response to this forthright letter could be a watershed between successful co-operation and disaster.

To Shaanxi and Shanxi   *May–September 1894*

On the international front dangerous developments were afoot. Anglo-Russian friction had arisen in protest against Russia's growing influence over China. The trans-Siberian railway began its Manchurian extensions after the inauguration on May 17, 1891, and the imperial edict of June 1893. But the power of Japan was becoming a greater threat as she rapidly modernised her armed forces and began sabre-rattling over Korea.

Korea lay uncomfortably between China and Japan, defensively significant to both. Historically China was the suzerain power, allowing Korea her independence while guaranteeing her against external aggression and internal disorder. This dual policy of non-interference and protection kept Korea as a buffer state.

China's suzerainty over the Ryukyu Islands, Annam, Siam and Burma had been whittled away. Only Korea remained. Her affairs were in the hands of Li Hongzhang and the Resident at Seoul, Yuan Shikai. But China's weakness meant that her only defence against Japan's progressive undermining of stability in Korea lay in treaties with the Western powers. At the same time Japan's best hope of being seen by the West as an equal power lay in military domination of China.

So provocation followed provocation in spite of the Tianjin Convention of 1885 between China and Japan.

The Empress Dowager had siphoned off huge allocations for strengthening the navy, to rebuild the Summer Palace. But as a sign of imperial favour when Li reached seventy years of age, the highest honour possible in the empire, the three-eyed peacock feather, was again bestowed on him in March 1894, the only Han Chinese ever to receive it.[26] In June Japan landed twelve thousand men in Korea, engineered a *coup d'état* at Seoul and made demands to which China responded by also shifting troops to Korea.

This was how things stood in May as Hudson Taylor travelled at the worst possible time of year. By then he was deep in the hinterland of Henan and Shaanxi, toiling painfully towards Xi'an. He, Jennie and their son-in-law 'Joe' Coulthard, a seasoned traveller, had set out from Shanghai in mid-May, up the Yangzi to Hankou, calling on the missionaries at each port.[27] While they were still there Howard and Geraldine arrived, alarmed to hear that his parents were intending to travel in such heat. It was too late to change plans. They had cabled ahead to call conferences at four cities. 'Then let us come, too,' Howard pleaded. So the family party of five left Hankou by houseboat on May 22, changing to wheelbarrows on the 24th. Zhoujiakou was reached on June 2, Xiangcheng on the 6th in springless carts, and Tongguan on the 22nd, jolted incessantly and well-nigh intolerably, sometimes in dust and temperatures of over 100°F in the shade, and sometimes in pouring rain. The armed confrontation in Korea had begun, but as yet no fighting.

Geraldine had started the journey ambitiously, keeping a diary.

> June 13. 6 am. This is indeed a moment of misery. We are sitting waiting in our carts in this filthy inn-yard, all ready to start – as we have been for an hour – while the rain pours steadily down and the carters are obdurate. For several nights . . . we have slept but little (bed bugs). Outside in the courtyard half a dozen fiery mules were fighting and braying all night long. . . . There being only one room, Mother and I occupied it; Father, Howard and Joe slept in the carts outside.

After that she could manage no more than mere notes. On June 14 a river barring their way was impassable and they had to return to a primitive type of inn. 'June 14. Dreadful-looking people – no inn – place dangerous. Had to return.'

'June 15. Quite an exciting moment! We are in the act of crossing a swollen river . . . One cart (overturned and was) washed away before our eyes (so) we felt it wiser to cross by ferry.' 'Our rough, rough journey' ended at Xi'an on June 26.

Since the Hunanese family's opposition in Xi'an (HTCOC Book 6, p 414) had been ended by friendly officials, houses for women missionaries had been secured in the west suburb and for others in the city itself. It seemed miraculous that now even a conference of foreigners could be held safely in what had for years been such a danger spot. Twelve Scandinavians of the first thirty-five (p 154), and four full members of the CIM (Easton, Bland, Steven, and another) had gathered for conference with Hudson Taylor. Four days' travel to the west, Thomas Botham was nursing his wife, at death's door with high fever. Howard set off for Fengxiang to help them – and found her recovering.

In Shaanxi there were none of the serious problems that awaited Hudson Taylor in Shanxi. He was impressed by the progress these Alliance missionaries had made in adaptation to China and by the success of their work. 'Very few of our men after three years in China are as competent as they have become, or as careful . . . Their plans for independent work seem so matured . . . they are looked on with much favour and get on well and wisely with the officials.' It was more a matter of organising co-operation in keeping with the P and P.

By July 2 satisfactory arrangements had been made. One of the Scandinavians, Henriksen, was to be recognised as 'Senior Missionary Associate' working with Botham as Assistant Super-intendent of the whole province of Shaanxi. Bland was to help Botham, and Botham would be responsible to G F Easton as superintendent of Gansu and Shaanxi. The complexity of this organisation reflected the great distances and growing numbers of missionaries involved. Others of their own Scandinavian Alliance, from Shanxi, Zhejiang and Jiangxi, would be found suitable loca-tions to occupy, but in no hurry. Real difficulties had been created for the single women by the two-year marriage rule, so Hudson Taylor simply waived it in the case of Scandinavians, putting the good of the cause before normal practice. This capacity for being master of the rules he made, instead of being mastered by them, stands out as one of Hudson Taylor's strong characteristics.[28]

On July 4 they set off by cart again, back to Tongguan and over the Yellow River on the 7th, making for Yüncheng, Erik Folke's base for the Swedish Mission in China. Conditions had been gruelling. A pocket thermometer in the shade of a covered cart registered 110°F. Outside it was considerably higher. When Howard Taylor caught them up his father was 'very seriously ill (with) cerebral congestion' although most of his head had been shaved. He recovered with treatment. After that they travelled by night to Qüwo for a third conference, this time with some of the restless Swedes. (An absence of records suggests 'the less said the better'.) Then on to Linfen (Pingyang) to be met on the road by Hsi Shengmo and Dixon Hoste.

The Linfen conference of thirty-five missionaries including eleven more Scandinavians and sessions for church members, lasted eight days (July 17–24). Personal consultation again secured agree-ment over where the Swedes could be safely deployed. And to general rejoicing Dixon Hoste and Gertrude Broomhall became engaged. After doing well in Shanxi as a missionary and in Britain and North America as a public speaker, she had only recently returned. (They travelled with the Taylors to Tianjin and were married at the consulate on September 6, 1894 – a partnership in what they could not have dreamed would come their way.)

From Linfen onwards the Scandinavian problems became overshadowed by CIM disorder. Travelling from city to city for meetings with Chinese Christians and missionaries who could not get to the conferences, Hudson Taylor found a disgraceful state of affairs. Two factions, for and against Hsi Shengmo, lived in a permanent state of friction which their unbiased colleagues could not overcome. At Taiyuan this 'dread of Hsi' was compounded by a recurrence of the 'Shanxi spirit' – the 'Christianised Confucianism' being offered in place of (rather than as a means of presenting) the gospel. Recognising a degree of spirituality in Confucian classics, the minds of some lost sight of the uniqueness of Christ and therefore of Christianity. In Latourette's assessment, 'as Timothy Richard pointed out, there were two ways of regarding the Gospel: as a means of saving the soul of each individual, and as a means of saving a nation through the collective efforts of regenerated souls.'[29]

At a more mundane level, distancing themselves from the heart of the CIM, some members showed the spirit of compromise in being 'loose on the dress question'. All too many of the CIM and Scandinavians in Shanxi were copying other missions and some who had resigned from the CIM, in compromising between Chinese and foreign dress, wearing a Chinese gown, but leather boots, pith helmet and no queue, a clownish hotch-potch scorned by the Chinese. The two doctors, some senior missionaries and Stanley Smith were among them.

'SPS's' vacillating loyalty to Mission principles and even to his beliefs had been one of the factors determining Hudson Taylor's return to China. They had already met (at Yokohama) and talked it over. This time Hudson Taylor wrote to William Cooper, 'It would be far better for him to retire from us and make his own arrangements with Studd' if both wished to work together. The doctors might resign anyway.

Two decisions faced Hudson Taylor. If he failed to nip this defection in the bud it would spread. 'Chinese dress' meant correct Chinese dress and deportment, unreluctant adaptation winning Chinese approval. That included the conventional hair style. Harmony and co-operation as a Mission team necessitated mutual respect and the end of dissension. He advocated courtesy to the Chinese by ceasing the charade of neither one proper dress nor the other, and won the compliance of most. Then with them he worked

out a division of Shanxi into separate areas under different superintendents. To southern Shanxi, Hsi's region, he appointed Hsi's
faithful companion Dixon Hoste. And to the central region one who
would be pleased to have no more dealings with Hsi. To rally Dr
Edwards, he offered him a seat on the China Council. By the time
Hudson Taylor left Shanxi all knew that proper *observance* of the P
and P was a condition of membership of the CIM. Some were
weighing whether or not to accept or to reject it. The debate among
missionaries of all societies, for and against Chinese dress, was still
very much alive, and the grass outside the CIM fence looked
greener. Opinions differed within the ranks of a mission, often
strongly held. The CMS failed to reach agreement and 'Salisbury
House' left it to individuals to do as they saw fit.[30]

All through July the possibility of war between China and Japan
over Korea had been degenerating towards probability. The *daotai*
of Shanghai informed the consuls on the 23rd that he intended to
block the entrance to the Huangpu River at the cost of strangling
half of China's coastal trade. To prevent this, the British representative in Tokyo secured an undertaking by Japan to 'regard Shanghai
as outside the sphere of its warlike operation', but Canton, Fuzhou,
Ningbo and other ports constructed barriers. War would drastically
affect missions, however far from the war zone. If Hudson Taylor
knew what was developing, he disregarded it. Rumour and alarm
were never far from the surface. Finally the sinking of the Chinese
troopship *Kowshing* on July 25 (while they were at Hsi Shengmo's
home) marked the start of major hostilities. But it was ill-health that
brought the Taylors' journey to an untimely end.

Unable to check the enteritis they had developed on their hard
journey, they decided to head for Shanghai while the way was open.
After the council meetings in September, Hudson Taylor himself
would come back, as the surest way of resolving the Shanxi disorder. So on August 16 they left Taiyuan, reached Shouyang in two
days and stayed with the council member who had resigned to do
things in his own way. They were Christian enough not to harbour
resentment over strong deviations of policy. Four more days' travel
brought them over the mountains to Huolu (Hwailu) and they
reached Tianjin on September 4 with no worse mishaps than Jennie
and Geraldine being 'ducked in the Sha River' and, near Tianjin, 'a
narrow escape, boat sunk in passing bridge'. But Jennie's dysentery
became dangerously worse and on September 5, after the Hoste's
wedding, they quickly took her on board a ship leaving at 1.00 am

for Shanghai, through the Bo Hai Strait and disputed waters between Shandong and Korea.

To Shanxi alone   September–December 1894

Three weeks later, the council meetings over, Hudson Taylor sailed north again (September 25) looking 'very aged and tired' to reach Tianjin on October 2. Before leaving Shanghai he had written to Walter B Sloan in London, 'Now the war has broken out, I am not sure that I ought to leave China . . . The authorities are diligently trying to protect the missionaries . . . but the greatest danger would arise from rebellion, should the secret societies think the government was so seriously embarrassed as to give them a good chance of success.' After consulting other missions in Shanghai about the prospects, since by then the Chinese had been driven out of Korea and fighting had reached beyond the Yalu River (map p 197) he started inland on October 5 with one employee companion.[31] Some sixty Japanese warships were reported at the mouth of the Gulf of Zhili and likely to blockade it. 'All seem to think . . . the dynasty unlikely to survive the shock.' He was carrying one thousand taels' worth of gold leaf and as much again in silver lest his communications be cut and a long enforced overland journey to the south become unavoidable. A letter to his daughter, Amy, reflects the fears at Tianjin.

> It may be that in a few days the war may shut the door by which I have entered; and some think . . . there may be a time of dangerous anarchy before order can be restored . . . I only know one thing, the LORD reigneth and under His reign *all* things work together for good to them that love God. This will be so if I am alive . . . to return to you in peace . . . But it will equally be so should this note be the last you receive from me.

Joe Coulthard, Howard and Geraldine were back in Henan, perhaps in great need of prayer when she received it, he said. He believed that revolution might break out any day and the lives of all foreigners, his own no less than others, would be in jeopardy. He sent it via Jennie who added a postscript: 'It is a time of strain . . . but God is over all and nothing can happen to us that has not first been sanctioned by Him who is Love.' In the event they had six more years before that protection was withdrawn.[32]

This time he had no son or daughter-in-law to see to his comfort.

He bargained with muleteers, rose at 3.00 am to see that they fed their animals in time for an early start each day, and had to find accommodation and food for himself. 'I confess I do not like crossing the (treacherous) rivers and pools . . . Part of this journey has been a time of great spiritual conflict, but the Lord has greatly helped me.' He was feeling too old and drained of energy for such travelling. And the purpose of this journey, to reinforce discipline among the still recalcitrant missionaries, could hardly be more distasteful. But he knew the power of personal friendship and frankness.

At Baoding, Huolu (Hwailu) and Shunde some were growing their queues again; not all. One had been impressed by seeing how pleased the Chinese were and how much notice had been taken of its absence. They were far from indifferent to the question, as some missionaries believed. At Shunde he found C T Studd and his wife 'in a beautiful spirit', on their way home to Britain. C T's asthma made it useless to stay longer. He hoped to return, but insisted on presenting to the Mission the fine large premises he had personally bought at Lu'an (Lungan, now Changzhi). 'I told him that dear SPS had so impulsively taken up views contrary to the platform of the Mission; that had he not . . . (retracted) all he had written on the subject, his continuance in the Mission would not have been possible.' 'Some sudden impulsive step' might yet sever the links.[33]

Going on by mule litter across 'a sea of mountains – solid waves', taxed his endurance. Often in the dry beds of mountain torrents broken up by large boulders, flash floods from distant cloudbursts posed a threat. At Lu'an he spent a day with Stanley Smith, vacillating again, but as charming as ever. He doctored and bandaged the injured leg of an enemy of the Christians, and later heard that he had become 'almost a friend'. Then on in snow, with icicles forming on his litter and the man-servant he had employed ill with typhoid and having to be carried. Through one mission centre after another, finding loyal compliance by most missionaries, but obduracy from others, he reached Taiyuan from the south. There he wrote, '(Edwards) agrees, thank God' – to live by the P and P.

The Hostes, back at Hongtong, had had a royal welcome from the church. A large banner of blue with gold characters for 'With one heart serving the Lord' greeted them, as well as flowery furniture and bright curtains. Pastor and Mrs Hsi presented them with a warm quilt covered with crimson silk, the bridal colour. At a church gathering of four hundred with Hudson Taylor, sixty-nine were baptised and several deacons appointed. This was the true Shanxi. 'I left Taiyuan glad this time, a load removed.' 'Nearly all I hoped for is accomplished.' 'Had I not been able to visit (Shanxi) and (Shaanxi) we should have lost a good many workers.'

But the war news was bad. Mukden fallen to the Japanese; the Taiyuan authorities afraid they would be the next, to become a bastion against reinforcement from the west before the kill at Peking. Rumours abounded. Yantai bombarded, Zhang Zhitong, a reformer, assassinated on the emperor's orders. Both proved untrue. Using a Chinese atlas he followed the Japanese advance through Manchuria. On November 20 he learned that two thousand Chinese troops were behind him. He must keep ahead or food and shelter would be hard to come by. Then a boat from Baoding to Tianjin through freezing temperatures and icy winds, not knowing whether the way was clear or Tianjin still free. It was. But all ships were full with people fleeing south. He reached Shanghai on December 4, having been on the move almost incessantly for seven months.

War with Japan[34]   *May 1894–1895*

The sinking of the troopship *Kowshing* on July 25, 1894, led to both China and Japan declaring war on August 1. But while the main Chinese army formed along the Yalu River, an advanced force at Pyongyang, halfway to Seoul, was routed by an overpowering Japanese army of 80,000. China's appeal for intervention by the Western nations had met with no success. The Korean royal family were seized and Korea declared war on China. Then on September 17 the decisive naval engagement of Haiyang Dao took place off the mouth of the Yalu. The Japanese established their control of the seas, and the remains of the Chinese fleet took shelter at Lüda (Dalian, Dairen, Port Arthur) and then at Weihaiwei on the Shandong coast east of Yantai.

Blame for the outbreak of war and this defeat were unjustly laid at the door of Li Hongzhang. Deprived on December 26 of his viceroyalty and two most prized decorations, the 'yellow jacket' and his three-eyed peacock feathers, he retained his unenviable responsibilities. And, after ten years 'in the wilderness', Prince Kong was recalled to head the government and 'piece together the smashed cup'. By the end of September Korea had been cleared of Chinese troops, and the Japanese crossed the Yalu River into

Manchuria on October 24. On the same day they landed above Lüda and by November 6 were investing the port, to the intense alarm of Peking, for it was just across the gulf from Tianjin. The wealthy began to transport their riches and womenfolk by the Grand Canal to the safety of the south.

The Empress Dowager's sixtieth birthday on November 7 (the 10th day of the 10th moon) passed almost uncelebrated, but the foreign envoys were received with ceremony and the British and American ministers presented her on behalf of China's ten thousand Christian women with an ornate *Wenli* New Testament measuring 13 by 10 inches. Bound in solid silver covers embossed with golden characters for 'Holy Classic of Salvation', it lay in a silver casket. Not long afterwards the young emperor sent a palace eunuch to the Bible Society asking for a copy of the Old and New Testaments for himself. The old Buddha's birthday was also her opportunity to recall Yong Lu from punitive disgrace and once again to put him in command of the palace garrison.[35]

When China had made a second appeal for foreign help, Britain could arouse no interest from the other powers, but Prince Kong tried again. This time the envoys asked Japan whether mediation would be acceptable. Not until China sued for peace, she answered. Overtures were then made through the American envoy for peace based on the independence of Korea and a negotiated war indemnity. These also failed. The Peking court petulantly meted out punishments to the unfortunate commanding officers and replaced Li Hongzhang as viceroy of Zhili.[36]

So ended the year, but not the war. The Japanese army continued to advance until on March 5, 1895, they held Yingkou (Niuchuang). No natural line of defence remained before Peking except at Shanhaiguan, the last barrier of mountains where the Great Wall runs down into the sea. Capture of the pass would open the way to both Peking and Tianjin. Manchuria east of the Liao River was theirs, the region of Liaodong, dynastic home of the Qing. Across the strait they bombarded Penglai (Dengzhou) west of Yantai, three times in January, and landed twenty thousand troops and ten thousand transport coolies east of Yantai at Rongcheng Bay on the tip of the peninsula, only thirty miles beyond Weihaiwei. The remains of the Chinese fleet anchored in the harbour at Weihaiwei were mauled by gunfire and torpedoes. So the Chinese admiral and other commanding officers committed suicide to save themselves from decapitation and their families from death and confiscation of

LI HONGZHANG IN 1896
showing the scar of the wound below his eye

their estates. Rumours of Yantai being bombarded on November 14 were unfounded.

Meanwhile, more confused attempts to negotiate peace came to nothing, and on February 19, 1895, the Peking court had no recourse but to restore to the incomparable Li Hongzhang all his honours before appointing him ambassador extraordinary to negotiate with Japan. With his son, Li Jingfang, two other emissaries and a suite of 135 attendants he met the Japanese delegation at Shimonoseki in south-western Honshu on March 20 and requested an armistice. Only on surrender of Shanhaiguan, Tianjin, the port of Dagu at the river mouth and the railway between these places, the Japanese arrogantly replied. On March 24 they met to discuss terms for peace and Li was told that an expedition was on its way to occupy Taiwan. Would Japan's aggression stop at nothing?

On his way back in his sedan chair Li was shot at by a Japanese fanatic, the bullet embedding itself in the cheekbone below his left eye. Fuming with rage he quietly walked from the chair to his room and for seventeen days negotiated through his son. International feeling was outraged and Japan humiliated. The emperor expressed his regrets and his nation their sympathy. They granted an armistice, reduced their demands, abandoned claims to exceptional privileges, and signed the Treaty of Shimonoseki on April 17. What war and diplomacy had failed to achieve, the venerable Li Hongzhang's personal suffering secured.

The terms, nevertheless, were harsh and humiliating for China: complete independence for Korea; cession of the large Liaodong region of Manchuria, of Taiwan and the Pescadores; an indemnity of two hundred million taels; more treaty ports and inland waterways to be opened to commerce; and Weihaiwei to be held until ratification was complete. But Russia, France and Germany jointly 'recommended' that all the Manchurian territory be returned to China. The Russian Mediterranean squadron was on its way, and by the time the exchange of ratifications was made at Yantai on May 8, the warships of many nations, including twenty or more flying the Russian ensign, had congregated there. Japan signed a subsidiary treaty on November 8, accepting an additional eighty million taels in lieu of Liaodong, which brought the total indemnity to about £40 million sterling, provided by loans from Russia, France, Britain and Germany, all secured by customs revenues.

On April 7, 1895, Sir Robert Hart wrote to his colleague E B Drew, 'Japan wants to lead the East in war, in commerce and in manufactures, and next century will be a hard one for the West.' Taiwan quickly fell to the expeditionary force after an abortive attempt to declare Taiwan a republic, when Britain and then France (close to war with each other over Siam) rejected a request from Taiwan to make the island a protectorate. 'The wires burned with telegrams.' The stakes were too high.[37] The only authentic flag of the Taiwan republic to survive was in the possession of H B Morse himself, customs officer at Danshui.

Alicia Bewicke Little wrote of the Chinese people being crushed and tearful and of some viceroys and governors baying for Li Hongzhang's blood. But for Ci Xi he would have been beheaded, she maintained.

Hudson Taylor had not needed to use his emergency gold-leaf. He had left Baoding for Tianjin the day after the port of Lüda (Port Arthur) was taken. Sailing from Dagu on the last day of November, his ship made straight for Shanghai, through the war zone, not calling in at Yantai. So he was back at Wusong Road when he wrote to Walter Sloan on December 6 of hopes of peace, but: 'There will be a time of danger while the troops are being disbanded. And if . . . they are defrauded of pay and given no means of returning home . . . the additional danger of rebellion or bands of banditti.' Two weeks later he wrote again of hoping to get up to Yantai where morale was understandably low, but he had heard of isolated missionaries in south-west China talking of resignation through sheer loneliness. If he took two years visiting all mission centres it could be time well spent, conditions permitting. 'Nothing but great urgency would justify my leaving China at present.' He himself was not well, but both Broumton and Stevenson were seriously ill again, so for the present he was anchored at Shanghai.

At Yantai the anxiety was justifiable when the two ports to east and west of them came under attack. The harbour was barricaded and plans made to evacuate all foreigners. The Japanese were reported to have landed at Ninghai only fifteen miles away. They had not. Dr Douthwaite quickly prepared his hospital under the Red Cross, and insisted that it was to receive the wounded whether Chinese or Japanese. His good relationship with the amazed Chinese general made it possible to convince him that the hospital could be neutral territory. But his point was never put to the test. Desperately injured men dragged themselves through the snow from Weihaiwei to reach Chefoo frost-bitten. Every bed was soon filled, and untrained missionaries assisted him in his surgical operations.[38] The schools had consular instructions to be prepared to leave at short notice, each child with his or her own bundle. For a mile from shore the sea was frozen. Farther out foreign ships waited to receive them. When word came that a body of five hundred famished Chinese stragglers were retreating towards the schools, the consul warned the Mission to be prepared for looting. But they straggled past, to be received by the mandarins.

The armistice restored calm and the ratification of the treaty at Yantai, with the bay filled with warships, brought new excitement. Cholera broke out in the city and on the ships. Two CMS missionaries attended a school prize-giving; one died of cholera before the morning. Yet the school escaped. Without warning the general and his staff arrived one day at Douthwaite's hospital on horseback, a brass band playing and soldiers bearing a large honorific tablet which they set up with great ceremony. When the foundations of the big new school (HTCOC Book 6, pp 207–8) were being laid, a company of soldiers brought eight hundred 'loads' of quarried rock as a gift. And when the Douthwaite family left Chefoo, the general and a whole regiment paraded at the hospital. As Dr Douthwaite came out they dropped on their knees while a speech of thanks was made for all he had done for them. And he was escorted with a guard of honour to the harbour. Not content with that, the emperor awarded him (and ten other missionary doctors involved in the war) with the Order of the Double Dragon.

Hosea Ballou Morse, eyewitness of some of these events, particularly in Taiwan, made the comment, 'Unable to make headway against the Japanese, (the Chinese) hit hard at the missionaries.' In every month of 1895 the American legation at Peking had occasion to report on the dangerous position in which American missionaries were placed. For Zhou Han, the evil genius in Hunan, surfaced again with more diatribes against foreigners in general and missionaries in particular.[39] This time the blood of missionaries was to be shed as had not happened for generations.

PART 3

'THE SLEEP AND THE AWAKENING'

1895–1905

CHAPTER SEVEN

CHINA IN CONVULSION
1895–97

Rebellion in the air *1895–97*

A new maritime nation had appeared almost overnight. In less than twenty years Japan had modernised sufficiently to rank with any Western nation on the Oriental high seas. With a two-thousand-mile coastline to defend, China's nucleus of a navy lay in fragments. Counting on intervention by the powers to curb Japan's aggression, China had been disillusioned. Her government had scorned Japan, made little effort to match her growing strength, and had been forced to her knees by a navy built on the British pattern and an army modelled on the French and Germans. Finding herself 'in a state of utter helplessness', China (or at least her thinkers) saw more aggression and dismemberment as her likely fate. Stunned shock gave place to anger. All knew that the obscurantist rulers at Peking were to blame. But, above all, they were most ready to find scapegoats and to crush criticism at source.

Hosea Ballou Morse, as a customs official at Danshui (Taiwan) when the Japanese walked in, felt the pulse of the nation. Until humiliation opened the nation's eyes, 'a few thousands at most' of China's intelligentsia could see that modernisation in the Western mould was their only hope. Once defeat became not fear but a fact, 'many myriads in number burned with indignation and looked for reform', while others turned on the only foreigners within reach, the missionaries.

'Marquis' Zeng, the ambassador to Paris, to St Petersburg, and to London had written in 1887 urging reform, in his book *The Sleep and the Awakening*. In 1894 the Western-trained doctor, Sun Yatsen, first graduate (in 1892) of the Hong Kong College of Medicine, at twenty-five formed a cell of the revolutionary Golaohui secret society at Canton. Before the start of the Sino-Japanese war he obtained the signatures of many educated Cantonese to a memorial to the throne on modernisation. In October 1895 he organised an armed raid from Hong Kong on Canton. It failed, and he fled to America and then London, organising revolt wherever he could. The Manchu secret service tracked him down, and in October 1896 kidnapped him in London. They held him prisoner at the Chinese legation until Lord Salisbury secured his release at the request of Dr James Cantlie, Sun Yatsen's professor in Hong Kong. For seventeen years he was hunted (1895–1912) with a huge price on his head, ready to be tortured and killed if only the Manchus could be ousted and replaced by a democratic republic.[1]

The other outstanding angry young man was Kang Yuwei, also a Cantonese of Guangdong. Not a revolutionary but a reformer, his goal was to convert the literati, the mandarins and the throne to 'the wisdom and the necessity of reorganisation of the machinery of government', as a constitutional monarchy. His books were widely read and in calling him 'the modern sage of China' admirers were saying he was 'a second Confucius'. In April 1895, he presented a memorial to the throne signed by over a thousand qüren (MA degree men) urging non-ratification of the treaty of Shimonoseki.[2] Both these young men were destined to share in the reshaping of the nation, but the spontaneous movement was widespread and growing stronger. Zhang Zhitong accepted the presidency of the Reform Association of China while viceroy of Nanjing before returning to Wuchang and being succeeded by Liu Kunyi.[3] The Hanlin Reform Club of Peking included some of China's élite. From all over China viceroys, governors and military commanders deluged the empire with memorials in favour of rejecting the treaty and continuing the war.[4] But this reforming spirit still clung chiefly to the coastal cities and along the Yangzi.

(The people's) pride has been wounded [Hudson Taylor wrote to all 630 of his missionaries]; their respect for their own rulers lessened; rebellion is in the air, turbulence and unrest are found everywhere . . . Rioting in (Sichuan) has been followed by riots against Christians (in Wenzhou and its neighbouring city of Bingyae) by the terrible massacre of missionaries in (Fujian), the attack on Fatshan near Canton, and by a tendency to revenge on Christians the losses from drought or flood or from other national or local disasters . . . The Secret Societies may seize the opportunity to try to overthrow the Government altogether, when anarchy with all its horrors might be the result.

[Calling for a day of 'waiting upon God' he continued] The counsel we have given in times past, as far as possible to remain at one's post strengthening the faith of (Chinese) Christians by our own restful trust in the Lord, we still recommend . . . The (Chinese) know that we possess no firearms, but rely on the living God alone for our protection . . . It behoves us . . . not to yield to the spirit of unrest . . . If filled with the Spirit we shall also be filled with love, joy and peace . . . Come what may, we are on the winning side.[5]

The Mission that faced the ultimate test five years later had been gradually prepared for it.

'Why *do* the heathen rage?' he asked Walter Sloan, not knowing from day to day what the next telegram would report. Why China raged soon filled the headlines. The journalist Alexander Michie wrote, 'China was defeated amid the applause of Europe and the whole world' – mistakenly glad in thinking that the inflexible Empress Dowager and her court could no longer live in the past and must face up to international realities. Mistaken, for nothing would change Ci Xi, but also because Japan and 'the lawless West' had already earned and would go on earning China's hatred as they 'sliced the melon'.

Convulsions widespread   *1895*

Hudson Taylor's letter was no over-reaction to events. In this year of 1895 alarm followed alarm. January saw the Japanese invasion of Shandong, and February the fall of Weihaiwei and surrender of the Chinese fleet. Chefoo lay in the path of extreme danger. In March a fracas between rival Muslim sects in the Gansu-Qinghai border regions was turning into full-scale rebellion with the defeat of a Chinese force sent to quell them. City after city, even Lanzhou, was reportedly in rebel hands. Nothing was heard of several missionaries, presumably engulfed (see pp 231–7). April brought news of the assassination attempt on Li Hongzhang, and then of peace at such a price that anger flared after tears of mortification. In May, Liu Pingzhang, the viceroy of Sichuan, fomented riots in his own province, affecting the CIM at his capital of Chengdu, at Leshan (Jiading), Yibin and Ya'an in the south, and (in June) at Langzhong (Paoning) in the north. But when 'the great province became a hotbed of mob violence with the suddenness of a tropical thunderstorm . . . more than sixty foreigners [sixty-one in fact] were driven out. [Their] work was completely broken up. [But] several tens of thousands of Christians (largely Roman Catholics) suffered, many being killed.'[6]

Xining in Gansu was under threat of siege, and the Ridleys (p

235) sent out word that they were staying to help if they could. Grim persecution of the Christians broke out at Pingyang (Bingyae) halfway between Wenzhou and the Fujian border.

By mid-July the homes and possessions of twenty-one families had been destroyed. Fifty-nine refugees fled to the mission house and chapel. A murderous attack on Dr D Z Sheffield of the American Board at Tongzhou (now Tong Xian in Zhili) left him nearly dead with thirty-four severe wounds. But it was not all one-sided. A Wenzhou Christian commented, 'In the New Testament all the best people went to prison.'[7] From Hanzhong, just north of Sichuan, came news of 'unmistakable signs of a great harvest' throughout the district. People came crowding simply to hear the gospel.

Then on August 1 the restraining hand of God was withdrawn and the worst massacre of missionaries in China since the mid-eighteenth century (HTCOC Book 1, p 82) took place in Fujian. The Xining siege was at its worst in the autumn and through December, until it was raised in January 1896. October brought news of ten CIM missionaries and Chinese at Wenzhou dead from cholera. In his review of the year Hudson Taylor only called 1895 'the most trying (year) experienced by (Protestant) missionaries in China.' The meaning of 'riot' to individual missionaries has been made clear in the earlier books of this series, but the Sichuan riots of 1895 taught new lessons and influenced the attitudes of the viceroys and governors of China, even if Ci Xi and her closest confidantes were unmoved.

Sichuan riots   *April–July 1895*

The CIM had eleven 'stations' in Sichuan. In the absence of Dr Herbert Parry from Chengdu, his wife and two single women and the J G Cormacks were there, with Joshua Vale of Yibin on a short visit, when rioting broke out. James Cormack's letter home gave the facts, amplifying his note 'written when we did not know if we should be alive the following morning'.[8]

In April a woman under treatment by Dr Hare of the Canadian Methodist Mission died, and the husband imprisoned the doctor, accusing him of murder. When a crowd gathered and set upon him, Dr Hare escaped and ran for his life. Vile stories about him were then circulated in the city. Again and again the magistrates were appealed to, but took no action to calm the people. On May 28 the

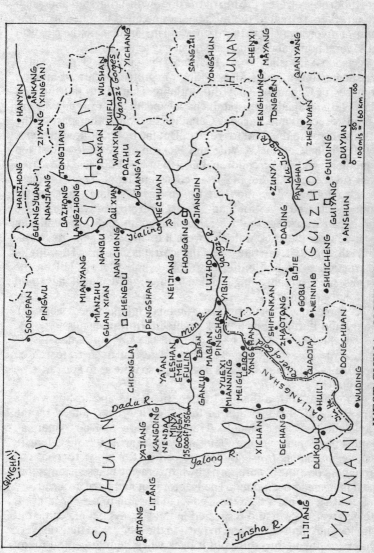

WEST CHINA: SICHUAN AND GUIZHOU

Canadian Hospital was surrounded and stoned. To impress the mob Dr Kilborne shattered the top of the door with a rifle shot and when the attackers retreated the missionaries escaped to a nearby army camp. Driven away from there, they hid in darkness on the city wall for several hours and then made their way to the CIM.

As soon as Joshua Vale heard of the rioting he too sent a messenger to the magistrates asking for protection for all mission premises in Chengdu. They did nothing. That night and through May 29, the Canadian hospital, chapel and all other premises were looted, wrecked and burned. Canadians from another part of the city also came to the CIM for refuge. But the rioters followed them. By 10 pm the Cormacks, Vale and Jackson of the CMS and seven Canadians, with seven children, knew their best hope was to escape. Four succeeded, hidden in curtained sedan chairs. The Cormacks were to follow. 'The mob set up an awful yelling', but *yamen* 'runners' cleared a way for them. As the mob burst into the premises and began wrecking, the five remaining adults and three children escaped over the back wall and were hidden by neighbours, 'huddled all together on one bed, the curtains drawn'. The din of destruction continued until 'not even a whole tile was left on the premises, everything being levelled to the ground and all that could be stolen carried off.'

The American Board's premises and six Catholic places were also looted and burned. For a week eighteen Protestant missionaries, eleven children and two Catholic priests were concealed in the nearest *yamen*. All had lost everything. The local magistrate treated them well, 'but higher officials have done so little as to appear to be accomplices'.

At Leshan, known then as Jiading, the Riries and Joshua Vale's fiancée, Annie Bridgewater of the CIM, had been joined by the Canadian Methodist doctors Hart and Hare and an American Baptist missionary when students and others arrived from Chengdu and began rabble-rousing. Posters calling for mobs to beat the foreigners on June 5 were torn down by brave Chinese friends, but the damage had been done. The lust for loot had been aroused.

Ben Ririe went over to the Canadian Mission to see for himself. He was well known and respected in the city. As people came out with loot he calmly told them to put it in the lobby, and they obeyed. Others removing furniture put it back when he intercepted them. When the magistrate arrived with soldiers he returned home, to find a mob of several thousands preparing to break in. He learned that neighbours had helped the women over the garden wall to hide so he rejoined them. The city prefect arrived, 'got knocked about a bit', and could only withdraw, leaving the house to be looted. 'Everything carried off or smashed.'[9]

After midnight they made their way to the *yamen*, and were treated as guests for three months. Housed in a beautiful cottage and garden built for the magistrate's son, and sent all their meals, 'very nicely done up', they were visited by 'the great man of the city' and urged to stay. 'Many asked us, if we went, to come back again . . . Our love for the people here grew as we saw how anxious they were for us . . . We are all of one mind, "don't go till we have to". We are . . . far better off than our Master who had nowhere to lay His head.' 'We were able to show the people that we can "take joyfully the spoiling of our goods" . . . I never knew I had so many friends in (Leshan) until yesterday.' 'All who had ever been in our service – carpenter, barber, etc, stuck to us right through and lost their own things.'

This experience became full of lessons for the Riries and for the Mission when the full story appeared in *China's Millions*. Love for the Chinese and contentment with whatever affected them themselves spoke more loudly than any preaching when the testing came. They learned that the inflammatory posters had said that they were not to be touched because they had no firearms, as others had. Heywood Horsburgh of the CMS also learned at Chengdu that the rioters there had been told to leave the CIM untouched – until they gave sanctuary to the armed missionaries. Horsburgh's own calmness and good humour seemed to influence the rioters so that they did not go beyond petty pillage at his place.[10]

Mrs Ririe told her parents that she saw the riots as Satan's show of anger for their 'working in his camp'; and as good preparation for 'greater trials than this'. 'We have only lost our homes' . . . 'What we do feel (aggrieved over) is that such accusations as eating children and other vile sins too bad to mention should be put down to the name of Jesus's followers.'

Three CIM women in Qionglai near Chengdu at the time of the riots were not only taken into the *yamen*, but were 'saved from a riot by the headman of a secret rebel society . . . The very men who helped to smash the RC mission to pieces took (the women's) things to the *yamen* for them.'[11]

At Guan Xian, Guangyuan, Yibin, Luzhou, Wanxian and other cities, the mandarins did 'all in their power' to protect the missionaries and their homes, but half-heartedly at Langzhong. And at Chongqing summary execution was promised to anyone who incited to riot or even spread wild stories.[12] A clear picture was emerging of the general situation. Much seemed to depend on the attitude of individual officials, with little encouragement from their seniors to protect the foreigners. The relative value of firearms and friendliness left no room for doubt. And as striking as the danger was the unrealised presence everywhere of many who had become truly friendly to the missionary.

Considered conclusions   *Autumn 1895*

After most of the dust had settled, Hudson Taylor summed up his impressions in a letter congratulating the Riries for their good spirit and wise behaviour.

> I am convinced that missionaries who are going in for forcible claims and demands for punishment are, as you say, missing a grand opportunity for witnessing . . . I doubt whether twenty years will make up for the practical misrepresentation of Christ which this action amounts to.
>
> It seems that the consul has made a great mistake in blaming you. You have acted according to the principles of your mission, which principles have received the official commendation of consul, consul-general, ambassadors, and have received at least the tacit approval of the Foreign Office . . . they have published commendation of the action . . . in the Blue Books . . . I should be thankful to believe that none of our missionaries under any circumstances would be induced to take any steps to seek the punishment of those who may have wronged them . . . Christ's commands to us are unmistakable – 'Resist not' and 'Resent not'. If obedience to Christ leads to martyr-dom, even, it is none-the-less our privilege and duty.
>
> I am very sorry for the under-officials who have been kind and done all they could for us and others. To treat them as if they were offenders is to make enemies and not friends . . . Express (to the magistrate) our gratitude and belief that the riots were as truly his misfortune as our own.[13]

John Stevenson had returned home to Britain, and Hudson Taylor at Yantai was very frail. William Cooper was at Shanghai in the administrative 'hot seat' when Hudson Taylor wrote: 'I would advise that a statement rather than a claim of losses be given to the consul . . . If the Emperor has ordered that losses be made good, then there seems no reason to refuse it.' But already the Leshan mandarins had given the Riries (unasked) 1,000 taels to repair their house, and 1,000 taels for personal losses.[14] However, some CIM Sichuan missionaries had written about the 'glaring neglect of the officials'. 'Plenty of others have written and spoken of that, and it is not the CIM role.' He also wrote to the editor of the *Chinese Recorder*:

It is a serious question in my mind whether our work suffers most or gains by (asking) the interference of our government in such cases as Chengtu and Kucheng. It is true that pecuniary compensation may be obtained, and the missionaries reinstated . . . but what of the effect of all this . . . Are such appeals even good policy? . . . Is it not that the missionary, if more dreaded, is also more disliked . . . and that his converts also are more hated? . . .

A former American Minister to China says, 'The theory of any body of men and women coming . . . to a strange land and enduring hardships for the good of the people was something that no Chinese intellect could comprehend, not even the intellect of Li Hung-chang. There must be some ulterior purpose. And he would insist on associating the gospel with the sword, and see in the devoted persons who . . . preached *Christ*, the men who had battered down the Taku forts [Dagu, 1860] and forced opium upon China.' Must not the effect of appeals necessarily strengthen the belief of the literati that missions are a political agency designed, together with opium, to facilitate the absorption of China by foreign Powers? . . .

A Chinese official must also necessarily look upon a foreign resident as a source of danger and difficulty. He never becomes a source of emolument, but he may become a cause of loss or ruin . . . If a mandarin can keep us out, it must appear to him good policy to do so . . .

The effect of appealing on the (Chinese) Christians: is it not to lead them to lean upon man rather than upon God? . . . The teaching of Scripture on the matter (leaves) no uncertainties. 'Christ also suffered for us, leaving us an example' . . . I submit that our Saviour's command, 'Be ye wise as serpents and harmless as doves' distinctly forbids the carrying or use of firearms or other deadly weapons for self-protection, if it is not intended to use them, then to display them is to act a lie . . . The Holy Spirit . . . distinctly teaches us (1 Peter 4) to do good; to suffer for it; and to take it patiently . . . No riot takes place without His permission; no persecution is beyond His control . . . 'The weapons of our warfare are not carnal' . . .

We have the example of St Paul in making known to the local governor a threatened danger and, therefore, have warrant for obtaining the friendly help of local officials . . . (and) in pleading his Roman citizenship, 1. to prove that he had been punished wrongfully at Philippi; 2. to prevent his being wrongfully beaten at Jerusalem; 3. for the protection of his life by appealing to Caesar; but in none of these cases did he demand the punishment of the wrongdoers. Should we fail, however, to secure the friendly help and protection of the Mandarin we still have God to depend upon; and may count on grace to enable us to bear whatever He permits . . .[15]

The Sichuan viceroy's order that telegraphic communication between Chengdu, Chongqing and Shanghai should be stopped, quickly gave rise to wild rumours of 'a fearful massacre of all missionaries . . . The China Inland Mission premises at Paoning [ie Langzhong] are said to be destroyed and its members hunted about like wild beasts.'[16] It was not true. Anxiety in the homelands led some to ask for more news. Hudson Taylor's laconic answer, among many matters connected with routine administration of several hundreds of members' affairs, was simply, 'Had any missionary been murdered I would have wired.'

On the British government's insistence, Viceroy Liu Pingzhang, of whose complicity there was no doubt, was degraded and transferred.[17] But widespread unrest continued and the consuls forbade foreign women to return to Sichuan. News of the sufferings of Chinese Christians tended not to be reported to the same extent. *The Times* of September 5, 1891, said, 'Men, women and children are murdered by scores, their little property is destroyed, and hundreds of them are refugees from mob violence.' The same was true of 1895. In contrast, Joshua Vale on returning to Chengdu found himself fêted by the mandarins.[18] Generalisation was equivocal. Light and shade chased each other across the face of China. But the massacre at Kucheng threw black shadow over everything else.

'Kucheng massacre'   *March–August 1895*

In almost ninety years of Protestant missions in China no atrocities like those in the Indian mutiny and in Africa had befallen the missionaries. Ones and twos had lost their lives by violence and many had narrowly escaped. In 1891 Dr John Rigg of the CMS in Fujian had been thrown into a cesspit and barely escaped alive. Two women missionaries had night-soil poured over them. Anything could happen in Fujian, where the expanding Church had thrived

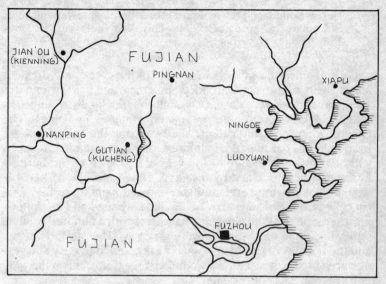

FUJIAN: SHOWING KUCHENG AND KIENNING

on frequent persecution. The Kucheng district (known now as Gutian, but honoured for all time as Kucheng) had a flourishing work of the CMS under Robert Stewart and his wife, and of ten single women of the CEZMS and two of the Victoria (Australia) Church Mission Association. All were under Stewart's supervision. Like the CIM women on the Guangxin River they lived in Chinese style, 'going in and out among the (Chinese) women'. Eugene Stock's account of what happened on August 1 needs little amplification.[19]

In March 1895 a religious sect of so-called 'Vegetarians' in rebellion against the authorities posed a danger to foreigners at Kucheng, eighty miles north-west of Fuzhou. On the consul's advice the women and the Stewart children withdrew to Fuzhou until the threat had receded in June. Twelve miles from Kucheng the mountain village of Huasang at two thousand feet offered relief from the great heat of summer. The missionaries had two small bungalows and met for conference coinciding with the Keswick Convention in the last week of July. In the final communion service on July 31 they all repeated together the words,

> Here we offer and present unto Thee, O Lord, ourselves, our souls and bodies, to be a reasonable, holy, and lively sacrifice unto Thee.

Early the next morning before some of the party were dressed, about eighty of the sect descended upon them and in a few minutes nine missionaries were dead, two small children fatally wounded, a fifth CEZ lady left for dead, and both houses in flames. The children's nurse, Lena Yellop, 'died covering the baby from the brutal blows', but two older children, one also wounded, escaped with two little brothers and the year-old baby from the burning house and fled to a nearby dwelling. Miss Codrington, 'terribly wounded', 'disfigured and mutilated', joined them there.[20] A doctor called from Kucheng arrived the same evening, and the following afternoon (sic) the Kucheng magistrate with a hundred soldiers – by which time the attackers were far away. The Stewarts' ashes and the remains of the dead woman were taken to the city and sent downriver to Fuzhou with the wounded. One child died on the way, and a second a day or two later.

Wherever the news arrived, a sense of horror seized the secular and Christian worlds. Cries for vengeance from Hong Kong were rejected by the CMS and CEZMS. Instead the Exeter Hall in London was crowded on August 13 with sympathising friends from fellow-societies. Theodore Howard and William Cassels, whose appointment as Anglican bishop in Western China had just been announced at Keswick, took part.[21] 'Not one bitter word was uttered; nothing but sympathy with the bereaved, pity for the misguided murderers, thanksgiving for the holy lives of the martyrs, fervent desires for the evangelisation of China.'

J W Marshall, father of one of the victims, preached to his congregation at St John's, Blackheath, on the words, 'Not unto death, but for the glory of God, that the Son of God might be glorified thereby.' The widowed mother of two Saunders sisters, trained nurses who died together, took her bereavement as an honour from God. She greeted two friends who called to comfort her with 'You've come to congratulate me, haven't you?' She determined to go to Kucheng as a missionary, to see for herself 'a memorial of precious living stones', Chinese converted through their sacrifice – and did so.[22] No clearer demonstration of forgiveness, love and heroism could have been given. 'Within a few months of the massacre there were more Chinese inquiring about Christ in the province of (Fujian) – in the Kucheng district itself – than ever before.'

D MacGillivray, in *A Century of Protestant Missions in China*, 1907, concluded his account with the words, 'Thousands of converts have come from this blood of the martyrs.' Not a hundred years later the truth is hundreds of thousands. On August 28, 1895, the remaining CEZMS missionaries issued a joint letter saying that for each of their four dead colleagues they were asking God for ten to replace them, forty in all.[23] Early in 1897 Miss Codrington herself returned to Kucheng, no less to the amazement of the Chinese, and stayed to become the senior missionary of the CEZMS.

'Throughout the foreign communities of China great excitement prevailed, since it was felt that the lives of no foreigners were any longer secure.'[24] Lord Salisbury's protest to the Chinese government resulted in the execution of some of the murderers, but when he asked the CMS and CEZMS what compensation he should demand, they told him they would accept none. Neither society wished to appear vindictive or to let compensation for wrecked property be regarded as indemnity for lives lost. The Zongli Yamen told Sir Claude Macdonald (O'Conor's successor as British minister at Peking) that this 'high-minded attitude commanded (their) profound respect and esteem.'

Hudson Taylor's encouragement to the CIM 'to remain at one's post' and 'rely on the living God alone for protection . . . not to yield to the spirit of unrest' was written in the shadow of this seeming tragedy; and it seems from letter after letter as the decade advanced, with a deepening premonition of a greater price to be paid for the soul of China.

Muslim rebellion and Xining siege[25]   1895–96

Eighteen years had passed since Yakub Beg died suddenly at Kashgar on May 1, 1877, and the great general, Zuo Zongtang, captured the city. His army was known to have halted to sow and reap a harvest on which to live, still far from Kashgaria. When they crossed the awesome Tianshan range by the almost unknown passes (used earlier by Colonel Nikolai Prjevalski), suddenly to appear before the walls of Aksu, they achieved complete surprise. The Muslim rebellion in the north-west had ended with the loss of millions of lives. In the affected part of Gansu only a tenth of the Chinese population was said to have survived, and one in three

ZUO ZONGTANG
conqueror of Kashgar; viceroy of Jiangsu, Jiangxi and Anhui

Muslims. For his part in Zuo Zongtang's campaign, William Mesny had been promoted to what he called in English 'Brevet-Lieutenant General'.[26]

Muslims were widely spread throughout China, but congregated in some regions. Hezhou (now Hezuo) in Gansu was the home of thousands of 'Salars' and the seat of Arabic-speaking scholars. In 1875 it had been the scene of an uprising, savagely suppressed. Xining, sixty miles east of the Qinghai Hu (Lake Kokonor), lay in a narrow valley at eight thousand feet, reached by two mountain passes from Lanzhou, another hundred miles to the east. A fine city with high, strong walls, it was the home of twenty to thirty thousand Han Chinese, who had expanded into a large west suburb. In the east suburb ten thousand nominally Muslim families, very lax in their religious observances, carried on the major trade in Tibetan and Mongolian wool. They despatched it by camel train through Ningxia to Tianjin, or by raft to Lanzhou and beyond when melting snows fed the Huang He (Yellow River). Chinese and Muslims lived contentedly side by side with Tibetans, Mongols and aboriginal communities until early 1895.

The long tentacles of 'the octopus mission' had reached Xining in 1885 when George Parker and W F Laughton first lived there in an inn, until able to lease a home of their own. The Cecil Polhills took over from them for three years while travelling and learning Tibetan, and then were followed by James C Hall. H French Ridley had spent three years at Ningxia before he married and took his wife to Xining. Every day Hall and Ridley preached in open places along the streets of the city and suburbs or in a shop front, to standing audiences of 100 to 150 friendly people. But none showed deep interest in the gospel.

For 250 years there had been two sects of Muslim Salars in Gansu, originating from Samarkand and related to the Turki-speaking Uighurs of Hami. At the time of the 1785 uprising at Hezhou they were either Shiite, known as Red Caps, or Sunni Muslims called White Caps. But at Xining the wealthier, more powerful Muslims were called Black Caps. Strict Muslim missionaries from Turkey and Arabia had concentrated on the Black Caps for nearly a decade, until friction between them and the lax White Caps resulted. But all alike were waiting for the Chinese empire to become embroiled in a foreign war, to avenge the holocaust of the 1870s.

The Sino-Japanese war was the signal. Hostilities began when the Salars wiped out a small city garrison. The Chinese responded

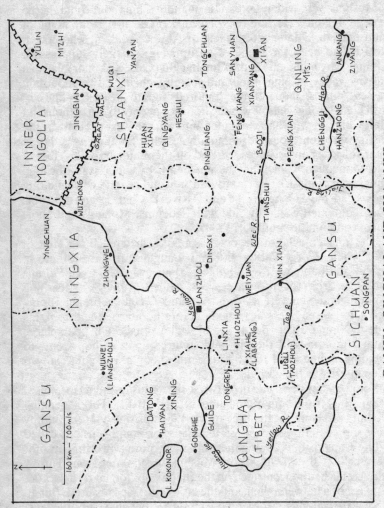

GANSU, QINGHAI AND SHAANXI

energetically. Ninety miles from Xining, only three days in the saddle, ten thousand Salars were routed early in 1890. Their defeat roused Muslims of all sects, and the cold-blooded slaughter of nine hundred old White Caps and women and children infuriated them further. Reports reached the coast that the Silk Road was impassable, Liangzhou cut off, Lanzhou fallen. This was untrue. But throughout Gansu the missionaries were isolated and Shaanxi expected to be involved. 'Take any action you may deem necessary,' Hudson Taylor instructed G F Easton, the superintendent. George W Hunter, apostle of Urumqi in later years, but already winning his spurs in Gansu, was away from home in Hezhou when the city fell to rebels. Many believed that if it had continued, the revolt would have swept across China to Peking.

From February the Chinese of Xining were asking the Ridleys and Hall to stay, saying they 'felt safe' with them there. So they went on preaching until July 23, while the Muslim rebels came closer and closer, destroying everything and everyone in their way. From the city wall Ridley watched village after village in the surrounding countryside go up in flames. July 24 was the day of decision. Floods of refugees filled the city; excitement became intense. The Ridleys had money enough and at first could have left, but felt sure it was God's will for them to stay – even though refugee children and babies 'terribly hacked about' made them fear for their own six-month-old infant. After that the roads became impassable. Every night four thousand men on the city walls kept watch for attackers.

It was no time for preaching, but what else could the missionaries do? After four days a beggar pleaded with them to go to the Confucian temple and see the state of the refugees crowded there. They found the temple filled with lacerated women and children who had been thrown into flaming buildings yet had somehow escaped, terribly burned. An indescribable stench kept ghoulish onlookers at a distance, their noses in their sleeves, doing nothing to help.

Without medical training the Ridleys set to work dressing the burns and wounds with cotton wool soaked in vegetable cooking oil, until darkness fell. The officials learned what they were doing and asked them to continue the next day. The city governor sent barley gruel for the patients. Day after day from morning to night they went from temple to temple and to public buildings, sewing up sword-cuts with silk thread and dressing burns, using what native medicines they could buy, sulphur, alum and borax, and 350 feet of calico for bandages. Smallpox and diphtheria broke out and took the lives of almost every child. In the first three weeks they treated 250 diphtheria patients. Soon it was nearly one thousand. Ridley himself nearly died of diphtheria. The dead were simply thrown into the streets. Yet the Muslim suburb remained apparently loyal and the city gates stayed open until a small city under siege only twenty miles away fell to the rebels and three thousand Chinese were butchered.

Then suddenly, one Sunday evening, September 1, when Xining was packed with fifty thousand people, the suburb joined the rebellion. Hundreds of wounded again thronged the Ridleys, brought on stretchers or carried on men's backs. Mrs Ridley stayed alone in the house with her child, treating those who came to her, while Hall and her husband went out to work on their two thousand patients. One day she 'cut out' three bullets before they returned, using a pocket knife. Some people changed the name tablet on their house from Good News Hall to Save Life Hall.

After an ambush and night attack on September 21, it looked as if Xining was lost. But a large Chinese force was on its way from Lanzhou and the Muslims turned to intercept them. Hudson Taylor (Jennie wrote) would lie awake praying about Xining. Then a telegram from Redfern in Lanzhou reported that the siege had been lifted. 'Xining open – letters arrived here – all well – no cause for apprehension – we are able to remit.' Ridley's sangfroid and Redfern's misunderstanding at Lanzhou together misled the directors. Ridley's messages had been carried at night by army couriers using circuitous mountain tracks. In fact the worst period was beginning. Redfern himself died of typhus on February 6, 1896. From September to January the relieving force were hemmed in among the mountains without sufficient food or clothing. Another force from Shanxi took more than four months to reach them. Supplies were captured on the way to them. A thousand men, half the force, were lost before General Tong Fuxiang's loyal Muslim cavalry from the eastern provinces, under a General Ho, broke through to the survivors and with them reached Xining on January 14, 1896. It seems also, from our documents, that at this point General Sun, Dr Douthwaite's Yantai friend, came on the scene and befriended the missionaries.[27]

Until then the mandarins of Xining had prevented the city people from slaughtering the Muslims in the suburb. At last the demoralised populace rebelled and turned on their rulers. The general had to rescue them, 'half dead'. But when a mounted Salar attack was made in February on defenceless Chinese, the troops and city people retaliated together. Thousands were slaughtered in the Muslim suburb amid horrendous scenes of cannibalism, and thousands of Muslim prisoners were beheaded daily in batches of fifty or more until October 1896. The toll of dead amounted to forty thousand Chinese, of whom ten thousand were soldiers; and forty thousand Muslims, including ten thousand who died of exposure among the twenty thousand who retreated westwards towards Kashgar.

For more than five months the Ridleys had no contact with the outer world and for nine months received no supplies. In April 1896 Mrs Ridley went out to Lanzhou for a few months, but returned to Xining in October 1896, this time to clothe and feed Muslim survivors through the winter, for all were reduced to beggary. The Ridleys themselves could barely find enough to live on until the governor discovered their sacrificial existence and supplied them with sacks of flour until they left, 'saying we had done so much for the people he could not take money from us'. The wife of another official insisted that Mrs Ridley go to her house for a meal from time to time.

After two years, February 1895 to January 1897, it was all over. 'All the country now opened up to us – everywhere we`go we find a warm welcome . . . "What, don't you know me?" they asked. "You saved my life in the rebellion!"' But the whole area had been devastated with hardly a house standing. Not in twenty years could it be restored to normality.

Tibetan Pioneer Mission[28]   1895–1904

Annie Taylor and her Tibetan Pioneer Mission were in trouble before the end of 1894 (p 166), unfortunately, trouble of her own making. Her colleagues rejected her leadership and she herself went up to Gnatong at 12,350 feet on the Sikkim-Tibetan border, with Pontso her Tibetan servant for company. 'We are the last hut on the way to Tibet,' she wrote, not far from a military outpost of huts within a stockade. Tibetans from all parts of Tibet came there to trade, and she spent her days among them. A Danish member of their team had died of typhoid, but Pontso, ill at the same time, recovered. Bonfires had to be lit to thaw the ground so that the grave could be dug. Instead of men she asked William Sharp to send women pioneers, saying:

The Tibetans respect women and do not even in time of war attack
them. The political parties of India and Tibet are not so likely to look
with suspicion on women missionaries . . . They must be ready to
endure all kinds of privation; to roll themselves up in blankets and
sleep out in the snow; to live at times on barley flour alone . . . to live
as much like the Tibetans as possible.

By January 25, 1895, William Sharp was writing to ask if Hudson
Taylor would take the Pioneer Mission team into the CIM. They
had signed the same P and P as the CIM when joining Annie Taylor.
And in April he asked him to visit Kalimpong to meet the team. The
tensions in China were too great for Hudson Taylor to be away, so
Cecil Polhill-Turner went instead, until October. The men impressed him. He suggested bringing them to China if the way to
Lhasa did not open by the end of the year. By June 6 Annie Taylor
had moved sixteen miles further in, to Yadong in the Chombi
valley, inside Tibet, welcomed by the Chinese officials to open a
medicine shop. Her courage could not be questioned.

At long last the Sichuan riots had simmered down, the Kucheng
massacre alarm had proved to be localised and not the first of
widespread attacks, and Tong Fuxiang's troops had put down the
Muslim revolt at Xining. Writing to John Stevenson in Britain,
Hudson Taylor said on January 18, 1896, '(Xining) is safe, thank
God.'[29] And in a note to Gansu in mid-October he showed how he
felt for the front line missionary. 'You have lived in our hearts daily,
almost hourly, and when awake through the night . . . may He
preserve you in safety at this time of peril.' That same day he and
Jennie boarded a ship to Calcutta. Robert Wilder and John R Mott
had asked him to speak at student volunteer conferences in Indian
cities, so before going up to Darjeeling he took part at Benares,
Agra and elsewhere. News of Redfern's death in raving delirium
followed him. As he daily prayed for all his long list of missionaries,
he knew the dangers nearly all were facing, and the difficulties from
inflation following the war. 'If we do all that we can and ought, we
can leave the results with (God)' he wrote to Walter Sloan as they
neared Calcutta. While he was there, on February 19, Hsi Shengmo
died, after a long illness, and David Hill of typhus on April 18.

In Darjeeling Hudson Taylor shared Cecil Polhill's impression of
the Pioneer Mission team. They showed great potential. Some
chose to stay in India; six were to come soon to China; the Polhills
and a young family would follow later. In China they were to be
known as the Tibetan Mission Band, an associate mission of the

CIM under Cecil Polhill's leadership.[30] The Taylors sailed away
again on March 10 and were in Shanghai to receive the six men,
Soutter, Neave, Moyes, Amundsen, Johansen and Sorensen, and to
send them up to Hankou en route for Sichuan. The Anqing language school had lost its principal, H N Lachlan, by a sudden
stroke.[31] 'We are utterly perplexed to know where to get anyone to
take his place,' Hudson Taylor confessed. When the Cecil Polhills
arrived they lived in one of the forty large Tibetan inns at Kangding
until they were able to rent a house and bring the team to Kangding
as their base. From there the gospel in print and by word of mouth
was sent, they believed, to widely scattered parts of Tibet from
which the many traders came.

Tibetan sequels[32]   1895–1905

The lure of Lhasa continued to induce men and women to
undergo the hardships of Tibetan travel. In January 1895 as the
Salar rebellion began and Annie Taylor occupied Gnatong, a
Berkshire landowner, St George Littledale, and his wife set out from
Kashgar for the same goal. Like everyone else they failed, but were
only forty-nine miles from Lhasa when they were turned back and
began the painful exodus to Ladakh. Henry Savage Landor entered
Tibet on July 13, 1897. But the strange drama of Petrus Rijnhardt
again breaks upon the Gansu and Tibetan scene at this time.

He married the Canadian doctor in 1894 and with her returned to
Gansu (p 194). They were at Kumbum, where William Rockhill had
lived for a month in the guise of a pilgrim, not far from Xining, when
the Salar rebellion reached them, and the epidemic smallpox and
diphtheria. Fearing for their safety, the abbot of the great monastery invited them to move in, and there they stayed through 'the
months of terror', learning Tibetan. With the return to peace they
transferred to Danka (Tankar) on the Tibetan caravan route to
Lhasa (now a motor road), and on May 20, 1898, set out in Tibetan
dress with three servants, five saddle ponies, twelve pack animals
carrying provisions for two years (with more they had sent ahead),
and their son Charles whose first birthday fell on June 30. The
hillsides were ablaze with flowers and 'we all sang for very joy',
Susie Rijnhardt wrote.

But soon two of their men deserted, the five ponies were stolen,
Charles died 'inexplicably' in Petrus's arms, and two hundred miles
from Lhasa they were intercepted and told to return. With

A TIBETAN LAMASERY

persuasion the outpost guards allowed them to make for the Tashi Gompa monastery on the head waters of the Lancang Jiang (Mekong River), known there as the Za Qü (Tsa-ch'ü). But on the way they were attacked and robbed. Across the river lay a Tibetan camp and Petrus waded in to parley with them. Then Susie saw him turn and start back. He rounded a big boulder – and was never seen again. When Susie gave up waiting and set off eastwards she saw that on the near side, not far up, lay another Tibetan encampment. She could only surmise that this was the robbers' lair and that Petrus had been killed or drowned. Whether she knew of his past history, we are not told. For two months she struggled on, to turn up at Kangding in November 1898, emaciated and frostbitten, to be nursed back to health by the Cecil Polhills.

The story must be ended without elaboration. Polhill, William Soutter and another, William Upcraft, travelled out, over the 15,000–16,000 feet passes crossed by James Cameron in 1877 and by Susie Rijnhardt more recently, to visit Batang. Later on, Soutter went again, fell ill with typhoid on the way, and Susie went to look after him. He died and was buried 'in full view of the glorious, dazzling, snowclad Mount Nenda'. Susie eventually remarried and returned in 1903 to Kangding in the Foreign Christian Missionary Society, but died three weeks after giving birth to another son. A colleague, Dr A L Shelton, established work at Batang, but years later was killed by robbers.[33]

Major H R Davies, author of *Yunnan*, 1891–1900, a notable traveller, turned up at Kangding on June 20, 1900, with two friends on their way from Yunnan via Litang to the coast. Who should he find living quietly in this out of the way place but Cecil Polhill? They had been at Eton together.[34]

In another category of traveller, a Japanese physician, Ekai Kawaguchi, entered Lhasa on March 21, 1901, purporting to be Chinese. No missionary attempted it again, but the gospel was given to Tibetans in the Moravian field of Ladakh, on the Sikkim frontier, through the work of the Scandinavian Alliance Mission and Annie Taylor, and along the border with Xinjiang, Gansu and Sichuan over the years, through the CIM and C&MA, small numbers of Tibetans came to faith in Christ.

In 1902 Russia's annexations, an unending story, led Lord Curzon to fear her intentions towards Tibet and India. On August 11, 1902, the British minister in Peking reported signs of an agreement whereby Russia would give China protection against other powers in exchange for her predominance in Tibet. Curzon briefed Francis Younghusband in May 1903 on what was to be a secret mission, but loud protests from Russia and China against his first moves drove the British government to strong, overt measures. Promoted lieutenant-colonel with one thousand soldiers, ten thousand carriers, seven thousand mules, four thousand yaks, six camels, two maxim guns and four field guns, Younghusband entered Tibet through Gnatong and Yatong on 'one of the most contentious episodes in British imperial history'.[35] The gallant Tibetans would only negotiate outside Tibetan territory, so Younghusband attacked and seven hundred Tibetans died at Guru on the way from Phari, at fifteen thousand feet, the highest town in the world, and more in the Battle of Karo Pass at sixteen thousand feet, the highest recorded battle.

The Dalai Lama withdrew from Lhasa leaving no one to negotiate. So, after fruitlessly waiting, Younghusband himself left Lhasa on September 23, 1904 (and was knighted for his achievement), but civilian Residents remained on friendly terms with Tibetan authorities, until they, too, withdrew in 1905. No proof of a Russian involvement with Tibet ever justified the invasion. But at the time high-handedness towards China seemed to be justified, after what had happened in 1900 to the legations in Peking and numerous British subjects throughout the Chinese empire.

CHAPTER EIGHT

NO TIME TO FALTER
1895–98

'My head, my head' 1895–98

A chronology of this post-war period is packed with more detail than most. The only way to present it intelligibly is to separate the main components of a kaleidoscopic jumble. Hudson Taylor's part in each story emerges incidentally, leaving an impression of a leader who has at last devolved the routine running of the CIM upon others while keeping his hand on everything. Standing back from detail he is sensitive to the mood of China and faint with apprehension of what he sees approaching. Yet, because the main task is still far from done, he believes that it must continue, 'if the Lord tarry' – however great the blood-price to be paid. We are left with a medley of matters which touched him intimately.

In April 1895 he and Jennie set off together to visit the main mission centres on the Yangzi, but she had to be left at Yangzhou with infection of a foot (erysipelas). His notes to her spoke often of being 'fit but feeble', or of resting and sleeping on the river steamer instead of working. He felt the need of 'the True Solomon's wisdom' for many hard decisions as he planned for the growing complexity of the mission. If missionaries' children could stay at Chefoo while their parents went on leave to their homelands, costs would be lower and furloughs more frequent, as urged by some advisers. So a 'preparatory' school for younger children was the answer.[1]

On his 63rd birthday, May 21, 1895, he was feeling years older mentally and physically, but wishing he could write 'a little sketch of the Mission', a 'chatty, readable book' on China and progress so far towards her evangelisation. He complimented Lindsay, the current sub-editor of the *Millions*, on a job well done and suggested that he put together the materials for such a book. When Lindsay fell ill, Hudson Taylor himself completed a pot-boiler, *After Thirty Years*,[2] as a factual, statistical statement of policy and fulfilment, to supplement Geraldine Guinness's 'chatty, readable' *Story of the CIM*. Conscious of a duty to report to donors and to keep the Church informed, because the will to contribute funds always existed, he

BENJAMIN BROOMHALL, CIM GENERAL SECRETARY,
UK, 1878–95

wrote for thinking Christians. And he corresponded at length with Walter Sloan instead of with Theodore Howard and Benjamin. For Howard had enough on his hands and Benjamin had formally retired in January after reaching 66.

On March 8 the Mission's offices moved from Pyrland Road to the new building at Newington Green, but Benjamin stayed on at No. 2 to pursue his anti-opium campaign until he died in 1911. Hudson Taylor wrote of 'our home', 8 Pyrland Road, having been sold for £570, a loss of £130 since the area had gone down in 'respectability' as the advancing tide of building engulfed it.

When John Stevenson was due to leave China to arrange for his family in Scotland he found it hard to go, for both Hudson Taylor and William Cooper were in precarious health. But he left on May 11, 1895. The news of Sichuan was 'not reassuring' and Hudson Taylor was painfully concerned for the missionaries in Gansu as the Muslim rebellion escalated. By mid-July he and Jennie were at Chefoo, both unfit for work, he hardly able to sit up. Henry Frost, visiting China to convalesce, was also seriously ill again. Many references to Hudson Taylor's head being unable to take more strain, or to neuralgia, stop short of a diagnosis in medical terms, unless as warnings of a threatened stroke.[3] When they intended to return to Shanghai, the cholera epidemic in Chefoo decided them to stay there, if only as a comfort to others. In this condition he dictated his general letter about 'rebellion in the air', calling for a day of prayer for China (p 220). 'On all hands there are evidences of a great internal upheaval,' he said, listing the major examples.[4]

But Chefoo always did him good. A month in the magic of 'Chefoo air' saw him 'at his best', alert and competent, finding staff for the schools and planning the new Boys', Girls', and Preparatory School buildings, with E J Cooper, the architect's assistant before joining the Mission. Not content with those major undertakings, they were at the same time planning the sanatorium and an isolation block. In mid-August 1895 workmen began on the schools, all together, and the foundations were in by mid-September. His mind was clear and his hand on the controls.[5]

After his return from Barclay Buxton's convention in Kobe, September 10–18, the Riries' fine spirit through the Leshan (Jiading) riot (pp 224–5 'We have only lost our homes') confirmed his belief that the Mission would rise to any occasion. 'If obedience to Christ leads to martyrdom even, it is none the less our privilege and duty,' he wrote. The foreign powers were uneasy about China's instability and kept naval vessels on the move from port to port to 'show the flag'. Then cholera struck at Wenzhou in October 1895 and the Taylors took the first possible steamer, to be with the shocked survivors. Nine Chinese and three missionaries had died in the CIM premises, leaving Bella Menzies bereft of her husband and child. 'How to shepherd the six or seven hundred Christians at Wenzhou and Pingyang (Bingyae) we do not know,' they wrote. 'The dialect is spoken nowhere else.' Charles Fishe went down for a month to do what he could, followed by the Coulthards. Again it was his own family whom he sent to the danger spots.[6]

'The most trying (year) that has ever been experienced by missionaries in China' came to an end with fifteen of the CIM dead from disease but not one from violence. And 1896 began with trouble from two familiar quarters rearing its head again. As Hudson Taylor was leaving for India on January 18, 1896, to help the disintegrating Tibetan Pioneer Mission, he asked Dixon Hoste to represent him in arranging for the CIM to hand over all its commitments in Taiyuan to Dr Edwards and the 'Shouyang Mission'.[7]Once that was done, the most urgent need was to return to Europe, to straighten out an accumulation of problems with associate missions.

The CIM was still in the throes of transition, of persuading the older members to accept the authority of leaders other than Hudson Taylor himself.[8] As for Dixon Hoste, the ten years spent with Hsi Shengmo while he supervised fifteen to twenty local churches with four ordained pastors, had done much to fit him for the years ahead as a leader of a mission to Chinese. Hsi's own tribute was, 'In all matters connected with Church or Refuges, Mr Hoste and I have united in prayer and consultation . . . We mutually help one another, without any distinction of native or foreigner, because the Lord has made us one.' Hsi's death on February 19, 1896, released Hoste to go on home leave, the last of the Cambridge Seven to do so.

Radical resolution of the chronic Shanxi problems led Hudson Taylor to observe, 'Come what may, we *ought* to have unity and peace among ourselves.' Sometimes surgery became preferable to palliative treatment. The same thought had decided him when he regained his own health and China was quieter, to return to Europe while John Stevenson was still there. He needed to work out with the continental associate missions some kind of uniformity in place of their existing diversity, 'to unite many bands into one CIM'.[9] If uniformity could not be reached, it would be better for each to go their own way, as the Bible Christians were doing. Where difficulties arose from one godly man's inefficiency as an administrator, a new appointment would be enough. Uniformity need not mean rigidity, he demonstrated repeatedly, for when circumstances differed he responded with flexibility. But there was strength in all sharing the same principles and basic practices.

For two months William Cooper would have to carry the burden of supreme leadership alone in China, but Hudson Taylor had full confidence in him. He did everything well and made no mistakes. The appreciation was mutual. 'Thank you for giving me the privilege,' Cooper wrote, 'of reading so many of your letters. It is quite an education to me, and I earnestly pray that God may give me more and more of the spirit that pervades your correspondence.' One particular feature of Hudson Taylor's letters won his correspondents' hearts, his familiarity with their children's names and progress. His caring betrayed his faithfulness in praying for them. This alone contributed largely to making the CIM a family. His love won him the following he received.

That the skill in letter-writing which Cooper referred to was infectious had become apparent in Jennie's letters, too. Years as her husband's amanuensis for confidential letters led her to her own style becoming almost indistinguishable from his when he was away from home leaving her to keep other directors informed. In spiritual counselling Jennie performed a valued service. Geraldine's sister Lucy Guinness wrote, 'I wish I were like her.'[10] Jennie also kept a close watch on the many births to young families, to be sure of writing and of remittances being adjusted to include them. Children of CIM missionaries by then exceeded two hundred in number, and by May 1895 several had become full members in their own right: Herbert, Howard and Maria Taylor, Gertrude, Hudson, Marshall and Edith Broomhall, three of James Meadows' daughters, others of the Rudland, Fishe, Baller and Williamson families, and more preparing to join in. Ernest Hudson Taylor, by then a chartered accountant, arrived in China on February 9, 1898, the fourth Taylor to join his parents.[11]

On May 2, 1896, the Taylors and Dixon Hoste sailed from Shanghai with the Eastons (free to leave the north-west once the Muslim rebellion was over), with the widowed Mrs Redfern of Lanzhou and her children, and several others. While still in the Huangpu River their ship came into collision with another, in which seven officers and three hundred Chinese were drowned. But an otherwise uneventful journey brought them to London on June 17. Hoste left them at Colombo to visit relatives, and barely survived a severe fever contracted there. Convalescing in Scotland, he then fell ill with typhoid and needed months of rest. Gertrude, his wife, was to visit Australia for a tour of meetings to speak about China, so Dixon joined her there before returning to China to become superintendent of Henan.[12]

This was Hudson Taylor's nineteenth voyage and tenth period in Britain. Uneventful journeys could never be taken for granted. In June 1897 the SS *Aden* was lost with the lives of four CMS and other missionaries on board. Two CIM travellers had tried and failed to get berths on the ship. In October the Ballers survived a fire on their ship, and a month later the SS *Kaiser-i-Hind* with a CIM party was nearly lost in a typhoon in the South China Sea.[13] Hudson Taylor's party were travelling at the time when every available berth was filled by people returning home for Queen Victoria's Diamond Jubilee celebrations. Hot, airless cabins and incessant noise and crowding on deck and in the saloons made it barely tolerable.

Too late for the annual May meetings he sent a written report of 'in many respects the most remarkable year we have ever experienced', of deliverances outweighing the setbacks. Growth and expansion of the Misson's work had continued in spite of all the upheavals. At the end of 1895, communicant Christians in churches served by the CIM had risen in number to 5,208 and mission centres to 135 with 126 substations. Organised churches had increased in the year from 149 to 155, with 461 paid and unpaid Chinese co-operating with 641 CIM missionaries. By May 1896 the number had become 672, and a year later 720, with income keeping pace in every home country.

On August 17, 1896, before visiting Germany, he began with another profitable tour of Norway and Sweden. The associate missions' leaders welcomed the invitation to become more closely knit to the CIM, agreeing to adhere to the same Principles and Practice, and Erik Folke of South Shanxi was made an associate superintendent with a seat on the China Council meeting each October.[14]

Two weeks after Hudson Taylor's return on September 10, John Stevenson sailed for China, again leaving his wife and family at home. Hudson Taylor sent him on his way with a note of sympathy and thankfulness that with William Cooper and Walter Sloan the four of them enjoyed strong links of confidence and love.[15] Stevenson, however, soon showed that he had been under heavy stress and was not really well enough to shoulder the burdens of his directorship in China. Before long he was at odds with Cooper, and Hudson Taylor was exhorting him to treat Cooper as 'a junior partner', not an inferior.

Through the autumn of 1896 an incessant round of speaking engagements kept Hudson Taylor on the move, working at full pressure, while news of one after another desperately ill or dead, kept coming to him. 'Headache and neuralgia' dogged him until in 1897 it became too much.

What of 'The Thousand'?   1895–99

Five years had passed since the Shanghai Conference and the appeal for one thousand men within five years, and also for women. Hudson Taylor as the originator of the call, and chairman of the permanent committee, in May 1895 issued a report.[16] Forty-five societies had sent a total of 1,153 reinforcements during the five years. Of these 672 were women (167 wives and 505 unmarried) but only 481 men. Of the 1,296 Protestant missionaries in China in May 1890, only 589 had been men. The number had not even been doubled, and 'not a few' had died or retired from China in the same period. So not half the goal of one thousand men had been reached. Nothing was to be gained by claiming success or satisfaction. The report therefore ended, 'Will not the Church arise and take immediate and adequate action to meet the pressing needs of this vast land?' The thinking of the Christian world was still back to front. Those in the front line should not be left to call for others to replace their casualties and extend their influence. The Church of every land, in its many forms and divisions but one in purpose, should be active in sending its best young men and women to the far corners of the earth – young, if they were to learn new languages and adapt to new conditions.

In May 1890 the CIM had 383 members, and in May 1895 had more than 620, an increase of about 240. By the end of 1899 the CMS had added 'more than Eight Hundred names . . . to the roll' of their members in Africa, India and China. Ninety-three went to China between 1895 and 1899. Those close to the need were right to ask for large reinforcements, and societies whose leaders took it up had no lack of offers to go. But some mission boards, committees and Churches in distant homelands seemed too remote and deaf. They needed more than an appeal.

What the historians have noticed was not an expansion of evangelism 'to every creature', though an effort was made, but a rapid expansion of 'Christianity' in China, which continued well into the twentieth century after the spiritually productive interruption by the Boxer Rising.[17] K S Latourette saw in this period a parting of the ways between orthodox missions and institutional societies, not that many of the theologically orthodox societies did not have ambitious schools, hospitals and presses. After twenty years, St John's College in Shanghai were teaching theology in English, with the whole range of Western learning in that language open to the graduates. By 1895, 143 Protestant doctors were running seventy mission hospitals and training 170 medical students, as well as serving opium refuges and widely distributed clinics. Well-meaning attempts to avoid overlapping succeeded to some extent, some missions being careful to consult with others before moving into already occupied districts and cities. Others saw room enough for all and a duty to present their own particular emphases, where exponents of different views of doctrine and church government were already established. Institutional societies, liberal, and foreign ways came more and more to share the field with the evangelists intent on first planting a spiritual Church.

Good relations between the CIM and the Anglican Church took a new turn in 1895. Nominally the bishop of Anglican missionaries and churches in West China, George Moule had found it impossible to go two thousand miles to fulfil his duties in Sichuan. His crook, he told Cassels, was not long enough to reach so far. Heywood Horsburgh and his CMS team in West Sichuan, and W W Cassels, E O Williams, Charles Parsons and the CIM in the eastern half were witnessing a Chinese Church enlarging on the Anglican pattern, but without a bishop. The CMS conceived the perfect answer. Without altering in any way Cassels' position as the CIM superintendent, informally advising the CMS team, his consecration as Bishop in West China would meet the ecclesiastical needs as well.[18] With Hudson Taylor's approval, consultations in London and in China by John Stevenson with George Moule, resulted in Cassels becoming a full member of both missions. On the CMS payroll, he could continue as a member of the CIM China Council with his home and office at Langzhong. The Archbishop of Canterbury agreed.

Cassels and Beauchamp were sharing the missionary platform at the Keswick Convention with Amy Carmichael and Dr Herbert Lankester, Medical Secretary of the CMS, when the appointment was announced. Supporters of both the CMS and CIM approved, but each society received protests against association with the other body, of which the protester could not approve.[19] The consecration by Archbishop Benson took place on October 18, 1895, in Westminster Abbey, and the Cassels family sailed for China a week later. A close neighbour during their furlough in England had been the mother of Elsie Marshall, one of the CEZMS missionaries murdered at Kucheng (Gutian) (map p 229). The Sichuan riots were barely over, the siege of Xining was at its worst. The 'progressive' phase of the work in Sichuan was merging into the phase of 'opposition'. The charge William Cassels had accepted at the age of thirty-seven was no sinecure.[20]

Hunan at last[21]   1895–98

Hunan and Guangxi were never far from Hudson Taylor's thoughts. Moving forward meant taking the gospel to those deprived of it. From the time of the Yangzi valley riots of 1891 until early 1896, Hunan seemed inaccessible. Whoever undertook to attempt the evangelisation of Guangxi became diverted by one thing or another. Even Shashi, Dorward's base with its nucleus of Christians, had to be worked as an outpost from Wuchang. Shishou on the Hunan border could only be visited from time to time, although a dozen believers were waiting to be taught. With Zhang Zhitong's return as viceroy, and a friendly governor of Hunan who set himself to eliminate public prejudice against foreigners, the prospects were brighter than they had ever been.

Early in 1890 a Presbyterian minister in the CIM, George Hunter (unrelated to George W Hunter of Xinjiang), came to China with Hunan as his objective, but the death of the Chefoo schoolmasters, Norris and Elliston, created an urgent need which Hunter was asked to fill. In 1895 when Frank McCarthy, John's son, arrived to begin his outstanding thirty-five-year headship (March 1895–summer 1930), George Hunter was free to begin. He took his family to Yichang and began travelling over Adam Dorward's old trails to Jinshi and Changde with his evangelist companions. He found the people friendly, wanting to know more about the outer world and Western progress.[22] In September 1897 Dorward's friend the evangelist Yao succeeded in obtaining a deed of rental at Changde

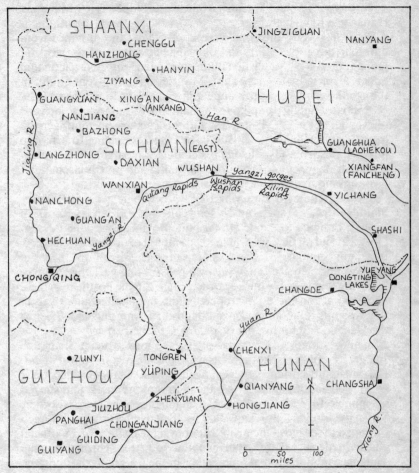

THE HUBEI AND HUNAN RIVER ROUTES
to Shaanxi, Sichuan and Guizhou

and T A P Clinton moved in. A month later two men of the
C&MA, Chaplin and Brown, gained a foothold at the other side of
the city. By the end of 1899 a church of thirty-five members with six
preaching chapels had grown out of the Changde root. But in March
1900 George Hunter had his baggage on a boat, ready to start
from Changde, when he fell ill with a high fever and died within

a few days.[23] Even at the turn of the century the price of opening Hunan was to be high.

By 1898 several missions were approaching the province from different directions. Griffith John appealed for men to work in Hunan; the LMS established outposts in the Hengzhou region and openly baptised converts. The CMS tried to enter from Guilin in the south. And when the appearance of electric lighting in the governor's residence betokened a change in attitude to new ideas, B Alexander of the C&MA tried again and again to get a footing in the capital city, Changsha.[24] But lasting success came to Chinese missionaries from Hsi Shengmo's church in Shanxi and his opium refuge strategy, and to Anna Jakobsen, the one-time housemaid of Kristiansand, Norway.

She had come to China in 1885 with Sophie Reuter (Stanley Smith's wife), and spent nearly ten years at Huo Xian (Hochow) in Shanxi. Longing to tackle Hunan, the province that defied Adam Dorward and all the men who had attempted to occupy it, she knew that being unmarried was a major obstacle. Early in 1893 she became engaged to marry an evangelist named Cheng Xiaoyu, believing that here lay the key to acceptance in the hostile province. She had not considered the repercussions upon other single girls in the Mission. John Stevenson and Hudson Taylor persuaded her to think again, and for five years she followed their advice.

In the summer of 1896, however, she moved from Shanxi to Jiangxi to join A E Thor and his wife, intent on going into Hunan. Hsi Shengmo's friend, the evangelist Ren, who had also been concerned about Hunan, went ahead to rent premises, and started an opium refuge at the village of Chenghuang on the Hunan border. When the foreign lady (Anna Jakobsen) arrived, Hunanese women thronged to see her. One invited her to visit the wife of an ex-official who wished to break free from his opium addiction. Through him she found accommodation at Shengguanshi, near Chalingzhou, on the main route from Jiangxi into south-eastern Hunan, and quietly moved in. Here, too, she was well received.[25] After three months she handed over to Ren and two other Christians from Pastor Hsi's area, and herself returned to Shanxi. This time she was determined to marry, to the alarm of John Stevenson and the superintendents, not through prejudice against inter-racial marriage – Minnie Parker had shown how successful that could be – but for fear of how her example would affect scores, even hundreds, of unmarried women missionaries, especially in the Guangxin River region of Jiangxi. So far they had been a phenomenon apart – no Chinese had looked on them as eligible for marriage. A Cheng–Jakobsen marriage could expose all the single girls to unwelcome attention by unsuitable men, if not to danger.

From England Hudson Taylor wrote to Stevenson, 'Mr Hoste told me that there was a great danger of her heading a party of (Chinese) and together breaking away from the Mission – that good woman as she is, she was becoming a source of danger since the death of Pastor Hsi.' Since single women in the CIM first went into the interior of China, criticism had been strong in secular and missionary publications. Even one case of such a marriage going wrong could justify the pointing of accusing fingers at the Mission. Parents in the homelands might feel justified in refusing to allow their daughters to join the CIM if it did not protect them from reduction to a position as subservient daughters-in-law in unsympathetic families.

Anna Jakobsen was unmoved by their persuasion and by the fact that most missionaries in Shanxi were firmly opposed, for an ordained member of an American society agreed to perform the ceremony. Hudson Taylor tried from a distance to dissuade him. Letters and even telegrams had no effect. A few CIM colleagues stood by her, weakly claiming afterwards that their motive was sympathy rather than approval. And as no church was open to them, the ceremony took place in a photographer's shop. The consul responsible for Norwegian affairs declined to recognise the marriage, and the American consul denied the right of the missionary to perform the ceremony. She had rejected all advice and had chosen to marry out of the CIM. What became of her subsequently is not apparent, but the work she and her Chinese colleagues had started in Hunan went on from strength to strength. The only clue lies in a note to 'A Jakobsen Cheng' asking them not to complicate the lives of sister missionaries by returning to Jiangxi.[26]

Towards the end of 1897 when A E Thor visited the city of Chalingzhou, he found a congregation of thirty, another solid result of the evangelists' efforts. Months later, on October 26, 1898, Frank A Keller moved into new premises in the city. Keller was an outstanding young German American physician, a travelling secretary of the Student Volunteer Movement in the States before joining the CIM. Friendly mandarins sent policemen to every shop in the city to say that the foreigner must be well treated, ensuring peace for a few months. But threats by the literati to kill Keller's landlord and destroy his medicine shop began to circulate. Keller's companion, a teacher named Li who had become a Christian through teaching the missionaries, proved to be like the devoted colleague who said to George Hunter, 'If you mean business, if you're going to preach and are ready to endure hardness, I will go with you,' not otherwise. Together Li and Keller went through the 'house-warming' the mandarins could not prevent.[27]

Big gifts bring problems   *1895–97*

The instability of China made nonsense of any plans for organised expansion and advance. But there was still plenty of scope. The country was wide open. George Andrew walked 2,432 miles in Yunnan, Guizhou and Sichuan in the course of his service as superintendent, without being molested. The Burma frontier agreement made Tengyue a trade centre, a good base between Dali and Bhamo for work among the many border tribes (map p 45). Sam Pollard at Zhaotong and James R Adam at Anshun could scarcely cope with the opportunities among the Miao of Yunnan and Guizhou. In spite of Montagu Beauchamp's indefatigable evangelism, large areas of Sichuan remained untouched. Hudson Taylor was thinking in terms of 'Spirit-filled Chinese' to reach 'This Generation' and of twenty men of the Botham and Ririe type, wholly given up to evangelism. Many worked steadily but not intensively as they did. They should devote five years to this work, without thought of marriage for five years at least. Jiangxi offered the greatest promise, and in Archibald Orr Ewing had the right leader for five new districts with training centres in each for Chinese evangelists.[28]

In 1895 Hudson Taylor had completed his reorganisation of the London staff. With Walter B Sloan as Hon Senior Secretary, after Benjamin's retirement; Miss Williamson of Shanghai in charge of accommodation at Newington Green; Graham Brown in Scotland; Marcus Wood in London for the male candidates and Henrietta Soltau for the women; and with William Cooper as Assistant Deputy Director in China helped by C T Fishe, 'Never before were we so well prepared for definite advance.' His emphasis on maintaining the pressure where it was possible received what he regarded as strong confirmation in two forms. In the three years 1894–96 the CIM received 221 reinforcements without special effort[29] and 1897 began with forty more asking to be sent. Among all these were a few of whom he had great hopes. At the same time several large gifts and legacies were made conditional upon advance in specified directions.

Back in April 1891 when John Stevenson arrived in Scotland to care for his ailing family, he had met a Mr Gregg[30] who took a close interest in China. This first link in a chain of events had immense consequences, for through Mr Gregg's contacts with a friend in England, he also became interested. This friend, J T Morton, had made a small fortune as a wholesale provisions merchant, and kept a yacht on which he wintered at Mediterranean ports, returning to Britain for the summer. At Dartmouth he met James Williamson, veteran of the *Lammermuir*, and questioned him about the CIM. As a result J T Morton began to send books and later ordered the despatch of crates of canned groceries to many CIM centres in China – in time for the Ridleys to survive the Xining siege by careful rationing of his bounty.

On June 15, 1895, J T Morton wrote to Hudson Taylor from 107–109 Leadenhall Street. If 'more extensively establishing schools in the different stations of the CIM (is in line with CIM's policy) it will give me great pleasure to assist you with pecuniary help. (Also) in training adult Chinese converts to act as evangelists, teachers and pastors,' he would like 'to help to initiate work of this kind where it does not at present exist'.[31] Three months later a pencilled note from the philanthropist Robert Arthington (p 47) read, 'You will receive within a few days a sum of money left by my sister for the China Inland Mission. I should like to see the whole of the aborigines of China embraced in a comprehensive well-arranged plan for evangelisation.'[32]

Specification of how donations were to be used created its own problems. Their use depended on the availability of suitably experienced missionaries, and care needed to be taken to avoid weakening the indigenous church by encouraging dependence on foreign aid. Hudson Taylor advised that rather than (ask) individual missionaries to correspond with Mr Morton about his allocation of funds, it should all be done through John Stevenson as China Director. J T Morton fortunately agreed and the missionaries simply reported to him on progress. In October he sent £5 for each station, requesting individual reports. Difficulties increased. The directors needed to know whether the money was being wisely used, and asked for copies or summaries of the reports. As money given for 'the work', not for personal use, it had to be accounted for, as with all mission expenses.

In forwarding Mr Morton's lump sum to China, Walter Sloan commented, not ungratefully, 'It does seem a pity when we so sorely need money for the very carrying on of the work, that a large sum like this should be . . . a difficulty in the hands of workers who do not know how to utilise it.' For months on end donations had been minimal for 'general' purposes – the insistent drain on travelling, rentals, language teachers and simply food. 'What lesson should we be learning?' William Cooper asked Sloan. 'May we have the grace and wisdom to learn (it) quickly.' Perhaps the chief lesson was for the Church at home to trust the experts overseas to apply funds wisely where advance could best be made. Somehow enough always arrived, often from unusual directions, and 'straitness' (as they called the thin times) taught the Mission that living 'off the land' instead of dependence on stores from the coast was not only salutary but more economical by far. Hudson Taylor had no doubt on this score. Donations for consolidation and advance came from God himself, whoever the donor.

Writing to William Cooper in August 1896 about the Morton money, Hudson Taylor stressed that Chinese schools should be opened only where the missionaries could commit them to really suitable Chinese teachers and not themselves be side-tracked by new responsibilities from evangelism and teaching of believers. 'I have further pointed out (to Mr Morton) the inadvisability of doing for (Chinese) Christians anything that they are able to do themselves, and that it is much better to make help given stimulate them to help themselves, and to assist them in doing so . . .' J T Morton quickly saw that the men on the scene were best placed to judge how to apportion the money, and accepted Hudson Taylor's advice.[33]

Meanwhile he was following the CIM's affairs with greater interest. Realising that epidemics of infectious disease in the Chefoo schools could become dangerous, he offered to pay for a site and buildings for an isolation block and sanatorium. On November 20 Hudson Taylor wrote to tell John Stevenson that Mr Morton was intending to make a substantial donation towards the new girls' school and building. Work on it had been halted when the building account ran dry, and in studying the accounts Hudson Taylor had pointed out that one of the missionaries in charge was consistently overspending. Some lessons in bargaining with contractors were needed. A retaining fee to all the workmen for not working on

Sundays could be met from other funds. Boundary walls could be deferred. Physically frail he might be, but mentally he was still alert. His letters were precise as to facts and figures, clear as to meaning, and careful to avoid misunderstanding between John Stevenson and William Cooper.

By June 1897 the pace had proved too fast and his strength unequal to demands. 'Great weakness and prostration' following 'mumps' and 'neuralgia' were preventing work altogether. Walter Sloan called it 'serious collapse from overwork'. Whatever it was, he recovered in time to face the stresses of September.[34] On December 18 the difficulty was over. J T Morton sent £400 and work resumed. The boys' school was a separate project, financed by Orr Ewing, but Mr Morton wanted a hand in that, too. His donation was received in February 1897. E J Cooper, the architect, reported to Hudson Taylor on September 1, 1896, that the roofs were going on and the final west wing being started. All work was being done 'in accordance with your desires, namely "*substantial* and characteristic (of the CIM, that is); at the same time *economical*."' (Illustration: Book 6, p 207.)

J T Morton's involvement became deeper month by month. On March 12, 1897, he instructed William Cooper to 'give me timely advice when you require additional money' for the sanatorium.[35] Plenty of surrounding land should be provided 'for seclusion and relaxation', at his expense. And on May 5 he suggested twelve houses with gardens for missionary families convalescing or on short leave at Chefoo. Each letter pressed William Cooper to get on without delay, not realising that in China urgency put up prices and apparently endless patience saved large sums. By June 11 Hudson Taylor told Stevenson that he had been given carte-blanche to buy up whatever land was necessary at Chefoo to allow the whole area to become one property. And after recovery from his serious illness and convalescence at Davos, he wrote that on September 1 the sum of £10,000 had come from J T Morton, without restrictions on how it was to be used.

The Morton legacy   *1897–98*

Mr Morton's health was in a precarious state. If he died within a year, Hudson Taylor pointed out to Stevenson, at least £1,000 would be returnable as 'legacy duty'. In fact he died the day after sending the cheque. The Taylors left Davos on September 22 and two weeks later he wrote again. 'The death of Mr Morton considerably alters the position of things,' regarding expenses at Chefoo. He had bequeathed his fortune of over £700,000 in equal amounts to four societies, the CIM, the Waldensian Church, the Moravian Mission, the Aged Pilgrims Friends Society, and further sums to others.[36] But inexplicably his will left his wife and one of his sons and his employees 'hampered'.

Hudson Taylor was asked to hurry home from Stockholm, where the Swedish Mission in China were facing crucial decisions. Mr Morton's son was preparing to challenge the will in court.

In a letter of October 29, 1897, to John Stevenson, Hudson Taylor revealed how his own thoughts were shaping. The possibility of an income of £10,000 annually from the legacy for 'forward movement' struck him not only as an answer to prayer, but as an emergency. The Mission was unready, even unworthy of it.

> We are sorely needing fresh life infused into every part of our work; without this, (the legacy) may prove the greatest misfortune we have had for a long time; while inapplicable to general fund, it might lead (other) donors to withhold (their gifts), thinking we were rich.

But also a misfortune if it led the Mission to neglect its dependence on God alone. Hudson Taylor planned to come out to China to discuss 'a well-concerted plan for definite evangelistic extension'. He intended inviting Dr A T Pierson and Mr Inwood of Keswick to tour China to 'stir up the Christians to evangelise their own people'. 'Spirit-filled' Chinese were China's best hope, but Pierson and Inwood would also gain from the experience, 'so that when they returned to Europe and America they may set the Churches on fire'.

In his editorial in *China's Millions* for December 1897, under the title 'This Generation of the Chinese', he reiterated George King's strong appeal for Shaanxi, applying it to the whole of China. When King wrote in 1883 he was alone at Xi'an and Easton alone at Hanzhong. Since then the two outposts had become twenty and the two missionaries, seventy-seven. From there being no Chinese Church at all in the province, a church of five hundred Christians had developed. This progress must continue.

In the *Millions* of February 1898, Hudson Taylor wrote again, plainly stating the facts of the Morton legacy – 'a share of the residue of his estate', an unknown amount, to be released by the trustees as not more than one-tenth in any one year, and to be used only in

China (not even for related expenses in Britain or for sending missionaries out). Before the needed evangelists could be sent, however, the greatest need was for revival among the eighty thousand Protestant communicants in China and the missionaries already there. 'We may be quite sure that the spirit of evil will also be active.' The opposition since the appeal for The Thousand has been 'as never before'. A new advance such as this legacy seemed to justify could be expected to meet with the same response, so all should pray 'that in every way Satan's power may be curbed'.

Writing to Walter Sloan and William Sharp on January 29, 1898 (about a Sunday spent with Matthew Henry Hodder, the publisher), Hudson Taylor expressed his opinion, 'that the question (of Mr Morton's legacy) is one of principle and not of expediency'. He knew his family's and his firm's circumstances when in good mental health he made his will, and once the Mission received a donation it ought to be used for the purposes specified. It placed the CIM in a difficult position, in which to accept a legal judgment would be quite different from arbitrarily dividing the bequest made for evangelism and educational work in China because of claims upon it. 'The loss of the whole legacy [in court] would not be so great an evil as the loss of a conscience void of offence.'

So the matter went to court and the CIM was awarded £187,500 in trust. Although contested until March 1899, payment began in September 1898 and continued until 1916 when the last sum of £250 was disbursed. At that point the 'Borden legacy' began to come in. Not only so, but word came in August 1898 of yet another will leaving £20,000 to the CIM.[37]

Before any of this money became available in China there were months of painfully low transmissions from the homelands. With the Mission growing all the time, in May 1896, for the sixth month in succession, less than £1,000 came from Britain. To be unable to respond to estimates of expenditure from all 'stations' 'is a great strain' on the China directors and treasurer, William Cooper admitted, 'but Jehovah Jireh! (the Lord will provide) we will not fear'. When £1,400 arrived in December he wrote, 'the Lord be praised. He is faithful!' If this phenomenon had not continued for almost a century since Cooper's time – of a large organisation being run on funds promised by God, but without human guarantee of any kind – we should scarcely believe it was true. But funds were forwarded when they became available, and belts were tightened and prayer became more realistic when, as sometimes happened, the message was, 'Sorry, but we have nothing to send you this month.' 'In some way or other the Lord will provide' has always stood the test. Large sums for special objects remained untouched, in keeping with the principle reiterated by Hudson Taylor: 'Nothing could be more contrary to the wishes of Mr Morton than to use his legacy as practically part of the general fund. Through years of correspondence with him I have never known him to propose giving one pound to that fund . . . God clearly gave us this money for a Forward Movement.'[38]

The 'Forward Movement' seemed on course for ultimate fulfilment, but restraints of one kind and another, and premonitions of approaching distress appeared more and more likely to the Mission's leaders as China's own agony deepened.

'On a volcano'   *1896–98*

At the annual meeting in May 1897, Hudson Taylor spoke of the growing number of Chinese church members, doubled in the last seven years to reach eighty thousand, and immediately went on to quote one of the Kucheng martyrs.

> 'What have we to face in China? God and the devil!' She speaks of what a solemn thing it is to be brought face to face with the great enemy of souls, and to know all the time that you are sitting, as it were, over a volcano which, apart from God's restraining power, may burst forth at any moment . . . God withdrew the restraint, and she and her fellow-workers were honoured with the crown of martyrdom . . . While we are meeting (here), it may be, some . . . in some part of China are in extreme danger.[39]

So far, still, in the thirty years of the Mission's history not one CIM life had been lost by violence. Daring policies and deep penetration into remotest China had been justified. But recently one mission and another had seen God's restraints removed. Hudson Taylor saw no reason why the CIM should be an exception. Writing from Frankfurt for his daughter Amy's twenty-first birthday, he thankfully observed that during her lifetime the only death in their family had been of one grandchild.

After the May meetings he was unwell for two months and confessed to John Stevenson he was finding the incessant demands on his strength more than he could bear. He ought to 'get away' and hoped to visit North America and China on the way to Australia and

New Zealand. *China's Millions* reported 'quite a serious breakdown in his health', asking readers to spare him unnecessary business. Jennie took him to Switzerland where he relaxed and soon recovered.[40]

But there at Davos he received a letter from William Sharp, the lawyer, urging him to name his own successor and to replace John Stevenson. Stevenson, he alleged, was alienating more and more members by unfeeling harshness in his administration. Sharp, it seemed, still had an ear for the disaffected. Then a cable brought news of Jennie's sister Nellie Fishe's death from 'heat apoplexy', leaving Charlie with five motherless children in China and five older ones in Britain. Maria (Taylor) Coulthard wrote on the same day to say that her year-old baby had died of dysentery at Wenzhou.

But in Stockholm a serious difference of opinion had arisen in the central committee of the Swedish Mission in China, and Hudson Taylor hurried over for two days' consultation. A baroness whose daughter wanted to join the Mission insisted on her being allowed to marry before going to China, and opinion differed sharply in the committee on whether the two-year marriage rule should be relaxed. Some thought their circumstances exceptional in view of her social status. So serious was the rift that the survival of the Swedish Mission was at stake, but to Hudson Taylor the case was clear. To make an exception to the rule on this ground alone would not be keeping faith with others who had been held to it. What was needed was a friendly search with the couple for a way out that did not involve compromising principle. Together they found it. They could marry and go out independently to join Erik Folke as associates. Only actual membership of the Swedish Mission would be sacrificed. In China they would be no less part of 'the family' of the CIM. To have guided the committee back to agreement was a greater achievement than finding the solution.

From Stockholm he crossed the North Sea to Edinburgh to keep some appointments, and to his surprise found Jennie waiting for him at Mrs Kalley's (HTCOC Book 6, p 326). She had news to break to him. Maria herself had died of dysentery shortly after her baby.

By November he could delay his return to China no longer. John Stevenson's apparent inability to work with William Cooper demanded his presence. Satan 'like a roaring lion' seemed insatiable in seeking whom next to devour. But William Berger was unlikely to live much longer, so Hudson Taylor paid a quick visit to Cannes (November 12–17) to say goodbye. After an express return journey his boat train back from Paris to Boulogne was travelling slowly from the town to the pier when it became derailed and his carriage thrown on its side. He was extricated with difficulty, but unhurt, and a week later (November 24) sailed with Jennie, Miss Hanbury (the hymn writer?) and Henrietta Soltau for New York.[41]

Henrietta recollected that on this journey, all the way to China, he spent hours talking with fellow-passengers, for he was always an evangelist. But at other times he sat for hours deep in thought, and when he spoke 'Forward Movement' seemed to preoccupy him. Litigation over the Morton legacy would only affect the ultimate amount. The central fact remained unaltered: God had provided a massive sum for advance when advance seemed thwarted by few men of the right kind being available, and by China appearing to be at flash-point. What was God saying? That setbacks were second-ary, delays immaterial and the devil's counter-blows to be parried or endured? How did the fulfilment of his dream of twenty years fit in with the opening of the Burma frontier, a British Commercial Resident and two CIM missionaries established at Tengyue and the Arthington bequest for the evangelisation of the aboriginal 'tribes'? (After J R Adam's successes among the Guizhou Miao, Hudson Taylor had thrown his arms around his neck and thanked him when they met in Scotland.)

With a succession of encouraging developments, the time looked ripe for advance. A Chinese Imperial Post had been created by Imperial decree. With an Anglo-German loan for China's recon-struction; with the Yangzi River open to foreign shipping as far as Chongqing, and steam-launches attempting to ascend the rapids in the gorges;[42] with an agreement signed with Russia for a Chinese eastern railway in Manchuria; with Belgium contracting to build a Peking-Hankou railway; and with the French demanding the right to engineer a Tongking-Kunming line – in a word with China opening up for freer, faster access and communication – the call for missions to move forward sounded loud and clear. Except for the volcano.

What did Li Hongzhang's humiliation mean, after his return from Europe? Representing the Empress at the coronation of the young Tsar, and honoured also in Germany, France and Britain, he had arrived back in 'remarkable vitality and spirits', only to be accused of 'trespassing' in the grounds of the Summer Palace, and fined a year's salary (37,000 taels) by Ci Xi, allegedly for remarking in her presence on the beauty of the Tsarina.[43] During his absence from the country the Emperor's mother had died in suspicious circumstances, the finger of accusation pointing once again at Ci Xi. What would this capricious woman be up to next? What threat to China's security lay in Russia's railways (even if called Chinese) with wide swathes of territory and their inhabitants each side under Russian control? And in French, Belgian and other lines to the very heart of China? The danger of China's dismemberment by Western nations struck Hudson Taylor as being a greater threat to the spread of the gospel than any opposition by the Chinese. At a stroke the Roman Catholic nations, or for political reasons the British, in control of a 'sphere of influence' could ban or hobble missionary activity as they were doing in their colonial territories elsewhere.

Even before the Taylors' journey started, the process soon known as 'slicing the melon' had begun. On November 1, 1897, two German Catholic missionaries of the Society of the Divine Word were murdered in Shandong. In retaliation a German force seized the port of Qingdao (Tsingtao) at the mouth of Jiaozhou Bay on the 14th, and to legalise their action, on March 6 wrested a ninety-nine-year lease of the city and environs of Jiaozhou (Kiaochow) and Qingdao, and obtained exclusive railway and mining rights in Shandong province.[44] On December 18, the day that the Taylors left San Francisco to cross the Pacific Ocean, Kaiser Wilhelm II informed Chancellor von Bülow: 'Hundreds of thousands of Chinese will quiver when they feel the iron fist of Germany heavy on their necks.' Bombast as it was, the speech made history and branded 'the lawless West' in the eyes of the world. At a time of her own choice China would wreak revenge.

Only a year before, twenty leaders of Protestant missions in China had submitted a memorial to the Zongli Yamen for presentation to the Emperor, asking for an edict banning slander against Christianity and reaffirming religious liberty. 'Instead of falling behind to rank among small nations,' they urged, '*China should rank among the greatest in the world.*' Hudson Taylor had joined his long-standing friends and younger men in signing it: Muirhead, Burdon, Griffith John, David Hill, Young J Allen, Timothy Richard and Gilbert Reid among them. After Timothy Richard had been granted interviews with the Zongli Yamen and with some ministers individually, he reported that,

> If these had their way there would be an end to our trouble at once.
> Indeed there was a general feeling for a few days among the mandarins and scholars of Peking that the memorial was approved of

by the Emperor, and that an edict would be issued within a few days.[45]

Unfortunately the Manchus were not of the same mind. 'They seemed to have made up their minds that Christians are all a bad lot . . .' So no more was heard of the gesture. After the volcano erupted the sinister hand of the Empress Dowager could be recognised behind the fate of the memorial. A sincere attempt at friendly dealings between missions and government had failed. In days to come friendship unsoured by treachery and bloodshed would succeed where words were impotent. But the mailed fists of nominally Christian nations would first make the word of all Christians seem untrustworthy.

CHAPTER NINE

THE REFORMERS
1898–1900

Reform and reaction *1898–99*

'The abasement of China . . . produced a profound effect on the educated classes' of China. Blind refusal to learn its lessons characterised the Empress Dowager and her coterie of mostly aged advisers. Enlightenment of the more open-minded, predominantly younger men, but not exclusively, set them on the course of reform as we have seen (pp 108–9). While Sun Yatsen (pp 219–20) and the impatient activists took to armed protest and attempts to seize power as revolutionaries, Kang Yuwei, 'the Erasmus of the reform movement', opted for constitutional reformation. Only a republic would satisfy Sun, but Kang worked for reform of government and nation brought about by the Emperor himself. Kang's published studies of *The Reform of Japan* and the *The Reform of Russia* (by Peter the Great) illustrated his aim, 'a republic with a nominal hereditary ruler', a constitutional monarchy.[1] The obscurants were to drive both into exile with a price on their heads.

By early 1898 there were few of the younger mandarins or literati who did not favour reform to some extent. Their attitude towards foreigners showed a marked change, which in places off the beaten commercial tracks benefited missionaries more than merchants, for 'missionaries were the largest and most widely dispersed body (of foreigners) in China'.[2] 'Even the younger members of the Manchu nobility were infected.' Every major city had its Manchu garrison quarter, and provincial capitals their powerful enclaves (like the British in India). On April 18, 1898, the *North China Herald* reported the presentation 'by a prince of the blood' of a memorial signed by 1,200 officials and recent *chinshi* (doctorate) graduates, protesting against the government's weak stand against the grabbing Russians in Manchuria and Germans in Shandong, 'slicing the melon' of the motherland. Even in Peking an outspoken weekly called *Chinese Progress* could count on selling 10,000 copies, and became a daily.

The Imperial Grand Tutor, Weng Tongho, had access to the

young Guang Xü emperor and the support of most Chinese government ministers in his patronage of reformers. Prince Qün, the emperor's father, had died in 1891, and Prince Kong died in May 1898, or the sorry events of 1898 to 1900 might never have happened. Li Hongzhang, on the Grand Council, but consigned to the political wilderness, had little influence except from the distant viceroyalty of revolutionary Canton to which he was posted.[3]

Early in June 1898, Weng Tongho commended Kang Yuwei to the thirty-year-old emperor, who began to read his books, was immediately impressed, gave him official rank, and summoned him to an audience on June 14. Guang Xü's 'introduction to Western learning, under the indirect supervision of W A P Martin, had been going on for some years'. He had been 'enormously impressed' by Timothy Richard's translation of Dr J K Mackenzie's 'hymn to the conquests of science and the dogma of progress', a *History of the Nineteenth Century*. A million bona fide and pirated copies were in circulation.[4] Already on June 11 Guang Xü had issued a decree that reform was necessary, but when another on June 13 deprived Weng Tongho of rank and dignities and ordered him home to his native place, the hand of Ci Xi cast its sinister shadow. Another edict commanded all high officials on appointment to appear before her as well as the emperor. And yet another made her old friend Yong Lu viceroy of Zhili and commander of China's best army. After the first decree the wily Old Buddha had scented the wind, had reacted immediately and was ready for more.

At this point in June 1898, Zhang Zhitong, the enlightened viceroy of Hunan and Hubei, produced a literary masterpiece entitled *Learn, an Exhortation to Learning*. Of this also a million copies were soon sold and read throughout the empire. From a platform of admiration of the Confucian precepts and the Qing dynasty, and rejection of republicanism which would encourage insubordination and destroy social stability, he advocated learning from the successful nations. 'Chinese learning for the essential principles; western learning for the practical application', summed up his argument. So retain the classics and add science. Learn how little Japan became strong. Learn how weak nations – India, Burma, Korea – fell into the hands of the strong. Learn how other nations govern themselves and grow in strength. Send students abroad to learn. Multiply schools at home. Translate books, tolerate all religions, build railways, maintain powerful armed forces. Much of what he advocated has its echo in our own day.[5]

The Hunanese quickly took 'a leading part in the march of thoughts'. From heading the anti-Christian movement by means of the outrageous Zhou Han publication, *Death to the Devil's Religion*, Hunan became for a time more peaceful than the rest of China. The Society for the Diffusion of Christian and General Knowledge (SDK) with Timothy Richard as secretary, could not keep up with the demand for books. At Changsha a new College of Reform had been established in 1897 and the SDK was asked to nominate a president for it. The sales of Bibles doubled, and foreign and Chinese scholars poured out translations and digests of Western books of learning. The contribution of missionaries became recognised as crucial to this awakening and development.

Timothy Richard, Young J Allen and Gilbert Reid, through his 'Mission among the Higher Classes in China', enjoyed their heyday.

Timothy Richard had been secretary of the SDK since 1891. Every book of any value was also being pirated extensively, and 'the Chinese names of men like Timothy Richard and Young J Allen were on people's lips throughout the country'. Kang Yuwei himself told a reporter in 1898 that 'he owed his conversion to reform chiefly to the writings of Richard and Allen.'[6] Through the SDK's *Review of the Times* Richard and Allen made their influence felt increasingly. Young J Allen's keen analytic mind, his ready wit and forceful expression were matched by his striking appearance. Born to be a statesman, he had devoted his talents to the service of missions. By his faithful marshalling of the facts month by month, and his emphasis on the essential weaknesses of China, he aroused public opinion, especially among the official classes, to a realisation that China must either advance or be destroyed.

In a different key, Western dress and rejection of the 'queue' (imposed upon the Han Chinese by their Manchu conquerors) were adopted by the daring. Zhenjiang had its foreign restaurant with knives, forks and spoons. (Singapore led the way with the first automobile, a Benz, in 1898, but Shanghai did not follow, with an Oldsmobile, until 1902.)[7]

When Hudson Taylor and his companions arrived at Shanghai on January 15, 1898, he quickly detected the new climate. China was seething with conflicting currents. A ferment of new ideas and new activity by both the Chinese and the foreign powers spelt instability, the seedbed of disaster. The daily newspapers reflected the anxiety of the foreign community. Blind avarice led nation to follow nation in stealing advantage from China's weakness. Resentment and desire for reform as conflicting emotions soured discussion among Chinese.

'Non-alienation' of the Yangzi Valley was agreed on February 11 and of Fujian on April 26, but a Sino-German convention about Jiaozhou and Qingdao on March 6, a Sino-Russian convention on March 27, confirming the cession of Port Arthur to Russia, took more slices from the melon. A French claim to a lease of the Bay of Guangzhouwan close to Tongking (Vietnam), and a spate of contracts to build railways, carried the tentacles of foreign power farther into China's heartland. A Franco-Russian scheme to link Manchuria with Tongking by a joint railway project like a sword-thrust through the heart of China came to nothing when the other powers called a halt. An American contract to build a Canton–Hankou line was signed on April 14, and for a British Shanghai–Nanjing line on May 13. Russia secured a contract for a line into Shanxi, and Britain to mine Shanxi's mineral wealth. On July 1 Britain leased Weihaiwei as an answer to Russia's Port Arthur and Germany's Qingdao, and on July 6 Russia concluded another agreement for railway extensions through Manchuria to Port Arthur. Britain disclaimed Shandong and Russia disclaimed Korea, but on June 9 a Sino–British convention extended the leased territories of Hong Kong. More was to follow.

April saw the Spanish–American war over Cuba spread to east Asia, when Admiral Dewey sailed into Manila Bay at 5.00 am on May 1, 1898, and destroyed the Spanish fleet. British colporteurs from Hong Kong had been garotted by the Spanish for taking Bibles into the Philippines. The Philippines were made vulnerable to occupation by any European power, but seemed unready for self-government. So the Americans stayed in control of Manila and Manila Bay. A brief war of independence ended with annexation on February 6, 1899, when the USA promised to hand over government after fifty years of preparation. In the event this took place after the liberation by General MacArthur at the end of the Second World War. The United States had become a colonial power with colonies in the Philippines, in the Pacific at Guam and Hawaii, and in Cuba and Puerto Rico. Suddenly the whole archipelago was free from the medieval grip of Rome and Protestant missionaries moved in. Agonising China saw her own autonomy at risk.

Sir Robert Hart's exemplary management of the Chinese Imperial Customs had so benefited the nation that at long last the collection of *likin* taxes on internal movements of merchandise was also entrusted to him. Revolt against this innovation almost broke out at Hankou (at a time when Hudson Taylor was there) for private pockets inevitably suffered by the curtailment of corruption. In Sichuan, on the other hand, revolt did erupt and was not finally suppressed until a year later. The Sichuan riots of 1886 had been attributed by the Chinese authorities to the expanding real estate and secular power of the Roman Catholics, and, as J K Fairbank put it, 'the arrogant, even unscrupulous behaviour . . . of converts', especially 'the grip on the local economy' some had gained.[8] During an attack on the leading Chinese Catholic's home in Chongqing a rioter was killed and the French consul failed to prevent the Catholic being executed.

At about the same time a wealthy Chinese, who became known as Yü Manzi, lost a lawsuit against a Catholic owing, it was believed, to intervention by a foreign priest. Yü's son raised a force and attacked the Catholics, but was caught and executed. Yü then became 'the implacable enemy of all Catholics'. By 1898 he had several thousands of men destroying Church property and making 'over twenty thousand Christians' homeless, according to Lord Charles Beresford in his book *The Break-up of China*. The brash manner of young Lord Charles's visit to China and the crudity of statements in his widely circulated book further incensed the nation against foreigners, Protestant Christians suffered persecution and annoyances, but were not the primary objects of attack as the Yü Manzi revolt continued into 1899.[9]

The dismemberment of China with regions coming under the rule of foreign powers, while a possibility in the early stages after the Sino-Japanese war, could not materialise because of jealousy and rivalry between those powers, and their preoccupation with commitments elsewhere in the world. But more dramatic events were about to startle everyone.

'The Hundred Days': too much too soon   June–October 1898

Between June 11 and September 20, 1898, the youthful enthusiasm of the emperor and the inexperience of the political philosopher, Kang Yuwei, together resulted in a rickety pyramid of seventy-three reforms. Edicts of increasing weight, each sound in itself and necessary to progress, poured out of the palace. But 'the pyramid stood on its apex' and fell in ruins. As Sir Robert Hart wrote to H B Morse when it was all over, 'They simply killed

Progress with kindness – they stuffed it . . . with food enough in three months for three times as many years.'[10]

For instance, a decree ordered the Zongli Yamen to encourage art, science and agriculture; another urged speed in constructing the Peking-Hankou railway; another reformed the examination system. The Manchu Bannermen were ordered to adopt Western arms and drill. July saw commands for every province to have its agricultural college, and every city its modern schools and colleges. Inventors and authors were to be encouraged, and protected by patent and copyright laws. Courts of law were to be reformed and merchants to be assisted. In August an Imperial university was established at Peking by decree with the seventy-one-year-old W A P Martin as head of the faculty under a Chinese chancellor and others, and he was honoured by elevation to the second civil rank with a red cap button as worn by viceroys. If disaster had not followed 'it is very likely that Richard would have been invited (on Kang Yuwei's recommendation) to join the inner circle of imperial advisers'.[11]

On and on the edicts flowed until at the end of August they struck at corruption and began to hurt. Sinecure boards at Peking and duplicate governorships were abolished, as were Salt and Grain Commissioners in provinces which produced no salt and sent no tribute of grain. In the first two weeks of September military conscription was begun, with abolition of the antiquated but honoured 'Green Banner' army. Uncultivated land attached to military garrisons was to be thrown open to the people, and the right granted to all subjects to memorialise the throne. Manchus were permitted to take up trade or a profession – which many understood (correctly it may be) as a threat to their idle lives. And annual publication of budgets, receipts and expenditure threatened the age-long corruption throughout the palace and people. For his reactionary attitude and perhaps because of his loyalty to Ci Xi, Li Hongzhang was dismissed from the Zongli Yamen on September 7 and for resisting the right to submit closed memorials to the emperor, high-ranking officials of the Ministry of Rites (including a relative of Ci Xi's) were replaced by reformers.

Reaction by the diehard conservatives became inevitable. They urged Ci Xi to resume power. The emperor decided to strike first. But during 'The Hundred Days' China's ferment broke out in rioting and rebellion, often unconnected with the emperor's reforms beyond the fact that the nation's weakness and a spate of reformation literature were the talk of the teashops. Railways were being extended urgently, without adequate negotiation to avoid disturbing the *fengshui*.[12] A rising in Guangxi quickly gained ground, and continued unquelled for five years. And in Sichuan, Yü Manzi captured two Catholic priests and held one, M Fleury, for six or seven months. 'Catholic villages were plundered and no priest was safe.' A local uprising had become rebellion against the government.[13]

Throughout this time, through the autumn and winter, anti-Catholic outbreaks in other provinces took a grimmer form. Riots in Hainan, Shashi, Songbu and Yangzhou heralded the return of the notorious Hunanese Zhou Han, urging the slaughter of Chinese converts. In Guangdong a priest and thirteen Chinese were killed, while in Hubei a Franciscan priest 'was tortured and beheaded after eight neophytes had been done to death before his eyes'.[14] Imperial decrees on January 15, July 12 and October 6, 1898, ordered special protection for Christians, but the mandarins' power to prevent outrages depended on local compliance. Too many riots took place to be given prominence in the papers. *China's Millions* recorded those that affected the CIM, with stories of great heroism by Chinese Christians.[15] Property was looted and destroyed at Changshu in Jiangxi, and at Nanchong (Shunking) in Sichuan. At Changshu a friendly magistrate was stoned for protecting the missionaries and an unfriendly one who refused to help nevertheless had his own *yamen* destroyed.

As Hudson Taylor explained in the *Millions*, most of this rioting was in protest against the transfer of inland customs duty (*likin* tax) to foreign administrators. 'Thousands will lose their squeezes and don't like it.' He himself wrote, 'There were riots at Huzhou the day before I arrived. Three men were beheaded . . . You will have learned that (Ningbo, Shaoxing and Wenzhou) have also had riots', from crop failure. Two weeks later he explained that he could not leave headquarters while anything might happen. 'There is serious rebellion in (Guangdong) and . . . nearly half (Guangxi) is in the hands of rebels. The authorities seem powerless to deal with it and France may take the opportunity to do something' – seizing territory. He himself was in better health than for the last three years, but Maria's brother, Samuel Dyer, the Bible Society secretary in China, was dying of high fever.

Part of the trouble was that officials aware of great changes taking place at Peking were feathering their own nests as fast as they could,

and the prestige of the Manchus had sunk to danger point. One riot
was entirely by disgruntled soldiers on the rampage. Disintegration
of the nation seemed a possibility. Drought had struck central
China, and famine conditions existed in a broad swathe from
Qingjiangpu in Jiangsu to Laohekou on the Han River in Hubei
province. George King, newly qualified as a doctor and back in
China, undertook the Mission's relief work.[16]

The Hundred Days came to a dramatic end when Old Buddha
decided it should. By then the merchants wanted stability under
which to trade; the *laobeixing* ('old hundred names', the prolet-
ariat) simply wanted to be left alone; the gentry clung to time-
honoured customs, and officials resented interference with their
privileges and profits; Manchus saw their ascendancy threatened
and the court felt the foundations of the throne shaking. With
reformers in one position of power after another, Ci Xi had begun to
fear for her life.

'The core of the matter'   1898

To run your eye down a chronology of this period (Appendix 2) is
to see its kaleidoscopic confusion in perspective. France's move
towards the Sudan, quietly checked by Britain, may explain to some
extent the fact that France did not slice off part of southern China
while it could in 1898. Britain's preoccupation with the Mahdi,
ending in his defeat at Omdurman on September 2 (with Winston
Churchill taking part), distracted her from the tempting fruits in
China. Sir Claude Macdonald, the minister at Peking, an evangelical Christian, preferred to arrange financial loans to help China's
reconstruction. The eclipse of the sun on China's New Year's Day
foreboded calamity, a fatalistic thought in the minds of prince and
pauper. For Hudson Taylor, holding the reins in Shanghai, it was
the year of tension, of danger in Sichuan from Yü Manzi, of the
Jakobsen marriage affair, of litigation over the Morton legacy, of
Hunan opening fast, of Rijnhardt back in Tibet, and of the very first
death by violence in the CIM. The year of the Hundred Days also
became the year of the unscrupulous Ci Xi's return to power.

Hudson Taylor's articles in *China's Millions* were as ever the
barometer of his thinking. As 'ROCK FOUNDATIONS' re-
affirmed the sure ground of truth on which the Mission stood, so it
also revealed his sense of approaching trial. Destitution, even
death, might be the price to be paid, but 'I will never leave you nor

forsake you,' remained God's immutable promise. With that foundation, the raison d'être of the China *Inland* Mission, 'the core of the matter' for which huge legacies had been given was 'forward movement' – Advance. Four instalments in the *Millions* kept attention on the subject. Suitable men were slow in offering to give five years to intensive evangelism, but a sensational start was made in Jiangxi under Archibald Orr Ewing's leadership. The owner of a house in Nanchang, Jiangxi, who merely agreed to sell land to Orr Ewing, received one thousand blows as punishment. Thomas Botham and the Scandinavians P E Henriksen and G A Carlsson continued their systematic ploughing and sowing of the Shaanxi plains. The pioneers out on the fringes of Gansu, Ningxia, Tibet, Yunnan, Guizhou among the Miao, and at last in Hunan, pressed boldly on. George Andrew went to Guizhou as leader of the dispirited team. Month after month the *Millions* repeated that Xinjiang (Sinkiang) remained 'almost untouched'. The George W Hunter of Xinjiang (distinct from his namesake in Hunan) had arrived in China, and Eva French also, but their own Xinjiang adventures were still years away.[17]

'The core of the matter', however, was not territorial advance or the dispersal of teams; to Hudson Taylor 'not by might, nor by power but by My Spirit' said it all. Missionaries of all societies needed help in maintaining their spiritual tone, dulled by drudgery or overstrain; help in opening their hearts to be 'filled with the Spirit'. Some had lowered their standards through pride of achievement. The colleagues of an individualistic veteran at Taizhou were waiting impatiently for him to go on home leave so that they could spring-clean the whole mission in the region. Hudson Taylor questioned whether one-third or a half of the people he had baptised were true believers. Only by bringing such men back to humility before God would their work become more than 'wood, hay and stubble'. He asked the Keswick Council to send speakers, 'missionaries to missionaries', and Dr and Mrs Inwood arrived in October to spend months in conferences for members of all societies and foreign communities in the north, south, east and west of China. Dr A T Pierson although invited could not come. (John R Mott's visit to Shanghai in the course of his world tour to students did not coincide with this period.) But since 1894 a more complicated problem had troubled Hudson Taylor. Increasingly he felt that God, by withholding 'general' funds month after month, and the best kind of men to take the gospel to 'every creature', was saying to 'Joshua', 'There is sin in the camp', something to put right.[18]

'Special support'   *1894–98*

A system of 'special support' existed, whereby the friends and home churches of some missionaries agreed together to provide their missionary representatives with regular amounts of money. 'Independent' (self-supported) members of the Mission also had their sources of supplies separate from the funds distributed to other members. No one took exception to the system, for all alike were trusting God for everything they might need, not least for health and protection. But big fluctuations in exchange rates sometimes resulted in those receiving 'special support' ending up with far more in Chinese currency – a matter of when the funds were available. In January 1894 a difference of 40 per cent occurred, affecting Australians more than others.

Another anomaly lay in the fact that overheads (in the form of premises, repairs, travelling expenses, training homes, business departments and Chinese employees) were met from 'general funds' to the benefit of all alike, although 'special support' missionaries' funds were not drawn upon. The Australian Council brought this state of affairs to its missionaries' attention, with the result that those on 'special support' agreed to receive for personal use the same monthly sums as others, the balance going to the general administrative expenses of the mission. On May 11, 1894, Hudson Taylor wrote to all concerned: 'Specially supported missionaries are asked to give thought to this subject while all may give thanks that while Mission income has decreased from home sources the change in exchange rates has greatly benefited the situation in China.'[19]

By 1896, when copper was becoming scarce in China and copper coins were being smelted down, the inflationary effect necessitated larger remittances to missionaries at a time when receipts were low. A serious financial crisis was looming. In July 1898 the China Council (meeting at an atmospheric temperature of 98°F in the shade) faced the fact that while the estimated 'apparent need' of the Mission in China amounted to £1,500 each month, for three months running only £500 had been transmitted each month from the United Kingdom. Belt-tightening and solemn reviews of expenditure saw them through, and a £2,000 legacy (unknown to them as yet) was coming in August. 'If we do all we can and ought, we can leave the results with (God),' Hudson Taylor remarked.

But beyond asking God to guide and provide, what lessons should they be learning? Both the China Council and London Council agreed that dependence by some missionaries on 'special support' was undermining their dependence on God, apart from their supporters. The time had come to consult both 'special support' donors and missionaries and to propose a change. The risk of losing some of each kind would have to be accepted, in the interests of unity in China and true adherence to the Principles.[20]

During 1898, when so many tensions took time and thought for the well-being of the widely scattered Mission, Hudson Taylor and the China Council grasped the nettle, obtained the approval of the London and North American Councils, and issued a carefully drafted letter to all members. In it they explained all that was involved and asked for 'hearty concurrence' in its solution.

Any fears proved unjustified. Letters poured in from 'special support' donors and recipients, so that by June 1899 Jennie wrote of 'great joy and thanksgiving' over acceptance of the proposals by *all* affected. They knew from observation and experience that the blessings from trusting in the Lord alone far outweighed the satisfactions of a regular income. Over the years of continued expansion, with nine associate missions and international developments, the Mission had tended to become fragmented. A need 'to unite as one mission, not separate bands' had become paramount. 'Unity involves diversity', Hudson Taylor said, 'the diverse members of one body animated by one spirit . . . heart unity, not uniformity.'[21] This unity and trust in God's faithfulness proved to be the cement. The fault had been remedied and the CIM made ready, it seemed, to move forward when peace returned.

'*After you die*'   *1898–1900*

Another issue on Hudson Taylor's mind during these fateful months in the summer of 1898 had been raised by William Sharp in June. 'For the future well-being of the work Mr Stevenson must on no account be entrusted with the principal oversight in China. I doubt if the Mission would hold together for six months after you were gone.'[22] Sharp's judgment was not always reliable, and this looked like a return to the fault of tales told in London by individuals from China being taken at face value, or of Stevenson's part in earlier controversies having delayed effects. The worst about Stevenson seemed to be brusqueness and sometimes indecision, according to some. No one could work harder or keep his finger more efficiently on a myriad matters at once. Paltry shortcomings mattered little in comparison when big men were scarce. In later years they were to accuse Dixon Hoste of indecision, but both men were imperturbable, waiting until they could see the target clearly before pulling the trigger.

But Hudson Taylor had to take seriously the question of his own successor. Sharp went on, 'I am a good deal struck with Mr Cooper's apparent fitness for dealing wisely and well with whatever may come before him . . . He has qualities evidently suited to the position you have given him.' Here they were of one mind without doubt. If Hudson Taylor were to die, 'who should take the initiative?' The only one Sharp could think of as General Director was Henry Frost, first-rate, but frail and lacking experience as a working member in China. Sharp's letters on this theme continued periodically through 1899 and into 1900. Stevenson 'must know that he is not liked,' and, 'If you *could* work in someone else – say Mr Hoste – it would probably be more agreeable to Mr Stevenson than if Mr Cooper were there . . . You know how willing (Cooper) is for anything – he would gladly go . . . if it would save friction or Mr S's feelings.' William Sharp was not surprised to learn from Hudson Taylor that John Stevenson 'commands esteem *outside* the Mission'. But after Hudson Taylor appointed William Cooper to deputise for him as 'Visiting China Director', to travel extensively trouble-shooting and encouraging the front-line missionaries, Sharp continued to criticise Stevenson. The matter, he said, *must* be dealt with. Dixon Hoste had 'very valuable qualities for leadership'. He and Cooper would work well together.

Taking note and replying non-committedly to the importunate lawyer, Hudson Taylor kept his own counsel. Whether he had a written deposition, a directive set aside for the event of his death, will never be known, but the evidence points to the probability that at this stage he had William Cooper and after him Dixon Hoste at least in mind. He showed no anxiety about the possibility of being taken unprepared, and had more serious matters to attend to. The ferment in China was taking a dangerous new turn. Young Guang Xü and Old Buddha were to strike simultaneously.

Plot, coup and counter-reformation   *July–September 1898*

While the emperor 'devoured (the Bible) with avidity' (according to Charlotte Haldane)[23] and poured out his reforming decrees, 'a constant procession of petitioners' besought Ci Xi to intervene and rescue them from the iconoclasts. Egged on by the young progressives, an increasingly powerful party. Guang Xü and his mentor, Kang Yuwei, became bolder, striking not only at the evils of weak and corrupt government but at their roots. This could not but excite the hostility of powerful men. Abolishing the sinecures hurt not only those unseated but their superiors who for personal gain had appointed them. Promoting modern military training and examinations in place of horsemanship and archery, brain instead of brawn, angered the old brigade. The venom of reform was stupefying not only the younger literati but the highest in the land.

While Liu Kunyi, viceroy of Nanjing, kept his distance from trouble, Zhang Zhitong dared to add to his doctrine of 'Learn' the accusation that the old conservatives were 'stuck in the mud of antiquity'.[24] Yong Lu went so far as to recommend for appointment a young reformer radical enough later to be executed. Even Old Buddha scandalised the purists by approving an edict declaring that on October 29 the emperor and she would 'travel by fire-carriage on the iron-road to (Tianjin)' (to quote Morse's literalism) to review the modern 'model army'.

But Ci Xi was too astute to be deceived. This thing could end in the taming of the Manchu tiger or even in the republicanism for which Sun Yatsen was on the run. She knew she had two loyal supporters in Li Hongzhang and Yong Lu. Li's dismissal from the Zongli Yamen had ostensibly been because he was too friendly to Britain and too weak in ceding Liaotong to Russia. He approved of modernisation, but opposed sweeping reform and belonged finally to Ci Xi's faction. On September 8 Sir Claude Macdonald reported to Lord Salisbury, 'Li Hung-chang has recently shown himself markedly antagonistic to our interests.' Yong Lu was not only viceroy of Zhili at the gateway of Imperial China, Tianjin, but commander-in-chief of the whole northern army. In 1895 Yüan Shikai, ex-Resident at Seoul, had been appointed civil-commandant of the crack foreign-trained Tingwu division of five thousand troops. Yong Lu's elevation to the viceroyalty and army command therefore made him Yuan Shikai's direct superior. Yuan was in his prime, and Yong Lu already in his late sixties.[25]

YONG LU, VICEROY OF ZHILI, GUARDIAN OF THE THRONE
commander-in-chief, the Northern Army

The rising head of steam behind the reform movement had already made it apparently an irresistible force. Domination of the antiquated Manchu system had become only a matter of time. But while the immovable object of the Empress Dowager's will power remained, a cataclysmic collision was inevitable. Both decide to pre-empt the issue. Control of the model army would settle it. Constitutionally the emperor, but actually the retired dowager held the key of loyalty. Yong Lu would obey Ci Xi's orders. Yüan Shikai favoured reform. Where did his loyalty lie? All her life Ci Xi had used time to her own advantage, while always ready to strike. She patiently played her reforming nephew's game, intending to consult Yong Lu privately on October 29 when they ventured to ride the fire-carriage to Tianjin.[26]

Guang Xü feared that at any moment she might veto his reforms and restrict his freedom. He knew her well. He decided to act. Whether on his own initiative or Kang Yuwei's advice he took the only course open to him and sent for Yüan Shikai, who 'convinced him of his zeal for reform'. He then gave him the brevet rank of vice-president of a ministry with responsibility for organising the army, making Yong Lu's northern army command subservient. Finally, on September 20 at a second audience, the emperor gave him a decree investing him with Yong Lu's offices of viceroy of Zhili and direct command of the northern army, and secret orders: he was to have Yong Lu decapitated and at once to bring the army to Peking, to surround and imprison the Empress Dowager in her Summer Palace, and to arrest the leading reactionaries.[27]

Between the two audiences Ci Xi had told Guang Xü to arrest Kang Yuwei for slandering her, but instead he warned Kang to flee for his life, armed with an imperial order to establish the official *Gazette* in Shanghai. Kang at once went into hiding and consulted Timothy Richard, asking him to enlist the support of the British and American envoys. Richard was later rebuked by Sir Claude Macdonald for interfering in affairs of state, but at this crucial moment he and other envoys and Sir Robert Hart were absent from Peking and unable to help.

It so happened that Kang Yuwei and Yüan Shikai with his fateful orders travelled on September 20 by the same train to Tianjin. And Kang, preceded by telegrams to arrest him, after several narrow escapes in which British ships and officials protected him, reached Shanghai and later Europe in safety, with a price of one hundred thousand taels on his head.[28]

According to Yüan Shikai (in 1911 when his own reputation was at stake), as soon as he met Yong Lu at his *yamen* at Tianjin, Yong Lu said, 'You have come for my head!' claiming that he had already been told of Guang Xü's orders. Either he was bluffing to delude Yüan Shikai, or palace eunuchs had moved to save Ci Xi. But in 1898 the common knowledge believed by the foreign envoys, the reformers and 'generally by historians' after investigation, was very different. By it he reached Tianjin before noon and at once re-minded Yong Lu that they were blood-brothers by a pact unknown to the emperor. Because of it he could not carry out his orders and instead revealed the whole plot. Yong Lu left immediately for Peking and the Summer Palace. Ci Xi called in her trusted advisers and with a full plan of counteraction decided, Yong Lu returned to Tianjin the same night. As commanded by the emperor the model army moved on Peking, but to surround the Forbidden City instead of Ci Xi in the Summer Palace.[29]

On the morning of September 22 the emperor was to give audience to Marquis Ito, a Japanese statesman, but was himself summoned by Ci Xi. 'Like a rabbit mesmerised by a snake' he cowered before her; 'his whole body trembled . . . and his powers of speech left him.' She forced him to sign a decree reinstating her as Regent and confined him to prison on a promontory jutting into the Winter Palace lake, the laughing-stock of lesser eunuchs. 'The Emperor being ill, the Empress Dowager has resumed the Regency' (for the third time) the world was told. 'This gave rise to considerable anxiety, since it seemed to suggest that with her aid 'Guang Xü would very soon mount the Dragon and go to join his ancestors.'

The real enemy, foreign devils   *September–December 1898*

Li Hongzhang was still China's most astute statesman. This trifling with emperors angered him. And Viceroy Liu Kunyi (p 265) bravely broke his silence to protest in a memorial against it. But Zhang Zhitong quickly played safe by urging action against the culprits. The British and other ministers left no doubt in the minds of the Zongli Yamen that they would take strong action if the emperor's life were endangered, for several navies immediately headed northward – another factor in his survival and possibly in the fate of the legations eighteen months later. Liang Qichao, editor of *Chinese Progress*, escaped by a hair's breadth to Japan, and a few other leading reformers, but six of the most notable were executed. Others suffered the even harder sentence of exile to the deserts. Yong Lu was elevated to 'a position of power unprecedented in the history of the dynasty', and a decree on September 26 swept away many of the reforms, restored the sinecures and anachronisms, including the hoary sword-brandishing military examinations, but retained some of the educational measures.

As soon as she had suspected what was afoot Ci Xi had sent for the 'coarse old rough-neck' Tong Fuxiang and his twelve thousand Muslim cavalry from Gansu, and thousands more troops from other frontiers to congregate near the capital. The uniform answer from Tong's men when asked where they were going was 'to drive the Germans at Jiaozhou into the sea'.[30] From then on, the unsettled state of the empire owed as much to this fact as to the palace intrigues. What was afoot? The riots of the spring and summer were followed by more at Canton on October 25, by the first CIM death from violence in November, and by attacks at Yizhou, Shandong, on a German and three Americans. In December two Catholic missionaries were murdered at Yizhou and their missions destroyed.[31]

But for miles around Peking itself the chief danger to foreigners lay in the teeming presence of the 'turbulent soldiery', of whom the most unbridled were Tong Fuxiang's horsemen, the savagery of the Xining siege fresh in their memories. When some of them attacked members of the American and British legations on September 30, the foreign envoys all sent for their marines to guard them. The approaching winter made early action imperative. In deep winter the frozen sea and land routes could make protection impossible. But on October 23 Tong's men again attacked some engineers and British legation personnel, without being disciplined. The attitude of troops and rowdies became so menacing that the envoys jointly demanded the removal of the Gansu troops to a distance. This placed the court and government in a dilemma, for while unruly troops were present in force the dynasty itself was at risk. Probably by filling the pockets of Tong and his generals, Morse thought, they withdrew a mere eighty miles eastwards, only to bring terror to the foreign residents of Tongzhou.

In late December 1898 a Tongzhou correspondent of a Shanghai paper summed it up with blood-curdling restraint. Tong Fuxiang's cavalry rode, he said,

> At a slow trot, in compact companies of fifty; with waving silk banners and fluttering scarlet cloaks and long red-tufted lances quivering in their hands like reeds . . . so conscious of their strength and their power to crush foreigners, when the word is given, that they look on them more with pitying contempt than with active dislike . . .
>
> Something unusual is under way; and if the Empress Dowager has undertaken the overturning of the whole Imperial policy towards foreigners, she has taken good care to gather troops enough to ensure the success of her policy, however ruthless. Everywhere, in both city and county, we hear the same tale, that all foreigners are to be killed

or driven out, and that our day is close at hand. These remarks are seldom made to us personally . . . but the ears of native helpers and converts are filled with them . . . The feeling of unrest . . . merely includes the dispassionate though agreeable conviction [sic] that our lives are drawing to a close.[32]

'Killed for the present'   *October 1898–99*

The Hundred Days were over; the reform movement looked dead. Its resurrection seemed to its sympathisers an impossible dream. But not to its promoters. Spurred on by the offers of blood-money, the hunters of Sun Yatsen, Kang Yuwei and Liang Qichao stayed hot on their trails. Uncowed they continued to work for the reformation and were rewarded for their courage only twelve years later. Far from being 'a Manchu family quarrel', as undiscerning foreigners chose to say, the clash between progressives and obscurants had exposed a major rift, a geological fault in the political bedrock of the nation. The old Manchus, in the ascendancy again for a few brief years, made audacity their policy. A show of strength, a scorn of aliens quickly became their attitude while they used them to press forward the modernisations of which they did approve. On October 10, 1898, in the heat of change, an Anglo-Chinese loan contract for railroad development in north China was signed. As late as December 2, 1899, a Franco-Belgian east-west railway across Henan received approval.[33] Seen from the side of imperialism, deep cuts in the melon were still being made, with areas of influence and exploitation in vogue until the American 'open door' policy, welcomed by Britain, restored the sanity of unrestricted competition.

The remarkable world traveller and author, Isabella Bird (1831–1904), (married at fifty to a Dr John Bishop (1881–86) but widowed) arrived at Shanghai in January 1896 as the guest of Hudson Taylor and the CIM at Wusong Road and travelled for most of the year through Sichuan to the Tibetan marches and back.[34] Ascending the Yangzi gorges and crossing Sichuan from Wanxian through Langzhong, she braved the terrors of crowds shouting 'Kill the foreigner' as well as the dangers of rapids and mountain tracks and Tibetan passes in the snow. Her firm conviction, supported by many good photographs, that China was far from breaking up or decaying, as Lord Charles Beresford declared, she based on observation of the strong personalities and industrious lives of the people. She could

THE CASSELS' HOME IN LANGZHONG, SICHUAN

see that China's economy was growing strongly and that humiliation at the hands of Japan and the West had been a spur to revival. Reaction took time to penetrate the empire. At Langzhong as the Cassels' guest she saw the need of a hospital and forthwith bought and presented to the Mission a Chinese mansion, in memory of her sister. The Henrietta Bird Memorial Hospital went from strength to strength until the end of the Open Century, and afterwards developed into a medical college at Nanchong (Shunking).

Writing on October 24, 1898, from Guangyuan near the Sichuan-Shaanxi border, Montagu Beauchamp said of the reform movement, 'In fact there is a widespread rumour that the Emperor has believed, and ordered the temples to be turned into schools. [The truth was that the edict merely ordered that schools be opened *in* temples.] Let me quote a FACT. We have proclamations in this city, coming from the Central Government, declaring that the ancient teaching of Confucius is out of date, and therefore Western learning must be taught in all schools, if China is to hold her own with other powers.' His own comment was, 'All this will attract more attention than ever to the Gospel.'[35]

The effect on foreign missions, Catholic and Protestant, took many forms, related to wide differences in their activities. The Roman Catholics largely stood aloof from the reform movement, although it had been the early Catholics at Peking who used Western science as an effective key to the heart of the empire. Instead, in 1899 they took a different sensational leap into notoriety with startling consequences, as we shall see. Western learning could be obtained almost solely in Protestant institutions, while the universities and schools projected by Guang Xü's edicts were in preparation.

In 1897 the Methodist Free Church at Wenzhou was teaching English in its high school,[36] and at Hangzhou the American Presbyterian high school became a college. The Canadian Mission Press was established in Sichuan in 1897, and the West China Religious Tract Society in 1889 as a product of the inter-mission conference at Chongqing convened by Hudson Taylor. The Presbyterian missions in Manchuria had more appeals for evangelists and teachers than could be responded to, yet church membership rose from under eight thousand in 1896 to almost twenty thousand in 1899. In Fujian a similar expansion took place, and in 1898 the CIM reported 1,029 baptisms, with the number in Shaanxi increased threefold and in Henan, another resistant province, by sixty per cent.

After John R Mott's visit to China, student groups connected with the YMCA grew rapidly. Germany's occupation of Jiaozhou (Kiaochow now Jiao Xian) led to three societies moving into the area, a short-sighted action which again stamped Christianity indelibly with the brand-mark of imperialism.[37] The favours shown to the reforming missionaries, and the subsequent demonstration of their success, went far towards substantiating the divergence between what J K Fairbank has called the evangelical and the 'secular' missionary. 'Professionalisation' of missions (especially in medicine and education) 'increasingly divorced from evangelical aims', resulted in about four hundred higher level institutions in the next eight years.[38]

On March 16, 1899, a growing trend in Catholic practice received imperial approval by the issue of a rescript on the access by Catholic missionaries to mandarins. Since 1860 the Catholic hierarchy in China had assumed official status by imitating the mandarins in dress and appearances in public. Official cap buttons, formal sedan chairs preceded by a formal 'thousand name umbrella', even the firing of cannon on their arrival at a town, and the issue of proclamations in the official form, had all appropriated to themselves the honours and dignities of officials. By the March rescript recognising these practices the Peking government was seen to wish to deal directly with the Church instead of through the French protectorate. Bishops were to have access to viceroys and governors and to rank with them, leading priests with *daotais* and priests with prefects and magistrates. The move miscarried terribly – unless Ci Xi's deep scheming anticipated the resentment which 'an empire within the empire' would stir up against the Church. 'Extra-territorial' rights already accorded foreigners greater freedom from the arm of the Chinese law than even the literate of China enjoyed (HTCOC Book 1, pp 265, 272–3).

When the *North China Daily News* of May 19 pointed out that under the 'most favoured nation' clause Protestants automatically enjoyed the same privileges as Catholics, Arnold Foster (HTCOC Book 6, pp 168, 171) addressed the editor in terms of this lapse by the Chinese government (in yielding to French pressure) as 'one of the gravest importance to the future of China as a nation, and also to the future of Christian Missions'. He spoke of 'the danger to the peace and well-being of the Chinese people, danger to the interests of all foreigners living in China and . . . danger to the very life of the Christian Church . . .' He quoted Sir Rutherford Alcock in *The Times* of September 13, 1886, in which he denounced the whole system of priestly interference in the political affairs of China. To it he attributed 'the perennial hostility towards Christianity and its teachers in every form, which now pervades the whole nation.' When the Chinese government made a determined stand against Catholic pretensions, Sir Rutherford said, 'It is in the interest of religion and of all foreign nations that they (the Chinese) should not fail.' Arnold Foster found it easy to imagine that the shrewd Chinese were trying to play off Catholics against Protestants as two rival religions, and France against the Protestant nations. Refusal of the same privileges would expose Protestant Christians and missionaries to persecution by pagan and Catholic alike, but it was vital that political status should be rejected if the purity of the Chinese Church was not to be compromised.

From the first, Protestant rejection of the actions and privileges was almost unanimous, though some were slow to understand.[39] In September 1899 the Anglican bishops in conference protested against growing Catholic interference in provincial and local government and courts of law. But the damage had been done.

Nationwide resentment already threatened the safety of Catholics and Protestants alike.

The CIM's first martyr   *November 1898*

Yü Manzi's rampaging in Sichuan led the consuls in Chongqing to send foreign women downriver to safety, but by November 1898 all seemed quiet. The Hudson Taylors set off up the Yangzi on November 15 with the Charles Inwoods of Keswick for conferences in Hankou and Chongqing. On the 18th a *North China Daily News* 'Extra' carried a telegram from Chongqing,

> MURDER OF MISSIONARIES. Mr W S Fleming, a China Inland missionary, and a native evangelist were murdered on 4 inst. at Panghai (Guizhou). (The Kueifu RC mission, Sichuan, was all burned down two days after the new viceroy passed.)

London papers quoted it on the 21st. After thirty-three years of courting danger, the CIM had lost its first member in this way.

A young Scotsman who had settled in Australia after five years at sea, Fleming had been in China since 1885, and at Panghai only a month (map p 223). He and two 'Black Miao' evangelists both named Pan were starting on a two-week journey together to Miao villages when they ran into trouble. Roving bands of robbers and rebels, said to be encouraged by Yü Manzi's success against foreigners, were pillaging the countryside. Fleming decided to return to Guiyang, but had ridden only ten miles on November 4 when armed men attacked them. Seeing one of his companions, Pan Shoushan, wounded, Fleming dismounted to help him, instead of escaping, and both were cut down by a cavalry sword. The other evangelist made good his escape and took the news to Guiyang.

Local mandarins fabricated a report that Fleming had been supplying the Miao with weapons, but after full investigation the verdict was reached: 'There is no doubt that the murder had been arranged by the leading men of the district.' Whatever the facts, confused and contradictory accounts could not conceal the truth that this was one of the earliest instances of deliberate violence against foreigners following the counter-reformation coup at Peking. When the consul proceeded to claim an indemnity, Hudson Taylor intervened, writing to W B Sloan in London,

We hear that the Consul here had kindly thought to help Mr Fleming's parents by claiming for them £2,500 . . . (Could you) use your influence with them not to accept this money as . . . the effect on the Chinese will be bad; in the Kucheng massacres the CMS refused all blood-money. To the Chinese it will seem as if the parents were quite satisfied to sell their son. It is a pity to encourage the idea that the lives of missionaries can be paid for.[40]

By December the lull had ended and 'unsettlement all over China' was causing greater anxiety than ever. The counter-reformation had gathered strength and ominous things were happening. When Alicia Bewicke Little quoted the Tongzhou correspondent's words, 'Our lives are drawing to a close' (p 282) she added, 'We all read it, and some of us – thought a good deal.'

PART 4

THE BOXER MADNESS

1898–1900

CHAPTER TEN

NO LIGHT BEYOND NEW YORK
1898–1900

The rise of the Boxers   *1898–1900*

'The times are too ticklish to go in for adventures . . . caution and discretion are everywhere necessary,' wrote Sir Robert Hart to his commissioner, Hosea Ballou Morse, on October 24, 1898.[1] Beneficial regulations for the control by the customs service of steamers on inland waters were resulting in greatly increased traffic. Cargo ships and launches towing trains of Chinese lighters were ruining the age-old sailing junk trade as railways were stealing the livelihood of carters and muleteers. In March 1899 the anger of the junk men, already incensed by the crop failure in central China, erupted at Zhenjiang and Yangzhou in anti-foreign incendiarism and rioting. Hunan, to the surprise of all who had known the bitter spirit of the province in the past, agreed to the opening of Yueyang (Yochow), at the entrance to the Dongting Lake system from the Yangzi, as a trading port (map p 251). As titular commissioner of customs at Hankou in 1899, Morse was responsible for establishing good relations with the gentry of the province. In this he had the backing of Zhang Zhitong and the wisdom and long experience of Griffith John to help him. Morse quoted John as saying as late as May 23, 1900, 'that the complete transformation of the Hunanese into friendliness still continued.' In comparison with the rest of China, Hunan was peaceful, but only relatively.

Risings in the famine-stricken areas of northern Jiangsu and Anhui and in western Hubei had their echoes south of the Yangzi. On January 20, 1899, W J Hunnex, his wife and three children were attacked at Nanyang, the capital of Jiangxi. Travelling past the city on a little boat, they suddenly 'saw boats full of excited men and women closing in on all sides . . . A number of women, who seemed beside themselves with passion, crowded on to our boat, and kneeling down knocked their heads (on the deck) before us, at the same time screaming violently and demanding that we should give up the *four dead children* whom we had stolen and were taking away.' The sight of foreigners had started a rumour. It had swelled into a battle-cry and instantly drew the crowds, crying 'Kill the child-stealers.' Their extreme danger ended as suddenly. Providentially rescued by missionaries of another society who were nearby in a larger boat, and by river police, they got away unharmed.[2]

In June and August Zhejiang, Fujian and Yunnan saw dangerous unrest. Sam Pollard was told that his name was on a hit-list of victims when the time became ripe. At Jian'ou (Kienning) in northern Fujian the CMS premises were burned and a Christian killed, three missionaries barely escaping with their lives.[3]

After Dr Keller's 'house-warming' at Chaling in Hunan (p 94) in March 1899, and insistence that his landlord should be compensated in full while he himself would take nothing, he struck up a warm friendship with the magistrate's son, Han Xiaoye. Then in May he was called to attend Han's wife, in obstructed labour for three days, and saved not only hers but their child's life, too. During June he had narrow escapes at Hengshan and Hengzhou, west of Chaling, where LMS and Catholic premises were destroyed and three Italian priests killed, mutilated and burned. But he was at Xiangtan, south of the provincial capital, Changsha, where 'great crowds followed me . . . two miles to the ferry. Shouts of "Beat!" and "Kill!" filled the air and some of the mob began to strike me. God raised up a friend for me; a man of evident power sprang to my side, shouted to the mob "Don't strike him; he is leaving; isn't that enough for you?" . . . This man stayed by me all the way to the ferry, constantly holding back the crowd.'

Returning to Chaling he and a colleague were told of a rumour being circulated that an imperial decree to kill all foreigners was on its way. Han Xiaoye was deputising for his father the magistrate and kept armed patrols on the streets to nip trouble in the bud. But a force of men from Hengzhou came through the city saying they were on the way to the coast to kill foreign devils. 'Why don't you kill (them here)? We have killed them all at Hengzhou, they are being killed all over China . . . Take us to their hall and we will do the job for you.'[4]

Han tried to persuade the men to leave Chaling, and took Dr Keller and his companion into his own residence, but he himself 'looked pale and worn (and) could not eat'. A copy of a decree from the Empress Dowager had in fact been received by the anti-foreign element at Chaling, and he expected the *yamen* to be destroyed and his father and himself to be killed. Keller at once insisted on leaving, so Han enlisted friendly members of the Golaohui secret society to escort them to the Yangzi, starting at midnight. 'An almost uninter-rupted tirade of threats and curses' accompanied them, but Keller reached Shanghai safely on August 31. Instead of his feeling relief, the extreme test of nerve had angered and embittered him. He arrived determined to demand compensation whatever Hudson Taylor might say.

The fact emerged later on that in Jiangxi and Hunan the Roman Catholics were being identified with the Taipings who had stormed through the provinces fifty years earlier (HTCOC Book 2, pp 78–9). In October the prefect at Changsha promised Edward Pearse to reinstate Keller at Chaling, and on December 6 he reoccupied his house, destroyed in June but rebuilt for him. Perhaps most notable in these events was the friendliness of the mandarins, from the viceroy to the junior magistrate, whatever the temper of the rabble rousers.

The history of events at Hengzhou also deserves more attention. In 1892 a native of Changsha named Peng, 'from being the wildest and worst of characters, had been transformed' after his conversion through Christians baptised by Griffith John. 'So remarkable was his conversion . . . that one of the leading publishers of the vile pamphlets of 1891 came to Hankou expressly to . . . learn what (had) produced the change in (Peng).' In 1897 Griffith John found twenty to thirty believers at Hengzhou asking for baptism, and left Peng to teach them, with the result that by 1899 out of hundreds of adherents 192 were baptised. But a year later they and their chapels became the target of renewed attack during the Boxer madness.[5]

Meanwhile, in Sichuan, Yü Manzi's fortunes had waxed and waned. From malice towards Roman Catholics his aim had become the expulsion or destruction of all foreigners. But on January 20, 1899, he was forced to release M Fleury and surrendered to strong government forces. Spared the executioner's sword he was even given parole, either in the hope that defeat and leniency would be enough of a lesson, or from sympathy with his aims. H B Morse, after long acquaintance with corruption, inferred that 'silver bullets played as great a part in the suppression as lead'. During a lull before Yü Manzi renewed his attacks, the eighty members of the inter-mission conference at Chongqing (to which we shall return) were able to disperse again to their homes. Then the uprising was renewed and spread widely with a big riot at Nanchong (Shunking) after Yü Manzi was re-arrested.[6]

The influence of Yü Manzi spread to neighbouring provinces and communities (engulfing Fleming and Pan) and extended to the Muslims of Gansu and Xinjiang who called for a *jehad*, to Hubei via the Golaohui, and to Shaanxi where 'a great conspiracy to exterminate foreigners' was reported. Riots and destruction in too many places to be named sometimes enveloped CIM missionaries. At Yangzhou secret meetings of the Golaohui and Dadaohui ('the Great Swords') planned rebellion against the Manchus, sensing that the opportunity had come to destroy the Qing and re-establish a Han Chinese dynasty. A clash between Russian Cossacks and Chinese in Manchuria resulted in ninety-four killed and 123 wounded. Russia had to pay full compensation, but too late. The hatred stirred up by this massacre took a greater toll. 'In every province in the empire there had been unrest, riot or rebellion through the whole of 1899 and continuing into 1900; mission stations had been attacked in every province, and railway engineers in Yunnan and (Shandong), the only classes of foreigners who were not ordinarily in the shelter of the treaty ports.'

High-handed action by Germany, and demands by Italy for a mid-China anchorage at Sanmen Bay in Zhejiang (map p 94) on the same terms as Qingdao, buttressed by four 14,000-ton cruisers with 110 guns, drove the Peking government to put the armed forces on a war footing. Italy backed down, but preparations continued throughout the year 1899, accompanied by hate-filled yet justifiable edicts from the dowager empress against alien intrusions. 'The various powers cast upon us looks of tiger-like ferocity . . . It behoves all our Viceroys, Governors and Commanders-in-chief . . . to unite together and act . . . so as to present a combined front to the enemy . . .' Foreign aggression and imperial reaction, therefore, fuelled the spreading anti-foreign feeling, while to the superstitious, drought and famine showed Heaven's displeasure at China's tolerance of such treatment. Ci Xi appointed Kangyi, as rabid a Manchu reactionary as existed in all China, to raise large sums of money for her coffers. With Gilbert and Sullivan holding the London stage, Kangyi became known by the press as the 'Lord High Extortioner'. Passed down from superior to inferior, his demands hit the common taxpayers most severely and intensified their resentments.

In Shandong tensions rose to snapping point after three German engineers were attacked by villagers and in retaliation German soldiers razed their villages and took five of the gentry as hostages. Military 'exercises' were mounted as a demonstration to the Ger-

A BOXER RECRUIT AT DRILL
from a drawing by Savage Landor

mans. Yüan Shikai with 5,500 men, Tong Fuxiang with 9,000 Gansu veterans, and 7,500 others like 'the brave old Duke of York' marched into Shandong – and returned to Zhili within a month. Anger and frustration at the foreigner largely out of reach could only be vented upon Christian villagers. A secret society or association of societies calling itself the Yihochuan came to the notice of the *North China Herald* in September 1899. Including the Dadaohui or Great Swords and many criminals and riff-raff, it had ostensibly been formed for the promotion of boxing and gymnastics.[7] Mystic rites of initiation and training made them invulnerable, they believed, to bullet, spear or sword. At a demonstration to Ci Xi one fired a musket at another who stood unscathed and 'spat the ball out of his mouth'. Ci Xi was impressed. Perhaps blank cartridges and this conjuror's trick were little known in the palace.

'*Yi-ho-chuan*' could be understood as 'Association for Justice and Harmony' (a euphemism) or as 'Fist of Patriotic Union', the truer sense, for after May 26, 1899, when the association had come into being, their banners carried four characters. '*Fan Qing Mie Yang*', meaning 'Overthrow the Qing; exterminate the foreigner'. Newspaper reporters then introduced the word 'Boxers', for the first time in print, but there was nothing flippant about the Boxers' intentions. Chinese officials and gentry aided and shielded the Boxers, and a military mandarin who arrested some was himself assassinated. Troops sent to control them were withdrawn on the orders of Ci Xi's henchman Yü Xian, the governor of Shandong since March, and their commander was dismissed although he was Yüan Shikai's brother.

In October a tell-tale and sinister change in the slogan to 'Uphold the dynasty; exterminate foreigners', betrayed collusion at the highest levels, the espousal of the Boxers for the palace's own ends. By the turn of the year the Boxer movement had spread far into Zhili. The new factor of alliance between anti-foreign officialdom and the Boxer movement looked convincingly like a device 'to prevent popular, anti-foreign feeling from being turned against them'. Certainly Ci Xi increasingly took their part and used them as her tools, perhaps with the foresight to think that if they were not destroyed in the approaching hostilities, she could complete the process herself when it suited her.[8]

On December 31, 1899, a twenty-four-year-old Anglican (SPG) missionary in Shandong, S M Brooks was attacked by a band of men wearing red headcloths – with red girdles the symbol of the Boxers soon to be feared far and wide. When he broke away mounted men chased and beheaded him.[9] The first Boxer martyr had fallen.

To Chongqing in spite of Yü Manzi   1898–99

Looking back to 1898, the strain on Hudson Taylor of political tensions from the time of his arrival in China on January 15, 1898, until he left for Australia on September 25, 1899, a year and nine months later, led him to develop his 'leisure interests'. When sapped by the heat or an excess of demands on his time and strength, he would go up to Chefoo or to one of the new hill resorts of Guling or Moganshan near Shanghai. For the first time he mentioned in a letter that they were boiling their drinking water as a precaution against disease. At Chefoo he enjoyed conferring with E J Cooper, building the schools and sanatorium. Jennie Taylor wrote that when he was doing this he was at his best in health and spirits. A note records his instructions for insulating ceilings with sawdust covered by two inches depth of sand as a fire precaution. Another asks for all his photographic equipment to be sent, and again of talking photography with a nephew. He planned to buy a quarter-plate lens. Others mention his veranda greenhouse and tropical plants at Shanghai. When John Stevenson drove himself too hard, Hudson Taylor wrote urging him to get regular exercise and fresh air, implying that he did so himself.[10]

But nothing suited Hudson Taylor better than travelling, away from the pressure and out among the Chinese he loved. When Yang Cunling (HTCOC Book 6, Index) brought his son to meet Hudson Taylor on the river-boat at Wuhu it was an emotional moment. Children always attracted him, and a prayer and patriarchal blessing would have been most natural in their relationship. 'To watch the head of the Mission entertain (Chinese) friends with simple, unaffected and expert politeness was an example . . .', the missionary at Ningguo wrote. Much more so his brothers in Christ.

In an unusually agitated letter to John Stevenson, Jennie complained that Hudson had gone up the Yangzi to Jiujiang and Jiangxi without a Chinese or missionary companion, knowing full well that dysentery or hostile people could endanger his life. Her distress was misplaced. He had soon found someone to travel with him and was in his element. Inspecting premises Herbert Taylor and his family were to occupy at Guangde, he saw that whoever had rented them in a quiet by-lane had failed to discover that the neighbouring houses were brothels. No respectable people would be seen near them. As a mission centre the premises were worthless. His accountant son, Ernest, volunteered to be a 'forward movement' pioneer, and joined Dr F H Judd at the newly occupied Jiangxi city of Shangrao (known then as Raochow). For nine months Howard Taylor had been acting as superintendent in Henan while suffering from intractable dysentery. When he asked to be replaced and freed to get proper treatment, his father confessed that he had no one available to take over. He urged Howard to stay on, for 'we ought to lay down our lives for the brethren'. Then he invited Dixon Hoste, at last in better health, to become superintendent in Henan instead of Shanxi.[11]

Returning by canal boat through Hangzhou and his 'old haunts' of forty years before, Hudson Taylor claimed to be in better health than at any time in the last three years. But only a few months later he was at Guling again, febrile and bewildered, troubled ubout the spiritual morale of the Mission being in decline at a time of deepening crisis in China. 'A fiery trial' might be what would do most good. Like Griffith John, certain that effort, zeal and organisation achieved little without 'a close walk with God', he was doing all he could to help members reach and live by conviction of this truth; '"Not by might, nor by power, but by My Spirit," says the Lord of Hosts.' And Henrietta Soltau was being so successful as a missionary to missionaries that he persuaded her to extend her time in China. It would be better to close the women candidates department in London than to lose opportunities to help those who 'are not spiritually equal to the harass and strain of the present crisis in China.' Other missions were sharing in the benefits her visit brought.[12]

As Dr A T Pierson could not come, the Keswick Convention council took up Hudson Taylor's request and not only sent Charles Inwood and his wife to China but other representatives as a 'Keswick mission to missionaries' in other continents as well. Societies in Shanghai and the south and north of China welcomed the Inwoods to conduct conferences for them, and on November 15, 1898, the Hudson Taylors and Inwoods started up the Yangzi to the far west. Wherever they held meetings the gratitude of widely differing types of missionary showed how timely and appropriate their teaching was. The 'perilous, long and difficult journey' up the Yangzi rapids brought them to Chongqing on January 7, 1899.[13]

There the inter-mission conference Hudson Taylor had convened drew up to eighty missionaries of seven Protestant societies from Guizhou, Sichuan and Yunnan, and members of the business and customs community. After a week of meetings (January 16–21) they asked for a second week. Many more were prevented from attending by the dangerous conditions in Sichuan. Out of it came not only spiritual renewal but a comity agreement on the division of Sichuan to avoid duplication of effort, a standing inter-mission 'committee on polity', and the West China Religious Tract Society, a monthly *West China Missionary News*, and a condemnation of the opium traffic 'by a rising vote'.

Before the conference ended, news came of Yü Manzi's first surrender, and on January 24 Charles Parsons set out for Lang-zhong (Paoning), expecting William Cassels to follow with the Hudson Taylors a week later. Parsons had come through unscathed when 'dragged and driven' out of Nanchong, and when rescued by the magistrate from a riot at Langzhong in 1895 (map p 223). But this time he came closer to losing his life. The prefect at Chongqing had sent four unarmed soldiers to escort him and a Chinese Christian by boat up the Jialing River. But on the way they were attacked by about two hundred men commanded by an adopted son of Yü Manzi. The Christian bravely defended Parsons, warding off the spears until wounded himself, so Parsons jumped into the river from which he was hauled by a government patrol and defended until dark. He arrived back at Chongqing still wet but none the worse for his experience. A week later he and Cassels tried again, hidden in a boat, and reached Langzhong safely. But the Taylors again had to abandon as untimely their long-deferred plan to visit the Sichuan stations.

Hudson Taylor had missed conference sessions through illness, and before the end of January developed 'influenza'. By February 10 he was 'more ill (with bronchitis) than Jennie had ever known him'. News and correspondence were kept from him. They were still in Chongqing on March 1, but back in Shanghai on April 6. He saw the Inwoods off to Britain on May 24 and went up to Chefoo, but incapacitating headaches and then dysentery limited the work he could do. Instead, Jennie carried his heavy load of correspondence, under his guidance but revealing her own efficiency and spirit. Typically she advised a fraught mother, 'Try praising because it is His way.' But the truth had become plain to them that at sixty-seven, looking and feeling much older, his active days were coming to an end.[14]

Cooper's worth   1898–1900

In 1898 when William Cooper was run over and seriously injured while away in Britain, Hudson Taylor had written to Walter Sloan, 'The Lord preserve his precious life.' And in March 1899 while William Cooper was conducting meetings in Canada at Hudson Taylor's request, 'his life is of priceless value to the Mission, far more so than my own.' 'More than my own'? Because Cooper had many active years ahead of him while Hudson Taylor's own end was in sight? Or is the inference that Hudson Taylor wished Cooper to be known in North America before promoting him further as a leader or the leader of the CIM?[15]

A few weeks earlier, in January 1899, William Sharp and the

London Council had again raised the matter of John Stevenson's alleged unpopularity. 'Think of the difficulty . . . if you were taken without having first installed an acceptable leader and director in China . . . Surely the *one* must be sacrificed rather than the *many*, and also rather than risk the break-up of the Mission.' Sharp went so far as to draft the wording of a letter for Hudson Taylor to send to Stevenson, asking him to retire. 'There is perhaps one other course . . . to place the responsibility of the matter on the London Council, who are in a better and more independent position for doing what is best for the Mission than anyone else'! The lesson of years of disharmony seemed forgotten.

Yet again, William Sharp and, so it turned out, Theodore Howard and the London Council failed to understand their role in the management of the CIM, their relationship to the other councils, or the principle that affairs in China were beyond their competence. W B Sloan, 'a rock of strength', and Marcus Wood were 'quite admirable' in Britain, and William Cooper had the full confidence of the council in London, but, as Theodore Howard wrote to Hudson Taylor in September over the signatures of Sharp and Richard Hill as representing the council, '(we) expect that you will not leave China (for Australia) without . . . Mr Stevenson retiring altogether from the post (of China Director). In Mr Cooper you have a tried man, loved, trusted and honoured by all his brethren and well qualified for the work. With him should be associated as his second in command a man of somewhat similar gifts, and proved ability, and one perhaps who has had a fuller educational training' – Dixon Hoste.[16] In the minds of some men the succession seemed clear.

Hudson Taylor kept his own counsel, but although 'London's' pressure verged on the unconstitutional, their thinking resembled his own – except for their unrelenting rejection of the faithful, wise and selfless John Stevenson, whatever some might say of him.

With the thermometer at 95°F the China Council met in July. Then the Taylors retreated to Moganshan. Although capable of less work, his grip on practical matters still showed no sign of diminishing and without question he knew what he was doing about a successor. But the time was not ripe to declare it. John Stevenson was 'open to God', had 'had a blessing' through Charles Inwood and was too valuable to lose. Hudson Taylor was content to watch developments. During these hot summer days the Hunan riots were taking place and Dr Keller was being hounded through Jiangxi, to reach Shanghai indignant and set on laying the matter before the consul-general. If the mission would not allow him to do so, he would resign and handle it himself. John Stevenson persuaded him to wait for Hudson Taylor.

> During our first interview [Keller recalled] Mr Taylor did not even refer to the subject. He discussed the work in general and asked my advice about the use of certain drugs, and when the dinner bell rang . . . asked me to call again at 3.00 o'clock. I felt guilty at taking up so much of his time and (at 3.00) said, 'Mr Taylor, I see the whole matter differently and am prepared to act as you may direct.' 'Thank God!' exclaimed Mr Taylor, . . . This experience was a turning point in my life; it taught me . . . how even strongly formed purposes can be changed, and how men's hearts can be influenced by prayer alone.[17]

By Dr Keller declining reparation in any form, while ensuring that his Chaling landlord was fully compensated, a lasting friendship with the city prefect was formed, to prove valuable when the Boxer madness flared.

Miracle in Toronto 1899

While missionaries and the Church in China were being tested and disciplined in many ways, the home countries were not immune. Since the beginnings in North America nine years before, the Toronto premises of the CIM had become inadequate for all that had developed. One hundred and thirty Canadian and American missionaries had been sent to China, apart from the Scandinavian associates. A move had to be made, and freehold ownership would avoid the constant drain of rental payments. But Henry Frost's bank balance was laughable. The ideal would be a large residence he had long known on the other side of the road, if ever it was for sale. Meanwhile, the CIM's landlord had raised the rent. Frost and his council prayed for a solution and in China Hudson Taylor prayed with them.

On the morning of January 9, 1899, the eighty-four-year-old William Berger dressed and came downstairs, sank on to a sofa and died.[18] By his will he left £1,000 to Hudson Taylor which he immediately passed on to Henry Frost – the largest single donation so far to come Frost's way. The next morning a 'FOR SALE' sign appeared on the property he thought suitable. Frost hurried to tell his colleague, Joshua S Helmer, and together they prayed that the place might become theirs. They then called on the owner, a Mr Somerville, who showed them round. It was as they thought, perfect in every way, with coach-house and stables which could become offices and a new billiard room large enough for meetings.

Mr Somerville knew nothing of the CIM, but when Henry Frost explained, he reduced the price to $13,000 and agreed to accept $5,000 in down payment. Hudson Taylor's £1,000 from William Berger was equivalent to $4,850. The balance of $8,000 they declined to secure by mortgage, on the Mission principle of not entering into debt of any kind. Instead Frost offered 'a unique proposition', that several well-known Council members would serve as trustees to pass on any sums received, acting for the CIM and for Mrs Somerville and her heirs. On payment being completed within thirty years, without financial obligation during that time, the deeds would be transferred to the Mission! To their surprise Mr Somerville signed a legal agreement on those extraordinary terms. Within ten days $2,000 more were paid, and the total sum within a year. What had cost the owner $23,000 he gave with all its carpets and fittings for $13,000. They called it Berger House. But 'Somerville House' would have been justified.[19]

Countdown to 1900   1898–1900

On September 11, 1899, Hudson Taylor wrote to Walter Sloan, 'The state of things in China is very serious just now – might I not say throughout the world . . . China weakened by insurrections within and torn to pieces by Romish intrigues will be powerless before any foreign power or powers who may attack her when England's hands are tied.' [The Boer War began on October 10.] And on September 23, two days before sailing to Australia, 'I am very sorry to leave China at this time; to miss Mr William Cooper and Bishop Cassels . . . but I feel it is now or never; for I cannot rush through all the work that urgently needs to be done in Australasia and be at New York for the (Ecumenical) Conference if I further delay.'[20]

His letter went on as fully, efficiently and to the point as any he had ever written. Franson, he wrote, had sent some of his first fifty 'on the strength of faith healing views, which their health record did not otherwise warrant; and very naturally these broke down and (died or) had to return [with advanced tuberculosis]. The proportion of them who have made really valuable workers is so good that

it compares very well with workers sent from (other countries).'
Sloan was preparing to visit North America and afterwards to
continue Charles Inwood's work of reviving missionaries in China.
Hudson Taylor continued by analysing the record of the thirty-six
of Franson's first American Scandinavians still in China, and by
statistically comparing all his men and women with the CIM's
reinforcements in the same period from Australia, North America
and Britain. The same number in each group had died, but fewer of
Franson's parties had withdrawn.

The loss of William Berger, a faithful friend of many years, could
not but move Hudson Taylor deeply, but during these months his
grief was renewed again and again. The death of eight or nine
members of the Mission (leaving 816 on May 25, 1899) compared
very 'satisfactorily' with the losses suffered by other societies and
with public health figures in the West. But the death of George
Müller at ninety-two on March 10, 1898, after seven decades of
Christian service, andArthur Douthwaite's distress after his second
wife died, were only the beginning. James Adam of Guizhou had
lost his wife from toxaemia, and in May 1898 was shattered by the
death in convulsions of his second wife from the same cause. In the
same month the Scandinavian Alliance lost both their leaders in
Shaanxi, Henriksen and Carlsson, from typhus. During the 'Hundred Days' of reform and the start of the Yü Manzi rebellion,
Hudson Taylor's brother-in-law, Samuel Dyer, the Bible Society
representative, died in Shanghai and two more old friends in
England: Montagu Beauchamp's mother and Mrs Grattan Guinness, Geraldine's mother, on November 3. In Australia his saintly
old friend Philip Kitchen, treasurer of the Melbourne Council, died
in October of pneumonia. On October 22 the 'indispensable'
Thomas Botham died of typhus at Lanzhou, and on November 4
W S Fleming was murdered at Panghai. William Soutter, of the
Tibetan Pioneer Band, died on the Tibetan heights in December.

It was almost as if Hudson Taylor like Job was being inured to
such news in preparation for worse. Frequently one or another, and
sometimes several missionaries together were fighting for their lives
with typhoid or typhus, some of Hudson Taylor's own family among
them. In 1899 four valuable leaders returned to China after home
leave. E O Williams died of typhoid in July, within six weeks of
reaching Sichuan; Dr Douthwaite himself of dysentery on October
6; and George Hunter of Hunan of malaria on March 12, 1900.
William Cooper was to be the fourth. For D L Moody 'Heaven

opened' on December 22, 1899. 'This is no dream,' he said. 'It is beautiful . . . so wonderful. If this is death it is sweet.' And later, 'I went to the gate of heaven. Why, it is so wonderful!'[21]

In the explosive atmosphere of those days, sad news had to be absorbed with the excitements – the frequent riots and escapes, the coups and counter-coups – and with the flood of good news constantly coming of the eight hundred missionaries and seven hundred Chinese colleagues in nearly two hundred centres. Archibald Orr Ewing reported two hundred baptisms in Jiangxi, with eight hundred to one thousand promising candidates under instruction. In Shanxi, a Church conference at Linfen (Pingyang) under Pastor Hsi's successor Elder Si, showed every sign of Christian maturity and readiness to face greater persecution if it were to come. Si's own example of maturity had echoed Hsi's under attack by his rival, Fan (p 65). An influential man, jealous of Si's preferment by the churches, opposed him bitterly. But when this enemy died, Si took his widow and three children under his own protection. In China as a whole sixty Protestant societies with 2,400 members reported a total of eighty-five thousand communicants. While CIM's 'forward movement' suffered from 'money but few men', the Church in China had begun to burgeon.[22]

Montagu Beauchamp, pioneer evangelist par excellence in East Sichuan, was facing a personal parting of the ways which many Anglicans have faced since his day. While his contemporaries in other provinces were drawing men and women to Christ and forming them into congregations, local churches under elders, deacons and pastors, Montagu being an unordained Anglican could neither baptise nor conduct a communion service. New Christians had to wait for an ordained man to visit them from elsewhere, and for William Cassels as bishop to confirm them. The system was a drag on the Sichuan church. Hudson Taylor sympathised, but could suggest only two alternatives, to be ordained and stay in East Sichuan, or to accept responsibility for an entirely pioneer field outside the Church of England area. The far south-western corner of Sichuan beyond the ranges where Colborne Baber and George Nicoll had explored (HTCOC Book 6 pp 142, 152, 415) still had no evangelist. With a base at Xichang (Ningyuan) he would have the whole Jianchang Valley as far as the River of Golden Sand (the Yangzi in the south) and the wild minority peoples in the mountains on each side, the Yi (or Nosu) in the Daliangshan and the Xifan, Naxi and Moso towards the Tibetan border. Beauchamp chose East

Sichuan and was famed as a prophetic and proverbial figure for decades to come. Xichang and the mountains had to wait until after the Second World War.

In the volcanic cauldron of China as 1899 ended anything could happen. No record has been found of any discussion or decision to continue in the hope of a return of peace as Peking regained control and prestige, or to withdraw (the women first) from any threatened region. Which region was more dangerous or more secure than any other? Chinese Christians could not leave. 'Stay on if you can, and by your calm confidence in God set an example,' seemed the right advice as it had always been. Henry Frost had put the Mission's united conviction into words when he declared in 1898,

> It is more than a possibility that not a few (of our fellow-workers) might be called to lay down their lives . . . Leave GOD out of account, and fear must possess and overwhelm us. Bring GOD into account and there is perfect peace . . . Satan is mighty, but GOD is almighty. Not one thing can man do which GOD does not allow to be done . . . Would He be less strong to keep in the hour of death than He has been in the days of life? . . . What is to be done for this generation (of Chinese) needs to be done at once, in spite of all danger. Let the cost be what it may, we must press quickly forward . . . Face to face then, with whatever the future has for us as a Mission . . . and because of threatenings, we ask the LORD's followers to go to those who threaten . . . since the very wickedness of their threatenings is the revelation of their need of CHRIST. We pray, therefore, for men and women whose lives have been cast by the SPIRIT into martyr-mould.[23]

A year later, when Hudson Taylor went to Australia, the threat had not diminished, but the Church had grown in strength and maturity. When rioters at Hekou on the Guangxin River destroyed and pillaged the Catholic and CIM premises, September 20–28, 1899, 'all the mandarins came' and took the women missionaries safely to the *yamen*; and the people of Hekou, indignant that outsiders had committed the outrage, rebuilt their home and welcomed them back.

'The great miscalculation'[24]

1900

An omen of disaster for the nation had occurred in the year of the hundred days of reform, a solar eclipse. Passing over Lhasa and

Inner Mongolia, its deep shadow had devoured five-sixths of the sun even at Peking, to feed the brooding fears of palace and people. Coming like a harbinger of doom before the fateful conjunction of an eighth intercalary month with the *gengzi* year of the lunar calendar (Appendix 8), an event last seen in AD 1680, the two ill-omens together promised calamity for dynasty and people alike. Ci Xi, the evil genius as shrewd as she was superstitious, chose to manipulate the omens to reassert the dominance of the Qing over both rebels and aggressors. In this she was not alone, for fatalism was the sure product of omens, and many chose to go down fighting. If the heavens foretold disaster, why not use disaster to some purpose? The secret societies set on restoring a Ming dynasty also took their opportunity to ferment civil convulsion. The food shortages from two years of drought across Hubei and North Anhui confirmed the omens and fired anger against the government and foreigners.

To deflect the anti-dynastic aims of the Golaohui and Yihochuan (the Boxers), Ci Xi chose to ride the tiger by aiding and abetting them against the hated barbarians. Proverbially, getting off a tiger becomes more dangerous than staying on. Memorials against the deposition of the emperor, and begging him not to abdicate were flooding in. Li Hongzhang, Liu Kunyi and Zhang Zhitong joined in the protests. But even as a prisoner Guang Xü remained a threat to Ci Xi and her faction. To eliminate him by death would bring trouble from Western nations, especially Britain, as much as from the great majority of younger officials and literati who admired him. When he was reported to be ill (like other victims before him), Sir Claude Macdonald warned that he must not 'die'. A French physician was allowed to examine him. Instead a decree in Guang Xü's name declared on January 24, 1900, that as he did not belong to the direct line of succession and had no heir, not only should a legal heir be appointed, but Pu Jün, the son of Prince Tuan, had already been selected as Prince Imperial. [See Ci Xi's plot to make the infant Zaitan emperor twenty-five years previously, HTCOC 5 pp 437–8.] Confronted by Ci Xi with a decree of abdication, Guang Xü was unwilling to sign it, until impelled by her menacing eyes and steely will to do so. Then with a blanched face he sank on to his chair, 'dyed his robe and the carpet with his life's blood from a burst blood vessel,' and was carried weeping all the way back to his prison.[25]

After the murder of S M Brooks in Shandong (p 296), those responsible were tried by a Chinese court and sentenced to death.

But Sir Claude reported to London that the governor of Shandong, Yü Xian himself, was the real culprit. While he and an ambiguous edict from the dowager empress encouraged the Boxers, no one could restore order. The American envoy, Major E H Conger, demanded Yü Xian's recall, and Yüan Shikai took his place. But Ci Xi received Yü Xian in audience 'with all the marks of favour'. When Yüan Shikai tried to suppress the Boxer trainbands he quickly learned to change his tune, by obstruction from Peking. The envoys of Britain, America, Germany, France and Italy then read the signs clearly and advised their respective governments that a joint naval demonstration was needed in the Gulf of Bohai, off Tianjin. It began on March 13. Ominously, three days later Yü Xian was appointed Governor of Shanxi. The envoys protested, but another two-faced edict against 'bad elements' in the Golaohui and Boxers successfully placated them and they withdrew the warships. Yü Xian arrived at Taiyuan on April 20, and Boxers began drilling in broad daylight, while posters declared, 'The Boxers' leader is a royal person.'[26]

Through the early months of 1900 tension increased all over China. Two British members of the Burma boundary commission were killed, and in Yunnan the message circulating through the bazaars and street restaurants was 'sharpen your weapons for the coming struggle', against the French in particular and their railway from Tongking. A Catholic missionary was wounded in clashes at Taizhou in Zhejiang, and reports of Ci Xi's ruthless ally, Prince Tuan, having sent eight thousand armed men to stiffen the Boxers in Zhili, gained credence.[27] The old statesman in Li Hongzhang despaired as he saw the way things were going. 'I have exhausted every reasonable resource of speech or writing,' he wrote in his diary. In one interview with Ci Xi 'he urged her to crush the Boxers. "In an instant she was alive with wrath and angry words, and I immediately withdrew."'[28]

Although German railway engineers were attacked in Shandong, a German newspaper in Shanghai 'ridiculed alarmist reports' as 'wild tales'. An extension of the French concession at Shanghai then desecrated the ancient cemetery in defiance of Chinese sentiment and beliefs, inviting retaliation sooner or later. Anti-foreign feeling had not been so high in Peking since the French and British looted and burned the Summer Palace in 1860.

A member of the family of Zeng Guofan and 'Marquis Zeng' strongly warned in a despatch to the *North China Herald* that a blood bath was imminent.[29] A scheme had been worked out, he revealed, to crush all foreigners and take back all leased and ceded territory. Behind it was an all-Manchu 'Army of Avengers' of ten thousand under Prince Tuan, 'a vicious and violent man'; thirteen thousand under Kangyi, 'Lord High Extortioner'; and fifty thousand under Prince Qing, an old adversary of Yong Lu. To his credit Yong Lu had remained loyal to Guang Xü and urged the viceroy of Zhejiang and Fujian not to act on Ci Xi's edict to enlist and train bands of criminal types to exterminate foreigners. In the north, Tong Fuxiang's Muslim horde and the Boxers were to be used as expendable tools against the foreigners, whether armed or unarmed. Bunkers were being built in the palace and the Eunuch Guard being armed. 'All Chinese of the upper classes know this, and those who count foreigners among their friends have warned them, but have . . . been more laughed at . . . than thanked.'[30] 'Wolf, wolf!' had rung in their ears for decades. The Boxers, this correspondent said, had increased tenfold since the new year, even in Peking and Manchuria. Indoctrination teams were touring the provinces enlisting and training Boxers to drive the invaders from their strongholds, and to kill foreigners scattered in the interior. Chinese Christians were to be the first attacked, leaving the missionaries unprotected.

Still the ministers of the various legations held their hand, not advising their nationals to withdraw to the coast, or to leave the ports or Peking. Retreat would be to play into the hands of their enemies. Sir Robert Hart, who knew China and the Chinese as well as any foreigner, wrote in retrospect, 'Those of us who regarded the movement as likely to become serious . . . put off the time of action to September; our calculations were wrong.' Others believed that the calculations were right, that the scheming dowager empress intended wholesale action throughout the empire in the ill-starred intercalary month (September), wreaking havoc upon the foreigners and turning ill-omen into victory for the Qing. While Britain celebrated the relief of Mafeking on May 17, more and more acts of violence were taking place in China. On May 20, Monseigneur Favier, the bishop in Peking and well informed, also warned that the explosion was nearer than the optimists believed.

The Boxers were impatient, chafing to begin. Before Ci Xi was ready, they precipitated the holocaust.

*Before New York: Australia
and New Zealand*   *September 1899–March 1900*

Nearly ten years had passed since Hudson Taylor's first visit to Australia in 1890. The one hundred missionaries within ten years, which he had urged the Melbourne Council to pray for and send to China, had been exceeded in September 1899. Four hundred had offered to go. The eighty-nine sent from Australia and twelve from New Zealand had already lost two by high fever and W S Fleming by violence in Guizhou. A fourth was dying as the Taylors set sail from Shanghai on September 25, 1899, to fulfil his long-promised return visit.

Since his arrival at Shanghai on January 15, 1898, for his tenth extended period in China, Hudson Taylor had carried the heavy end of the administrative burden and all its major stresses. While John Stevenson handled the routine administration, no light task, the hammer blows had fallen to Hudson Taylor's lot. Through 'the Hundred Days of reform' and the crises of Ci Xi's coup, the Yü Manzi rebellion, Fleming's murder, the death of leading missionaries, many riots and the ominous movements of troops and Boxers in the north, he had been largely single-handed. Dissension in the mission, 'Special Support' negotiations and the Morton legacy litigation, with his frequent illnesses and much travelling had taken their toll. William Cooper had left on March 29, 1898 for Britain, and after recovering from his accident had spent two months in Canada. He did not reach Shanghai again until October 21, 1899, the day on which the name 'Boxers' first appeared in print.

Hudson Taylor's approaching keynote address at the great Ecumenical Conference of Foreign Missions in New York, in April 1900, was the fixed point upon which all his movements had to hinge. To allow for two months in Australia and two in New Zealand, a thousand miles distant from each other, and then the long ocean journey to North America, had meant leaving China on September 25.

The moment for this uprooting had seemed woefully inappropriate. The volcano threatened to erupt. The anti-foreign fever was being fostered from the palace. Farther afield, after years of skirmishing the Boer War had started in earnest. The United States had proposed the 'Open Door for China', a policy of fair trading between the nations in place of spheres of influence and the competitive land grabbing that had started. But Russia was believed to be waiting only for Britain's hands to be tied before extending her grip on Manchuria.[31]

Ci Xi's tragic prisoner, the Guang Xü emperor, had 'begged permission' on September 4 to abdicate; Yü Xian and the Boxers, far from being in disgrace for attacks in Shandong and the murder of S M Brooks, were flaunting their welcome to Peking and appointment to Shanxi with chilling elation. At the heart of the CIM, the influential Stanley Smith's disruptive espousal of the eccentric 'Dowie sect' and 'universal restoration' in place of the 'annihilation' theory he had previously favoured, had led Hudson Taylor to call him to Shanghai for a frank discussion. Dixon Hoste (back from his long recuperation in Australia) was 'answering him well', but 'SPS' this time was adamant. He chose to leave China rather than to adhere to the Mission's principles. C T Studd's intractable asthma had decided him not to return. Instead he took his wife and four beautiful daughters to Ootacamond in India, to serve as pastor of the community church.

John Stevenson had been left in charge at Shanghai, with dark clouds looming on a close horizon, but William Cooper's return in October would allow some sharing of the strain. Loath to go, Hudson Taylor had been sure that 'duty called', as he explained in an open letter to the Mission after meeting for five days with the China Council, September 11–15. Duty to God, to be doing his will, mattered supremely. 'Pray that we may be kept near to God, walking with him, with the eye kept single and the heart pure and simple in these dangerous days . . . Satan will try to unsettle us and subvert us, and the weak will go to the wall.' Had he delayed his departure it would quickly have been far harder to get away. As it was Jennie (or more often 'Jenny' now) seems to have sensed a finality in their going. She had become a mother-figure to the predominantly youthful members of the mission, but in writing from the ship to all her 'sisters' to say goodbye, without any other hint of premonition, the tone of her letter was one of farewell for the last time.

The voyage was what they needed, and Hudson Taylor was 'at his best' off the Australian coast, taking photographs and developing them himself. They hoped to visit each colony in turn, were met by John Southey at Brisbane and stayed with a niece. At Sydney they received a 'very cordial' welcome from Archbishop Saumarez Smith, and Hudson Taylor spoke at meetings almost every day. Then on November 11 they boarded a ship to Melbourne.[32]

Meeting the Melbourne Council was his chief purpose, but a hundred ministers came to hear him on November 17, two hundred friends of the Mission attended the Saturday prayer meeting and on the 22nd he addressed fifteen hundred. In ten days he gave twelve addresses. And both John Southey and the Howard Taylors who were accompanying him took his place on other occasions. Correspondence kept him in touch with China. He replied to Stevenson that it was urgent for William Cooper to visit Chefoo and Shanxi if four or five resignations were to be prevented.

In Britain, although Robert Scott was the London treasurer and R C Morgan a member of the council, their popular 'weekly', *The Christian*, strongly criticised the principle of what they called 'faith missions'. (The misnomer was to take root, emphasising 'faith' instead of God's faithfulness.) Yet again the importance of referees and members of council having a sound understanding and approval of the root principles of the mission was being demonstrated. This time William Sharp replied for the CIM, rightly saying that its members were 'an association of missionaries' who themselves chose to live in daily dependence on God's promised provision, and did not want the kind of 'assured support' which the editor anonymously advocated under the pseudonym Quartus.

After ten days at Adelaide where he was 'brisk and well, for him', and two at Ballarat, with Jennie also speaking with 'power' at her own meetings, they sailed from Melbourne to Tasmania on December 22. 'Almost daily meetings' and the inexorable round of social events, as in every place, brought them to the end of the year and the voyage to New Zealand. Still accompanied by John Southey and the Howard Taylors, they sailed from Hobart on January 5, 1900, bound for Invercargill, on the southernmost tip of New Zealand.

China was never far from their thoughts or public speaking. On Christmas Day Hudson Taylor had remarked, 'How many men we have lost this year and last!' And on December 30 Jennie wrote apprehensively, 'One wonders what next year may bring.' Her fears were justified the very next day, when S M Brooks' murder heralded the coming storm. And on board ship Hudson Taylor, writing again to Amy on January 6, said they might have to return direct to China 'if any very serious complication arose there'. 'One cannot tell what this sad African war may lead to. I have no *light* beyond New York.' But they would probably be in England by July. 'Till the Lord gives us His light I must not fix anything for myself, or may lose His light and guidance.' Utter submission to the will of God and dependence on his leading must govern every decision and plan.[33] The way ahead was no clearer on January 30 when they had spent three hard-working weeks in the South Island. From Christchurch he wrote again, 'We cannot at present make plans and have no light beyond New York.'

In China the ill-omened *gengzi* year (Appendix 8) was about to begin, with the evil powers about to have their heyday. (January 24 was the fateful day on which Guang Xü was forced to abdicate (p 306), bursting a blood vessel under stress – and Pu Jün, son of the extreme Prince Tuan, was by decree appointed Heir Apparent, Prince Imperial.) But Hudson Taylor's sense of Satan having more rein to harass the Church, to which he had referred in his farewell letter to the Mission, turned his thoughts increasingly to the truth that whatever God might permit, '*power* belongeth unto God'. During 1899 forty-seven new members had brought the CIM to a total of 811 members, many of whom were comparatively young and inexperienced. To carry anxiety for them would be too much to bear. To be the servant, the instrument of God their Lord and Father, was altogether another matter. Satan could not go beyond the limit set for him by the One who held the power.

To Hudson Taylor's disappointment, John Stevenson, outstandingly efficient in other ways, was failing again to let William Cooper share his responsibilities 'as a partner'. So Hudson Taylor wrote on January 8 to announce at the next meeting of the China Council his appointment of Cooper 'as Visiting China Director in place of his former appointment as Assistant Deputy Director'. And to Cooper himself, 'I am convinced that you need to visit and know the whole mission', especially in Shanxi. 'In visiting feel you have full power as China Director to do whatever is necessary, but as far as it is possible let it be felt that you and JWS are one – as two wise parents are one in managing their children.'[34] If practicable, Cooper should return from Shanxi via Shaanxi, Gansu and Sichuan, as Hudson Taylor had hoped to do, but if not, through Henan.

In the event, even this arrangement did not satisfy members of the London Council. William Sharp wrote on March 10 urging again that William Cooper and Dixon Hoste should actually replace John Stevenson. But events were transpiring which made the experience and ability of Stevenson irreplaceable. God had other plans for both Cooper and Hoste.

An equally busy month in the North Island, with a visit to the hot lakes as guests of the government, brought them to March 20, their date of departure to San Francisco. New Zealand's position close to the international date line on longitude 180° E and W, meant that they sailed on the first of two days called March 20. Plague at Honolulu prevented their going ashore, and they landed at San Francisco on April 5.

In China tension had mounted increasingly. Wholesale initiation ceremonies and drilling were daily adding to the Boxers' strength. The worst anti-foreign feeling in Peking since 1860, forty years previously, made the foreign community and Chinese Christians fear for their lives. In mid-April eight thousand followers of Prince Tuan, evil genius with Ci Xi, joined the Boxers. And on April 20 when Yü Xian arrived at Taiyuan and set Boxers on to enrolling new members, he began collecting church membership lists. The Empress Dowager's ambiguous edict of April 17 blaming 'bad elements' in the Boxer movement was being interpreted as intended – as approval of the majority of Boxers.

William Cooper and John Stevenson himself were anxious about Stevenson's health, so although Cooper was on his way to Shanxi, he meant to return early to Shanghai and to complete his long journey to the west at a later date. From Baoding on April 6 he proceeded to south Shanxi.

The Ecumenical Conference of Foreign Missions in New York was to run from April 23 to May 1, so the Taylors travelled first to Los Angeles for three days of meetings arranged by George Studd, and on to the Moody Bible Institute at Chicago, preaching in what had been Moody's church. More meetings followed at Cleveland, and they reached New York on April 20. A letter from the President of the Union Theological Seminary, Charles Cuthbert Hall, welcomed Hudson Taylor. 'I beg to ask that you will preach or deliver an address in the Chapel of the Seminary on Sunday afternoon, April 29 . . . The work of the China Inland Mission is dear to our hearts . . .'

New York and beyond   *April–June 1900*

'The immense Carnegie Hall', seating 3,500, was filled to capacity with large simultaneous overflow meetings to accommodate the enthusiastic public who joined the 1,845 official delegates. Of these 779 were missionaries of 108 societies, including the Hudson Taylors, Howard Taylors, Henry Frost, Walter B Sloan, George Graham Brown and six other members of the CIM. The President of the United States and the Governor of New York State 'attended to welcome the conference on its assembling', thereby attesting its significance.

Initially a two-hour session was exclusively devoted to prayer. The published subject of Hudson Taylor's opening address was 'The Source of Power' for 'Foreign Missionary Work', and the impact of his address made itself felt from his first words: '*Power* belongeth unto GOD.' The futility of attempting to take the gospel to the whole world, apart from being the channels of that power, must govern all consideration of methods, personnel and message.[35]

Thirty-two years later Henry Frost wrote,

> I am still meeting men and women who declare that Hudson Taylor's address that morning radically changed their lives. [And again] The impressions produced by Mr Taylor were nothing less than phenomenal . . . There at the front of the platform, (he) stands a moment in silent prayer . . . As he begins to speak his voice takes on a kindly, companionate quality. A hush which can be felt falls on the vast audience . . . When Mr Taylor finished, there was almost an audible sigh of spiritual relief, so many of his hearers realising that they understood as never before the will and way of God.

A New York minister who attended the Adams Chapel service at the Union Seminary wrote to Howard Taylor after his father's death,

> As I listened to Mr Taylor I kept constantly comparing the idea of sainthood expressed in the paintings (of the four evangelists) above his head with the living man who addressed us. (These thoughts) gave rise to a sermon on 'The Reality of Saintliness in Daily Life', which I have repeated a number of times since. Mr Taylor was, I believe, one of the noblest and greatest leaders whom God has given to the Church in our times.

In addition, Hudson Taylor preached twice on the same day at the Central Presbyterian Church, after attending 'as many of the conference meetings as his strength would allow.'

In view of Oberlin College having its representatives in Shanxi alongside the CIM,

> The whole tenor of an address by Dr J H Barrows, its President, on 'The Right Attitude of Christianity toward the non-Christian Faiths'

met with general approval. He pointed out that these other religions were entitled to be dealt with in a kind and respectful spirit, but that there simply could be no compromise whatever between faiths which were merely the products of the human heart reaching out in its darkness after God and this Gospel of redemption, which had come to men as the only revelation from heaven.

Such an answer to the liberalism colouring the statements of some missionaries in China and from such a source was timely. To Henry Frost the conference was 'one of the major events in the history of the Christian Church', and certainly its widespread influence placed it in the same rank as the great Edinburgh Conference of 1910, but in a different way.[36]

The Howard Taylors were to give the following winter months to the Student Volunteer Movement in universities and colleges throughout North America, so on May 1 they sailed for Britain, leaving his parents in the care of Henry Frost. They spoke at Princeton on May 2 and 3, and reached Toronto on the 5th for meetings of the CIM Council, saw Berger House, to which he had contributed and fulfilled more preaching engagements. For the frail old man the pace was too great.

Walter Sloan had addressed the Ecumenical Conference on 'The basis of admission to Church membership, and Church Discipline', in which he had referred to the problem of polygamy. After Sloan's return to Britain, Hudson Taylor was challenged on the subject, and on May 16 wrote 'a weighty letter' in reply. His conclusion as it concerned China, he said, was the same as the official view of the Moravian Church:

> that while no Christian could be allowed to contract a polygamous marriage, a heathen who had two wives, when converted could not, without great injustice and scandal, be called to put away either of them, as this would put an innocent woman in an impossible position, and render the children illegitimate.[37]

In the evening of the same day, May 5, after consultation with Henry Frost they took the night train to Boston. A restless journey and the usual sociabilities before going on to a public meeting soon after arrival left Hudson Taylor more fatigued than others realised. Dr A T Pierson had come on ahead of them and shared the platform with him. As Hudson Taylor was speaking, his doctor son, Howard, later wrote, 'he lost his train of thought, I think,' and A T Pierson 'immediately came to the rescue', taking over the meeting from him. Pierson added that he repeated the same phrase several times. Geraldine Howard Taylor, not present, conjectured, 'Recovering from the threatened stroke, Mr Taylor continued his journey . . .' But no mention has been made of any other signs or symptoms, so the word 'stroke' was hardly justified.[38]

He was advised to 'knock off work altogether for a time', and did no more public speaking, but attended a communion service at Germantown, probably on May 29. 'In all my twenty-five years' ministry I never saw anyone so moved at the mention of the love of God, and in receiving the emblems of our Lord's body and blood as your dear father was that morning,' D M Stearns recalled. Aware perhaps of having reached the end of his active life, did Hudson Taylor see himself that day as no better than an 'unprofitable servant'?

They cut short their time in America and booked a passage to leave a month sooner than previously planned, while a very humble Henry Frost took Hudson Taylor's place at his engagements. On May 29 they travelled to Northfield to visit D L Moody's widow and on June 5 went to Pittsfield, after working on a paper to be read for Hudson Taylor. From there to Boston again to join their ship. They sailed for Liverpool on June 9 and reached London on the 19th.

Eleven societies met at the Exeter Hall on the 20th to pray for China in crisis, but whether the Taylors were present is not clear. They spent the weekend of the 24th with Jenny's father at Tenterden. But the laconic entry in her diary the next day read, 'News serious'. Ci Xi's wolves had been unleashed. The legations at Peking were already under attack. Atrocities were multiplying. After a family consultation in London on July 2 they decided that the peace and seclusion of Switzerland would give Hudson Taylor the best hope of recovery. He himself wrote on July 6 to John Stevenson, 'If my head were in a condition to do mental work I should certainly have been on my way back to China before now. We are just preparing to go to Davos as that seems the quickest way of getting fit for work.' They arrived there on the 10th.

News from inland China travelled slowly, taking weeks to reach Shanghai. Even in late July cables from John Stevenson still told of danger, but as far as was known all were still safe. This was far from the terrible truth. Massacres had, in fact, been taking place since early June. Special concern for William Cooper was mentioned in letters, but Hudson Taylor had no inkling of how serious the situation had become. He even suggested that a hospital should be opened in Henan at the first possible opportunity, to break down prejudice.

Long after it was all over, the true story was still being pieced together. Eyewitnesses were difficult to find and slow to relive their bitter experiences. Some of the accounts of identical events differed widely, as seen from different viewpoints in the heat of excitement. Memories varied in reliability, and a comparison of printed sources makes a unified version of some incidents difficult and at times impossible to achieve. As always, the firsthand statements are best, within the limitations of exhaustion, of euphoria after deliverances from death, or of ability to express what remained all too vivid in their minds.[39]

Martyred Missionaries of the China Inland Mission was in print well before the teams of mission representatives returned inland to learn what lay behind terse telegrams listing all too many names and ending 'murdered'. The *Chinese Recorder* carried only what came to its editor.[40]

If the Christian world was staggered by the extent of suffering permitted by an omnipotent God, how much of what was known could be endured by the sick old man who loved his CIM family as dearly as his own children? Until the worst was over they kept it from him, but in the early days few had any concept of the horrifying truth, or that Cooper's headless body lay where it fell on July 1, outside the Baoding city wall.

CHAPTER ELEVEN

THE WOLVES UNLEASHED
May–July 1900

'Alarms and excursions'   *May–June, 1900*

The leader and human inspiration of the CIM had been set aside incapacitated at the moment of supreme crisis. John Stevenson never lost the sense of horror as, virtually alone at the CIM headquarters in Shanghai, he bore the battering of desperate reports from place after place in China. In one way or another he was responsible for the welfare of eight hundred men and women, hundreds of children, and many more Chinese Christians under threat of persecution and death. Looking for the help or advice he often could not give, they tried to maintain contact with him and each other, until uprooted and overwhelmed, many fleeing for their lives, or destitute and tortured they suffered until the end. As the reports came in, weeks or even months after the events, Jenny Taylor[1] in her strength kept from her husband all that she judged to be emotionally unbearable. Told bit by bit what was happening, he reached the limits of endurance and had to be spared any more. 'I cannot think, I cannot pray, but I can trust,' he said at the height of the inferno. Like Job and like the victims in China he clung to the faithfulness of God, saying, 'Though he slay me, yet will I trust in him' (Job 13:15 AV).

We pick up the threads of 'the great miscalculation' in May 1900, when the unthinkable took the foreign community by surprise and the Empress Dowager championed the Boxers. 'Had the crisis not been precipitated before the plans of the Chinese Government had been completed . . . in all probability few foreigners would have escaped to tell the sad story.'[2] Of eighty-nine missionaries of the CIM and other societies in the province of Shanxi at the time, forty-seven were known to have been killed by October, and their children with them. On this scale what would the toll have been throughout China, had brave viceroys, governors and court officials not risked decapitation and worse to negate the edicts of the evil Ci Xi? In the view of contemporary writers, 'nothing can be gained by the narration of harrowing details'. But in our day full knowledge of

HUDSON TAYLOR UNDER STRESS DURING THE
BOXER RISING
'Though he slay me, yet will I trust in him.' (Job 13:15)

the facts is deemed necessary to true understanding. In most cases death came quickly, but the protracted sufferings of others carry their own timeless message.

Events had led inexorably to this calamity. On her return to Britain after her eight-thousand-mile journey in China and 'outer Tibet', Mrs Isabella Bird Bishop (p 663) observed, in a paper read to the Church Congress at Newcastle: 'Everywhere an increasing hostility to foreigners was apparent.'[3]

The seizure of Qingdao Bay and Jiao Xian (Kiaochow) by the Germans, and the policy it engendered of land-grabbing by other powers, had roused a storm of anger against foreigners. The Empress Dowager was fully justified in saying in her edict of November 1899, when she called upon all her officials and armies to resist any further attempts to invade Chinese soil, 'There are certain things to which this empire can never consent. Let no one think of making peace.' The author of *Martyred Missionaries of the CIM*, himself in Shanxi when Tong Fuxiang's horde of Muslim cavalry were passing through the province towards Peking, was invariably told in answer to his questions, 'We are going to drive the Germans out of Kiaochow!'

Wherever the Roman Catholic Church acted on the edict of March 15, 1899, granting official rank to each order in the priestly hierarchy (p 284) – the privileges categorically refused by all Protestant Christian bodies in concert – anti-Catholic feeling and resistance were aroused. When the rains failed and famine threatened, the desecration of graves, and disregard of *fengshui* were blamed. Between Peking and Baoding where the Boxers were recruiting and drilling, the flash-point of violence was particularly low as May progressed, while in Shanxi the newly-arrived governor, Yü Xian, was waiting for no one.

Towards mid-May (about the 12th) armed Boxers raided three Roman Catholic villages near Baoding, the capital of provincial Zhili, eighty miles south-west of Peking and Tianjin (HTCOC Book 3, p 216), 'killing and burning alive some seventy' converts. On May 17 Sir Claude Macdonald, British minister, reported sixty-one killed in three villages. Two days later, halfway between Baoding and Peking, two largely Protestant Christian villages in Laishui county and the LMS chapel at Gongcun were attacked and destroyed (map p 345). In the carnage the pastor perished heroically.[4]

Meanwhile William Cooper had passed through Baoding to

WILLIAM COOPER AND DAVID BARRATT LEAVING
LINFEN, 1900

Shanxi, visiting Taiyuan and 'a large number of stations' before
meeting thirty-two missionaries of the 'south-central region' in
conference at Linfen (Pingyang) on May 17 – the day after Hudson
Taylor succumbed to exhaustion at Boston. William Cooper had
already detected the oncoming of the storm, when reports began
coming in that Elder Si of Hongtong, (p 304) the worthy successor of
Hsi Shengmo as leader of the churches, had been attacked and
severely wounded. Yü Xian, the provincial governor, had sent
mounted Boxers from Shandong through the length and breadth
of Shanxi to recruit and drill reinforcements in three categories:
to fight for the empire – these were sent to Peking; to fight for the
gods – these were to attack Christians and missionaries; and to
fight for their homes – 'defending' their own villages, even against
destitute refugees on the run.[5]

The Hongtong Boxers had announced on May 14 at a public
parade that they would begin by killing Elder Si, and at once went to
his home, plundered it and gave Si a fatal sword-thrust through his
side. Dr Millar Wilson rode out to his village home at once, but Si
suffered for months before dying. His assailants went next to Linfen
where the missionaries were congregated. William Cooper there-

fore spoke on Hebrews 13, verses 5 and 6: 'I will never leave thee, nor forsake thee. So that we may boldly say, The Lord is my helper, and I will not fear what man shall do unto me.'

When the Boxers took no action he moved on, to Lu'an (now Changzhi), Yüwu and Lucheng, and again this was his theme in speaking to Chinese Christians and missionaries alike. It was likely that all would be called upon to suffer for Christ, and in sharing the lot of the Chinese, the foreign missionaries could set an example of fortitude and peace of heart. The first attack on Lu'an came two weeks later.[6]

He had intended to follow Hudson Taylor's wish, as Cooper regarded it, and to return to the south through Henan. But John Stevenson needed him without delay. So he made instead for Baoding, to go by sea from Tianjin to Shanghai. He walked straight into trouble. The attack on Si had coincided with the attacks on the Christian villages between Baoding and Peking. And a week later the Boxers plundered Pastor Hsi's home, declaring that they had come by imperial orders through General Tong Fuxiang to exterminate foreigners. They severely beat Pastor Hsi's wife and old mother, and distributed the family's possessions among hundreds of onlookers. When the Boxers had gone, some people returned the loot to the family.

During the last days of May, the railway and telegraph lines had been cut between Baoding and Peking and between Peking and Tianjin. When thirty Belgian, Greek and Italian engineers fought their way through to Tianjin, 'for three days fighting all day long, closing round and at last carrying their women folk', in their final extremity they were rescued by sixty mounted volunteers who rode out to meet them. Nine of the original party were missing, and only nine remained unwounded.[7]

When William Cooper reached Benjamin Bagnall's home at Baoding all appeared quiet, and some Boxers said they bore no ill will towards Protestant missionaries. But to continue towards the coast was impossible. Two SPG missionaries, Harry V Norman and Charles Robinson, had repeatedly warned the consul at Tianjin that Boxers were massing near Yongqing, and urged the Christians to escape to safety. While any were in danger they themselves refused to leave. On June 1 they were attacked. When they took refuge in the magistrate's *yamen*, the right thing to do, the Boxers demanded that they be handed over. The magistrate let them escape through a back door and they sought asylum in a Confucian temple, but were turned away and caught. Robinson was killed instantly, but after a brief evasion Norman was carried off and murdered in cold blood the next day.[8]

The gravity of the situation at last impressed the allied envoys and on June 4 an appeal was sent to Europe for adequate protection. It would take weeks to come. At any point in May or early June all foreigners in Peking could have been wiped out, but until the Boxers forced her hand Ci Xi had more far-reaching intentions. As she and her prisoner, the emperor, returned from the Summer Palace, she issued her decree justifying the Boxers' action, and the increased activity around the capital at once flared into riot and the massacre of eight Chinese Christians at Tong Xian. The fuse had been lit. The last trains from Peking to the coast pulled out; a dangerously vulnerable party of fifteen Tong Xian missionaries at last braved the fifteen miles to the safety of the capital; the missionary communities in the city rapidly congregated for greater safety; those in the Methodist Episcopal Mission premises formed committees including one for defence; and Sir Claude Macdonald, a seasoned soldier, requested a relief force of British marines from Tianjin without delay.

By then (the weekend of June 9 when Hudson Taylor was leaving Boston for Britain) the forced exodus of missionaries from their homes in many provinces had begun. A 'rain procession' at Lu'an, trying to break the drought, attacked the mission premises on June 6, doing little damage, but prompting A E Glover to take his pregnant wife to the coast while he thought he could. Such was their isolation from reliable news. They started north on June 9, in mule litters, on a journey which was to cost them a thousand miles of suffering, death and deliverance. By the time they reached the Martin Griffiths at Shunde, the countryside of Zhili was seething. After eleven days in hiding, there remained no choice but to return to Lu'an and try a southern route through Henan. Only 'ten miles from (Shunde) we were stoned and captured and given over to death . . .' But 'a thousand miles of miracle' had begun.[9] The Martin Griffiths also set out separately for Lucheng, but failed to arrive. For months there was no news of them.

Massacre and mayhem[10]   *June 10–24, 1900*

Two fateful weeks began on June 10 with the final severance of the telegraphic link between Peking and the outer world. The last letter out was dated July 14, and the last from Tianjin reached the Peking legations on the 18th. Ill-founded optimism in the cushioned diplomatic circle suffered a sequence of shocks as the Boxers burned the grandstand at the race-course only six miles from the city walls on the 9th and the legation hill resort the next day. Also on the 10th the extremist Prince Tuan was appointed President of the Zongli Yamen (the Foreign Office). Within hours of receiving the requisition from Peking for more marines, Admiral Sir Edward Seymour set out from Tianjin with a quickly mustered defence force of 2,000 men of various nationalities. Expecting them to arrive the next day, or at least by the 12th, a number of legation diplomats rode out to welcome them; but the resistance Seymour had encountered was too strong and no reinforcements arrived. Instead, to the diplomats' alarm, Chancellor Sugiyama, secretary of the Japanese legation, returning to the city was dragged from his carriage by Tartar cavalry and clubbed to death.[11]

The 13th became more fateful still: an imperial decree commanded the viceroy of Zhili and the commanders of the northern army to 'resist any further foreign reinforcements and to stop the Allied force from coming to Peking'. Admiral Seymour had reached Langfang (map p 345), only forty miles from the capital, but as fast as his men repaired a sabotaged stretch of railway line, Boxers wrecked another. Food, drink and fuel supplies dwindled and the relief force was encircled. Fighting to retreat, and twice suffering costly defeat, they had not yet regained Tianjin when the Empress Dowager's worst edict, of June 24, stunned the world.

She, the Boxers and irregular armed bands each ran wild in their own way. A demonic horde of fanatics, criminals, drought-starved peasants and ill-disciplined troops, all wild with blood-lust and a passion for plunder, stormed into Peking brandishing whatever weapons they could lay hands on. Most horrific were their flaming torches, seeking out and destroying every foreign house and all Chinese property in any way connected with foreigners. Starting with a Methodist Mission chapel, the flames engulfed the most prosperous quarters, not sparing innocent Chinese whose homes and businesses happened to stand alongside the objects of hatred. Even Sir Robert Hart's Imperial Maritime Customs Inspectorate, the Chinese Imperial Bank, and postal and college premises suffered the fate of the French and other European legations. The Greek Orthodox Church, the Roman Catholic East Cathedral, the LMS and American Board establishments went up in flames.[12]

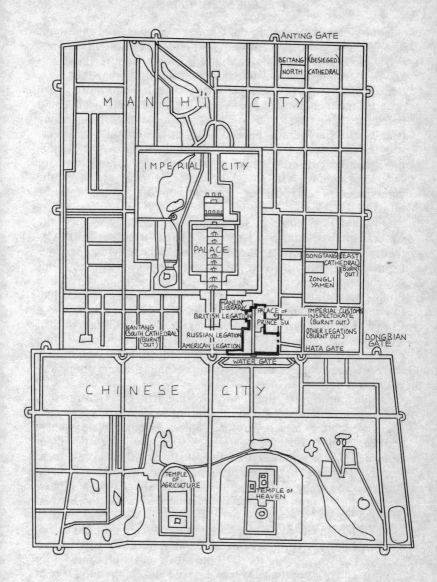

AN OUTLINE PLAN OF BEIJING (PEKING)
the Manchu City, Imperial City and Chinese City with the Palace
and Legations

None suffered more than the Chinese Christians and their families. Without distinction between Catholic and Protestant converts and adherents, all were hunted and if caught were tortured and killed. Crowding into the churches or cowering at home they were burned alive. Any who escaped often wounded and burnt, were rounded up and thrown back into the flames. All who could barricade themselves in defendable buildings did so. The Beitang (the North Cathedral), packed with three thousand refugees, was 'held by forty-three French and Italian marines and some five hundred converts armed with spears and a few rifles' for two long months. In the Methodist Episcopal Mission the committees of defence and 'general comfort' prepared to be attacked.[13]

On June 14 a posse of Frenchmen dramatically rescued the Catholic priests, nuns and Sisters of Charity from the South Cathedral before it was put to the torch. And on the 15th rescue parties from the American, Russian, British and German legations searched for Chinese Christians in the southern quarter. They found 'women and children hacked to pieces, men trussed like fowls, with noses and ears cut off and eyes gouged out. Chinese Christians (accompanying the rescuers) ran about in the labyrinth of streets calling upon the Christians to come out from their hiding places . . . Boxers were even now caught red-handed at their bloody work.' Some refugees succeeded in reaching the remaining legations and were taken in.

On the following day the *Times* correspondent, Dr G E Morrison, with an international troop of thirty-five marines under the Japanese military attaché, Colonel Shiba, searched the east city. His report (of October 15, 1900) described how cries reached them from a Daoist temple used by the Boxers for their occult rites. Forcing their way in, the patrol found Christians bound hand and foot, waiting to be tortured and executed. Shockingly mutilated bodies lay still warm and bleeding, sacrificed as part of the Boxers' frenzied ritual.[14]

The Chinese city of Tianjin, close to the foreign business settlement, similarly fell into the Boxers' hands, and all Christian premises were destroyed. On the 16th the settlement itself came under gunfire. D J Mills of the CIM took his wife and children to Dagu at the river mouth, and returned at once by armoured train to attend the wounded throughout the week-long assault from all sides. 'Bullets . . . entered every window and shells damaged the CIM house', but neighbouring fires were contained and the settlement held out until relieved.

When the Dagu forts fired on allied ships offshore, the admirals demanded their surrender, and at dawn on the 17th took them by assault, before pressing on to the relief of Tianjin. Lord Elgin's feat of 1860 had been repeated. Ci Xi was furious, and Prince Tuan seized his opportunity to sway her opinion from following Yong Lu's counsel of moderation to one of belligerence. At a meeting of the Imperial Council, Tuan presented her with a forged ultimatum purporting to be from the allied envoys. Its crudity should have condemned it as spurious, for it demanded that the emperor be restored to power, with a proper place of residence, that all revenues should be collected by the foreign envoys and all China's military affairs should be under their control. So outrageous a document – for she 'never for a moment suspected its authenticity' – left her with no alternative but to do as Prince Tuan intended. She sent three of her ministers to challenge the envoys to haul down their flags and leave China under safe escort. Far from having hostile intentions, Sir Claude Macdonald pointed out, the Allied forces were bent on restraining the excesses daily devastating the capital, Tianjin and other cities. Unmoved, Ci Xi ordered the envoys out of Peking within twenty-four hours. And they were prepared to comply, until suspicions of perfidy were confirmed. Prince Tuan had offered 'five hundred taels for every dead foreigner.'[15] At any point in May or early June all foreigners in Peking could have been wiped out, but Ci Xi had more far-reaching intentions – until the Boxers and their powerful patrons forced her hand.

Meanwhile unrest in the provinces was taking conflicting forms. On June 14 Boxers arrived at Datong between the two arms of the Great Wall in northern Shanxi, an outpost of the CIM. (Map p 339) Stewart and Kate McKee and their two children, Charles and Florence I'Anson and three children, Margaret Smith and Maria Aspden were stationed there. They could but wait and pray as the Boxers drilled and recruited. It was too late to escape even to Mongolia.[16]

Away to the east in Manchuria, Boxer agitation and attacks on Christians had been building up, held in check by the viceroy but encouraged by his Manchu deputy. Their private power struggle ended on June 19 when the viceroy, recognising that his rival was in direct touch with the Peking court, quietly capitulated by gently urging good Boxers to keep the peace. Farther and farther afield the prospects for foreigners and Christians were daily becoming worse.[17]

Between Datong and Guihuacheng on the Mongolian border, Soping was a centre for the Swedish Holiness Union, the associate mission of the CIM. Each year they and their colleagues in other cities met in conference on June 24. In 1900 the ten members were joined by two C&MA couples and their children, and Chinese delegates from each local church. As soon as they set out for Soping, mobs wrecked and burned their homes at Hunyuan and Zuoyün, driving the Christians into the flames. So, as at Baoding and Datong, the fourteen missionaries, two children and 'many' Chinese Christians at Soping were cut off, unable to find any way to escape.[18]

The point of no return   *June 20–24, 1900*

On June 20 a secret meeting of the Manchu Grand Council formally decided at 5.00 am on outright war. But for their characteristic inertia, they could have annihilated the scattered foreign community within hours. Instead the hardening of their attitudes became apparent. When the envoys requested an interview they were snubbed, and some serious incidents at last convinced them that decisive action must be taken immediately for the protection of all under threat.

Against his colleagues' advice, Baron von Ketteler, head of the German legation and 'a very passionate and excitable man', set out at 8.00 am with his secretary, Herr Cordes, and an escort of marines for the Zongli Yamen. Meeting an apparently friendly squad of Manchu soldiers, von Ketteler sent his escort back and proceeded with the Manchus. Cordes, bringing up the rear, saw one of them take aim and fire point-blank at von Ketteler from behind. The baron was killed, and soon afterwards Cordes himself was severely wounded in both thighs. He managed to escape to where he could be rescued. A strange rumour had already been circulating at Tianjin for a week, that Baron von Ketteler had been killed.[19] No explanation was found.

The alarm spread rapidly and foreigners of all kinds poured into the strongly walled legation with their Chinese dependants. At the same time the Catholic Beitang (Cathedral) entered a true state of siege. And two thousand other Chinese Christians, whom Sir

Claude Macdonald described as 'survivors of a massacre intended to be complete', crowded precariously into unsuitable premises elsewhere. The dozen or so buildings of the British legation were crammed to capacity, but seeing how vulnerable the two thousand Chinese were, Dr Morrison of *The Times* and Professor Francis Huberty James, of the 1878 CIM famine relief team (HTCOC Book 6, pp 175, 186), succeeded in persuading the allied envoys to allow them also into the precariously defended legation. They negotiated with a Prince Su to guard and preserve his adjoining palace if he would allow the refugees to occupy it, and courageously led them through the streets to its relative safety. There Japanese marines and other volunteers manned the perimeters. Into the confined space under siege the troops of Tong Fuxiang began at 4.00 pm to pour shells and rifle fire in 'a fusillade which was generally constant and furious, at times interrupted by periods of quiet'. They had a vantage point on the city wall, so a daring sortie under full observation had to be mounted to drive them off.

From the first the Christians made themselves indispensable, doing the manual labour of digging, carrying and sandbagging the defences, and driving mine shafts under the attackers' positions. But seeing how heavily the odds were weighted against them, some took their own lives, among them the father of Wang Mingdao, a month before his son was born (p 660). The child's grandmother prophetically named him Tiezi, 'Iron'![20] Apart from 'some thousand of Chinese converts', the lives of 473 foreign civilians were at stake – 245 men, 149 women and 179 children. International jealousies made co-ordination difficult, but with the experienced soldier Sir Claude Macdonald as commander, 451 guards including seventy-nine marines and seventy-five civilian volunteers fortified and held the legation against almost incessant attack for eight long weeks. A missionary was put in charge of fortification and another of 'general comfort'.[21] At the end they were highly commended for their outstanding success. After Sir Claude, the most distinguished of the military men, and most admired by the defenders, was the Japanese attaché, Colonel Shiba, 'reckless in courage, unceasing in his vigilance, and fertile in plans'.

No one knew why Francis James left the legation alone, an hour after firing started. He had resigned from the CIM in 1881, preferring to have a regular income, and for a few years joined the BMS. At the Shanghai Missionary Conference in 1890 he had read a paper on the secret sects of China. But in 1898 after an appointment with the Imperial Arsenal near Shanghai, he moved to Peking as a professor in the Imperial University. At 5.00 pm on June 20, 1900, well knowing of von Ketteler's death that morning, he set out perhaps to enlist the help of influential Chinese colleagues, but was seen to be arrested and led away. Later reports claimed that he was beheaded and his head exhibited on a spear, recognised by passers-by.

On June 22 a proclamation offered fifty taels for any foreign man taken alive, forty taels for a woman and thirty taels for a foreign child. This incentive was later found to have contributed to the sufferings of many missionaries in Shanxi and Zhili in the ensuing weeks.[22] Much of what is known of events in Peking, in court and government circles, has come from the personal diary of the Manchu aristocrat Jingshan, a high government official who himself had a hundred Boxers billeted at his mansion.

The 'primary devils', he wrote, were barricaded in the legation, but on June 24 the 'secondary devils' (Chinese friendly to foreigners) received the full force of Manchu anger and Boxer bloodlust. By decree, Prince Chuang and the 'Lord High Extortion-er', Kangyi, together were given command of the Boxers, and Prince Chuang presided over the execution outside his palace of 'many hundreds of Chinese Christians'. 'There was no mercy shown . . . innocent people perished with (those called) guilty.' A week later another batch of 'over nine hundred people were summarily executed' outside his gates. The Empress Dowager congratulated and rewarded the Boxers for their gruesome work. Then, on June 29, a tiny note from Sir Robert Hart dated June 24, probably sewn into the clothing of a daring courier, was received by the Allied commanders at Tianjin. 'Besieged in British Legation. Situation desperate. MAKE HASTE.'[23]

For the 'primary devils' outside the partial protection of the legation defences, June 24 had become the blackest day of all. The Empress Dowager issued a secret decree 'of savage ferocity'. No copies survived to be held as proof of her guilt, but reliable evidence in time emerged to implicate her incontrovertibly. 'Its authenticity is well established,' Hosea Ballou Morse stated, citing the evidence. On July 4 Jingshan recorded that 'ten days ago' she had sent Yü Xian, governor of Shanxi, a secret decree: 'Slay all foreigners wherever you find them; even though prepared to leave your province they must be slain.'[24] Of Protestant missionaries alone there were eighty-seven in Shanxi, but also many Catholics. In

Henan a friendly official in the military mandarin's *yamen* confidentially handed to a CIM missionary a copy of a decree 'in the appalling and unexampled words':

> *Yang ren bi sha, yang ren tui hui ji sha* – Foreigners must be killed, even if they withdraw (or escape) they must still (or instantly) be killed.

A H Smith in his book, *China in Convulsion*, wrote that warning of the edict was,

> brought to missionaries and others by friends in the *yamens*, friendly telegraph operators and by officials – some of them of high rank – in at least three provinces and in numerous places hundreds of miles apart, almost simultaneously. Twice at least the original despatch was seen by foreigners.

The fact that people and places were not named in these contemporary reports testifies to their veracity; for Ci Xi remained the tyrant even in defeat, afterwards taking revenge on some whom she learned had thwarted her commands. The supreme heroes were two of her own ministers in Peking, Yuan Zhang and Xü Jingcheng,[25] who intercepted the decree about to be telegraphed and changed the word *sha* (kill) to *bao* (protect). Other, unaltered, copies despatched by courier were received and 'obeyed ferociously and without hesitation'.

But enlightened viceroys and governors took their stand on the amended imperial decree they received by telegram, and later rejected 'unsubstantiated reports of a different intention'. Outstanding among them was one of whom the *North China Herald* later carried this account. On receiving the command by courier, he defied the Empress Dowager's madness even without benefit of Yuan Zhang's alterations.

> The interim Manchu Governor of (Shaanxi), Tuan Fang, has so protected the lives and property of some eighty foreigners that . . . it is owing to his care that they are now alive. When the Edicts of the 20th to the 25th of June, that gave imperial sanction to the murder of foreigners, reached (Xi'an), that humane governor was so distressed that he wept in the presence of other high officials, and could neither eat nor sleep for some time. He immediately suppressed these drastic Edicts, and issued stringent orders that at any cost and all hazards order was to be maintained.

In so doing he condemned himself to execution, but before long found he had the support of powerful viceroys who shared his own convictions. He beheaded Boxer ringleaders, replaced inflammatory posters with his own counter-proclamations, sent cavalry at the gallop to protect a Swedish missionary, and his own bodyguard to escort others travelling to the safety of Viceroy Zhang Zhitong's protection at Wuhan.[26] Altogether he was credited with saving the lives of two hundred foreign residents and their families, and others passing through his jurisdiction.

The viceroys intervene[27]   June–July 1900

The admirals at Dagu were in a quandary. By June 20 nothing had been heard 'from Peking since June 10, from the Seymour force since June 14, or from (Tianjin) since June 16'. They notified their respective governments that they were assuming responsibility to safeguard their national interests, and all received official approval. Reliable word of Count von Ketteler's murder and the start of the legation siege did not reach them until a week after the strange rumour about him had been in circulation (p 328). They acted on the known facts of mayhem in the capital, Seymour's predicament at Langfang and the Boxer holocaust in the Chinese city of Tianjin, threatening the adjoining foreign settlements. On June 20 (the day of the Grand Council's decision on war), therefore, to reassure the Chinese government and people they jointly announced their intentions. They would use force only to rescue their fellow-countrymen from Boxers or any others who threatened them or resisted the rescue attempt.

Several viceroys were already predisposed to welcome such a declaration, and the Chinese ambassadors to Western courts shared their views. Li Hongzhang had been appointed to Canton ostensibly to control the reformers, but largely to remove him from Zhili. The belief became general that had he remained at Tianjin, the Boxer rising would have been stamped out. On June 21 he informed the Chinese envoys that if the Western governments did not consider themselves at war with China he himself would go north, take steps to suppress the Boxers, and then negotiate with the powers for a settlement. The response was mixed and Li did not go.

The Yangzi basin viceroys, Zhang Zhitong at Wuhan and Liu Kunyi at Nanjing, regarded the secret societies as a menace sworn to the subversion of the Manchu dynasty, and therefore to be resisted. Early in June Liu had ordered the execution of apprehended members of the Dadaohui (the Great Swords), and on June 16 with the support of the governors of Jiangxi, Anhui and Shandong memorialised the throne by telegram begging the Empress Dowager to recognise the Yihochuan (the Boxers) as revolutionary, not patriotic. To ride this tiger was to invite disaster. But the Boxers and their powerful patrons had already forced her hand.

When the admirals' declaration reached him, Zhang Zhitong, the classical scholar, issued a proclamation in poetic *wenli* (see Glossary): 'Obey decrees; arrest rebels; keep the peace; rumour-mongers and disturbers of churches will be executed.' The diarist Jingshan noted that Liu Kunyi's refusal to send troops to help Ci Xi massacre helpless foreigners had 'excited her wrath'. Liu's neutrality towards reform during the Hundred Days (p 269) now contrasted strongly with his 'sturdy resistance to reaction'. Four fifths of the empire's officials were Han Chinese loyal to the dynasty, who in the current crisis suspected the empress and insisted on their loyalty to the emperor, still nominally on the throne, as well as to her.

On July 3 the viceroys together proposed to the Chinese envoys that agreement be negotiated guaranteeing 'protection in accordance with the treaties to the lives and property of people of all nationalities within their respective jurisdiction', in exchange for the foreign powers agreeing not to send foreign forces into the interior of Jiangxi, Zhejiang or the Yangzi valley, whatever might transpire in the erupting north. Visions of the dismemberment of China in retaliation for widespread atrocities against foreigners clearly prompted the proposal, but the adoption of America's 'Open Door' policy had already halted the race to carve up China into acquisitive spheres of influence. The powers agreed, the two viceroys Zhang Zhitong and Liu Kunyi issued proclamations to the nation,[28] and Li Hongzhang accepted the pact in principle, agreeing 'no longer to recognise the Peking government' – to quote Consul Warren to Lord Salisbury on June 29. Yuan Shikai telegraphed from Shandong, 'My views are the same as those of the viceroys.' And Tuan Fang, the brave governor of Shaanxi, was found to have adopted the same course of action independently. In this way,

> all the high officials in the southern and central provinces had allied themselves with the foreign powers, on the basis of the declaration that this was an insurrection and not a foreign war, and that the powers sought no acquisition of territory.

In the remoter provinces of Guizhou, Yunnan, Sichuan and Gansu, hesitation due to poor communications delayed conformity with the rest, but with persuasion they too left the Boxer 'rising' to fulminate only in the provinces north of the Huang He (Yellow River). Henan and Zhejiang proved to be the tragic exceptions. Such facts were not public property. As 'the great flight' of many hundreds of foreigners from the interior of China to the coast proceeded, it was in ignorance of what fate lay ahead of them. Only the bitter experience of fear and differing degrees of suffering would enlighten them.[29]

Crescendo of horror   June 21–26, 1900

On the day after the Peking siege began and the court declared war (June 21), Ci Xi issued an apologia in the name of the Guang Xü emperor, in defence of her action. Foreign encroachments and insults to the gods in return for extreme kindness by China had evoked indignation and riot by patriotic people, she claimed. The nation of four hundred millions was united in choosing to fight rather than to be eternally disgraced. Hundreds of thousands of patriotic volunteers (the Boxers) had taken up arms, even children carrying spears 'to vindicate the dignity of our country'. She could only approve, deviously saying nothing of the armed forces already driving Admiral Seymour back to Tianjin and battering at the frail walls of the legation enclave. Those 'patriots' were unthinkingly setting fire to the ancient Hanlin Academy adjacent to the legation, intent only on igniting the legation buildings. The timeless Hanlin library, filled with immeasurably precious manuscripts, went up in flames leaving the legation buildings intact.[30]

Shandong province under Yüan Shikai had remained relatively peaceful since S M Brooks's murder. But with events in neighbouring Zhili becoming desperate, all Shandong missionaries fled to the protection of the ports, those from the provincial capital Jinan to Yantai and from Wei Xian to Qingdao. F H Chalfont held off an attack at Wei Xian single-handed with a revolver until the mission premises were ablaze, and then escorted his colleagues to safety. The missionary community as a whole was divided between those who were prepared to use firearms in self-defence and those who would not in any circumstances.[31] With their exodus, fearful persecution of the Shandong Church broke out. Faced with the torture and death of many members at Qingzhou, two pastors publicly recanted in the name of all Christians in their congregations, saying afterwards, 'The sin was ours and ours alone' and 'I decided to take on myself the shame and the sin', 'so that old and young would be spared the terrors of a massacre'.

At the same time, June 21–25, in Manchuria the viceroy was keeping secret the anti-foreign edicts, to allow time for foreigners to escape. Russian railway engineers took the Mukden (now Shenyang) women, children and younger missionaries to safety at Yingkou (Niuchuang), and when 'the streets everywhere resounded with the unearthly shouts of the Boxers, "Slay!" and "Burn!" the Christians insisted that the three male missionaries who had stayed behind should escape while they could.'[32]

Five members of the American Board fleeing from Zhangjiakou (Kalgan) and three Swedish families who had joined them in Mongolia (p 402) found the magistrate at Harausa unfriendly. He ordered them to leave at once, saying that a force of Boxers was only ten miles away. What were they to do? The fearsome Gobi Desert lay between them and Siberian Russia (map p 45). It happened that the British consul at Shanghai had planned a journey, now impossible for him, and a caravan of twenty camels, six camel carts and nineteen horses was available. They decided to take the plunge. Then, before they started, four more Swedes arrived. One of the women had been 'almost clubbed to death' and one of the men 'presented a frightful spectacle, covered with blood and dust'.[33] Together the twenty-two refugees set off to cross the desert northwards making for Urga (Ulan Bator) and the Russian border at Kiakhta. Bandits, dry water-holes and Boxers would endanger their lives until they were in Russia. 'For eight days there was nothing to be seen but sand . . . The heat was intense . . . We all suffered greatly . . . Day marching was impossible . . . We ineffectually tried to snatch some sleep in the daytime, drawing up our caravan in horse-shoe formation, and keeping the necessary lookout. We were completely isolated' for thirty-eight of the fifty days of such travel.

By June 24 all hope of a peaceful conference of the Swedish missions in Soping (p 328) had vanished. When threatening placards appeared on the walls in the city and hostile crowds chanted, 'All foreign property has been destroyed in other cities; burn this place down!' two of the Swedish men went to consult the friendly magistrate. He confessed he was powerless, but urged them all to take refuge at his *yamen*. He would send them safely to Zhangjiakou (Kalgan) when he could. As soon as the missionaries moved out, however, their premises were put to the torch and all the Christians, employees and friendly neighbours were herded into the inferno and burned to death. In the commotion a doorkeeper named Wang Lanbu fainted and somehow escaped the fate of the others. When discovered he was flogged and left for dead, but before daylight recovered enough to go into hiding. Eventually he made his way to Tianjin, gathering information about the atrocities in place after place from which the conference delegates had come.

From the massacre by fire the mob went to the *yamen* and demanded that the foreigners be handed over to them. To win time the magistrate had five of the men shackled, and announced that all would be sent to Peking 'for execution'. At first this seemed to satisfy the ringleaders. But when an escort of soldiers took them out through the city gates on the morning of June 29, all sixteen were ferociously dragged from their carts and stoned to death.[34] One of the children was literally 'torn asunder by the violence of the mob'. In the mêlée two of the young men broke free, only to be caught, killed and their bodies burnt; but all the rest were decapitated before being burnt, and their heads displayed on the city walls. On the same day the Christians at Yingzhou were burnt alive.

Three engineers prospecting for new railway routes had travelled unhindered from Canton through Hunan and Guizhou to Sichuan and Gansu before heading east to Tianjin. On June 24, that fateful day, their raft on the Yellow River was wrecked and one, John Birch, was drowned. Another, Harry Matheson, somehow made his way alone to Tianjin. But Captain Watts-Jones, RE, the leader, continued on to Ningxia and 'was later subjected to a lingering death by torture'.[35]

In Zhili, Shanxi and Manchuria the Boxers systematically called upon Christians to recant and deny the faith, and afterwards often killed those who complied. But some magistrates whose own lives depended on placation of the Boxers, especially under the authority of Yü Xian, 'the Butcher of Shanxi' (see p 377), attempted to avoid confrontation and to protect the people under their jurisdiction. They made recantation appear as innocuous as possible. A mere formality, representative recantation by one or two pastors on behalf of a community, as in Shandong, or simply signature to a document undertaking 'no longer to practise the foreign religion' would secure freedom from action against them. Many convinced themselves that Christianity was no more a foreign religion than Buddhism or Islam, and took refuge in the play on words. Proclamations then announced that they 'had returned to their position as Chinese subjects'.[36]

The subtlety of such wording often made the temptation to comply more than unlettered countrymen could resist. One devoted old Christian afterwards told with chuckles of delight how he had hoodwinked the Boxers with the greatest of ease. But if many hundreds, thousands, saved themselves and their families from atrocious suffering, as many (if unsubstantiated generalisations are to be accepted) chose to suffer and die rather than to yield at all. Often 'adherents' not yet accepted as true believers or baptised, proved as staunch as mature Christians when confronted by a terrible death. Large numbers of Catholics and Protestants so proving their fidelity were honoured after the holocaust ended, but the records at best were incomplete. Those who not only died 'as partakers of Christ's sufferings' but would not leave their foreign friends in the last extremity have a place of their own in the history of Christian martyrs. R C Forsyth gave example after example, of men, women and children who died by the sword rather than deny their Lord, and missionary survivors had many stories to tell of Chinese companions who would not leave them. 'Liu Mingjin, a chapel-keeper, was bound to a pillar in the temple (but) kept preaching to his persecutors . . . One of the Boxers in a rage cried, "You still preach do you?" and slit his mouth from ear to ear.' A 'Bible-woman' named Wu was taken to the same temple, bound to a pillar and flogged, without uttering a cry. The flesh was burned off all her face, and her hands and feet were cut off before she was taken out, hacked to pieces and burned. The appalling sufferings of many missionary men, women and children even compared favourably with what their Chinese brothers and sisters endured.[37]

'Escape!' – but how?   June 26–30, 1900

June 26 was the day the southern and central viceroys promised protection within their jurisdiction. The north was beyond their power and given up to obeying Ci Xi's every whim. On that day also Dr Millar Wilson, suffering he believed from 'peritonitis', rejoined his wife and son Alexander in Taiyuan. And on the same day the mission at Pingyao (forming an arc with Taigu, Jiexiu, Xiaoyi, Fengzhou (now Fenyang) and Yongning south-west of Taiyuan) was attacked and looted.[38] A R Saunders at once took his wife and

four children, Alfred Jennings and a single woman named Guthrie
under official escort to the supposed safety of the provincial capital.
None of them yet knew that on the 24th the Empress Dowager's
command to kill had been received and relayed on the 25th by Yü
Xian to his officials in each county as 'withdraw protection from all
foreigners'. Boxers would do the rest.

Only seven miles from Taiyuan, Saunders and his companions
met a Christian who told them that the Schofield Memorial Hospital
and the Shouyang Mission premises in Taiyuan had been burned
down, that Miss E A Coombs had been burned to death, and that
twenty or more foreigners, including children, had taken refuge in
the still standing home of George Bryant Farthing of the BMS.
Several thousands of people were surrounding them and in spite of a
military guard round the house were preparing to raze it to the
ground with its occupants that same night.

Saved in the nick of time from walking into the lion's mouth,
Saunders decided to head south again and make for Lucheng, miles
away to the south-east. Their escort deserted them, and after three
attacks by Boxers, Saunders succeeded in 'buying' the protection of
the officer in charge of the imperial couriers' stables for the rest of
the way. But tension was building up to a riot in Lucheng itself when
they arrived there eight days later.

The destruction of the Schofield Hospital and mission premises
on June 27 had been without warning. Dr and Mrs A E Lovitt, G W
Stokes and his wife, and James Simpson and his wife forced their
way through the crowd and, although separated, all succeeded
eventually in reaching G B Farthing's house. But Edith Coombs, a
nurse, seeing the hospital on fire returned to rescue a child patient.
On leaving the building she was 'struck on the head with a piece of
iron' and, according to Dr Millar Wilson quoting an eye witness,
was stoned to death before being thrown back into the burning
house.[39] Attempts by Farthing to get protection by the authorities
failed so blatantly that with chilling probability their connivance had
to be assumed. From this time the city gates were kept closed to
prevent any foreigner or Christian from leaving. On June 28 young
Dr Lovitt, formerly of the London Hospital and Mildmay Mission
Hospital, wrote, 'We cannot but hope for deliverance (hope dies
hard) and our God is well able . . . even to save us . . . There is not
much time. We are ready.'

The six young women (p 645)[40] who had moved to Jiexiu, as a
quiet country town less likely to see disturbances, had been there

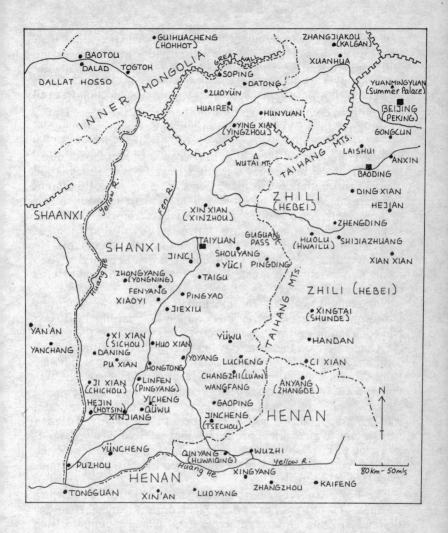

THE KILLING FIELDS: GRUESOME SHANXI
bordering Mongolia, Zhili, Henan and Shaanxi

only three weeks when news of the riot at Pingyao precipitated an attack on the mission house. Annie Eldred had gone to stay with the A P Lundgrens at Fenzhou (Fenyang), but the five others, led by Eva French, escaped to the *yamen*. The friendly mandarin told them he was forbidden to protect them, but sent them concealed in carts with an escort to Linfen. For this he was later cashiered by Ci Xi on her flight to Xi'an, 'and dismissed for ever from the public service', but ostensibly 'because he encouraged the Boxers'. On the way, at Hongtong on June 30, unruly crowds tried to break down the doors of the house they were in, so Eva French, showing the courage and initiative that made her a great apostle of the Gobi Desert in later years, as she wrote, 'called for a cart and went myself to the *yamen*'. Again the mandarin proved as friendly as the one at Jiexiu, told her about the fire and Miss Coombs's murder at Taiyuan, and that their only hope lay in escaping to Hankou. He told the church elder who accompanied her that he would have to recant and worship idols, and shortly before midnight sent carts to take them on to Linfen.

Not content with all her inflammatory edicts, the Empress Dowager promulgated yet another on June 28, 'praising the Boxers and commanding all viceroys and governors to support the rising'. As it happened, on that same day the viceroys and governors of the southern and central provinces declared Ci Xi's extremist adviser, Prince Tuan, a rebel and united to resist him. Her goading was unnecessary in the north where destruction and slaughter were already out of hand, and futile in the rest of China where restraint was being applied. In the two provinces of Zhejiang and Henan neither course met with absolute compliance. Before July was out, Zhejiang was to taste supreme tragedy, but as early as June 29 (the day the Yingzhou Christians were burned alive) the first exodus from Henan began.[41]

The Canadian Presbyterians had been advised by the British consul at Tianjin to withdraw from Zhangde (now Anyang) [close to the Henan-Zhili border and across the Taihang mountains from Lu'an (now Changzhi)] and to make their way north-eastwards to Jinan, capital of Shandong. From there they could travel concealed in canal boats to the coast and be picked up by steamer. Two doctors and their families, with one single lady, had already succeeded in this. But when they applied to the prefect for an escort he refused to do anything for them. They therefore cited the treaties, saying, 'The foreign powers have seized Dagu and a settlement of this trouble must come.' At this he changed his tune, but only to allow them to travel southwards, deeper into Henan (map p 359).

A large party of them left Anyang on June 28. Jonathan Goforth and his family, four or five other families and three single men were stoned on one occasion, but crossed the Yellow River (the Huang He) safely, and on July 1 met three armed British railway engineers of the Peking Syndicate with an official Chinese escort.[42] All stayed together and made good progress until ten miles from Nanyang. There they learned of danger ahead. The engineers took the Slimmon and Mitchell families with them to obtain escorts for the rest of the party, and reached Nanyang safely. But here also the prefect refused protection on the pretext that China was at war with Britain. Risking attack, the Goforth, Mackenzie and Leslie families with three single men, McIntosh, Douw and Pike, came on without a proper escort and reached Nanyang late on July 7. Then their real troubles began.[43]

Cornered, with nowhere to go   *June 27–July 8, 1900*

The county town of Shouyang lies eighty miles east of Taiyuan, about halfway to the Guguan Pass. When T W Pigott withdrew from the CIM and by agreement with Hudson Taylor continued to work at Shouyang and Taiyuan, he retained a young tutor, John Robinson, for his son, Wellesley, and a governess, Mary Duval, welcoming other children to be educated with him. Two Oberlin missionaries of the American Board named Atwater entrusted their two daughters to them, and they were in Shouyang on June 29 when desperate events began.[44]

The Shouyang magistrate informed the Pigotts that by order of Peking through Yü Xian, the provincial governor, protection was being withdrawn from foreigners. He offered to escort them to the county border, but could do no more. While they were considering what to do, word came of the destruction of the hospital and the murder of Edith Coombs in Taiyuan on the 27th. Immediately they began preparing to escape.

It happened that a Christian from the country was visiting them at the time. He invited them to go out to his home in an isolated hamlet of ten families in loess-cave dwellings. Darkness had fallen by the time they all arrived there. But the next morning word of their coming quickly spread and a stream of curious villagers flocked to see them, openly discussing what the Boxers were doing elsewhere.

As soon as they had left Shouyang, a crowd led by a renegade church member plundered their home, carrying away even the doors and windows. And two days later some Christians were killed only a few miles from the hamlet. At once a crowd collected and began to pillage the Pigotts' few possessions and the home they were staying in. They therefore returned to Shouyang.

At midnight, when they reached the magistrate's *yamen*, asking for sanctuary, they found that his attitude had hardened. They were all put in the guard house and soon afterwards sent to Taiyuan with Pigott and Robinson in handcuffs, all together in a large uncovered farm cart, escorted by fifty soldiers. At roadside halts for watering the animals, Pigott and Robinson preached to the crowds that surrounded them, and heard people say, 'They are going to be killed for preaching, and yet go on doing so.' In the evening of July 8, two hundred more horse and foot soldiers met them about three miles from Taiyuan and took them, not to join the other foreigners as they requested, but to the common gaol.

Forty-five miles north of Taiyuan, at Xinzhou on the Datong and Soping road, was a BMS mission centre staffed by Herbert and Mrs Dixon, William and Clara McCurrach, Bessie Renaut and Sidney Ennals.[45] On June 29 when they heard that the Schofield Memorial hospital and homes had been destroyed and Edith Coombs killed, visitors from Taiyuan, Thomas Underwood and his wife, were with them. News of the Soping massacre (p 335) had not yet reached them. Immediately they all decided to flee.

They left Xinzhou unhindered, in two carts and a mule litter, with two riding horses, but had covered only ten miles when a messenger caught up with them. They were wanted by the Xinzhou magistrate. They pressed on all the faster, to the cave dwelling of a Christian 'at the head of a narrow valley with high, steep sides on either side'. After two weeks their hiding place was discovered by men who had been out searching for them, and the friendly villagers on whom they had depended for food and water had to go into hiding themselves. As the missionaries were known to possess firearms, in an easily defended defile, no attempt was made to capture them until soldiers came out from Xinzhou. They put up a brief resistance but were outnumbered and Dixon surrendered. The whole party were then thrown into the common gaol in Xinzhou, among all the filth, stench and vermin for which such places were notorious, especially in the heat of high summer.

The Chinese who had left Xinzhou with them were the first to suffer. Ho Cungui, one of the first to become a Christian in that area, also became the first martyr. Caught by young Boxers when looking for an escape route for the missionaries, he was beaten with a thousand strokes on the magistrate's orders and thrown into prison in manacles and the stocks. Another Christian prisoner cared for him until he died on the fourth day. Two others, An Xügan and Zhang Lingwang, a boy of sixteen, had stayed with the party until supplies ran low, when they were persuaded to return home. But on the way they were taken by Boxers, interrogated, hacked to death and burned, young Zhang refusing to leave his friend when offered the chance.[46]

In a strong account by F C H Dreyer of events with which he was concerned around the time of his successful escape to Hankou, is the passage:

> We destroyed all (Chinese) and foreign Church registers, collection books, lists of children, Chinese letters, etc, and reminded others to do so lest they fall into the hands of the Boxers . . . having been told that the Boxers at (Xiaoyi) got the names of many Christians from a silk banner which had been presented to the ladies and hung on the chapel wall.[47]

News from Xiaoyi, in the arc of cities south-west of Taiyuan, had been minimal, as after the massacre no one was left to pass it on. But on September 19 (sic) a letter to Erik Folke from the shadowy figure known to the CIM as 'CCH' lest he be caught and punished, contained the words, 'At (Xiaoyi) the two ladies and many of the Christians have been killed, and many have had to flee. Their houses have all been destroyed.' Eventually a Christian teacher named Wang Yinggui, who narrowly escaped the slaughter referred to, told the full story; but even the *Last Letters* of December 1901 could only say (mistakenly) that they had died on June 30.

On June 28 a messenger had brought news of rioting and plunder at Pingyao (p 337) and Fenzhou (p 403) and on his way to inform Emily Whitchurch and Edith Searell had thoughtlessly spoken about it in the town. A hostile crowd quickly gathered at the mission door, battering at it while the two women and loyal Chinese inside prayed together, and a leading Christian, He Xiaofu, climbed over the back wall, ran to the *yamen* and rang the great bell kept for life-threatening emergencies. The magistrate hurried to the mission, found nothing in his opinion to justify the appeal and punished He Xiaofu for raising a false alarm. He told the local constable to guard the door. But when he had gone, the rioters returned, smashed the heavy gate and began stoning the missionaries.

This time the magistrate took the threat more seriously and told them to leave Xiaoyi, saying he could not protect them. Again his control of the rioters was short-lived. Early the next morning, June 29, they forced their way in and battered the two women to death as they knelt together to pray. They then 'stripped, exposed and defiled' their dead bodies and piled all their possessions in the courtyard to be carried off.

The magistrate sent two cheap coffins such as were used for pauper criminals, and the two disfigured bodies were deposited in the chapel. Then began the witch-hunt for all Christians in Xiaoyi, and the looting and destruction of their homes and property.[48]

The Baoding massacre   *June 25–July 1, 1900*

A fortnight had passed since William Cooper joined the Bagnalls at Baoding in Zhili (p 322). As late as June 25 he managed to send a telegram to John Stevenson in Shanghai, saying it was still impossible to travel, but he thought there was no cause for anxiety. A month later Stevenson cabled to London,

> Authentic information has been received that all missionaries have been murdered in (Baoding). We apprehend the worst for Mr and Mrs Bagnall and Mr William Cooper.

Letters were subsequently found in the viceroy's *yamen* at Tianjin saying that Europeans and Americans had been massacred at Baoding on June 30 and July 1. The facts were known to the highest mandarins, but treated as unimportant, a mere incident in the nationwide extermination that had been planned.

To the outer world, events even in the previous provincial capital of Zhili remained unconfirmed and indistinct, and not surprisingly at Wusong Road, the headquarters of the largest Protestant mission in China. John Stevenson lived until August 15, 1918, but never lost the sense of horror that he suffered day after day as the responsible leader in China during the Boxer rising – and for months afterwards, until everyone was accounted for.

Not until May 1901 did the *Chinese Recorder* print such meagre

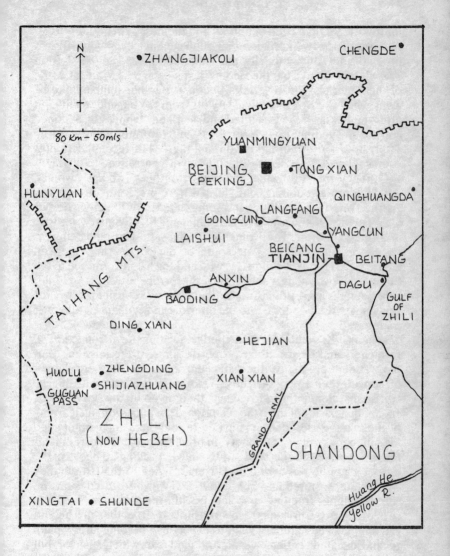

ZHILI: SCENE OF THE SIEGES
and sufferings of Norman, Robinson, the Greens and J Gregg

information as had been obtained, and the *Last Letters and Further Records of Martyred Missionaries* published in December 1901 had little to add. But gradually the truth was pieced together from eye-witnesses and from the victims' last messages. J Walter Lowrie of the American Presbyterian Mission at Baoding happened to be away when the Boxers cut the city off from the outside world. But after the Peking siege was lifted and an allied commission assumed control at Baoding, Lowrie served as an interpreter-adviser during the restoration of normal conditions there. His reconstruction of events formed the basis of Robert Forsyth's narrative.[49]

Of the normal Protestant community of thirty-two men, women and children at Baoding, only fifteen were present in June, 1900. At the American Presbyterian premises north of the city were Dr G Y Taylor, Dr and Mrs C V R Hodge, and F E S Simcox, his wife and three children. The Roman Catholics also had a fine church, residences and schools. And south of the city at the American Board were Horace T Pitkin (his wife and son having returned to the States) and two single women, Mary S Morrill and Annie A Gould. The Bagnalls lived close by in charge of the CIM business office for relaying funds and supplies to the interior, and William Cooper was their guest.

When Ci Xi's edict was made public, inciting the nation to kill all foreigners and destroy their property, some of the missions' employees fled, but many others stayed or returned and were slaughtered with their foreign friends. Among the Presbyterian Chinese Christians alone, thirty-five gave their lives in this way. Meng Jixian, first pastor of the American Board congregation, on learning of the missionaries' danger, hurried to join them and commanded his son to make his way to safety, in order that he might carry on his father's work. On June 28 Meng Jixian was packing up books in the chapel when he was seized by Boxers, carried to the temple they were using, tortured and beheaded. The word 'tortured' sums up the appalling cruelties associated with their human sacrifices (p 326). Daring Christians recovered his body from the ditch behind the temple. The nature of what to expect had become luridly plain to all. Educated gentlemen came and shed tears with Dr Taylor, but could do nothing to protect him. Fair-weather friends among the literati kept well clear, and officials known to have been friendly went into hiding to preserve their own lives.[50]

As always, Boxers were joined by street rabble bent on plunder when they came to the north suburb on June 30, heaped stubble against the outer gate of the Presbyterian premises and quickly reduced it to ashes. Breaking in, they looted the missionaries' homes and set fire to them. Two faithful gatekeepers and other employees, with their women and children, were either killed or driven into the well to drown. The foreigners all took refuge in the Simcox home. Two armed with a rifle and shotgun tried to drive the mob back. They killed the leading Boxer, but the rest surged on. 'Mr Simcox was seen walking to and fro, hand in hand with his two little sons, as the flames enveloped them.' Dr Taylor from the window of his own room pleaded the many kindnesses they had all done as missionaries, but also died in the flames of his own house. His medical assistant, refusing to escape, was buried half alive in a shallow grave after being brutally wounded.

The American Board and CIM in the south suburb soon heard of the massacre and prepared to die. Horace Tracy Pitkin, given his life purpose at Moody's Northfield conference and serving first as one of the best secretaries of the Student Volunteer Movement, wrote a note to his wife and gave a verbal message to a Chinese Christian. At Pitkin's request the Christian scaled a wall and escaped, eventually to deliver the message: 'Tell little Horace that his father's last wish was that when he is twenty-five years of age he should come to China as a missionary.' He did.

In pouring rain on the morning of July 1 the main gate of the American Board was broken open by the mob and imperial soldiers. Pitkin and the two ladies retreated to the chapel and, firing from its windows, he tried to defend them until his ammunition ran out. They then hid in an outhouse, but were soon found. With one sword stroke 'Mr Pitkin's head was severed from his body' and 'the ladies were rudely seized by the brutal mob'. In horror, Annie Gould sank limply to the ground. Her hands and feet were roped together and she was carried suspended from a pole between two men, like a pig being taken to market. Mary Morrill walked alongside, exhorting bystanders to prepare for the life to come by trusting in Jesus Christ, and even 'gave some silver to a poor creature in the crowd'. They were taken to the infamous Boxer headquarters in the temple.

Hearing the commotion at the American Board a few hundred yards away, William Cooper and the Bagnalls with their little daughter quickly collected up their money and valuables and decamped to the imperial military cantonment nearby, in the faint hope of a safe escort to Tianjin. Instead the colonel relieved them of all their valuables and handed them over to the provincial judge. He delivered them to the Boxers, and they were taken to join Mary Morrill and Annie Gould in the temple. A few hours later (hours of terror to any who could not face death with the Christian confidence and composure of these missionaries), the Boxers roped the hands of each one very tightly to his and her head and neck and to each other. With little Gladys Bagnall walking alongside, they led them out in single file to their execution. On February 22, 1901, when their remains were exhumed, it was found that Mr Bagnall and Mr Cooper had both been tightly bound round the head with a rope which passed over the eyes. 'So tight was it that when removed it left quite a distinct mark on the skull.'[51]

At some point, probably as they walked to the south-east corner of the city wall, outside the city, Mary Morrill, aged thirty-six, tried to persuade the Boxers to be satisfied with taking her life and sparing the others. A young imperial soldier, aged twenty, heard what she said. Thirteen years later, at an evangelistic meeting in Peking, addressed by John R Mott on a visit to China, Major Feng Yüxiang made a profession of faith in Christ.

> A forthright man of towering physique and great energy, he gave himself wholeheartedly to his new faith as he understood it. Feng rose rapidly in rank and in influence and by 1922 was a national figure . . . He encouraged missionaries (especially Goforth) to preach to his troops. Thousands (of them) received baptism. Many of his officers were professing Christians . . . In the army . . . a daily religious meeting with Bible reading, prayer and hymns was usual. (General) Feng himself often preached to his soldiers.[52]

As the Baoding victims stumbled to their execution, 'guns were fired and demonstrations (of sword play) made'. Intended to celebrate a Boxer triumph, they were more than that. They marked the triumph of life over death, for 'it is not death to die', and 'from the ground there blossoms red, life that shall endless be'. All were beheaded, Gladys after being thrust through with a sword. And after lying exposed overnight, all were buried in one grave.

What then of 'Cooper's worth'? Often sick and partly deaf since having typhoid, his character had seemed refined by hardship so that W B Sloan could quote a tribute to him: 'One of the very few blameless lives that I have ever come into contact with', and add, 'confirmed on all hands by those who were Mr Cooper's co-workers in . . . the Mission'.

WHERE WILLIAM COOPER DIED
outside the city wall, Baoding, Zhili

No hiding place   *July 1900*

That another edict from the dowager empress should have been issued on July 2, ordering the expulsion of foreigners and persecution of Christians, was as perfidious as any of her actions during these days of the Boxer madness. The government was to be seen as expelling foreigners, with the implication of doing so for their protection. That they should be deliberately driven into the hands of Boxers and ruffians waiting for them outside city walls was left unsaid. The Boxers bore the guilt of massacring them.

All through Ci Xi's erratic career as emperor's concubine, regent, and dowager empress, she had practised the wily art of covering her traces, to safeguard the possibility that events could turn against her. She could always lay the blame on someone else. The Boxers were to do most of her butchery, but while using them she took care to refer on July 1 to 'wanton murder and robbery committed by persons feigning to belong to the Yihochuan.'

That on the next day she should appeal in the name of the emperor to the Western powers for help to restore order was duplicity in the extreme. The legations were under constant attack, yet her appeals attributed the 'upheavals' in China to dissension between 'Christians and the people of (Zhili) and Shandong'. The current hostilities she blamed on the seizure of the Dagu forts. But to each ruler the appeal was addressed in different terms, calculated to yield the best results. The concept of psychological warfare was not generally exploited at this phase of history, but Ci Xi's intelligence may be credited with measures to weaken resolve and delay counter-action.[53]

It resembled the extraordinary events in the palace on June 25. Sixty Boxers, led by the extremist Prince Tuan and Prince Chuang, burst in, 'clamouring noisily for the emperor, "the foreigners' friend"'. An irate dowager empress confronted them, expostulating that she alone had the power to create or depose the emperor and for that matter the heir apparent, Prince Tuan's son, whom she had arbitrarily appointed. In fury she ordered that 'in accordance with imperial commands to protect the foreign envoys' all fighting in Peking be stopped, and that Yong Lu should negotiate terms of peace at a bridge north of the British legation. When a legation representative under a white flag came to the bridge, however, he faced levelled rifles and withdrew. No communication from the government was delivered, but after a short interval 'the attack was renewed more furiously than before'.

Sir Robert Hart wondered whether the episode was to throw the defenders off their guard or to put some 'friendliness' on record for future use. Ci Xi, the court and government were at sixes and sevens. The 'furious sound of rifle-shot' against the legation defences was sometimes punctuated by 'the shell of field pieces'.

> During the two-month siege it was calculated that 2,900 shell fell within the legation area, but it was one of the miracles protecting the besieged that the shell fire was not more abundant or more accurate. Credit for this is given to (Yong Lu) . . . He would not allow (his) artillery to be used 'so near to the imperial palace', and he refused point-blank to sanction the use of his reserve guns – beautiful new pieces, not yet even unpacked. [Yong Lu even dared to memorialise the Old Buddha, warning her that] 'the persons of envoys are always held inviolate within the territories of any civilised state' and that 'This attack on the legations is worse than an outrage, it is a piece of stupidity which will be remembered against China for all time.'[54]

This then was the climate at the seat of power when the foreigners widely scattered throughout the empire realised their danger and began to withdraw to the coast. In Manchuria parties of missionaries, merchants and engineers profited by the warnings given them and accepted the protection of Russian troops through many attacks and considerable hardships until evacuated to safety by railway and river steamer. But their property was destroyed. F S W O'Neill of the Irish Presbyterian Mission at Fakumen (map p 197), made his escape with five to six hundred Russians, French Catholics, and Protestants, witnessing pitched battles on several occasions before reaching Harbin on July 20. At Mukden (now Shenyang) on July 3 the Roman Catholic bishop, priests, sisters and hundreds of Christians were burned to death in their church.

> Three hundred Chinese Protestants were slaughtered, some with great cruelty. One preacher, on his refusal to recant, had his eyebrows, ears and lips cut off and his heart torn out and exhibited in a theatre . . . A native sect, the 'Fasters' (*Tsaili*), joined the Boxers and the government in an orgy of extermination . . . In all Manchuria fourteen or fifteen hundred Christians are reported to have been massacred.[55]

Huolu and the Greens   *July 1900*

On July 2, the day T W Pigott and his party returned to Shouyang from their hideout (p 342), and Eva French and her companions at

Jiexiu joined the Dreyers at Linfen (p 340), Charles Green and his wife and Jessie Gregg at Huolu in Zhili (near the entrance to the Guguan Pass) received the unsettling news of the Baoding massacres less than a hundred miles away. But that was not all. A riot had taken place at Shunde (now Xingtai) where their nearest CIM neighbours, the Griffiths, had lived, and the much feared Yü Xian was soon to arrive at Huolu with his Shanxi troops and Boxers.[56]

A prolonged drought had ruined the previous autumn's harvest and prevented sowing in the spring. Placards then began to appear saying that there would be no rain until all foreigners were exterminated, but a friendly mandarin promised to protect the Greens. Most Christian Chinese in and around Huolu were the only Christians in their families and came increasingly under persecution. Night after night intruders disturbed the missionaries' sleep, until the mandarin posted guards round the premises. These facts, and rumours about the fate of foreigners elsewhere, became the talk of the town; and couriers employed by the various missions in Shanxi began to be intercepted and killed by Boxers when caught carrying foreign mail.

From June 30 rain fell for several days, enough to allow of sowing to avert famine. But on July 3, after news of the Baoding atrocities arrived, 'a shouting, howling mob' began to pelt the Greens' front door with stones. At once their landlord urged them to leave Huolu, lest his property be damaged. Hearing that mission property in Taiyuan had been destroyed and lives lost, they began to plan their escape. A few days earlier a temple-keeper had offered them a room on a nearby mountain, and they decided to put themselves in his hands, but when?

Their city of Huolu was already in a ferment of excitement when a messenger arrived saying that after the CIM at Shunde had been rioted, the Martin Griffiths and R M Brown had gone into hiding; the Glovers (p 323) trying to return to Lu'an had been robbed; and no magistrate would lift a finger to help any of them. Another messenger then came in. The Shouyang mission homes had been wrecked and the occupants taken away in chains (p 342). The Greens and Jessie Gregg at once took a change of clothing, some bedding, essential food and cooking utensils, and left under cover of darkness for the temple.

As soon as they had gone, on July 5, their Huolu house was stripped by the landlord of anything he coveted, and thrown open to looters. They were homeless. And worse still, they were seen and the big village gong was sounded to call everyone to decide what to do. On the 8th, the local bully came and told the fugitives to leave at once or be driven away. They had nowhere to go to. But as soon as the bully had gone, the temple-keeper said, 'Don't be afraid; I have . . . a natural cave high up on the face of the mountain; plenty of room inside, but a very small entrance; few know of its existence.' 'Shouldering a giant's share of our things, he then led the way', each of them carrying a load up the difficult, stony pathway. At last a steep 300-foot climb away from the track and they crawled into their 'cool, new home'. The only patch of dry ground for three adults and the children aged five and two to lie down measured five feet by three. The children were already crying piteously for water, but the only available water would have to be fetched from the foot of the hill after dark; and other voices could be clearly heard across the valley on the opposite hillside. The children's crying would give them away.

Brave Chinese friends in two small groups began searching for them as soon as they learned that the temple was empty, and met a party of Yü Xian's Boxers who asked, 'Are you looking for the foreign devils, too?' But the cave was well hidden. 'This was the first of our (nine) wonderful deliverances from death.' Meanwhile the temple-keeper had gone to tell the Huolu Christians where to find and supply them. He led one to the cave after nightfall. 'What a meeting! How we praised God together!'

Two days and nights 'chilled to the bone and huddled together' were enough in that cave. So they were glad when six friends arrived late on the third night and carried their children and belongings by moonlight to an isolated farmhouse, a mile from any village. They left them in the care of Farmer Gao, an influential man and his wife, with an alert watchdog and two small children whose voices would mask those of Vera and John. But by day the terraced hillsides were worked by labourers who came to draw water from the well – alongside their room. They were to live under constant strain lest their presence be discovered. Even so Charles Green managed to get a telegram sent from Huolu to Shanghai, giving Stevenson the first news of rioting at Taiyuan and a hint of their own dilemma. Their home in Huolu was being used to train twenty men and youths in Boxer mysticism and trances, to make them invulnerable to sword and bullet. Dysentery, abscesses or neuralgia were weakening each of the family.

Then to their distress word came of the Griffiths and R M Brown having turned up at Huolu almost destitute.

The mandarin at Shunde had sent them to Shanxi, but the Pingding mandarin, near Shouyang (map p 339), told them that Pigott was dead and it would be certain death to go any further west. Moneyless, they had had to walk the seventy miles back to Huolu, intending to return to Shunde, eighty more miles away. By then Mrs Griffith and her baby were too ill to go farther, but, still without encountering Boxers, they struggled on as far as Zhengding, twenty miles to the east. The cathedral premises in Zhengding had been successfully defended against Boxer attacks and, almost uniquely, the brigadier commanding the imperial troops had decided to protect them, banning Boxers from entering the city. Hearing of the Griffiths' plight, the bishop invited them to move in. So from then onwards, through Christians who took their lives in their hands, the Greens near Huolu and Griffiths at Zhengding were able to keep in touch – until suddenly Boxers searched the Greens' farmhouse.

CHAPTER TWELVE

THE GREAT EXODUS
July 1900

'Go south!'   *July 1900*

Silence or vague rumours of what was happening in the north, by July was being replaced in the Yangzi valley by authentic reports of atrocities. The consuls were calling all their nationals to head for the coast or to leave the country by whatever route they could. From Yunnan they went south to Tongking (Vietnam); and from Guangxi and Guangdong, even from Canton, to Hong Kong and Macao. From Manchuria and Mongolia they made for Siberia, or eastwards to Vladivostok, or southwards to Yingkou (Niuchuang). From the Yangzi River provinces, including Sichuan, they passed through Chongqing, Yichang, Wuhan and the river ports, congregating in great numbers in Shanghai and being dispersed as soon as possible to Japan, to Singapore or their homelands.

Telegrams to Europe and America at first reporting only riots and tragedy, began increasingly to say 'friends safe', meaning the missionaries from places named.[1] But soon among the lists of those who 'arrived safely, all well' were the names of others 'recovering' or 'murdered' or 'feared dead'. Week after week the whereabouts of many was unknown. Some found themselves guarded and escorted through hostile regions to the safety of territory under the enlightened viceroys. Others set out almost empty-handed only to be robbed of what little bedding, clothing, money and food they had with them. Destitute, wounded, cursed and pelted with stones like pariah dogs they stumbled, often barefoot and half naked, without covering from the sun, on and on for hundreds of miles, dramatically re-enacting the last few verses of Hebrews 11, a comfort to those who recalled them:

> They wandered in deserts, and in mountains, and in dens and caves of the earth.
>
> And these all, having obtained a good report through faith, received not the promise . . .
>
> (Heb. 11:38–40 AV).

Their stories are scattered in fragments through old copies of *China's Millions*, newspapers and books long out of print. But they belong to the deathless history of the Church. What could fill these volumes can only be given here in outline. Any less detail would not do them justice.

On July 6 Dr J W Hewett left Yüwu, north of Lu'an and Lucheng to consult E J Cooper (the architect) and A R Saunders, and found them at Lucheng threatened by hostile crowds. While he was away his colleague David Barratt was forced out of Yüwu, so Hewett returned there, hoping by his presence to delay the destruction of their property. Instead he found himself fleeing for his life from place to place for a month, never sleeping under the same roof for more than two or three nights, yet never more than ten miles from Yüwu. Neither he nor the Christians who harboured him could stand the strain, especially after a proclamation threatening death and destruction to any family taking him in, but a safe escort to the coast for any foreigner giving himself up. Having nowhere to turn, Hewett decided to risk consulting a friendly headman: he took Hewett to the police station.[2]

An enlightened magistrate and chief secretary agreed with him that the proclamation was a trap and by their own admission spent sleepless nights working out some way of saving his life. They told him they would put him on trial, and he must go down on his knees and bow to the ground before the magistrate, pleading that he preferred to die in custody than to be turned loose, at the mercy of the merciless. He would then be sentenced to prison, shackled for all to see, and locked away, but must not be afraid; he would be unchained and kept out of sight until it was safe again to travel.

He did as he was told, and to his amazement was treated kindly even by the prison underlings, was sent extra food by the secretary's family, and was brought a few books by the village headman. The mandarin even sent for Hewett's clothes and language study books which he had left in the care of Christians, so that he could learn to write Chinese and amuse himself by sketching.

No one knew where he was. John Stevenson cabled as late as on September 6, 'Dr Hewett, no information', and on October 8, 'apprehend the worst for . . . Dr J W Hewett'. Not until November 1 was it safe for Hewett to report that he was heading for Hankou.

His case, like the Griffiths', was another remarkable exception. David Barratt and Alfred Woodroffe of Yoyang (between Hongtong and Yüwu), still in their twenties, both individually fled

BEFORE THE MAGISTRATE
how Dr J W Hewett acted the part

HEWETT'S PRISON YARD
his sketch with Chinese brush and ink

to the hills, not knowing where the other or Hewett was. Each succeeded in evading the Boxers, but, destitute, died from their privations during the summer months.[3]

A few parties travelled to safety even from southern Shanxi, passing through hostile territory with documents and escorts from high mandarins. Members of the Swedish Mission in China (p 153) were the first to be favoured in this way, as citizens of a neutral nation. But Ci Xi later degraded the *daotai* responsible. It happened that a large sum of money had been committed to them shortly before they had to leave their base at Yüncheng. So they entrusted about £200 (thousands today) to an elder in the church (one of the first believers in Shanxi) for distribution to missionaries in distress.

With skill and daring this 'CCH' organised a secret cell of Christians who travelled through the mountains trying to keep in touch with those in hiding or making their way out of the province, and supplying their needs. Until long after the rising ended he continued to be referred to in the Mission correspondence and publications as 'CCH', lest Ci Xi should establish his identity and take revenge.[4] The danger to his family became so great that after his home was looted he took them to Xi'an and directed the cell from there, himself making hazardous journeys back into Shanxi. In Xi'an the Scandinavian Alliance gave him £145 more, to use in the same way. Without his help several groups of fugitives could not have survived. The story of his undercover contact men should be researched and published. Ten pages are to be found in *Martyred Missionaries of the CIM*.

Knowing that Christians were being hunted, tortured and killed, three of these men attempted to penetrate even into Taiyuan and the surrounding danger zones. Their search for information and for the one or two Christians in hiding who knew where each group of fugitives was hidden, and their circumstances, was in itself highly dangerous. Eva French eventually wrote: 'Elder Chang Chih-heng (Zhang Zhiheng, in *pinyin*) looked us up twice on the road as we were fleeing from Shanxi, and helped us and others with money' (p 417). In some cases faithful Chinese refused to leave their foreign friends and suffered with them. At other times the evanescent presence of 'unknown' Chinese, preserving their own lives in order to keep watch on the travellers and help them whenever possible, must have heartened the most hopeless.

The acting-governor of Shaanxi, Tuan Fang, was making his province safer than Shanxi, Zhili, or Henan. So Shaanxi was the

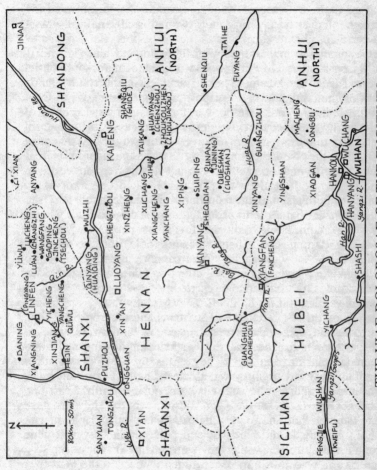

THE VIAE DOLOROSAE OF THE FUGITIVES
to show their flight paths from South Shanxi, Shaanxi and Henan

better place to make for. But several parties from Shanxi had to pass through Henan. Although out of Yü Xian's jurisdiction, some Henan mandarins were strongly anti-foreign and menacing to refugees within their grasp. None could know this when planning their routes. And the hard attitudes of Henan people that had broken the spirit of at least two early pioneers, made the long, agonising journeys of desperately sick men, women and children almost unendurable.

Three young women of the Swedish Mission in China (E Anderson, S Engstrom and M Pettersson) worked at Xin'an, south of the Yellow River, the Huang He, but included in the south Shanxi 'field' of their mission. To escape the great heat they were on holiday, living in cool cave-houses, but drawing large crowds of country folk. Alarmed that they were so conspicuous, the mandarin sent an escort and asked them to leave. On the way, via Xiangcheng (map p 359) they were threatened several times by Dadaohui (Great Sword Society) men and robbed of their few possessions, even to some of the clothing they were wearing. When one swordsman ordered M Pettersson to kneel down for him to decapitate her, 'she smiled, put her hand on his shoulder and looking up into his face said, "We are not afraid to die, but first let us speak a few words to the men escorting us."' Their assailants looked at one another, smiled and went away, saying, 'You cannot die because you are devils.' When they had gone, M Pettersson fainted, 'lost her voice for the whole day' and had to be carried.

For days they hid in the fields or in haylofts, helped by some, betrayed by others, rescued by Christians and seen on their way, only to be sent back and threatened again. Walking twelve miles at night, twenty miles the next day, eight the following night and fifteen in pouring rain on muddy roads the second day, they eventually reached a *yamen* and asked for help. The kindly mandarin and another in the next city, 'provided us with a cart and would not let us start until we had had some food'. They also gave them some clothes and money and sent them on to Taihe in safe Anhui. This made the hardship and persecution they had gone through bearable. But while they were resting on the shore of a large lake, a ferocious hurricane suddenly wrecked the boat they were travelling by, drowned people in thirty other boats, and 'drenched and bruised us'. What would Satan be allowed to do next? 'We felt that we could not go through any more.'

At last they reached Qingjiangpu on the Grand Canal, where the

Christians overwhelmed them with kindness and saw them on to a
canal launch on the way to Shanghai. Their ordeal had lasted more
than a month.

To the hills[5]   *July 1900*

The missionaries at Qüwu, south of Linfen, had very different
experiences. Within a few days of the conference at which William
Cooper had prepared the delegates for suffering, they found a
marked change in the way people treated them. Duncan Kay was in
charge at Qüwu and greatly loved by the Christians for miles
around. As death-threats increased, he sent for his colleagues to
come to the relative safety of the city. 'Here we remained,' one of
them wrote, 'for five weeks in great suspense, expectir.g every
minute to be called into the presence of the King.' When the
mandarin said he could no longer protect them, they decided to
separate into two parties and hide in the mountains until the danger
passed. Duncan Kay, his wife and child and some Christians were to
hide in the mountains of Jiangzhou while Graham McKie, Marion
Chapman and Matilda Way and other Christians went to the
Yichang range[6] (map p 339).

McKie's party set off on the night of July 4, dressed in men's
clothes, and by 4.00 am had covered ten miles and had some sleep in
a mud hut, when they heard that the Boxers were searching for
them. Hiding by day they walked twenty miles into the mountains
on the second night and lay low in a hay loft for six weeks, able only
to speak in a whisper. A devoted youth named Yuan'er brought
them food three times a day. By then, mid-August, their 'whereabouts seemed to have leaked out' and they decided to walk by night
to Hankou, six hundred miles away. Only once between July 4 and
October 21 did they venture out in open daylight.

Duncan Kay and his wife and child waited two more days before
starting on the forty-mile journey to their chosen hiding place. Too
great a distance to cover in the dark, it meant that they were seen
and talked about. Their colleague in Linfen, F C H Dreyer, even
heard from the magistrate that their whereabouts was known. He
also heard that 'CCH' had given Kay 200 taels and the promise of
more should he need it. In such difficult days there were non-
Christians prepared to house and feed people in exchange for
payment. They could be relied on because once they sheltered those
whom the governor was hunting, their own lives were at risk. But

Duncan Kay was a marked man, hated by the Boxers for speaking against them. For two months he and his wife and child dodged from place to place before being caught.[7]

As we saw in the previous chapter (p 338), A R Saunders and his family and colleagues, saved from 'the lions' mouth' at Taiyuan, had changed direction and travelled a hundred and fifty miles to Lucheng, arriving on July 5 (map p 339). Even then they thought they might be the bearers of the first report from Taiyuan and wrote to tell William Cooper what they knew – Cooper who unknown to them had died on July 1. Saunders's own story was given in full in *The Times* of September 29, 1900, and in his booklet '*A God of Deliverances*'.[8] After only one day to rest at Lucheng they were caught up in a riot. The Lu'an mission had been attacked that same morning. Bloodlust and greed for plunder were in the air. This could only be the prelude to worse attacks the next day, so at midnight all the missionaries in each place set out 'secretly' upon a nightmare journey towards Hankou, in their case seven hundred miles away.

The Lucheng party was large: the Saunders and their four children, with Alfred Jennings and Miss E Guthrie, now joined E J Cooper, his wife and two children, and two single women, Mary Huston and Hattie Rice – fourteen in all. They put their essential

HATTIE RICE AND MARY HUSTON
the last photograph before they fled

baggage on two donkeys and starting walking, carrying the small children. One donkey disappeared almost immediately and was not seen again. An opportunist had guessed their plight. Soon after daylight they hired more donkeys at a village, for the women to ride, but had gone only a mile or two when they met two hundred armed men and were robbed of all they had, even their clothes.

> Most of us were left with only a pair of Chinese trousers on, the upper part of our bodies and our heads being entirely unprotected from the awful burning of a July sun . . . All that and the following two days . . . Although we were now almost naked, without either shoes or stockings, the people would not believe that we had no silver secreted about us, and we were beaten most unmercifully (to) bring some confession as to where the silver was (concealed). The people of one village would follow us to the boundary of the next, stoning us . . . and beating us on the back and head . . . from village to village . . . Mr E J Cooper was dragged to the outside of (one) village by a rope and left by the roadside as dead. [They believed that if he died in the village his ghost would haunt it.] If we sat down anywhere to rest awhile we were stoned and beaten all the more, and the only rest we got was under cover of darkness, (in) some lonely spot (when we) slept on the hard ground . . .
>
> The first two days we had nothing to eat and no one who would even give us water to drink . . . (In one village) we refused to go on (until) they at last gave us some bread and water . . . When we had gone about two miles a man, altogether unknown to us, came up (and gave us) three dozen hard-boiled eggs, even at this unfriendly time in China . . .

A magistrate gave them money to buy food, and provided a cart and escort for a few miles, but within a mile they were robbed and left without food or money. At another stage they were stripped of some of the scanty clothing they still had. Alex Saunders was left stark naked until a single remnant was handed to him. At another, more hostile, village Hattie Rice could go no farther. When the others were driven on with sticks and whips, Mary Huston doggedly stayed with her, saying they would come on more slowly. The others had no choice, being beaten till they moved.

Saunders and E J Cooper hoped the mandarins at Jincheng (Tsechou) would send a cart back to fetch the women; and they did, but too late. On July 13 Hattie was beaten to death at the roadside and as Mary Huston lay already terribly injured 'they even ran a horse and cart over her to break her spine'. When the mandarin returned her to the others at Wuzi, near the Yellow River she was alive, but had a head wound exposing her brain.[9]

The Glovers' 'thousand miles of miracle'   July 1–9, 1900

Archibald Glover had been at Oxford and a colleague of Prebendary Webb-Peploe before joining Stanley Smith at Lu'an. Flora his wife and two children, Hedley and Hope, had joined him there in 1897. So they were relatively junior to Caroline Gates, a stalwart of fifteen years' experience in China.[10] In June a Boxer placard had been posted on a city gate at Lucheng blaming Christians for the long drought and saying that the gods had come down to give supernatural powers to any who would exterminate Christians. It claimed that all foreign ships in Chinese waters had been destroyed and most foreigners had been driven into the sea. All good Chinese must join in completing this work. But when another 'rain procession' attack was threatened at Lu'an after the Glovers left for the coast (p 323), a friendly high mandarin had not only sent troops to protect the mission, but himself went with a civil magistrate and a military mandarin – the three highest officials in the city – to stand outside the house as thousands roaring hate streamed past. Inside, Caroline Gates and five Christians who would not leave her spent the day on their knees, at first praying and then praising God for his protection.

After the Glovers returned from their mauling at Shunde, and several other terrifying brushes with death the same magistrate sent word to Archibald Glover that he had orders to withdraw all protection from foreigners. Violence against foreign nationals was to be seen as part of a people movement with no demonstrable link with the government. Boxers had been training in the neighbourhood and were expected soon to start their gruesome work, so the mission's employees had been sent home and before the Glovers' return Caroline Gates had decided to escape to the hills. Two faithful Christians, Zhong Shengmin and Bao'er, had refused to leave her. They were going to take her to a mountain cave and care for her there.

The date for the foreigners' execution was fixed for the tenth day of the sixth moon. It was time to go. In his daily reading of Scripture Glover had come to Joshua 8 (AV). On the morning of July 5 his attention was caught by the words 'Flee before them . . . flee before them' (vv 5, 6) and 'See, I have commanded you' (v 8). And when

THE GLOVER FAMILY AT HOME
before their '1,000 miles of miracle'

the household met for family prayer, the Scripture for that day (about David in 2 Samuel 15:14 AV) read, 'Arise and let us flee . . . make speed to depart.' With it came the conviction to each of them that God's will was for them to lose no time in going. With difficulty they found two men willing to take them by mule-litter to Zhou-jiakou, where they could find a boat down the Huai River to safety. Had they reached Zhoujiakou (now Zhoukouzhen) they would probably have been killed, but sufferings almost worse than death were to save them from that.

Near midnight they lifted the sleeping children from their beds and carried them to the litters, hoping to put some distance between themselves and the city before daylight. But one delay followed another, deliberately, they were to discover. Armed men in league with the muleteers gave chase and soon they realised that they were no more than prisoners. After a little food at noon on July 6 they were denied anything except weeds for two days and nights. From then onwards, in fact for forty days and nights, they 'were never free from storm and tempest and the shadow of death'.

A detachment of Boxers arrived and Shengmin, hearing their conversation in an inn courtyard, came in, and said, 'We are all to be killed,' leant his head on Caroline Gates's shoulder and wept – that he had been unable to save them. The strain of trying to protect his friends was already as much as he could bear, yet their journey had only begun. Faced with death, Glover afterwards recalled, 'The peace of God took possession of our hearts,' and even the children's terror was calmed as their mother taught them to say, 'I will trust and not be afraid.' They said goodbye to each other and 'rejoiced in the thought of so soon meeting the Lord.' Shengmin and Bao'er were free to escape and save their own lives, but refused to go.

A night of threats and taunting in a crowded inn room ended with a mock trial and an all too serious sentence of death. Taken in their mule litters 'in a kind of sacrificial procession' they ran the gauntlet between lines of spearmen who at a signal fell upon them – and fought like wild beasts to pillage their few possessions. The strong litters were wrecked and their occupants 'seemed almost buried under a frantic mass of struggling humanity from which it seemed impossible that they should come out alive'. But the Boxers were nowhere to be seen, apparently bought off by the robbers, expecting a profitable haul. And their victims were uninjured.

At the next village a mob tore their clothes off them, leaving Glover in almost nothing and Flora and Caroline Gates in their underclothes. Again they were physically unharmed. Bao'er gave Glover a pair of trousers, and 'someone in the crowd threw (him) a beggar's coat of filthy rags', himself appearing later in Glover's clothes.

Again they struggled on, surrounded by abusive crowds, yet still with the faithful Shengmin and Bao'er beside them. Told to take a certain road, but sensing from the steady beat of a gong that it led into a trap, they turned down a side path – and the whole crowd stopped dead in their tracks. No one followed. Glover did not know why, but suspected that as night had fallen fear of evil spirits near a graveyard could have been the explanation. In bright moonlight they met four Boxers who called others to help and 'fell savagely on them', stripping the women to the waist, but scorning the beggar's rags. When Glover chided them for being so shameless, they sullenly threw the women's clothing back and moved off so deliberately as to suggest more ominous plans. The fugitives fled for their lives.

After escaping down a dry torrent-bed and sleeping until midnight in the graveyard, they tramped across open country and through undergrowth to hide in the hills near by. More Boxers loudly searching for them passed close by, but on the bare top of one of the hills they found a depression deep enough to sit in, shivering with cold. When the sun rose, however, on Sunday, July 8, the heat became unbearable. Their thirst was intense and the children wailed, 'Water, water!' So Shengmin went down to find water. He failed to return. 'A great sense of loneliness came over us.' Their mouths became dry. Flora Glover showed signs of exhaustion, panting and gasping for breath, until by the end of her struggle she cried, 'Oh, God has forsaken us!' At once,

> God put into Miss Gates's mouth the most wonderful song of praise I have ever heard. Kneeling by (her) side and holding her hand, she poured forth passage after passage, promise after promise from the Scriptures exalting His name, declaring His faithfulness and proving His unchanging and unchangeable love sworn to us in the everlasting covenant and sealed to us in the blood of His own beloved Son. Never shall I forget the music of that heavenly utterance. Instantly the darkness was past and the light was shining again. The expression in my wife's face (was) of joy unspeakable . . . Then together we repeated right through – with parched lips . . . but with hearts that had tasted the wine of heaven – the beautiful hymn: 'How sweet the name of Jesus sounds in a believer's ear!'

Hotter and hotter the day became under the merciless sun, and still no sign of Shengmin. Bao'er had gone ahead and failing to find them again made his own way home. Then Caroline Gates fainted. They must get water. In the distance they could see a small stream shining in the sunlight. They stumbled down the hill and across ploughed fields and plunged into it, drinking on and on. Only then did they notice that their mouths were coated with mud – the stream was laden with silt. From there to the burial ground again with cypresses to sleep under, and their sunburnt faces and bodies blistered and peeling.

A procession passed by and they were seen. To their amazement the sub-Prefect of Lu'an had come with *yamen* underlings and a cart to look for them and take them on towards Hankou. Had they waited on the hilltop the mandarin would have gone his way. But Shengmin failed to find them, so he too went home. The sub-Prefect ordered them to climb in, showing them a safe conduct pass and a bundle of clothing. So, taking the risk that he was lying and would deliver them to Boxers, they obeyed and were carried to the next town, Wangfang, and given a meal. 'Shall I ever forget the fragrance of the savoury pork dumplings set steaming hot before us!' After all that had happened it was still Sunday, July 8, only the third day since they left Lu'an. But the pork dumplings were deceptive.

Soon they discovered that Wangfang was full of Boxers, hundreds wearing their insignia. They were not mistaken. It was a trap. A guard was placed at the door of their room and great activity outside showed that preparations were being made for some event. A little old woman hobbled in on her bound feet and told them, 'They are piling wood all round you to burn you to death in this room. The Wangfang evangelist's wife is to die with you.' And with, 'I feel very sorry for you,' she hobbled away again. 'Once again we were face to face with the king of terrors.' The room was then emptied of furniture, even the bed mat, confirming the old woman's message. So they cried to God who had delivered them time after time already.

Apart from the miraculous, their only hope seemed to lie in the fact that the sub-Prefect's mule was still tethered near the cart outside. Suddenly Glover saw a man untethering it. 'Now or never: come at once!' he cried, and together they dashed past the sentry and into the cart, taking the Boxers and the *yamen* escort by surprise. They were under the safe-pass and in the sub-Prefect's hands. He must hand them over or the Boxers must snatch them

RUTS IN THE SOLID ROCK
torture to ride in springless carts

back. 'Burn them in the cart,' some suggested. But the mandarin
had been worsted and (to save his own face) he 'mounted his horse,
the soldiers tore at the mule's mouth and off we dashed . . . pursued
by hundreds of local Boxers, shouting, "Death to the foreign
devils!"'

Deposited for the night at an open theatre stage where homeless
beggars slept, in the next town, they were told they were to be killed
in the morning. All hope seemed again to have forsaken them, when
four-year-old Hedley said, 'I think Jesus must have slept in a place
like this when he had nowhere to go! We ought to be glad that we are
like Jesus, oughtn't we?' Very well, they thought, if this was where
their Father God allowed them to be, they would be content. A man
risked death by giving them food and water, and an old woman
supplied a needle and thread. But the official and escort were
nowhere to be seen until noon the next day, when two mounted
soldiers with drawn swords rode past them – their executioners,
they were told. 'Thus our minds were directed perpetually to the
thought of death.' Then the sub-Prefect reappeared, led them
through the city gate and told them to mount two springless
coal-carts of a type known as 'mountain tigers'. 'What else could this
mean than that we were common felons riding to a felon's death?'

Glover protested that his pregnant wife could not endure such treatment, but without effect. The mandarin who could let them be burned alive by the Boxers could not care less for their comfort. They drove on, bumping and crashing from boulder to boulder over the pass, their escort telling onlookers that they were to be executed at Gaoping. Sure that this time they were going to their death, Glover suddenly thought of the words 'Mighty to save', describing Jesus. He ran forward to tell the others, and Flora reminded him that her hopes were pinned to Job's declaration, 'I shall not die, but live, and declare the works of the Lord.' In the shadow of death they feared no evil as they reached Gaoping – and kind treatment in the *yamen*.

The magistrate sent his son to reassure them and gave them money for clothes and the next day's travel. One *yamen* gentleman gave Glover a clean gown and removed his beggar rags. 'A beautiful supper' was served them and a supply of rice, bread and eggs for their journey. They thought they would soon be out of nightmare Shanxi and into a more peaceful Henan. But across the Yellow River half-a-dozen groups of refugees were in the same predicament, and in central Shanxi on that same day 'no fewer than fifty' missionary men, women and children, and unnumbered Chinese Christians, were being put to the sword – a prelude to many more.

Escape to Hankou[11]   *July 1900*

Two hours after the Canadian Presbyterians reached Nanyang on July 7 (p 341), the innkeeper told them that seventy armed men were on the way to take the inn and everything in it. The Canadians sent word to the magistrate that they held him responsible for their safety, and prepared to defend themselves. Barricades of carts and household paraphernalia, and heaps of stones, were made ready. But he sent an escort and they set out the next morning through massed thousands of townsfolk and 'two bands of several hundreds armed with swords, spears and guns'. 'We had only three revolvers amongst us,' Jonathan Goforth wrote. 'The whole crowd came on us with a rush . . . We had to defend ourselves. I got nine wounds on my arms and hands, the only serious one being . . . at the back of the skull; I also got eight blows with clubs.' But they escaped, robbed of almost all their possessions, and pressed on southwards towards

Fancheng (now Xiangfan). At a Muslim village 'the men said they would fight' for (them), but when the attack was renewed, the travellers fought alone. Dr Leslie had his revolver hand nearly severed by a sword-cut, and a tendon of one knee cut through. Some cited Ci Xi's edict that all foreigners should be killed, and attacked them repeatedly – until they reached the Han River at Fancheng. There the leading engineer in their party, Jamieson, sent a telegram to the viceroy, Zhang Zhitong. He sent two gunboats and soldiers to see them all safely to Wuhan, where two American consuls came out in a tug to meet them (map p 359).

Passing Sheqidian on July 7, the Canadians had sent a message to the CIM there, warning them to escape.[12] Dr Whitfield Guinness, H S Conway, his wife and month-old baby and W Wilson, a young single woman, wrote to the Nanyang mandarin for help, but the few soldiers who came to guard them soon melted away. When 'a vast crowd' assembled and began breaking through the main gate, the household climbed a wall and into the neighbour's loft. Their Chinese teacher, 'pale and nervous', said, 'Hide! It does not matter if you are killed, but I fear worse things may happen to you!' In the loft among all the dust and lumber they lay listening to 'the crash and falling of masonry and timber, (and) a crackling of flames', waiting for the child to cry and give away their hiding-place.

Time and again men came searching for them and each time their neighbour managed to deter them from searching the loft, and a second loft to which he moved them. As they lay in a dark corner for four days, men stacked straw and timber round the whole house, saying, 'We will burn them out and kill them if they run.' Whitfield Guinness wrote a letter to his parents on the back of some sermon notes, telling how they planned to escape. At last the neighbour could protect them no longer. He appeared at the trap-door and said, 'Fly! They have come with swords to kill you!' The debris of their own home remained the only place to flee to, and there they crouched under a blazing sun. A man came over the wall. It was impossible to avoid discovery. But he said, 'They have gone!'

Five days after the riot friendly Chinese disguised them and took them through the streets to large business premises where they were hidden in a strongroom and the chief merchant himself, armed with a gun, a sword and two daggers, 'a man of power', stood guard to protect them. Then one night their friends took them secretly to a small boat on the river and escorted them downstream, all together in one cabin for two weeks. Thirty days after their home had been destroyed and, a month since they had had a change of clothing, they reached Hankou.

C M Lack was alone at Sihua, an outpost of the Zhoujiakou mission, when a mob attacked it after dark on July 7.[13] He and a Chinese companion fled to the *yamen*, and thirty soldiers were sent back with him. 'Reaching the place, the soldiers rushed in with a yell, and what a sight!' Everything of any value had been looted and the place was a shambles of discarded waste. As the crowd scattered, Lack and the evangelist slipped away and in spite of being trailed by four men 'armed with swords and guns', reached Zhoujiakou on Sunday, July 8, unharmed. There he had two days' respite before being rioted out again.

An Italian-born member of the CIM, Alfonso Argento, was the only missionary in the city of Guangzhou, 140 miles south of Zhoujiakou on that Sunday, July 8, when a mob armed with knives attacked the mission premises.[14] The street was 'packed from one end to the other', and there was no other way of escape. Manhandled by a dense crush of attackers in the guest-hall, Argento struggled out of his Chinese gown by which they were holding him, dived to the ground and reached a corner where he crouched out of sight. As everything was being wrecked, a screen fell, partly covering him, until he could crawl under a table. The house was wrecked and broken timber was being piled in the centre of the main room and soaked with kerosene, when a man with a burning firebrand looking for more fuel saw Argento. 'With a rush they . . . dragged me from under the table and on to the pile of wood.' Others used benches to batter him. 'They poured kerosene on my clothes and set them on fire.' Neighbours tore off his burning jacket and dragged him outside by his hair. At this the rioters struck at his head with a pole and knocked him unconscious. When the mandarin came that night and found him lying in the street in a pool of blood, he had him moved into the ruined chapel. There, some Christians took turns to stay with him until he regained consciousness on the fourth day, Wednesday, July 11.

Hearing that plans to decapitate Argento were being discussed, the mandarin, in spite of threats against himself, had him put on a bamboo stretcher and carried the 140 miles to Zhoujiakou. 'Take him away,' he said, 'I don't want him to die here.' An escort of fifty foot-soldiers and twenty mounted men, all well armed and led on the first day by the mandarin himself on horseback, protected him from repeated assaults on the way. But on Sunday July 15 while the stretcher-bearers and escort were resting at an inn, he was left in the open for an hour at the mercy of 'thousands' who crowded round him, pulling his hair and knocking him about although he feigned death. Finally a local mandarin, only twenty-five miles from Zhoujiakou and friends, refused to let him go further and forced the cavalcade to return to his starting-point at Guangzhou. On the way, at place after place he was maltreated, being left for a whole night in the rain. And 'because a bamboo stretcher was too grand' he was transferred to a springless wheelbarrow, in spite of his wounds and bruises.

Hearing that he was lying abandoned in a *yamen* yard, a gentleman came and took him home, put him to bed and gave him three good meals each day for three days while it poured with rain. He even urged him to stay until he could send him safely to Hankou, but the choice was not the victim's to make. To the many visitors who came to sympathise with him, Argento explained the gospel. But finally the mandarin sent for him and sent him under escort to Guangzhou.

There again the mandarin left him in the *yamen* yard for four hours 'at the mercy of large crowds of enemies who abused me and mocked me, saying, "God has brought you safely back, has he? Your God cannot save you. Jesus is dead" . . . They spat in my face . . . and others expressed themselves in the most vile way.' The magistrate's chief concern was to prevent Argento from being killed while in his custody. So after dark he sent him on towards Hankou, with an escort who abandoned him at the roadside. He stayed where he was until daylight and, walking on, took refuge at a little inn. When some thirty armed men came looking for him, saying they were hunting a 'foreign devil' to kill him, the innkeeper denied having seen him. Argento was lying on the ground with his face to the wall and his arm over his head, and was not recognised although they stayed until first light before setting off again.

He continued his journey alone, later in the day, feeling too weak and despondent to do more than stagger painfully along. A man coming towards him stopped, looked closely at him, and went on. Then he stopped again, turned and said, 'Are you not Mr Ai?' Cautiously Argento answered, 'Who are you?' and was told 'Lo of Wulidian'. Then Argento remembered meeting him at Runan two years before, and said, Yes, he was Argento. At that the man shed tears and offered to take him all the way to Hankou.

As good as his word, Lo collected money, food and clothing from his home and for a week they travelled on together. Three times their 'lives were at stake', but they reached their journey's end on July 31; as Argento put it in another understatement, 'glad to have the dangers and sufferings over, and to be able to rest and get medical treatment'.

Heartless Henan was exacting a high price from its victims. Their experiences varied greatly and were still far from over.

Escapes through Anhui   *July 1900*

C Howard Bird, an Australian, had been away on a preaching trip for six or seven weeks when he returned to Xiangcheng on July 7 to find 'frightful reports' circulating, and his colleagues preparing to leave at short notice.[15] Amid great excitement the townsfolk were making human effigies of dough and boiling them, to shouts of 'Boil the foreigners!' 'The engineers of the Peking Syndicate with their retinue' and Canadian Presbyterians had already passed through, and the Christians were urging the Gracies and John Macfarlane (on a visit from Tasmania) to go north to Zhoujiakou or they would be killed. Howard Bird chose to stay with the Xiangcheng Christians if he could.

The others left early on July 8, but on arrival at Zhoujiakou found large crowds converging on the mission. Their mules were seized and led into an innyard where hundreds surrounded them, shouting 'Kill the foreigners!' In this extremity they succeeded in persuading some officials to escort them a few miles south-eastwards towards Taihe in Anhui where they could hire a boat to take them by river to the Grand Canal. After several brushes with death they reached Zhenjiang on the Yangzi on August 4.

A general spirit of unrest had seized the country-folk, as in the worst regions of the drought. They began looting the granaries of the wealthy. Soon, they believed, they were going to need everything they could lay hands on, to buy food. At Xiangcheng the evangelist and others came to Howard Bird with reports of foreigners being killed farther south. He must escape while he could.[16] He set off with one companion carrying some bedding, silver and small change. People were friendly but guessed from the absence of baggage that they were in trouble. After the first night they were told that all the foreigners at Zhoujiakou had been killed. It was untrue. But while Bird hid in the fields by a river bank, his

Chinese companion went to find a boat and took him to it. Bird hid under a mat covering but was discovered by an inquisitive youngster and a crowd that quickly gathered robbed him of everything but his trousers. *Yamen* underlings then dragged him down the street of the nearby town by his hair.

Desolate and helpless, Bird was befriended by an unknown Muslim who gave him food, hid him for two days and then hired another boat on which Bird hid below the deckboards all that night and the next day. And when they reached Zhoujiakou and learned that the Chinese Christians' homes had been pillaged and most were in hiding, the boatmen lured him ashore and left him destitute 'in a great city full of enemies'. A gatekeeper let him sleep in his hovel, and he left at dawn and trudged unharmed to the next city. But again the *yamen* would not move a finger to protect or help him. Still destitute, he wandered on until a passer-by directed him to a village where Christians took him in, gave him a tub of hot water and a meal, and made him lie down and rest. Two of them went on with him, but only forty miles from Taihe they fell into the hands of robbers. 'Three great ruffian-looking fellows . . . led me to a field . . . produced three great swords and began swinging them about just above my head . . . I really thought my last moment had come. I just lifted my heart up to God. I had no fear, only joy that I should soon see Jesus. But it was not to be.'

That night, half a dozen or more of the gang encircled him and his friends and all settled down to sleep. Bird whispered to one of the Christians that he was going to escape. He crept away 'and then ran for dear life, not resting till I was some six or seven miles away'. Nor did he eat or rest properly until he had covered seventeen miles to the city of Shenqiu and reached the *yamen*, not knowing what reception he would be given. His surprise at a kindly hearing was no greater than the officials' amazement at his story. They took him in, gave him a good breakfast and sent him on by cart under escort. At about 10 pm on July 24 they reached Taihe. 'The city gates were shut, but on sending in the mandarin's letter they were at once opened, and a great array of officials and soldiers with big lanterns ushered me into the city and escorted me to the (mission) house. What a welcome I had!'

One after another had almost reached Zhoujiakou from the north, south and west, only to find such danger that to go nearer would be foolhardy. So each party had bypassed the city, only sending messages to the two couples, two single men (Charles Lack and Robert Powell) and four single women trapped inside.[17] The pro-Boxer mandarins in the main city of Chenzhou (now Huaiyang) and at Zhoujiakou itself prevaricated, while rumours spread that on July 24 first the Christians and then the foreigners were to be killed. On the 9th they refused to see Powell and in the hearing of a crowd said they could not protect them – an admission as good as a licence to kill.

Early the next morning the mission was attacked at its three entrances simultaneously, and all the missionaries had to climb over a high wall to take refuge in an unwilling neighbour's home. The mandarin then came with soldiers, but merely said to the mob, 'Take what you like but don't hurt the foreigners,' and went away. So when their hiding place became known there was no alternative but to take the great risk of brazenly walking out into the crowd. They found them so busy carrying off all their belongings that with the help of some well disposed onlookers they reached the *yamen* of the chief of police. To their delight Yan Dalao, a Hunanese, took their side and gave them his best room to use. But he said he could do no more than help to make arrangements for them to travel to Anhui. More than once he returned, unable to persuade boatmen to take the risk, and even wept with concern for his guests.

With reports of hundreds of men waiting to intercept them if they should leave the city, they succeeded in arranging for an escort of soldiers, but half of them decamped, afraid of the consequences. At that Yan Dalao said, 'If God does not help you now, we can do nothing.' They were all in the act of praying together when, outside, a shout announced the arrival of a force of soldiers from Huaiyang, the prefecture. And more were following behind them. The date was Friday July 13. An order had been received, it was said, from the great Li Hongzhang on the 12th, that all foreigners were to be protected. But possibly it came from Liu Kunyi and Zhang Zhitong (see p 333).

Li had been reinstated on July 9 to the viceroyalty of Zhili, and Senior Guardianship of the throne, and had left Canton for Hong Kong and Shanghai without delay. He had been honoured with the privilege of wearing on the official square on his chest back and front a five-clawed dragon, such as only the emperor wore on a circular plaque. The Western communities were unimpressed. They wished to keep him in the south to protect the Yangzi agreements. He did not resume his viceroyalty in Zhili until October 1.

Whatever the truth, the effect of a report that he had ordered the protection of foreigners everywhere had immediate effect when it was received and made public. But where telegraph lines were lacking, wilful delaying tactics appear to have been employed by anti-foreign officials in Henan, Zhejiang and, predictably, in Shanxi. Some parties escaping from Shanxi to Henan suffered no more physical injuries after July 16, but were shown undisguised hatred by the Chenzhou mandarin as long afterwards as the 22nd. After all that had happened, Shanghai was still in the dark, and John Stevenson could only send his first tentative crisis cables to the homelands on July 21 and 23.

'The Butcher of Shanxi'   July 9, 1900

If little mercy had been shown before Li Hongzhang intervened in the south, none at all could be expected from the military, the Boxers, the riff-raff or the anti-foreign mandarins in Governor Yü Xian's Shanxi. July 9 was the worst day of horror and the signal for atrocities continuing until September.

The twenty missionaries and children (called thirty in error) crowded together in G B Farthing's home in Taiyuan (p 338) well knew the danger they were in. After the destruction of the old CIM premises (taken over and expanded by the Shouyang Mission) and the Schofield Memorial Hospital, the survivors had fled to the BMS. All were 'protected' by armed guards, but as it later proved, were themselves under house arrest.[18] Dr Lovitt's words 'We cannot but hope for deliverance' were echoed by Millar Wilson in a note to F C H Dreyer at Linfen: 'It's all fog, but I think, old chap, that we are on the edge of a volcano, and I fear Taiyuan is the inner edge. I'd rather be where you are.' In spite of this, after the hospital went up in flames, Wilson wrote asking for medicines and surgical instruments to be sent to him.

As early as June 21 G B Farthing had written to Herbert Dixon of the BMS in Xinzhou (pp 342–3) saying that the Taiyuan telegraph clerk had told him about Ci Xi's secret edict, that all foreigners were to be killed. 'If it is true, I am ready and do not fear; if such be God's will I can even rejoice to die.' Dixon's comment to an evangelist named Zhao had been, 'I feel just the same.' It was no secret. Even before making an official announcement, Governor Yü Xian talked in public about it.[19]

Reports from the rest of the province added to their fears. Dreyer had heard of one thousand Boxers being expected 'to clear the province of Christians', and four hundred were soon at work. The Soping and Xiaoyi murders had been a foretaste. After a disturbance at Fenzhou (ten miles from Xiaoyi), the prefect and city magistrate took energetic action to control the attackers, and urged the missionaries to fire on them if in danger. At the time the A P Lundgrens and Annie Eldred of the CIM were staying with two Oberlin College couples of the American Board. When the edict arrived, withdrawing protection from foreigners, like other good men in authority this mandarin also wept. With such friends in office the missionaries were still hopeful when preparations for an escape came to nothing, and were still there in August. But in Taiyuan stories were being put about that missionaries were poisoning wells. The rumour was widespread, often to the effect that hired renegades and beggars did it for them. As a result many innocent people were being accused, tortured and killed.

Troops had been passing through Huolu, Zhili, for several days, going they said, 'to stop the Russians', when the Greens (p 352)

YÜ XIAN, THE BUTCHER OF SHANXI

learned that Governor Yü Xian himself was expected. He and a regiment of soldiers had been summoned by Ci Xi. But a display of reluctance by the people of Taiyuan to let him go (a customary ploy possibly staged this time by Yü Xian himself) led to his deferring his departure long enough for him personally to direct the events of the next few days. He boasted of his subtlety when he claimed his reward from the dowager empress.

On July 3 all foreigners, Catholic and Protestant, were told to congregate 'for their protection' at the previous headquarters of the Railway Bureau alongside the magistrate's *yamen* in the Boar's Head Lane (Zhu Tou Xiang) near to the governor's *yamen*. After well-justified hesitation they moved in on the 6th. All mission property was immediately wrecked and ransacked by the mobs, another portent. There at the Bureau they were kept waiting in suspense for death that could come to them at any moment.[20] The Catholic bishops, Gregory Grassi and Francis Fogolla, two foreign priests, the Sisters of Mary who ran five orphanages, and a lay brother were accompanied by Chinese priests, students for the priesthood and nine servants. The BMS was represented by G B Farthing and his wife, with three children, their governess E M Stewart, and Hudson Taylor's one-time personal secretary, Frank Whitehouse, and his wife. Dr and Mrs A E Lovitt and an infant, and the G W Stokes and J Simpsons, were joined by Dr and Mrs Millar Wilson and their baby, Jane Stevens and Mildred Clarke of the CIM, and by Alexander Hoddle and the W F Beynons of the B&FBS with their three children. T W Pigott and his party had not yet arrived from Shouyang.

The first eye-witness account of events in Taiyuan came from Yong Zheng, a reliable Christian who escaped and carried the news to Dr J A Creasey Smith of Peking (see p 428). On July 8, Yong Zheng was in a village about three miles from the city of Taiyuan when he saw two carts containing the Pigotts and other Shouyang foreigners, John Robinson, Mary Duval and the Atwater girls, with an escort of seven or eight soldiers (p 342). The men were in manacles so Mrs Pigott was feeding her husband. To the astonishment of the crowd that gathered, Pigott and Robinson proceeded to preach the gospel to them and Yong Zheng heard some say, 'You're going to be killed for preaching, yet you go on doing so.' After the main escort arrived (p 342), Pigott asked that they might be taken to join the others at the Bureau, but his party were all thrown into the common prison for the night.

Governor Yü Xian had netted his victims. On the morning of July 9 he sent for them all to be brought to his *yamen* 'before being sent to the coast'. His motive may have been less cat and mouse than to ensure their coming quietly. Accounts of what followed are largely based on Yong Zheng's statement:

> The next day I was on the street near the Governor's *yamen*; I saw a big crowd and went to see what it was they were following. I found it was the foreign pastors and their wives and children and Roman Catholic priests and nuns and some Christians. I heard people say they were going to be killed, and I tried to get out of the crowd, but could not, so stayed and witnessed with my own eyes the killing of all the foreigners.
>
> [Forsyth added: They were all ranged in line outside the *yamen* entrance in the open space next to the street.] The whole number of men, women and children were then stripped to the waist like common criminals, and were made to wait in this degrading condition till the Governor came out to inspect them. [He asked their nationality, laughed scornfully at their answer, and at once gave the order for their decapitation.]
>
> The first to be led forth was Pastor Farthing. His wife clung to him, but he gently put her aside, and going in front of the soldiers, himself knelt down without saying a word, and his head was struck off by one blow of the executioner's knife.
>
> He was quickly followed by Pastors Hoddle and Beynon, Drs Lovitt and Wilson, all of whom were beheaded with one blow by the executioner. Then the Governor (Yü Xian) grew impatient and told his bodyguard, all of whom carried big beheading knives with long handles, to help to kill the others. Pastors Stokes, Simpson and Whitehouse were next killed, the last one by one blow only, the other two by several. When the men were finished, the ladies were taken. Mrs Farthing had hold of the hands of her children who clung to her, but the soldiers parted them, and with one blow beheaded their mother. The executioner beheaded all the children and did it skilfully, needing only one blow; but the soldiers were clumsy, and some of the ladies suffered several cuts before death. Mrs Lovitt was wearing her spectacles and held the hand of her little boy even when she was killed. She spoke to the people, saying, as near as I remember: 'We all came to China to bring you the good news of salvation by Jesus Christ; we have done you no harm, only good; why do you treat us so?' A soldier took off her spectacles before beheading her, which needed two blows.
>
> When the Protestants were killed, the Roman Catholics were led forward. The Bishop, an old man, with a long white beard, asked the

Governor (Yü Xian) why he was doing this wicked deed. I did not hear the Governor give him any answer, but he drew his sword and cut the bishop across the face one heavy stroke; blood poured down his white beard, and he was beheaded.[21] The priests and nuns quickly followed him in death.

Then Pastor Piggott and his party were led from the district gaol which is close by. He was still handcuffed; so was Mr Robinson. He preached to the people till the very last, when he was beheaded with one blow. Mr Robinson suffered death very calmly. Mrs Pigott held the hand of her son, even when she was beheaded, and he was killed immediately after her. The lady and two girls [Mary Duval and the Atwater girls] were killed also, quickly. In all on that one day forty-five foreign people were beheaded – thirty-three Protestants and twelve Roman Catholics. A number of native Christians were also killed; I did not see them all, but I was told there were thirteen . . .

All were surprised at the firmness and quietness of the foreigners; none cried or made any noise, except two or three of the children. [Taken down from Yong Zheng's words by J A Creasey Smith.][22]

Hosea Ballou Morse, using Forsyth and quoting Yong Zheng's accounts in the *Chinese Recorder*, emphasised that the order was carried out,

first on the Protestants of Taiyuan, then on the Roman Catholics, then on the Protestants from Shouyang . . . So perished . . . under the eyes of (Yü Xian) the governor and by his orders, 34 (British Protestants and 12 Roman Catholics – 15 men, 20 women, and 11 children; in addition, the heads of six American missionaries killed at Taigu were, according to his own report to the Empress Dowager, sent to this governor (Yü Xian), now 'infamous for ever'. [But the Taigu massacre happened three weeks later.]

Discrepancy exists between the eyewitness Yong Zheng's figures; forty-five foreign people (thirty-three Protestants), and Forsyth's summary, by name including Edith Coombs: 'Forty-six Europeans – thirty-four Protestants and twelve Roman Catholics . . . besides Miss E Coombs, who died on June 27.' But Forsyth's own summary in *China Martyrs* (p 140) includes Miss Coombs in his total of forty-six. Morse's total follows Forsyth's, omitting his observation that 'This made the full tale of fifty-one (not counting Miss Coombs) for which it was afterwards found (Yü Xian) had claimed a reward from the Empress Dowager in Peking.'[23] What may well be the explanation was found in the diary of Jingshan, the Peking court official, on July 16:

> (Yü Xian) has memorialised the throne, reporting that he cunningly entrapped all the foreigners, cast them into chains, and had every one of them decapitated in his *yamen*. Only one woman had escaped, after her breasts had been cut off, and she had hidden herself under the city wall; she was dead when they found her.

This could also throw light on Yong Zheng's statement about some ladies receiving several sword-cuts, although he was referring primarily to the soldiers' inferior ability.[24]

Another enigma has no explanation or sequel. 'CCH', the organiser of the Christian 'secret cell', a careful observer and correspondent, also wrote on July 26 to Eric Folke, 'I heard a rumour that in Taiyuan, on the 12th of the 6th moon (July 9) thirty-seven foreigners and thirty Chinese were massacred. I have heard the same report from five different *yamens*. I cannot vouch whether this rumour is true or not.'[25]

'CCH' left his family five days later on one of his mercy missions in Shanxi, learning all he could of what was happening to his fellow-Christians and missionary friends. On his return he wrote again, factually and precisely. He gave no hint of unverified rumour in saying, 'The Prefect of (Puzhou), returning from (Taiyuan) brought a foreign child; sex unknown. We do not know to whom the child belongs.' Such a report would certainly have been investigated when the uprising ended, and much would have been made of it if the child had been recovered. But on this there is silence.[26]

Yong Zheng's report continued:

> The bodies of all were left where they fell till next morning, as it was evening before the work was finished. During the night they were stripped of clothing and other things, such as rings and watches. Next day they were removed to a place inside the great South Gate, except some of the heads, which were placed in cages on the gates of the city wall. On the 11th July the remains were temporarily buried outside the great South Gate, to the west side. On the 10th July there were also killed many Catholic Christians, I heard six, and during the next few days a few more Protestants were also killed.[27]

Another source of information was an Evangelist Zhao, from Shandong, who had spent eighteen years at Xinzhou, north of

Taiyuan. Because he was well known he lay low while a companion, Wang Xiyo, the son of a general, gathered information and reported to him. Trustworthy people who were not eye-witnesses supplied him with all that they learned. Understandably, their accounts differed in several respects from the other sources.

To deviate a little from the chronological presentation; during the months of July, August and September, 'CCH' collected the names of many Chinese Christians who had suffered and were suffering still for the faith, and reports of recantations. He revealed his own standing with officials and Christians alike in making such references as,

> I sent (Cao Qingho) to (Qüwu, Linfen, Hongtong, Hezhou, Fenzhou and Taiyuan) to obtain information . . . I also sent Lui San to ascertain . . . the whereabouts and condition of the missionaries. [Owing to the extreme danger they did not reach all their objectives] . . . Many of the magistrates are afraid . . . and are desirous that the Christians should write a paper saying that they have ceased to practise the religion. Magistrates speak to me personally in a very friendly way . . . (The Boxers) are pressing the magistrates to assist them to ferret out all Christians and inquirers, that they may either be forced to recant or be murdered . . . I have sent men to tell the Christians to leave their homes and go into the country, and those near (Shaanxi) to cross over into that province . . .
>
> Near Linfen the people rose up and got hold of all the (remaining) Christian men and women, with a knife cut a cross on their foreheads, and they afterwards tortured them before killing them, throwing their bodies into the Fen River . . . The villagers then destroyed all their properties and homes . . . My own home has been looted. I have in consequence taken my whole family to (Xi'an), barely escaping with our lives . . . I write the letter with tears; and my family, after hearing the above news, were unable to eat for three days . . . The persecutions of the Christians in Shanxi are indescribable . . . The wives and daughters of the Christians have been shamefully treated and tortured.[28]

Late in October Matilda Way wrote, after her eventual escape,

> Our hearts are filled with joy when we think of the faithfulness of the Christians at Taiyuan. The missionaries were beheaded first, and then the (Chinese) Christians [those brought for execution] had to kneel down and drink their blood, and as they knelt, were killed – not one denied Christ. The schoolgirls were taken to the *yamen* and the

Governor said to them, 'You follow the foreigners'; they answered
'No, we follow Christ.' He then said, 'You read the foreigners' book';
to which they replied, 'No, we read God's Book.'

These schoolgirls were martyred with their fellow Christians in
Taiyuan. After this butchery a new wave of persecution and bloodshed swept through Shanxi with the loss of many lives. Among the
mature believers who refused to recant or pretend to do so, were
children who would not be moved by threat or torture.

Miracles continued, and withheld   *July 9–13, 1900*

The Glovers and Caroline Gates (p 369) learned late of Yü Xian's
order that all foreigners in Shanxi be sent to Taiyuan.

> Why, therefore, we were not sent north instead of south is a mystery,
> (but) we were sent on under arrest with nothing but a criminal's
> passport and at the mercy of each magistrate . . . We never knew
> when we left one city what awaited us in the next. More than once we
> were on the point of being sent back to Lu'an, and once it was all but
> decided to send us direct to (Yü Xian) himself. Of the nineteen
> *yamens* through which we passed, fourteen were so anti-foreign that
> it was a moot point with each whether we should be passed on, sent
> back or executed there and then.[29]

After spending the night of that bitterest of days, July 9, sleeping
the sleep of the exhausted on a stone platform, they were taken for
thirty miles on the same springless coal-carts, bumping and crashing
from boulder to boulder, 'a terrible journey', as far as Jincheng
(Tsechou). At each market town they passed through, hostile
crowds surrounding them discussed in their hearing how they were
to die.

> Foreign blood must be spilled by reason of the drought. But . . . how
> much? Should all our party be put to death, or only one? . . . A child
> or an adult? . . . Finally (it was) decided to put the ladies to death on
> the spot . . . The thought of having first to witness and then to survive
> the murder of my wife was insupportable . . .

But no one raised a hand against them. They arrived at traditionally anti-foreign Jincheng (Tsechou) to be mobbed and
threatened, but not injured, while the Roman Catholic mission was

set on fire. All the next morning, crowds which 'seemed to spring from nowhere' as they continued the journey, chanted the Boxer song, 'Foreign blood must be spilled e'er the rain can fall.' Spiritism and the ancient fertility rites had reared their ugly heads in a wholesale submission to the powers of evil. Blistered and wailing from unrelieved exposure to the July sun, the children's misery even moved the callous escort to lend an old straw hat to shade them. But no allowances were made for Flora Glover's pregnancy, or dysentery.

Near Huaiqing, close to the Yellow River, they were locked into a room with five stark naked, opium-smoking guards while a mob outside yelled for their execution to end the drought. As Glover listened, he remembered the words of Scripture, 'And call upon me in the day of trouble: I will deliver thee, and thou shalt glorify me' (Ps. 50:15 AV).

> Accordingly, kneeling up on the bed we poured out our hearts before Him, in Chinese so that the gaolers might know exactly what we were doing and what we were asking . . . Scarcely had we risen from our knees when . . . down upon the howling mobs swept the sudden fury of a torrential flood of waters. In a few seconds the street was deserted and not a sound was heard but the . . . rushing rains.
> The effect upon our gaolers was immediate; something akin to awe took the place of their hard incredulity . . . The rain fell in sheets . . . all that day and far into the night.[30]

The door was unlocked and an official came in, ordered the guards to kill their prisoners, and withdrew. Thereupon an attempt to stupefy them by poisonous fumes barely failed. In the morning the guards explained, 'These people have been praying to God, and we could do nothing against their prayers.' Instead they were taken on, past people too busy in their fields to pay attention to doomed prisoners. They crossed the Taihang mountain range and the Henan border – out of Yü Xian's jurisdiction – only to find the Dadaohui, the Great Sword Society, still active in Henan and more crowds as merciless as ever. But it was July 13, the day after Li Hongzhang's order had been circulated. It was also the day that Hattie Rice and Mary Huston were separated from the Saunders and E J Coopers, and fatally attacked near Jincheng where the Glovers had just been spared (p 363).[31]

The Datong six   *June 24–July 12, 1900*

While the sieges at the Beitang cathedral and the legations in Peking kept their imprisoned thousands in constant danger, the consolation of being in it all together made their suffering in some ways more tolerable than for the isolated individuals and handfuls in the provinces. And terrible as were the long drawn-out sufferings of those trying to escape to the south through Henan, the terrors of being at the mercy of Yü Xian's indoctrinated Boxers were more acute.

Away to the north of Shanxi, between the two arms of the Great Wall, the CIM had two couples and two women at Datong (map p 339) serving a thriving church. Charles and Florence I'Anson of Grattan Guinness's Harley College and Cambridgeshire, and Stewart and Kate McKee of Glasgow (to be distinguished from Graham McKie and the Duncan Kays of Qüwu), had as colleagues two young women, Margaret Smith and Maria Aspden. Unconfirmed news of the massacre of six missionaries at Datong reached the coast early in 1901; but hope was slow to die that they might have escaped through Mongolia to Russian Siberia. Not until June 1901 did eyewitnesses arrive at Tianjin to tell the full story.[32]

Boxers had appeared at Datong on June 14, 1900, and began drilling recruits in public. But eighteen new Christians had dared to be baptised four days later. The long-expected attack came on the 24th, and the missionaries, with three I'Anson children and four-year-old Alice McKee fled to the *yamen* under a hail of stones. The apparently friendly prefect took them in, and when they returned home a few days later for the birth of Kate's baby, he posted guards to protect them. Meanwhile, the atrocities at Soping, Zuoyün, Yingzhou and Henyüan had fed the lust for blood in the prefectural city.

Three days after the Taiyuan massacre, a minor official came to take their names, a cold-blooded act 'for the record' and rewards, and three hundred horse and foot soldiers surrounded the house to prevent their escape. All were killed by the sword and flung into the flames of their burning home. Thirty-two Chinese Christians met a similar death, including five of those newly baptised. When the Roman Catholics in Datong shared the same fate, the toll of victims rose to more than one hundred – another heyday for the devil. When teams of investigators eventually arrived, eyewitness accounts confirmed the first hearsay reports.

Daning and Hejin   *July 12–16, 1900*

Enlightened mandarins somehow maintained the peace at Linfen in 'south-central Shanxi'. But over the mountains to the west, semi-isolated on the western flank, were country churches in the cities of Xi Xian and Ji Xian (then known as Sichou and Chichou), and in the smaller towns of Daning and Hejin (spelled as Ho-tsin at that time). Daning and Xi Xian had been pioneered by Montagu Beauchamp and William Cassels in 1886 when the first church was formed (HTCOC Book 6, pp 403–8). As late as July 7 John and Alice Young at Ji Xian and on July 8 the Nathan sisters, Edith and May, and Mary Heaysman at Daning wrote of feeling safe, unthreatened, and well cared for by local Christians. Four days later the news of Emily Whitchurch's and Edith Searell's brutal murders at Xiaoyi on June 20 reached them, and they fled to the hills with three trusty Christians.[33]

Not knowing whether her letter would ever reach her family, Edith Nathan wrote,

> My heart bleeds for the Christians . . . They will have to suffer much . . . Our hearts are sick and sad . . . Truly these 'child Boxers' are devilish and a device of the devil. We in England know little of what the power of Satan can do over the mind of a child. God deliver us from a like fate . . . I happened to say to (our dear old Pastor) 'We are pitiable!' He said, 'There is One to care for you better than all earthly magistrates.' (His face is full of light and brightness, not born of earth but from constantly looking into his Master's face.) Could you but see our Christians . . . you would think as I do; it is quite worth while coming to such a pass, to find out how much they love us. Last night some of the men almost cried . . . We know our times are in God's hands. Don't grieve as those without hope!

For a month they waited in a mountain farmhouse, tense and ready for the worst at any moment, yet often bored except when Christians met with them to pray or the approach of strangers forced them to scramble up the hillsides and hide. Still the Boxers did not come.

Roughly fifty miles to the south, Hejin (Ho-tsin) was home and workplace to George and Bella McConnell, their son, and two young women, Annie King and Elizabeth Burton, still struggling to learn the language. John and Alice Young of Ji Xian were with them when warning of danger arrived. They decided to head for the

Yellow River without delay. By crossing into Shaanxi or getting a boat down to Tongguan they could go on south, they hoped, to safety.

On July 16 a troop of mounted soldiers overtook them, saying they were from the *yamen*, presumably an escort. On reaching the river bank they said they had not come to protect them but to murder them, unless they recanted. They refused. 'McConnell was then dragged from his mule and despatched with a sword,' and his wife and child after him. Annie King embraced Elizabeth Burton and both died together in the same way. The Youngs were then killed in each other's arms and their attendant, Ke Tianxüan, also refusing to recant, 'met with a violent death'.[34]

An unsigned letter from a Hejin Christian to another later said, 'Men's hearts are shaking with fear. We cannot rest night or day. All Christians and inquirers are being persecuted.' On July 22 May Nathan wrote her last letter to her mother:

> Edith met me and said, 'All the Young's party are killed.' (p 387) I said, 'What?' in high falsetto. It was such a shock. I wanted to cry, but the pastor said 'Don't', so I sat as in a dream while he read out the letter . . . All of them young, married a little over a year . . . and oh, such a death! It makes one shudder – hacked at with knives, I suppose . . . I don't want to die, and such a death, but if it comes, well . . .
>
> Many will say, 'Why did she go? – wasted life.' Darling, No. Trust – God does His very best, and never makes mistakes . . . Dear, it may be the deliverances will come through death, and His hands will receive . . . the incorruptible, glorified spirit . . . Now we are called to endure, perhaps, extreme bodily suffering. But, darlings, *death is but the gate of life*, we shall see His face, and, darling Mother, I'll wait and long for you there! . . . Now is the hour and power of darkness . . . How long, O Lord, how long? . . . It is rather like the hare being hunted by the hounds. Stones (for pillows) are not soft.

[The pastor, Zhang Zhiben, wrote to their families]:

> On (August 12) Yang Dequn (p 387) was killed . . . After he was dead the three ladies were seized (beloved sisters, alas, alas) dragged to a temple outside the city (of Daning) where it was difficult either to stand, sit or lie down, hungry and thirsty, with no one to look after them, and surrounded by a gang of evil men. At early dawn on the morning of (August 13) the three were killed . . . News of the victories of the foreigners reached us during the second intercalary

eighth moon (September 24–October 22). On (November 1) the Daning magistrate and gentry placed the corpses in coffins and deposited them in a temple in the western suburbs . . .

Happily I was seized a few days later (August 21) with my son. The edict of the Governor Li, who succeeded Yü Xian, which saved our lives, came to the *yamen* on (August 20 or 21).

The Linfen refugees

July 2–16, 1900

When the Swedish Mission in China were issued with safe-conduct passes early in July and all left the Yüncheng district under escort (p 358), F C H Dreyer and his wife were in charge of Linfen, with the Hoskyn sisters. Albert Lutley, his wife and two children and their colleagues, E Gauntlett and Edith Higgs, were with them from Hongtong; and Eva French's party of young women (p 645) had also arrived on July 2 from Jiexiu (p 340). Both Lutley, the most senior, and Eva French had high qualities of leadership, but he was ill with high fever and she naturally deferred to the missionary in charge. All fourteen looked to Dreyer to deal with the authorities and prepare for whatever action they would have to take. He showed himself well able to do this.[35]

It happened that one of Elder Si's attackers (p 321) and five Boxers had been imprisoned in the stocks at Linfen for a major robbery. On their capture a large crowd of townsfolk had ridiculed them, shouting 'Hello! We thought you could ride the clouds! That you were invulnerable!' After Yü Xian intervened to free them, 'the mandarin sent word that Linfen was full of wild rumours', and ordered the missionaries all to leave, promising an escort for a few days' stages. But for the wisdom and courage of Dreyer, Lutley and Eva French all might have joined the sad procession of destitute victims southwards through Henan. They knew nothing of that yet; simply that a mere 'road pass' could land them in deeper trouble. So they refused to yield until an official pass (a *wenshu*) of the highest status was issued by the highest officials to ensure their safe conduct all the way to Hankou. 'We told them plainly that unless everything was satisfactory we would not move. Rather than go to Henan and perish among strangers, we were prepared to wait for our doom in (Linfen) if need be.' From that time their doors were guarded and no troublesome crowds molested them.

When the Roman Catholics hired 'athletes' to escort them to Hankou, the officials urged Dreyer to join them. Again he refused on the ground of propriety, for his party were mostly unmarried women. China should protect them. Then came the news of the murder of Emily Whitchurch and Edith Searell at Xiaoyi, and of the difficulties the Kays and McKie were in among the hills beyond Qüwu, the Nathan sisters at Daning and McConnell's party at Hejin. Woodroffe, too, alone on the run, sent a message that he would like to join them, if only to die with them. But he could not get into the city. News of the Taiyuan massacre on July 9 only reached them on July 20 when they were travelling towards Xi'an, but the officials knew earlier and put pressure on them to go. Impossible, Dreyer answered. With ten women, two children and Lutley so ill, they could neither hide nor divide up into smaller parties. They must be openly escorted under official protection. At that the mandarins told the guards on their gates that they could disperse, an open invitation to plunderers, but Dreyer 'gave the (guards) a few (good) reasons in the shape of copper cash' for staying until his negotiations with the prefect ended.

Boxers had been drilling and boy and girl recruits learning to become possessed, 'foaming at the mouth and lying . . . as in a trance' until given orders. There was no time to be lost. On July 14 the officials became insistent and agreed to all their demands: to supply a document giving all fourteen safe conduct, and an escort to Hankou. They agreed to pay the cost of passage, but could not find carters willing to go the whole way. So in their anxiety to avoid responsibility for imminent bloodshed in the city, they decided to provide 'government carts' instead. A mob was said to be waiting outside the south gate already, and an attack was to be made the next day; so a midnight start was agreed.[36]

Four Christians set off with them (Sang Sifu, a well-known courier, Liu Baolin, a Hongtong deacon, and two young men, Go Wangde of Xi Xian and Li Wenhuan of Linfen), brave men determined to do all they could to help, well knowing that they made themselves the objects of bitter hatred. Within 'three hundred paces' one was violently knocked off a cart, another was flogged at the city gate and all four were reviled as 'secondary devils' and 'false foreign devils'. Go Wangde and Li Wenhuan when prevented from leaving Linfen climbed over the city wall before daybreak and rejoined the party ten miles away. On the first day Dreyer and Eva French were dragged out of the carts by their hair (evidence that they were at the front, shielding others farther in), robbed and threatened with swords at the neck, to say where their silver was concealed. Enemy underlings had planned it in advance, but could do no more.

'The remainder of the journey was less adventurous (though) frequently the Lord allowed us to get almost to the point of despair . . . with apparently no possible way of escape.' The intense heat in tightly curtained carts, so that they 'could scarcely breathe', resulted in nearly everyone becoming ill, 'and several were in so critical a condition that we almost despaired of their reaching the coast alive.' The Lutleys' two girls died.

After the adventure ended, Dreyer paid tribute to some mandarins and,

> men of all ranks who sympathised and showed us kindness. Even (at Linfen) there were those who would have helped us if they had dared. One man of position and influence told us he had been ill with rage at the utter stupidity of his Government. 'While you,' he said, 'are the ones to suffer now, the tables will be turned, and China's turn of suffering will come within a very few months.'

SANG SIFU, HERO COMPANION OF THE
DREYER–FRENCH PARTY

He promised to do all he could in secret to help them. Their escape in such favourable conditions, with effective safe-passes, could well have been his doing.

Eva French cited another mandarin in a city they passed through, who came to sympathise with them and afterwards sent them seventy eggs and a basket of apples. Another sent the sick man, Lutley, two bottles of stout, cans of condensed milk and marmalade and four packets of cakes. Such kindnesses were shown at great personal risk. But the chief credit belonged to the four Christians, Sang, Liu, Go and Li who stayed doggedly with the party, finding them food and shelter, and speaking up for them in threatening situations.

The Qü Xian tragedy[37]   *July 21–24, 1900*

A bitter bungle by the governor of Zhejiang was to cost the lives of the county magistrate of Qü Xian, of thirty of his family and followers; and of two CIM families and four single women. These eight adults and three children and an uncertain number of Chinese Christians paid the price of the governor's irresolution. Until the following year the atrocity was believed to have been unconnected with the Boxers, but this was disproved. It stemmed directly from Ci Xi's edict of June 24, 1900, that all foreigners were to be exterminated (map p 94).

Widespread unrest had resulted in armed 'marauders' congregating near the provincial borders, traditionally the regions of loose control and ease of escape by criminals from one jurisdiction to another. Since the days of the *Lammermuir* party's early pioneering up the Qiantang River the successful planting of a church at Qü Xian (HTCOC Books 4–6, *passim*) and consolidation by Arthur Douthwaite, had led to daughter churches springing up – at the border cities of Changshan, Jiangshan and many places across the border in the Guangxin region of Jiangxi. Ostensibly to protect Qü Xian against these banditti, but in fact an extension of the Peking policy of mobilising the masses against foreigners, the literati raised a militia who quickly became an even greater danger to both citizens and missionaries. Encouraged by the county magistrate, however, David Baird Thompson and his wife and colleagues stayed where they were.

When the provincial governor, Liu Shutang, received the dowager empress's original edict to kill, he already knew of the altered version adopted by the viceroys, and reinforced by their own orders to protect foreigners. So he vacillated – until his Manchu provincial judge prevailed on him to publish the edict. The Nanjing viceroy, Liu Kunyi, at once reprimanded and threatened the governor, so he countermanded his own proclamation, but too late. The militia and 'brutal soldiery' had lost no time. They seized the magistrate and all his household, dragged them to the prefect's *yamen* and in his presence murdered all thirty-one of them. On the same day, July 21, a mob encouraged by the military mandarin, who should have protected the mission, broke in and plundered it, even removing bricks from its walls. The evangelist Chen Tianfu escaped and appealed at the *daotai*'s *yamen* for help, but was rebuffed. David Thompson had received a head injury in the riot, so his wife Agnes and Josephine Desmond tried again, only to find the county magistrate being beheaded in the *yamen* court.

Under the treaties the mandarins were duty bound to give asylum and to defend foreigners in trouble. There was nowhere else to go. David Thompson, therefore, took his wife and children and Josephine Desmond back to the *yamen*, the highest to which they could appeal. The door was closed against them, showing incontrovertibly that this was no random rising, but premeditated action by the authorities. At this signal the mob seized Thompson, dragged him into the street and 'stabbed him to death with knives and tridents'. They then stabbed his two sons before their mother's eyes, and finally the two women.

Etta Manchester and Edith Sherwood lived elsewhere in the city, and both were severely wounded in an attack on them the same day. Neighbours hid them in a temple until they were discovered on the 24th. Pushed and dragged through the streets to the Roman Catholic chapel they, too, were stabbed to death and their bodies flung into the chapel.[38] As the militia and people had been declaring that all Christians were to be killed, Chen Tianfu, the evangelist, and his family went into hiding.

At Changshan, near the border thirty miles to the west, the danger had seemed even greater, so on the friendly mandarin's advice George and Etta Ward and Emma Thirgood left home on July 21 to join the Thompsons in Qü Xian. The women and the Wards' child with his amah travelled by boat, while Ward and two Chinese companions followed overland. Ten miles from Qü Xian the boatmen anchored, but seeing 'an angry red glare in the sky in the direction of Changshan,' the women persuaded them to press on. When they reached the city at daybreak on the 22nd and found it barred against them, they rightly hired another boat to take them downstream to Hangzhou. As they were loading their goods on board in full view of six Chinese gunboats with their officers and men, soldiers arrived, killed both mother and child at the breast with one sword-thrust and beheaded Etta Ward with the next. Emma Thirgood sank to her knees in prayer and also met her end. The gunboat crews did nothing to intervene.

The marauders had entered Changshan after the women left, and George Ward had escaped on foot with the local evangelist and Mao Liyuan, an 'inquirer'. Five miles short of Qü Xian a mocking crowd surrounded them and clubbed them to death, except for the evangelist, who feigned death and crawled away under cover of darkness to report events to James Meadows at Shaoxing.

Across the provincial border, only 25 miles from Changshan, in the Jiangxi town of Yüshan (of great historic interest to the CIM),[39] Kate Lachlan (see p 170) had returned to the work she was doing before her marriage and bereavement. As Kate Mackintosh she had pioneered the first stages of the Guangxin River experiment, and in 1900 was the senior missionary to seven junior women. When 'the marauders' became more and more powerful, many Chinese families left Yüshan, among them a solicitous mandarin, Zhang Laoye. 'He told us we were in a twofold danger from the Empress Dowager's edict and the rebels, but we felt it best to remain.' Still he urged them to escape at any time to his large house in Guangxin (now Shangrao) 20 miles downriver.

On July 24 Yüshan became agitated by news of the murders at Qü Xian, and although many people protested against what had happened, both Zhang Laoye and the mandarins in office at Yüshan and Guangxin feared for the women and repeatedly offered to escort them to safety. Again they chose to stay, till one day 'we quietly left the city (with) a good escort' and eventually reached Jiujiang.

At this very time the Martin Griffiths, reduced to destitution, were being taken in by the Catholic bishop at Zhengding, Zhili, under the brigadier's protection. And Alfonso Argento destitute and wounded was being befriended by the stranger Lo (p 373). Others, in Shanxi, were vainly trying to evade capture, and party after party was in desperate straits crossing Henan. How much had happened in those few frightful weeks!

CHAPTER THIRTEEN

THE FINAL PHASE
1900–1901

'From prison to prison'   *July 15–October 25, 1900*

One of the most poignant episodes in the whole sad saga of the Boxer Rising belongs to this period. From Caroline Gates's careful narrative, sparing of emotion, and Archibald Glover's expressive detail, as if the vivid memory were etched indelibly on his mind; from A R Saunders's restrained letter to *The Times* and E J Cooper's terse notes, and letter to his mother; and from C F H Dreyer's factual report, a picture of incredible suffering emerges. But the suffering is borne with such Christian fortitude that an impression is given of more than acceptance of the lash permitted in God's wisdom. A vein of gladness in being 'partakers of the sufferings of Christ,' runs perceptibly through each page, even through the death of those dearest to them. This is the miracle as much as that of deliverance from death time and again.[1] The Glovers' and Saunders' parties were in a far worse plight than Dreyer's (p 385).

'Friday, July 13, was the eighth day of our second flight from Lu'an and the week seemed like a year, so much had been crowded into it of misery and suspense,' Glover wrote.[2] Flora Glover and Caroline Gates and the children were in a disintegrating mule-litter, and Archibald Glover had to choose between the agony of riding on an unpadded wooden saddle-frame or walking in calico socks and one cloth shoe, or barefoot. Although out of Shanxi and in Henan, their persecution by evil mobs continued hour after hour. While the escort rested, their prisoners out in the glaring sun could neither rest nor persuade anyone to get them food or water. 'The children kept sobbing with hunger, terror, sores and utter weariness. My wife, overcome by her great fatigue . . . fell heavily sideways and struck her head violently.' And when they moved on towards the river they had to flounder through quagmires until they reached Huaiqing – and a great surprise. Treated as criminals they were made to cross the city on foot behind the prefect's sedan chair. To 'follow the chair' was defamation akin to condemnation. But he did it in self

defence. He took them to a good inn, good food and free access to a
privy (an open cesspit but such luxury) and to a water butt, a chance
to wash. Glover's mention of such things revealed the depth of
degradation in which they (and all such victims) had been forced to
exist. Mats on the ground to sleep on and bricks for pillows
completed the hospitality.

As if physical suffering were not enough, at Wuzhi mental torture
was added. They were told by a young mandarin flaunting his
authority that all foreigners had fled from Hankou and Shanghai
and none was left in the whole of China. But the mandarin's wife
gave the children some cast off clothing and, asking many questions
about the gospel, gave them the opportunity they welcomed to tell
her about Jesus. Cruelty and kindness alternating were almost
harder to bear than sustained hardship. On Sunday July 15 they
again faced death – at the hands of their escort. This time it stared
them in the face more vividly than ever before. Then after hours of
menacing the hapless family, the men thought better of it and
allowed their prey to cross the Yellow River to Zhengzhou – the seat
of a rabid mandarin.

Progress became more settled then, but for eleven days they
travelled about thirty miles each day by agonising cart and barrow,
always treated as prisoners. Their route was to take them due
southwards through Zhengzhou and Queshan (Choshan) (where M
Henry Taylor had met with such reviling that his spirit was broken)
(HTCOC Book 6, pp 83–4). It seemed as if officials cared for
nothing more than to get rid of them, each callously passing them
on to the next city. The suffocating crowds and animosity continued, flaming at times into terrifying vehemence. At other times
kindnesses almost too much to bear reduced them to tears. The
prefect at Zhengzhou

> stormed and raved, hurling invective and anathema with an ex-
> haustless energy that could only be of the devil . . . Wheeling
> suddenly upon me, he said or rather shrieked into my face: 'You
> devils ought to have your heads off . . . there is an Imperial Edict out
> for your destruction', and with the edge of his hand (he) chopped and
> sawed my neck so violently that it felt tender for hours afterwards.[3]

A week later this same mandarin treated the Saunders–Cooper
party to the same performance.

Lodged in a guard-room or 'in a cell immediately adjoining that occupied by convicts', in the darkness they knew the nature of their unlit, filthy quarters by the clanking of fetters and the stench of excreta on the ground where they must sleep. Yet *yamen* ladies sometimes sent for the children, Hope and Hedley, and treated them generously with gifts of 'sweetmeats', clothing or a wadded quilt to lie on. At last, on July 26, they reached Xinyang, near the Hubei border, and were delivered to the *yamen*.

A young official greeted them in English and led the way to an inner courtyard where they were received so kindly by other officials that it 'quite broke me down'. A barber was called and gave Glover his first shave for three weeks. Housed in a temple within the *yamen* grounds, among the idols and without a stick of furniture, they were kept hidden from public view for eight days of as blissful a rest as sleeping on 'mother earth' allowed. Soldiers were on the march to join in the defence of Peking against the foreign allies, they were told. It would be too dangerous to travel on. The third day saw a large parcel delivered to them, containing five complete sets of brand-new clothing. At last they could discard their verminous beggars' rags except to use them as pillows. Sunday worship for the first and only time on their long journey lifted their spirits to be ready for anything. But the shock they received on the fourth day was unimaginable.[4]

Alex Saunders' matter-of-fact description for *The Times* of his party's journey left too much to the imagination.[5] Glover supplied what he left out. They crossed the Yellow River, but the magistrate on the south side spurned them and forced them back to Wuzhi (p 364) saying their pass was invalid. There they found Mary Huston, sent on by the Jincheng (Tsechou) magistrate. To her, alone and dreadfully injured, with Hattie her companion dead, their arrival was a breath of heaven.

Together they were all taken to the river again and discarded on the north bank with no travel passes. So the ferries could not take them. At last on the third day a semi-official courier boat took them across and, a week behind the Glovers, they walked the thirteen miles to Zhengzhou. At the *yamen* the viceroys' directive to protect foreigners had just arrived. So the same wild mandarin who 'chopped and sawed' at Glover's neck could go no further. Resentfully, he abused them, saying, 'An edict has come today ordering that all foreigners be sent under escort to Hankou. Had you come here yesterday I would have had you all killed!' Treating them as common criminals he had the whole party of men, women and children thrown all together into the revolting gaol, separated from the chained prisoners only by wooden bars.

Night after night, as they continued the journey, they received the same treatment. By day they trundled on, grimly enduring the torture of their comfortless carts or barrows. Then, prosaically, Saunders wrote, 'We reached (Xinyang) on Monday, July 30, were treated well and clothes were given us . . . It was here, too, that we overtook Mr and Mrs Glover, two children, and Miss Gates, who . . . had met with similar treatment to ourselves' – so restrained as to obscure the truth. But Glover's account of their arrival told what Saunders left out.

> Shall I ever forget the sight? Slowly and painfully they were descending from the carts – three men, four women and five children . . . in their rags, emaciation and utter woebegoneness, more like apparitions than beings of flesh and blood . . . the Lucheng-Pingyao party, recognisable still though so pitiably changed . . . My dear wife ran to (Margaret Cooper) and with a tender embrace led her gently in. She just lifted her eyes and smiled wearily as she greeted me, 'Oh, how

FROM PRISON TO PRISON
'separated from the chained prisoners only by wooden bars'

nice to see somebody clean!' Next came her husband, his arms around a litter of loose dirty straw [anything to soften the carts and hard ground], then the Rev. A R Saunders and Mr Jennings in like manner – followed by Mrs Saunders, Miss Huston and Miss Guthrie, leading or carrying the children, though scarcely able to support their own weight.

Truly it was 'a time to weep' . . . Stretching themselves on the ground as we had done five days before, (they) gave thanks to God . . . for rest after weeks of torture. But oh, the sadness of that sight! The earth floor of the room was covered, every yard of it, with sick and wounded . . . Mrs Cooper's (rags and tatters) revealing gangrened sun-wounds about the breasts, and with ulcerous sores where the cruel (coal-carts) had galled her limbs, (and) the pains of dysentery. By the incense table was stretched Miss Huston with a broken jaw, a gaping scalp wound that laid bare the brain, flesh wounds in either forearm deep to the bone, and her whole body a mass of contusions – the work of the Boxers. Next to her was Mrs Saunders, terribly reduced by dysentery; and near the door Miss Guthrie, apparently in the last stage of the same disease . . . The children, who in their painful distress looked the personification of misery, to which their moans and sobs bore continual witness . . . were all in the throes of dysentery; and . . . in the agony of undressed sun-wounds. Jessie Saunders and Edith Cooper perhaps suffered the most. Their arms from the shoulder to the elbow were gangrenous sores, alive with maggots.[6]

Two of the party, Hattie Rice and the Saunders' baby, had already died and been buried. When Mary Huston had recovered consciousness during the night after their lynching at Jincheng, and found her own and Hattie's faces plastered with a mask of mud, she knew they had both been declared dead. Realising it was true of Hattie, she had warded off the hungry dogs, 'waiting for her own expected end', until the *yamen* people sent her on southwards to die somewhere else. Even as she rested among friends in that temple room, 'a haunted, hunted look' betrayed her thoughts. She spoke little except to her friend Caroline Gates, the only one not physically ill. Outside the room, 'under the fierce heat . . . the latrine just below the window (the only provision for seventeen people of whom nine and soon twelve had dysentery) had become a foetid mass of reeking corruption; while within, wounds and bruises and putrefying sores fouled the atmosphere.'

When Miss Guthrie lay apparently dying, she asked Archie Glover 'to pray over her "the prayer of faith" . . . and from that time she received strength to recover'. They gave their 'pest-house' the name 'Christ's Hospital', though water was almost their only remedy, and washing each other's putrid clothes and bodies their main service. From watching the uncomplaining fortitude of its patients, suffering as much from their memories as from their pain, Glover 'saw a new meaning in the words, "The *noble* army of martyrs praise Thee."' 'The ministry of mutual cleansing . . . was beautiful to see.'

At last, on August 3, the Glovers' ninth day and the Lucheng party's fourth at Xinyang, they were sent on by cruel wheelbarrow, with Flora Glover (within days of her confinement) and Margaret Cooper in stretcher chairs. A discarded pair of trousers, stuffed tight with the filthy straw, made a serviceable bolster, and two quilts softened 'the excruciating pain' of riding 'the long file of barrows with their screeching wheels and dislocating boards'. All were surprised, however, when little Jessie Saunders quietly died at an inn that night – put out in the street by the landlord, for fear of her homeless spirit, and buried on a hillside at sunrise.

They ran into an unexpected column of troops who cried, 'Army and Boxers are one' and were only kept from killing them by the courage of the party's escorts with the army officers' support. Mary Huston and Caroline Gates were roughly manhandled, and a spear levelled at Hope Glover reduced her to a 'terror that now settled upon (her)'. At Yingshan an LMS evangelist named Lo greeted them, took them all in and did all he could for them, refusing to leave them until he had delivered them to a hospital in Hankou. But a hundred miles from their destination Margaret Cooper died, on August 6, and on the 11th Mary Huston died at sunset. 'More than once (on Sunday, August 12) I thought my wife was dying,' Archibald Glover confessed, but they reached the LMS church at Xiaogan and received from the Christians 'a foretaste of the love of heaven'. Sent on by boat and nearing the end of their journey, 'the old dreadful yell went up, of curses for the foreign devils, and they pelted us until we were out of reach.'

At last on August 14 they were safely in Hankou and under medical care. Only Caroline Gates was thought fit to go on to Shanghai, but no sooner had she started than she succumbed to a terrible reaction . . . with critical nervous prostration'. Ceaseless tears could not wash away the memory of such weeks in which she had been a tower of strength. Brainerd, the Coopers' youngest, died on the 17th; Flora Glover's baby was born the next day, their fourth day in Hankou, and died on the 10th day; Hedley Glover nearly died in fever, and Hope could only scream. But by mid-September the Glovers were well enough to go by ship to Shanghai.

Flora's last letter to her parents said little about their sufferings, but instead 'it is better to dwell on the glory side', and then, '*my heart longs to return to Lu'an as soon as possible*'. Reduced to the point of having no resistance to disease, she died on October 25 of what they called 'peritonitis', aged only twenty-eight, 'the last of the martyrs of 1900 to pass from the cross to the crown'.

In those months, August through October, the agony for many others was prolonged, in their shared experience illuminating the hymns of Heaven:

> *Who shall separate us from the love of Christ?*
> *Shall trouble or hardship or persecution or famine*
> *   or nakedness or danger or sword?*
> *As it is written, 'For your sake we face death all day long;*
> *   we are considered as sheep to be slaughtered.'*
> *No, in all these things we are more than conquerors*
> *   through him who loved us (Rom 8:35–7 NIV).*

> *These are they who have come out of the great*
> *   tribulation . . . Therefore, they are before the*
> *   throne of God*
> *   and serve him day and night . . .*
> *   Never again will they hunger;*
> *   never again will they thirst.*
> *   The sun will not beat upon them,*
> *   nor any scorching heat.*
> *   For the Lamb at the centre of the throne*
> *   will be their shepherd;*
> *   he will lead them to springs of living water.*
> *   And God will wipe away every tear from their eyes (Rev.*
> *   7:14–17 NIV).*

The Oberlin martyrs and others   *July–August 1900*

Good mandarins in Shanxi had a hopeless task. By retaining office they could control to some extent the savagery of the madness at large. By helping the hunted they could endanger not only their own lives but those of their families and friends. That some protected the missionaries for as long as they did, and secretly advised and helped their sympathisers, such as 'CCH' and his 'wanted' men, stands to their great credit. That as close to Taiyuan as Taigu and Fenyang (Fenzhou) the Oberlin College members of the American Board could stay in their homes until July and even August is remarkable.

On July 30, another day to be remembered, the five American Board and twenty-two C&MA Swedish refugees from Zhangjiakou (p 335) reached Urga (map p 45) after thirty-eight days crossing the Gobi Desert from south to north. The Russian consul-general welcomed them hospitably, but with the news that ten thousand Mongols were gathering for a festival and two thousand Mongol soldiers in the area might be hostile. He was waiting for three hundred and fifty Cossacks for his own protection, and urged the travellers if they valued their safety to leave as soon as possible. They met the Cossacks on their second day out, reached Kiakhta on August 13, and St Petersburg on September 18.[7]

July 30 had been the day the woebegone Saunders–Cooper party joined the Glovers at Xinyang, that Argento was nearing Hankou with his God-given companion 'angel', Lo, and in Shanxi and Zhili several groups of refugees were hiding in the hills. The Nathan sisters and Mary Heaysman of Daning (pp 387–8) were still in the care of Christians, and somewhere in the same mountains the CIM team from Xi Xian (Sichou), William and Helen Peat and their two little girls aged seven and three, with Edith Dobson, a hospital nurse, and Georgiana Hurn, only two years in China, were hiding in a remote natural cave. Three hundred Boxers, furious that they had slipped the noose, destroyed their home and were searching the hills for them. 'Are we to be saved – a remnant for the glory of God?' Peat wrote in his last letters to his mother, 'or are we to be taken . . . ?' Then two days later, 'The soldiers are just on us, and I have only time to say "Goodbye" . . . We shall soon be with Christ, which is far better for us. We can only now be sorry for you who are left behind . . .'

And Helen: 'At the last moment I say, "Goodbye!" Our Father is with us and we go to Him . . .' while 'Georgie' Hurn wrote, 'After this time of trial China will be a very different land . . . God ruleth over all, and He must have some wise purpose in allowing all this to come to pass . . . It would be nicer to be taken and be with so many who have laid down their lives; but for (your) sake and for the sake of the many heathen who are still without Christ, one would like to stay . . . We have heard that the people are coming, so we are going to our Heavenly Home.'

Instead they were dragged before the magistrate and 'regarded as the off-scouring of the earth; they were refused protection; and were sent in the usual squalor from city to city.' Some officials tried to befriend them and send them to Hankou, 'but after weeks of weary wandering and imprisonment, they were attacked by two Boxers fifteen miles south of (Qüwu) . . . and all the party were put to death on August 30.'[8] No more is known.

While friendly mandarins were able to protect the Oberlin missionaries they carried on their work, but from July 16 after news of the Taiyuan massacre on July 9 reached them, hope faded. Yet they stayed where they were, safer with friends than among strangers. At Taigu eight Chinese Christians stood by them, waiting for the end.[9] It came on July 31 when the yells of a mob, 'Kill! Kill!' became louder and louder, and the gates were broken in.

Elder Liu was seen calmly sitting in the courtyard when he was attacked and killed. The missionaries, D H Clapp and his wife, Francis Davis, George Williams, Rowena Bird and Mary Partridge, retreated with some of the Chinese to a flat roof from which they fired on the three hundred Boxers and soldiers sent against them. 'But their ammunition soon gave out, and they were easily overpowered and beheaded. The heads of them all were sent in a basket to Taiyuan to the governor. Their bodies were thrown into the flames of the burning houses, and were speedily reduced to ashes.' Now Yü Xian felt ready to go up to Peking for Ci Xi's congratulations. His personal tally of missionary heads had reached fifty-one.

The Oberlin missionaries at Fenyang (Fenzhou), Ernest and Elizabeth Atwater with two daughters, and Charles Price with his wife and one girl, had been on good terms with their prefect and magistrates, and knew they would continue to be protected. When other cities became unsafe, and Emily Whitchurch and Edith Searell were murdered at Xiaoyi, only ten miles from Fenyang, the Prices invited their CIM friends, the A P Lundgrens of Jiexiu and a newcomer, Annie Eldred, to come and stay with them. Nowhere else offered even a hint of the protection they enjoyed. At this point Eva French and her companions in Jiexiu had decided to join the Dreyers at Linfen. From city after city the tragic trail of fleeing missionaries was clinging precariously to life or falling to the Boxers' swords. For two weeks after the tragedy at Taigu, no change took place at Fenyang, but hope of escaping alive forsook the seven missionaries. 'Lizzie' Atwater wrote to her brothers and sisters:

> I have tried to gather courage to write . . . [about the massacre at Taiyuan, when her stepdaughters had been beheaded, and the second massacre at Taigu]. We have tried to get away to the hills, but the plans do not work . . . The people know we are condemned . . . I long for a sight of your dear faces, but I fear we shall not meet on earth . . . I was very restless and excited while there seemed a chance of life, but God has taken away that feeling, and now I just pray for grace to meet the terrible end bravely . . . My little (unborn) baby will go with me . . . Dear ones, live near to God and cling less closely to earth. There is no other way in which we can receive that Peace from God which passeth understanding . . . My married life, two precious years, has been so very full of happiness. We will die together . . . If we escape now it will be a miracle.

Ten days later, on August 13, the friendly prefect died. Only fifty miles from Taiyuan, he was quickly replaced by an anti-foreign mandarin. At once he demanded of the subordinate magistrates, Why had the Americans not been driven out? He flogged the dispenser at the mission clinic with three hundred blows and sent him to collect the foreigners' firearms, two pistols and two shotguns or rifles. 'Lizzie' Atwater's confinement was expected very soon, but the prefect had no mercy. They must 'leave for the coast' the next day.

A young Chinese schoolmaster from Zhili, Fei Qihao (Fei Ch'i-hao), educated by missionaries of the American Board at Tong Xian, near Peking, and speaking English, had faithfully stayed with them.[10] On August 15 he accompanied their carts on horseback through thousands of ghoulish spectators crowding to see them go. But when he saw that he himself was attracting unwelcome attention from the soldiers escorting them, he joined the Atwaters on their cart. His suspicions had been aroused. Talk of the coast was a ruse.

They had covered thirty-seven miles and were approaching a small market town when one of the soldiers said to Fei, 'Escape for your life! We are about to kill the foreigners!' He jumped down and ran. But ahead were twenty more soldiers. They robbed him of almost everything he had, but let him go. Then as the travellers reached them an official gave the signal and all seven missionaries and the three children were killed with swords and bayonets, stripped of their clothing and (on the insistence of the villagers) buried in a nearby pit. Every last member of the American Board in Shanxi had been slaughtered – five men, five women and five children, and nearly half the Chinese Christians associated with them.

Fei Qihao was destitute and uncertain what to do. His decision to escape from Shanxi as soon as he could and take the news to Tianjin brought the first authentic reports of these events to the outer world. There is also a strong probability that he played a significant role in saving the life of Charles H S Green of the CIM. And of interest to missions is the link Fei had with the Kong family, descendants of Confucius. On Fei Qihao's flight from Fenyang, he visited a teacher named Kong at Taigu, a well-to-do country gentleman, who tried to persuade Fei to 'leave the foreigners, come back and worship (his) own gods'. Kong had a nephew also at the Tong Xian College of the American Board, who like Fei 'refused to apostatise and escaped after great perils'. This Kong Xiangxi (K'ung Hsiang-hsi) later graduated from Oberlin College, became principal of the Oberlin school in Shanxi and later a prominent member of the Guomindang to the end of the 'open century'.[11]

The 'Peking sieges' lifted   June–August 1900

Since mid-June the foreign communities of both Beijing (Peking) and Tianjin had been held at gun-point. Worse still, China had the power to overrun the legations and the foreign settlement at Tianjin. The Chinese city of Tianjin was already in Boxer hands, and the settlements were being shelled. After being fired on from the Dagu forts, the allied ships offshore landed marines, who took the forts on June 17 and advanced to the relief of Tianjin. At once the Chinese attacks on the settlements were intensified on three sides.[12]

At Beijing the British legation and Prince Su's adjoining palace were packed with Chinese and foreign refugees, under shellfire from June 20 and hopelessly undermanned. Should Tong Fuxiang set his Gansu army and the Boxers on to swamping them with attacking waves, they would soon be overrun. In this extremity Sir Robert Hart sent his cryptic message, 'Situation desperate, MAKE HASTE!' by secret courier on June 24. By then about eight thousand marines from Dagu had relieved the Tianjin settlements, and Russian troops had rescued Admiral Seymour's retreating force in its last stand at Xigu. On June 27 the Chinese eastern arsenal of Tianjin and on July 9 the western arsenal fell to determined Allied assaults. Ten thousand Russian, German, Japanese, American, French and British men captured the walled city of Tianjin after a costly all-day battle on July 14. As a direct result threats to Yantai and Shanghai receded.[13] The Boxers and after them imperial troops had already 'slaughtered, burned and plundered freely' in the old city. Now the foreigners took their turn, smashing fine porcelains and shipping tons of silver ingots abroad. On one day alone, 1,400,000 taels in silver were landed at a Japanese port. 'Military raids were made in all directions and . . . it is certain that the three shortest of the Ten Commandments were constantly violated on an extensive scale.' On July 14 some Russian shipping on the Amur River had been fired on, and the next day a Chinese battery bombarded the Russian settlement of Blagoveshchensk. For this the Russians exacted a terrible revenge. The corpses of many thousands of Chinese men, women and children floated down the Amur. In Beijing after the siege the worst excesses were attributed to the Russians. Certainly China had few reasons to love the foreigner.

Defeat weakened the Chinese commander Yü Lu's resolve, but any prospect of the Allies breaking through the massing forces between Tianjin and Beijing depended on strong reinforcement from overseas. On the Dagu-Tianjin front their combined strength totalled fourteen thousand, of whom ten thousand were Russians and Japanese. The Russian admiral judged '20,000 to 30,000 men' to be required for the relief of Beijing, in addition to twenty thousand guarding communications. But the council of admirals set the figure at 'at least 60,000' apart from the guards. The international cable still ended at Shanghai, and internal telegraphy was unreliable. Ships took three days at least to reach Tianjin, so the capitals of the West were always slow to receive up-to-date news, and slow to respond. The relief of the legations looked impossible.

Meanwhile, in Beijing, three almost inexplicable truces gave some respite to the legation thousands in their bunkers;[14] the first on the day after the infamous edict to kill (June 24) when the *North China Herald* reported 'an imperial decree on June 25 ordering that the foreign envoys in Peking be protected at all costs'; and firing stopped at one point while carts laden with vegetables and melons (not even poisoned) were delivered by order of Ci Xi to the severely rationed inmates. Such 'double dealing' was unfathomable to any who did not know Ci Xi's wiles.

A month after Yüan Zhang and Xü Jingcheng heroically changed her telegram 'Kill' to 'Protect', they were savagely executed. 'This morning my son Enming witnessed their death,' Jingshan wrote in his diary. They were cut in half and beheaded.[15]

Each brief respite was followed by renewed attacks but, Sir Robert Hart commented, 'that somebody intervened for our semi-protection seems probable; attacks . . . were never pushed home, but always ceased just as we feared they must succeed . . . Probably (due to) a wise man who knew what the destruction of the legations would cost empire and dynasty'. Yong Lu was thought to be that man.[16]

Weeks were passing as the Allied governments faced the practical difficulties of distance and other commitments (the British in South Africa and the Americans in the Philippines). The estimate of needed troops then rose to eighty thousand. Only Japan could provide unlimited thousands, and decided to increase her expeditionary force to twenty thousand. America sent seven thousand from Manila and British Indian troops reinforced the two thousand already in north China.[17] Delay was becoming crucial. As missionary refugees had found, Chinese troops were on the march from distant provinces to defend the capital. Even the British commander at Tianjin who advocated a daring advance, with Lord Salisbury's support, thought a relief column of twenty-five thousand essential. 'Fear that a reverse would imperil the lives and fortunes of all foreigners in north China,' prolonged the delay. Such was the lack of 'intelligence'. Every single foreigner in North China was already in direst peril or dead. An urgent message from Major E H Conger, the United States envoy, then succeeded in showing that action had become more urgent than full preparation. And the arrival of the American General Chaffee gave timely support to the British General Gaselee. Together they persuaded the other nations' reluctant generals (whose men formed two-thirds of the whole) to advance on August 4.

By an extraordinary stroke of mischief or mishap, a report found its way into the *North China Herald* on July 18, claiming that the Director-General of Telegraphs at Shanghai had received a telegram from Yüan Shikai announcing the massacre of all occupants of the Beijing legation: 'No one left alive.' And the Chinese servant of a foreigner escaped from Beijing was quoted as confirming the report. 'The startling news had already been telegraphed to all parts of the world' when the director-general, too late, denied having received such a telegram. Charlotte Haldane in *The Last Great Empress of China* attributed the 'story of the so-called Peking massacre' to the Shanghai correspondent of the *Daily Mail*, who picked up sensational fiction from the vernacular newspapers and embellished them from his own imagination. Whatever its origins, *The Times* of July 17 carried two-column obituaries of Sir Robert Hart, Sir Claude Macdonald and Dr G E Morrison, and a solemn memorial service was ordered at St Paul's Cathedral for July 23. Only 'the urgent remonstrances of Mr J D Campbell' of the Imperial Maritime Customs secured its postponement. Then a small boy disguised as a beggar was let down from the Beijing city wall and carried confirmation of the survival of the legations to the Allies.

Meanwhile, the Zongli Yamen received an enquiry from the Chinese ambassador in Washington, Wu Dingfang, as to the situation of the beleaguered United States envoy, Major E H Conger. They cabled Conger's coded reply that he had been besieged for a month, supplies of food and ammunition were low, and 'quick relief only can prevent general massacre'. The other envoys were denied the right of sending messages in code and instructed to state *en clair* that all was well with them. The Beijing government then told Wu Dingfang that all the allied envoys were safe and well, provisions were being supplied to them, relations were 'most friendly', and the envoys were to go to Tianjin for negotiations. But Major Conger's statement that to leave the legation would be 'certain death' convinced the powers that the need for action had become more urgent than preparations.

Jingshan's diary for August 5 (Diary p 295) confirmed that the envoys would have been murdered on the way.[18] Wiles and perfidy had failed. 'A storm of shot and shell, and . . . all the privations and dangers of a siege' resumed on July 29.

The siege of the Beitang cathedral continued uninterrupted and at Xian Xian, a hundred miles south of Beijing, thirty thousand other Catholic converts, of whom twelve thousand were armed, were successfully defending themselves. But twenty miles closer, at Hejian, over a thousand were slaughtered by troops accompanying the fanatical Li Pingheng (previously governor of Shandong) to Beijing.

In the legation, as the ammunition stock fell lower and lower, ears were straining to hear the sound of an approaching army from

Tianjin – even before the capture of Tianjin city. But at last, on August 4, the field force of sixteen thousand moved out, the Russians and French Annamese as a right wing following the east bank of the river, and the Japanese, British (mostly Indian) and Americans as the left wing on the west bank. Beicang fell on the 5th and Yangcun (now Wuqing) on the 6th and the viceroy of Zhili in command, Yü Lu, shot himself in shame on the 8th. The column reached Tong Xian on the 12th. With the enemy only fifteen miles from the capital, the court prepared to flee (map p 345).

By imperial decree Li Hongzhang was appointed plenipotentiary to negotiate with the powers and tried by diplomacy to halt the allies at Tong Xian, without success. Behind the advancing allies swarms of disorganised Chinese soldiery and Boxers were scattering. But a nation faced with defeat could resort to desperate acts. 'At Shanghai and along the (Yangzi River) much apprehension was felt.' A thousand volunteers stood ready to defend the Shanghai Settlement, backed by fifteen to twenty warships.[19] Three thousand Indian troops were sent from Hong Kong to defend Shanghai, reaching Wusong on the 12th, and each allied power sent detachments to join them.

At Beijing 'the night of August 13–14 was marked by the most furious and persistent assault that the legations had experienced', but the 14th dawned with the Allies only five or six miles from the city walls. Co-ordination between the allied troops broke down as the Russians, disregarding agreed strategy, attacked and took the Dongbian Gate (see diagram p 325). Some Americans then cleared the top of the Tartar city wall and unfurled the Stars and Stripes. South of the British legation, however, was a water-gate under the wall of the Tartar city, through which secret couriers had succeeded in passing from time to time. Sir Claude Macdonald now sent a cipher message to advise General Gaselee of this easy access to the city. At 3 pm on August 14 Sikh troops were the first to enter.

Inside the legations the defenders faced incessant firing from the Chinese lines, in spite of a torrential downpour of rain,

> Lead was simply poured into us . . . We thought (they) were preparing to assault . . . Suddenly (a Japanese) called out, 'Listen! Do you hear the machine-gun outside the Hatamen? The relief force is outside the city.' We laughed, we joked . . . Soon after tiffin (lunch) . . . Konavaloff rushed in with a shout – 'The relief force is in! The Sikhs are in the legation! Listen to the shouting . . .' Men, women

and children, everyone out on the lawn, cheering, yelling, crying, mad with excitement and delight, and there coming in, line after line, waving their turbans and cheering, real, live, big, burly Indian troops . . . I rushed up to the first one I saw; I clapped him on the back; I shook his hand; I yelled, I cheered . . . I was at last saved![20]

For eight weeks one thousand foreigners accustomed to great comfort and three thousand Chinese had survived on rationed rice and occasional horseflesh; 458 marines and seventy-five volunteers had suffered, seventy-six killed and 179 wounded, 255 casualties in all, but very few among non-combatants. No child had been hit, and the only woman to be injured received her wound after the liberation. The next day Psalm 124 verse 7 was cabled to the outer world: 'The snare is broken and we are escaped.'

Also on August 15 General Chaffee and the American troops cleared Chinese troops from the imperial city, from which they still threatened the legations. Forcing gate after gate into the Forbidden City they reached the last before the imperial palace when they were stopped by an imperious intervention by the Russian general. His troops and the Japanese were burning and sacking the Tartar city, where a heavy pall of black smoke rose from the huge conflagration, but he insisted on having a hand in the richest prize.

The Roman Catholic Beitang was crowded with three thousand Chinese converts. About five hundred of them under forty-three marines had been armed with improvised spears and a few rifles, and the attacks had been 'more furious than on the legations'. Rations were five ounces of food per head from August 1 and three ounces from August 8. Altogether four hundred Chinese and eleven French marines were killed before their siege was at last lifted on the 16th.

Confusion reigned in the Court from August 12 as Ci Xi weighed Yong Lu's advice to stay and 'prove her innocence' by executing guilty Manchus, against Prince Tuan's and Kang Yi's persuasion to flee. But at 4 am on August 15 she and her hostage, the emperor, both in peasant clothing, left secretly in a common cart for the Summer Palace of Yüanmingyüan. 'Mistress of the situation to the last', before leaving she ordered the emperor's favourite concubine to be thrown down a well and drowned. A body of troops escorted them from the Summer Palace to Zhangjiakou (Kalgan) from where she was to travel southwards to Taiyuan on the way to Xi'an.

After the sieges   *August 15–October 1900*

Five days after the relief of the legations, a service of thanksgiving was held on Sunday, August 19, addressed by A H Smith of the American Board. Under the title 'The Hand of God in the Siege of Peking,' he reviewed ten remarkable aspects of the experiences they had been through:

1 The fact that the foreign community was not annihilated before the first marine guards arrived;

2 the guards' arrival just before all access was made impossible;

3 the immunity from attack on widely scattered groups coming through the city to the legations;

4 the Methodists' success (under semi-siege for twelve days before moving to the legations) in working out ways and means of defence and survival, and in training personnel who were ready when the move was made;

5 the late addition of the two thousand Chinese Christians and of the palace of Prince Su, both of which factors became essential to survival;

6 the discovery of 'mountains' of wheat, rice, corn and much else in shops within the periphery of the defended area, of an exceptional number of mules and ponies in the stables, of ample water in eight wells, and more than enough coal and timber;

7 apparently inexhaustible sources of clothing, curtains and calico for about fifty thousand sandbags, and even a smithy and raw material for the armourers to use;

8 the restraining hand of God on the attackers, who seemed afraid of coming to close grips with the defenders – shelling ceased just as the right range was found, and between a million and a million and a half rifle rounds fired into the legation killed and wounded so few;

9 many diseases, including typhoid and smallpox, occurred while overcrowding was excessive, yet no epidemic developed;

10 while the attackers seemed confused and irresolute, in spite of rivalries and jealousy between nations, defenders and defended enjoyed 'a spirit of unity rare to see' with Greek, Roman Catholic and Protestant Christians fraternising as never before.[21]

But Christian unity and thanksgiving were only small glimmers of light in an otherwise sombre situation. Unbridled sacking of Beijing by the victorious troops followed the city's occupation, and continued for a week or two until a semblance of control was gradually restored. By making strong representations to the commanding officers, Moir Duncan of the BMS was able to save the Beijing mansion of Tuan Fang, the enlightened Manchu governor of Shaanxi, from destruction. The shameless rape of Tianjin was exceeded at Beijing; 'the troops were out of hand and looked on Peking and all it contained, persons and property, as prize of war, subject to their will'. During those days 'countless thousands of women put an end to their lives (and) many thousands of men were killed in a wild orgy of slaughter.'[22] The common people had suffered similar treatment, first from the Boxers, then from the soldiers, and finally from foreigners 'with a sordidness more despicable than the madness of the Boxers'. The dowager empress had brought it all on her people and herself, but the bloodlust of baying mobs and vicious Boxers had been matched by their victims' 'rescuers'. Quickly the parts of the city occupied by certain of the allies were drained of Chinese, fleeing into other parts policed by the more civilised conquerors, among whom the Japanese had a good record.

The Forbidden City was not occupied until the German Field-Marshal von Waldersee set up his headquarters in the emperor's palace in October. But on August 28 detachments of foreign troops marched through the sacred courtyards, and the envoys and senior officers 'inspected the imperial throne rooms and chambers'. China had been humiliated to the depths, and the western powers rode roughshod over the devastated capital and countryside. Where only eight hundred 'French' Annamese and no Germans had had a part in the victory, by September 10 the *North China Herald* reported two thousand Germans and 1,500 French troops in occupation of segments of Beijing assigned to them. The fact that the German envoy had been murdered was enough for the other powers to grant Germany a predominating influence in dealing with the Boxer revolt. On the day after news of Baron von Ketteler's murder reached Germany, the German emperor had ordered the formation and despatch of 'an expeditionary force' of seven thousand, in the words, 'When you meet the foe you will defeat him. No quarter will be given, no prisoners will be taken.' Citing Attila the Hun, he declared 'that no Chinese will ever again even dare to look askance at a German'.

But where some co-operation had existed in lifting the sieges, the allies were at sixes and sevens from then on. In exchange for a free hand in Manchuria, Russia entered into negotiations with Li Hongzhang to secure the withdrawal of foreign troops from the capital and restoration of Chinese control in conquered territory.[23] Britain and America refused to go along with the scheme, and Sir Claude Macdonald reported to Lord Salisbury on September 7 his opinion that 'a general massacre of Christian converts and of all Chinese who have shown themselves friendly to foreigners would most certainly ensue if all foreign troops were to leave now.' The glaring mistake of such a withdrawal as had happened in 1860 and on other occasions (interpreted by the Chinese as inability to hold what had been captured) must not be repeated. The allied powers then welcomed 'so distinguished and experienced' a soldier as Count von Waldersee to head the international forces in north China. In this capacity of commander-in-chief he set up his head-quarters in the imperial palace and began punitive operations into the surrounding countryside.

Retreating Boxers and demoralised troops were heavily defeated by Yüan Shikai's Shandong troops, and on August 28 the siege of Xian Xian was relieved from Baoding by the guilty, and now devious, acting-viceroy of Zhili, pending Li Hongzhang's return (p 376). But the organised imperial armies retreated south-west to Baoding and Shanxi, and north-west to Zhangjiakou (Kalgan), from where Tong Fuxiang and his Gansu Muslims accompanied the court via Taiyuan to Xi'an. The countryside surrounding the capital for hundreds of miles was still being terrorised by those marauding Boxers and disorderly soldiers. So although essential control of communications between the coast and Beijing was maintained by foreign troops, missionaries who had so recently been besieged needed courage to go out to the relief of Christians in distress. Armed foreign escorts who went with them levied fines in the most culpable places, to provide food for destitute Christians who would have starved in the approaching winter.

As soon as troops could be spared from the cities, punitive expeditions destroyed Boxer centres and pockets of resistance, to restore a free flow of market produce and provisioning of the cities. The coastal forts at Shanhaiguan, Qingwangdao and Beitang (near Dagu) were occupied, and on October 8, one thousand French troops marched south to relieve the Catholics holding out in several places against the Boxers. Another French column relieved those being protected at Zhengding by the friendly brigadier (p 354), and another column from Xian Xian entered Baoding unopposed on

October 13 to find the Greens and Jessie Gregg (p 429) being held prisoner.

An international column of 3,500 from Beijing and four thousand from Tianjin also reached Baoding on October 18, and formed a tribunal to investigate the murder of foreigners on June 30 and July 1. As a result, the acting-viceroy, the Tartar-General and the camp commandant who had refused sanctuary to the CIM and Presbyterian missionaries on July 1, were executed. The city gates and a corner of the wall were blown up and the Boxer temples demolished. Heavy fines were exacted for the relief of survivors in distress, and 3,200 Germans and French remained in the city for the winter. J Walter Lowrie, the American Presbyterian who happened to be away from Baoding when disaster struck, and returned as interpreter-adviser to one of the generals with the international column (p 346), by his influence was credited with saving hundreds of Chinese from the vengeance of the vindictive expedition.[24]

Territorial ambitions and land-grabbing by the occupying powers risked clashes between them, with scheming Russia the chief menace to harmony; but pacification of the country continued. Between December 12, 1900, and the end of April 1901, forty-six expeditions, thirty-five of them German, were sent out. One of the first by German troops reached the Guguan Pass, signalling a panic evacuation of Taiyuan by officials and wealthy gentry. In Beijing itself, by the irony of an imperial decree, various princes, dukes and leading officials were deprived of rank and office and committed to trial, while the evil genius of massacre and mayhem no longer in disguise went her way to the ancient inland capital, Xi'an, meting out punishments as she went.

At Taiyuan she 'lingered for a short time' and left her imperial clansman, Yü Xian, 'infamous for ever', in office as governor. In his *yamen* courtyard he demonstrated to her how the foreigners had been beheaded.[25] She arrived at Xi'an on October 28, and not surprisingly 'every act of administration ordered from (Xi'an) only served to accentuate the continuance of anti-foreign and pro-Manchu tendencies of the court'. The allies protested at her worst moves, such as the appointment of the notoriously anti-foreign governor of Henan to be governor of Hebei with his seat at Wuchang, a threat to the wise viceroy Zhang Zhitong. She countermanded the appointment, but it was believed that Tong Fuxiang, the tiger she had chosen to ride and could not dismount, was dominating her. When under pressure from the Allies an imperial decree condemned the barbarous princes Tuan and Chuang (p 330) to imprisonment for life and Yü Xian to banishment; Tong Fuxiang's punishment was 'reserved for consideration'. His fifteen thousand battle-hardened men were there with him. As a ruse, Yü Xian was reported dead by suicide while he left Shanxi, but the subterfuge was transparent and the Allies insisted on his execution. A new decree ordering the death penalty was put into effect at Lanzhou, but by having his throat cut instead of decapitation. 'By a stroke of superlative hypocrisy Her Majesty ordered that all her pro-Boxer Decrees and Edicts be expunged from the records of the Qing Dynasty.'

Negotiations to bring the court back to Beijing began almost as soon as they escaped in August, and intensified when the influence of 'pernicious advisers' made diplomatic progress difficult. But the heavy-handed occupation of Baoding and execution of its rulers frightened the imperial court into keeping its distance at Xi'an until October 1901. Beijing, Tianjin and the province of Zhili were therefore under the command of the official plenipotentiaries, Li Hongzhang and Prince Qing, joined by the two Yangzi viceroys, Liu Kunyi and Zhang Zhitong, in negotiating reparations. On August 25 they made a proclamation that all killing must stop.[26] But it took weeks to take effect. The rest of the empire remained nominally under Ci Xi's control. All too slowly the Boxers and bloodthirsty soldiery learned that their licence to kill had expired. Numberless Christians and helpless missionaries were yet to succumb.

The Shanxi toll continues   August–September 1900

On August 22 'CCH' (the secret cell leader) (p 358) wrote again to Erik Folke reporting on his activities. His businesslike letters cannot disguise his anguish and anxiety. 'The hiding-place of Mr and Mrs Duncan Kay of Qüwu has become known (p 361). Some local rebels, pretending to be Boxers, captured him and are holding him to ransom. Elder Shang Guan and the evangelist have had to flee . . . therefore we have no means of communication with Mr Kay.' Nor was there any word from the Kays after the end of July, but he was seen alive on August 17. Then only the news that they and their child were 'cruelly put to death on September 15'.

'CCH' also wrote that on August 7 Yü Xian had 'issued a proclamation ordering the people in every town and village to practise the Boxer arts, and now all are practising. The persecutions of the native Christians in Shanxi are indescribable.'[27] Two days later, on August 9, the Baptist missionaries imprisoned at Xinzhou north of Taiyuan (p 342) were told they were to be taken to the coast, and a guard of ten soldiers sent by Yü Xian took them out of the city in four carts. As they reached the gates they were set upon, stripped of their clothing and immediately killed by blows to their heads with swords. For some days their bodies lay unburied outside the city until their friend, the literary chancellor, hired men to wrap them in mats and bury them at the foot of the city wall.[28] Yü Xian then set out, on August 11, for Beijing, and entered the experiences of the Greens and Jessie Gregg (p 379).

When the flight of missionaries from Zhangjiakou (Kalgan) and Guihuacheng across the Gobi Desert took place, two former members of the C&MA, Mr and Mrs Helleberg, and a new colleague named Wahlstedt succeeded in covering two hundred miles before being murdered by Manchu soldiers. At Guihuacheng itself seventeen adults and twelve children of the C&MA delayed their escape across the Gobi until one member's confinement was over. As they travelled they were robbed repeatedly even of clothing, and accepted the invitation of four Catholic priests to join them. But C L Lundberg wrote that Boxers and soldiers were coming: 'Tell our friends we live and die for the Lord . . . The way He chooses for me is best, may His will be done. Excuse my writing; my hand is shivering.' And on August 22, 'the soldiers have arrived, and will today attack our place. The Catholics are preparing to defend themselves, but it is vain. We do not like to die with weapons in our hands; if it be the Lord's will, let them take our lives.' Emil Olsson, the leader, and Lundberg escaped, but were caught and beheaded. 'The whole place was burned and the missionaries perished.'[29] Out of thirty-eight members of the C&MA in the whole of China, twenty-one and fourteen children died in the Boxer rising.

One of the Scandinavian missions to Mongolia (p 614) known as the Scandinavian Alliance Mission of Chicago consisted of three men and three single women devoted to rough pioneering from Mongol tents with no settled home until after several years.[30] On September 1 Boxers murdered D W Stenberg and the three women at Dallat Hosso near the Yellow River in the Ordos desert region, and C J Suber ten or twelve days later, but N J Friedstrom escaped. In the same Ordos area the Roman Catholic Bishop Hamer 'after a valiant resistance, was captured, his fingers and toes were cut off, and he was taken from village to village until death ended his sufferings'. Elsewhere in the same region two priests were executed and their heads exposed. And in another place three were burned to death in a church. Four thousand more Catholics survived the siege of one mission centre, and fifteen Catholic missionaries escaped across the desert to Siberia, taking forty-two days. Altogether nine Catholic missionaries and three thousand converts were killed, and many died of privation in Mongolian territory alone.[31]

F C H Dreyer's party (p 391) had been driven to despair by hostile people, and almost suffocated in their closed carts by the time they reached Zhengzhou in north Henan on August 3. The first of the Lutleys' two daughters, Mary, died that evening, and the second, Edith, on the Henan-Hubei border on the 20th. Each night they were all thrust into the same foul prisons as the Glovers' and Saunders' parties had occupied, and heard tall stories of their plight. But even then a sense of humour did not forsake them. Noisy crowds blocked doors and windows in their eagerness to see the 'foreign devils', denying the prisoners the fresh air they desperately needed. 'It was most comical seeing them holding their noses and yet breathing through their mouths the bad and poisonous smells which they thought emanated from us!'[32]

Because of the dangers in Henan, 'CCH' who had twice met and encouraged them on their way with money when they needed it, shed tears when the *daotai* of Tongguan forced them to take the Henan route instead of through safer Shaanxi. Yet the same official's commissioner congratulated them on safe travel so far, and at other cities, including Queshan (Choshan), they were given generous supplies. LMS and Methodist Christians in Hubei did all they could for them, as for the earlier parties to pass through, and on August 28 they reached Hankou. After Erik Folke's Swedish Mission, theirs were the lightest sufferings of those who escaped from Shanxi. The experiences of the Greens and Jessie Gregg and of the Ogrens were to be many times more heart-rending.

Caught! The Greens and Jessie Gregg[33]   *August 1900*

Charles Green, his wife and children and Jessie Gregg had been sheltered in the isolated farmhouse for three weeks when the Boxers suddenly searched the place (p 353). Farmer Gao had heard whispers among the villagers that the fugitives' presence was suspected, but instead of sending them away, for the sake of his own family, he tried to hide them more securely. He dug a tunnel through the loess cliff behind his home, to link it with two derelict caves where they could hide. The very small tunnel entrance was easily hidden behind household chattels. But a Chinese Christian named Geng came to invite them to move to his home forty miles away, and an invitation had also come from the Catholic bishop in Zhengding to join the Griffiths there.

On the morning of Thursday, August 9, while they were half-dressed and in the act of discussing which offer to accept, the alarm was raised. Men were approaching. They all crawled through into the cave, joined by Geng, and Gao's wife hid the tunnel entrance as the Boxers arrived. There was 'a tramping of many feet' and 'a banging of utensils, then a shout of triumph!' To the minds of each adult came the words, 'Thou art worthy!' but the children's cries '"Are they going to kill us now?" pierced deeper than any Boxer's knife . . . We could only tell them that very soon we should be with Jesus.'

Charles Green crawled along the tunnel to plead for the women and children, and as he emerged a Boxer fired a shot gun from close range. 'By the dull heavy thud on my head I knew I was wounded, and was conscious of falling through the entrance, then rising to my feet I seemed to spin round two or three times (and) leaned against the wall for support.' He staggered from room to room, blood streaming down his face, and as the Boxers outside tried to fire at Green again, Geng crawled out and escaped. Green then rejoined the others and together they decided to surrender. As they came out of the house into the courtyard, men on each side of the doorway brandished 'their huge ghastly swords' and laid them on their necks while they robbed them of everything they possessed except what they were wearing – and a pocket Bible which they handed back to Jessie Gregg, saying, 'If you read that you can get to heaven.' Seeing the children's distress, they said they would not kill any of them. But they spoke with a Baoding accent, so were they the men who killed William Cooper? They then led them off in procession to the city, each under a sword, with the firearms bringing up the rear. Enormous crowds lined the streets, many showing real sympathy. When Jessie Gregg saw the tear-stained face of their own house-help, she called out, 'We are not afraid; God is with us!'

They were taken to the wreck of their own home in Huolu, and when the men began to whet their swords it looked as if their hour had come. But the Boxers left for their daily ritual and a policeman friend of the family said, 'Don't be afraid; the mandarin will be here directly.' A hand passed a pot of water to them through a broken window. They were not alone. The mandarin arrived with an escort of two hundred soldiers, and thousands lined the streets as the prisoners, 'too faint and giddy to care', were taken on foot all the way to the *yamen*.

The mandarin told them he would send them to safety at Zhengding or Baoding, and had them lodged in the *yamen* temple. At last the women could examine Charles Green's gunshot wounds. Because of his crouching position as he crawled out of the farmhouse tunnel, not only had his head but his 'face, shoulders, arms and back had taken their share of No 1 shot.' 'As blood, hair, and clothing were now firmly clotted', they decided to leave it to be dealt with properly at Zhengding. But bricks for pillows and the pain and stiffness made sleep impossible.

Early in the morning Mrs Liu, the house-help, came to the *yamen*, even though told they had been executed singing hymns! She took the children in her arms and embraced their mother and Jessie Gregg, oblivious of the onlookers. 'Her calm, strong faith in God and loving, helpful words . . . enabled us to share St Paul's joy over his converts, "I am filled with comfort; I am exceeding joyful in all our tribulation." ' A soldier escort took them to Zhengding, but the Baoding Boxers, wearing Green's clothing and carrying bundles of booty, followed, always within reach of them. At the sight of the Boxers, the Zhengding mandarins were adamant that neither they nor their prisoners could enter the city; the wounded man would have to wait for treatment.

This time the Boxers' bundles and weapons were piled on the prisoners' cart as they headed for infamous Baoding only six weeks after the massacres. The provincial governor had more recently declared by proclamation that all foreign teachers of religion were devilish deceivers, and all Christians must recant or be killed. They covered fifteen miles by midnight and twenty-three more by daylight, but after an hour and a half's rest and only some millet gruel and bread rolls to eat, were sent on another twenty-mile stage. Their road took them through Boxer territory where every Catholic had been killed. 'It seemed so improbable that we should be allowed to pass through alive, but our hearts were kept lifted up to God . . . that He might be glorified in us, whether by life or by death.'

At Ding Xian they were put into the *yamen* prison for a few hours, with ten or more chained prisoners in a cage at one end, and given some food. But at 3 pm they started off again on another twenty-three-mile stage, much of it up to the axles in mud and water. This time the ten Boxers were outnumbered by *yamen* soldiers and officials, and the journey took until midnight again, when they reached another prison.

After travelling for forty hours with little food, and no sleep for three nights and days, nothing could keep them awake. In the morning a subtle change of attitudes towards them raised their hopes. They had their first wash since Huolu, and the prison warder told them that the emperor had ordered the protection of missionaries. ('Missionaries and merchants have nothing to do with the war.') It was August 12 (cf p 619). The allied expeditionary force had reached Tong Xian, fifteen miles from Beijing, and the government was protecting its own interests. An engine and one coach were running on the line to Baoding, but moved off as the forlorn party came within sight of them. Another forty miles of jolting in a springless cart brought them to Baoding at daylight, 'understanding as never before how Jesus must have felt as He went up to Jerusalem for the last time.'

Suddenly, before they realised what was happening, the women and children were taken to the women's lock-up, and Charles Green found himself alone 'in a filthy yard among some twenty prisoners in various stages of dirt and wretchedness'. His exhaustion overcame him, and he lay on the ground and wept at being separated at such a moment, so that they could not die together. But after half an hour he was taken out again – to find them refreshed and combed, by the kindness of the women's warder. The magistrate, however, refused to receive them and was bent on sending them back where they had come from.

> A fast increasing and excited mob was surging about the cart, and a number of the city Boxers appeared with their guns and great swords, and took up their position all around us . . . The heat became intense, and we sat like that for at least two hours . . . I heard the spokesman of our (original) Boxer party say, 'There will be trouble here very shortly.' To that man, under God, we undoubtedly owe our lives on this the third wonderful deliverance from death. He had gone to the mandarin and pleaded for us, showing him that we should certainly be killed as soon as we got out of the city, even if we were allowed that far.

The mandarin relented and they were returned to their prison quarters. Charles Green was then taken before him and treated kindly. The current troubles were Britain's fault, he said, but as Green and the others had come to Baoding they would be protected, and as a favour Green was allowed to rejoin his family. At last with a broken penknife and a needle they began cleaning his wounds and removing the lead shot. Most were embedded too deeply.

Miracles one after another[34]   *August–September 1900*

On August 14, when the legations were relieved and the imperial court were preparing to become fugitives themselves, the Greens and Jessie Gregg were told they were to be sent by boat to Tianjin. Two carts came to take them to the riverside and they were given cash for travelling expenses. But four or five local Boxers with drawn swords and eight of their first Boxer escort joined them on the boat, with no representative of the mandarins. What could this mean? Three miles out, the local Boxers left them, and by sunrise the boat had covered thirty miles. Perhaps they were going to Tianjin after all. They tied up at the river bank and the two leading Boxers went ashore.

> My wife cried, 'Oh, Charlie, something is wrong; do ask the others what it is.' I spoke to one of them, but he only wrung his hands and said, 'This is terrible! terrible!' Then the two men returned, and the leader said, 'It is all a lie about you being taken to Tianjin. It is impossible to get there. The river is held by Boxers at several points . . . Our orders from the Governor were to bring you so far down the river, and then kill you.' As he spoke he pointed to his long ugly knife, which I had seen him sharpening . . . Then he went on, 'We don't intend to commit such a sin; we have no quarrel with you; but you must leave the boat now and make the best of it for yourselves.'

They were advised to hide in the tall reeds until the evening and then go to Anxin (then called Hsin-an), the city they had passed, and see what the mandarin would do for them. 'We were simply stunned as if in a dream.' They took what food and bedding they could carry, and were soon among the reeds and undergrowth. Either to think or pray was too difficult. For a fourth time they had escaped death as by a miracle.

> Our God had delivered us from a cruel death, touching even the hearts of these Boxers for us . . . All the way from (Huolu) we had maintained a quiet, respectful demeanour towards them, and they played with the children . . . Tears came into the eyes of the spokesman when, on stepping from the boat with John in my arms, I turned and, putting my hands together in the Chinese manner, thanked him.

Most of the day among the reeds they spent praying, holding their breath at the sound of footsteps on a nearby path. Charles asked 'what the Lord was saying' to his wife. 'Delivering thee from the people . . . unto whom I now send thee,' she replied. And Jessie Gregg? 'I have been waiting all day for a little bird to bring us a letter,' was her surprising answer. [I, AJB, cannot write this without a vivid sense of our friend Jessie Gregg's personality; it is so typical of her, like an old-time prophet with a sixth sense.][8] They laughed at the time, but their troubles were far from over. A boy saw them and,

> with a scared face gave me a wide berth. I must have been an object with dirty, bloodstained undercoat and trousers, no gown, worn-out shoes, unshaved, wounded face and dishevelled hair of six months' growth . . . No wonder he was frightened.

Boxers came searching for them, 'shooting off guns into the reeds', but went away again. Then a thunderstorm drenched them and chilled them to the bone. 'O Lord, was there ever a more helpless, hopeless, desolate band of Thy little ones?' Green added to his narrative. They were still half dressed as they had been when surprised by the Boxers at the farm. They decided to do the right thing and go to the *yamen* in the city. On the way they came to a cottage, asked for help, and were told to wait while a man with a boat was called. This looked promising.

> Suddenly we were startled by an unearthly sound . . . With a slash of a drawn sword the reed curtain at the door was dashed down, and we were again face to face with a crowd of fierce Boxers . . . I was seized by the hair, dragged to the ground, and was conscious of blow after blow (and) then of being trampled on by many feet as others rushed over me to seize my wife and Miss Gregg. I remember a pang as I heard the heart-rending shrieks of the children, and then a sweet calm filled my soul as I committed my spirit to God . . . We have each been able to testify that this was the calmest moment in our lives . . . never doubting that we should immediately be killed.

Now we were dragged outside and thrown down in the mud, then bound hand and foot. Suddenly I missed the cries of the children and was glad that (they) were spared more of these terrible sights. Miss Gregg was hauled by the hair into a kneeling position, and her head pressed down on to a stone (incense table). One cried: 'Who will strike?' But other voices overruling cried: 'No; take them all to headquarters first.' As we lay there bound in the mud, one and another struck us heavily again and again with the backs of swords or the handles of spears . . . As blow after blow fell on (Miss Gregg) no sound escaped her lips, only a long, deep sigh.

[The command was given to carry them off.] The handles of two spears were put under my left arm, two men taking the ends on their shoulders, and I was taken off hanging between them by one arm, with hands tied to my feet behind me . . . about a quarter of a mile (in) excruciating pain . . . My wife (similarly suspended) by both hands and feet, (Miss Gregg) by one arm and one leg. (The children were tied hands and feet, John carried and Vera made to walk.)

The Boxers would not believe their story, convincing themselves that they had captured Roman Catholics from the nearby mission who had shot two of their number. But they moved Mrs Green's head out of a pool of dirty water and eased Jessie Gregg's thongs at Charles' request. Lying there on the wet ground (and later in the Boxers' temple building), still trussed like fowls, they said, 'For Jesus' sake' and prayed together. For three or four days they were held, bound more reasonably and cross-examined, until Charles Green's 'mouthful of Huolu dialect' and 'two wives and children' convinced the Boxers that they spoke the truth. At last their ropes were removed.

From the 16th to the 18th they were on show to curious crowds of hundreds of Boxers 'carrying their ghastly weapons, and by their looks thirsting for our blood,' while messengers went to Baoding to discuss their fate. On their return with the news that the governor was angry when told that the foreigners were still alive, and had ordered their execution, a consultation of civilian Boxers, superior to the armed gangs, was held in the temple. These literati and tradesmen (playing the part, it transpired) decided to hold them until it was safe to send them on to Tianjin. In explanation they said that Charles Green must have 'accumulated so much merit that heaven itself had intervened on our behalf (to save us again and again).'

Two meals a day of the coarsest food became their next hardship.

> Don't be afraid for
> Chinese robbers nearly all
> have been killed by both
> Chinese & foreign soldiers
> Peking + Tientsin belong to
> European now I will go to
> Tientsin + tell your armies
> to protect you
>
> You may tear it into pieces when
> you have seen

THE 'LITTLE CRUMPLED TUFT OF PAPER'
Fei Qihao's (?) message of hope to the Greens and J Gregg

Dysentery struck the children and Mrs Green, but their bedding and the little Bible were again returned to them, and occasional gifts of cash by sympathisers provided odds and ends more suitable to eat. After a week they were allowed to wash themselves and their verminous clothes.

Then, early one afternoon, Charles Green was fanning the sleeping women and children to keep the flies away, and looking through the open latticework of the door at their slumbering guard and a solitary sightseer. A 'little crumpled tuft of paper' fell through the lattice to the floor at his feet – an act of contempt, Green thought, and went on fanning. The young man had moved off, but stopped, came back, and pointed at the floor. Green unrolled the paper and read in English, 'Don't be afraid . . . Peking and Tientsin belong to Europeans. Now I will go to Tientsin and tell your armies to protect you. You may tear it into pieces when you have seen.' 'Looking up I motioned my thanks, and my unknown friend left hurriedly . . . I was so excited that I woke the ladies to show them. Miss Gregg at once claimed it as the "little bird" letter she had looked for . . .' – and kept it (p 422).

Three weeks passed. The month since they left Huolu seemed like months and months. Then on Monday, September 3, a large hostile company of Boxers arrived, and for two hours crowded into the prison to see them. 'One thrust the muzzle of his gun into my wife's face and said . . . they were "going to begin business today"'. They declared that they were coming to kill them. But 'the whole town and neighbourhood were in an uproar about us' – determined to protect them! Leading gentry were negotiating with the Boxers, and plans being made to hide the foreigners and hold the city against any attack. They were moved into a little storage room, 'overrun with rats and vermin', while shouting and much excitement went on outside. The Boxers were told they had been sent down river, and a 'monster meeting' succeeded in persuading them to call off an attack. But the prisoners in the storeroom had been overlooked.

> Sick, ill, tired, cold, hungry and uncertain, the black pall of despair was settling down on my soul . . . [Charles Green wrote]. With tears I implored my wife and Miss Gregg to pray for me, when suddenly there was quiet and music in my heart. I listened to catch the tune (and) sang,
>
>> Praise the Saviour, ye who know Him,
>> Who can tell how much we owe Him?
>> Gladly let us render to Him
>> All we have and are.
>
> As the Lord's own peace flowed again into our hearts, we did not try to keep back the tears that would come.

At last they were brought food and told that the British consul had heard of their plight at Anxin, and demanded a safe escort for them to Tianjin. But the countryside was full of Boxers, so they were to be taken back to Baoding at once. They called this their seventh deliverance from death, but heard later of others unknown to them at the time. Just after they were taken from Huolu to Zhengding, Yü Xian himself had arrived at Huolu and made minute inquiries about them. The fact that they were in Boxer hands already was probably what saved them from his further attention. And while they were being kindly treated in the women's prison at Baoding, ruthless Boxers had only been prevented by a strong guard from breaking in and killing them. As in God's words to the ocean (in Job 38:11 AV), 'Hitherto shalt thou come, but no further: and here shall thy proud waves be stayed,' they recognised that evil men with the worst intentions could go no further than God allowed.

Fei Qihao to their rescue[35]   *August–October 1900*

On the day that the Oberlin staff at Fenyang were massacred, August 15 (p 402) – the day that the Greens spent in the riverside reed bed and Jessie Gregg's 'thought from God' was of 'a little bird' bringing them news – the young schoolteacher, Fei Qihao, made his escape to Pingyao. But as he prayed about what he should do, as a destitute fugitive without friends, he became convinced he should return to Fenyang at all costs.

After dark he arrived and crept by a back street to the home of a Christian courier, on the point of fleeing. They left together and went to a poor Christian who out of his poverty gave Fei an old garment and some cash. Fei then made his way to Taigu where an old gentleman of the Kong family (p 405) gave him more clothing and cash. Going on to Yüci, he was told of the Boxers having killed one hundred church members in July. Doing thirty miles a day, and amazed that he was given the strength for it, he crossed the mountains and arrived at Huolu, hoping to find someone at the CIM. Instead he found Yü Xian and two thousand soldiers in the city, and the missionaries already taken as prisoners to Zhengding. So Fei Qihao pressed on.

'Every day as he passed between (Huolu) and (Baoding) he met countless hordes of (Tong Fuxiang's) troops . . . escaping after their defeat. They marched along, looting all the way, but poor Fei in his destitution had nothing to fear.' At Zhengding he went to the cathedral and found 'a bishop, three priests, five foreign sisters, five railroad people and others; in all nineteen foreigners', including the Martin Griffiths and H M Brown of the CIM. Five couriers had been killed near there so they did not ask Fei to carry letters, but sent an oral message to the consuls.

Again he travelled thirty miles and stowed away in a railway freight-car until near Baoding. There he joined a boatful of defeated soldiers and Boxers, and an old man looking for his soldier son. With him he lay low when they encountered boatloads of Boxers, still with their swords and red sashes. Day after day the rain poured down, and in the misery of being wet and cold he inadvertently said aloud in English, 'Oh, dear, dear!' but no one noticed it. In Mrs A H Smith's account there is no mention of his passing through Anxin, on the direct route between Baoding and Tianjin, or of seeing the Greens; but when she questioned him he had not yet seen the consul. He was a discreet young man.

He reached Tianjin on August 30, only fifteen days since leaving Fenyang. Passing French soldiers, Russians, Sikhs and Japanese, he made himself known to an American who took him to his captain. Fei produced a little rag given him by C W Price, the Fenyang martyr, on which were the words 'What this man says *is true!*'[36] He was interrogated at length, and at midnight, worn out, was taken three miles further to face a British officer. The officer told him to go and get some sleep. Given a bed of clean sheets and blankets, Fei 'felt as if he was in heaven'. The next day he had interviews, one with Mrs Smith of the *Tientsin Times* and others, and one with the British consul for an hour. Finally he went to the American Board college where he had been educated. At the sight of his rags and dirt and long hair some shed tears. But what news of the 'Oberlin Band' he had to bring to them!

Only then could he start hunting for his wife and family. He found his village home a heap of rubble and a solitary man alarmed by his arrival began to run. Instinctively Fei called out his brother's name. The man stopped and turned towards him. They wept and wept together. Their parents were dead and what was left of their family had scattered. Their elder brother had become a Boxer, the rest had fled in abject terror of the frightful Hindu soldiery, 'who took the men as carriers and outraged the women, old and young indiscriminately'.[37] Large bodies of Boxers were in the neighbourhood. They had to flee, first to Tong Xian and then, with Sikhs who beat him, to Beijing. As they entered the city he saw E G Tewkesbury, his friend and tutor, and A H Smith. His wife was rescued and brought to him, and his adventure had ended.

The timing of Fei Qihao's journey and of the Greens' movements, as well as the contents of the crumpled note and the behaviour of the one who brought it, leave little if any doubt that Fei Qihao was the one who told the consul about the prisoners at Anxin. The Greens were there from August 15 until September 5; and Fei Qihao covering thirty miles a day and the last forty miles by train to Baoding could well have reached Anxin by the 23rd. The Greens and Jessie Gregg were betrayed and captured at Anxin on August

15 and held there for their own safety until September 5. The 'little crumpled tuft of paper' incident was on or about August 23–24. On September 5 they were told of the consul's demand for their protection, and were taken to Baoding. Fei Qihao left Fenyang on August 15, reached Huolu *circa* August 20, Baoding *c* August 22 and Tianjin August 30. So he would have been at Anxin on August 23 or 24. August 31 he told the consul, who would have acted promptly to tell the Baoding mandarins what he knew.[38]

The report Fei brought of the massacres in Shanxi was, according to Robert Forsyth, the first to reach his mission in Tianjin and, it seems, the first accepted by the consuls.[39] 'When the news was telegraphed to England . . . Queen Victoria instructed Lord Salisbury to write, on September 20, 1900, to the Emperor of China' in protest. (This suggests that the account by Yong Zheng of the Taiyuan massacre (p 379) was literally 'the first eye-witness account', not the first report.)

Another Christian who arrived at Beijing on September 19 from the horrors in Shanxi was Wang Lanbu, the door-keeper at Soping who escaped after being flogged and left as dead on June 24 (p 336). His own mother and his little daughter had been burned alive at Yingzhou and he had taken two months to complete the journey. But of all his hardships, one of the most distressing was being robbed of what little money he had left, by European soldiers after his arrival. His report on the atrocities in the northern cities, near the Mongolian border, was substantially confirmed by another, Zhang Rufeng, when he reached Tianjin on October 19.

When bad weather prevented the boat conveying the Greens from Anxin to Baoding from arriving when expected, the now anxious officials sent two boatloads of soldiers to search for them. They all reached the city together on September 7. A high-ranking commissioner who came to meet them asked how the consul knew they were at Anxin, and it was easy enough to say that a complete stranger on his way to Tianjin had told them he would report their plight. How Baoding had changed! Apart from soldiers, the streets were empty and many shops were closed. A rumour that foreign troops were on the way had panicked many who stood to lose by staying. The viciously anti-foreign mandarins were trying to play safe, ending the siege of Xian Xian and protecting the Greens on the one hand (p 425) and still harbouring Boxers on the other. They feared for their own future.

Once again their prisoners were taken to the women's lock-up, but a marked change in their treatment began. Cheap bedding was provided. The mandarins' own barber attended them. The 15th of the 8th moon, a feast day, saw them provided with a good meal from the mandarin's own kitchen and gifts for the children. Their rags were removed, and clean new clothing, even though the cheapest, was provided. The next day they were taken to clean rooms in a *yamen*, with a courtyard and garden for their own use, a cook and four soldiers under an official exclusively to guard and serve them. Eventually they learned that on September 7 at John Stevenson's request the consul-general in Shanghai had called on Li Hongzhang to draw his attention to their conditions. Three Christians were allowed to visit them, and told them the harrowing truth about the Baoding massacres of June 30 and July 1. At the acting-governor's expense Charles Green broke the silence of four months with a telegram to Shanghai, and towards the end of the third week received a letter from the Tianjin consul. But they had not yet been given their liberty.

Here Charles Green's account ended, for he fell ill. His wife and Jessie Gregg were mournfully discussing their situation when Vera looked up at them and said, 'Auntie, the Lord looseth the prisoners', and went on playing – the words that had encouraged them during their long anxiety at Anxin. For weeks Vera and others of them at different times had been suffering from painful dysentery. On October 8 her pain increased and at 4 am on the 10th she died.

> We did not sorrow as those who had no hope [Mrs Green wrote], for we know that those who sleep in Jesus, God will bring with Him . . . Her bright loving ways had touched the hearts of people and led them to spare us; her life was laid down for Jesus' sake and for China . . . Each day found (Charles) decidedly weaker. We heard rumours of French troops approaching, which filled us with hope and thankfulness, but we could not understand why the officials left us so much alone these days.

On October 13 the French entered Baoding, but not until the 16th did the colonel hear that there were English prisoners in the *yamen*. He sent an ambulance to bring them to his camp, although the mandarins told him that they did not want to go to the coast. In fact they had been holding them as hostages for use in negotiating with the allies. Then on the 19th other allied troops arrived from Beijing (p 407), General Gaselee came to see them, and transferred them to the British field hospital under an army surgeon. 'With grateful adoration too deep for words, we praised God.'

Then Martin Griffiths and H M Brown arrived from Zhengding on the 21st, after twelve weeks' protection by the Zhengding brigadier, and on the 23rd all were taken in the care of the doctor by boat to the coast. At Anxin Surgeon-Major Thompson invited the leading townsman, a Mr Zhao, who had befriended the prisoners, to come aboard, and took the names of others instrumental in saving their lives. He then gave Mr Zhao a document promising them rewards, and addressed a crowd on the river-bank. Ten days later at a public meeting the British commander from Baoding thanked the whole town, gave $100 to each of the leading men, and a Union Jack for them to display if troops of any nationality should trouble them. The names of Farmer Gao, who had sheltered the fugitives for a month, and the temple-keeper who first hid them were also given to the authorities at Tianjin for reward in due time.

But Charles Green had typhoid fever, contracted in the *yamen*. On the way downriver he became delirious and was still unconscious

THE C H S GREENS AND JESSIE GREGG
survivors safe in Shanghai

when they reached Tianjin on October 27. He recovered consciousness two days later. 'So many had been called to lay down their lives,' they wrote. Why then had they been spared? They had no answer, but 'often turned to Acts 12', where they read, 'Herod . . . killed James . . . and proceeded . . . to take Peter' (vv. 2–3 AV), but God brought Peter out of the prison.

Vera was buried at Tianjin. Then Mrs Green and little John became critically ill. A month later the rivers and northern seas were about to freeze and be closed to shipping for three months. So they decided that even in their condition it would be best to go south. The Russian general in charge of the railways provided an ambulance car; Jardine Matheson and Company put a steam launch at their disposal and gave them privileges on board their ship; and on the tenth day they were welcomed at Wusong Road, Shanghai. Dr F H Judd, one of the first Chefoo schoolboys then removed the remaining shot from Green's arms, head and face, and on January 5, 1901, they sailed for Europe.

> But thanks be to God, who in Christ always leads us in triumph, and through us spreads the fragrance of the knowledge of him everywhere (2 Cor 2:14 RSV).

Alfred and Olivia Ogren[40]   *July 13–August 1900*

A wealth of impressive writing about the Boxer rising has somehow obscured Olivia Ogren's inspired record of her own and her husband's experiences. It ends this summary on the note that scores of others sounded, yet with a potency of its own. This twentieth-century fulfilment of the words of Jesus in Matthew 10 makes them as relevant today as to the listening disciples and to the despairing fugitives of the Boxer nightmare.

> *I am sending you out like sheep among wolves . . .*
> *On my account you will be brought before governors and*
>   *kings*
> *as witnesses to them . . . But when they arrest you,*
> *do not worry about what to say or how to say it . . .*
> *for it will not be you speaking, but the Spirit of*
> *your Father speaking through you . . .*
> *All men will hate you because of me,*
>   *but he who stands firm to the end will be saved . . .*

> *When you are persecuted in one place, flee to another . . .*
> *Do not be afraid of those who can kill the body*
>   *but cannot kill the soul . . .*
> *Whoever loses his life for my sake will find it* (Matt. 10:16–39
>   NIV).

In a word, 'We are more than conquerors through Him who loved us', for 'It is not death to die!'

Alfred and Olivia Ogren were a young couple from Jönkoping in Sweden, but full members of the CIM. After six years in north Shanxi, they had pioneered Yongning (now Zhongyang) in 1899 – across the high Luliang range from Fenyang, and about five days' travel from Taiyuan (map p 339). The 'bold and independent' people of Yongning had been 'well disposed' towards them, until drought and threatened famine revived their superstitions and made them look for scapegoats. Even then the magistrate secretly asked the Ogrens to pray to the God of heaven and earth for rain. In May 1900 strangers with Shandong accents arrived, and awe-struck countrymen saw how they, the Boxers, could kindle fire from magic buttons – of celluloid. Rumours multiplied, and one that foreigners were poisoning wells was seen to be true when the water in a well near the Ogrens turned red.

On July 5 word came of the murder on June 29 of the ladies at Xiaoyi, only fifty miles away. The friendly magistrate told the Ogrens to escape while they could; supplied them at midnight with one hundred taels of silver; and took charge of their premises. They had already cut and disguised a secret exit through the big back door of their garden. Before daylight on July 13 they and the evangelist mounted a mule litter to take them under guard the twenty-five miles to the Yellow River. There they were confronted by people armed with clubs and openly hostile, blaming them for the drought. But the local official helped them to hire a small boat to Tongguan in Shaanxi, three hundred miles to the south. Because of the strong current and rapids, boats only travelled downstream and were sold on arrival. But hiring one, and a change of escort, were expensive, so that they had to send to Yongning for more money. The *yamen* secretary himself brought it four days later, with 'a cordial letter of recommendation by our friendly mandarin'.

Halfway to Tongguan they came to three miles of impassable rapids where a porterage had to be made, and heard of the massacre of the McConnells and Youngs (p 388) on the river-bank not far away. No testimonial could help them against such ferocity. An old ex-mandarin, who proved to be a friend of the Yongning magistrate, invited them to his home in Shaanxi and protected them from a troop of Linfen soldiers who suddenly appeared with orders to drive them away. But soon after they started towards the old man's home they 'saw men skulking among the rocks ahead' who leapt out at them brandishing weapons and began rifling their baggage. One with a great sword 'began whetting it with the strange Boxer movements, shouting "Kill" at the same time. We thought our last hour had come, and expected that soon our dead bodies would be hurled into the rushing river.' But they were spared and crossed into Shaanxi before another squad of soldiers arrived on the Shanxi bank to arrest them.

After two days of weary tramping over the hills, carrying their infant Samuel, they reached the old man's village, only to be turned away by the villagers and robbed again by two gangs of men. They found shelter in a small cave deep in the mountains, but starvation drove them back. Alfred Ogren's 'awful agony from hunger' distressed his wife, but he said, 'It is no matter what we suffer for Jesus' sake,' and, 'I rejoice that through these sufferings the Church will be awakened into new life. The field is being watered with blood; what a harvest there will be!'

The Boxers had offered a hundred taels for every foreign head, and the villagers had to hold back a villainous young man among them who raved like a madman and rushed at the Ogrens with raised sword. But they were not given food. What could they do? Not knowing that Governor Tuan Fang had made Shaanxi a safer province, they decided to walk back to Yongning and the kind mandarin. Without money and with only the infant's coverlet and pillow, a saucepan and some flour on which to feed the child, the clothes they wore, a Bible and a pair of scissors to offer to a ferryman, they could not buy food. But Jesus had said, 'So do not worry, saying, "What shall we eat?" or "What shall we drink?" . . . your heavenly Father knows that you need them' (Matt. 6:31–2 NIV). 'However it be, I felt that to die of starvation for Jesus who died for me was easy.'

Following bypaths and scrambling up and down hills they came upon people who treated them kindly, so that they had at least one meal a day and a roof over their heads at night. An old man took them by the hand to ford a big river, and led them to his home. But after another long day on foot, two rogues searched them, emptied the feathers from Samuel's little pillow and burned them, and took the Bible. 'The vehemence with which I declared I could not and would not part with that Holy Book' made him hand it back. The rogues forced the ferryman to take them all over the Yellow River and delivered them to the Boxers on the Shanxi side. While Alfred was being questioned, a crowd surrounded Olivia and with a sardonic grin a man put his head on one side and remarked, 'The Daning missionaries have gone back to heaven.'

The Boxers then marched them fifteen miles to their leader in a temple, and Alfred was taken in while Olivia and Samuel sat in the outer courtyard. She recalled,

> I could hear (him) pleading, telling them who we were . . . when he was quickly interrupted by a loud shrieking voice. Then came the sound of the sharpening of swords, followed by a weird moaning, as of someone being tortured. My feelings were indescribable. I could only pray God to cut short my husband's sufferings, and fill his heart with peace, and give me grace to meet my lot without fear. [She did not know that the Boxers were only going through their weird ritual – but in preparation for his execution.]
>
> (Again she heard her husband pleading.) Again he was interrupted, and again came the same moaning as before. Then all was silent! My husband was killed, and I was left alone with my helpless babe.

It was dark and she was six months pregnant. But she tried to escape. The original two rogues saw her, and dragged her behind a wall saying,

> 'The General is coming, and he can't abide the sight of a woman.' There was a great firing of guns and shouting, and the whole crowd came out of the temple yard carrying, as I supposed, my husband's corpse. (As they approached) I thought, 'It is my turn now' . . . though I wished to rise, I could not. A man . . . taking my hand led me down to the side of the river. At some distance . . . I saw lanterns and heard a great uproar . . . After a long while some men came along and said my husband had run away. It seemed strange to me . . . as I thought him dead.

Olivia alone[41]   *August 1900–February 1901*

They locked Olivia in a tomb-vault for the night with only a bowl of water, but brought her some rice in the morning and led her away. Suddenly they cried out, 'Hide! the big man is coming!' So she hid, but when she peered out, even the two men had gone. 'So I was alone with my little Samuel. Yet not alone. Oh no! Had He not said so distinctly to me, "Fear not, I am with thee"?' Bravely she set off walking to Daning where the Peats were said to be in prison, 'for to be with friends in prison was better than this awful freedom'. 'At times Boxers pretended to be about to kill me; at other times some women would come round me and give me food.' She tried to wade across a river with Samuel in her arms and was being carried away, when strong men pulled her up the bank, only to jeer at her 'widowhood'. Wet through, she settled down as she was, to sleep in the open, but long after dark two other men led her to a cave and left her 'with a "God bless you"' – they were Christians, but they could do no more.

Before daybreak she started towards Daning again, only to be caught by Boxers. A village headman rescued her, gave her food and a pair of socks, and sent two men to escort her to the Daning *yamen*. 'The Boxers stamped and jumped in the frenzy of their rage', but she was safely put in the common prison. The Peats had passed through two days previously, before being murdered near Qüwu.

In the morning the warder passed some bread and half a water-melon to Olivia through a hole in the iron-clad door of the prison yard, and told her to say her child was a girl, as all males were to be killed. But when asked she told the truth. So in the afternoon when the door was opened and she was ordered, 'Bring out the boy!', 'terror seized me as if I had been struck by a thunderbolt'. She was made to kneel before the magistrate and sternly questioned about her husband, who, he said, was still alive. She did not believe him, thinking he could not admit to the murder in his county. But gradually he began to speak more kindly as if pitying her. After-wards, the county secretary's wife told her she had offered a reward for finding Alfred and bringing him in. Then Olivia was led back to prison.

The bed was alive with vermin so she lay on the ground outside. For days one of her eyes had been badly inflamed, painful and swollen. She could not sleep. At daybreak she was dozing off and thought she heard Alfred's voice. She leapt up. 'Again that longed-for, tender voice, "Olivia! Oh, Olivia!" But it came from the hole in the prison door.' She ran to the door and looked out. 'His clothes hung in tatters and his head was bound up with a piece of some garment . . . I could see Boxers running wildly about in the *yamen* yard.' Someone opened the prison door and took them both to where she could dress his wounds. She washed the blood from his shirt and tore it in strips as bandages.

> What a sight! A great piece of the scalp hung loosely down; one ear was crushed and swollen; his neck bore two sword gashes; near the shoulder were two spear cuts, one very deep; and all his back was red and swollen from beating.

Crowds flocked to stare at them until the evening. Then they had quiet enough for him to tell his story.

In the temple the Boxer 'general' had had him bound with his hands behind his back, and everyone had kicked and beaten him. Then they led him to the riverside, to kill him, they said.

> They forced me down on my knees and set upon me from all sides, but as their weapons clashed one on another they did not kill me. Loss of blood made me feel faint, but I was so happy! . . . I felt no pain . . . heaven seemed open, and one step would take me there.
> Then came to me suddenly . . . the thought of my wife and child . . . I leapt from the midst of the crowd (of thirty or forty men) into the (deep) water. I managed to get out on the other side, and with my hands still bound behind my back, started to run . . . barefoot over the rocks. Under cover of darkness I got out of sight, (and) after about fifteen miles I dared to stop and free my hands by rubbing the cords on a stone.

Heading again for Yongning, he several times lost his way and to his distress found himself back on the Daning road, until someone told him his wife was there. Entering the city, he was seen by Boxers who gave chase, but he ran for his life and reached the *yamen*. They let him in, protected him, and took him to Olivia and Samuel.

Two days later, on August 30, in spite of their condition they were put on donkeys with unpadded pack-saddle frames and sent towards Linfen, escorted by an officer with four soldiers and four brutal Boxers. Riding was such agony that Alfred preferred to walk. But at Pu Xian, halfway to Linfen, they were sent back to Daning. The Linfen officials had refused to have them.

Prison at Daning was a relief. But privations too much for Samuel to bear reduced him to 'a limp little body too weak to cry'; Olivia's second eye began to swell painfully, and she could only sit and endure. Alfred became delirious with fever, struggling to escape his terrors, so that he had to be tied to the verminous bed.

'God only knows the horror and misery of those hours,' Olivia wrote. 'After that awful night' each of them recovered slowly. But when Olivia shared her scanty ration with her child and husband, they punished her by stopping her own rice and milk supply.

'Harder than all weariness were the filth and vermin. The very sight brought scalding tears to my eyes.' But that no one could prevent her from escaping to 'the God of all comfort' consoled her. A *yamen* 'gentleman', knowing that the other prisoners abused the Ogrens for their quiet faith in God, even in such circumstances, asked if they still prayed. 'At my simple assurance of the peace of those who have the comfort of God's loving presence, he seemed much impressed and listened respectfully.' And with Alfred able to talk rationally again, they thanked God for the training he was giving them, and its effect on the official.

'After a month of misery and untellable sufferings' until October 4, they were taken to Linfen. ('CCH', who knew as much as anyone, on September 19 still had no idea of what had happened to the Ogrens.)[42] But four miles short of the city they heard that the Empress Dowager and retinue were passing, *en route* to Xi'an. They had to lie low, and the week in a temple on the coarsest of food left Alfred very weak. But on October 12 the politeness of their reception of Linfen and the news that some missionaries had escaped, distracted them from their own extremity.

Olivia failed at first to realise that Alfred was dying. On the 14th,

> a terrible fear seized me . . . Oh, how I cried out to God in the anguish of my soul! . . . No human words are full enough of sadness to tell my awful loneliness. No tears were bitter enough . . . A storm of grief overwhelmed me, until God gave me comfort . . . To my heart came the words (of Jesus) outside the gates of Nain, 'Weep not!'

A young Christian widow kept her company in the *yamen*. Her husband had been the Linfen mission courier, imprisoned by the magistrate in an attempt to protect him. But the Boxers had dragged him out and beheaded him. His head, along with those of many other Christians, had been nailed to the city wall, until she was released from prison and took it down. Her own physical sufferings had been relatively light. Some Christians had been maimed for life. One grey-haired old man had been strung up by his thumbs for half a day. Others were scarred by the cross cut into their foreheads. Terrible as the sufferings of missionaries had been, they were a fraction of the anguish the Christians had endured. But peace and security were returning.

Before Alfred Ogren died they heard that four Roman priests had held the Boxers at bay in Hongtong and survived; and Graham McKie with the two young women, Marion Chapman and Matilda Way (p 361), were still hiding in the hills near Qüwu. At midnight on August 19 (five days after the end of the Peking siege) they had started walking with six Christians towards Hankou, six hundred miles away. Captured and released again, they lived in caves for six more weeks, evading the Boxers, and in a loft above two children with smallpox, until on October 1 they were taken safely back to Qüwu. For five months they had not taken off their clothes. But when the Linfen magistrate sent soldiers to bring them to him, 'the (Qüwu) Christians wept bitterly when (they) left'. Even in October no one could ever be sure what might happen.

So Olivia Ogren 'had the glad surprise' on October 24 of being joined by Graham McKie and the two girls. 'I could not speak as I pressed their hands.' They were with her when her baby was born on December 6, and on the long journey to Hankou (from January 6 to February 16, 1901) under the protection of two officers, sixteen mounted and two foot soldiers. Dr J W Hewett, in spite of his long imprisonment (p 356), had arrived there on November 6, three and a half months sooner.

Olivia ended the story of her sufferings with the words, 'After all that the Lord has given me to bear I can yet say from my heart – "Bless the Lord, O my soul, and all that is within me, bless His Holy Name."'

She and her companions had been the last of all the fugitives to reach the comfort and security of the outer world again. Mutual admiration of each other's qualities through the long weeks of suffering and danger had soon developed into love, and led to the marriage of Graham McKie and Marion Chapman. In a euphoric narrative, Matilda Way wrote of the Linfen Christians,

> Nearly all have a large cross on their forehead, inflicted by the Boxers . . . I rejoice to think of the glorious harvest yet to come. I heard that the Taigu Christians had met for worship, and the Boxers had come and killed them all but two . . . My first twelve months in China have been full of a wonderful experience . . . I am hoping to have a rest, and return to my work in Shanxi.

She did, with Eva French.

PART 5

A NEW CHINA
1900–1950

CHAPTER FOURTEEN

TO BURY THE RISING
1900–1901

Directors' dilemma   *1900–01*

There was nothing new to Hudson Taylor or the China Inland Mission in being forced, helpless, to their knees. The division of labour at Shanghai between John Stevenson and William Cooper that satisfied both had defied solution until Hudson Taylor took decisive action. His gift, of seeing through the brushwood of confusion to recognise the jungle trail to open fields beyond, had shown him a way out. So Cooper, as an equal partner with Stevenson in responsibility in China, was to have supplied the personal touch, the sympathy and understanding that the dour Scotsman did not lack but found hard to show. As travelling director Cooper was to get close to the men and women of the outback, see their circumstances, listen to them, sense their spiritual morale, and give them advice and support.

The darkening thunder clouds of early 1900 had intensified the need for consultation between the leaders and with the rank and file. So William Cooper had gone north to Shanxi and Zhili, and Dixon Hoste, superintendent in Henan, was called to Shanghai to share Stevenson's load. He dealt with the day-to-day matters, the visitors with little concept of the pressure of such work, and missionaries with grievances or problems they wished to discuss at length. What needed to be referred to Stevenson he presented concisely, with his recommendations. The system worked well. Stevenson welcomed and valued him. Both kept in touch with Hudson Taylor, fully occupied with international commitments, who frankly stated his opinions but left decisive action to the men in China.[1]

The correspondence during these years reveals their loyalty and affection, and that of Frost, Sloan and Marcus Wood among others. James Meadows's recollections of Hudson Taylor's 'affectionate reverence (for God) which made the godliness of the good man stand out conspicuously', in a marked degree expressed these outstanding men's own attitude to their human leader. It is not only apparent in their letters but expressly stated in their own words.

Although prostrated by the Boxer despatches, Hudson Taylor still exerted strong leadership, and the Mission welcomed it. Physical and mental fatigue, culminating in the 'lapse of memory' at Boston, had cut short the General Director's active life and brought him home to Britain just as alarming news of developments in north China plunged Stevenson and Hoste into the crisis without precedent in the mission's experience. But Hudson Taylor's retreat to the comparative calm of Switzerland had been expressly for him to recover his vitality as quickly as possible.[2]

In the States, in London and increasingly in Switzerland concern for William Cooper's safety found expression in letters that could only generalise while factual detail was unknown and newspapers for lack of information were fictitiously sensational. John Stevenson warned the home country directors to believe nothing until he could confirm it.[3] The fabricated 'massacre in the legations' soon justified his caution. For some weeks no foreign casualties had been reported, except in the north. But unrest everywhere in China, with riots erupting in place after place, had been enough to lead the consuls to call for a general evacuation of all foreigners from the interior. Soon the safety of the treaty ports came into question and additional allied troops and warships came for their protection. Volunteer defence forces were formed, and tension in the international settlements increased.

After long delays, reliable news of the atrocities in Zhili and Shanxi began coming in and was relayed by cable to the homelands of the missionaries most affected. In and around Beijing hundreds of Christians were savagely slaughtered. The legation siege began. William Cooper was trapped, then unable to communicate with Stevenson, and finally reported dead. Four weeks after the massacre of all missionaries in Baoding, it was only possible to say that 'the worst' was feared for them. William Cooper's death was not confirmed until October 29. Emily Whitchurch of England and Edith Searell of New Zealand were brutally bludgeoned to death on June 30. Word of it took a month to reach Shanghai and was the first to be cabled home.

Gradually the truth emerged, with strong implications that much more was happening of which little if anything was yet known. The cables received in Britain revealed the difficulties that Stevenson and Hoste faced in Shanghai. No more missionaries were to be sent out; and for some in the interior it would be more dangerous to travel than to stay where they were.[4] Available funds had been distributed to all members and associates as soon as the crisis was recognised, but transmission to some soon became impossible. How could adequate help be given to any, let alone to so many in dire straits?

Not until September 8 did reports from Chinese sources tell of the Taiyuan massacre of July 9, but (revealing a black hole of ignorance of almost all that was going on) it was September 17 before Stevenson could relay Charles Green's telegram from macabre Baoding that he, his family and Jessie Gregg were relatively safe in the *yamen* after repeated brushes with death. The murder of the ten members of the Swedish Holiness Union on June 29, and even fears for the Datong six could not be cabled until October 3. Anxious relatives waiting to be put out of insufferable suspense learned on October 8 that the Duncan Kays, Graham McKie and the Misses Chapman and Way had met their death on August 30, only to learn four days later by another cable that the report affecting McKie, Chapman and Way had been contradicted.

The Foreign Office co-operated closely with the societies in Britain, as the consuls and (after the siege was lifted) the minister in Beijing worked confidently with the missions in China, passing on such information as each received. In this way Stevenson cabled on November 26 that Alfred Ogren had been killed, but Graham McKie and the two young women and Olivia Ogren were safe in 'Taiyuan' – a synonym for horror. The Foreign Office passed the same report to the CIM in London. But in fact they were in Linfen. That more misinformation did not complicate affairs at such a time was remarkable.

R Logan Jack, an explorer crossing China 'from Shanghai to the Irrawadi', illustrated the problems faced by Stevenson and most missionaries in remote places. On June 6 at Xichang (Ningyuan, in Sichuan) the prefect told him about the Boxers, but not until July 29 did 'a bombshell (fall) into our camp' – a telegram from Chongqing dated June 30, 'Go to Burma. Europeans and consuls ready to leave Chongqing at a moment's notice . . . Probable that all foreigners at Pekin have been killed.' And a July 27 telegram received on August 10 said, 'Foreign Office London instructions (to) remove all British subjects from China.' Other messages to 'keep west' told Logan Jack of Lieutenant Watts-Jones's fate in Ningxia (p 336). The same advice reached the Cecil Polhills at Kangding, but the children had measles and could not travel. Eventually the family travelled to Chongqing and all the way down the Yangzi to safety.

As news reached London it was relayed to Hudson Taylor at Davos. Having set himself to rest and regain strength he was taking graded exercise and enjoying his hobby of photography, developing and printing his own exposures. By June 9 he was 'gaining ground', and did what he could as General Director to advise John Stevenson. As he would do all in his power to help the missionaries and Chinese Church, how much more would their 'heavenly father do in His love and wisdom and power!' On July 16 he wrote to say that as refugee missionaries arrived in Shanghai they should be sent to Japan or Singapore or home.[5] The lavish Morton legacy was for evangelism and education, but 'in an emergency it would be quite justifiable to use any of (it) for travel expenses'. It could be replaced later on. Money on deposit in the banks was at risk of looting, even in Shanghai, and better put to use. Transmissions from Britain of Morton funds would be restricted until required for use.

Then on July 27, after hearing of the Whitchurch–Searell murders 'and doubtless Chinese Christians with them', and unconfirmed news of a massacre at Taiyuan, he wrote and wired advising the withdrawal of all women from the interior. The Chefoo schools could go in a body direct to Japan. War at Tianjin might make all the provincial viceroys act against foreigners, all banks freeze their funds and all means of transmitting money be closed. The time was ripe to 'make free distribution' rather than have large sums blocked and unusable. 'All willing to take the risk of travelling should be allowed to come to Shanghai . . . Chinese Christians would probably be safer if the missionaries were absent.'

To Marcus Wood at Newington Green he suggested 'an early day for united fasting and prayer', preferably with all societies joining in. 'The advance on Peking might mean the death of thousands of missionaries' if the viceroys withdrew their protection. '(Benjamin B) might be able to get the Archbishop to act promptly in the matter', to make it a national observance. 'Though all human power seems so unavailing, it is still true that the LORD reigneth.' Where in all this was the crumpled casualty from Boston? But the tax on his emotions soon sapped what vitality remained.

A long 'unnerving telegram' came from London on July 31. It must have been the one about Taiyuan, the Glovers, Greens, Henan escape attempts and finally 'the worst' for the Bagnalls and William Cooper. Jenny had it in her hand and was going to break its contents gradually to Hudson, but 'he came across my path and so had to know of it'. 'Where will the end be?' he asked, alive to the horrific consequences of unchecked anti-foreign action. He reeled, and Jenny feared lest shock after shock should be too much for him. Writing the next morning to Marcus Wood she said, '(He) felt as if he must get out or he would go crazy, so Amy (their daughter) and he went up a mountain.' And to John Stevenson: 'We are suffering with you all so much that I don't think we could feel more.'

Hudson felt his reason would go if he did not tire his body out, so he was walking as much as possible. Jenny herself felt too drained of strength to go out with them. But had not 'the Lord said, "Fear not them that kill the body and after that have no more that they can do"'?

That anyone could have taken a photograph of him at such a time is puzzling, but gives us an insight into his sufferings (p 319). Someone wrote on one copy, 'Tho' he slay me, yet will I trust in him' (cf Job 13:15).[6] He felt he should be in China where the decisions had to be taken, but knew that in his state of health he would be more in the way than useful. So as the reports came in, long after the events, Jenny told him only what he could endure.

The ubiquitous Howard and Geraldine Taylor came over from London on August 6 to support his parents for two weeks, but found them coping with the crisis. Made aware that the strain on John Stevenson could prove too much, and that his own condition was precarious, Hudson Taylor had come to the conclusion that no time must be lost. A successor must be worked in without delay. A letter to Shanghai could take too long. Anything might happen, any day. The niceties of procedure mattered less. He cabled to Stevenson that morning, 'expressing sympathy and concern for him' and appointing Dixon Hoste 'to act as General Director . . . during my incapacity' . . . 'so that the responsibility may be shared'.

He then wrote lucidly to Theodore Howard as director in London, saying in confidence what he had done. Announcement of the move could follow when it had been accepted by all councils. 'Cooper is probably gone and Stevenson alone with all this burden of responsibility. It seems to take all my strength away and to defer indefinitely my being able to go out and help.' Cameron, Dorward, Hunter, Lachlan – so many outstanding men of whom he had had high hopes had died. But Hoste was in Shanghai, and difficult though it was to bypass the faithful veteran of pre-*Lammermuir*

DIXON EDWARD HOSTE, SUCCESSOR TO HUDSON
TAYLOR

days (HTCOC Book 4, p 81), John Stevenson, the nettle had to be grasped.

Stevenson was invaluable as senior administrator, the managing director in China, but lacked essential qualities required of a general director, the international leader and inspiration of the Mission. Sooner or later he would have to face the fact and accept a younger man in office over him. Hoste's personality and ability had impressed him. Now the time had come for Hoste to be more than merely his assistant. As William Cooper had already found, Stevenson was not good at working in partnership as equals. He had to be told candidly of Hoste's promotion, and be trusted to weather the blow. Acting for Hudson Taylor would work Hoste gradually into the saddle and ease the transition for John Stevenson. If Cooper should return from the dead, as it would seem if somehow he survived, the way would still be open for reconsideration of who should become General Director. (Final confirmation of his death did not come until October 29.) So 'after much thought and prayer' the cable had been sent. Hudson Taylor concluded to Theodore Howard, 'What a blessing to know that God is king above the water floods and that nothing can be done without His permission,' and ended 'Yours in deep sorrow'.

The graphic events of those days failed to close his mind to other things. The CIM had come dramatically into the limelight again, and the public would be looking for information. 'People will read about China now especially and the Mission needs an increase of funds (perhaps £50,000 or £100,000) which will not be obtained without seed being sown.' America and the Colonies were asking for Geraldine's books, *In the Far East* and *The Story of the China Inland Mission* to be reprinted. The sanity of his balance between dependence on 'God alone' for all the Mission's immense and recurring needs, while recognising that people respond to knowledge of the facts, impressed his friends and colleagues. His shoulders were broad enough to bear any charge of 'money-raising'. It took more than reprinting books to 'raise' so many thousands of pounds over and above the forty thousand normally required.

But the tragic news continued to come in, and the stress of work, however slight, was making Hudson Taylor giddy and exhausted. Jenny 'after prayer concluded to act on Dr (J L) Maxwell's advice and keep all letters from (Hudson) except those I feel will help and not hinder his health' – for . . . 'his heart's action was impaired and power of walking almost left him.' 'We heard that *all* the Shansi missionaries were murdered. Thank God for all who are spared.' 'A German paper (stated) that nineteen missionaries had been murdered in Hankow' of all places, secure under Zhang Zhitong's eye. Both stories were false. In Shanghai the nightmare of those days and weeks seared and scarred John Stevenson as he read reports and lived through the imagined plight of those unaccounted for. He never lost the sense of horror.[7] Yet somehow Jenny remained optimistic. 'Some may be in hiding who have been reported murdered.'

Reluctant successor   *August 1900–March 1901*

Hudson Taylor's cable on August 6, 1900, struck both John Stevenson and Dixon Hoste between the eyes. Neither had any inkling of such a possibility. Hoste would not be forty until July 23, 1901. After the initial shock and two days of thinking and praying about it, he wrote declining the 'appointment by telegram'. His letters to Hudson Taylor and Stevenson, and their replies, kept the issue unresolved until the end of the year, during which time the China Council and Home Directors were consulted. The correspondence illuminates the personalities concerned.[8]

Hudson Taylor needed to appoint as his potential successor one whose wisdom, ability and acceptance by his colleagues were beyond doubt. Above all he had looked for the man who 'walked with God', one to whom God would make known his will. He had found these qualities in both William Cooper and Dixon Hoste. On August 8 Hoste wrote that in July Stevenson had spoken appreciatively to him and wished him to stay and help with his advice 'as he might ask for it . . . during the present difficult times'. Because of his respect for Stevenson he was glad to do so, acting as a go-between, he said, and doing all in his power to strengthen Stevenson's position. When all was eventually settled, Archibald Orr Ewing wrote candidly, 'I fear if some such step as this were not taken, soon the love and harmony in the Mission would have been seriously affected; numbers have spoken to me of the very unsatisfactory way in which their matters had been dealt with.' But Dixon Hoste had come to a different conclusion.

> Effects of an opposite and very grave character, which both Mr Stevenson and myself agree in thinking most likely (would) follow such an appointment . . . It would have the effect of weakening and, to a certain extent discrediting Mr Stevenson . . . without inspiring confidence. (Stevenson had done well in his direction of affairs in the crisis, members of the China Council were agreed.) . . . My appointment to act now on your behalf (during your present incapacity) would come as a complete surprise, and is one to which they would not agree, and . . . would be calculated to weaken and even produce disruption in the Mission . . . PS. I have not touched on the point of my own unfitness, mental and physical . . .

John Stevenson also wrote, '(Mr Hoste's) help at the Council meetings was most valuable and I thank God for his prayerful sympathy and advice. I consult him very freely.' But on September 20 Hudson Taylor replied to Stevenson confidently and forthrightly as usual,

> I have been most grateful to recognise how God has helped you in this unparalleled crisis, and have (wanted) to take some of the grave

responsibility off your shoulders and also off my own. I felt that I had a responsibility which I was unable, here and in my state of health, to bear, while my known previous judgment as to remaining quietly in the stations in times of difficulty might hamper you, hence my two telegrams. [The final authority should not be distant from the scene of action.]

You have correctly read my wire as to the wording, but it left your position the same as it has so long been; it was not my wish to put Mr Hoste into it. My own health is precarious, and the terrible news from China caused my strength to fail so fast that I felt it was urgent to appoint someone to take *my* place pro tem. I knew your esteem for Mr Hoste, and that if I were removed he would be accepted in London, America and Australia, and that no one else would be so accepted. I knew . . . that he would be the last one to take advantage of his position to weaken yours. Everyone has recognised the indefatigable, self-denying service that you have so long rendered the whole Mission . . . but not a few . . . have feared that it would break up unless some change were introduced by which the members . . . could be bound to it by a uniform expression of sympathy that you are unable to show. I thought my appointment of Mr Hoste would help in this way, and also that acting with you in Shanghai he would be gaining in the necessary experience for becoming General Director at my death. (To leave the appointment of a successor to be made by others would not be for the good of the Mission or Stevenson's own comfort.)

Another thought in my mind . . . was the fear that you might break down under the long, heavy strain, and that then no one would be empowered to act . . . . I made the appointment temporary, for I feel that all such important appointments should be so in the beginning, and in doing so I did not abdicate my own position.

I am remaining here (in Davos) feeling quite unfit to return to England.[9]

Frail and under strain Hudson Taylor might be, but still fully in command.

Crossing that letter came one from Dixon Hoste protesting his strong feeling not only of being unworthy and unequal to the demands of acting for Hudson Taylor but unfit. It troubled him to go against his wish and so 'to grieve or disappoint' him, but he was glad of the telegram, as

It may serve as an indication to Mr S of your mind, which it may be well for (him) to accustom his mind to assimilate. I think it came as a great surprise and even shock . . . to him. [Hoste expressed his deep sympathy for Hudson Taylor in the 'avalanche of suffering' being reported constantly to him.] A telegram (received) last night tells of the Home-going to Christ of eleven more dear ones from Xi Xian, Daning and Yoyang. I feel Shansi is honoured, and my heart beats for her more than ever, and the fears come too, as I think of so many friends of early manhood, gone in blood and tears.[10]

Henry Frost responded characteristically to Jenny on being told of Hudson Taylor's action.

The choice seems to me, as far as I can judge, an eminently suitable one . . . I say all this with deep sadness. My love is fixed presently on Mr Taylor, and it is hard to have any person come between himself and myself . . . Please let me urge once more, however, that Mr Taylor may not give up his office, and that no person may be asked, so long as he lives, to be more than an assistant to him . . .

As telegram after telegram reaches us reporting the deaths of our loved ones, and as letter after letter comes to hand describing the terrible suffering . . . it seems sometimes as if the heart could hold no more, and at all times the mystery of God's providence comes upon one in almost overwhelming force. But . . . 'perfect love worketh no ill' . . . I never dreamed that God would allow us to pass through such bitter sorrow. But it is all right. Our Father is teaching us new lessons regarding our privileges, for He has written: 'For unto you it is granted (as a privilege) in the behalf of Christ, not only to believe on Him but also to suffer for His sake.'

Then Dixon Hoste went down with typhoid, so often lethal, and a month later Gertie, his wife, told Hudson Taylor that although it had been a mild attack, 'the old trouble of clots in the veins has developed'. 'November 5; Both arms and legs are affected, so he is quite helpless,' 'I think so often of you, dearest Uncle, and plead your need of help when I ask God to spare my beloved Dick.' The risk of the thrombosis spreading and of emboli (clots) breaking loose kept them on a knife-edge of danger. Her prayers were answered in his complete recovery, but even more in his helpless dependence on night and day nursing being a parable to him and shaping his thinking about the future. On November 14 'Dick' dictated to her a long letter for Hudson Taylor.

I was in the Lord's hands . . . and I now feel that I should, when restored to health, take steps to carry into effect your wishes; and in the event of Mr Stevenson or others of importance demurring, leave the possibility . . . upon them . . . (I) hope the Lord may yet raise you up more speedily than anticipated, and render the necessity of my appointment void . . . I could conceive of no higher honour and privilege than being your helper, much more your representative or successor.

[November 23] . . . I need the strong love of Christ to constrain me to spend and be spent for others . . . The thrombosis in the forearms has disappeared and so far as Dr Judd can perceive, in the upper arm also. (In) my legs . . . the clots remain . . . My present purpose is, when I get up again, to tell dear Mr Stevenson that in the light of your letters I feel it my duty to accept the appointment. But that I equally feel *his* heartfelt acceptance and happy concurrence in it, is a necessity.

On December 15, for the sake of clarity, Hoste put his conclusions in writing for John Stevenson also. 'I feel I ought to accept the appointment; if, however, you do not see your way to agreeing . . . I shall feel free from responsibility.' But Stevenson told him 'of his decision to agree'.

It . . . cost him a great deal, and I have been not a little impressed with the eminently Christian spirit and largeness of mind which he has displayed . . . I . . . shall endeavour to act upon your words as to my appointment not being intended to supersede Mr Stevenson in his present position . . . Pending your promulgation the matter is being kept quiet.

[December 26] Dear Mr Stevenson called me into his office a few days ago and, with tears in his eyes, told me that the Lord had given him not only peace about it but joy in the assurance that it was of God and would be for blessing. I think Cassels was specially a help to him . . .

Then on March 22, 1901, John Stevenson released an open letter from Hudson Taylor to the whole Mission in China, presenting in full Hudson Taylor's decision made known on January 24,

to appoint Mr D E Hoste to act as General Director during my present incapacity through ill-health; of course this appointment does not in any way supersede Mr Stevenson in his position or work, but will supply him with the help which I would gladly afford him myself did health permit . . . Matters that might otherwise need to be referred to me can be dealt with without delay in China, by Mr Hoste, and I shall not have the mental strain of feeling that I am not adequately attending to my part of the work. A few months' freedom from responsibility may be God's means of restoring me to . . . permit of my once more visiting you.[11]

The China Council, with Henry Frost and Walter B Sloan also present, 'unanimously and most cordially concurred' in the appointment. Frost and Sloan had come specifically to spend a few months among the hundreds of refugee missionaries filling the Wusong Road premises and several additional rented houses in Shanghai. The potential danger of crowded conditions and emotional reaction against severe hardships and personal losses being exploited by the old enemy Satan, needed to be faced decisively. These two men were singularly gifted as counsellors and public speakers, Sloan in expository preaching on 'victorious Christian living', and Frost, by choice on this occasion, in systematic teaching of Biblical theology.[12] Their presence proved timely for Hoste and Stevenson also. Hoste wrote of feeling bereft when they had to return home.

A discreet note from Orr Ewing to Hudson Taylor said, 'There is no one in our midst so well fitted to take the position' – 'a great many who were hoping that Mr W Cooper would take a more prominent part in the work, were terribly disappointed when the Lord saw fit to take him home.' And on April 4, 'this decision has cost Mr Stevenson days of prayer . . . I am deeply thankful (for) the manifest grace of God seen in (him). He has throughout shown himself to great advantage; he could scarcely have been in a more trying position . . .' Even then, at the public meeting in Shanghai to announce Dixon Hoste's appointment, it was emphasised that it was 'a temporary measure' to hasten the recovery of Hudson Taylor.[13]

The trauma of this harrowing predicament had fallen on each man during and because of 'the avalanche of suffering' through which so many of the rank and file were passing. The end of the killings was the start of an almost equally heartbreaking phase of recovery.

How many died? 1900–01

The *Chinese Recorder*, a mirror of events and opinion, vaguely reflected the uncertainties of early 1900. Among the social and academic contents to be expected came an article on the Society for the Diffusion of Christian and General Knowledge; a comparison of methods leading to the goal of Christianity in China; the difficulties of Protestant Chinese Christians opposed by 'non-Christian and Roman Catholic power', moral and political; and then the first rumblings of the Boxer storm. The bones of the reformer Kang Yuwei's ancestors were reported exhumed and destroyed on Ci Xi's orders; S M Brooks' severed head was 'offered to the wayside god' by his murderers; the Beijing *coup d'état* and proclamation of Pu Jün (Pu Chün), son of the vicious Prince Tuan, as heir to the late emperor Tong Zhi, left the imprisoned Guang Xü out of account; a price of one hundred thousand taels was placed on the heads of the reformers Kang Yuwei and Liang Jichao (Liang Chi-ch'ao) dead or alive; the walls of Beijing were placarded with denunciations of the Boxers – while the two-faced court was encouraging them and the Manchu nobility joined the 'Boxer Association'.

Then at last came an editorial on the Boxers, on the murder of Norman and Robinson (p 322), on Prince Tuan adopting 'all the pomp and authority of an emperor' and, suddenly, that the consuls in Shanghai had assumed the role of acting-ministers of their respective countries. The legations had been cut off from the outer world. The main organ of Protestant missions in China was groping for the facts.

A list was given of missionaries under siege and of others 'safe' because absent for one reason or another from their homes in Beijing, Baoding and elsewhere. The friendly ex-*daotai* of Shanghai, promoted to be the governor of Sichuan, was doing all he could to protect foreigners in his province. The consuls had great confidence in him, but the people were unpredictable and the viceroy, Gui Zhun, a Manchu reactionary, was persuaded with difficulty by the provincial treasurer, Zhou Fu, to suppress the imperial edicts. According to Professor W E Soothill, the viceroy thrust the edicts 'into the privacy of his high boot', denying their existence to his anti-foreign officials.[14] And then in the September issue, still haphazard, Psalm 2 appeared in full, 'The Imperial Decree': 'Why do the heathen rage . . . ?' followed by a spate of horror stories from the Canadians of Henan; of the relief of the legations; from A R Saunders; George Parker on how he was shown the edict to kill and then given a running start to safety only just ahead of his pursuers.

Between the news of more than thirty allied men of war at Shanghai to defend the foreign settlements and an account of the Peking siege, came an article by Dixon Hoste on the future of Chinese Church-Missionary relations, with 'Possible Changes and

Developments in the Native Churches arising out of the Present Crisis'.[15] His long-sustained reputation as a thinker and statesman had begun; the point of his essay: that the upheavals and sufferings of the Church had thrown up God-given leaders who should be respected and not hampered by the returning missionaries. To go back expecting to take control again would be perverse. Foreign missionaries should return prepared to work with and under the Chinese church. Ten years with the powerful man of God, Hsi Shengmo, had proved to Hoste how it could be done as equals, neither subservient to the other, yet control belonging to the Chinese.

Teams of investigators would soon be going out, looking for survivors, distributing relief, and re-establishing shattered congregations. The opportunity for doing it on right principles could so easily be lost. Readers would not miss the significance of a related article from Korea, clearly demonstrating that J L Nevius' influence had launched the Korean Church on its successful course of self-government, self-support and self-propagation.[16]

On September 7, 1900, four hundred missionaries of twenty societies, many of them refugees, meeting in Shanghai, appealed to their 'Home Governments' to make a lasting settlement for the good of the Chinese people, restoring the Guang Xü emperor to the throne, punishing the guilty and safeguarding the Church, without alienating officials or citizens by demands too heavy to be borne without resentment. The debate on reparation and indemnities had begun.[17]

China's Millions for the first few months of 1900 had little to say about the Boxer menace beyond noting a 'critical state of affairs'. Too little was known for certain. General news was in the papers. Long, long lists of missionaries and their locations carried the occasional note 'Absent' – on home leave while their colleagues were dying or 'being reviled – persecuted – defamed – made as the filth of the world – the offscouring of all things' (1 Cor. 4:12–13 AV). The Christian perspective was maintained by reminders that 'unto you it is given in the behalf of Christ, not only to believe in him, but *also to suffer*' (Phil. 1:29), 'that Christ shall be magnified in (my body), whether it be by life, or by death' (Phil. 1:20 AV). And prayer was asked for those fleeing the country, with no hint of the horrors that cliché implied, until at last in October and November it became possible to publish authentic martyr and refugee news.

An editorial, urgent and deeply understanding, insisted, 'that there must be no cry for vengeance. Let us not forget the provocation that China has had.' It lamented 'the incessant and almost incredibly ignorant talk about partitioning China'; and the opium trade. 'We have sown the wind; can we wonder if we reap the whirlwind?' The western nations were not less to blame than the Manchus and their Chinese subjects.

News from Shanxi came piecemeal: the Xiaoyi ladies dead, but many, (named) whose whereabouts or fate remained unknown even so late in the year. All twenty-eight Henan missionaries were reported alive and safe after varying experiences. A policy of understatement seemed preferred. The secular press supplied more than enough exaggeration and fiction. Then the 'Latest Telegrams'. September 17: the Greens and Jessie Gregg safely in the care of the provincial judge – one of the last episodes, but here among the first to be publicised; September 20: the Youngs and McConnells killed; September 21: the Swedish Mission in China, none missing, arrived safely, all well – among the first to reach safety, but only now confirmed. So it continued, with hundreds, thousands of relatives waiting to know the worst or at least to end the suspense. The circumstances were without precedent.[18]

Calculations followed one on the heels of another, some right and some mistaken. At first a tentative report that 'no fewer than eighteen were massacred' filled all with alarm. Soon more telegrams dwarfed such figures. The November *Millions* reported the CIM death-toll to have reached fifteen adults and fourteen children, but 'Hewett safe' – the doctor hidden incommunicado in an inner gaol for his own safety. With the restoration of calm and civil order, although the guilty imperial court was still at Xi'an, 'final figures' began to appear in print. John Stevenson's 'official list of killed and missing to 29th September' (submitted to the British Consul-General on September 15 and amended to date for publication as a supplement to the *Shanghai Mercury*), gave a total of fifty-five adults and twenty-two children dead in Shanxi alone, and thirteen adults and four children in Zhili. The grand total for Shandong, Shanxi, Zhili and Zhejiang had reached seventy-seven adults and twenty-nine children.

But no less sombre was his tally of quite as many 'missing and unaccounted for'. In Shanxi forty-three adults and eight children of all missions, added to those in Zhili and Scandinavians on the Mongolian border, brought the total of missing persons to eighty adults and twenty-seven children. The scale of horror had become unspeakable, as descriptions by Glover, Saunders, Argento, Bird and others followed one after another. Eventually the list of missionary martyrs numbered *135 adults and 53 children, 188 in all, of whom 159 were in Shanxi* (see Appendix 7).

Most poignant, perhaps, of all the appalling results of the Boxer rising was the plight of the orphans, away at school in Chefoo or the homelands, and the smaller societies wiped out of existence or left with one or two missionaries absent on furlough. Ten members of the Swedish Holiness Union were killed, leaving one man. The Scandinavian Alliance Mongolian Mission were annihilated with one exception. The Swedish Mongolian Mission died to a man. The Baptist Missionary Society in Shanxi suffered the same fate so that two retired missionaries returned to replace them. Of what had been the Shouyang Mission all died with the exception of Dr and Mrs E H Edwards, in Britain at the time. And the Christian and Missionary Alliance of its total force of thirty-eight in China lost twenty-one and fourteen children, its whole strength in the north. By contrast, with deaths from 'natural causes' the CIM lost sixty-three members in 1900, ending the year with 745 alive if not all well.

A rash of speculation   1900–01

When the siege in Beijing ended, the onslaught in Shanxi became more ferocious than ever. But when Li Hongzhang's command to stop killing reached throughout the province and sympathetic officials replaced the vicious and weak ones, the general reaction among survivors at the coast was less of relief than a long, deep sigh, from a sense of having barely escaped. On all sides people were saying, What if the wind of change had veered so very little against the foreign community in China? The intended holocaust in every province and every city, in Shanghai and Canton as much as in Hankou and Chongqing, would have cost thousands of lives. Every one of those half-naked fugitives would have died. What if the courage of the southern and central China viceroys and governors had failed; if they had literally safeguarded their own necks, obeying the inhuman Empress Dowager instead of anticipating the world's outcry and retaliation? What if Yong Lu had not played his secret game of keeping the modern artillery in its crates and restraining Tong Fuxiang's attacks on the legations? What if they had fallen, as could have happened at many points of time? Thousands of defenders and defended would have died at a stroke.

What if the Boxers had not struck at the hottest time of year, when many were away on holiday at the coast, but after they returned? Or conversely, what if the consuls and envoys had judged differently and ordered an early evacuation of the interior, instead of being caught out by incredulous speculation on the ill-omened inter-calary month? Such conjecture deepened gratitude to God.

The spirit of reform among the literati of China was already so advanced and widespread that even if Ci Xi and her reactionaries had had it their own way, they would only have won a delay in the inevitable reformations. Most were elderly and their cause would die with them. Had the missionaries been ordered out by their consuls or directors, the Christians would have had to face the same attack alone. The example set by missionaries old and, mostly, young – and of their children to no small degree – would have been denied to the Church. Then why did some try to escape? Because the time came when their presence could do no further good, and their Christian friends exhorted them to hide or flee. In this a precedent was set, to be followed when the nation turned its fury on the Manchus in 1911, and civil war found its scapegoats and suspects in the late 1920s and 1940s.

The Boxer rising had been an imperial fiasco. The intended holocaust had in its very concept been a display of Manchu weakness. Ci Xi's failures sprang from the wisdom and sanity of the provincial rulers, their loyalty to the throne, nation and people exceeding loyalty to the fallible 'Old Buddha' (the sobriquet for Ci Xi). Superstition accounted for much of the origins and nature of the rising. Some Christians were chopped into small pieces and scattered on running water – to ensure their failure to rise again, as they claimed they would.[19] But the seed sown in agony was to reap a harvest beyond expectation. Hudson Taylor's preface in October 1901 to *Last Letters and Further Records of Martyred Missionaries of the CIM* drew the parallel of Christ's deliverance from death being through death. 'He asked life of thee, and thou gavest it him, even length of days for ever and ever' (Ps. 21:4 AV). The martyrs' prayers were answered in God's own way. 'As for God, his way is perfect.' As one wrote, 'If my Lord offered me my choice . . . I would prefer what He chose for me.'

At home again in England, A R Saunders addressed the crowded 'Meeting in Memory of the Martyred Missionaries' on February 12, 1901, at which several survivors of the rising spoke. Using St Paul's declaration as his own, he said:

'We would not . . . leave you ignorant of our trouble which came to us in Asia, that we were pressed out of measure above strength, insomuch that we despaired even of life. But we had the sentence of death in ourselves, that we should not trust in ourselves but in God which raiseth the dead, who delivered us from so great a death, and doth deliver.'

Such words as these were a comfort to us many a time on that long journey from Shansi to Hankow . . . We could not tell why GOD should permit such suffering. We could not see how GOD could in any way get glory to His name by such humiliation of His servants. But we rest in the blessed assurance that it was GOD's way. He makes no mistake . . . We think of those dear friends who are now in the presence of our LORD JESUS CHRIST . . . Perhaps thousands have seen their triumphant *death, which yet is not death* to the child of God . . . [And he continued:]

Under GOD we owe it to those viceroys and to those consuls that so many . . . escaped . . . If (the Yangzi River) had been closed, and if the country on both sides of it had been thrown into a state of anarchy, as the northern part of China was . . . the martyrs today would have been far more than a thousand . . .[20]

The miscarriage of Ci Xi's plans was among the factors considered miraculous by observers of the whole grisly affair. No less remarkable and 'attributable to an exceptional intervention by God' was the consistent exhibition of his grace in the courage of the martyrs, Chinese and foreign. That they could experience peace of heart and mind, show consideration for others at the extremity of their own ordeals, and calmly preach the gospel until the moment of death had an immeasurable influence on the Church and on pagan observers.

The nation swung within months from indifference or opposition to curiosity and outright admiration. Sir Robert Hart allowed the elation of deliverance to prompt his prophecy of China becoming a Christian nation within fifty years. Inevitable reforms went hand in hand with openness to foreigners and receptiveness to their recommendations, technological and religious. A new China was being born. But before the dying and the crying had ended, the foreign nations were planning punishment, reparations, indemnities and territorial domination – and the reinstatement of Ci Xi, instead of the Guang Xü emperor as the missions urged.

Reprisals or statesmanship?   *1900–01*

After all that had happened, settlement of the tensions between China and 'the powers' claimed priority. New envoys took the place of those who had been through the Peking siege, and the representatives of China who had tried to fill the gap left by the flight of the court, Li Hongzhang and Prince Qing, attempted to open negotiations in August and September, 1900. Li, the 'grand old man' of China, who had carried the main burden of statesmanship ever since the Taiping rebellion, confided his grief to his diary:

> Oh, if my hand were not so weak and my cause so much weaker! The Court is in hiding and the people are distracted. There is no government and chaos reigns. I fear the task before me is too great for my strength of body, though I would do one more thing before I call the earthly battle over. I would have the foreigners believe in us once more; and not deprive China of her national life; and I would like to bring 'Old Buddha' back to the palace, and ask her if she had learned her lesson.

At first they failed. The allies were reluctant to recognise their credentials. And the Germans insisted on the surrender for punishment of those 'whose guilt in instigating or committing the crimes there is no room for doubt'. These could be named, but most had fled. And proof could not be established within months. To nail responsibility where it belonged, on Ci Xi herself, could prove impossible. Not that the envoys would attempt it. Like Nelson, they chose to turn the blind eye of diplomacy in her favour and to dictate her tacit exoneration and reinstatement, while using her to punish the instruments of her own infamy.[21]

The American government held that no punitive measures could be as effective as 'punishment of the responsible authors by the supreme imperial authority itself'.[22] But negotiations dependent on prior punishment by sovereign or government might be deferred interminably. Negotiation would therefore have to go ahead and include punishments in its terms. Surprisingly, an imperial decree of September 25 removed this difficulty by ordering the trial and sentencing of some leading Manchus. But were they the right ones and were their sentences severe enough? Co-ordination of action by the erstwhile allies became confused as the Germans took punitive strikes into their own hands; Russia proceeded to absorb Manchuria and grab control at Tianjin; and Britain for diplomatic reasons

affecting German military supplies to the Boers concluded an
Anglo-German agreement on October 16.

After some indecision the foreign powers matched the imperial
court's manoeuvring to minimise its concessions to their demands.
On October 15 Li Hongzhang approached the powers with an
admission of China's culpability for attacking the legations contrary
to international law, and her liability to indemnify the injured
parties, and proposed that hostilities should cease. Guilt and liability were the premiss of negotiation, so this attempt 'fell still-born'.[23]
On December 24 the envoys telegraphed a joint note to Xi'an,
embodying 'irrevocable decisions', which Ci Xi accepted by wire
two days later, followed by an acceptance in writing for each power,
sealed with the imperial seal. Penalties acceptable to them were
ordered by imperial decrees in February 1901, and for the next eight
months the envoys sought agreement among themselves on the final
Peace Protocol signed on September 7, 1901. Meanwhile, the
Germans were prevented with difficulty from pressing their military
advantage to 'operations on a large scale', understood to have Xi'an
as their objective.

An imperial prince of the first rank, young Prince Qün (Ch'ün),
had already gone to Germany to express China's regrets for the
murder of Baron von Ketteler, and another went to Japan for that of
Chancellor Sugiyama. Punishment of the provincial literati taxed
the envoys' ingenuity, for they were less readily identified than the
mandarins had been for execution, exile, imprisonment or cashier-
ing. To satisfy the foreigners an imperial edict on August 19 decreed
what Ci Xi in her cunning way may well have recognised as
counter-productive, 'the suspension of official examinations for five
years in all cities where foreigners were massacred or submitted to
cruel treatment', six in Manchuria, twelve in Zhili, twenty-two in
Shanxi, two in Henan and one in each of Zhejiang, Hunan and
Shaanxi. Suspension of official examinations meant closure of the
door to the most sought-after careers for thousands of innocent and
often progressive scholars. For those five years the most intelligent
and educated young men were penalised for the guilt of a minority
of others. Their deep resentment was understandable. Missionaries
returning up-country frequently encountered it, and while sympathising could do nothing to help them.

But the imposition of indemnities outstripped in folly the dis-
crimination against the literati. At first the American envoy wisely
urged a demand for 'a lump sum within China's ability to pay',

perhaps three hundred million taels (£140–50 million).[24] The claims of each power could then be scaled down to realistic figures. The fire-breathing envoys led by Germany saw no need to be considerate of China, and 'the urgent need of Britain to maintain her entente with Germany' forced her hand. China's annual budget showed 'reported receipts' as approximately one hundred million taels which could be increased to 118 million by recovering from the tax collectors and their mandarin patrons the sums they habitually diverted.

Although an aggregate of claims by the powers amounted to 450 million taels, an imperial decree on May 29, 1901, accepted this demand. Again, did Ci Xi see the foreigner bearing the brunt of criticism for such coercion? Payment would be slow. With interest at 4 per cent the total sum payable by 1940 would exceed 982 million taels – with a legacy of resentment calculated to pay bitter dividends long before that.[25]

With two exceptions the atrocities had been limited to the north-eastern provinces, but additional taxation would weigh heavily on every province. The innocent, including many who had protected the victims, would suffer resentfully for the guilty, and blame the foreigner. Statesmanship had been forgotten in the lust for retribution. Britain and Japan submitted only moderate claims. But the United States provided the notable exception, declining any more than $25 million, and in 1908 remitting part of this indemnity in favour of education in China. Neither did these indemnities take into account the huge quantities of bullion seized at Beijing and Tianjin.

Other articles in the protocol provided the right to maintain legation guards in the capital of the empire, and greatly expanded legation territories. The coastal forts were to be demolished and the route from the coast to Beijing kept open. 'China had reached a stage of national degradation so low that she retained few of the attributes of a sovereign and independent state.'[26]

When Li Hongzhang signed the Peace Protocol on September 7 his days were already numbered. He died on November 7 in his seventy-ninth year. Strong, able, unscrupulous and immensely wealthy from acquisitions during forty years of high office, his wisdom and service to the empire deserved 'the highest posthumous honours ever accorded to a Chinese subject of the Manchus'.

The greater of the two Yangzi viceroys, Liu Kunyi of Nanjing, died on October 6, 1902, and the legendary Manchu bannerman,

Yong Lu, on April 11, 1903. 'The service of the state was left to be carried on by lesser men.' Zhang Zhitong returned to the viceroyalty of Nanjing, and Yuan Shikai replaced Li Hongzhang as viceroy at Tianjin. With the signing of the Peace Protocol and the withdrawal of foreign troops, apart from legation guards, Ci Xi felt able to return to the palace in Beijing. 'An early return was imperative if the dynasty was to be preserved.'[27] The court left Xi'an on October 6, 1901, but halted at Kaifeng until December 14. So Li Hongzhang failed to see the 'Old Buddha' again. She was at Kaifeng when he died.

Statesmanship had conspicuously failed. The supreme opportunity to distinguish between the true villains and the true China, and the true justice for each, had been lost. 'Behind the destruction which followed in (the Boxers') train there was a small Manchu clique, and not the Chinese nation.' The *Chinese Recorder* drew the hypothetical comparison of Finland dominating Russia for three hundred years.[28] But the Western powers in their own interests chose to label the dowager empress the victim of the clique and of the Boxers. For the sake of even temporary stability and the advantages it would bring them, they left the emperor and China's reform at her mercy. The evil genius returned to the palace with the emperor still under her heel. And the impositions of 1901 played their own part in subsequent anti-foreign nationalistic movements, including the banishment of all but a few foreigners at the close of the 'open century'.

The missions debate indemnities   *1900–01*

Not only the world powers saw China's instability as their opportunity for expansion and profit. Church and missions foresaw a change of attitude towards them and their teaching. Both had suffered severe losses and faced determined efforts by the secular powers to obtain substantial reparations for them. But these were being made at the same time as they claimed for the destruction of legations and the cost of naval and military operations. In spite of a new rift between France and the Vatican, the French worked strongly to reinstate the Catholic Church. The Tianjin Notre-Dame des Victoires, rebuilt after the massacre of 1870 (HTCOC Book 5, pp 241–3, 271), again lay in ruins, as did the four cathedrals at Beijing and many provincial churches.

Imperious behaviour in making local settlements reinforced the resentment against foreigners in general. A different attitude could have served to distinguish Christian from secular standards, Church from State, with lasting benefit. But, as the *North China Herald* reported of reparations at Taiyuan,

> The Roman Catholic . . . claims are not so easy to settle. As their cathedral was destroyed, they demanded that one of the public buildings should be given them – either the Governor's *yamen* (at the outer gate of which the massacre took place) or a large college (called the Provincial College). The Governor said he was unable to give away public property, and eventually they (declared that) they would go and occupy the college, and if they were opposed and there was trouble, they would hold the local officials responsible [in accordance with the peace protocol] . . . The authorities induced the resident staff and students to leave (and the Catholics moved in).[29]

By March they promised to withdraw within two months, reduced their claims to 2¼ million taels and gave up their demand for two named market towns to be surrendered to them. It had become imperative that Protestant and Catholic Christianity should be recognised as distinct from each other. Again and again missionaries on the run had saved their lives and those of their companions by convincing their tormentors that they were neither engineers nor Roman Catholic priests. 'Could the engineers speak Chinese? But you understand what I am saying in your own dialect. Did they have short or long hair? You well know that I could not grow a queue as long as this in under a year. Do the priests have wives and children as you see we have?' Their defence was convincing. The anti-foreign anger of the people had been as much as anything against the assumption of official rank and intervention in judicial processes. In the matter of indemnities the Protestant church adhered to Biblical principles, distinct from current secular and Roman attitudes.[30]

The efforts of the new envoys to press claims on behalf of the hard-hit missions met with a varying response from the different Protestant societies. Not all approved of being part of the pretext for teaching the Chinese government a lesson. Some tried to disassociate themselves from aspects of the foreign governments' action, and from being linked with the Roman Catholics under the general term 'missionaries'. On September 7, 1900, the four hundred missionaries of twenty societies assembled in Shanghai appealed to their home governments to recognise Ci Xi's responsibility for the Boxer rising, which she had 'instigated, ordered and encouraged', and to work for China's benefit in the eventual settlement of differences. 'No settlement can be satisfactory or permanent which does not aim to secure the real good of the Chinese people and the rightful interests of all foreigners resident in China . . .' Therefore any settlement should aim at the restoration of the Guang Xü emperor to the throne, protection of missionaries in their legitimate work and residence, protection of law-abiding Christians from persecution, just punishment of the murderers, and adequate proclamation throughout China of the historical facts.[31]

Compensation for losses of life or property did not come under debate until November, in a series of articles in the *Chinese Recorder*. Bishop George Moule recognised the basic right to require of the Chinese government full compensation for both loss of life and of property, but held that it would be good policy not to press such claims. 'Blood money' could not be accepted for the life of a Christian martyr. The LMS found in later years that reparations did more harm than good, and renounced all claims after a fresh outbreak of troubles.[32]

Each mission came to its own conclusions. The American Board submitted no claim for damaged mission property, but actively requisitioned land and fined guilty Chinese on behalf of the Christians of Tong Xian. In twenty-three villages 166 Christians had been killed and 184 homes been destroyed. The fines were used to relieve distress; ninety-six acres of land and small plots for cemeteries were confiscated; and the guilty were made to rebuild nineteen chapels.[33]

In spite of all the sufferings of foreign missionaries, far more Chinese Christians had suffered and to a far greater degree. In this, too, each mission followed its own judgment in presenting its claims, in every case through their foreign governments. But the American societies made a united presentation of their claims to the Department of State. The governments 'included in their demands indemnities for societies, individuals and Chinese who had suffered "in person or in property in consequence of their being in the service of foreigners."'[34] 'In consequence the indemnity paid to Chinese Christians (did injury) by sowing the seeds of a mercenary spirit.'[35]

'A military presence' at the funeral at Baoding compounded the confusion in Chinese minds. French and German military bands playing hymns after punitive action against the city had no justifiable place in the settlement of such rifts between two races. But at the reburial of Chinese Christians at Tong Xian, the voluntary presence of a Chinese army commander and 1,500 troops clearly

THE BAODING MARTYRS' MEMORIAL PROCESSION
a photograph by Dr E H Edwards

expressed regret and apology.[36] While some took advantage of the presence of foreign troops (as at Tong Xian) to obtain just compensation for Christians and missionaries alike, others took trouble to prove their independence from foreign secular influence, and worked as far as possible through the Chinese authorities.

J W Lowrie, an American Presbyterian of Baoding, and Dr E H Edwards, sole survivor of the Shouyang missionaries, had searched without success for remains of the Presbyterians who had died in their burning premises to the north of the city. But in the south suburb where they looked for graves of the American Board and CIM martyrs, they found on February 22 what was left in shallow pits outside the city wall. 'These remains had been much disturbed and were seemingly indistinguishable' when the first punitive expeditions had uncovered them, Dr Edwards wrote. 'We found only the skeleton of one headless body, recognised by some garments . . . as that of Miss Gould . . . In the same pit were seven heads, six foreign and one Chinese . . . all recognised by some distinguishing mark . . . Most of the coffins will contain only a skull.'[37]

Memorial services on March 23 and 24 were attended by Chinese officials and representatives of each society, including H M Brown of Shunde for the CIM. The coffins of eight foreigners and 'nearly twenty' Chinese Christians, representing forty-two martyred for their faith, stood in a pavilion beside a cross surmounted by a crown and the inscription '*Le bei ku jia*' ('They carried the cross of suffering with joy.') After the service in Chinese the coffins were all borne in procession through the streets to the site chosen for a cemetery, and buried in one long line of graves.[38]

In Shanxi an unusual development paved the way for exceptionally satisfactory solutions to be found. The enlightened governor, Ceng Chunxüan (Ts'eng Ch'un-hsüan),[39] who replaced the 'butcher' Yü Xian, in his admiration of Timothy Richard consulted Li Hongzhang and with his approval invited Richard to Shanxi. In April 1901 Li Hongzhang and Prince Qing asked the British minister to enlist Richard's help in settling all the complex cases facing the governor in Taiyuan, and Richard hurried north from Shanghai. At Tianjin, Li conferred with him for an hour and a half. They were no strangers to each other. Often during Timothy Richard's periods in Tianjin and Beijing and at other times, they had had occasion to meet. Viceroy Zhang Zhitong very possibly had spoken favourably of Richard's work and advice in Taiyuan. An old friend named Zhou Fu, *daotai* of Zhili, future governor of Shandong and viceroy at Nanjing and Canton, also joined in the interview.

Richard was ideally placed to influence the leading officials in north China after the Boxer rising. In May he telegraphed on behalf of Governor Ceng to invite representatives of the main Protestant societies to join them in settling the most numerous and widespread incidents of the Boxer holocaust. And the governor set aside two hundred thousand taels to be divided between Catholics and Protestants. A party of eight representatives was quickly formed. On June 26 they set out from Baoding (three months after the funeral) under an escort sent by the governor to bring them safely to Taiyuan.[40]

By choice nothing for the CIM   1900–01

Every one of the Mission's eight hundred members was personally affected by the upheavals of 1900. Least disturbed were the Nicholls of Dali in far western Yunnan. (Pioneers among the minority peoples of the province, they are to be distinguished from the George Nicolls of Sichuan.) They scarcely heard of the Boxer rising until it was all over and carried on their work throughout the crisis. A drastic drop in British donations to the CIM appeared to have a scarcely credible explanation. The Boer War and Peking siege held the headlines; and had not missionary work all but ceased? But a single large gift of £5,000 and more from other sources compensated for the shortage, so that members received almost as much as usual.[41]

Most were uprooted from their homes and possessions and spent a year first on difficult journeys and then in crowded refugee conditions. Hundreds came and went from Shanghai, but most stayed. Many were distressed and needing comfort and special care. But morale was high, and with time on their hands they spent it in consultation together and in preparation for their return to work. The Mission's leaders had to listen and advise on an endless stream of personal problems. Provincial superintendents, refugees themselves, absorbed most of this, but much came to John Stevenson and Dixon Hoste, crushed by the awfulness of the Boxer tragedy and their responsibilities. The year 1900 was the hardest in the Mission's history. Disorganised, it had to face an uncertain future. After providing for the flood of fugitives arriving at the river ports and Shanghai, the directors began planning reorganisation and return to the interior. Their task increased as missionaries who had been on leave in their homelands began to come back to China, bringing new members who had offered to take the martyrs' places. In the words of Johann Ludwig Krapf on the death of his wife in East Africa in 1844, 'The victories of the Church are gained by stepping over the graves of her members.'[42]

Dixon Hoste's appointment by Hudson Taylor 'to act as General Director' had come at the peak of the crisis. The announcement to the CIM on March 22, 1901, and to the public on the 26th, came only a few weeks before the governor of Shanxi's surprise call for help in resolving the reparation problems of his province. No one was better fitted to go than Hoste himself. Ten years as a colleague of Hsi Shengmo had won for him the confidence of the Shanxi Church. Scores, hundreds of the persecuted and martyred Christians were personally known to him. Archibald Orr Ewing, 'Mr Glory-face', (HTCOC Book 6, p 412) waiting for Jiangxi to reopen to his team in exile, was ideal as a companion, to stay on and implement decisions after Hoste had to return.

In November 1900, Stevenson had spoken of soon filling up the houses at the treaty ports, among them the language schools and Zhenjiang. And on January 30 Hoste told the Taylors that reoccupation of cities in the Yangzi valley was proceeding.[43] Shanxi, Shaanxi and Gansu would 'present considerable dangers and difficulties.' But by April he was able to give the whole mission lists of missionaries returning to Sichuan, Guizhou, Yunnan, Zhejiang, Anhui and Jiangxi. In Jiangsu all but one centre was already occupied, and soon the Guangxin River team would be on their way back. After little more than a year from the outbreak of the Boxer rising and five months since the last death, the work of the mission had been re-established in most of the empire. The most resistant places opened up soon afterwards. Shanxi remained one of the most sensitive provinces.

Some funds were available, but in each location throughout China great wisdom and tact were needed in dealing with officials, landlords of premises left vacant for so long, and local Christians who had handled all affairs of the churches in the missionaries' absence. Mission income from all sources in 1900 had been 2,780 taels lower than in the previous year, while travelling and rentals in China had cost 3,504 taels more. At the same time passages by sea had cost 22,833 taels, an increase of nearly ten thousand taels. Return to the interior and rebuilding wrecked premises would inflate expenses. So the talk of indemnities was highly relevant.

The elderly, indecisive governor of Zhejiang whose vacillations had cost the lives of the eight missionaries at Qü Xian (Ch'üchou), had been the first to raise the matter of reparations with the CIM. Sensing the approach of a tidal wave of similar circumstances, John Stevenson and the China Council referred the subject to Hudson Taylor for his opinion on the principles. And Dixon Hoste wrote (on a river steamer between Yichang and Hankou on January 30, 1901, personally investigating the security of those regions) saying he thought official recognition and reinstatement of each 'station' to be desirable; but he personally would be prepared to forgo it. In Chinese eyes the important matter of 'face' was involved. After degradation and expulsion the process ought to be publicly reversed. What did Hudson Taylor think? He replied, through Marcus Wood, secretary in London (and, it may be assumed, to each homeland), advising that the CIM should

> CLAIM FOR NOTHING, but to accept, where offered, compensation for destroyed Mission premises and property, as I feel we hold these on trust for God's work.
>
> For private property, we must leave each missionary free to accept or decline, *through the Mission only*.

> For injury or loss of life, to refuse all compensation.
> The Mission, likewise, should be responsible for the orphan children of Missionaries.
> For native Christians . . . I think we should do what God enables us to help them, and to care for bereaved relatives.

Compensation to Christians was regarded as a separate matter between the Chinese government and its own subjects. They were not 'in the service of foreigners' or under the 'protection' of the Mission, although everything possible would be done to help them.[44]

In a fuller letter to Shanghai, Hudson Taylor pointed out that to *claim* compensation for loss of life, injury or loss of property, whether private or belonging to the Mission, would contravene Article 15 of the Principles and Practice, which stipulated: no appeal and no demands. Accepting compensation offered by the Chinese would be left for each individual to decide in view of circumstances in their own locality, but in Hudson Taylor's opinion it would as a rule be wiser not even to accept compensation lest its acceptance have a harmful influence on the Christians. In February this was all conveyed to each member and associate of the CIM, and the first part to the consuls and Sir Ernest Satow, British Minister at Beijing.

Relatives of some members of the CIM had applied direct to the Foreign Office 'making long claims for compensation for lives (lost)'. So the London Council had in December conveyed to Lord Lansdowne the wish 'that this Mission should be entirely disassociated from all claims for life, or bodily injury, that may be put forward by (relatives or friends)' of members.

When unvarnished news of the atrocities committed by allied troops in and around Beijing reached Hudson Taylor he was appalled and protested to Theodore Howard about the atrocities being seen by China as perpetrated by 'Christian' nations. The contrast between nominal and true Christianity must be stressed, or hatred of foreigners and Christianity would be intensified.

> It (is) imperative that we should dissociate ourselves as missionaries as far as possible from government action. I have . . . advised Mr Stevenson to inform the consul-general that as a Mission we will not accept any money compensation. Thousands of Chinese as innocent as our missionaries seem to have been ruined and robbed of their all, and large numbers slain, through the action of the allies, for which

China will not be compensated . . . It therefore seems better to me now that we should trust in God to enable us to rehabilitate our stations when the time comes to reopen them. Though it will mean many thousands of pounds to restore all that was destroyed, He is able to provide.[45]

His change of mind, Hoste pointed out, was in part attributable to his rapid ageing.

Ten days later Jenny told Marcus Wood that Hudson was 'at his best just now', and in June they were in Britain meeting family, friends and survivors of the rising. There was nothing in his change of mind to apologise for. He had accepted advice, and his conclusion was lucid, deliberate and progressive, in the fighting spirit most characteristic of him. A money-conscious nation like the Chinese could be counted on to recognise such a clear-cut distinction between the motives of the secular powers and those of missionaries 'as witnesses to Christ and the Gospel'. It would show 'the meekness and gentleness of Christ'. And so it proved. At the end of February the CIM formally decided 'not only not to enter any claim against the Chinese Government, but to refrain from accepting compensation even if offered'. There was no need to publicise the fact, for the reasons could not very well be given without giving offence. Provincial superintendents passed the word on, acting on this policy, and D E Hoste applied it meticulously in Shanxi, with startling results.

Back to Taiyuan   *June–July 1901*

After the relief of the Peking legations and the return to Baoding, with their secular overtones, the official welcome back to Shanxi stands supreme. The spontaneous action of Governor Ceng Chunxüan in inviting Timothy Richard and other mission representatives to negotiate with him in person required no little courage. The scale of public ceremonies and the generosity of his proclamations and memorial tablets are as much a historical highlight as they made him a marked man. His liberal attitudes and wisdom are honoured in this triumphal story of the return and reinstatement of Christian missions and the Church. Heavy indemnities were expected and justified in law, and he was intent on fair settlements for each atrocious action of his predecessor, Yü Xian, but he was to meet with surprise after surprise.

It was right that D E Hoste, Acting General Director, and Archibald Orr Ewing, with their intimate knowledge of Shanxi, should lead the party of investigators, for major decisions lay ahead. Erik Folke's colleague in the Swedish Mission from south Shanxi, C H Tjäder, went with them to represent the associate missions. And Hudson Taylor's accountant son, Ernest, won commendation for his role as Hoste's assistant. Large sums of money were to be involved. They left Shanghai on June 1 with no more arranged than 'a respectful welcome' and safe conduct assured by the governor, and the request made to him for an official funeral for the martyrs as at Baoding. At Beijing, Hoste and Orr Ewing had an hour's consultation with the minister, Sir Ernest Satow, who showed 'an intelligent interest in missions', but remained unyielding about single women returning to 'the interior'. They were joined by Moir Duncan and Dr Creasey Smith of the BMS, by Dr E H Edwards, sole survivor of the Shouyang missionaries, and by Dr Atwood of the American Board, who were to enquire into the annihilation of their missions in the province; and by Major Pereira of the Grenadier Guards 'travelling for pleasure' but perhaps an official observer. A government 'deputy' was appointed to make all arrangements for them on their long journey.[46]

Starting by train on June 22, via Baoding where they hired mule litters, they received 'a very cool reception' at Huolu on the 29th by the same mandarin as had put the Greens into the Boxers' hands. But when the investigators responded by declining to pay their respects to him, and their sponsorship by high-ranking officials dawned on him, he sent local gentry to apologise. When their long cavalcade set out for Taiyuan, he came with a full deputation of officials and gentry to see them off. Heavy new fortification of the Guguan Pass showed that strong resistance would have been offered if the Germans had attempted to break through into Shanxi. Hoste's party, however, was received by an escort from the governor and at every resting-place a feast was ready at the official inn. Outside each city the magistrate met them ceremoniously, and when they left made his bow after accompanying them for a respectful distance along the way.[47]

At Shouyang on July 4, Pastor Qü, Elder Xü and Elder Si (Hsi Shengmo's brother-in-law, still suffering from the sword-thrust from which he was to die) met them to plan their movements in the province. Rain for three days preventing travel gave them more time to hear about the sufferings of the Church and missionaries.

PASTOR QÜ IN HIS M.A. ROBES

The magistrate of Shouyang, who had collaborated with the Boxers in sending Pigott and his family and friends to die at Taiyuan, the men in chains, had nominally been banished by imperial edict, but was there in the same capacity as before. Men who had so recently been commended by the Empress Dowager could not be deposed in a hurry – unless named in the Protocol.

Thirty miles from Taiyuan outriders enquired when the travellers would arrive at the city. Ten miles farther on, the trumpeters of Governor Ceng's own bodyguard 'blared out their welcome and unfurled their standards'. Ten miles from the city fresh cavalry joined the escort, and after two more miles mounted police saluted them. Three miles from Taiyuan they were transferred from their litters to official passenger carts and taken to the great South Gate where 'an immense crowd' was waiting. Among them stood many delighted Christians, their faces showing 'clear traces of their sufferings'.

A *daotai* of the Foreign Office (Shen Dunhe, who had spent a year at Cambridge) and high mandarins and civil dignitaries of Taiyuan received them with refreshments in a pavilion before they were conducted into the city. At the official quarters they were to occupy, the Provincial Treasurer, Provincial Judge, the Tartar General, City Prefect and other mandarins (HTCOC Book 4 App 5, p 415; 5 p 448) welcomed them 'with all politeness and cordiality', repeatedly expressing their regrets for the events of 1900. This was not the obsequious deference of guilty men, but a dignified admission by reasonable gentlemen that the Emperor's representatives must redress the excesses of that year. Without design, it happened to be July 9, the exact anniversary of the massacre by Yü Xian. And, providentially, a heavy rain fell shortly after their arrival, for this was regarded by the common people as a favourable omen. With timely rain they could sow their grain and reap before the hard winter.

The governor himself had sent formal documents to greet the deputation at Huolu, but on the day of their arrival was 'laid up with a rather serious illness'. He had talked with Elder Xü Puyüan a few days earlier, and before that had spontaneously offered and distributed forty thousand taels to Christian victims of the persecution who were in danger of starving.[48] On the 10th (through a representative) he gave 'a very elaborate dinner served in a large, beautifully carpeted hall'. Then, after two more days of courtesy calls and returning the compliments, formal discussion of compensation and rehabilitation of Christians and missions began. Meanwhile fifteen or twenty leading Christians were waiting for Hoste and his companions to be free from official obligations to work on Church affairs. After ten days Hoste wrote to Hudson Taylor,

> Shansi has been convulsed from end to end, first by the Boxer movement, and then latterly by the fear of foreign invasion. There was a general stampede (of guilty officials) from this city . . . Numbers of the more prominent Boxers have been put to death or committed suicide; many more are in hiding. [And a few days later:]
>
> It has been a time of great strain both in the quantity and the kind of work . . . Satan was let loose in Shansi last summer, and it is sober fact to say that for two or three months it was like hell on earth.
>
> The sufferings of the Christians have been frightful, and it is almost overwhelming to hear them at firsthand, and to be living in this place where so many were massacred. Never before have I felt so utterly unequal to the responsibilities on me . . . One great comfort is that some of the (Church) Elders have developed much since I last saw them, notably (Xü Puyüan). His powers as an administrator are remarkable, and all the others, including Pastor (Qü), seem gladly to recognise him as the moving spirit.
>
> Very capable, and stronger than Si, [Xü showed] a robustness and capacity for responsibility.

The pastors and other elders of the Church in the CIM districts of Shanxi had unanimously asked him to take the lead.[49]

'The most painful experience'   July–August 1901

The Foreign Office *daotai* had already chosen a good site for a walled cemetery, on a hillside overlooking the city and plain, and had had the missionary victims of the massacre buried there. No official funeral could be held, but official gestures were adequate. In the centre of the burial ground stood an attractive hexagonal tiled pavilion with flower gardens on each side; and each grave was marked with a cross on a stone pedestal.

On July 18 sedan chairs with four bearers for each came for the missions' representatives, and at the Prefect's *yamen* mandarins of the highest rank received them. With nineteen tall banners of red satin bearing the Chinese and foreign victims' names, surmounted by a canopy, and with many wreaths from the governor and leading officials and literati, all then went to the governor's *yamen*. On the site of the massacre outside the main gate a temporary pavilion had

ELDER XÜ PUYÜAN AND ATTENDANT
in Beijing to consult about destitute Shanxi Christians

been erected, and there Dr Edwards conducted a brief memorial service.

A procession then formed, to march through the crowd-lined streets and out through the East Gate to the cemetery. Men with gongs led the way. Behind them came the mandarins, followed by the wreaths, two hundred infantry and fifty cavalry, the foreign deputation in sedan chairs, Chinese Christians, the scarlet banners and more soldiers. At the cemetery a mandarin read out an address in classical *wenli* by Governor Ceng. The mandarins then returned to the city and Dixon Hoste conducted a Christian memorial service. Among the Chinese government's undertakings was the promise to erect a granite memorial tablet in honour of the Taiyuan martyrs. A few years later it fell to the lot of Amelia's youngest son to see it fulfilled at the rebuilt hospital.[50] In every city and town at which missionaries had been martyred this pattern of public apology and commemoration was followed during the next two months.

Most of the Christians had accepted the governor's offer of compensation for their losses, waiting for the deputation's advice on how to proceed. The governor and Foreign Office *daotai* therefore asked Hoste's help in organising the collection of particulars and distribution of indemnities. 'We drew up a list of trustworthy men in each district' – such was the confidence of the missionaries and Church leaders, Qü, Xü and Si, in their integrity. Each claim was to be investigated and confirmed locally and then by the elders. Finally all claims were to be submitted to the governor. But to the mandarins it was inconceivable that claimants would submit accurate calculations and that their representatives would not inflate the figures to their own advantage. The wheels of the empire ran on that principle. To get the right amount, ask for more and expect a reduction. From Taigu on August 8, Hoste wrote to Stevenson:

> The (*daotai*) wished to take twenty or thirty per cent from whatever was claimed, but to this I demurred, as I felt that compliance was virtually admitting that the Christians were exorbitant in their estimate. The Christians were not making charge for the loss of their crops, nor for the loss of time or expenses of travelling in connection with their flight . . . Precautions are being taken against possible exorbitant claims . . . The (*daotai*) looked rather blue when I declined his proposition . . . On our return (to Taiyuan) we (the CIM) shall present a carefully made-out estimate, and then tell him that we do not want any of it, and I shall endeavour to explain the grounds for this action.[51]

The team of investigators then split up and toured the province to learn all they could and to consult with church leaders in each place. Finally a letter addressed to all churches linked with the CIM set out the standard of action to be taken. 'The Lord's honour and not simply your own affairs' should be safeguarded.

> Christians who have had relatives murdered and are willing that they should have laid down their lives for the Lord's sake, and do not wish to report the case to the official, will be following the best course . . . Those who have been wounded and are maimed or disabled, but who have property and are able to support themselves, and are willing to forgive their enemies and therefore do not wish to report the matter to the Official, will do well. (Others should follow the normal process of law for 'the action of the temporal Government in vindication of law and order is also recognised as being of God') . . . There must be no carelessness or overstating, lest by your falseness the Lord's name be dishonoured before your enemies; and the Official and the Church will then have nothing to do with your affairs . . .

The matter of recantation posed another problem for missionaries and Church elders to face together.

> The ground we have taken is that anyone recanting places himself by his own act outside the Church, and it remains for those concerned to consider the question of his readmission. We find that there have been great varieties in the degree and manner of recantation. In many cases certificates were received from the Mandarin as a temporary expedient for averting extreme penalties while the storm lasted. Many Local Officials shrank from carrying into effect the sanguinary orders of the Governor (Yü Xian) and hit upon this device (to) tide over the difficulty. Other cases (present) varying degrees of conformity to idolatry. You can understand how extremely difficult our position is . . . by any want of sympathy and love, nothing could be easier than to quench the smoking flax and simply drive the poor, disheartened, suffering Christians to despair . . . Not to deal clearly and decidedly with the matter would mean the end of all discipline and Church order in the future.[52]

Paul himself had exhorted the Corinthian church, 'you ought to forgive and comfort him [a repentant believer], so that he will not be overwhelmed by excessive sorrow. I urge you, therefore, to reaffirm your love for him' (2 Cor. 2:7–8 NIV).

Hearing in place after place the grim details of torture and maiming, terror and coercion, shame and bitter grief over denying Christ, Dixon Hoste endured what he called 'the most painful experience of my life'. After Taiyuan, Taigu and Pingyao, he and Ernest Taylor toured the eastern cities of Lucheng, Lu'an and Hongtong, while Orr Ewing took the western route and Tjäder went to Yüncheng in the south.[53] Meeting at Qüwu they returned up the central plain through Linfen to Taiyuan again. Nowhere could they spend as much time as the Christians wished. There was always more to be said and done. They had to move on. A veiled report about one missionary woman's body having been sexually abused, to the deep distress of relatives, they carefully investigated and found it to be untrue. Even in such circumstances the Boxers had shown restraint far exceeding that of some foreign soldiers.

Chinese deacons were to take relief funds to Datong and the northern region, pending the arrival of more missionaries, as soon as John Stevenson could send them. Shen *Daotai* of the Foreign Office was pressing for not only men but women to return. Only the minister's and consuls' restrictions kept them back. Cassels had taken his wife home to Langzhong, to Sir Ernest Satow's alarm and Hudson Taylor's concern. But more women and children were being held in the oven of Chongqing at greater risk from illness than from harm in their country homes. To change the envoy's mind, Hoste visited him and wrote persuasively, citing Shen *Daotai*'s assurances until given a free hand again. By the end of 1901 all refugees had left Shanghai and either returned to their work or home on leave. Very few 'stations' were still closed.[54]

The Shanxi Church were more than ready for the help and comfort of missionaries, not least those who had been their friends before the crisis. Eva French and Matilda Way soon won permission to wait on the doorstep at Huolu, ready to re-enter Shanxi. Hoste hoped that when experienced missionaries returned they would do nothing to take control or exercise too strong an influence over less mature Christians – 'not that we lord it over your faith, but we work with you for your joy' (2 Cor. 1:24 NIV). 'The former basis of full independence', assisted by missionaries, led to a stronger Church than joint leadership and responsibility by Chinese and missionaries together.[55]

Governor Ceng and Timothy Richard   *June–October 1901*

With his summons to help the governor of Shanxi, Timothy Richard's great opportunity had come. Reparations should include the establishment in Shanxi of the university he had dreamed of for years. When he discussed with Dixon Hoste in Shanghai the formation of an inter-mission team to settle indemnities in Shanxi, Hoste told him the CIM's decision to accept no compensation for lives lost, bodily injury or loss of property. Applying indemnities to even as good an object as setting up a university would have the CIM's approval, but could not be in the Mission's name. Money obtained by taxation and fines could rightly compensate Chinese victims in the normal process of law, or be devoted, at Richard's instigation, to a Chinese institution for modern education in the province, but must not be levied to indemnify the CIM. So great a crime against her own people as well as foreigners could not be ignored by China's government. A university built by the government with funds declared to have been declined for the best motives by injured parties could only benefit the country by dispelling ignorance and prejudice, while acknowledging official liability.

Timothy Richard proposed to Governor Ceng and the emperor's plenipotentiaries (led by Li Hongzhang) that a fine of half a million taels (about £100,000 at that time) spread over ten years should be imposed and used for educating the province's ablest young men in Western learning. China's hope lay in a new generation alive to a progressive world. 'Fifty thousand taels a year for ten years would be a trifling sum for so large a province' to spend on the cream of its own people – especially while the classical examinations were in abeyance under the Peace Protocol. The plenipotentiaries at once approved the plan and put all administration of the funds, appointment of university staff and choice of curriculum into Richard's hands for ten years. But the implied insult to the governor and a strong party of officials at Taiyuan soured his relationship with them. They also resented the emphasis on Western learning, and launched a rival college of Chinese classics.

Richard's diplomacy was put to the test. After long negotiation they adopted the compromise that both disciplines should be combined in a secular university, and harmony was restored. Moir Duncan was installed as Principal and taught comparative religion, while Christian activities were carried on as an extra-curricular optional alternative.[56]

When D E Hoste submitted a statement of the CIM's losses to Shen *Daotai* and Governor Ceng, and added that no compensation would be claimed or even accepted by the CIM or the associate missions for whom he could speak, they were incredulous. He explained the Christian thinking behind this decision and suggested that a statement by the governor to be hung in each newly-erected chapel, would be enough. The result was extraordinary – a proclamation by the governor on October 11, 1901, placarded wherever the CIM had worked and suffered, throughout Shanxi. It 'went a long way to re-establish friendly feelings when the missionaries returned' and went further than years of preaching to acquaint the educated and uneducated with 'the teaching and spirit of Jesus'. In the proclamation the name of Jesus was honoured each time it was used, by being raised above the next (vertical) line.

> The Mission, in rebuilding these Churches with its own funds, aims in so doing to fulfil the command of the SAVIOUR OF THE WORLD, that all men should love their neighbours as themselves, and is unwilling to lay any heavy pecuniary burden on the traders or on the poor. I, the Governor, find . . . that the chief work of the Christian religion is in all places to exhort men to live virtuously. From the time of their entrance into China, Christian missionaries have given

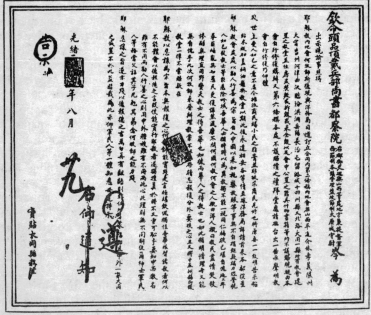

GOVERNOR CENG'S PRO-CHRISTIAN PROCLAMATION

medicine gratuitously to the sick and distributed money in times of famine . . . They regard other men as they do themselves, and make no difference between this country and that. Yet we Chinese . . . have treated them not with generous kindness, but with injustice and contempt, for which we ought to feel ashamed . . . contrasting the way in which we have been treated by the missionaries with our treatment of them, how can anyone who has the least regard for right and reason not feel ashamed of this behaviour? . . . JESUS, in his instructions, inculcates forbearance and forgiveness, and all desire for revenge is discouraged. Mr Hoste is able to carry out these principles to the full; this mode of action deserves the fullest approval. How strangely singular it is that we Chinese, followers of the Confucian religion, should not appreciate right actions, which recall the words and the discourses of Confucius, where he says, 'Men should respond with kindness to another's kind actions.'

I charge you all, gentry, scholars, army, and people, those of you who are fathers to exhort your sons, and those who are elder sons, to exhort your younger brothers, to bear in mind the example of Pastor Hoste, who is able to forbear and forgive as taught by JESUS to do, and, at the same time, to exemplify the words of Confucius . . . Let us never again see the fierce contention of last year . . . to enforce this on all persons, soldiers or people, is the aim of this special proclamation, which let all take knowledge of and obey.[57]

The governor also allocated another ten thousand taels to the relief of Christians.

Dixon Hoste returned to Shanghai, leaving Archibald Orr Ewing, Tjäder and Ernest Taylor to help the churches to return to normal life, and missionary replacements to find their feet in Shanxi. Geraldine's brother, Dr Whitfield Guinness, was one of these. But not until late 1902 did the foreign governments allow single women to re-enter the province, when the Greens returned to Huolu and released Eva French and Matilda Way to do so. Floods of new and returning missionaries were by then filling the Shanghai premises and dispersing 'over the bodies of the slain' (in Ludwig von Krapf's phrase) to every corner of China.

The *Chinese Recorder* carried long lists of arrivals from each continent, to reinforce each mission. In September 1901 it also quoted from the close of Tertullian's 'Apology' before pagan judges: 'The Christian blood you spill is like seed you sow, it springs from the earth again and fructifies the more' – conventionally reduced to the familiar words, 'The blood of the martyrs is the seed of the Church.'[58] The martyr T W Pigott had written in May 1896,

When I first reached this province there was not one baptised Christian here. Now there are many hundreds . . . and a large number of stations where thousands are brought under Christian influence. How shall we look on the investment of our lives and labour here; even from the near standpoint of one hundred years hence? . . . The work pressed home now will make all the difference a few years hence.[59]

Only four years later he laid down his life, and the Church in Shanxi went on from strength to strength. 'How shall we look on the investment of our lives and labour' one hundred years later?

CHAPTER FIFTEEN

CHARIOTS OF GOLD
1900–12

Return of the 'fat puss'   *1901–08*

If Ci Xi's sharp mind, sharp tongue and sharp claws were the essence of her strong personality, 'a certain cosiness' also characterised her. Her love of flowers, of silks, of porcelain and jade, of carpets, of decorum and of opera were as much part of her. The lap of luxury and her innate cruelty earned her the epithet 'fat puss'. She could make emperor, prince and minister tremble, and fussed over domestic detail as well as 'any thrifty housewife'.[1]

After the court's arrival at Xi'an on October 28, 1900 she quickly amassed gifts, tribute and her own replacements for lost antiquities and furniture from her Peking palaces. Operatic performances by three large troupes amused her; she fed well while the people were close to starving, and with generous make-up she looked twenty-five years younger than her true age. The Guang Xü emperor, meanwhile, took responsibility for the disasters of 1900 and looked worn and unhappy, anxious and sad, 'one of the most pathetic figures in history'.[2]

She could afford to wait until the Peace Protocol was signed on September 7, 1901, and foreign forces withdrew from Beijing before the advance guard of her court set out for the capital on October 6. Her advisers had impressed on her the importance to the stability of the empire and dynasty of an early return, but she alone would decide how and when. That decision rested upon her astrologers' notions. She and her entourage followed on October 20. But at Kaifeng, another ancient capital, she delayed to celebrate her 66th birthday on November 14 with more theatricals, and chose the auspicious 7th of January, 1902, to re-enter Beijing.

The loyal old statesman, Li Hongzhang, died on November 7 in his seventy-ninth year, hoping she had learned her lesson. She had his name engraved with the greatest of China's statesmen in the Temple of Faithful Ministers where it would be venerated, and elevated him posthumously to marquess of the first rank.[3] Too late to change appreciably, she saw that China must adapt to a·fast-changing world, and carried her Imperial Council with her. But the most they could attain was a few relatively futile measures dictated by the old aim of preserving Manchu domination in China. An imperial decree from Kaifeng established state education in Western learning, and banished her puppet Heir Apparent, Pu Jün, a rampant young lecher, to join his father, the disgraced minister Prince Tuan in exile. In his place she named Pu Lun, a grandson of the Dao Guang emperor. But to cover the traces of her guilt she honoured the Pearl Concubine posthumously for 'committing suicide in loyalty to the Empress Dowager and Emperor when unable to catch up with the court on their departure'! Ci Xi had not changed.

More genuinely she conferred on Sir Robert Hart the distinction of Junior Guardian of the Heir Apparent for his advice and assistance in the peace negotiations – having unleashed the wolves against him only eighteen months earlier. His home and library, and the lifetime's diaries of an intimate observer of the Chinese scene, had gone up in flames, searing his spirit inconsolably. The honour was poor consolation for the underlying wish to exterminate him with all other foreigners. Elevation in 1908 to the brevet title of President of a Ministry added little comfort in the year when he received doctorates from Oxford and Dublin universities and the freedom of the Cities of London and Belfast and Borough of Taunton to add to his baronetcy and high honours from thirteen other nations.[4]

Li Hongzhang was only one of Ci Xi's influential men to die (p 414). Kang Yi died during his flight from the capital, on his way to join her. As for Yong Lu, during his last two years he was in effect the prime minister and ruler of the empire, for if he disapproved of any action she might take, she would reverse it. The news of his death moved her deeply – at once she looked tired and worn; her clenched hands, a tear brushed away, and a change of subject betrayed more emotion than she liked to show. Since their youth Yong Lu had remained her dashing hero (HTCOC Book 3 *passim*; 6 p 25), and in his prime and maturity had closely resembled Li Hongzhang in astute wisdom. As soon as possible after the fall of Beijing he had rejoined her. Without him and Liu Kunyi she was left with two irresolute men to look to, Prince Qing and the scholar viceroy Zhang Zhitong – and the ambitious Yüan Shikai replacing Li Hongzhang as viceroy of Zhili, elder statesman and leading member of the Imperial Council.

The anti-foreign clique of Manchus and swashbucklers had finally been shaken off when she left Xi'an, Tong Fuxiang to banishment in the north-west, and Yü Xian to have his throat cut at Lanzhou.[5] She was free to pursue a policy of 'benign affability' towards her conquerors. The Foreign governments had taken the grotesque position of pretending that their troops were helping the Chinese government to put down an insurrection, even while their armies were routing Chinese generals and capturing Chinese cities. Instead of reinstating the emperor and curbing Ci Xi as press and missions urged with one voice from long experience in China, the reverse had become the diplomats' choice.[6]

Her message sent ahead from Kaifeng welcomed the foreigners to watch her arrival at the Tartar City and the ministers to be received in the Central Throne Hall in the palace as soon as she arrived.

She and the emperor crossed the Yellow River in a specially constructed dragon boat, resplendent in gilt and lacquer. From Zhengding they completed the long journey by that once diabolical fire-carriage, the train. Luxuriously furnished compartments decorated with imperial silks for the emperor and dowager empress made the return triumphant. Foreign onlookers on a high balcony at the great gate into the Tartar City watched as the procession approached and 'finally the Imperial palanquins (of yellow silk flashing with gold) advanced at an almost incredible speed between two lines of kneeling soldiers'. They 'seemed to move as fast as Tartar cavalry'.

At the gate they stopped for simple rites of home-coming and the emperor and dowager empress alighted – the emperor 'sad, silent and self-contained'. The rites over, the 'Old Buddha' looked up to the balcony, raised her small hands together under her chin and made a few little bows – to a burst of applause. 'All was forgiven and forgotten! – by the magic of Old Buddha's gesture.' 'Something told us that the return of the court to Peking marked a turning point in history.' The sacrifice of a few anti-foreign notables and a purr from the 'fat puss' and all was affability for seven more years. Parties for the diplomats' womenfolk, photography, even sittings for an American portraitist, and then back to normality, as nearly as could be, with many familiar faces missing. 'A corrupt and cankered Court had been preserved at the expense of the nation . . . There does not appear to be much hope for China now,' wrote Alicia Bewicke Little, ending her biography of Li Hongzhang.

A turning point in the history of China it certainly was. But Ci Xi's *coup d'état* against Guang Xü had been 'the bomb that destroyed the dynasty'. No empire could hold together with its emperor a captive, its reigning family disrupted by repeated disregard of the true line of descent, and flouting of tradition. 'Like any convict on parole, obliged daily to visit the police', Guang Xü still had daily to perform the ritual *ketou* of obeisance to Ci Xi until he died.

Changing China – changing world   1902–08

The Victorian era ended with the queen's death on January 22, 1901, and the ascension of the sixty-year-old Edward VII. Her Diamond Jubilee in 1897 had been marked by 'a vast military thanksgiving parade in London, with proud contingents from every continent (and) the little old lady in black . . . driving (in an open carriage) through dense, cheering crowds' to St Paul's Cathedral. Her sense of vocation had found expression in new moral standards for her nation. But colonialism in the guise of moral obligation had reached its peak, and her successive governments had been deaf and blind to the national conscience about Britain's opium curse on China. King Edward's brief hedonistic reign and achievement of the *entente cordiale* in Europe then supplied a new climate for relations with China, co-operation in her strong drive against opium in ports, cultivation and consumption, and for the missionary movement.

Yehonala (Yehe Nara), who became Ci Xi, born on November 3, 1835, and an empress for decades, outlived Victoria by seven years, long enough to see the changes she had fought to prevent. Her own change of mind (not belief) on reform began in January 1901 when she solicited advice from her ministers, viceroys and envoys abroad. Self-seeking and 'precedent', die-hard conservatism, had brought the nation close to ruin, she confessed, and modernisation had so far proceeded to no greater extent than the 'skin and hair', the superficial aspect of Western technology. How should China become rich and powerful again? Memorialists led by Liu Kunyi and Zhang Zhitong had quickly responded, but with nothing new. No new solution existed. Foreign study and travel would make up for deficient education at home; that outworn education must be reformed to include western learning alongside the Chinese classics. Corruption, sinecures, the official sale of appointments and fatuous military examinations based on physical prowess must all be eliminated.[7]

It was all so clearly true, though it had provoked a dynastic crisis and *coup d'état* in 1898. This time Ci Xi declared, 'There is no other way out,' much as she hated it. But the changes must be gradual. Zhang Zhitong detected duplicity, 'a noisy demonstration without substance', compounded by the appointment of incapable Manchus to implement the changes and ensure slow progress. But other startling edicts in Ci Xi's name took all by surprise: 'the customs and beliefs of Manchus and Chinese are now alike' – so after 250 years of the Qing dynasty's strict prohibition, intermarriage was to be permitted; the cruel custom of foot-binding (by which Chinese (never Manchu) girls' feet were tightly bandaged from infancy, to turn all but the big toe under the instep) was denounced; and selected Manchu clansmen were to be educated abroad. The Imperial University of Peking was re-established with a Chinese chancellor and W A P Martin as president of the foreign faculty – a phoenix from the Boxer bonfire.

Timothy Richard's University of Shanxi became a resounding success, a state institution under foreign control, but a model for other provinces. His dream of such a college or university in each provincial capital was slow in coming to fruition. Neither funds nor faculties of sufficient calibre could be mustered at short notice. The Russo-Japanese war of 1904–05 brought progress to a halt. But the portentous exhibition of a small newly-modernised Asian country crushing the mighty Russian forces on land and sea drove the Chinese nation to acquire the knowledge that made it possible.

From undisputed military possession by Russia of the whole of Manchuria at the dawn of 1902, and a Russo-Chinese Convention signed on April 8 providing for Chinese authority to be re-established in stages, Russian dominance was challenged by Japan in the autumn of 1903. Russia in Manchuria threatened Japan's hold on Korea, and also Japan's intended expansion of trade with Manchuria. On February 8, 1904, Japan broke off diplomatic relations with Russia and war broke out – to decide who should dominate the three Manchurian provinces of the Chinese empire, the home of the Manchu rulers of the subject Chinese millions! So low had the Qing dynasty sunk. Russia was worsted on land and sea. The Russian Baltic fleet reached the war zone on May 27, 1905, and was practically annihilated by Admiral Togo's fleet in the Sea of Japan the next day.

China had declared her neutrality, and the foreign powers obtained from Japan and Russia an undertaking not to cross the Zhili border, lest the Beijing court and government panic and take to 'the Imperial Chariot' again. On June 8, 1905, President Theodore Roosevelt urged both nations to talk peace, and the Treaty of Portsmouth, New Hampshire, was signed on September 5. Manchuria was to be evacuated by both powers and taken over by China, except for the Liaodong peninsula and ports which Japan was to lease. Chinese sovereignty and an 'open door' to other nations were recognised. No indemnities were claimed, and Japan returned to Russia the northern half of Sakhalin Island. Japan had settled the old score from 1894 when a Russian general menacingly laid his sword across the Sino-Japanese treaty at Yantai, and forbade its ratification.

Japan's victory 'electrified' China.[8] A new sense of nationality seized reform-minded Chinese. Thousands of Chinese students in Japan, hundreds in America and scores in Europe reacted strongly. In China itself 'student agitations swept the country, and the government took action'. 'Young China imposed its will on old China', and a new commercial, cultural and educational 'invasion' of China by Japanese began.

Before this, sporadic anti-foreign outbreaks had punctuated the relative peace following the Boxer rising – relative because demobilised troops and outlaws resorted to widespread brigandage. A neo-Boxer movement in Sichuan cost the lives of 1,000 Catholics and posed a serious threat from 1902–04. Yet Cassels called for thirty more missionaries; the requests for their teaching were more than could be met. On August 15, 1902, a mob, not politically motivated, murdered two young men of the CIM, J R Bruce of Australia and R H Lowis of Britain, at Chenzhou (Ch'enchou) in Hunan. A cholera epidemic had been attributed to the medicines they dispensed. But a strong gunboat reaction by the British led to a fine of £10,000 being exacted and offered to the CIM, who declined it.[9]

The two most obdurate provinces, Henan and Hunan, had in fact opened up after the Boxer fever ended. An editorial in the *Chinese Recorder* celebrated 'a hearty welcome (to missionaries) almost without exception' by both officials and people throughout the empire, so that 'a positive danger' had arisen 'that soon there (would be) more difficulty in keeping people out of the Church than getting them in'.[10] Popularity and false motives went hand in hand. The refugees from Henan were received back with deference and apologies. Howard Bird and Alfonso Argento (pp 372–5) met wide-eyed astonishment. Everyone 'knew' they had been 'killed'.

In 1905 Bird learned that at 'the place (Xiao Yao) where I was set upon and robbed of all my clothing . . . there is quite a little band of Christians and nearly fifty enquirers . . . They (repeatedly) say that my sufferings were the beginnings of their interest in the gospel. One man is the opium sot in whose room I hid . . . now broken off opium.' Robert Powell (p 376) of Zhoujiakou waited until the dowager empress had left Kaifeng and then with considerable courage 'occupied' the city, the first to do so since Henry M Taylor made his risky reconnaissances in 1875 (HTCOC Book 6, pp 53–5, 63, 84).[11]

An official had said to Griffith John, 'When Peking wants Hunan opened it will open.' The appointment of the right governor was the key. In May 1901 Governor Yü Liansan lent his steam launch to Griffith John, and everywhere on the way to Hengzhou and back to Wuhan he and his LMS companions were received 'with every demonstration of respect' and friendship. 'The old opposition is dead, the city (of Changsha) is open . . . We met with nothing but civility.' The highest mandarins asked the LMS to move in.[12] Also, in May 1901, Dr F A Keller of the CIM moved from Chaling to Changsha and with the authorities' help ('they have been *extremely kind*') was installed in good premises on June 11, the start of his celebrated hospital. But in November 1902 inflammatory proclamations by a provincial commissioner led to several hundred volunteering to rid the province of foreigners again. Change involved instability. When Ci Xi ordered the arrest of reformers in Beijing and one was 'most brutally beaten to death' in 1903, she revived terror such as they had suffered during the *coup d'état* in 1898. Reactionary violence lurked wherever progress was to be found.[13]

The Spectator hailed the Christian survival of the Boxer holocaust, and the reasonable approach to compensate, as 'a pure cause nobly vindicated'. But 'blind prejudice, lies and rumours' about missionaries calling for vindication of their wrongs were aired in the world press. The *Chinese Recorder* replied with the proverb, 'A lie will go round the world while truth is putting its boots on', expressing missionary concern that false accusation, like anti-foreign indoctrination, was not easily reversed. The end of the Boxer outbreak was not the end of the story. The greatest change in the CIM's experience and another test of resolution, unlike the Boxer years but potentially disastrous, was approaching.

Switzerland: building strength to return   *1900–02*

For the first year in Switzerland Hudson Taylor kept the one aim before him, to get fit enough to return to China. He was only sixty-eight and had more fight in him. The pace of life had over-strained him. Incessant responsibility, travel, public speaking and the tidal wave in China mounted to terrifying heights. But rest and exercise had often done wonders before. He knew how to shelve the stresses and relax with the glory of mountains and Alpine meadows, botany and photography, walking-stick and ice-axe as his companions.[14] When the Boxer wave broke over the men, women and little children he loved, Chinese and missionary, the agony of heart had been as much as he and Jenny could endure. The poetry of Geraldine Howard Taylor's chapter on this period gives what she observed through being with them while completing her biography of Hsi Shengmo. Escape to the mountainside, to come home tired out, kept him sane and soon would give him strength to get back, he hoped. If only to weep with those who wept, his presence might help to bring the Mission through.

So for the first six months they stayed at Davos-Dorf in eastern Switzerland, where the calm climate and relatively constant sun-shine had made it a popular health resort. By January 1901 the nightmare in China was over and the Mission was reoccupying 'safe' territory. Hudson Taylor was little better in health, but they were cold in Davos and William Berger's widow was ill at Cannes, so they went to be near her for three months, and to see the C H S Greens, convalescing from their Boxer ordeal and typhoid. By April Hudson Taylor had recovered so far as to visit Britain, and met survivors of the grim death marches through Shanxi and Henan.

While in England they received a letter from Lord Northampton, President of the Bible Society (the sixth marquess who with the Marquess of Aberdeen bought 'Gordon's Calvary' and garden tomb), offering to make Hudson Taylor a vice-president, as 'an expression of our sympathy with the China Inland Mission and our admiration of its Founder and Director'. He accepted gratefully. Jenny's father, Joseph Faulding, eighty-four and in retirement at Tenterden in Kent, showed them his considerable geological collec-tion, a lifetime's hobby.[15] Then briefly to Germany and back to Geneva on May 23.

While Dixon Hoste and his team were in Shanxi, W B Sloan and Henry Frost came to Geneva for two weeks of intensive consultation about Mission affairs. Hudson Taylor thought highly of both men and they found him still mentally well able to advise on complex and thorny subjects. Geneva in July became too hot for comfort and the Taylors moved across the lake to Chamonix on the French side and to the hamlet of Tréléchant at the head of the valley, below Mont Blanc. A letter of August 13 tells of his walking and climbing again, still intent on recouping strength to get back to China. Amelia, his beloved sister, and her surgeon son came to stay with them in September, and Ben borrowed Hudson Taylor's well-worn ice-axe to visit the glacier with a guide. Bought in July, it had already seen good use. On August 15 Hudson had 'startled' Jenny by saying, 'I must have had a slight stroke', for one side of his body was 'weak', but a fall when his foot slipped on pine needles might explain it, they decided.[16]

When Amelia left, they returned to Geneva for six weeks of 'the greatest mental effort of recent years', ploughing through 'voluminous pages' from Stanley Smith, and from Handley Moule, Bishop of Durham, refuting Smith's views on 'conditional immortality' and 'final restoration of unbelievers'. The Evangelical world had become less dogmatic about interpretations of Biblical statements on this subject, and in August Hudson Taylor remarked to William Sharp that if the CIM were being organised in 1901 instead of 1865, the clause in the P and P on 'the eternal punishment of the lost' might have been worded differently. It was not that his own attitude had changed, but that 'the Mission having been formed as it is, should not now be altered, our workers having joined it on this basis'. It would also be unfair to donors who supported the Mission with this understanding.

The historic principle of the CIM, unity on theological fundamentals and mutual tolerance of different views on lesser issues, made harmony and co-operation possible while wide variation existed along denominational and eschatological lines. Stanley Smith wrote, 'I admit that final restoration is not *clearly revealed* in Scripture, hence I cannot preach it. Any hope I may privately hold concerning it, is based on premises which are open to question.' On this undertaking his return to China in the CIM was agreed by the London Council.[17]

Geneva proved restless, and wanting peace and quiet they retreated to Château d'Oex for the three months of November 6 until mid-February, deliberately not settling anywhere. During part of January and February 1902, Hudson Taylor was 'at his best', but after another visit to London with full days and jolting vehicles, he became 'very exhausted and feeble' (the word they used for 'frail') with a recurrence of pain in his spine. Returning by gentle stages to Switzerland, they stayed for three weeks at Vevey and Veytaux before moving to Geneva until early July. In May his extreme frailty often made Jenny 'very concerned' and for four months he depended on a 'Bath chair' whenever he left the house. May 21 was his seventieth birthday. But weak or strong he was still General Director of an expansive international society. They faced the sad truth that his active days were over; he could never return to China as Director, if at all. He must act without delay to provide for his decease.[18]

Painful transition   June–December 1902

The frailty that threatened to end Hudson Taylor's life was poor preparation for winding up his part in Mission affairs and handing over to others. Jenny wrote of 'both head and legs so powerless'. But his capacity for bracing himself to face the inescapable came to his rescue again. Before he could relax he must steer the transference of his responsibility to Dixon Hoste through several stages. First, a contingency measure in case of his own early death. By the end of June he had provisionally appointed Hoste to succeed him in that event, 'subject to the approval of the various Councils', and had begun consultations about the substantive appointment.[19] The time had also come for Walter B Sloan to be recognised as assistant or associate Home Director with Theodore Howard. And agreement needed to be reached on procedures for the appointment of future general directors, should any die or be incapacitated before naming their successor constitutionally. This had then to be legally incorporated in Mission documents. And the scintillating, much-loved but frequently trouble-prone Stanley Smith's relationship with the CIM had to be clarified once and for all. On arrival in China he had returned to expounding his views in terms of a 'larger hope' disrupting the community at Chefoo.

With an indefinitely prolonged period of ill-health ahead of them, the time had come for the Taylors to make a more settled home somewhere. The difficulty of access by jolting coach excluded Château d'Oex, so they took rooms in the Pension La Paisible at Chevalleyres above Vevey, which they could reach by boat from Geneva. The *pension* suited them ideally. Facing south across the lake, with a 'glorious outlook over the Savoy Alps and up the Rhone Valley', their rooms had the added boon of a glazed veranda such as they loved, idyllic for an invalid. The proprietors, M et Mme Bonjour, did all they could for their comfort, sending their meals up to them. They quickly became good friends. So this was home for the next two years.

Within a week of their settling in, news came of the Mission treasurer James Broumton's wife having died at Chefoo. A raging epidemic of cholera was spreading from port to port up the China coast and Yangzi River. Danger of infection threatened all exposed to it. A few days later a letter came from Walter Sloan, whose brother-in-law, in business in Swatow, had just died of cholera. But he had 'appalling news' to give them. 'Be alone before you read on,' he told Jenny. In the Boys' School at Chefoo, Amelia's grandson, Gershom, the only son of Hudson Broomhall and 'so promising', had fallen ill with what was thought to be ptomaine poisoning, and died within four hours. They buried him beside Mrs Broumton. Nine others then died in quick succession on the same day, and three later. Charles Fishe's son, Howard (Jenny's nephew); Duncan Kay's son, Stewart; Dr Parry's son, Herbert; and Gray-Owen's two sons, Hugh and Norman, at one blow – these all belonged to the CIM family. Worse still in one respect, the remaining seven had been committed to the Mission's care by other societies, by imperial customs officers and by merchant homes.

'Even in this . . . calamity (God) is putting to the proof our confidence in His love and faithfulness,' Sloan wrote. Hudson Broomhall acknowledged the Chefoo news by telegram: 'God makes no mistakes,' and in a letter echoed Hudson Taylor on the death of his daughter, Grace, in 1867 (HTCOC Book 4, p 365): '"Who plucked this flower?" said the gardener. "The Master", was the answer. And the gardener held his peace.' (On the first anniversary of Gershom's death another son was born to them.) There happened to be a ringleader of disorder in the school who escaped when the others died. Driven to think deeply by his brush with death, he turned to Christ. This, too, softened the blow. A full consular investigation soon established with the help of bacteriologists in Shanghai that cholera, a cause regarded as less avoidable even with utmost care, not food poisoning, had been to blame.[20]

When case after case of typhoid fever in the mission followed the cholera, Hudson Taylor urged Stevenson to insist that missionaries eat or drink no uncooked food of any kind. 'All our people ought to know this.' He was still reading widely.

A letter from the saintly Francis Coillard of the Upper Zambesi came as strong comfort to Hudson Taylor.

> From the very beginning of all the trouble and calamities in China, I have suffered with you as much as the human heart is able, we ourselves here passing at the same time through deep affliction . . . Your sorrows, your bereavements are ours, they are the sorrows and bereavements of the Church . . . They will, by the example of those modern martyrs, stimulate a spirit of truer and more joyous consecration . . .
>   I count it one of the greatest blessings . . . not only to have *seen* you, but to have been in personal contact with you.[21]

When Stanley Smith had agreed that his views on 'eternal punishment', 'conditional immortality' and 'the final restoration of all' were philosophical and could not be shown positively to be taught by Scripture, he had undertaken to keep them to himself. But like an obsessive hobby, Hudson Taylor commented, they brought 'SPS' back again and again to mull over the same tendentious reasoning, closing his mind to Biblical revelation. He could see no incongruity between his ideas and his membership of the Mission. As long as he vacillated, doubting his own arguments, and did not confuse Chinese Christians or colleagues, endless patience and persuasion in dealing with him, a lovable friend for seventeen years, seemed the right policy. The apostle's advice 'Accept him whose faith is weak, without passing judgment on disputable matters' (Rom. 14:1 NIV) had its relevance to SPS. But when he wrote 'declaring himself a positive believer in the final restoration of all', he distanced himself from the CIM and the Principles and Practice he had signed. Hudson Taylor still hoped against hope to bring him back to Biblical realities, but Dixon Hoste and the China Council were less sanguine. He was doing too much damage. Another missionary had resigned over the issue.

Worse still, Henry Frost was 'greatly distressed' that 'SPS' had gone back to China with strong reservations. And Walter Sloan shared his objections. Howard and Geraldine in America as travelling speakers for the Student Volunteer Movement for a year already, wrote urgently to Hudson Taylor. In America and Canada, the CIM would be condemned even for leniency towards Stanley Smith. If he remained in the Mission, Frost himself might feel it necessary to resign from his position as Home Director, but as quietly and inconspicuously as possible. The issue was becoming one of disruption of the Mission rather than one of Smith's beliefs.[22]

Howard and Geraldine Taylor were fulfilling their undertaking for the SVM with outstanding success, Frost reported. And the CIM was benefiting greatly. Could they be spared for another year to continue the good work? But behind the scenes their rôle as mediators was no less valuable. The 'extreme gravity' of this confused situation justified their staying, and merited Hoste travelling halfway round the world to meet with Frost and the North American Council before travelling on to Switzerland. His coming would give Hudson Taylor the opportunity he needed to go over a hundred and one other mission matters with him before responsibility for them descended on his shoulders.

In October 1902 Henry Frost visited the *pension* for two weeks of conversations with Hudson Taylor. Much as he admired Dixon Hoste, his devotion to Hudson Taylor still made the thought of his proposed retirement difficult to accept. Robert Wilder and his sister Grace, the initiators of the SVM, were in Switzerland for their health and, joined by his mother, wife and children, moved into La Paisible during Frost's visit, until they left for Norway in April 1903.

In the company of these two outstanding men, Hudson Taylor's state of health improved, until writing to point out to Stanley Smith that he had taken the decisive step himself, 'cost him (JHT) so much'. It meant that Stanley could no longer remain in the Mission. Then Hudson Taylor relapsed, but rallied to continue four days of consultations with Hoste and Sloan together and nine more with Dixon alone. In January he had written to 'Dick': 'Dear Stanley may be led but cannot be driven . . . ought not to be driven.' In the end even 'mild and inoffensive' dealings with him had failed.

The business with Hoste and Sloan then covered a wide range of other matters. Formal appointment of Dixon Hoste as General Director in place of Hudson Taylor came first. The American Council had been impressed with Hoste as 'a man of God and a person of unusual intelligence and gifts'. And he himself could see that the time had come, when the consultations sapped Hudson Taylor's strength so that he was 'pretty well done up, with bad headache'. While Dixon plied him with questions, the old man, physically ten years older than his age, paced slowly up and down the room, sharing his wisdom and experience with his Elisha.

On November 11 Walter Sloan returned to London to become

Assistant Home Director.[23] And on November 17 before Hoste headed back to China on the 20th, Hudson Taylor gave notice to Theodore Howard of his intention to declare Hoste General Director as soon as he received confirmation from the Council. All were unanimous in welcoming him, and on January 1, 1903, Hoste's appointment and Hudson Taylor's retirement became official. At the Anniversary meetings in May the announcement was made generally public. Hudson Taylor himself, after some discussion, was to be known as Founder and Consulting Director. On November 21, 1902, he wrote at length to Theodore Howard, giving his 'mature thoughts on the future conduct of the Mission', almost a last will and testament. A few quotations will show its nature, and his mental ability.

> The CIM is not a Church, nor a section of the general Church, but a voluntary union of members of various denominations, agreeing to band themselves together to obey the Saviour's last command in respect to China; holding in common the same fundamental truths, accepting the directorship rule of the Mission, and receiving where needful such ministration as God may make possible from its funds . . .
>   In my judgment the Holy Scriptures do not hold out any hope for those who die impenitent . . .
>   If the Directors and Members of our Councils are godly and wise men, walking in the spirit of unity and love, they will not lack divine guidance in important matters, and at critical times; but should another spirit prevail, no rules could save the Mission, nor would it be worth saving. The CIM must be a living body in fellowship with God or it will be no further use and cannot continue.[24]

He was frail but not decrepit. Even so, Hoste found oversights in the letter to correct. The load off his shoulders, the strain of hard mental work over, and news of single women at last re-entering Shanxi in October coming as a bouquet of joy to him, Hudson Taylor was 'quite at his best again' by Christmas. On New Year's Day, 1903, Jenny wrote to their adopted daughter, 'Millie' (Duncan), 'He finished reading his Bible through in a year for the 40th time yesterday.'

The new 'GD'   1903

His duty done, and a man of such qualities wearing his mantle, Hudson Taylor regained strength. A succession of visitors to

Chevalleyres continued through the year, among them Sister Eva of Friedenshort,[25] and from time to time he and Jenny made short journeys, together to Thun and the Bernese Oberland, and separately to Zermatt or to see the invalid Mrs Berger in Geneva. Stanley Smith pressed for his case to be reconsidered, but all councils of the Mission were united in seeing no merit in reopening the matter. That the controversy continued at all, with Henry Frost pressing his unwilling colleagues for a more explicit mission 'Basis of Faith', was enough.[26]

On July 6 Hudson Taylor wrote reminding Frost that God did not allow David to build the temple 'because he was a man of war'. The time and energy spent on disagreement could lead to disaster and would be better used positively. To Hudson Taylor another aspect of the matter applied, as it had often done with others in the past (and still applies today), though he did not raise it with Frost – they joined the Mission on its existing constitutional basis, which satisfied hundreds, and should not try to change it.

Dixon Hoste had taken firm hold of his leadership, modifying Hudson Taylor's proposed measures for appointing directors, and encouraging the missionaries to launch out confidently in their work, whatever the past history or present opposition. He invited the two outstanding men at the 'Home' end, Frost and Sloan, to come and resolve the so far intractable dispute together with the China Council. (John Southey, their equivalent in Australia, had not yet become Home Director.) At first, when they met in February 1904, it looked as if a disastrous mistake had been made in laying all cards on the table. Failure could polarise opinion irreparably. Dixon Hoste wrote forlornly to Hudson Taylor that at one point he had prayed, 'Lord, I admit all my blunders and folly and sins, but that is just the reason why I count on Thee to undertake the matter.' Then on the third day the whole picture changed. Henry Frost's account to Hudson Taylor revealed his own amazement.

> It looked for a time as if agreement would be impossible and that disruption must follow. (Then) we found ourselves seeing eye to eye and the danger passed . . . We fell on our knees to praise the Lord, and rose to sing the doxology. Now we feel we can give ourselves anew to our work . . . as never in the past.

The truth was that Dixon Hoste as Chairman had shown the God-given skill and wisdom that impressed Governor Ceng in

Shanxi and were to become a byword in the missionary and secular community in China. He had no easy task. One of his first duties had been to dismiss a provincial secretary for embezzling large sums of mission money. He was not to be prosecuted if he packed up and left immediately. In contrast, an author-traveller named W E Geil, after crossing China to Burma wrote to Stevenson,

> Never have I seen the people's money made to go so far as under your wise administration. My own accounts without exception were promptly, politely, properly attended to. In an age of commerce and high-pressure commercial enterprises . . . it is good to find equally wise methods applied to the gifts of the Church . . . Among the CIM workers (I was impressed) by a spiritual atmosphere saturated with . . . kindness and commonsense . . . Your missionaries receive very small pay, but . . . never has salary been mentioned but the ready reply has come, 'It is sufficient.' God bless the self-effacing missionaries of Inland China.[27]

With all districts reoccupied since the return of the imperial court to Beijing, ample funds coming in, and good news of progress, Hoste had thoughts of renewing the advance (the 'forward movement') interrupted by the Boxers. Between May 1902 and May 1903, 132 members had returned and fifty-seven new reinforcements arrived, 189 in all. But the potential for many more suggested putting the subject to the Church at large. The first step was to bring the existing Mission to its knees before God. Walter Sloan and Henry Frost, already well known and admired, were the right men to lead them in conference after conference 'for the deepening of spiritual life' at convenient centres.

The Chinese Church was growing strong. The number of members in the whole of China at the end of 1902 was about one hundred thousand, with two hundred and fifty thousand adherents not yet baptised. Within four weeks, three hundred carefully vetted baptisms had been reported, and in 1903 a total of 1,688, nearly seven hundred more than in 1902, had included some distinguished literati. One was the son of a literary Chancellor. In Shanxi, 250 repentant former members had been reinstated, and 150 families in Pastor Hsi's district had professed faith in Christ and destroyed their idols. One of the poignant instances of reinstatement after recanting had been none other than Elder Si before his death on July 2, 1902. Still suffering from his sword wound and weeping on his bed over the sufferings of the Christians and their missionaries, in 1900 he had been menaced again and shrank from the pain. But his recantation had been a lie. He cringed in shame. When pitied and forgiven by his fellow-Christians, he had besought them to stop calling him 'Elder', he was so unworthy. But they insisted, and cared for him until he died. One congregation had managed to continue worship throughout the rising. Others as late as 1903 were still too terrified to begin again. In the Hongtong area the Christians built a chapel seating one thousand, and at Yüwu eight hundred attended a church conference.[28] The greater danger had become the admission of false applicants.

In Sichuan a unique development highlighted the change for good in the political climate. Governor Ceng (Ts'eng Ch'un-hsüan), who had dealt so strongly with Yü Xian's Boxers in Shanxi, executing their leaders, was promoted to Viceroy of Sichuan, to stamp out the neo-Boxer outbreak there.[29] When his son immolated himself beside his mother's coffin, an imperial commendation and monument eulogised his filial piety – such was the underlying ambience of a nation grasping uncertainly at reform. But when the missionaries in Sichuan presented the new viceroy at Chengdu with an address of welcome, he replied,

> . . . I earnestly hope that this insurrection may be speedily suppressed, and that both the people and the Church may enjoy tranquillity.
>
> Regarding my management of affairs in Shanxi, it was entirely owing to the fact that all the leaders of your Church were truly able to act according to the precept of the Save-the-World religion, 'Love men as thyself.' Therefore, the honour should be divided between us . . .
>
> I earnestly hope that . . . there may be between us (also) mutual confidence and sincerity.[30]

After only eight months, during which the neo-Boxers were recruiting members and a thousand Roman Catholic Chinese and twenty Protestants were killed, with the destruction of chapels in six places, a difficult time for the viceroy, he was promoted to Guangzhou (Canton). Again the Protestant community in Chengdu wished him well, presenting him with a replica of the New Testament given to the Empress Dowager in 1894 (p 212). He answered,

> . . . my talents are few and I am not worthy of your praise . . . I have barely suppressed the disaffected, and have but roughly pacified the

country. Besides this I have scarcely made a beginning to all the reforms that are necessary . . .

. . . Chinese and foreigners are coming more and more into cordial relations, and the country enjoys a lasting peace. This fills me with joy and hopefulness . . . My hope is that the teachers of (British and American Missions) will spread the Gospel more widely than ever, that hatred may be banished and misunderstanding dispelled, (creating) boundless happiness for my people of China . . . My thoughts will be with you . . .

May the Gospel prosper!

The Literary Chancellor of Shaanxi in addressing five hundred Chinese graduates declared that missionaries had come to China to do good, and stories to the contrary should not be believed. Urging them to cultivate the acquaintance of Protestant missionaries, whom he complimented on their Christian literature and on not intervening in litigation to gain 'advantage for their converts', he said, 'If you wish to enter the Protestant Church you are at liberty to do so.' That 'one who had obtained the highest degree in the Empire, and occupied such a position, should speak so fearlessly and favourably of Christianity' was unheard of. The graduates could hardly believe their ears. China was changing dramatically fast.

Instability was also in evidence. To replace Governor Ceng in Shanxi, the friendly governor of Hunan, Yü Liansan, who had lent Griffith John his steam launch in 1901, was appointed to Taiyuan. But because Bruce and Lowis had been murdered in Hunan (prompting strong-arm action by the British in sending a gunboat), the foreign envoys objected. Yü Liansan's appointment was withdrawn. But Shanxi was to enjoy years of peace and prosperity under the 'model governor', Yan Xishan (Yen Hsi-shan, p 537).

Dixon Hoste knew well enough when he accepted the directorship that it was no bed of roses. In the thirty-three years he was to serve as General Director, the CIM was to grow to 1,360 members, and the Qing dynasty was to founder, while revolution and massacre of the Manchus were to bring back the fears of 1900. In republican China warlords were to fly at each other's throats, militant nationalism was to be directed against foreigners again, and the emergence of communism in China and of Japan's imperial ambition were to herald the greatest upheavals yet.

YAN XISHAN, 'MODEL' GOVERNOR OF SHANXI
in the new Republic. Note his Western-style uniform but full
mandarin-style sleeves

'To the City Gate'   1903–04

Late in July 1903, Jenny was found to have an abdominal tumour. She had been losing strength for ten months. When a surgeon on the North American Council, who was visiting Switzerland, came at Howard Taylor's request to see her, examination under chloroform showed the tumour to be inoperable. Somehow she and Hudson Taylor understood that it 'would not need to be removed', and no one disillusioned them. She remained free from pain well into 1904. Howard expected 'obstruction' and a slow agonising end to her life, but not until nine hours before she died on July 30, 1904, did she suffer greatly, and then from respiratory distress.

In these circumstances the past mattered little. Jubilee celebrations would have been incongruous. Neither September 19, 1903, the fiftieth anniversary of Hudson Taylor's sailing from Liverpool on the *Dumfries*, nor March 1, 1904, the anniversary of his reaching Shanghai, deserved to be celebrated, except in a jubilee number of *China's Millions*. 'If I had a thousand lives, China should have them,' (HTCOC Book 3, p 198) had been fulfilled as he had never dreamed when he first wrote the words. More than 1,300 men and women had joined the CIM, and unnumbered others had gone to China in other societies through his urging; 1904 was also the centenary year of the British and Foreign Bible Society. But with Jenny so ill these milestones were barely noticed.[31]

To be within reach of medical help the Taylors moved to Lausanne for the winter, but were back in their *pension* home when news came of eighty-five-year-old Joseph Faulding's death on March 25, 1904.[32] From April Jenny was on liquids only and by June her diary was recording 'bad days'. On July 16 she told Geraldine, 'I only live by the day now', but continued making entries and on the 25th wrote her last letter. The next two days' diary entries were simply 'Tired all day.' A French friend who called to see her commented on her 'tranquil serenity'. Asked if she thought about the joys of heaven ahead of her, she answered characteristicaily, 'The Bible says more about Him than it does about heaven. No, I do not often think of heaven. He is here with me, and He is enough.'[33] Another friend wrote to Grace Wilder of Jenny's forgetting herself to the last, 'always bright and patient, enquiring about one's health, et cetera'.

On the 29th she dictated goodbye letters to members of her family and friends, and towards midnight 'began to sink rapidly'. Fully conscious until the last quarter hour, she said repeatedly for Hudson's sake, 'No pain, no pain.' But her difficulty in breathing increased. 'For about two hours at daybreak (her 'fight for air') was so terrible that she begged (him) to pray the end might come quickly.' Afterwards he confessed that this was the hardest prayer to pray, but as he himself was suffering intensely with her he found words to ask the Lord 'to take her from me to Himself'. Again 'Never did I feel more gratitude than when my prayer . . . was answered within five minutes.'

'Death' had come, but, 'precious in the sight of the Lord is the death of his saints' (Ps. 116:15). 'She is not dead, but entered into life,' Theodore Howard wrote, 'not death but life immortal', for only her mortal body had ceased to live. Bunyan's imagery of the passing of Christiana over the last 'river' expressed Jenny's strong faith and her family's. 'Behold, all the banks beyond the river were full of horses and chariots, which were come . . . to accompany her to the City Gate. So she . . . entered in . . .'

In private, Hudson Taylor was 'heartbroken and desolate that the dear person was out of reach', but at the funeral services, while others wept, he rejoiced that Jenny had 'entered into the joy of her Lord', and was composed. At the cemetery he shook hands with everyone and thanked them for coming. She had chosen the place for her grave, near the creeper-clad church tower of La Chiesaz at St Legier, in a beautiful position looking out over woods, hills and the mountains of Savoy across Lake Geneva. After Howard and Geraldine had taken him up the Rhône Valley for a brief change of environment, he often visited 'the sacred spot in the little churchyard', 'sacred until the Resurrection morning'. And, all stresses ended, he steadily regained his health.

'O Greatly Beloved': back to China   February–June 1905

Returning strength revived in Hudson Taylor his hope of visiting China again, and 'the Mission leaders' freed Howard and Geraldine to travel with him. The Hostes were due in Europe before long, so he planned to reach Shanghai before they left. The old zest had returned and he 'set his heart on a visit to Changsha, the capital of Hunan'.[34] For decades Hunan had been 'the most violently anti-foreign province', and after it Henan. But conditions had greatly changed since the Boxer year. He could sail up the Yangzi in April, visit Henan by train in May and Changsha by ship, and be back at Shanghai by mid-June.

They crossed the Atlantic on the 24,000-ton White Star Line ss *Baltic*, one of the biggest ships afloat, sailing on February 15; and dodged the blizzards in the northern States and Canada by taking the southern route. On the way they heard news of Russia's defeat by the Japanese at Mukden, quickly followed by the loss of her fleet. The voyage from San Francisco on May 18 via Honolulu to Japan and through the 'inland sea' brought them to Wusong on April 17. The long calm journey had been a tonic to him.

A tender took them up the Huangpu River to Shanghai, as a pilot boat had taken him fifty-two years before. Then, his 'heart felt as tho' it would burst from its place'. This time all the sights, sounds and smells were familiar, charged with memories. Then, he did not know a soul in China. Now John Stevenson and friends without number thronged to welcome him at the Wusong Road mission home and offices he had planned and built. The China Council was in session, and photographs had to be taken of all together, and of Hudson Taylor with the two most senior members, Meadows and Stevenson – historic photographs, for the Council had decided in 1904 that the wearing of Chinese clothes in the ports should be optional. In 1907 the option was extended to other cities with large foreign communities.[35] In an open letter thanking all who had written to welcome him, he said, as if thinking of hard times in the past and the unknown ahead, or perhaps of God's patience with his own shortcomings and unfulfilled aims: 'He does not expect or require anything in us that He is not willing and able to impart.' And again, in the simple terms he had come to use in his old age, reminiscent of his remark sometimes expressed as, 'God looked for someone weak enough to use, and found me' he wrote: 'We cannot do much, but we can do a little, and God can do a great deal.' The greatness of God, his growing realisation.

At Zhenjiang he visited the graves of Maria and his children in the little cemetery among the hills, 'where he had always hoped that he might some day rest himself', and spent Easter Sunday at Yang-zhou, scene of the first great riot in 1868. Speaking to young missionaries at Zhenjiang, soon to scatter inland, he said,

> You do not know what lies before you. I give you one word of advice: Walk with the Lord! Count on Him, enjoy Him . . . He will not disappoint you – [echoing words he had used about two years before]

'For forty years I have made it the chief business of my life to cultivate a personal acquaintance with the Lord Jesus Christ . . . No (trifling) with self-indulgence or sin – and there is no reason why the Holy Spirit should not be outpoured.'

On a new, fast river steamer they made the journey to Hankou, and in Griffith John's home the two veterans again sang hymn after hymn together as they had often done since 1855. Fifty-one years had passed since they had cut their milk-teeth together as newcomers to Shanghai.

W A P Martin came over from Wuchang on April 29 to welcome his colleague of Ningbo days, and historic photographs of the three veterans mark the occasion.[36] The weather had been exceptionally cool, and all three were wearing overcoats. Hudson Taylor looked well. Martin had arrived in China in 1850, Hudson Taylor in 1854 and Griffith John in 1855. Joseph Edkins had reached Shanghai in 1848, but news of his death in Shanghai on April 23 came while his three good friends were together – the Joseph Edkins with whom Hudson Taylor had made his first inland journey, and 'who had forgotten more about China than most of us ever knew', the learned A H Smith was to write. W A P Martin, so highly honoured by China (p 270), had returned in 1902 from America, to confer with Viceroy Zhang Zhitong, about establishing a University of Wuchang. But after nearly three years as President, during much of which time Zhang was absent at Nanjing and Beijing by imperial command, 'the University existed only on paper', so Martin returned to Beijing.[37]

The heat of summer was approaching. On May 1 Hudson Taylor, Howard and Geraldine boarded the Belgian train on the Hankow –Beijing line, and six hours later (instead of weeks of heat, dust and jolting by springless cart and wheelbarrow as in days gone by) they thundered in a cloud of smoke through a long tunnel into Henan.

At Xiangcheng, where Charles Bird had suffered so appallingly (p 374), at Zhoujiakou and the Howard Taylors' old home at Chenzhou, they met and worshipped with survivors of the Boxer atrocities and with others newly Christian. And at Taikang (another city 'opened' by the Howard Taylors) they met Bird and Ford, working as if they had never been the victims of such hatred and superstition. At place after place the venerable old man with his long white beard was fêted and honoured. Scarlet satin banners with golden Chinese characters hailed him as 'Benefactor of Inland

THREE VETERANS IN HANKOU, APRIL 1905
W A P Martin, Griffith John and Hudson Taylor

China' and 'O Greatly Beloved!' Red bunting draped the pavilions and platforms erected to refresh him. Someone tucked a copy of *Punch*, the satirical magazine, into a basket of food for him, and amazed bystanders cried, 'See, what an example to us! The venerable teacher must be at least a hundred and there he is still storing his mind with wisdom.' To Howard it seemed that 'happier days there could hardly be on earth!'

Back at the railroad and joined by Jane af Sandeberg, whom Hudson Taylor had known as the child of his first hosts in Sweden, they reached Hankou on Friday May 26, the thirty-ninth anniversary of the sailing of the *Lammermuir*. After travelling for three and a half weeks he needed to recuperate for a few days. So Griffith John, W A P Martin and the leaders of several missions, the Methodist Episcopal Bishop Roots, Arnold Foster of the LMS and others came to see him at the CIM the next day, and more photographs were taken in the garden. Griffith John in particular seemed drawn to his old friend. Their attachment had always been at a deeply spiritual level, and but for his mission's insistence on a different strategy, he also would have been a trail-blazer. In the event he had become a model of the effective, city-based church planter and author of powerful Christian literature in immaculate Chinese. Of Hudson Taylor he wrote, 'I never felt more attached to him than I did . . . before he started for Changsha. I was longing to see him again on his way to Shanghai and home.'

The Japanese ship on which the Taylors were hoping to travel cheaply, ran aground, and reluctantly they had to go by 'saloon class' on the largest steamer to Changsha, with the whole accommodation to themselves. Always ready to help lovers hindered by unfavourable circumstances, Hudson Taylor invited Jane af Sandeberg and Geraldine's doctor brother, Whitfield, to travel with them. Within two days and still on board, they were engaged.

Since Charles Judd's first attempt in 1875 to gain a foothold in Hunan, and Adam Dorward's journey with Yang Cunling, his ex-soldier friend, in 1879, many persistent efforts had been made and suffering endured, until Dr Keller succeeded at Chaling. Until eight years previously not one Protestant missionary was resident in Hunan. In 1905 there were 111 of thirteen societies, and many Chinese colleagues, working from seventeen central stations. For Hudson Taylor to stand on Hunan soil and set foot in CIM premises in the last but one citadel of China to yield to the gospel, marked in a sense the crowning moment of his life. Hunan was the last province, and Kaifeng the last capital to be occupied. Simeon's prayer might well have been his own, 'Now let your servant depart in peace.'

'And all the trumpets sounded'   *June 1905*

On Friday, June 2, the first full day in Changsha, Hudson Taylor climbed without difficulty to the upper storey of the pavilion on the highest stretch of the Changsha city walls. It commanded extensive views of the great Xiang River valley and surrounding hills, and in the city the handsome temples and mansions of the rich and powerful. The governor had offered to present a site of several acres to Dr Frank Keller for a hospital, so they went to inspect it. In the afternoon the Imperial Customs superintendent and his wife invited the visitors to their home. Hudson Taylor was feeling the humid heat and had not been sleeping well, but when Chinese Christians from several churches – churches in Hunan! – came to meet him the next morning he addressed them in the Mission chapel – another high point, his son thought, of his father's missionary career.[38]

He would not start a journey or even travel on the Lord's day if it could be avoided, but if the steamer captain would postpone leaving until early Monday morning, he would walk to the jetty on Sunday evening, though it would take him an hour. Otherwise he would wait for the next Thursday boat. No answer came to a telegram asking the shipping company to authorise the delay. Storm damage had cut the wires. What could they do? At this point Hudson Taylor said that he had 'always been accustomed to think that circumstances must be made to bend to the requirements of God's law, and not God's law to our convenience'. The ship's captain agreed on his own authority to wait; and an hour or two later the company's wire came through authorising the delay.

A reception for all missionaries in Changsha and his Customs friends was planned for 4.00 pm on Saturday, so as he was tired he spent a quiet day, reading in a long-chair. At four he came downstairs looking fresh and well in a newly-laundered suit of Shandong silk, and chatted with the thirty or more guests from six societies over tea in the garden. Dr Keller enjoyed seeing the pure joy on Hudson Taylor's face. Then informal photographs were taken, and no one appears to have noticed that Hudson Taylor was exhausted. A photograph caught him looking drawn and supporting his head on his hand. As soon as most had gone he went up to his room, and a Dr

EXHAUSTED: THE RECEPTION AT CHANGSHA
shortly before Hudson Taylor retired to bed and died. Note:
Howard Taylor already dependent on a strong hearing aid;
Dr Keller chatting in the doorway

Barrie joined him. In conversation, 'I remarked that the distinction between small and great things frequently came into my mind . . . at times of prayer . . . After a pause . . . he said, "There is nothing small and there is nothing great; only God is great, and we should trust Him fully."' If 'nothing is too hard for God', all is equally within His power, the sparrow and the universe. 'Only God is great.' A lifetime of proving this truth had shown him that a half-sovereign in a glove (HTCOC Book 2, pp 50–1) or an empire opening to the gospel against the wishes of its rulers, were neither here nor there, only God's will and God's action.

He did not feel ready for another meal, and decided to retire early for the night. Howard brought him a tray of 'good things' and prepared to read to him while Geraldine encouraged him to eat a little. Howard went for something missing from the tray, and Geraldine stayed chatting. She was in mid-sentence when Hudson Taylor 'turned his head on the pillow and drew a quick breath'. She disregarded it until he caught his breath again, 'gasping'. Then she saw he was not conscious. She called out, and Howard and Dr Keller came, in time to see him draw his last breath. 'No cry, no word, no choking or distress.' In *Daily Light* for that evening was the verse, 'And Enoch walked with God . . . and God took him' (Gen. 5:24 AV). 'It seemed more like translation than dying, and to the stricken son came the words, "My father, my father! the chariots of Israel and the horsemen thereof!"'[39]

The Chinese Christians of Changsha insisted on buying the best coffin they could find, lining it beautifully, though this was normally the son's duty, and on paying for it to be taken to the ship. They gathered round his bed to say goodbye, and one old woman whispered, 'Tens of thousands of angels have welcomed him.' At Hankou, Griffith John grieved as for a brother. 'I was longing to see him again.' 'What a wonderful life your father's life has been! What a work God has enabled him to do! . . . Eternity alone can show how much China owes to Hudson Taylor.'

The Yangzi ship's captain flew his flag at half-mast. Flowers and wreaths were brought aboard at every river station, till the coffin was hidden. John Stevenson met the boat at Zhenjiang, and Dixon Hoste came up from Shanghai to conduct the funeral and commit the loved body to the ground beside Howard's mother, sister and brothers, Grace, Samuel and Noel, 'in sure and certain hope of a glorious resurrection'.

After the 'Liberation' of China in 1949 the little cemetery largely disappeared beneath industrial buildings, but in 1988 Hudson Taylor's great grandson made a discovery. The former British Consulate, scene of many episodes in this history, had become a museum. There, preserved, were the monument stones, the inscriptions all intact.[40] Only his 'dust' lay buried. His true monument is still alive and growing.

There at Zhenjiang, after the funeral, Geraldine wrote to Theodore Howard, 'Surely this is not death! He is gone from us. We know it . . . But *life* it is that has come suddenly into our midst, not death. He was caught away from us; he did not seem to die . . . We look up rather than into the grave, and cry instinctively – "My father, my father! – the chariots of Israel and the horsemen thereof!"' No one really mourned. The passing of Hudson Taylor was 'promotion to higher service'. No cortège but a simple Chinese procession of Chinese Christians and family and friends had been enough. The 'sound of trumpets' was on 'the other side'.

'More like translation than dying,' echoed Bunyan's concept of crossing the last river. When Valiant-for-Truth's turn came, Bunyan put into his mouth the immortal words spoken in effect by every valiant contender for the truth to follow him.

> My sword I give to him who shall succeed me in my pilgrimage,
> and my courage and skill to him that can get it.
> My marks and scars I carry with me
> to be a witness for me that I have fought his battles,
> who now will be my rewarder . . .
> 'Death, where is thy sting?' . . .
> 'Grave, where is thy victory?'
> So he passed over,
> and all the trumpets sounded for him on the other side.
> *'IT IS NOT DEATH TO DIE!'*

In Memoriam: the tributes agree 1905

Although the primary purpose of this biography is to bring as much as possible out of the archives, our summary has now to be even more selective, especially of tributes. Two days after the coffin bearing all that remained of Hudson Taylor to await the resurrection was transshipped at Hankou, the missionary community together honoured him with 'spontaneous and informal' tributes. It was not a time for criticism. Arnold Foster spoke of his having stimulated the zeal and exertions of all missions in China. W A P Martin, who recorded the occasion, recalled that in his *Cycle of Cathay* he had dubbed Hudson Taylor 'the Loyola of Protestant Missions in China'. And added that like Martin Luther he needed no honorific title. It was enough to know them by the names their mothers used. Griffith John remembered how a Shanghai missionary had denounced Hudson Taylor's enterprise as extravagant when seventy men and women were about to be sent inland. 'How many have you now?' John asked the Hankou secretary. 'Eight hundred,' he replied. 'Faith and prayer gave Hudson Taylor power with God,' John continued. 'Firmness and love procured nim a moral sway over the hearts of men.'[41]

A memorial article in *China's Millions* for July 1905 agreed. That over a million pounds sterling should have been contributed to the Mission without solicitation was only one indication. A column in the *Guardian* newspaper 'stated with striking precision the object and aim of Mr Taylor in his lifework: "He had but one aim – to preach CHRIST to China by any means that came to hand . . .

There was nothing so real to him as the individual soul, and GOD in CHRIST for its salvation."' 'Above all things his life exemplified the power of prayer; the value of faith in God . . . in a manner the simplest and most natural . . .' A member of the Society of Friends (the Quakers), remarked 'I regard his life as one of God's best gifts to humanity . . . not to China only, but in as real a sense to the Church of Christ in all lands.'

At a CIM memorial service in Shanghai, the Mission could be allowed some hero worship, but most tried to be objective. Dixon Hoste struck a note which he and others frequently repeated,

> (Hudson Taylor's) complete concentration on the fulfilment of his divinely-appointed trust and calling. He laid aside every weight (yet) he was no ascetic, putting (aside) pleasures for the sake of doing without them, (but) to live in the world as Christ lived . . . We can witness to his beautiful character . . . the sources of his influence lay . . . in his humility, love and sympathy. He never suggested that others should go into difficulty and danger while he remained in ease and safety. He led the way. And always with a contagion of love.

Griffith John knew him well enough to give an off-the-cuff biographical review.

> He loved the Chinese with a Christlike love . . . He lived for China and he died for China . . . Today the Mission (has) 200 central stations, 450 outstations (with) since its foundation a total of nearly 20,000 baptisms . . . It was ridiculed as the offspring of ignorance and religious frenzy; it is now universally respected as a grand civilising as well as evangelising agency . . .
>
> It was impossible to come into close contact with Mr Taylor without feeling that he was not an ordinary man and that as a Christian he towered far above most men . . . God and His love; Christ and His Cross, the Gospel as God's *one* remedy for China and the whole world, were realities to him. His trust in God was implicit . . . He lived in Christ and Christ lived in him . . .
>
> His heart was full of love . . . His love for the Chinese was manifest to all, and they knew it. His influence over men, and especially the members of his own Mission, was very remarkable (due) in great measure to his kindliness of heart, his humility and self-denial. He was the *servant* of all . . .
>
> Then he was a man of consummate commonsense . . . It was emphatically so . . . He knew how . . . to bring the best out of them . . . God had given him this work to do, and he did it. 'This one thing I do.'

On June 13 a memorial service in London at the Mildmay Conference Hall so closely connected with Hudson Taylor and the CIM drew representatives of many societies, not only to honour the Founder's memory but 'to re-examine the foundations of the work and . . . to rise with the assurance that the foundations are of God and stand secure'.

Excerpts by definition omit much else. Theodore Howard did not hesitate to draw the parallel of the apostle Paul in his many journeys, perils, sufferings, privations and 'the care of all the churches'. On Hudson Taylor's last journey in Henan the Christians of Taikang came out to meet him, only to learn that he was too weak to come further. At once they knelt in the road and prayed, 'What have we done, Lord, that our great archbishop who brought Thy gospel to inland China, should come so many miles, and stop just one day short of our city?' He came. Of his practical competence Theodore Howard wrote much as Griffith John had spoken:

> Hudson Taylor was gifted with remarkable powers of organisation. He paid the greatest attention to detail. He was extremely particular that the funds of the Mission should be dealt with in the most economical way, and that the accounts should be kept with scrupulous exactness . . . His humility, his tenderness, and his sympathy endeared him to all.

J E Mathieson, who had followed William Pennefather as director of the Mildmay Centre, introduced himself as 'a neighbour and friend of dear Mr Taylor'.

> You must remember [he said] that the great provinces of China are as big as many of our European kingdoms. With a pointer in his hand and a large map of China on the wall, he would take us from province to province and city to city, and name . . . the cities, towns or stations in which the China Inland Mission was working; and not only so, but name by name he would mention every missionary in every part of those vast provinces all over China [for he constantly prayed for each and for their children] . . . Because Hudson Taylor remained lowly in his own eyes, God was able to take that beloved man up and to make him a prince . . .

Eugene Stock, 'only one of the three Secretaries of the Church Missionary Society on the platform', took up Bishop Cassels' prayer of praise to 'the Lord and not men'. ' "He that exalted the humble and meek" – describes exactly what the Lord has done with Hudson Taylor.' On the Monday the newspapers had announced his death, and 'the first eulogy', published on Wednesday in the *Guardian*, had been written by a High Church bishop – 'in praise of the Lord for His grace in the man'. Eugene Stock continued:

> I have tried to think which of (the great missionary pioneers) our dear friend was like . . . John Eliot . . . Carey and Duff, Morrison and William Burns . . . and Gilmour . . . John Williams . . . and Allen Gardiner . . . Moffat and Krapf and Livingstone . . . some of them, as the world would say, much greater than our dear friend; but I do not find one among them exactly like him, and I am much mistaken if we shall not in the course of years . . . begin to see that Hudson Taylor was sanctioned, enabled and permitted by the Lord to do a work, not less than any of them, if, indeed, one might not say greater in some respects . . . He did a mighty work for China, and he did a mighty work for the Church at home . . . He was a man who saw visions, but . . . they were not fulfilled quickly . . . Ten years passed before more than two provinces had been occupied. But the day came . . . He braved the criticisms of the smoking-rooms of Shanghai, and let the women go . . . into the interior . . . What a work the women have done . . . and we owe it to the China Inland Mission which set the example! . . .
>
> It was not for the China Inland Mission that Hudson Taylor pled. I have heard him plead many times. It was China, and not China only but the world. It was just as much joy to him when men went to Africa or to Japan, or to India . . . Persia . . . South America or the islands of the sea . . . (George) Pilkington (p 63) had first intended to join the China Inland Mission; and yet without any hesitation whatever . . . dear Taylor would say to me, 'The Lord send you many more such men.'

R Wardlaw Thompson's tribute, as secretary of the LMS, was from one who had only met Hudson Taylor on public occasions.

> I felt that the oldest Protestant missionary society in China ought not to be backward in expressing to the largest and most remarkable missionary organisation in that country, its sympathy on . . . the loss of . . . a great missionary, a great leader of missions, and in a very profound sense a prince in the Church of Christ . . . The name and influence of Hudson Taylor have steadily grown and spread, even among men who have . . . criticised (his) methods severely. All great men must be criticised . . . They had to recognise the wonderful work God permitted him to do . . .

Doctor Harry Guinness, brother of Geraldine and Whitfield, and honorary director of the Regions Beyond Missionary Union, recalled visiting the Taylors in Switzerland. 'I noticed that in his prayers he was always praying for South America.' His friends, Dr and Mrs Kalley of Edinburgh, had long since won his support for their venture, 'Help for Brazil'. And Walter Sloan, who had known Hudson Taylor intimately for many years, referred to

> perhaps the most wonderful thing we have in the Mission . . . that family feeling that exists . . . Essentially one thing originated it. It was that large measure of God-given sympathy that Mr Hudson Taylor was able to afford everyone of the workers with whom he came into contact . . .

Walter Sloan then quoted from the story, fresh from the hand of Elder Cumming himself, of his conversation with Hudson Taylor in the train (p 114), and added

> God must have looked (for) someone weak enough to do such a work . . . and said, 'This man is weak enough. He will do.' Those of us who knew Mr Taylor most intimately, know that that was the genuine expression of the feeling and the thought of his heart, as he came into the presence of GOD concerning this work.
>
> Mr Taylor . . . in Chinese dress, came down to the side of a river in China one evening when the light was beginning to fade, intending to cross, and he hailed (a) boatman . . . A (Chinese gentleman), dressed in silk, when the boat came near . . . not seeing that Mr Hudson Taylor was a foreigner . . . struck him a great blow on the side of the head and knocked him over into the mud. I heard Mr Taylor say himself how the feeling came to him . . . to smite that man, and how God immediately stopped him . . . The man went to get into the boat, but the boatman said, 'No, I came across at the call of that foreigner.' The (gentleman) said, 'What! You a foreigner, and . . . you did not strike me back?' . . . Mr Taylor stepped into the boat and replied . . . 'Come in and I will take you . . . where you want to go.' On the way . . . he (told him) the gospel of salvation which had made him . . . treat in this way (one) who had struck him.[42]

An 'Appreciation' by John Stevenson carried weight after all they had gone through together.

> His meekness and lowliness of mind, which were so characteristic, made him pre-eminently gracious, gentle, and courteous in his bearing to all . . .

Besides his long seasons of private devotion in the stillness of the night or early morning . . . 'Pray without ceasing' was his constant habit in considering any question or difficulty that came up in the course of the day . . . His courageous stepping out in faith and definite committing of himself for this stupendous undertaking . . . marks the beginning of a distinct epoch in Church history . . . [And again:] No thoughtful person can seriously contemplate the history of the China Inland Mission . . . without being impressed with the statesmanlike tact and wisdom . . . in all the arrangements.

The variety of sources with one voice testified to the same truths. But what would be said after months or years had passed? The historian A H Smith of the American Board wrote in 1907, 'His name will never be forgotten as long as Christianity lasts.'[43] Eighty years later we have a wider and perhaps deeper perspective. After Hudson Taylor's death a meditation in his hand was found, dated 1874, when he was forty-two. It puts the praise into perspective, where it belongs, to God. In the period when he and the 'adolescent' CIM were at their lowest ebb, in Eugene Stock's words, 'pathetic in the extreme'; when Hudson Taylor was bedridden and apparently forgotten by many of his friends; when the Church's interest in China seemed non-existent; he had many lonely hours in which to think and pray. He opened a window on his soul, on the true Hudson Taylor who wanted to be like Christ, cost what it might.

If God has called you to be really like Jesus in all your spirit, He will draw you into a life of crucifixion and humility, and put on you such demands of obedience that *He will not allow you to follow other Christians*; and in many ways He will seem to let other good people do things that He will not let you do. Other Christians and ministers who seem very religious and useful may push themselves, pull wires and work schemes to carry out their schemes, but you cannot do it; and if you attempt it, you will meet with such failure and rebuke from the Lord as to make you sorely penitent. Others may brag on themselves, on their work, on their success, on their writings, but the Holy Spirit will not allow you to do any such thing; and if you begin it, He will lead you into some deep mortification that will make you despise yourself and all your good works.

Others may be allowed to succeed in making money, but it is likely God will keep you poor, because He wants you to have something far better than gold, and that is a helpless dependence on Him, that He may have the privilege (the right) of supplying your needs day by day out of an unseen treasury. The Lord will let others be honoured and put forward, and keep you hidden away in obscurity, because He wants some choice fragrant fruit for His coming glory which can only be produced in the shade. He will let others do a work for Him and get the credit for it, but He will let you work and toil on without knowing how much you are doing; and then to make your work still more precious, He will let others get the credit for the work you have done, and this will make your reward ten times greater when Jesus comes.

The Holy Spirit will put a strict watch over you, with a jealous love, and will rebuke you for little words and feelings or for wasting your time, over which other Christians never seem distressed. So make up your mind that God is an infinite Sovereign, and has a right to do as He pleases with His own, and He may not explain to you a thousand things which may puzzle your reason in His dealings with you. He will take you at your word and if you absolutely sell yourself to be His slave, He will wrap you up in a jealous love and let other people say and do many things which He will not let you say or do.

Settle it for ever that you are to deal directly with the Holy Spirit, and that He is to have the privilege of tying your tongue, or chaining your hand, or closing your eyes, in ways that He does not deal with others. Now when you are so possessed with the Living God, that you are in your secret heart pleased and delighted over the peculiar, personal, private, jealous guardianship of the Holy Spirit over your life, you will have found the vestibule of Heaven.[44]

CHAPTER SIXTEEN

TWILIGHT OF THE QING
1906–1912

Flood tide of reform   *1906–08*

A few quiet years remained to Ci Xi and Guang Xü, but very few. Reform movements were gaining strength and deepening gloom was descending on the centuries-old dynasty (1644–1912). Ci Xi could 'see in the dark', but the best Manchu leaders left to her could not. On her return to Beijing she had soon replaced the abundance of priceless *objets d'art* with which she liked to be surrounded. 'The wanton destruction of irreplaceable works of art, in (the) search for the Empress's hidden treasure' angered her still, but the gold plate, jewels and bullion bricked in at the bottom of a well had not been discovered. After her death the value was assessed as 99 million taels of silver and 1,200,000 taels of gold (about £22 million sterling in 1900) apart from wealth in kind.[1]

After the Russo-Japanese treaty signed at Portsmouth, USA, a boycott of American trade expressed the resentment of the people, especially of Canton and San Francisco over restrictions on immigration into the States; and Americans were murdered in Guangdong. But Anglo-Chinese agreements in 1906–07 provoked little resentment.

A new expression of nationality took the form of moral protest against the evil of opium smoking. The student generation 'imposed its will on old China', and the court seized its opportunity to assert itself. Thousands of Chinese students who flocked to Japan saw the benefits of an absolute ban on opium and and attributed Japan's dramatic ascendancy to immunity from its curse. And hundreds of thousands who had been under foreign influence in mission schools and colleges since the Boxer Protocol shared in the protest.

A strong, even daring imperial decree of November 21, 1906, ordered that all land planted with the opium poppy be converted to grain within ten years, that smoking by government officials cease, and that negotiations bring to an end the import of foreign opium within ten years. All such opium was shipped from British ports.

The timing at last was appropriate. The conscience of Britain had at last awoken. In December 1906 the British government agreed to restrict Indian exports by one tenth each year; an international convention (called by the United States and chaired by Bishop Brent of the Philippines) in 1909 resolved to limit smuggling and overt shipping of opium by other powers. When China reduced her production more radically than planned, Britain agreed at another convention on May 8, 1911, to end all imports by 1917; and in January 1912 another international convention at The Hague agreed on all controls needed to suppress production, trade and smuggling of opium. Opium smokers abandoned the habit by millions, but millions more found means to gratify their addiction. The price in loss of revenue was borne by China and Britain.

In two articles in *The Times*, Dr G E Morrison, the Peking correspondent, pointed out that three things 'had made it practically impossible for the British Government to continue . . . the gradual process (towards the abolition of the opium trade) by an annual 10 per cent reduction': 1. the resolution passed at the Edinburgh Conference of 1910 (in response to Benjamin B's strong pressure); 2. the Day of National Humiliation and Prayer arranged for October 24, 1910; and 3. the resolutions passed by the Chinese National Assembly. When Benjamin on his deathbed was shown *The Times* and the words, 'The agreement means the extinction of the opium trade within at least two years', he gathered up his strength and said with an effort, "A great victory. Thank God I have lived to see it."' He died on May 29, 1911. On May 7, 1913, 'the British Government announced, "We are in the satisfactory position of saying that the (opium) traffic is dead."' This admission that it had been 'traffic' rather than trade would have given the old warrior added satisfaction.[2]

The long, long campaign for 'national righteousness' to stop Britain's guilty trade had at last achieved its aims. Parliament had twice pronounced the opium trade 'morally indefensible', without taking action. So belated steps to end it by gradual stages had left no room for pride. Until the cultivation of the poppy was suppressed, Christian farmers had a losing battle on their hands. The income from sowing grain was far less than that from opium; and the birds of vast areas converged on grain fields to feed. When revolution weakened and removed government control, the country reverted to growing opium.

Desperate to regain its hold on the nation, the Manchu government introduced reforms designed to strengthen its own position.

Railways were extended in all directions; Western education was encouraged, and selected Manchus were sent overseas to study science, including political science. *The Times* of April 15 and 16, 1908, reported the cancellation of the imperial rescript of 1899 which granted official rank to Roman Catholic priests (p 284), a heavy blow and 'loss of face' to forty-six bishops and over a thousand priests.

Diehards of the old school had to be placated. In spite of her edicts, Ci Xi herself remained one of them. Manchu interests had to be protected if the dynasty was to survive.[3] And conservative attitudes among the literati and *laobeixing*, the Old Hundred Names (a term for all the people), had to be conciliated. On December 30, 1906, an imperial decree raised 'the sage Confucius from the level of the Sun and Moon, to which the high ministers of state paid worship, to the level of Heaven and Earth, to which the Emperor alone made ceremonial offerings'. And a college was established at his birthplace to perpetuate his teaching. When a move was made in 1914 to recognise Confucianism as the national religion, Protestants, Catholics and representatives of other faiths saw to its rejection. Japan sent strong Buddhist representations and funds to restore temples and teach Buddhism. The strong tide in favour of Christianity after the Boxer attacks had strong opposition to contend with.

Constitutional reform, however, became the decisive current in the floodtide of change. Constitutional government became the goal of thinking Chinese, literati, governors and viceroys. Liang Qichao, in exile, advocated the sovereignty of the people, with liberty and equality, but with a constitutional monarchy, at any rate at first. Zhang Zhitong still favoured retention of the dynasty, reformed. But Sun Yatsen stood squarely for revolution and a republic, and ridiculed Liang Qichao. Ci Xi was forced to resist him by favouring moves towards a constitutional monarchy – the crime for which she had been holding the Guang Xü emperor captive for years. The Japanese model looked preferable to Western concepts of monarchy.[4]

On September 1, 1906, she approved proposals made by an imperial commission, but typically specified no date for their promulgation. They would centralise government in favour of the Manchus, and curb the power of the predominantly Chinese viceroys. She formed a new Ministry of the Army, by which Yüan Shikai lost four of the six divisions in his foreign-trained Beiyang

(Northern) army. And in August 1907 she transferred Zhang Zhitong and Yüan Shikai, the two most powerful viceroys, to Beijing as Grand Councillors under her own eye. In September she enacted a National Assembly of Ministers.

Pressure for a constitution became so strong, with young Manchus supporting it, that Ci Xi drew up an Outline of Constitution in August 1908 by which an elected parliament would advise the emperor in whom legislative, executive and judicial power would reside in perpetuity. Provincial Assemblies were to be organised and inaugurated in 1908–10, and in 1910–11 a National Assembly. Implementation of government from 1911–15 and abolition of the distinction between Manchus and Chinese in 1915–16 would then bring in parliamentary rule by two houses. By then the nation should be educated in constitutional government subordinate to the throne. At seventy-three (in 1907) she appeared to believe she would live to see the new constitution implemented.

But the first declaration in her published draft fuelled the fires of revolution: 'The Great Qing dynasty shall rule over the Great Qing empire for ever, and be honoured through all ages!' Her reform began at the apex of the pyramid and left the broad base of the nation's millions almost where they were, without equal justice, protection from tax extortion, or from officials (not least herself) diverting huge sums into their own coffers. But by then she had only three months to live.

One hundred years since Robert Morrison　　　　　　　*1907*

'And so, Mr Morrison, you really expect that you will make an impression on the idolatry of the great Chinese Empire?' 'No, Sir,' he replied, 'I expect God will' (Book 1, p 119). Robert Morrison landed at Canton on September 4, 1807, and died on August 1, 1843, with a bare dozen converts to his name. 'The unsectarian unity of Morrison, Elijah Bridgman and others was not achieved. Each mission and each denomination started its own work. Even the two Anglican Church societies, American and British, went their own ways . . . "Unfriendly and wasteful competition" caused confusion in the minds of the Chinese, but "by no means as much as might be supposed"' (Book 1, p 306). The first General Inter-Mission Conference met at Hong Kong in August 1843 and initiated the translation of the Bible into literary Chinese. 'Despise not the day of small things!'

By 1905 the Protestant missionary community in China had risen to 3,445 with 178,000 communicants, and five years later to 5,144 with 15,500 Chinese colleagues and two hundred thousand communicants. The (wrongly named) 'Third' General Inter-Mission Conference of 1907 (after those in 1877 and 1890, discounting 1843) drew a total attendance of five hundred delegates and 670 others, including representatives of home boards. Convened for 1900 it had been postponed on account of the Boxer upheavals. But while Shanghai was filled with missionary refugees an informal conference had been held in 1901. More than twice as large as in 1890, the 1907 conference was still a forum of foreign missionaries with only six or seven Chinese delegates present. The Chinese Church remained fragmented by the denominational differences of the west.[5]

The conference also reflected a growing concern with organisation and education, in the name of the gospel but overshadowing it. Co-operation between the missions and the Chinese churches included plans for turning over the control of the Church to the Chinese – beginning with the union of churches of similar ecclesiastical order. The slogan 'China for the Chinese' was being heard, and a committee to consider the formation of a Chinese National Missionary Society was proposed. Again the old arguments for toleration of ancestral rites, including worship, were advanced. The conference held that the ultimate judge of the issue and what substitutes could be introduced must be the Chinese Church. But they agreed as before that 'the Worship of Ancestors is incompatible with an enlightened and spiritual conception of the Christian Faith'. 'Reverence for parents and affectionate remembrance of the dead' must be encouraged, but not worship. This time Hudson Taylor was beyond the reach of criticism.

On the proposition by Dr Thomas Cochrane, the conference recommended a Christian Federation of China composed of Chinese and missionary delegates in each province and meeting at national level at least once in every five years. This quickly led to developments such as the adoption of the goal of 'One Protestant Christian Church for West China'. But how were Anglicans, Baptists, Methodists, Presbyterians and others to agree on modes of baptism and admission to Holy Communion? Delay in the implementation of the 1907 agreement became permanent when three years later the continuation committee of the World Missionary Conference at Edinburgh superseded it. A common name 'to manifest the unity that already exists among all faithful Christians in China', the 'Christian Church in China', came into use.[6]

The 1907 Inter-Mission Conference also gave Richard a platform. John King Fairbank remarked in his volume on the Late Qing (*Cambridge History of China*, vol.10), 'The Chinese names of men like Timothy Richard and Young J Allen were on people's lips throughout the country. And had the *coup d'état* of September 1898 not taken place, it is very likely that Richard would have been invited (on Kang Yuwei's recommendation) to join the inner circle of imperial advisers.' W A P Martin, and Gilbert Reid by his 'Mission among the Higher Classes of China', focused their attention on the scholar-gentry of the empire and met with 'massive unresponsiveness' to the spiritual message of Christianity. 'The message (they) finally succeeded in conveying to Chinese of prominence turned out to be secular rather than religious in content.'[7]

Fairbank's essay on 'The professionalisation of missionary work' focuses on the difficulty the CIM faced after the turn of the century, with the hunger of educated Chinese for western learning and science. Schools, colleges and medical institutions had been used in the nineteenth century as adjuncts to the Christian gospel of Christ. But muting of this message to accommodate the objections of some students and officials, and its exclusion from the curriculum as in Richard's University of Shanxi (although permitted on the premises 'out of hours'), led to its gradual neglect and replacement. 'A significant shift towards professionalisation' developed as the subject and the missionaries themselves 'became increasingly divorced from evangelical aims'. 'Medical missionaries were beginning "to plan for the health of the entire Empire", and for many the creation of a healthy China was starting to assume as much importance as the creation of a Christian China.' The means of presenting the gospel was replacing the gospel itself. The CIM, among many missions, rejected this trend in the face of growing criticism and earned the label of 'unco-operative'.

That phrase 'the creation of a Christian China' summed up the shift in emphasis. 'Christian nations' had waged war on China, forced opium on China, wreaked vengeance on China. The concept of 'Christianising' the nation had seductively misled missionary thinking away from Christian truth. Timothy Richard maintained in the *Chinese Recorder*[8] that the gospel could be seen in two ways, as a means of saving the souls of individuals, or 'as a means of saving a nation through the collective efforts of regenerated souls'. But his understanding and use of the words 'souls', 'saving', 'regenerated' and 'conversion' no longer meant to him what they meant when he heard them in the Second Evangelical Awakening, nor what they still meant to most missionaries in China.

So much is heard of Timothy Richard that a paragraph by way of illustration is not out of place. At the Shanghai Conference in February 1901 he gave a long discourse on 'How a Few Men may make a Million Converts'. Because one soul is more valuable than the whole world and many were open to adopting a new religion, he reasoned, while the Student Volunteer Movement was aiming at no less than 'the evangelisation of the world in this generation', an acceptable gospel offered in an acceptable form could see millions accepting it. Change mission methods and change the appearance of the gospel. So he summarised the leading religions of the world to show features they had in common. One of them, Christianity, he subdivided. Early Christianity 'had higher ideals than Judaism' and other religions. 'By making God universal instead of merely national, by substituting faith for old ritual and higher ethics for lower, by mystic union with God and consequent immortality, Christianity was an advance on other religions.' But 'Reformed Christianity', still higher than early Christianity, he claimed, was conquering the world by substituting individual liberty of conscience for papal authority, by improved education, by letting the people have more voice in government, 'by enlightened uplifting of all nations and races' – still with no mention of Christ. The religions of the world must be studied, for 'the power of the Holy Spirit is believed in by them all. Not that they use our phraseology, but they have the same ideas.'

'When (the missionary) has given an outline of the material, social, intellectual, and religious advantages . . . and has persevered till they thoroughly understand, then the conversion of China will be accomplished as suddenly as the explosion of a mine . . . Why should we follow antiquated methods of mission work when the new produces results a thousand times better?' Richard asked. The gulf between him and orthodox missions had become unbridgeable; a gulf of his own making. 'A thousand times better' in his view could only refer to the hunger for education and reform, for 'uplift'.

Without any wish to be at odds with any others in the missionary community, the orthodox societies and individuals by continuing the 'foolishness' of preaching 'Christ crucified' with profound effect, found themselves accused of schism and failure to co-operate in the 'better, wiser' way. 'Mass conversion', 'conversion by the million', through persuasion and the intellect should come first, they were told. 'Conversion' of individuals would follow in great numbers. Education, reform, progress, literature, health, good servants of the gospel if rightly used, became all important to 'progressive' colleagues. Christianising and 'uplifting' China became the gospel – substitutes for 'the glorious gospel of the grace of God' in Christ, and 'the offence of the cross'.

Nearly seventeen thousand Protestant schools in 1890, had become nearly fifty-eight thousand by 1906, four hundred of them higher level institutions. In the interests of consolidating local churches, the CIM also multiplied its Christian schools, purposely restricting their size. Propagating the gospel of reconciliation with God through the death of Christ could not but result in social reform.

Kang Yuwei and Liang Qichao became Richard's true friends, and only the violent collapse of Guang Xü's reforms during the Hundred Days kept Richard from the inner sanctums of the empire. But Kang Yuwei himself went no further than to adopt a Christianised Confucianism, and later tried to make Confucianism the national religion. The Christianity that he and others embraced was largely nominal. As secretary of the Society for the Diffusion of Christian and General Knowledge (SDK), later the Christian Literature Society (CLS), Richard poured out material for publication faster than his printers could produce it. But (as J K Fairbank points out) in the first decade of the twentieth century national reforms sped away from missionary influence, 'the Chinese quickly discovering that they could reject God and still have progress'.[9]

As we have seen in earlier volumes (HTCOC Book 6, Index p 518), the 'indigenous principles' of self-government, self-support and self-propagation had for long been discussed by missionaries, and practised with varying degrees of success by those who grasped the meaning of them (HTCOC Book 6, p 411 note 14). John McCarthy at Hangzhou (HTCOC Book 5, pp 293, 333–5) and Dixon Hoste with Hsi Shengmo in Shanxi (HTCOC Book 6, pp 411–12, 419, 476) had clung to Hudson Taylor's guidelines, while all too many doubted the maturity of their Chinese colleagues and fellow Christians and kept control of them, sometimes with a heavy hand. Church members welcomed both kinds of care, patronage and financial props as much as liberty with responsibility. Then drastic removal of foreign supervision during the Boxer period taught many churches to stand on their own feet, and Hoste tried hard to inculcate a preference in them and returning missionaries for Chinese autonomy with missionary help. As every community has its leading members, so the Church no less reveals its potential if given the chance. In many regions he failed. In some he succeeded. In most of China the missions returned to preside with loving condescension over Christians who only lacked the opportunity to mature in action.

The CIM – 'a rope of sand'   1905–12

The epithet 'a rope of sand' was applied to evangelical Christianity in the nineteenth century to express its intellectual weakness. 'Thank God it is so,' Henry Venn would say; 'so is the seashore,' able to withstand the buffeting of waves. When Hudson Taylor, the moving spirit of the CIM, began to fail, some recalled the phrase and spoke of the Mission's approaching disintegration.[10] In Griffith John's words, 'It was predicted that the retirement of its founder from active control would be the death of the Mission; but the Mission has never shown greater stability, vitality and force. To this Hudson Taylor replied, "If it be of God it will last; if it be 'my work' the sooner it goes the better."'

The gradual relinquishment of control to a deputy who proved himself while acting for the General Director was the first explanation of survival. The readiness of the founder to stand by his principle that control in China must be exerted by directors in China, and to trust his deputies, was the second. The humility he had shown, continued by D E Hoste in leading from the front rather than imposing control on the Mission from a base, ensured a smooth transition.

Hoste's letters to the rank and file, finding encouragement from the limitation of massacres to three provinces, rather than harping on the sufferings endured, inspired his colleagues. He led and they followed, though he remarked to Hudson Taylor at first that a 'GD' seemed to be the Mission's 'whipping boy'. A godly, strong man, he looked beyond the disaster of 1900. That was over. A new, changing China offered unprecedented promise as a field for evangelism, and he grasped it. His policy from the start became advance, expansion, with consolidation of churches already founded. Pioneering of remote regions continued, especially among the minority 'tribes' of West China, with striking success. But the original strategy (Book 5, pp 373–4, 412–3) of starting in the chief cities and spreading from them to smaller cities, towns and villages was pressed home. While mission centres increased in number, their outposts multiplied. Instead of travelling in circles looking for a welcome, missionaries met with more invitations than they could accept. W W Cassels on a one thousand-mile itinerary through eleven counties of East Sichuan found 'a great movement towards Christianity'. In twenty to thirty different places he found any number from a handful to one or two hundred wanting to 'enter the church'. This proven strategy had to be followed against the current of the 'modern' alternative policy.

Those who speak and write of conflict between Timothy Richard and Hudson Taylor over Richard's philosophies too often show confusion over the chronology and only partial knowledge of the facts. Their spoken disagreement ended in 1890, and Hudson Taylor retired at the turn of the century. Stevenson and Hoste had to answer the new reasoning. They did it not by debate but by the largest society in China quietly treating it as contrary to divine revelation, and continuing to work effectively as before. In this they had the unquestioning support of the Church in the sending continents, with steadily increasing numbers of reinforcements, of mission stations, organised churches, Chinese church workers and believers baptised. By the beginning of 1908 members of the CIM exceeded nine hundred, and one thousand by 1912. Communicants numbered more than nineteen thousand in 1908 and four years later over twenty-six thousand.[11] By 1905 the annual total of baptisms recorded by the CIM had risen from hundreds to thousands, seven hundred in 1895, 2,500 in 1905 and 2,800 in 1908, and rose to 4,500 and five thousand in 1913 and 1914. The 'rope of sand' was never more than a figment of imagination.

'At the Shanghai Missionary Conference of 1907 a resolution was unanimously adopted calling for united prayer that God would raise up men with special evangelistic gifts whom He could use in reviving the life of the Churches, and in gathering in the tens of thousands who already had some knowledge of the gospel.' A great spiritual awakening was in progress in Korea. After the conference Jonathan Goforth (Personalia p 667) travelled through Korea to Manchuria 'spreading the flame of revival' there also. And in 1908–09 Albert

Lutley and Wang Qitai, an evangelist, preached in Shanxi a call to repentance, confession, forgiveness and response to the sufferings of Christ, 'very quietly, without demonstration or excitement'. From there they carried it to Shaanxi and then Sichuan. Everywhere 'the sense of God's personal presence (was) frequently so real that the whole congregation would fall on their knees with their faces to the ground' in prayer and confession. The wave of 'revival' continued to sweep from province to province until in 1911 public meetings became impracticable when the empire became convulsed by armed revolution.

The legacy of Hudson Taylor's resolute 'contending for the faith that was once for all entrusted to the saints' (Jude 3 RSV), continued by the Mission, paid rich dividends decade after decade. No vocal opposition to the exponents of 'another gospel' was needed. Persistence in preaching 'Christ crucified' and in 'well-doing' ensured a harvest as great as could be gathered and conserved at the time, and contributed to the ultimate millions of believers in China today.

The CIM also undertook social service on a wide scale. In 1907, only thirty years after the appalling drought and famine in North China which took the lives of between nine and twenty millions (Book 6 pp 181, 466), abnormal rains and flooding devastated an area as large as England in Jiangsu, Anhui and Henan. Relief committees raised large sums of money, and to allay the fears of the viceroy, Tuan Fang, Protestant missionaries promised not to claim indemnities for lives lost in distributing relief. Instead of providing money for the starving refugees to buy food, a policy of supplying flour in payment for work was adopted.

Ten or more members of the CIM among others took part. The report of one, O Burgess, assisted by a woman recorder, graphically described his achievements at Qingjiangpu. Using 1,500 men they first filled up a three-acre swamp to a depth of eight feet to make dry land. They then surrounded an area of inundated houses with a raised road linked to a highway and continued through the city, isolating lakes of water later to be drained dry. Meanwhile three thousand more men dug out ten miles of river bed and a new canal, to drain away the flood water. They enclosed the city with a raised road and nine connecting roads, some of which they paved with stone, widened and deepened all main drains, and made ramps over the city walls for the thousands of men carrying earth into the city. Four large and nine smaller stone and timber bridges and a stone canal lock completed the major work. By the end Burgess was controlling eleven thousand workmen in addition to his three thousand to four thousand mud carriers. 'Men, miles and mud' filled his memories of those months. His assistant recovered from typhoid fever, but Dr J E Williams of the CIM, Dr J Lynch, the Zhenjiang port doctor, and two American Presbyterians gave their lives.[12] Care of the whole person, not only the soul, took different forms. Hospitals, opium refuges and leprosaria began to play a greater part.

The medical arm of missions   1807–1912

Even amateur knowledge of Western medical methods gave unskilled missionaries the means for helping the sick. Many instances in these books have shown in passing how it was put to good use. The Ridleys' extraordinary success with locally bought materials at Xining during the Muslim rebellion (pp 231–7) had its humbler counterpart through the years wherever missionaries were at work. But the development of medical missions was slow in coming, largely because medical men and women were slow in venturing out to China. Ten medical missionaries in China of all missions in 1874, forty years after Peter Parker, and nineteen in 1881, was the pace of the CIM's experience too. If enough of the right type of doctor had joined the Mission, great progress would have been made (HTCOC Book 6, pp 317–20). But of all societies, sixteen hospitals in 1876 and sixty-one in 1889, with forty-four dispensaries, gave the measure of how ambitiously those who did come aimed high with little equipment. Motivation was consistently Christian, and orthodox Biblical teaching was given in parallel with treatment. Relief of physical suffering and disarming prejudice were accompanied by the gospel for patients' spiritual needs.[13]

Hudson Taylor's two years' apprenticeship at the London Hospital had made him enough of a doctor to be able to take over William Parker's hospital in Ningbo (HTCOC Book 3, pp 187–91) and perform amputations, but even after graduating as a member of the Royal College of Surgeons in 1862 and forming his own mission with a score or more of colleagues, all medical care of them and of his own family devolved upon him. In the 1870s came a transition period in which two or three doctors shared the responsibilities with him. Then Harold Schofield arrived in China in June 1880, followed by William Wilson and E H Edwards in 1882, and several experienced missionaries took short courses and qualified as doctors, Douthwaite, Cameron, George King and George Parker among them.

We can only speculate on what Harold Schofield might have achieved at Taiyuan, had he not died of typhus. And, for that matter, Howard Taylor with his high qualifications in medicine and surgery if severe deafness had not handicapped him increasingly after his missionary career began, and if Hudson Taylor had not recognised that Geraldine's value as an author far outweighed whatever service she might have given in an inland city. The part they played in the Student Volunteer Movement and in non-medical rôles probably outweighed in effect what they would have been able to do medically.

Dr Millar Wilson, the Taiyuan martyr, had opened another hospital at Linfen at his own expense. Dr William Wilson developed one at Hanzhong in south Shaanxi and later at Yibin (Suifu) in Sichuan. After Kaifeng reluctantly opened its gates to missionaries (the very last provincial capital to do so, not excepting Changsha) Drs Whitfield Guinness and Sydney Carr began medical work there in 1902. The only Jewish colony in China was to be found in Kaifeng, and a Chinese Jewess became their first patient. In 1891 the rising star of China, Yüan Shikai, a Henan man, called Dr Howard Taylor to attend his mother, dying of cancer. In recognition of his services no less than Li Hongzhang presented Howard Taylor with an honorific tablet, and as a result he occupied the city of Chenzhou (pp 376–7) in 1895.[14]

The Henrietta Bird Memorial Hospital began work at Langzhong Sichuan in 1903 and the CIM opened another hospital at Taizhou, Zhejiang, in 1904. In Changsha, Drs Keller and Barrie began their influential hospital on the site bought with the viceroy's gift (p 508). Other hospitals on a smaller scale were opened by Dr F H Judd at Shangrao (Guangxin), Jiangxi, by Dr W L Pruen at Chengdu and Guiyang, by Dr E S Fish at Anshun for the aboriginal Miao people, at Lu'an in Shanxi, at Zhenjiang by Dr G A Cox, and at Dali, Yunnan, originally by Dr W T Clark. The Borden Memorial Hospital and leprosaria followed at Lanzhou, Gansu, in memory of William W Borden who died in Cairo while studying Arabic in preparation for work among the Muslims in north-west China.

By 1906 the CIM had seven hospitals, thirty-seven dispensaries and 101 opium refuges. As action progressed against opium production and smoking, refuges decreased in number, but in 1912 there were still fifty-seven in action. Three years later there were ten

CIM hospitals, sixty-eight dispensaries and fifty refuges (and, incidentally, 135 boarding-schools with 4,295 students and 237 day schools with 5,412 pupils). Medical work by other missions expanded more rapidly. Of 3,445 Protestant missionaries in China in 1905, 301 were doctors of medicine, of whom 94 were women, in 166 hospitals and 241 dispensaries. The (British) Baptist Missionary Society sent Dr H Stanley Jenkins to Xi'an in 1904 and Andrew Young in 1905. Dr Cecil Robertson joined them, and these three were in Xi'an during the fighting and massacres of Manchus and missionaries in 1911. Young was in Britain in 1912 when Jenkins and Robertson died of typhus, so he returned at once to replace them.

The medical profession as a whole did not recognise the overriding importance of primary health care and preventive medicine until another seventy or eighty years had passed. So the emphasis remained on curative medicine and surgery. Even Western medicine was still a young science when the cataclysmic changes of 1908–12 once again threw China and missions into turmoil.

Death of a Grand Dowager 1908–12

When the emperor died on November 14, 1908, and Ci Xi on the 15th, suspicion of foul play was inevitable. Accounts of what happened in the palace varied with their sources. The Times' own correspondent in Beijing attributed the dowager empress's death, immediately following the emperor's, to foul play against her. 'The more natural explanation' appeared to the historian Hosea Ballou Morse to be action in keeping with her character during her long reign. Realising that her own death was approaching, and unwilling that Guang Xü should outlive her, to guide the destinies of 'her' empire at so critical a time, 'she took the steps necessary to avert the calamity'.

Charlotte Haldane in The Last Great Empress of China gave first a more lenient account and then the inside story from the diary of Der Ling, Ci Xi's longstanding lady-in-waiting on whom Charlotte Haldane constantly drew for inside information. Der Ling was the daughter of a Manchu nobleman and a secret Christian, partly educated in France. She claimed to have received the confidence of Ci Xi and on occasion of Guang Xü also. Charlotte Haldane frequently used her statements because of 'the ring of truth' in them. In 1908 Der Ling was no longer at court, but stated that the details had been given her by a former principal eunuch.[15] Sudden deaths and palace intrigues were always carefully covered by plausible versions of what took place, and the royal deaths were no exception.

In August 1907 when Ci Xi was seventy-two she suffered a slight stroke, affecting her face, but 'her mind and tongue remained as sharp as ever'. The emperor, a prisoner since 1898, was deeply depressed and ailing, but not seriously ill. 'I feel in my heart that I shall outlive the Old Buddha,' he indiscreetly wrote in his diary. But Ci Xi told the chief eunuch, Li Lianying, that the emperor's illness was incurable. In that world of fantasy, this had a clear meaning. As he became weaker she relaxed some of the restrictions she had imposed on him, no longer requiring the long ritual obeisance on his knees in her presence.

In 1908 his condition deteriorated considerably. She was well enough to celebrate her seventy-third birthday picnicking on the palace lake, but bouts of dysentery were dragging her down. On November 10 Guang Xü's condition degenerated further and she summoned Prince Qing to attend her appointment of the emperor's successor.

For a third time she violated dynastic law. She summoned the Grand Council, ascended the throne and 'spoke with all her wonted vehemence and lucidity'. Again overriding the Council's views and the rightful succession she named Yong Lu's grandson, Pu Yi, the two-year-old son of the young Prince Qün by Yong Lu's daughter, as heir apparent in place of Pu Lun. The child was doomed to become the last tragic occupant of the dragon throne. Finally on November 14 when the thirty-eight-year-old Guang Xü lay dying, Ci Xi came to see him, and showed no emotion unless of relief. When she herself died the next day, it became 'very widely believed' that she had committed or caused to be committed the murder of yet another emperor before taking her own life.

Der Ling's account was explicit, based on details given her by Zhang De, the former assistant to the chief eunuch, Li Lianying. When the chief eunuch had heard of Guang Xü's belief that he would outlive Ci Xi and be able to avenge himself on his enemies, not least his eunuch jailers, he told Ci Xi, 'It would be beneficial to all concerned were His Majesty to die before Old Buddha.' At once she understood and replied, 'His Majesty is desperately ill . . . Those preparing his medicines have perhaps been careless. Hereafter, Li, you will personally administer them to Guang Xü.' She had given him the licence he had intended. Systematically he poisoned his prisoner. Der Ling wrote that Guang Xü died in agony after being dressed in burial clothes while still conscious.

Edicts announced the child emperor's reign title as Xüan Tong, and he was placed on the Dragon Throne with Ci Xi's own status in future to be Empress Grand Dowager, retaining final authority over all others. On November 15 she fainted at her midday meal and after recovering summoned the Grand Council. In their presence she declared that she was dying, and transferred all power to Prince Qün as regent, 'subject only to my instructions', thereby retaining supreme power to the last moment. She dictated a long, lucid justification of herself and her lifetime of misdeeds, and died at 3.00 pm.

Death of a dynasty   *1908–12*

The Mongol Yüan dynasty had lasted only eighty-nine years, and the Qing dynasty 268 (by 1912). After the decadence of the late Ming empire, the early Manchus, Kang Xi, Yong Zhang and Qian Long, did well. But by 1800 'the sun had begun to set and the moon to wane', as the proverb put it. 'Domestic rebellion and foreign invasion' to which decadent rulers could not adapt, doomed the dynasty to extinction. While Meiji Japan initiated far-reaching reform and became a modern state, Qing China in the lifetime of Ci Xi disintegrated and foundered.[16]

The whole Protestant missionary enterprise in China had been set in a climate of turmoil. From Morrison in the Canton 'factory' to the martyrs and fugitives of 1900, the penetration of China by the gospel had been precarious or hazardous at best. Opium wars, Taiping and Muslim rebellions, Tianjin and other massacres had found Manchu rule either inadequate or conniving in persecution. But the Chinese people recognised Manchu inflexibility and Manchu weakness as the chief cause of China's vulnerability – and at last, China's hope for the future. Only an oversimplified epitome of a long, confused mêlée is possible here.

Kang Yuwei's campaign for progressive, constitutional reform, and Sun Yatsen's avowed revolutionary campaign for the overthrow of the dynasty, germinated in good soil. When the Manchus, after the dowager empress's death, tried to strengthen their own position against the ethnic Chinese, they sealed their own fate. No Chinese in the empire held a higher place than Yüan Shikai as Senior Guardian of the Heir Apparent and member of the Grand

Council concurrently with Zhang Zhitong – until on January 2, 1909, the regent, Prince Qün, ordered him to resign and return to his home province of Henan. (Zhang Zhitong died on October 5 the same year.)[17] Wealthy and astute, Yüan knew he had alienated the reformers by betraying the reforming emperor in 1898, and the reactionaries by opposing the Boxers. He saw the approaching end of the dynasty and had the grandest personal ambitions. So he bided his time until the reformers needed him to fulfil their aims.

Ci Xi had set her constitutional reforms in motion, designed to gratify reformers while consolidating Manchu power. The provincial assemblies met in October 1909, 'little more than debating societies'. But collectively they demanded that the national *parliament* should be convened within two years, only to be rebuffed by a decree of January 10, 1910. The first national *assembly* opened at Beijing on October 3, 1910, and it also demanded that the first parliament be summoned early, with the Grand Council responsible to it! No inspired Ci Xi remained to wave the magic wand, and Prince Qün, the regent, in his early thirties had no experience behind him.

On May 8, 1911, an imperial decree went so far as to abolish the Grand Council and two others, creating a Cabinet and Privy Council in their place, with old Prince Qing, president of the defunct Grand Council, as prime minister. This cosmetic move, under 'a decrepit, irresolute, wily, corrupt and inefficient old man', was transparently doomed to failure. The national assembly was called for October 1911, but on October 10 armed rebellion broke out at Wuchang, spreading to Hankou and Hanyang. Risings in other principal cities of the empire succeeded with little fighting in central and southern China.[18]

But in some of the provincial capitals with large Manchu garrisons and 'Manchu quarters' occupying many acres, resistance led to massacre. At Xi'an rebellion was interpreted as licence to rob, burn and kill.

> The massacre of Manchus in the city lasted five days. Even though they fell on their knees and begged for mercy, they were slain, excepting some of the women and children . . . Others roamed about till they died of hunger. Not reckoning those who jumped into wells or were buried alive in underground passages, there was . . . a funeral expense for 21,000 corpses, many of them being Chinese. Even at the lowest estimate, 15,000 Manchus lost their lives, these five days . . . The rich were robbed without mercy. The highest Chinese official in the city had to pay a million taels to be permitted to live.

Mutinying soldiers were mostly to blame.[19]

E R Beckman of the Scandinavian Alliance Mission of North America escaped with his youngest daughter when his wife and two other girls of eight and thirteen were massacred in Xi'an. With them died one other missionary schoolteacher and four children between ten and fifteen years of age. 'They passed through severe suffering. Their (stoned and) pierced bodies were found buried in a field.' An instructor at the Military Academy at Xi'an, C T Wang, escorted the survivors to Hankou, and other missionaries escaped unharmed from Xi'an and other Shaanxi cities, although 'robbers' in thousands were bent on attacking them. C T Wang reported to 'His Excellency the President of the United Provinces of China' and the Vice-Minister of Foreign Affairs wrote personally to E R Beckman in July 1912.

Ten years later the Xi'an Manchu quarter still lay devastated. Looking out from my home at the Jenkins-Robertson Memorial Hospital, separated only by a high wall from the ruins, I (AJB) could see the great city wall away on the other side and everywhere between, a battlefield. No house appeared to stand higher than a few feet, and every yard of earth had been deeply dug, probably in the search for valuables. Skulls and bleached bones still littered the ground, a lasting image of the frenzy of 1911.

The court recalled Yüan Shikai, giving him sweeping powers to save the dynasty. He retained command in the north and retook Hankou, but too late. Kang Yuwei's brand of reform, favouring a constitutional monarchy, had been made hollow by Manchu rejection of parliamentary sovereignty, and Sun Yatsen's followers took control of the revolution. On February 12, 1912, 'the emperor' abdicated and the court retreated to the palace refuge in Jehol, last used in 1860 (HTCOC Book 3, pp 216, 257). The empire and dynasty had fallen apart.

Rise of a republic[20]   *1896–1912*

'Sun Yatsen', the name by which the West knows the architect of the revolution, was secondary to his personal name, Sun Wen. Chinese use his revolutionary name, Sun Zhongshan (Sun Chungshan). After his kidnapping and release in London in 1896 (p 220), he stayed in Europe studying social and political developments, and enunciated his Three People's Principles, the famous San Min Zhu Yi: Nationalism or National Consciousness; Democracy, or

People's Rights; and Socialism or People's Livelihood, which he liked to compare with Abraham Lincoln's 'of the people, by the people, and for the people'. When he returned in 1897 to Japan and was joined in exile by his rivals Kang Yuwei and Liang Qichao – refugees from the coup that ended the Hundred Days of reform (p 269) – his attempts to find common ground failed. His republican aims and their 'Emperor-Protection Society' clashed 'like water and fire'. So he turned to plotting armed action, with little effect. But when an independent uprising at Wuhan in 1900 was disclosed prematurely, Sun came to be seen as no longer an outlaw but a patriot.

In 1905 he organised a revolutionary party, the Tong Men Hui, which adopted his Three Principles. As a rallying-point it received strong support from literati and progressive army officers in all provinces, and risings multiplied between 1906 and 1911. A major attempt to take Guangzhou (Canton) failed in April 1911, but six months later success came at the Wuhan conurbation of three cities. Great unrest followed the nationalisation of railways in which many had invested savings. On August 24, 1911, more than ten thousand demonstrators clashed with troops in Chengdu, Sichuan, and fighting between the government and people of Sichuan intensified. The two issues, the railway controversy and outright revolution, 'fused into one'.

As the Sichuan imbroglio became more serious, part of the Hubei 'New Army' was sent to maintain order, leaving Wuchang vulnerable. On October 9 the accidental explosion of a bomb betrayed the existence of secret arsenals, and rebel army units attacked the offices of the governor-general and army commander, controlling the city on the 10th. The former chairman of the Hubei provincial assembly then urged other provinces by telegram to declare independence of the Qing court and persuaded the foreign consuls in Hankou to maintain strict neutrality. Within six weeks 'fifteen provinces, or two-thirds of all China seceded from the Qing dynasty'. Shanghai was lost to the revolution early in November, and Nanjing on December 4, 1911.

Sun was in Denver, Colorado, when he read a newspaper report of the Wuchang revolt. He suppressed his desire to hurry back to China, and embarked on ambitious but successful diplomacy with Britain and France to check aid to the Manchus and prepare for recognition of a new government. He reached Shanghai on Christmas Day and on December 29 was elected provisional president of the Republic of China. His government-to-be 'adopted the solar calendar in place of the lunar one and named January 1, 1912, as the first day of the republic'.

When the helpless Qing court turned to Yüan Shikai, he named his own terms, four measures to please the revolutionaries and two to make him the most powerful man in China. The regent capitulated. The Qing cabinet was replaced by a 'responsible' one, and control of the army and navy and adequate funds passed to Yüan. Shanxi seceded on October 29, Prince Qün resigned as regent and Prince Qing as prime minister. Yüan Shikai replaced him, and showed his power by recapturing Hankou and later Hanyang. But two divisional commanders and Yan Xishan (Yen Hsi-shan), the revolutionary leader of Shanxi, prepared to march on Beijing to prevent Yüan's return. He foiled the attempt, formed his cabinet, ensured military control of the capital and began negotiations with the revolutionaries. Only the presidency would satisfy him. He threatened to fight for a constitutional monarchy. But when the Qing diplomats abroad on January 3, 1912, urged the abdication of the emperor, Yüan told the revolutionary Nanjing government that he 'would induce the voluntary abdication of the Qing throne' if the presidency were offered to him.

To avoid civil war Sun stepped down, adroitly telling Tuan that he had accepted the honour of *provisional* president until Yüan could replace him. But he used the news media to make Yüan's appointment conditional upon declaration of his support for the republic, and provisional election by parliament. Yüan obtained the court's compliance, with Nanjing's offer 'to treat the deposed Qing emperor with the same courtesy as a foreign sovereign', to let him use the Summer Palace, and give him four million taels annually. These 'generous' concessions were later modified. The abdication was made public on February 12, 1912, 'and with that . . . the last of China's twenty-five dynasties came to an end'.

But that was not the end of the Ci Xi story. Her funeral a year later was the costliest in living memory. And her mausoleum, containing rich treasure, was so strong that dynamite was used by titled looters in July 1920 to break it open. The imperial remains were hacked in pieces and scattered, and the loot found its way to the markets of the world. After she died the fragile Qing dynasty had survived for only three years. And the tragic figure of Pu Yi, 'Henry Pu-yi' as he became, drifted from place to place, patronised by changing masters.

CHAPTER SEVENTEEN

DAWN OF A NEW CHINA
1912–89

Yüan 'sows the dragon's teeth'[1]   *1912–16*

The Hudson Taylor story has been told. But has it? In 1989, a long lifetime since his death, we find him again the butt of hostile criticism. Why? Called a blackguard, an enemy of China 'masquerading as a servant of God', the real Hudson Taylor does not fit the description. No one has ever been a truer friend or given his life, health and family more entirely for China's millions. So, if the allegations are to be understood, we must add a sweeping bird's eye view of China, the CIM and the Chinese Church after the Revolution of 1911–12 and under the People's Republic.

In 1912 the doomed dynasty had foundered, but the 'rope of sand' had held. The national banner of hope, in horizontal bands of red, yellow, blue, white and black (for the five constituent elements of the nation), waved over the new Republic of China. Christianity seemed to stand for progress, and a spirit of enquiry was abroad. But the tables had turned and Christians, not least the missionaries in their rebuilt premises, had become cities of refuge for hunted Manchus.

Protestant Christians were being brought into local, provincial and national government. Vice-president Li Yüanhong, fresh from capturing Nanjing, said: 'China would not be aroused today as it is, were it not for the missionaries.' And Huang Xing, one of the leading republican generals, replied to Bishop J W Bashford of the American Methodist Episcopal Church:

> Christianity is far more widespread than you realise. Its ideals have largely pervaded China . . . it brings a knowledge of Western political freedom, and . . . inculcates everywhere a doctrine of universal love and peace. These ideals appeal to the Chinese; they largely caused the Revolution and they largely determined its peaceful character.[2]

Amazingly, April 27, 1913, was set aside by the ruling cabinet as a day of prayer when Christians worldwide were asked to pray for

China and the government. Services were held throughout China and in many churches in Europe and America.[3] The grounds of the historic Altar of Heaven were opened for evangelistic services where formerly the emperor prostrated himself on behalf of the nation. Although a minority in the population of China, by the time of the revolution 'an élite of educated, alert (men of) integrity and resolution' were ready to take responsibility. The expectations of all missions in China had become greater than they had ever been. And it was no dream.

Looking back to Robert Morrison, risking death simply for learning the language, we marvel at what was achieved in a brief century. During the first half of it China was a closed land. But history moved on inexorably, from anti-barbarian dynasty to pro-Western republic. Within two years the result proved to be hollow. The first enthusiasm waned in 1914, reaction set in, reaching full force after 1922, and republican China became fragmented. In this debacle the Church faced even more difficult times than at any time during the dying dynasty.

The story of the CIM through the twentieth century has been graphically presented by Leslie T Lyall in *A Passion for the Impossible*. Even a summary would be out of place here. The 'open century' merges with the heyday of missions and ends with the eclipse which looked to some like the end of both Church and mission in China. Far from the Revolution of 1911 or the Second Revolution of 1916, forty years of upheaval ended in greater turmoil than even the Second World War. For missions the 'open century' ended in 1950. For the Church, the body of Christ in China, another valley of the shadow of death proved yet again the seedbed for new life, growth and maturity.

But another glance at the perspective of the few decades under the Republic may broaden our vision and understanding. For it reveals a nation groping for self-government and stability, and missions polarised in their day of opportunity by dissension over motives and methods. Four decades of greater political instability under fumbling politicians and revolutionaries, and of personal insecurity during years of civil war and brigandage, still saw greater expansion and progress than under the dynasty. Most painful and regrettable was the divergence and distrust between the two schools of thought, the theologically mutable and the conservative orthodox who continued under criticism and pressure, unchanged in loyalty to the unchanging gospel. Mutual respect, friendship and

comity to avoid overlap and competition were constantly sought,
but compromise on irreducible essentials was unthinkable. Bishop
Stephen Neill understood the dilemma when he wrote in his *History
of Christian Missions* (p 431):

> . . . Scores of Christian schools could record that every single student
> had been baptised before leaving school. This rising Chinese Chris-
> tianity . . . was little interested in the question of personal salvation.
> Not 'How can I be saved?' but 'How can China live anew?' – this was
> the burning question. It had little to do with the Churches. Most of
> these young people . . . had a very real loyalty to Christ and to His
> message (but) what they stood for was 'the Christian movement in
> China'.

The two currents of missionary emphasis were like oil and water.

The first phase of the Republic lasted from 1912 until 1916, typical
of revolutions in which thought and energy had concentrated on
taking power, but relatively little on applying it to government. A
middle-class intellectuals' revolt had largely left the peasant pro-
letariat out of their reckoning. The people wanted peace. A medley
of strong men, reformers and generals jostled for influence and
power, and each failed through personal inadequacies, inexperience or selfish ambitions.

Yüan Shikai, last of the great viceroys, secretly inserted in the
imperial rescript of abdication a clause to show that he personally
derived the provisional presidency of the Republic from the Qing
emperor. After forty-five days in that office, Sun Yatsen resigned in
Yüan's favour, and Yüan's inauguration took place on March 10,
1912.

After some hesitancy the provisional parliament made Nanjing
the capital, but Yüan stayed at Beijing. From the Wuchang rising on
October 10, 1911, the 'Double Tenth', to the establishment of the
Republic on January 1, 1912, only eighty-three days had elapsed.
But to Sun's grief few showed concern for reconstruction and the
welfare of the people. His three-stage plans for reconstruction were
ignored, and the way was paved for two attempts to restore the
monarchy and for the chaos of rivalry between warlords.[4]

As provisional president, Yüan Shikai at once made a travesty of
the Republic. 'He stamped out the tender shoot of democracy' and
in less than a year rescinded the constitution. He appointed his own
henchmen to the ministry of foreign affairs, internal affairs, war and

navy. By turning on his charm, Yüan disarmed potential opponents. Only minor ministries went to the architects of revolution. Sun Yatsen and Huang Xing, 'the Napoleon of the Chinese Revolution', were made directors of a national railway system. The cabinet had become Yüan's puppet.

But by December the revolutionary Tong Men Hui and four satellite parties had amalgamated as the Guomindang, the Nationalist Party (KMT: Kuo Min Tang), which won a landslide victory in the parliamentary elections. A chain of assassinations followed, leaving Yüan Shikai heavily under suspicion. When troops surrounded the parliament in session and Yüan dismissed Nationalist provincial governors, six southern provinces declared independence. Yüan crushed this Second Revolution within two months and left his generals in control of the Yangzi area – as little more than warlords.

Yüan's personal ambitions knew no limits after that. With a crowd of ill-disguised men of military bearing in mufti surrounding the parliament building and shouting, 'Elect the president we want or do not expect to leave!' Yüan on the third ballot became substantive president. He dissolved the Nationalist Party, revoked the credentials of 358 members of parliament, and eighty more later, and contrived to become 'legally' the lifelong president, ruling without a cabinet and with the right to appoint his own successor. 'On December 23, 1914, (he) performed at the Altar of Heaven the immemorial rites which have been the sole prerogative of the emperor. The journey from his palace to the temple grounds was made in an armoured motor-car!'

So by 1915 he was ready to be made emperor. He accepted Japan's infamous Twenty-one Demands which would have robbed China of all remaining freedom, and secured the publication of an article by the president of Johns Hopkins Uniuversity favouring a monarchy in China on the lines of the constitutional monarchy of Japan. 'Yüan himself remained conspicuously aloof', denying any wish to be made emperor. But a 'representative assembly' of his choosing approved the reintroduction of a monarchy and petitioned Yüan to accept the nomination. He 'reluctantly' acceded on December 15 and the next day decreed that his reign would begin on January 1, 1916. He had misjudged the nation.

Sun Yatsen had fled to Japan after the Second Revolution and in 1914 organised a Chinese Revolutionary Party to fight Yüan and his betrayal of the Republic. In exile he worked on the implementation of his Three Principles, the San Min Zhu Yi. War began with the capture of a government naval vessel; an ultimatum was delivered to Yüan; an anti-monarchist army came into being in Yunnan; and on December 25 the province declared its independence. Guizhou and Guangxi followed suit; in Shandong another anti-monarchist army was formed; and two of Yüan's strongest generals declined to lead armies against his opponents. Yüan's dream evaporated.

Trying to revive a cabinet he watched helplessly as five more provinces declared independence and prominent citizens of nineteen provinces also refused any longer to recognise him as president. Such utter loss of face was insufferable. 'Overcome with shame, anxiety and grief, Yüan suddenly died (of uraemia) on June 6, 1916, at the age of fifty-six.' But he had 'sown the dragon's teeth', the seeds of warlordism – power to him who seizes it. Vice-President Li Yüanhong took over the presidency, and the 1912 constitution was restored.[5]

Ill winds blow some good[6]   *1912–16*

A bias in favour of Christianity at a time of such fluctuation added momentum to Church and missions. All factions had this attitude in common. Sun Yatsen to his dying day professed to be a sincere believing Christian.

The CIM had passed the membership mark of one thousand including associate members, with 2,500 Chinese colleagues in 1,200 centres and secondary schools largely for the children of Christians. Many missions frowned on sending Chinese students abroad to study theology. Too many who went chose not to return or came home unable to readapt to the conditions they found. So small theological and academically lower training colleges sprang up in China.[7] The CIM saw the identical problem in taking potential church leaders out of their natural environment and making scholars of them in an age of politically militant students. And, too readily, zeal to equip themselves for service in the Church became blunted by academic study. The genius of training men and women 'on the job', by systematic teaching and example as had been practised by the pioneers for decades, was capable of unlimited expansion.

Acknowledging the good work being done by Christian universities and theological colleges, the CIM chose to retain the method used by Jesus with his disciples, Paul with his companions and

Hudson Taylor, Dorward and many others with their Wang Lae-djüns and Yang Cunlings.

Educationists looked for academically trained Chinese in the churches connected with the CIM and many like-minded missions, and saw few. But the majority of missions, among them the CIM, saw the institution-trained clergy, pastors and evangelists preaching over the heads of their hearers or lacking 'heart knowledge' of basic Christian truth.

A strong letter to the *Chinese Recorder* from an American Southern Baptist, 'an ardent educationist', stressed that huge sums of mission money were going into secular education, that the colleges were not producing evangelists and ministers but business-men and government officials, cultured but not Christian graduates. The Chinese Church could not take over the colleges and were pauperised by dependence on foreign funds. It must be shown by missionary example that preaching the gospel is the primary object of the missionary's calling, and familiarity with the Word of God the first tool to be mastered.[8]

The orthodox societies deliberately equipped peasant leaders for peasant churches and educated men and women for the type of town and city churches they were to serve. 'Bible Institutes' produced men and women by the hundred, well fitted for their particular work. This policy was misunderstood by critics, but has stood the test of time and adversity. The survival of the Church in China through years of attempts to exterminate it is attributable to its grass-root leadership with the encouragement of the few heroic intellectuals. Dr Frank Keller's 'Biola' travelling Bible school,[9] in boats on the Hunan waterways, studying while they evangelised, had its counterparts in several provinces.

These early years of the Republic also saw undreamed-of access to Chinese schools, colleges and army camps. The experience of Arthur R Saunders, the tortured fugitive of 1900 (p 399), at Yangzhou, the scene of the Hudson Taylor family's trial by riot in 1868 (HTCOC 5, pp 77–104) is an example. Fifteen thousand troops under General Xü Baoshan were stationed in and near the city, potential recipients of many thousands of pamphlets and New Testaments. Saunders consulted a junior officer and was summoned to an interview with the general. 'Preach to them too!' Xü told the astounded Saunders, and appointed his brother, the military gov-ernor of the city, to accompany him from camp to camp. 'We were received with military honours at each camp, and (had) personal conversation with the regimental officers.' The officers themselves then distributed the booklets to the men and Saunders preached for half an hour. General Xü gave Saunders a pass to admit him to any camp at any time. It bore the general's seal and the words, 'A deputy of Jesus to preach the Gospel'. A month later General Xü invited him to preach every Sunday to his officers and afterwards to the troops, saying, 'Get the officers and you've got the men.' The first year of such work ended on April 27, 1913, the day of prayer called by the government in Beijing.[10]

During the next decade, and often afterwards in the other parts of China, missionaries had similar experiences. Between the eruptions of violence, calm periods permitted exceptional freedom for the Church to expand in strength and influence. But by 1916 the First World War had been raging for two years and the spectacle of so-called Christian nations at each other's throats disillusioned China. Meanwhile a renaissance of Confucianism and Buddhism, abetted by Japan, returned the nation to its previous religious imbalance.

A decade of warlords[11]   1916–26

Yüan Shikai had at least maintained some order. After his death and Li Yüanhong's assumption of the presidency, chaos and disorder engulfed the nation. Li was a soldier, the captor of Nanjing, but not a statesman. His premier, Tuan, declared war on Germany without consulting parliament or president, so he dismissed him. In Tuan's support the encircling provinces of Zhili, Shandong, Shanxi and Shaanxi and others declared their independence and prepared to march on Beijing. So President Li called on the swashbuckling military governor of Anhui, Zhang Xün, to come to his rescue, and on his insistence dissolved parliament. Zhang Xün then threw off restraint, and restored the ex-emperor Pu Yi to the throne, on July 1, 1917. On the 12th, Zhang himself was driven out with his twenty thousand troops, so ending the hapless Pu Yi's brief 'reign'.

Such disregard of the Constitution of 1912, as much by the president as others, led Sun Yatsen to launch a Constitution Protection Movement under a military government at Canton in August 1917, while Premier Tuan again took control in the north. By declaring war on Germany again, Tuan naïvely secured a loan from Japan in August 1918 'to sustain the war effort', and sent troops to curb Sun Yatsen's 'revolt'. But clashes within Tuan's own political 'cliques', as they were called, sabotaged his campaign and brought about his fall. In the process, 'the former bandit', Zhang Zuolin (Chang Tso-lin), came into prominence, in 1922 holding Manchuria against the Beijing regime. And another warlord, Wu Peifu, emerged in support of the in-and-out of office President Li.

By 1923 'disgusted with politics in the north, public morale hit rock bottom'. The only hope lay in the south. But in 1918 southern warlords had again driven Sun Yatsen in deep frustration to Shanghai. Frustrated but not despairing, he reorganised his Revolutionary Party and revived the name Chinese Nationalist Party (Zhongguo Guomindang). By skilful manoeuvres he regained power at Canton, and formally established a republican government on April 2, 1921, only to be thwarted by a turncoat who forced him once again to escape by warship to Shanghai. His Constitution Protection Movement had so far proved abortive.

During 1923 and 1924 fierce in-fighting between the warlords of several provinces compounded the chaos. When Wu Peifu, commanding a Zhili army of 170,000 men, went north to confront Zhang Zuolin who was already advancing on Beijing, the Christian general Feng Yüxiang occupied Beijing with his own 'National People's Army' on October 23, 1924. He forced the usurping president (Cao Kun) out of office, reorganised the cabinet, and with others invited Sun Yatsen to Beijing to discuss peace and reunification.[12]

Sun had cancer and his strength was failing, but he arrived on December 31, 1924, to a spontaneous welcome by a crowd of one hundred thousand. Within three weeks his condition worsened and he died on March 12, 1925, a disappointed man, apparently unaware of his high place in history. The Republic had brought the nation more suffering from lawlessness and war than misrule by the Manchus. But he was soon to be honoured as Father of the Revolution and the inspiration of opposing factions for decades to come. His embalmed body was buried at Nanjing four years later, and he was canonised as Lenin had been.

Within the Nationalist Party a small group of men (Sun among them) had begun studying the Russian Revolution of 1917 and Marxist-Leninism. The First World War had shaken his faith in Western democracy, and he looked to Russia for advice and example. A delegation under Mikhail Borodin came to Canton at his request, and helped him in the reorganisation of his Guomindang on the Comintern model. Sun had also established a military academy with German instructors on the island of Whampoa in the

Canton river, under young General Jiang Jiaishi – to be known to the world as Chiang Kaishek. Sun and Chiang had married the beautiful Soong sisters, Chungling and Mayling, daughters of a Methodist minister, and were close allies. In 1926, after Sun's death, Chiang embarked on his 'northern expedition' which, after an historic rift with the communist party, was to break the power of the northern generals. After fifteen more years he was to preside with Churchill, Roosevelt and Stalin at the overthrow of Hitler and Tojo. Then the tide of success was to turn.

K S Latourette's droll comment on missionary life under the warlords, that it was 'an extra-hazardous occupation', was an understatement.[13] Among many deaths from disease the CIM suffered the loss by typhus of W W Cassels and his wife in 1925, a major blow. Until 1926, being a foreigner still conferred some protection in some circumstances; but the kidnapping and murder of missionaries by bandits or unruly troops or looting mobs occurred all too often. The shooting of demonstrating Chinese students by Shanghai police on May 30, 1925, intensified nationwide agitation. And the inept shelling of Wanxian in Sichuan by a British gunboat aggravated the indignation.

'China for the Chinese' increasingly became the spirit of the Church as well. Foreign prestige slumped dramatically. The consuls called upon their nationals to withdraw to the coast, and by the end of 1926 fully half the large missionary force had complied. Two hundred CIM centres remained staffed and active, and in some regions more Christian 'literature' was sold than previously. New believers with the courage to be baptised in 1925 numbered 4,577. The National Christian Council of China was formed in 1922, and in 1927 the Church of Christ in China, a minority organisation with the strongest influence. Membership 'on the basis of a simple confession of faith in Jesus Christ as revealed in the Scriptures' satisfied some and left the interpretation of the words too wide open to reassure others. Neither the Anglican nor Lutheran Churches became members.[14] Nor did the churches connected with the CIM. But the new tide of xenophobia was rising.

The Two Hundred   *1927–32*

For Christians in China, whether foreign or Chinese, 1927 was most alarming, 'the hour of apparent disaster'. Always an embarrassment and anxiety to their consuls, whose responsibility was to avoid international incidents and to maintain prestige, missionaries had a predilection for trouble. Newspapers called them 'trouble-makers'. A London daily ran the headline 'Millions Wasted in China. Missionaries' Dreams Shattered', and another stated, 'Hardly a trace remains in China today of all those vast missionary enterprises to which so much money has been subscribed by the British and American public' – journalists' fantasy.

In fact attacks increased and at Nanjing several foreigners were killed, missionaries among them. So the American and British ministers urgently ordered the wholesale evacuation of all in the interior. Memories of 1900 were still too fresh. At least nine-tenths complied. Of 8,300 Protestant missionaries, nearly four thousand left China for furlough, two thousand never to return. Two-thirds of those remaining congregated in eight port cities with no foreseeable prospect of returning to work. Less than 1,500 remained inland. Of the CIM's 1,185, over 213, mostly Continental associates, were free to stay up-country and did so. Many of the rest believed that to stay would have been less dangerous than to leave their friends and travel. One father and child were shot dead on the way from Guizhou and the young mother wounded and held hostage with other companions. But if they had stayed, the persecution of Christians, 'running dogs of imperialism', would probably have been worse.

Schools, hospitals and homes were destroyed, others were taken over by troops for billets. Dr Whitfield Guinness died of typhus. And the magnificent Dr George King Jr, tall, powerful, gifted and popular, after organising the evacuation of the Gansu missionaries by five rafts on the Huang He (Yellow River) from Lanzhou to the railhead at Baotou on the Mongolian border, was swept away by strong currents and drowned. In the crucible of suffering, the Church in China had been brought closer to destruction than in 1900. But again God knew what he was doing. A stronger Church emerged.

Contrary to Latourette's mistaken understanding of the CIM's strategy, church-planting and church-building were basic policy from the beginning. Frank Houghton, a future General Director, wrote in 1932,

> Hudson Taylor's intention from the very first was to establish self-governing and self-supporting churches, but gradually there had been a tendency . . . to look upon the indigenisation of the Chinese

Church as a goal to be aimed at rather than as the foundation of all our policy as a Mission . . . If the Chinese leaders, whose development had been inevitably arrested by the very competence . . . of their foreign friends, were enabled . . . to demonstrate that (God) had indeed given gifts to His Church, then the evacuation would prove to be a blessing in disguise.

So it proved. The uprooting from preoccupations, and the involuntary crowding together at the coast, also led the CIM to pray and consider the future in a series of conferences. Had the work of consolidating the expanding churches led to neglect of 'preaching Christ where His name is not known'? Hudson Taylor's catchword, 'Always advancing', was recalled. Xinjiang had received no missionary reinforcements for twenty years. Unevangelised regions still abounded. Walled cities stood waiting. Tibet, Mongolia, the aboriginal 'tribes' were hardly touched. We might be 'an army of contemptibles', but was this not the time to get ready to advance again?

Dixon Hoste, 'a quiet man (and) most of all a prayerful man and therefore a wise man' 'was calmly directing operations' with the 1,185 missionaries and over four thousand Chinese colleagues. He called for a careful calculation of how many new recruits could be deployed as soon as the way opened. The sum total of 199 led him to express the China Council's conclusion as 'some two hundred new workers are required within two years'.

Three missionaries were murdered in Jiangxi just before the appeal for the Two Hundred was made known. And in the same week as the General Director was writing, hopes of the reunification of the country were shattered by the outbreak of a major civil war. Within a few months eight foreigners were murdered, thirty were held to ransom, five in Henan alone. Many more were robbed or captured briefly. Yet 1,200 or more men and women approached the Mission with a view to going to China.

The first party sailed in 1929 when the evacuees were returning inland, 185 by November 1931 when peace was restored in many regions, and the last of 203 on the last day of the year. Among them were six doctors.[15] Others became gifted evangelists and Bible teachers. Fourteen became superintendents, one the Mission treasurer from 1941–71, and another the Deputy China Director and Overseas Director in South-east Asia. A price had to be paid. Some died in their first year, others before they could achieve much. And Hudson taylor's 'bombshell' policy was followed – the Two

Hundred were deployed with little language or experience, to learn the hard way in pioneer conditions. Some found it too hard. Others thrived on it.

In 1932 Dixon Hoste at the age of seventy-one laid down his directorship. The China to which the Two Hundred came was still a' sad travesty of the true China. Opium growing had become widespread again, an anodyne for the intolerable distresses of the tormented populace. The 'wars of the ricebowls' had left them hungry. To pay their troops the warlords taxed the people, and when they could mulct no more, the disbanded soldiers 'lived off the land'. China had sunk into an abyss of misery.

The advent of Mao   1927–36

As the revolutionary troops of Sun Yatsen entered Changsha in 1911, a young man of eighteen stood watching. Mao Zedong joined the army for a year before becoming a student. He read widely and by 1920 was a committed Marxist. The first secret congress of the Chinese Communist Party founded on July 1, 1921, four years after Lenin came to power, saw Mao present. Its policy of infiltration had already begun. Mao joined Chiang Kaishek and Zhou Enlai (Chou En-lai) with Sun Yatsen's Nationalists at Canton, and with his fellow-communists began to dominate the Guomindang (KMT). In 1926 he took part in the Northern Expedition of Chiang Kaishek's five hundred thousand-strong army to quell the warlords and unify the nation. But after the pacification of Hunan and the fall of the three cities destined to comprise Wuhan, the Communists with the help of three or four KMT generals they had won over, challenged Chiang's leadership. The irreparable rift between them and the Nationalists took place, and a life-and-death struggle began.[16]

During 1927 Stalin's influence was strongly felt in China, and revolutionaries went to be trained at a Sun Yatsen University in Moscow. Several uprisings in south China showed the nature of things to come. After one setback Mao found a haven in the Jinggangshan (Ching Kang Shan), a remote mountain range in Jiangxi close to the Hunan border, and in 1928 was joined by Zhu De (Chu Teh) and others. While Chiang completed his northern expedition, the Communists created a strong base and set up a Soviet of Jiangxi peasants organised for revolution and guerrilla tactics against Chiang's Nationalist garrisons (map p 552).

Chiang Kaishek recognised this as his greatest obstacle to the unification of China, and embarked on a policy of 'encirclement and extermination'. In the north he had broken the power of Zhang Zuolin, last of the warlords, and on August 4, 1928, transferred the capital from Peking to Nanjing, in keeping with the 1912 Constitution. All restrictions on missionaries' travel in the interior were removed. On October 22, 1930, when Christianity was still despised as an alien religion, Chiang astounded China and the world by being publicly baptised. He never denied the faith, and his funeral in Taiwan in 1976 testified strongly to his Christian convictions.

In 1931 and 1932 a Japanese invasion of Manchuria (when Pu Yi was made puppet emperor of 'Manchuguo'), with a second front attack on Shanghai, gave enough respite from Nationalist pressure for the Communists to score some successes. Other Soviets were formed in south-western Fujian and in Hunan between Changsha and Yichang. But a truce with Japan allowed Chiang to return for his campaign against them with seven hundred thousand men in October 1933. Encircled and deprived of necessities, the Communists had to break out or be overcome. But ideological power struggles within their own ranks threatened their survival, until they embarked on their historic 'Long March' on October 15, 1934. Pounded by the Guomindang, they outdistanced the Nationalists, trained for positional warfare, and crossing into Guizhou they reached Zunyi (Tsunyi) in January 1935.

Mao's personal struggle had been against Chiang Kaishek, but also against the Communist Party (CCP) politburo. His guerrilla tactics using rapid mobile units to confuse the enemy and 'pick them off one at a time' had been singularly successful, but until the break-out he was virtually under arrest by his political opponents. Their military 'adviser', in command as 'Li Te', was a German Communist named Otto Braun. The Long March officially began with eighty-five thousand soldiers, fifteen thousand civilian officials and the wives of thirty-five high leaders, but heavy losses had been sustained. In vehement speeches at Zunyi, Mao nailed responsibility for the debacle on Braun and the extremist politburo, won the argument and became head of the CCP and Secretariat.

Mao eliminated 'Li Te' and his own rivals, chose north Shaanxi as the strategic destination of the thousands now under his command (another Soviet base had been established there), and set off for the wild regions of far western Sichuan. In July 1935, a veteran of the party, Zhang Guotao, challenged Mao's choice of destination and led a column of his own towards the Tibetan borderlands and possibly Xinjiang. All endured extreme hardships on the march northwards through the mountainous border regions and Gansu until finally eight thousand survivors under Mao reached Wuqi, north-west of Yan'an (map p 552). In October, they joined the local Red Army corps of seven thousand. Other columns arrived later, including Zhang Guotao's, to bring the total strength under the undisputed leader Mao Zedong to thirty thousand. On the Long March they had tramped and fought over six thousand miles. They captured Yan'an and moved their headquarters there a year later, in December 1936.

The CIM on the Long March[17]   1934–35

Marxist-Leninist doctrines carried to extremes caused intense suffering to the people of China. Even Mao Zedong resisted the liquidation of landlords, large and small, and redistribution of land to the very poor only, excluding any better off. China's Bolshevik politburo meted out death and destruction wherever they took power. Mao favoured levelling down the more prosperous peasants and small landlords, but only to equality with the upgraded poor. The politburo alienated millions by their atrocities. In Jiangxi alone one hundred thousand homes were destroyed, 150,000 so-called 'bad elements' were exterminated, and one and a half million refugees fled to other provinces. Changsha was sacked and the CIM's Bible Training Institute became the Communists' temporary headquarters. Henry S Ferguson, a CIM flood-relief worker, was put on show in place after place as a hated imperialist, for weeks indomitably preaching Christ until executed. Sichuan suffered similarly in 1933.

Two of the Two Hundred, John and Betty Stam, were taken prisoner at Jingde (Tsingteh) in south Anhui on December 6, 1934, by a sudden advance of thousands of Communists. Condemned to die as 'imperialist spies', they wrote, 'We praise God, peace is in our hearts . . . May God be glorified whether by life or death.' A Chinese who pleaded for their two-month-old baby to be spared, received the retort, 'Your life for hers,' and was killed where he stood. On the morning of December 7, John and Betty Stam were stripped of their outer clothes, tightly bound and led out barefoot to be executed. A Christian medicine-seller pleaded on his knees for them and shared their fate. John was beheaded first. Betty quivered, fell on her knees beside him and the great sword flashed again.

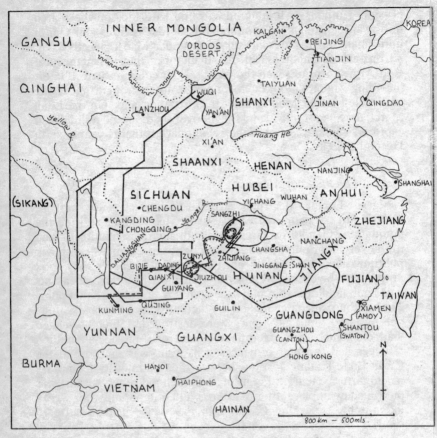

CAUGHT UP IN THE LONG MARCH
Hayman and Bosshardt learn the hard way

Their calmness throughout, and the look of joy seen on John's face afterwards impressed bystanders. The baby and the headless bodies were found by an evangelist thirty hours later.[18]

At Jiuzhou (Kiuchow) in Guizhou five more members of the CIM and two children had been captured on October 1 and 2. Alfred Bosshardt, of Switzerland, and Rose, his English wife, Arnolis Hayman, an Australian, Rhoda his wife, and two children, and Grace Emblen were 'tried' and a ransom of Mex $700,000 demanded. The women and children were an encumbrance to an army on the march, and were released, but Grace Emblen only when exhausted by a week of forced marches. The men were held captive and repeatedly threatened with death. They could not be silenced. Hermann Becker of the Liebenzeller Mission, a German CIM associate, had been on friendly terms with Ho Long, one of the Communist leaders, and acted as go-between to raise the ransom money. And three Chinese named Chai, Yang and Ho, who doggedly persisted as messengers in finding and gaining access to

THE BOSSHARDTS BEFORE THE LONG MARCH

the 'Red' leaders, won the praise of the Communists for their courage. They took their lives in their hands each time.

For over a year, while still together, Hayman and Bosshardt trekked north-eastwards into Hunan at Sangzhi (Sangchih). There they parted company. When Arnolis Hayman was released on November 18, 1935, after 413 days' captivity, Bosshardt said, 'Pray that I may recklessly preach Christ.' He was taken by a different route all the way back and on through mountainous Guizhou to Dading and Bijie before heading south into Yunnan. Not until Easter Day, 1936, five months later, after 560 days as a prisoner, was Alfred Bosshardt also set free near Kunming, with dangerously advanced beri-beri.

They had shared the exciting life of their captors, under Xiao Ke (Hsiao K'eh), the twenty-five-year-old 'general'. Always on the go, harried by the Nationalists, suffering scarcity and privation, and brutally flogged when they tried to escape, they won the Communists' admiration and sympathy by their cheerfulness and transparent love not only for each other as Christians but for their captors. Fifty years later, in 1985 when Xiao Ke, head of the Peking Military Academy and the last surviving general of the Long March, was in Paris, he read in a newspaper about Alfred Bosshardt and asked his embassy to make inquiries. He was put in touch with the ninety-two-year-old veteran, and gratefully ordered that Alfred Bosshardt's inspired account of their experiences (dictated from his sick-bed in Kunming and published by Hodder and Stoughton in 1936) be translated into Chinese. Devoid of rancour, *The Restraining Hand* is a timeless classic of missionary literature to be read and re-read.[19]

Too many missionaries suffered at the hands of the ubiquitous Communists before and during those years for the full story even to be summarised here. Russian influence and outright intrusion into Xinjiang, making the area an economic satellite, provided a strong rearguard to Mao's forces in north Shaanxi, and directly threatened the CIM's distant pioneers. In 1935 'the intrepid Trio', itinerant pioneers of the Gobi Desert oases and Xinjiang from June 11, 1923 to August, 1936, were arrested and held prisoner for months. These women were inseparable: Eva French of the Boxer rising in Shanxi, the leader of the three, Francesca French, Eva's younger sister, and Mildred Cable, the youngest, the author and platform figure, called 'our star' by the others.[20]

From Huzhou in Shanxi to Suzhou in Gansu took fifty days'

travel; from Suzhou to Urumqi (Dihua) thirty-six days; from Suzhou to Chuguchak sixty-two days, from Suzhou to Kashgar ninety-six days (map p 45). They covered the Suzhou–Urumqi route four times and the oasis area six times. Their books about their own decades in the Gobi Desert, and biographies of George Hunter[21] and Percy Mather of Urumqi (Dihua) are classics of exploration and adventure, as well as of missionary pioneering in Central Asia between Gansu, Kashgar and Chuguchak, far, very far from fellow Christians and colleagues. Eva was sixty-seven when they were forced out of Central Asia. They picknicked on her birthday in the open Gobi, on a precious jar of meat paste and 'the last lick of Chuguchak honey'.

Seven of the Two Hundred had crossed the Mongolian Gobi by Ford truck to Hami with Hunter in 1932 – a journey plotted for them by the great explorer Sven Hedin. They joined Percy Mather on November 12, in time to be with him through the next Muslim uprising.[22] When the storm burst upon them in January, ten thousand Qazaqs (Kazakhs) and Turkis attacked Urumqi, and the nine missionaries were overwhelmed with more wounded and typhus-ridden patients than could be handled. Worn out by incessant work, Mather and Emil Fishbacher, the only doctor, had no stamina to resist typhus when it claimed their lives.

The loss of Percy Mather stabbed George Hunter with greater pain than all his other experiences. 'When I knew that he must die I gave one loud cry to God for mercy, but then . . . I stilled my heart to accept His decrees.' Even so, 'in his loneliness he sometimes called aloud for his friend'. When the Russians took control, the young men were told to leave Xinjiang, and Hunter's greatest ordeal began. He was held prisoner by the Russians for eighteen months, deprived for one year of a Bible, and tortured by the NKVD, the Soviet secret police (1934–43), before being deported by plane to Lanzhou. [I write with feeling, for after his torture and deportation I saw him as a patient at our hospital in Lanzhou.] A shattered old man, he set off for the Xinjiang border again to re-enter when he could, but died a few weeks later among Chinese Christians at Ganzhou (now Zhangye) on December 20, 1946.

Decade of war and opportunity   *1936–46*

About fifteen years of the 'open century' remained; years in which Roman Catholic and Protestant foreigners could snatch

GEORGE HUNTER IN URUMQI
before the KGB took control

opportunities to continue their work, wars and rumours of wars permitting. Their success in this period is another epic of resilience. Unrelenting civil war between the Nationalists and Communists continued, while a New Life Movement to heal and strengthen the tortured nation was pursued. The firm policy of 'Generalissimo' Chiang Kaishek and the KMT, to break the power of the Communists, consolidate the nation, and then, but only then, to lead a unified China against the Japanese aggressors, called first for a determined offensive against the Yan'an strongholds. A north-western army was to attack from Gansu and a north-eastern army from Shaanxi and Shanxi, under the 'Young Marshal' Zhang Xüeliang (Chang Hsüeh-liang), son of the old warlord Zhang Zuolin (p 545).

The rise of the German Nazis, Italian Fascists and Japanese militarists had alarmed the Soviet Comintern. National Communist parties were urged to form alliances with other anti-Fascists against the common enemy. To be free to fight the Japanese, Mao needed a firm assurance of safety from the KMT. He launched a propaganda campaign with persuasive slogans: 'Chinese must not fight Chinese', 'War with Japan, not Communists', and popular pressure mounted. Mao's men infiltrated the two KMT armies and led the generals to favour a 'United Front'. On December 3, 1936, Chiang flew to Xi'an to restore morale, and on the 12th was put under arrest by Zhang Xüeliang and mutinous troops. They demanded among other things an end to civil strife, the release of political prisoners, the right of assembly and freedom to organise a people's patriotic movement. Asked what he required for his captivity he replied, 'A Bible only.'

The world was stunned, Chiang was needed to fight the Japanese. And faced with mounting Fascism in Europe, Moscow needed friendship with China to preserve stability with Japan, and could not stand aside while the Nationalists avenged themselves against Zhang Xüeliang and Mao. 'Chou En-lai emerged from behind the mountains to offer mediation.' From 'anti-Chiang, anti-Japan' the Communist party line changed overnight to 'Ally with Chiang against Japan'. A repentant 'young marshal' flew back to Nanjing with Chiang, on Christmas Day, to be spared all punishment except house arrest. And the Nationalist campaign against the Communists was called off, though the blockade of northern Shaanxi continued. The United Front against Japan consisted of two distinct and uncooperative parts, Communist in the north and Nationalist elsewhere. But while civil war ceased under the truce, subversion increased on a large scale. Communist cells in Nationalist China multiplied, and Nationalist morale declined.

By 1937 Japan's ambitions overflowed from Manchuguo. Control of the five northern provinces, isolation of China from Russia, domination of China's policies at home and abroad, and an East Asian Hegemony and New Order embracing all of south-east Asia were only beginning. After the Marco Polo Bridge incident at Beijing, when a Japanese soldier was killed, Japan's army swarmed over north China. Then Shanghai was occupied and Nanjing taken with the massacre of forty thousand and bestial excesses against survivors. Wuhan fell in October 1938 and Yichang at the mouth of the Yangzi gorges soon afterwards. Japanese control extended one or two hundred miles each side of the river.

Chiang Kaishek made Chongqing his wartime capital and spurned peace offensives, fighting where he could. But all ports were seized and the necessities for war prevented from reaching the west except by the French railway from Vietnam to Kunming, by air from Burma and by the hastily made 'Burma Road'. Missionaries surreptitiously left Japanese territory and crossed the Yellow River floods to reach 'Free China'. One convoy of cars and trucks driven by new missionaries travelled north from Haiphong in Vietnam to Chongqing, taking the octogenarian Sir Montagu Beauchamp with them. He died at Langzhong on October 26, 1939.[23]

There were times when China trembled on the brink of collapse. After Japan had attacked the US Pacific Navy at Pearl Harbor, Hawaii, on December 7, 1941, bringing America into the Second World War, the seemingly unstoppable Japanese war machine swept over south-east Asia, occupied Burma, and pressed south to the gates of Australia before being halted. Backward, under-developed west China received forty to sixty million refugees among whom were tens of thousands of migrating high school and university students and staff from the east, trekking thousands of miles on foot. And thousands of displaced Christians carrying the gospel with them.

Industrial equipment hastily dismantled before the advancing Japanese was reassembled, and unexploited sources tapped to provide essentials. The survival of China and containment of the Japanese verged on the miraculous. Unbridled currency inflation was somehow adapted to. At its worst the populace resorted calmly to barter. But widespread profiteering and corruption undermined the sincere efforts of the government. Mail not carried by air over 'The Hump' from India came through Tibet by yak, taking three months. The postage on one home letter cost me Mex. $23,500 in local currency, but a year after the Japanese surrender inflation stood at three to four thousand times the pre-war figures.

By 1944 and the end of the Second World War the Communists had a governmental machine of nine hundred thousand including a well trained army of six hundred thousand which, with their plans well laid, they insisted on retaining. On August 8, 1945, after the Hiroshima bomb had been dropped on August 5, Russia declared war on Japan, one week before she surrendered to the victorious allies; and prevented the Chinese government from occupying Manchuria. But Mao's troops were freely allowed possession and established their new base. Henry Pu Yi was carried off to Russia for indoctrination, and sent back after five years 'almost crazy' with humiliation and anger. After ten more years of 're-education' he was made a gardener, but later engaged in historical research.[24]

The membership of the CIM had climbed to 1,368 in 1934, and in spite of world recession in the 1930s, income at nearly £160,000 was higher than five years previously. Until 'Pearl Harbor' when Japan went to war with America and the European allies, foreign missions were free to take Chinese refugees into their premises and had endless scope for helping and comforting displaced people, receptive to the gospel. Plans for the CIM were all in terms of advance. Recorded baptisms in 1939 although incomplete were 9,364, but probably exceeded ten thousand in churches connected with the CIM alone. But under war conditions missionaries able to work fell to only seven hundred in Free China, leaving 250 in Japanese occupied China – and these were soon interned, unless from axis or neutral nations.

In 1940 the General Director George Gibb's health failed and he appointed Frank Houghton, Bishop of Eastern Sichuan since January 1937, to succeed him. Hardly could a General Director have had a worse moment to take responsibility. Frank Houghton's complete tenure of office was to be in the most desperate of times. Before the year was up, emergency headquarters of the CIM were established at Chongqing. He redirected the CIM's emphasis to self-government, self-support and self-extension by the Chinese Church where adherence to the policy had lapsed; 'not to try but to do it'. The Mission must always be auxiliary to the Church. The

price in terms of his own health led to his having to hand over the
leadership in 1951, without naming a successor.

Strong Chinese Christian leaders emerged to steady and
strengthen the tormented churches, and disruption of remaining
dependence on foreigners, prepared the Church nationwide for
meeting the greater ordeal after 'Liberation' by the Communists.
Leslie Lyall's biography of the great evangelist John Sung, and
biographical sketches of Yang Shaotang, Wang Mingdao and of Ni
Tuosheng should be read.[25] But what of Andrew Gih, Jia Yüming
and the rest? Before it is too late to collect first-hand information,
someone must write an unbiased, documented history of the gallant
Church in China. During and after the war years zealous Christians
were called to serve in the highest councils and ministries of Chiang
Kaishek's government. Many outstanding Christians in commerce
and education also deserve to have their contribution to the Church

JOHN SUNG, THE GREAT EVANGELIST

recorded. But not only the leaders who have hit the headlines. The history of the now burgeoning Church among the minority peoples of China deserves to be chronicled, to the glory of God.

The first intensive work among the many ethnic groups of Hmong or Miao (the Chinese term) began in 1896, nineteen years after James Broumton led the first one to Christ in 1877. (HTCOC Book 6, pp 241, 275). W S Fleming and his He Miao companion, the evangelist Pan Shoushan, were murdered in 1898. But by 1909 James R Adam knew of thousands of believing Miao and Nosu (Yi) in Guizhou alone. The farthest away towards Yunnan he referred to Samuel Pollard at Zhaotong, and soon the ten thousand Christian Miao and Nosu (Yi) of the Shimenkan (Stone Gateway) area were more than Pollard could shepherd adequately. Thousands more in the Gobu, Jiegou region (including 3,300 communicants) built themselves a chapel for a thousand to worship at a time. When Adam was killed by lightning at his own front door many superstitiously believed it to mean that he was secretly evil, punished by God, but the Church stood firm.[26]

Christians from the Zhaotong area migrated to the Wuding mountains north of Kunming, and there thousands more turned to Christ. Believing Miao at Sapushan and Yi at Salowu soon numbered thousands, the spontaneous product of testifying Christians among their own people. And yet more among the Lisu, Lahu and Gopu people near them. Arthur G Nicholls and Gladstone Porteous of the CIM served them for decades, and G E Metcalf farther west. Numbers have swelled in the intervening years. On a visit to China in 1988 I met three university students from one of these minority areas and asked, 'How many Christians are there in your region?' They looked surprised and answered, 'We don't know. We speak of how many are not Christians.'

Far off in western Yunnan another minority race, the Lisu, heard the gospel from James O Fraser, a graduate engineer with a flair for music, and a genius for establishing a strong indigenous Church. Taken into Yunnan by John McCarthy (who ended his days serving in the province he had crossed on foot in 1877), J O Fraser arrived in 1910 and six years later began to see Lisu turning from animism to Christ in increasing numbers. Lisu Christians won other families by the hundred. By 1918 sixty thousand tested believers had been baptised. A team of effective missionaries was built up over the years.

John Kuhn, an Elisha, joined Fraser in 1928. A strong, well-

taught, self-governing, self-supporting, and self-propagating
Church became the model for future church-planting ventures in
other regions and other lands. But Fraser died of malignant malaria
on September 25, 1938. He was only fifty-two. His dust lies on a hill
overlooking Baoshan (map p 45), but the apostle lives on 'in the
Glory' and in the hearts of the Lisu. They are designated a Christian
community by the Communist government. The Lisu Church now
spans the mountains from the Lancang Jiang (Mekong River) to the
Irrawaddy in Burma. The Salween valley sides still resound with
Christian singing.[27]

In the autumn of 1944 the Japanese drove strongly westwards to
threaten Guiyang and the Burma Road. Urgent evacuation of
women and children and many men, reduced the CIM to a few
hundred, in Yunnan, Sichuan and the north-west. Associates of
neutral and Axis countries continued under difficulties in Japanese
territory in eastern China and valiantly did all they could to ease the
lot of fellow-missionaries in the crowded internment camps. But
surrender in Europe on May 8, 1945, and then in the Pacific arena,
was the signal for missionaries in hundreds to flock back to China.
Six hundred filled the holds in tiers of canvas bunks on the ss *Marine
Lynx*, a US Navy transport ship. A golden age appeared to lie
before us. The signal was sent for new reinforcements to come and
begin language study. 'No one' realistically foresaw the sudden
bursting of the dam that released a flood of conquering Communists
upon the nation exhausted and demoralised by so many years of
civil and global war.

The 'gates of brass' slam shut[28]   1946–53

With world war ended and China apparently on the way to
recovery, the national government returned to Nanjing and the
CIM's administration to Shanghai. The Japanese vacated the headquarters buildings and the CIM moved in, not dreaming that in only
five years' time they would be occupied by Communists. Drought
and famine affected tens of millions of Chinese, at a time when the
wheels of government and missions were least geared to relief of
such distress. Teams of missionaries and Chinese Christians returned to comfort and help old friends. The indigenous movement
known as the 'Little Flock', led by 'Watchman' Ni Tuosheng (Ni
T'uo-sheng), flowered into new life, as did other Christian bodies
with no foreign connection – not least the Jesus Family. They

migrated in family groups to set up as Christian communities in devastated and remote regions.

Most remarkable and promising for the new China was the flame of spiritual life among China's students. In the 1940s it spread widely from west China to the eastern provinces vacated by the invaders. National conferences of Christian students, in Chongqing, Nanjing, Shanghai, faced the increasingly strident voice of Communism and its implications. 'Christ or Communism' had become the issue looming larger and larger before all Chinese Christians. Commitment to Christ posed no hypothetical risks but the decision to testify and suffer for him. Together with the YMCA, thoroughly infiltrated by Communist agents, the China Inter-Varsity Fellowship (CIVF) met attempts to take control and use it for political purposes. True spiritual life in an individual could not be feigned, and wolves in sheep's clothing could be recognised. The influence of those true student Christians of the 1940s on the Church in China is incalculable.

In 1948 a member of the Swedish Mission in Shanxi, Miss Lenell, and a church elder were taken before a 'people's tribunal', condemned and shot. If missionaries were to be vulnerable to that extent, hundreds were at risk. And what of the hundreds of thousands of church members? Should all the CIM be withdrawn, or each region be treated according to the threats against it? The northern provinces were in Mao's hands, though the KMT still held Beijing. In June Kaifeng, Henan, was threatened. Would the CIM hospital be safer than non-medical centres? It was handed over to a courageous Chinese doctor who offered to run it, and the missionaries were withdrawn before the city was 'liberated'. The Nationalists (KMT) seemed incapable of checking the advance.

A North China People's Government was declared on September 1, 1948. By Christmas the People's Liberation Army (PLA) had reached the Yangzi and by mid-March 1949 were massed and ready to cross. Nanjing fell on April 23 and on the 25th Chiang Kaishek and his government sailed for Taiwan, their cruiser laden with all the gold bullion in the Bank of China. British and American warships moved to the Yangzi estuary; HMS *Amethyst* made her dash under fire from the banks of the Yangzi. Beijing fell on May 5, the attack on Shanghai began ten days later and ended on the 25th. On October 1, 1949, the People's Democratic Republic of China was proclaimed at the Tian An Men, the Gate of Heavenly Peace, in Beijing.

Of all Protestant missions more than four thousand had remained in China (4,062), and as many Roman Catholics. Only 185 members of the CIM were advised to withdraw. The year ended with 737 and many children still in China, 119 in associate missions.

May 1950 showed the shape of things to come. A 'Christian Manifesto' was drawn up in Beijing by Zhou Enlai and pro-Communist or crypto-Communist members of Christian organisations, and on June 30 this was presented at a meeting of Christian leaders and missionaries summoned and addressed by high Communist government officials. Subsequently thousands of church members were enlisted to put their signatures to it. 'While China is putting its house in order,' Zhou Enlai said, 'it is undesirable for guests to be present.'

The meaning was clear. But 'fair words before the true face' of what Christianity in China was up against, meant that no expulsion order against foreigners would be issued; the Church was to rid itself of all traces of 'missionary imperialism'. 'Love Country, Love Church' had become the priorities. [While my own colleagues, my family and I were under house arrest for several months with fixed bayonets at our doors, we were assured that we could stay as long as we liked.] The CIM perhaps naïvely felt innocent of the imperialist label. Neither foreign hands on the purse-strings nor control of the churches could be held against them. Any hope of being tolerated died a quick death. 'It became clear not only that the missionaries would be allowed to do nothing, but that their continued presence in the country would bring danger to their Chinese friends.'[29] One by one the societies instructed their members to withdraw.

Two remarkable events connected with this period stand engraved in the history of the CIM. The first: in 1930 when the Wusong Road premises became inadequate for the expanding mission, the sale of the site and properties more than covered the erection of two large multistorey buildings at Sinza Road. Residences, offices, hospital and public rooms met all needs when the move was made in 1931. Second, in 1950, at a time of greatly increased expenditure, the power-play between two strong Communist government organisations ended dramatically in one paying three years' rental in advance for the Sinza Road mission home – where it could have been commandeered.[30] Enough cash suddenly in hand, but restricted to use in China, allowed all members of the CIM still up-country to travel out by any means available. And large Mission

ONE OF THE SINZA ROAD HEADQUARTERS
BUILDINGS, SHANGHAI 1931–53

incomes in 1950 and 1951 covered the inflated costs of dispersal once they were out.

God's provision convinced the Mission's leaders that even the apparent end, not only of the 'open century', but of the existence of the *China* Inland Mission was no more than the end of a phase. Forty years later the transformed Mission continues to work on the unchanged principles – forty years of constant, adequate provision for work in a dozen other East Asian countries by over one thousand active members from twenty-seven nations, as well as hundreds of superannuated members, children of missionaries and longstanding salaried colleagues.

To those of us who worked in the remotest regions it seemed impossible that the Communist Party, so recently blockaded in the sterile north of Shaanxi, should take control of more than a limited area of north China. When their armies reached the Yangzi, they appeared to be overstretching their resources. Astounding organisation, training and control of newly enlisted or conscripted reinforcements, consolidated each achievement. A period of anarchy or numb waiting for the unknown descended after the KMT officials melted away into anonymity and began the hazardous process of working their way to the coast and beyond.

Then the 'liberation'. And after a few days or weeks of charm and public entertainment with acrobats and music the rapid tightening of *baojia* control (see Glossary), by which the responsible member of every ten units (individuals, families, factories, streets, towns and so on) answered for the acts or thoughts of those under him or her. No one could move without official authorisation. Regimentation, parades, mass meetings, for indoctrination, for accusation, for denunciation and sentencing to imprisonment or firing squad were well under way before we left. Our colleagues' truck halted while eight were executed by the roadside. It then went on. Christian accusing Christian, congregations accusing their pastors, children their parents, madness erupted on a vast scale. A reign of terror began, soon to be exceeded when Mao unleashed the children of the Red Guards to smash, burn, assault and even to kill in the name of a 'cultural revolution'.

The role of China Director passed to Arnold Lea. What he could do for Mission members travelling out, or held for investigation, or committed to prison, was limited. But his long list of those still in China slowly dwindled. At the beginning of 1951 it held 627 names. By April, 371 and as June ended, 203; ninety in September, and thirty-three as the year ended. The sufferings of the last missionaries to leave, 'harassed, humiliated, reduced to penury, denied the necessities of life' and imprisoned, may be read in *A Passion for the Impossible*, *Green Leaf in · Drought* and *China: The Reluctant Exodus* (see Bibliography). On May 22, 1952, eight remained, and on January 1, 1953, four: Dr Rupert Clarke, Arthur Mathews and his wife and daughter. Clarke was accused of murder.

Harry Gould, a member of the CIM, had succeeded in finding employment in Butterfield and Swire, a foreign shipping firm still tolerated at Shanghai, and found ways to transmit funds inland. On March 24, Wilda Mathews and her child were escorted out, and on July 20 the two men. A few months later, the Goulds left Shanghai – one hundred years since Hudson Taylor first sailed off to China. A few men of other missions were kept in prison for several years. But not until April 1959 did Helen Willis, an elderly, independent lady missionary, follow them out, the very last Protestant missionary to go. Of all the CIM's many members involved in this great evacuation, not one life was lost, not one limb – or as one put it, 'not a hoof or a husband was left behind'. The gates had slammed shut on the brief 'open century'.

The people of China stand up 1949–89

A few broad strokes of the brush bring this epic to the present day. The 'open century' ended with the exclusion of foreigners from China, with the exception of the chosen few. Slowly the gates slid ajar again for some who could help to fulfil the Communist Party's aims, and increasingly for tourists bringing foreign currency. But to Christian aid for the Chinese Church they remained barred and bolted. The impact of Communism on individual Christians and their corporate life has been devastating for many and profound for all. Temporary relaxation has sometimes raised hopes, but Marxist dogma on religion underlies all government policy. The elimination of all religion is the strategic aim. The Christian Manifesto (p 564) was designed to eject all missionaries, to shackle the Church and to direct it towards ultimate extinction. At first appearing drastic but tolerable, it ushered in years of bitter persecution.

When Mao Zedong declared the inauguration of the People's Democratic Republic of China from the Gate of Heavenly Peace, the Tian An Men, on October 1, 1949, he made the historic statement, 'The Chinese people have stood up.' With the end of the Second World War China had become a 'new' nation. After all the oppression and exploitation of the Qing dynasty and by foreign aggressors for more than a century, the renunciation of extraterritorial rights and a new dignity in the family of nations justified Mao's words. He used them with a new defiance.

With the expulsion of the Nationalist government, the Communist Party's attention turned to consolidation of power throughout China. Anti-Communists of all kinds, 'counter-revolutionaries', Nationalist agents, other 'class enemies' and politically naïve employers, landlords, and landowners, found themselves the victims of vindictive accusation meetings. The 'people' were drilled for hours and taught party songs and slogans. (To this day they ring in the ears of all of us who were threatened by them.) Massed audiences yelled in unison the verdicts and penalties, in self defence. The predominant emotion of the largest nation on earth had become Fear. In the first six months of 1951 between one and three million executions took place. Mao himself admitted to eight hundred thousand. A 'Three Anti-' campaign directed against corruption, waste and bureaucracy was followed by a 'Five Anti-' campaign against bribery, tax evasion, fraud, theft of government property and theft of state economic secrets. The net was flung wide. Mao's control was absolute. The year 1954 saw the adoption of a Constitution of the

People's Republic of China, but in 1957 the independent judiciary was swept aside. Might was right.

The first five-year plan launched in 1953 led in 1955–56 to the regimentation of the nation in co-operatives of one hundred to three hundred families. Overconfident of support, the 'Great Helmsman' embarked on three great gambles. Each in turn miscarried tragically. By 1957 Mao judged that he could allow some freedom of expression – or set a trap for unwary opponents. Quoting from the classics he called on them to 'Let a hundred flowers bloom and a hundred schools of thought contend.' A storm of protest and accusation against the actions of Party and government poured in. Mao reacted with a 'rectification' campaign against what he called 'stinking intellectuals' and 'rightists'. Blind to the value of professionals, intellectuals, writers and students, he banished thousands to labour camps. For twenty years the services of the nation's most needed able men were lost.

Worse things lay ahead in the second decade. Dissatisfied with China's economic progress, Mao then took the 'Great Leap Forward' in which the millions, in his commitment to permanent revolution, were marshalled into communes, work brigades and production units. By 1962 eighty per cent of the people were in communes. The entrepreneurial genius of the Chinese people was fettered at a stroke. Great engineering feats were performed by mass labour. But by 1975 the gradual dissolution of communes had begun. Natural calamities combined with the repugnance of the people at being denied their individual or family independence to produce a disastrous famine. After Mao's death in 1976 the government acknowledged that twenty million had died of starvation. But meanwhile the campaign against students and intellectuals continued until by 1965 forty million had become farm labourers. Ironically their exile saved many of them from a worse fate. Mao's ideological dreams of a Communist Utopia of his own design lured him into his third and worst gamble.

In 1964 Mao abolished the United Front Works Department and everything under it, including the Religious Affairs Bureau and Three-Self Patriotic Movement. Then, on July 13, 1966, he closed all schools and called upon all children to serve the motherland as Red Guards.[31] Himself wearing the uniform red armband, Mao addressed a succession of massed thousands, 114 million in nine rallies, on the vast parade ground at the Tian An Men. He commissioned them to rebel, to flout the law, to destroy the 'Four Olds'

– old ideas, old customs, old culture and old habits. Inspired or hysterical, with the Little Red Book of 'The Thoughts of Chairman Mao' and the haunting chant 'The East is Red' to marshal them, millions ran wild. In a 'gigantic frenzy' nationwide they destroyed, tortured and killed, more viciously and more extensively than had the 'child devils' of the Boxer nightmare. According to Hu Yaobang, General Secretary of the Communist Party, they publicly humiliated and assaulted thirty million victims. Many were maimed for life, and 1,600 were executed. By October 1967 this so-called Cultural Revolution that vandalised the nation's treasure and best brains had appalled its originator. Mao used the army to call a halt, disbanded the Red Guards and sent eighteen million 'bourgeois' students, including Red Guards, to work on the farms. He substituted a new phase of 'Struggle, Criticism and Transformation'. During five years of madness and economic dislocation, the outer world had been cut off, in almost total ignorance of events in China, while a whole generation of young Chinese found themselves in 'the vacuum of a lost hope'.

As unpredictably, the third decade saw Mao and his doctrinaire 'leftists' yield to pressure from more liberal colleagues. There followed the relaxation of controls to allow an influx of tourists and specialists. Without them China would have taken decades to recover from her economic destitution. But defying the dangers, perhaps 280,000 Chinese fled the country between 1972 and 1978 to find sanctuary in Hong Kong. In 1976 the old hardliners received the blow from which they have not recovered. Zhou Enlai, the statesman and premier, died; then Zhu De, the veteran marshal of the army, and on September 9, Mao Zedong at the age of eighty-three. Mao's estranged wife Jiang Qing and her three extreme leftist collaborators in the 'Gang of Four' failed in an attempt to seize the initiative. They were arrested on October 26. Since then a left–right seesaw of political pressures has made the work of Deng Xiaoping's more liberal régime uncomfortable. But the Four Modernisations of agriculture, industry, science and defence have progressed, and the lot of Christians became not easy but easier than during the thirty years between 1950 and 1980.

The Chinese Church stands up[32]   *1949–89*

Even before the foreign 'scaffolding' was removed (in Hudson Taylor's phrase, HTCOC Book 5 pp 373–4), the Chinese Church could see the shape of things to come, and prepared for repression. Communist spokesmen give the total number of Protestant Christians in China at 'Liberation' as seven hundred thousand. One million is probably a more realistic figure, even after nominal 'Christians' by attachment rather than by faith have been discounted. If not, the record of their multiplication is even more remarkable.

The reign of terror begun in 1951 against 'spies, counter-revolutionaries, landlords and capitalists', caught up many Christians among those brought to summary trial, pilloried, imprisoned, executed or driven to suicide. Congregations were coerced into denouncing their pastors, fellow-Christians and foreigners with whom they had been associated. Hudson Taylor, Timothy Richard and other notable missionaries were and still are made the objects of attack for 'spreading the poison of imperialist thought' and serving the purposes of imperialist aggression.

Chinese Church leaders bore the brunt of denunciation. Ni Tuosheng, the influential leader of the 'Little Flock' Assemblies, was sentenced to fifteen years' imprisonment as a counter-revolutionary and died shortly after his release. Wang Mingdao of Beijing received a life sentence but was released in 1979, twenty-three years later. The government agency responsible for their elimination boasted that 'the counter-revolutionary rings headed by Nee and Wang had been smashed!'[33]

Persecution increased until the Cultural Revolution erupted in 1966, when Christians dared not show recognition of each other in public. Church life was completely suppressed and Christian books of all kinds destroyed. Whispered prayer in secret with one or two others became the only Christian fellowship still possible. In Amoy, to take one instance,

> Every pastor was made to 'walk the street' with a dunce's hat on his head and a placard around his neck announcing his crimes . . . One woman was beaten to death. Communist cadres and Red Guards . . . forced (twenty YMCA and YWCA secretaries) to kneel in front of a pile of burning (Bibles, hymnals and other books) while a large crowd stood around . . . As the flames radiated their heat towards them, the victims cried out in excruciating pain . . . Tormented by their excessive burns, most of them . . . committed suicide by jumping from high buildings.[34]

Marxism is dedicated to the extinction of religion and superstition. Temporary tolerance of the religions of China, with 'freedom

WANG MINGDAO: PREACHER, AUTHOR, SURVIVOR
of imprisonment, 1956–79; now in Shanghai

of religious belief', is part of the strategy for achieving the goal of
extinction. Control of a social phenomenon too powerful for control
by other means has proved to need a lighter rein than was at first
applied. Suppression of Islam in China began to provoke armed
risings, so thousands of mosques have been built at government
expense and Islamic practice tolerated. Attempted suppression of
the Christian Church was counter-productive. They did not suffer
or die in vain. Persecution purified the Church from false and weak
elements, and demonstrated its indestructibility and vitality. New
believers were attracted to it, even from the ranks of the Party. As a
result the million Protestant Christians have become five or more
millions by reluctant government admission, and twenty or more
million by conservative estimate from an abundance of testimony
and evidence.

The strategy of the Chinese Communist Party (CCP) is public
knowledge. It works through the government's United Front Work

Department (UFWD), with units throughout China, to co-ordinate and unify all aspects of national life, in fulfilment of Party policy. The United Front works through the Religious Affairs Bureau (RAB) centrally and locally, by 'patriotic organisations' in each religion. In the case of Christianity, the official arm of the government began as the Three-Self Reform Church, but was never a church in structure or function. This was soon changed to Three-Self Patriotic Movement (TSPM), adapting in name the familiar 'indigenous principles' of self-governing, self-supporting and self-propagating churches (HTCOC Book 6, Notes p 477). The Three-Self Movement, both centrally and wherever it is represented locally, is answerable to the Religious Affairs Bureau and as a government body calls upon the Public Security Bureau to enforce its will. In parallel with the administrative TSPM since 1980 is the China Christian Council (CCC). To it is delegated the pastoral aspects of the churches.

Launched in April 1951, the Three-Self Movement conducted a prototype 'accusation meeting' in Beijing and carried the method to Shanghai and throughout China. In 1955 it conducted a nation-wide accusation campaign against Wang Mingdao, who had become the leading evangelical preacher in Beijing. Its first chairman, Wu Yaozong (Y T Wu), until then the general secretary of the YMCA, was an avowed Marxist and committed Communist. He quickly wound up all other Protestant Christian organisations, to leave the TSPM the sole government-recognised representative, and in 1958 'consolidated' city churches in a form without denominational distinctions. In Beijing sixty-five were reduced to four, in Shanghai fifteen survived for a while out of two hundred. Rural churches had already been closed during the land reform period.

But the Three-Self Movement was also religious. In 1966 when Mao through the Red Guards and Cultural Revolution attacked religion in any and every form, even the government-sponsored Three-Self churches and personnel came under the same lash. Silence fell on the religious scene until 1972. Marxism seemed to have triumphed. 'The church is extinct,' the enemies and pessimists croaked. Believing that 'religion is the opiate that lulls the spirit of the people,' and that 'all worship or veneration of supernatural forces can be called superstitions; religions are also superstitions but not all superstitions are religions,' only the abolition of religion was acceptable to the purists. After the death of Mao and the return of Deng Xiaoping to power in 1978, a policy of uniting to heal the wounds of the Cultural Revolution revived the TSPM (moribund for fifteen years) to regulate the measure of religious freedom permitted.[35]

Even in the first decade of severe repression, strong evidence of Christian survival occasionally emerged. In 1957 Christian students were meeting to pray and study the Bible together in nine universities. Wherever they scattered they went as leaders. Following the Great Leap Forward of 1958, the 1960s saw the number of Christians in the communes increase dramatically. Successful work units even came to be known with approval as 'Jesus Production Team No 1'. With the dangers of the Cultural Revolution removed, and Christians showing their colours again in 1978, the complete failure to extinguish the Church became apparent. In contrast, it had grown stronger in numbers and spirit. Under suffering, faith and loyalty had been tested, spiritual maturity had deepened. A stronger, buoyant, indomitable Church emerged. After the release from prison and labour camps of many undaunted Christians, a new confidence became evident. 'Revival' took place in province after province, with every evidence of God's Holy Spirit using remarkable men and women to turn whole communities to Christ. The growing edge of the Church was in this spontaneous expansion, unrelated to the regimented churches. To harness it became the government's priority.

On July 28, 1954, Wu Yaozong (Y T Wu) delivered a long report at a conference of the Three-Self Patriotic Movement (TSPM) in Beijing.[36] After summarising the part played by missionaries in the early history of nineteenth century Sino-International relations he said:

> We have always thought that China Inland Mission founder Hudson Taylor was a warm-hearted evangelistic 'missionary'. But in 1888 at the London Centennial Missionary Conference he spoke greedily of the mineral resources of China. He said, 'These resources can make western nations rich.' He was afraid that China would wake up; he approved the special privileges which the unequal treaties gave to the 'missionaries', saying, 'Now under the protection of these treaties we can take our passport in our hand and go comfortably by road or river boat into every province in China.' He wanted foreign 'missionaries' to take advantage of the opportunity, and through preaching the gospel to extend imperialistic aggression against China.
>
> It is just these mission boards and these 'missionaries' who for over a hundred years have controlled the personnel, government, finances

and work of the Chinese Christian church, misinterpreted the Scriptures, perverted Christian doctrine, nurtured unspeakable renegades within the church, created dissension and division within the church, and made Chinese Christians unconsciously breathe in the poison of imperialistic thought.

The Centennial Conference to which Wu Yaozong referred was the one we outlined (pp 70–73) at which Hudson Taylor and the CIM pleaded strongly for China and against Britain's opium traffic. The two-volume report of the conference[37] gives Hudson Taylor's address verbatim. Referring to China he said:

If you will think not only of the number of people who live there, but of their capacity, you will see that we have a mighty nation to deal with, who deserve, as has been well said, our best prayers and our best efforts. They are an intellectual people. Where is the government that has surpassed China in diplomacy? Where are the merchants that have exceeded the Chinese in their ability or in their success? . . . Allow him to compete at our universities, and he will not only secure our academic degrees, but will take them with honours. This people is a great people, and they are capable of great things. The purposes of God with regard to them, moreover, must be great purposes . . . We have seen the rise and the fading away in succession of Egypt, of Assyria, of Babylon, Persia, Greece, and Rome; but China is neither old nor effete; today she is a living nation, young and vigorous and full of power . . .

We all believe in the God of whom we have been hearing as the Creator of heaven and earth. Is it by accident that beneath the broad acres of China the greatest mineral wealth of the world has been stored? Had God no purpose in view in those immense coalfields, which would supply the world with coal for two thousand years? Had God no purpose in view in giving China everything in the shape of mineral wealth which has made any country in the west to be great or prosperous? Surely, these things are not by accident. God surely has great purposes for China in the future . . .

They are on the move. Telegraph lines now span the empire . . . Railways are being surveyed for and prepared, and China is on the move . . . China will soon be a factor in the world's history, if we mistake not the signs of the times.

Now what has Christianity done for this great people? . . . After eighty years of missionary labour we are thankful for thirty-two thousand communicants; after eighty years of commercial labour there are more than one hundred and fifty millions of opium smokers in China (corrected by Hudson Taylor to 'opium smokers and their families who are suffering directly from the evil.')

We have given China something besides the Gospel, something that is doing more harm in a week than the united efforts of all our Christian missionaries are doing in a year. Oh, the evils of opium! . . . I entreat you to pray to the mighty God that He will bring this great evil to an end. Do we not owe China, then, by the wrong we have done her, and by her great needs, the Gospel? Now is the time of opportunity . . . I need not tell you the whole country is open to us. Now by treaty-right, with passport in hand, we pass into every province with safety and comfort, travelling along the great highways and the rivers of China.

'God surely has great purposes for China in the future.' With transparent admiration and love for China Hudson Taylor was emphasising her greatness, with endless resources to make her greater still. He stressed the moral debt the West owed her, to give her the gospel. Only two explanations of Wu Yaozong's interpretation are possible. Either his understanding of the English language and of Hudson Taylor's meaning was too limited; or he deliberately distorted Hudson Taylor's words and fabricated others. Did Hudson Taylor speak 'greedily of the mineral resources of China'? that 'these resources can make western nations rich'? Quite the reverse. China's vast resources were God's gift to China to make *her* rich and great. Quoting Marquis Zeng's *The Sleep and the Awakening* Hudson Taylor praised China's awakening and openness in 1888 as her great opportunity to hear the gospel. Frequently found in the Hudson Taylor archives are references to Napoleon Bonaparte's alleged remark, 'China? There lies a sleeping giant. Let him sleep, for when he wakes he will move the world.'[38]

Over the years others have used Wu's words and added to them, for their own purposes, accusing Hudson Taylor of a lifetime of deliberate fact-gathering for the consuls and merchants. Knowing as we do from so much evidence, that the CIM avoided dealings with both, such allegations could be amusing if they did not deceive the uninformed.

Wu Yaozong died in 1979 and was succeeded by Bishop Ding Guangxün (K H Ting), as chairman of the Three-Self Patriotic Movement, and of the China Christian Council.[36] Following Deng Xiaoping's visit to the States and the resumption of diplomatic relations, it became safe again for about two years for Christians to meet in each other's homes. The Three-Self Movement gave expression to a new policy: to restore so-called religious 'liberty subject to control'; to return confiscated properties to so-called 'open churches' under the TSPM and CCC; and to unite all Christians under the TSPM and CCC. Christians who for good reasons chose not to register as individuals or congregations with these agencies became the objects of special attention. However, reassured by the prospect of freedom to worship together under government protection, many former pastors and church members of the best type registered in the 'open churches'. In spite of the 'Love Country, Love Church' emphasis and regular political indoctrination received, they see membership as the way forward. If regarded as a crescendo meaning 'Love Country, Love Church, Love Christ', the slogan is acceptable.

The record of the TSPM before the Cultural Revolution, and suspicion of its motives and fair words kept many more away. In large and small groups, depending on the presence or absence of leadership and teaching, they embrace the majority of Christians in China today. Some adopt church structures with pastors or elders and deacons, baptisms and communion services. Others, 'taught by the Holy Spirit' though lacking human leaders, cling together for prayer and singing, and Bible reading if they possess any Scriptures. Whether meeting in homes or outgrowing them and meeting in the open or in other buildings, they are 'independent', 'unregistered' congregations which have come to be called (often inappropriately) 'house churches'. Many number hundreds and, linked up with each other, thousands, whom the government (after seeing how repression backfires) rightly hesitates to regiment by force. International awareness and published concern for them are also known to contribute to their protection.

The presence of crypto-Communists in the Chinese Church before 1951 is well documented. Li Chuwen, a notable Shanghai pastor, when about to be beaten by Red Guards, escaped by revealing that he was a party activist. In 1983 he was appointed Deputy Director of the New China News Agency in Hong Kong. Another elsewhere told them to read the proof in the United Front Work Department that he too was an infiltrator. A high-ranking official in the Religious Affairs Bureau has spoken frankly about members of the TSPM deputations to western countries. The favourable front presented to Archbishops and other church dignitaries and through the media has been designed to mislead. The Roman Catholic Church has its own story to tell. 'Religious liberty' as understood in the West is a very different matter from the frayed thread of 'liberty subject to control' conceded in China for political reasons. The *raison d'être* of the Three-Self Movement has been to 'rally all Chinese Christians under the leadership of the Chinese Communist Party and the People's Government'. And 'the CCC religious policy sets definite limits to the enjoyment of religious freedom beyond which believers step at their peril.' A leading member of those who maintain their independence asks, 'Should the Body of Christ be led by the atheistic Communist Party?' even if its leaders have been 'consecrated' as bishops?

From the earliest days political opponents accused missionaries of sinister and repulsive motives. But from the end of the warlord period until the present day, criticism and attack have been in terms of imperialism, spying, and fantasy. The inextricable involvement of missionaries with their aggressive governments has been recognised in each volume of this series. They still suffer the penalty of that involvement every time they are called the religious arm of the imperialists.

Accusations that Hudson Taylor and the CIM engaged in prospecting for coal and iron are only part of the modern propaganda by falsehoods. The recent misuse of quotations from CIM publications (such as *China's Millions*) and condemnation of the Mission's innocuous telegraphic economy code of 1907 are only examples of distortion of the facts for the same purpose. When Hudson Taylor protested to a consul that using force against China was futile but goodwill shown by famine relief gained friends, he was sincere. But his words have been manipulated to mean that aggressive intentions were better served by the relief of suffering. Hudson Taylor himself was described in lectures at the (TSPM) Nanjing Theological Seminary in which Bishop Ding Guangxün took part, as 'masquerading as a servant of God while actually representing colonial imperialistic foreign interests' and having 'a materialistic interest in the vast coal and mineral deposits of China' by which 'the capitalists can fill their mouths.'[39]

In 1981 a book by Yan Changsheng on *Missionaries and Modern China*, published in Shanghai, said:

> Besides doing missions, Hudson Taylor also aimed at offering intelligence information to the British aggressors, and exerting himself for British businessmen in the economic exploitation of inland China. Every CIM missionary carried a secret telegraphic code book, compiled by the CIM itself. Taylor collected information wherever he

went, and, using the secret code, he despatched telegraphic messages
to the CIM Shanghai office, whence the information was then
transmitted to London. Some of the economic information was
passed on to British merchants in Shanghai. These British merchants
in coastal China regularly authorised the inland missionaries to sell
commodities and investigate the market. Thus the missionaries
offered a great deal of help to the merchants (p 117 ff).

Another, in 1988, edited by Ma Chaoqün, *Two Thousand Years
of Christianity*, takes up the same falsehoods and amplifies them.

> The British missionary Hudson Taylor founded the China Inland
> Mission in 1865. He supplied the British forces, in their aggression in
> China, with enormous supplies of intelligence. Each CIM missionary
> had hidden beside him a secret telegraphic code book. Thus, at any
> time, they could use the code to send intelligence reports they had
> made, from all parts of our country to the CIM office in Shanghai for
> transmission to London (p 242).

Hunan's Zhou Han has equally imaginative successors. Certainly
'the father of lies' and 'accuser of the brethren' is as busy as ever.

The facts are simple. Hudson Taylor founded the CIM in 1865. So
neither he nor CIM missionaries worked in the theatres of either
opium war, of 1840–42 or 1858–60! Even in 1900 only one young
family was in Tianjin when Chinese troops and Boxers besieged it.
'Enormous supplies of intelligence' is pure fantasy. 'Each (or every)
CIM missionary had hidden beside him (or carried) a secret telegraphic code book . . . compiled by the CIM . . .'? This too is wide
of the mark. During Hudson Taylor's times the commercial economy code known as 'Unicode' was available for use by the general
public. 'Lammermuir' and 'Inland' were adopted as telegraphic
addresses from about 1904, but the CIM's own comprehensive code
book was collated by J J Coulthard, T G Willett and Charles T Fishe
in 1907, after Hudson Taylor's death. He never used one, let alone
to despatch information from wherever he went for transmission
to London. Such allegations are unworthy of intelligent Chinese
authors.

Revised and enlarged in 1929 by Frank Parry, as a private
(copyright) mission handbook, it was used by many other missions
and by business firms. Based on messages actually received and sent
in the normal course of things, it was in no way secret. Quite long
sentences could be represented by a single word. 'Homuriyupu'

with the help of the code book tables meant 'Mr and Mrs J R Sinton and children are leaving by Butterfield and Swire's Line on the 9th.' The 1929 edition weighed 1.5kg. Far from every missionary carrying one with him, a copy was kept for use at each Mission centre in cities and towns with a telegraphic office. They may be searched in vain for subversive or suspicious words or phrases such as secret agents would need; or, in the same way, any with economic, commercial, significance. An analysis of the contents clearly shows it to have been primarily for domestic and administrative communication, while making provision for reporting emergencies such as occurred all too frequently. It simply reduced the cost of telegrams to a fraction of what it would have been if spelled out in full. In wartime its use was of course banned.[40]

If any answer to all these accusations is needed, it must be that the burden of proof lies on the accusers to substantiate their suppositions. Meanwhile it is significant that the attitude of foreign governments, consuls and merchants towards Hudson Taylor and the missionaries belies the allegations. In his lifetime and since, only a handful of honours for famine, earthquake, flood relief and social service have been awarded to individuals, but never anything at all to the alleged arch-offender himself. But the *Chinese* government before and since the 1911 Revolution did award high honours, though not to Hudson Taylor. No, in this 'spiritual warfare' the 'father of lies' fears the truth, while Hudson Taylor has since 1905 been far removed from all attempts to condemn him. Attacks on him are attacks on what he taught.

This review has brought us to the present day, and as we go to press the winds of change blow hot and cold. Bishop Ding in mid-February 1989 stated (in an interview with News Network International, Los Angeles) that the Three-Self Patriotic Movement is to be dissolved by the end of 1991. Since then much has happened, and the future is unpredictable. But while the weather vane may swing, 'GOD reigns!' and 'holds the key of all unknown.'

The sufferings and continuing difficulties of Christ's Church in China are by-products of its life, of the life of Christ in them. They may be 'a rope of sand' in vulnerability, but 'sand like the seashore' in withstanding the waves. Since Robert Morrison and William Milne rejoiced over the first Chinese to respond to their 'good news', in not much more than a century and a half Protestant Christians alone have multiplied to many millions. On July 16, 1814, Morrison wrote in his journal:

> At a spring of water issuing from the foot of a lofty hill by the seaside, away from human observation, I baptised [Cai A-fu, the first convert after seven long years]. May he be the firstfruits of a great harvest; one of the millions who shall believe and be saved . . . (HTCOC Book 1, p 134).

Nearly five thousand 'open churches' and thirty thousand registered 'meeting points' are now acknowledged to exist, while governmental concern is apparent over the innumerable but probably one hundred thousand or more independent, unregistered meeting points in the cities and countryside. Official figures represent the tip of the iceberg. The persecuted Church in China had burgeoned to ten, twenty or more times its numerical size of one million when 'liberated' (in 'new-speak') at the close of the 'open century'. Where does it stand now?

The International Bulletin of Missionary Research's 'Annual Statistical Table on Global Mission' for 1987 (compiled by David B Barrett, of the Church Missionary Society since 1956 and research officer for the Anglican Consultative Council and the Lambeth Conference since 1970, currently to the Foreign Mission Board, Southern Baptist Convention) commented:

> Suddenly, by 1986 China has become the fastest expanding nation for church growth ever. This year's surveys indicate that China has a total of at least 81,600 worship centers (churches, congregations, house groups) with 21,500,000 baptised adult believers, and a total Christian community of 52,152,000 Christians affiliated to churches, including children. Thirteen large cities have baptised church members numbering over 10 percent of the population. House churches are now known to exist in virtually every one of China's 2,010 administrative counties. A vital evangelising church has come into existence almost everywhere throughout the nation.

If such spontaneous growth can take place under conditions of repression, what would full liberty result in? Given true freedom of belief *and expression*, what golden prospects will lie before China in a new 'open century' ahead! 'China evangelised by the Chinese!' And overseas? Already there is a strong body of Chinese Christians dedicated to worldwide evangelism.

The crown of life

From beginning to end this sketch of the Church in China and Hudson Taylor's part in it have reflected the story of the New Testament Church. The seed must die to release its life. Scripture consistently rates the physical below the spiritual. 'Do not be afraid of those who kill the body but cannot kill the soul,' were the words of Jesus himself (Matt. 10:28 NIV).

> Blessed is the man who perseveres under trial, because when he has stood the test, he will receive the crown of life that God has promised to those who love him (Jas. 1:12 NIV).
> Be faithful, even to the point of death, and I will give you the crown of life (Rev. 2:10 NIV).

When Hudson Taylor, the CIM and their fellow-Christians of all kinds treated life as on trust to be spent to the full, as part of continuing service for God in the life to come, its fruit 'the Church that will not die' sprang up. War, hatred, persecution, death, as incidentals formed the climate in which Christ's promise was fulfilled. 'I will build my Church' (Matt. 16:18 NIV). After Peter's strong defence, 'We must obey God rather than men!' (Acts 5:29 NIV) the advice of Gamaliel to the rulers enshrined another undying principle which China will do well to heed:

> I advise you: Leave these men alone! Let them go!
> For if their purpose or activity is of human origin, it will fail.
> But if it is from God, *you will not be able to stop these men*;
> You will only find yourselves fighting against God (Acts 5:38–9 NIV).

Perhaps we are still near the beginning.

A KEY TO SOME CHINESE PLACE NAMES

Pinyin	Wade-Giles	Postal, Press
Anhui	An-hui	Anhwei
Ankang (Xing'an)	An-k'ang	Ankang
Anqing	An-ch'ing	Anking
Anxin	Hsin-an	
Baoding	Pao-ting	Paoting
Baotou	Pao-t'ou	Paotow
Beijing	Pei-ching	Peking
Chalingzhou	Ch'a-ling-chou	Chalingchow
Changzhi (Lu'an)	Ch'ang-chih	Changchih, Lungan
Chengdu	Ch'eng-tu	Chengtu
Chenzhou	Ch'en-chou	Chenchow
Chongqing	Ch'ung-ch'ing	Chungking
Datong, Tongling	Ta-t'ung	Tatung
Dihua (Urumqi)	Ti-hua	Tihua
Dongchuan	Tung-ch'uan	Tungchuan
Fujian	Fu-chien	Fukien
Fuzhou	Fu-chou	Fuchow
Gansu	Kan-su	Kansu
Guangdong	Kuang-tung	Kwangtung
Guanghua, Laohekou	Kuang-hua	Laohokou
Guangxi	Kuang-hsi	Kwangsi
Guangxin (Shangrao)	Kuang-hsin	Kwangsin
Guangzhou	Kuang-chou	Canton
Guan Xian	Kuan-hsien	Kwanhsien
Guide (Shangqiu)	Kwei-teh	Kweiteh
Guiding	Kuei-ting	Kweiting
Guihuacheng (Hohhot)	Kui-hua-ch'eng	Kweihwacheng
Guilin	Kuei-lin	Kweilin
Guiyang	Kuei-yang	Kweiyang
Guizhou	Kuei-chou	Kweichow
Hanzhong	Han-chung	Hanchung
Hangzhou	Hang-chou	Hangchow
Hebei (Zhili)	Ho-pei (Chih-li)	Hopeh (-pei) (Chili)
Hejin (Ho-tsin)	Ho-ts'in	Hotsin
Hezuo	Ho-tso	Hochow

Hongjiang	Hung-kiang	Hungkiang
Hongkou	Hung-k'ou	Hongkew
Hubei	Hu-pei (-peh)	Hupeh (Hupei)
Huizhou	Hui-chou	Hweichow
Hunan	Hu-nan	Hunan
Huolu	Huo-lu	Hwailu
Huozhou	Huo-chou	Hochow
Jiading (Leshan)	Chia-ting	Kiating
Jiangsu	Chiang-su	Kiangsu
Jiangxi	Chiang-hsi	Kiangsi
Jilin	Chi-lin	Kirin
Jinan	Chi-nan	Tsinan
Jincheng (Tsechou)	Chin-ch'eng (Tse-chou)	Kincheng (Tsechow)
Jiujiang	Chiu-chiang	Kiukiang
Langzhong (Paoning)	Lang-chung	Langchung (Paoning)
Lanzhou	Lan-chou	Lanchow
Leshan (Jiading)	Lo-shan (Chia-ting)	Loshan, (Kiating)
Linfen (Pingyang)	Lin-fen (Ping-yang)	Linfen
Lishui (Qüzhou)	Ch'ü-chou	Chüchow
Lu'an (Changzhi)	Lu-an, Lu-ngan	Lungan
Lüda, Dalian	Lü-ta, Ta-lien	Dairen (Port Arthur)
Luoyang	Lo-yang (Honanfu)	Loyang
Luqü (Taozhou)	Lu-ch'ü (T'ao-chou)	Taochow
Nanchong	Nan-ch'ung	Nanchung (Shunking)
Nanjiang	Nan-chiang	Nankiang
Nanjing	Nan-ching	Nanking
Ningbo	Ning-po	Ningpo
Ningxia	Ning-hsia	Ningsia
Puzhou	Pu'-chou	Puchow
Qiantang	Ch'ien-t'ang	Tsientang
Qianyang	Ch'ien-yang	Chienyang
Qingdao	Ch'ing-tao	Tsingtao
Qinghai	Ch'ing-hai	Tsinghai
Qingjiangpu	Ch'ing-chiang-p'u	Tsingkiangpu
Queshan (Choshan)	Ch'ueh-shan, Ch'o-shan	Choshan
Qüwu	Ch'ü-wu	Chüwu
Qü Xian	Ch'ü-hsien, Ch'ü-chou	Kiuchow
Runan (Runing)	Ju-an (Ju-ning)	Runing
Shaanxi	Shan-hsi	Shensi
Shandong	Shan-tung	Shantung
Shangrao (Guangxin)	Shang-rao	Shangrao (Kwangsin)
Shangqiu (Guide)	Kweiteh	Kweiteh
Shantou	Shant-t'ou	Swatow
Shanxi	Shan-hsi	Shansi
Shenyang	Shen-yang	Shenyang (Mukden)

Sheqidian	She-chi-tien	Shekitien
Shunde (Xingtai)	Shun-teh	Shunteh
Sichuan	Szu-ch'uan	Szechwan
Shijiazhuang	Shih-chia-chuang	Shikiachuang
Songjiang	Sung-chiang	Sungkiang
Suzhou	Su-chou	Suchow
Taibei	T'ai-peh (-pei)	Taipei
Taizhou (Linhai)	T'ai-chou	Taichow
Tianjin	T'ien-chin	Tientsin
Tianshui	T'ien-shui (Ts'in-chou)	Tienshui (Tsinchow)
Tong Xian (Tongzhou)	T'ung-chou	Tungchow
Urumqi (Dihua)	Ti-hua	Urumchi (Tihwa)
Wanxian	Wan-hsien	Wanhsien
Wenzhou	Wen-chou	Wenchow
Wuxüe	Wu-hsüeh	Wusueh
Xi'an	Hsi-an	Sian (Singan)
Xiamen	Hsia-men	Amoy
Xiangfan	Hsiang-fan	Fancheng
Xiangcheng	Hsiang-ch'eng	Siangcheng
Xichang	Hsi-ch'ang	Sichang (Ningyuan)
Xin'an	Hsin-an (An-hsin)	
Xinchang	Hsin-ch'ang	Sinchang
Xing'an (Ankang)	Hsing-an	Hingan
Xining	Hsi-ning	Sining
Xinjiang	Hsin-chiang	Sinkiang
Xizang	Hsi-tsang	Tibet
Yan'an	Yen-an	Yenan
Yangzhou	Yang-chou	Yangchow
Yibin (Suifu)	Yi-pin	Ipin (Suifu)
Yichang	Yi-ch'ang	Yichang (Ichang)
Yingkou	Ying-k'ou	Niuchwang
Yueyang	Yueh-yang (Yoyang)	Yochow
Yuexi	Yueh-hsi	Yohsi
Zhangjiakou	Chang-chia-k'ou	Kalgan
Zhaotong	Chao-t'ung	Chaotung
Zhejiang	Che-chiang	Chekiang
Zhengzhou	Cheng-chou	Chengchow
Zhenjiang	Chen-chiang	Chinkiang
Zhenyuan	Chen-yuan	Chenyuan
Zhili (Hebei)	Chih-li (Ho-pei)	Chihli
Zhoujiakou (Zhoukouzhen)	Chou-chia-k'ou	Chowkiakow
Zunyi	Tsun-yi	Tsunyi

A CHRONOLOGY
1886–1986

(See also HTCOC Book 6, pp 444–5)

1886	
	First baptisms in Korea
April	JHT plans CIM business centres in Shanghai, major Yangzi ports
June	Wusong Rd site bought
	Outlaw Yü Manzi begins anti-RC violence in Sichuan
1887	
	Year of The Hundred
	Ambassador Marquis Zeng publishes *The Sleep and the Awakening*
March	Erik Folke, first Swedish associate, arr Shanghai
July	George and Minnie Parker begin crossing Gansu-Xinjiang; arr Gulja, 1889
	Francis Younghusband crosses N China, E to W
	Henry W Frost in UK invites JHT to N America
	Josef F Holmgren invites JHT to Sweden
1888	
June 9–20	International Missionary Conference, London; *National Righteousness* launched
Summer	Annie Royle Taylor to Luqü (Taozhou), springboard for Tibet
September 24	JHT forms nuclear N Am Council of CIM
September 27	Chefoo headmaster Herbert Norris dies, hydrophobia
October	Adam Dorward dies
	Discord between London Council and JHT over N Am
1889	
	Guang Xü emperor ends regency, assumes government

	Construction begins on Wusong Rd HQ, Shanghai
April 12	JHT dep Shanghai to UK
May 3	First Anti-Opium resolution before UK Parliament succeeds
July 6	JHT dep UK to N Am; August 4 arr UK
September	UK 'Ladies Council' and Scottish Auxiliary Council inaugurated
October	JHT writes *To Every Creature*; inspiration of F Franson and associate missions
November 1	JHT and F Howard Taylor (FHT) to Sweden, Norway
1890	
	Korea adopts J L Nevius' 1861 'indigenous principles', great success
February	Wusong Rd HQ, first occupants move in
March	CIM Deed of Constitution signed (legal incorporation)
March 17	JHT dep UK; arr Shanghai April 27
April 29	C H Parsons, first CIM Australian, arr Shanghai
May 1–6	CIM preparatory conference
May 7–20	General Missionary Conference, Shanghai
May 22	First session of Australian Council
June–July	JHT tours Yangzi R centres
July 19	JHT, M Beauchamp dep Shanghai; arr Sydney August 26; dep Brisbane Nov 20 with first Australian party; arr Hong Kong Dec 13
October 28	First US Swedish Alliance missionaries arr Shanghai (see Feb 1891)
1891	
	Hunan inaccessible, until early 1896
	London Council bid for administrative voice in China
January	*National Righteousness* against opium trade sent to 60,000 national leaders in UK Church and Parliament
February 17	Franson's first 'expedition' of N Am Swedes arr Shanghai
March 5	Guang Xü emperor receives foreign envoys in audience
March 9–11	UK National Anti-Opium Convention
April 14–21	H W Frost and N Americans in China vote for full membership of CIM
June 5	Argent and Green murdered at Wuxüe

	Yangzi valley riots through summer, into 1892
	T Richard became Soc of SDK
October 22	London Council ultimatum
1892	
January 31	Sun Yatsen graduates MD at Hong Kong
	C H Spurgeon dies
March 25	Arrest of Zhou Han, anti-foreign agitator, ordered
May 10	JHT and JET dep Shanghai to Canada, UK; in UK July 26–Feb 14, 1894
July 29	Cecil Polhill family and team flogged at Songpan
September 2	Annie R Taylor enters Tibet
October 6	Second National Anti-Opium Convention
November	Rebellion threatening in China
1892–93	Anti-opium pressure on Gladstone maintained
1893	
	Sven Hedin aged 28 begins Central Asian travels
January 3	Annie R Taylor near Lhasa, expelled, arr Kangding April 12
January 4	H W Frost, Helmer, Nasmith arr UK
February–March	Agreements reached with London Council
February 15, 23	A B Simpson's International Alliance Mission parties arr Shanghai
May	Newington Green, London, offices and home planned; work begins
June	H W Frost appointed Home Director, N Am
June 30	Parliament supports Gladstone's Opium Commission evasion
July 1	Two Swedes murdered at Songbu, Macheng, Hubei
July 7	Revised Principles and Practice accepted; discord ended
October 19	J L Nevius dies at Yantai
November 10	JHT speaks of planning advance, the 'Forward Movement'
1893–94	Rijnhardt's hornets' nest
1894	Sun Yatsen forms a revolutionary cell
February 14	JHT, JET, Geraldine Guinness dep UK via USA, arr Shanghai April 17
February 28	Second International Student Convention, Detroit

May 11	JHT raises 'special support' question; settled June 1899
mid-May	Hudson Taylors, Howard Taylors, J J Coulthard to Shaanxi, Shanxi, for Swedish conferences, June 26 Xi'an, Sept 5 dep Tianjin
July 25	Japanese sink Chinese troopship *Kowshing*; Sino-Japanese war
September 25	JHT alone dep Shanghai to Shanxi, Dec 4 arr Shanghai
November 7	Empress Dowager's 60th birthday; Christian women present NT
December 26	Li Hongzhang degraded after Japan defeats China
December	J A Wylie, Presbyterian, murdered in Manchuria
	Annie R Taylor's Tibetan Pioneer Mission, Sikkim
1895	
	China in convulsion
	Tibetan Pioneer Mission breaking up
	J T Morton's gifts begin
February 19	Li Hongzhang's honours restored
February	Xining, Gansu, besieged by Muslim rebels
March	B Broomhall retires to pursue anti-opium campaign
March 24	Li Hongzhang survives assassination attempt in Seoul
April	Newington Green office building occupied
April 17	Li Hongzhang signs Treaty of Shimonoseki, ratified May 8
May	Sichuan riots begin
August 1	Kucheng massacre, Fujian
mid-August	Chefoo schools building begins
Autumn	Xining siege extreme until January 14, 1896, qv
October	Ten cholera deaths at Wenzhou
	Sun Yatsen's first armed raid at Canton fails; hunted 1895–1912
October 18	Wm Cassels consecrated bishop
1896	
	Anti-Footbinding Society formed
	Isabella Bird Bishop travels in West China
	JHT pays return visit to Sweden
early 1896	Zhang Zhitong returns as viceroy to Wuhan;

	governor opens Hunan to missionaries
January 14	Xining siege lifted
January 18	JHT-JET dep Shanghai to Calcutta, Darjeeling
February 19	Hsi Shengmo dies
April	Reformer Kang Yuwei submits an anti-Shimonoseki memorial
May 2	JHT-JET, D E Hoste dep Shanghai; to UK, arr June 17
June 15	Chefoo schools foundation stone laid
August 17	JHT dep UK to Scandinavia, Germany
October	Sun Yatsen kidnapped in London, released

1897

June 22	Queen Victoria's Diamond Jubilee
July 13	Henry Savage Landor enters Tibet
August	J T Morton gives £10,000 to CIM; dies
September	T A P Clinton obtains Changde, Hunan, deeds; moves in
November 1	Two Germans murdered in Shandong
November 14	Germans seize Qingdao
November 24	JHT-JET, Henrietta Soltau dep UK to USA; Dec 18 dep San Francisco

1898

January 15	JHT party arr Shanghai
March 6	Germans lease Jiaozhou
March 10	George Müller dies
April 21	Spanish-American war
May 1	Admiral Dewey, USA, destroys Spanish fleet in Manila Bay
May 20	Rijnhardt and wife enter Tibet
May	Swedish leaders Henriksen and Carlsson die in Shaanxi
June	Question of JHT's successor raised
	Kang Yuwei becomes advisor to Guang Xü emperor
June 9	Sino-British Convention; Hong Kong leased territories extended; July 1 GB leases Weihaiwei
June 11	The Hundred Days of reform begin
September 20	Emperor promotes Yüan Shikai in plot against Empress Dowager
September 22	Empress Dowager takes power, imprisons emperor
September	J T Morton legacy payments begin; annually till 1912

October 22	Thomas Botham dies
October 26	Dr F A Keller occupies Chalingzhou, Hunan
Autumn–Winter	Yü Manzi outlaw active in Sichuan
November 4	W S Fleming, Pan Shoushan murdered in Guizhou
December	Tong Xian (Tongzhou), Hebei, foreigners sense coming storm
1899	
	All 1899 into 1900 unrest, riot, rebellion throughout China
	Italy demands Sanmen Bay, Zhejiang; rebuffed
	Yü Manzi uprising worse
	Marconi begins wireless telegraphy
January 9	W T Berger dies
January 16–21	JHT attends Chongqing conference; Feb 10 very ill
February 6	Philippines war of independence ends
March 15–17	Imperial rescript grants RC hierarchy official status
March	Yangzi R junk men revolt against steamships
	Dr Keller given a 'house-warming' riot
May	'Boxer' units formed in Shandong
June	Unanimous agreement on 'special support' in CIM
August	Dr Keller driven out of Chaling, to Shanghai
September 25	JHT-JET dep Shanghai to Australia, New Zealand
October	Boxers adopt slogan 'Uphold dynasty, exterminate foreigners'
October 6	Dr A W Douthwaite dies
October 10	Boer War begins
November	Empress Dowager's edict 'Resist aggression!'
December 22	D L Moody dies
December 31	Boxers murder S M Brooks, SPG, Shandong
1900	
January 5	JHT-JET dep Hobart, Tasmania, to NZ
January 6 & 30	JHT writes of 'no light beyond New York'
January 24	Emperor deposed, Pu Jün made heir apparent
March 13	Allied naval demonstration in Gulf of Zhili
March 16	Yü Xian appointed Governor of Shanxi
March 20	JHT-JET dep NZ arrive San Francisco April 5
April 20	Yü Xian arr Taiyuan, recruits Boxers
April 23–May 1	Ecumenical Conference of Foreign Missions, New York

May 5	JHT unable to finish an address at Boston
May 17	Mafeking siege relieved
June 9	JHT-JET dep Boston to UK, arr London June 19
July 10	JHT-JET arr Davos, Switzerland
June–November	BOXER CRISIS (see Appendix 6)
December 24	Allies present 'irrevocable demands'
December 26	Xi'an Court accepts Allied terms
1901	
January 22	Queen Victoria dies
January	CIM reoccupying Yangzi ports; D E Hoste on Yangzi R tour of inspection
February 22	Wm Cooper, Bagnall, remains exhumed, Baoding
February	Imperial edict inflicts penalties on guilty mandarins
February	Shanghai conference of evacuees
February end	CIM decide no claims, no compensation to be accepted
March 21	Ekai Kawaguchi enters Lhasa
March 23–24	Baoding funerals
March 24	JHT appoints D E Hoste acting-General Director
April	JHT-JET visit UK; JHT made a vice-president of B&FBS
April	Li Hongzhang and Prince Qün request T Richard's help in Shanxi
May	Governor of Hunan lends launch to G John
May 29	Imperial edict agrees 450 million taels reparation to Allies
June 1	D E Hoste team of investigators dep Shanghai to Shanxi
June 8	Dr Keller to Changsha by governor's invitation
June 26	D E Hoste investigators dep Baoding with governor's escort; received coldly at Huolu
July 4	DEH investigators meet Pastor Qü, Elders Xü, Si at Shouyang
July 9	Anniversary of massacre; pageantry on arr at Taiyuan
July 18	Ceremonies at Taiyuan massacre site and cemetery
August 8	D E Hoste team at Taigu; separate to each martyr city
August 13	JHT walking and climbing, but August 15 a fall or 'slight stroke'

September 5	Prince Qün presents regrets at Potsdam
September 7	Boxer Peace Protocol signed; Shanghai missions' advice rejected
September	Wang Lae-djün dies
October 6	Imperial Court except imperial party dep Xi'an to Kaifeng
October 11	Governor Ceng of Shanxi issues proclamation
October 20	Empress Dowager and emperor dep Xi'an
November 7	Li Hongzhang dies, aged 78
November 14	Empress Dowager celebrates 66th birthday at Kaifeng (born Nov 3)
December 14	Court dep Kaifeng
December end	All CIM refugees have dispersed inland or to homelands
1902	
1902–03	Russia in undisputed military possession of all Manchuria
1902–04	Neo-Boxer rising in West China
January 7	Imperial party re-enter Beijing
January 28	Foreign envoys received in audience
May 21	JHT 70, frail, provides for decease, moves to Chevalleyres, Vevey
May 31	Boer war ends
July 2	Elder Si dies
July 6–9	Thirteen boys at Chefoo school die of cholera
August 15	J R Bruce and R H Lowis murdered at Chenzhou, Hunan
October 1902– April '03	Robert Wilder family join Taylors at Vevey
1903	
January 1	JHT finishes reading the Bible, 40th time D E Hoste, General Director on JHT's official retirement
January 20	King Edward VII and Pres Theodore Roosevelt in wireless communication
April 11	Yong Lu dies
May	F Younghusband appointed to lead force to Lhasa, to counter alleged Russian moves
July	JET found to have an inoperable tumour
Autumn	Japan challenges Russia's dominance of Manchuria
1904	
February 8	Russo-Japanese war begins
March 1	Jubilee of JHT's arrival at Shanghai 1854
March 25	Joseph (Wm) Faulding dies

July 30	JET dies
August 3	British force reaches Lhasa
September 7	Anglo-Tibetan treaty signed; Younghusband withdraws
1905	
	Sun Yatsen organises Tong Men Hui (revolutionary movement)
February 15	JHT and Howard Taylors dep to China via San Francisco, arr Shanghai April 17
April 29	Three veterans, W A P Martin, Griffith John, Hudson Taylor, meet at Hankou
May 1	Taylors by train to Henan, arr back May 26
May 27	Three veterans meet again at Hankou
May 28	Russian Baltic fleet defeated in Sea of Japan
June 1	JHT arr Changsha
June 3	JHT dies after Changsha reception
September 5	Russo-Japanese Treaty of Portsmouth, USA, signed
1906	
	Crucial Anti-Opium debate in UK Parliament
	Conversion of many racial minority people in S-W China
	George Hunter settles in Urumqi, Xinjiang
April 18	San Francisco destroyed by earthquake and fire
December 30	Status of Confucius elevated to that of Heaven and Earth
1907	
	Robert Morrison centenary missionary conference
	Flood and famine in Jiangsu, Anhui, Henan; CIM relief team
August	Empress Dowager suffers a slight stroke
1908	
April	Imperial rescript of March 1899 re RC status, withdrawn
August	Empress Dowager issues an Outline Constitution with projected Parliament and Assembly to advise the emperor
November 14	Emperor Guang Xü dies in suspicious circumstances
November 15	Empress Dowager dies; Prince Qün regent for infant Pu Yi
1909	
October 5	Zhang Zhitong dies

1910

	J O Fraser arr China; by 1918, 60,000 West Yunnan tribal Christians
	World Missionary Conference, Edinburgh
October 3	First national Assembly and October 24 Day of National Humiliation and Prayer in UK, persuade Britain to end opium traffic

1911

April 6	Revolutionary uprising at Canton
April 19	British Parliament decides opium traffic to end within two years
May 8	Manchu Grand Council abolished
May 29	B Broomhall dies after Anti-Opium Campaign succeeds
August	Revolt at Chengdu
October 9	Accidental explosion at Wuchang triggers revolution
October 10–11	Rebellion at Wuchang, Hankou, Hanyang: 'Double Tenth'
	Xi'an massacre of 15,000 Manchus, many Chinese
	Swedish Mrs Beckman, Norwegian W T Vatne, six children murdered
November	Shanghai falls to revolution
December 4	Nanjing falls
December 29	Sun Yatsen becomes provisional President of Republic of China

1912

	Membership of CIM exceeds 1,000
February 12	Child emperor Pu Yi abdicates; Qing dynasty ends, Republic established
March 10	Yüan Shikai inaugurated, President
December	Tong Wen Hui and KMT (Kuomindang) amalgamate; landslide victory for KMT in national elections
	Yüan crushes Second Revolution in South

1913

| April 27 | World Day of Prayer for China called by Chinese government |
| May 7 | Indian opium traffic 'dead' announced in UK Parliament |

1914

| | Reaction to Chinese revolutionary enthusiasm sets in |
| August | First World War begins |

December 23	Yüan Shikai performs emperor's rites at Altar of Heaven
1915	
	Yüan accepts Japan's Twenty-one Demands
	T Richard retires, 'his dreams frustrated'
December	Yüan Shikai's 'Representative Assembly' petitions him to accept nomination as emperor
	Yüan declares reign to begin on January 1, 1916; widely rejected
1916	
June 6	Yüan Shikai dies; 1912 Constitution restored
1916–26	Decade of warlords
1917	
July 1–12	Pu Yi's abortive restoration to the throne
August	Sun Yatsen's Constitution Protection Movement
1919–20	Treaty of Versailles favours Japan, slights China
1921	Chinese Communist Party founded
1923	Chinese nation sick of politics
	Wars between warlords begin
1924	
October	Marshal Feng Yüxiang's National People's Army occupies Beijing
December 31	Sun Yatsen arr Beijing
1925	
March 12	Sun Yatsen dies
May 30	Shanghai police shoot a student demonstrator; anti-foreign feeling exacerbated: 'China for the Chinese'
November 7	W W Cassels dies of typhus; Nov 15 Mrs Cassels dies
1926	
	Chiang Kaishek launches his Northern Expedition
1927	
	Stalin's influence strong in China
	Many foreigners murdered or held to ransom
1927–32	CIM's 'Two Hundred' selected from over 1,200
1928	
	Chiang Kaishek subdues remaining Northern warlords
August 4	Chiang moves capital to Nanjing

1930	CIM sell Wusong Rd, buy Sinza Rd properties
1931	CIM HQ moved to Sinza Rd
1931–32	Japanese invade Manchuria; Pu Yi made puppet emperor of 'Manchuguo'
1932	
	The 'Two Hundred' completed, CIM membership over 1,300
	Seven men travel with George Hunter via Gobi Desert, arr Urumqi November 12
1933	
January	Muslim rebellion in Xinjiang, Urumqi besieged, Percy Mather and Dr Emil Fishbacher die of typhus
1934	
	Henry S Ferguson, CIM, captured, executed
October	Start of Communist Army's 'Long March' to Shaanxi
October 1–2	Haymans, Bosshardts, Grace Emblen captured; women and children released, men join the Long March
December 6	John and Betty Stam executed in South Anhui
1935	
	'The Trio', Eva, Francesca French, Mildred Cable, held prisoner for months in Russian dominated Xinjiang
November 18	Arnolis Hayman released in N W Hunan
1936	
Easter Day	Alfred Bosshardt released near Kunming
June11–August	'The Trio' evangelise Gobi Desert cities and oases
October	Communist Long March survivors arr Wuqi, N Shaanxi
December	Yan'an becomes Communist HQ
December 12	Chiang Kaishek held prisoner at Xi'an by 'Young Marshal' Zhang Xüeliang
1937	
	Japanese invade North China
1938	
September 25	J O Fraser 'apostle of the Lisu' dies
1939	
	Second World War
	Sir Montagu Beauchamp travels in CIM convoy from Vietnam to Chongqing; dies at Langzhong Oct 26

1942	
December 7	Japan attacks US Navy at Pearl Harbor, Hawaii; US enters WW II
1945	
May 8	Victory in Europe; 'VE Day'
August 6	Hiroshima atom bomb dropped
August 8	Russia declares war on Japan, enters Manchuria
August 14	Japan surrenders, 'VJ Day' celebrated Sept 2
1948	
	Miss Lenell, Swedish Mission, Shanxi, and church elder executed
September 1	Communists declare North China People's Government
December end	Armies reach Yangzi R
1949	
March–April	Communists cross Yangzi R
April 23	Nanjing falls
April 25	Chiang Kaishek and National Government to Taiwan
October 1	Mao Zedong proclaims People's Democratic Republic of China at Tian An Men, Beijing
1950	
	'Christian Manifesto' initiates withdrawal of all missionaries
	Whole of mainland China 'liberated'; controlled by *baojia* system (see Glossary p 19)
1951–52	
	Wholesale evacuation by CIM and other societies; last of CIM left July 20, 1953
1951	Great purge by 'Three Anti' and 'Five Anti' campaigns
April	Three-Self Patriotic Movement (TSPM) launched to control Christians
1953	Five Year Plan: co-operatives
1954	Constitution of People's Republic
1957	Independent judiciary abolished
	Mao encourages free speech; follows with rectification campaign
1958–61	Great Leap Forward; 80 per cent of Chinese in communes
1966	Schools closed; 'Red Guards' released for Cultural Revolution
	Christians including TSPM silenced until 1972

1972–78	Some liberalisation; thousands escape to Hong Kong
	Dramatic growth of Christian Church revealed
1975	Communes dissolved
1976	
September 9	Mao Zedong dies, aged 82; radicals led by 'Gang of Four' arrested
1977	
	Deng Xiaoping rehabilitated
1986	Chinese Church reaches 21½ million baptised members; over 52 million including Christian families and adherents

A SEQUENCE CHART OF HUDSON TAYLOR'S LIFE
21 May 1832–3 June 1905

UK 1

Barnsley	21 May 1832–May 1851
Hull	May 1851–24 Sept 1852
London	26 Sept 1852–19 Sept 1853

> *Dumfries* voyage
> 19 Sept 1853–1 March 1854

CHINA 1

1 March 1854–Dec 1855	Shanghai	Taiping Rebellion
	Ningbo	Muslim Rebellion
Dec 1855–5 July 1856	Shantou (Swatow)	
Aug 1856–20 Jan 1858	Ningbo	2nd Opium War
19 July 1860	Ningbo marries Maria Dyer	

> *Jubilee* voyage
> 19 July–20 Nov 1860

UK 2

Westbourne Grove	20 Nov 1860–9 Apr 1861
1 Beaumont St	9 Apr 1861–6 Oct 1864
JHT graduates MRCS	29 Jan 1862
JHT, F F Gough begin Ningbo N T translation	Oct 1863
30 Coborn St (No 1)	6 Oct 1864–26 May 1866
'CIM' a/c audited	3 June 1865
JHT undertakes 'CIM'	25 June 1865

> *Lammermuir* voyage
> 26 May 1866–1 Oct 1866

Lammermuir party sail	26 May 1866	Muslim rebellion in N-W China

CHINA 2

22 Nov 1866–1 June 1868	Hangzhou	
1867	CIM deploy inland	

1 June 1868	Yangzhou
22, 23 Aug 1868	Yangzhou riot
July 1869	Zhenjiang
21 June 1870	Tianjin massacre
23 July 1870	Maria dies

> Messageries Maritimes
> *Volga & Ava* voyages
> 5 Aug 1871–25 Sept 1871

UK 3

Mildmay	Oct 1871
JHT marries	
Jennie Faulding	28 Nov 1871
6 Pyrland Road	January 1872

> M M *Tigre* voyage
> 9 Oct 1872–28 Nov 1872

CHINA 3

November 1872	Shanghai
	Nanjing; CIM circuit travel

> Messageries Maritimes
> 30 Aug 1874–14, 15 Oct 1874

UK 4

JHT party arr London	14, 15 Oct 1874
6 Pyrland Road	October 1874
JHT 'paralysed' appeals	
for eighteen pioneers	Dec 1874–Jan 1875
	21 Feb 1875 Margary murdered
	April 1875 First of 'the nine' provinces entered

> Messageries Maritimes
> 8 Sept 1876–22 Oct 1876

CHINA 4

22 Oct 1876	Shanghai
13 Sept 1876	Chefoo Convention signed
Oct 1876–1880	JHT's 'bombshell' scatters CIM
1877	Zhenjiang: JHT 'at large'

CIM incessant
travelling

Messageries Maritimes
9 Nov 1877–20 Dec 1877

UK 5
6 Pyrland Road   1877–79   Great Famine

JET dep UK to China   2 May 1878–13 June 1878   Famine relief

23 Oct 1878   Taiyuan

JHT dep UK to China   Messageries Maritimes
24 Feb 1879–22 April 1879

CHINA 5

Aug–Sept 1879   Yantai (Chefoo)
Yangzi valley cities
Oct–Dec 1879   Yantai base, Chefoo
planned
1880   J L Nevius expounds
indigenous principles
13 Oct 1881–1 Dec 1881   JET dep Yantai arr UK
10 Feb 1883   JHT completes 15,000
miles administrative
travels

Messageries Maritimes
6 Feb 1883   dep Yantai
10 Feb 1883–27 Mar 1883   dep Hong Kong to UK

UK 6

Pyrland Road base   27 March 1883
UK travelling
Cambridge Seven   1884–85
First associate   1884
missions

Messageries Maritimes
20 Jan 1885–3 March 1885

CHINA 6

3 March 1885   arr Shanghai
Women's Guangxin
R field opened

		JHT extensive travelling
	15 June 1886	Wusong Rd HQ site bought
	1886	China Council; The Hundred decided

Messageries Maritimes 9 Jan 1887–18 Feb 1887

UK 7

Newington Green site bought	19 July 1887	The challenge of Tibet
'The Hundred' sent	1887	The Hundred deployed
H W Frost to UK	Nov–Dec 1887	
London International Missionary Conference	9–20 June 1888	
Anti-Opium Union and *National Righteousness*	26 June 1888	

Voyage 23 June 1888–1 July 1888

JHT dep UK to N America

Voyage 5 Oct 1888–30 Oct 1888

First N Am party dep Vancouver with JHT   arr Shanghai

CHINA 7

Discord over N Am council   1888–89   preparing for expansion

Voyage 12 April 1889–21 May 1889

dep Shanghai to UK

UK 8

London   21 May 1889–6 July 1889

Voyage 6 July 1889–14 July 1889 17 Aug–24 Aug 1889

dep UK to New York
dep USA to UK

To Every Creature   1889
dep UK to Sweden,   1 Nov 1889–5 Dec 1889
  Norway and back

                    18 Feb 1890   Wusong Rd HQ occupied

dep UK

Voyage P & O
17 March 1890–27 April 1890

CHINA 8

27 April 1890	arr Shanghai
7–20 May 1890	General Missionary Conference

Australia

Voyage	dep to Australia
26 Aug–20 Nov 1890	
21 Dec 1890	arr Shanghai, JHT-JET reunited

Discord with London   1890–92
British Govt Opium   1891
   Commission

Voyage	JHT-JET dep Shanghai
10 May 1892–26 July 1892	to UK

UK 9

via Canada arr UK   26 July 1892
   for 2 years

dep UK

Voyage
14 Feb 1894–17 Apr 1894

CHINA 9

in N America   23 Feb–March 1894

17 April 1894	arr Shanghai
mid-May–4 Dec 1894	Shaanxi-Shanxi journeys
1894–95	Sino-Japanese war
	China in convulsion
1 Aug 1895	Kucheng massacre
	Muslim rebellion; Xining siege

Voyage	
2 May 1896–17 June 1896	dep Shanghai

UK 10

arr London	17 June 1896	Hunan open
J T Morton legacy	Sept 1897	

	Voyage	
dep UK	24 Nov 1897	
dep USA	18 Dec 1897	
	15 Jan 1898	arr Shanghai

CHINA 10

	15 Jan 1898	arr Shanghai
CIM 'special support' members choose to pool funds	June–Oct 1898	'The Hundred Days' of reform
	4 Nov 1898	First CIM death by violence
		Yü Manzi uprising
	26 May 1899	'Boxers' organised
	September 1899	Coup and counter-coup

	Voyages	dep Shanghai to
	25 Sept 1899	Australia

arr Brisbane	16 Oct 1899	
Sydney	27 Oct	
Melbourne	13 Nov	
Adelaide	4 Dec	
Tasmania	22 Dec	
	31 Dec 1899	First Boxer martyr

	Voyages	
dep Hobart to N Z	5 January 1900	
dep N Z to San Francisco	20 Mar–5 April 1900	
Ecumenical Conference of Foreign Missions	23 April–1 May 1900	

	Voyage	
dep USA arr UK	9 June–19 June 1900	

arr Davos, Switzerland	10 July 1900	

UK 11

Switz	19 June 1900–Feb 1905	
	20 June 1900	Peking sieges begin
	24 June 1900	Imperial edict to kill
	9 July 1900	Taiyuan massacre
	14, 16 August	Peking sieges lifted
		Court flee to Xi'an
JHT appoints D E Hoste to act as Gen Director	24 March 1901	

	July 1901	D E Hoste investigators to Shanxi
	7 Sept 1902	Imperial cavalcade enter Peking
D E Hoste becomes Gen Director	1 Jan 1903	
JET dies	30 July 1904	
	1904–05	Russo-Japanese war

| JHT, FHT-MGT dep UK via San Francisco | Voyage 15 Feb–17 April 1905 | arr Shanghai |

CHINA 11

| | 3 June 1905 | JHT dies at Changsha, Hunan buried at Zhenjiang beside grave of Maria and children |

'A THOROUGHLY CHINESE CHURCH'

From Hudson Taylor's early days in Ningbo and the conversion and training of Wang Lae-djün, his 'indigenous principle' was practised – though he did not formulate it until later. 'A thoroughly Chinese Church' was his declared aim.

In this sequence of quotations from the earlier books of this series we see: that he would not let James Meadows return to Bridge Street, Ningbo, and deprive the Chinese of their autonomy (HTCOC Book 5, p 279); that after no more than one year at Hangzhou he dared to leave Wang Lae-djün and the fledgling church under the guidance of the beginners John McCarthy and Jenny Faulding (who understood the principle); that Wang, the interior decorator, became the 'chief shepherd' of a score of local churches, while in 1868 Hudson Taylor went 'inland' to Yangzhou with women and children; and how in 1871 McCarthy expressed the 'indigenous principles' in his own words (HTCOC Book 5, pp 333–5).

I hope this evidence will help to correct the impressions received from that friend of the CIM, the late Professor K S Latourette. His sympathetic accounts of Hudson Taylor and the CIM suffered from limited access to the sources from which these passages are taken. Had he seen them he could not have failed to record that these applied principles unerringly gave rise to a steadily growing Church. He wrote, 'The purpose of the China Inland Mission was not to win converts or to build a Chinese Church, but to spread the knowledge of the Christian Gospel throughout the empire as quickly as might be' (*A History of the Expansion of Christianity*, vol VI, p 329). The way he put it has proved misleading. Spreading the knowledge of Christ is inseparable from its effects. As the following excerpts show, Hudson Taylor from 1854 onwards worked to win and to nurture those who believed. The CIM did the same, building them up as local churches; teaching and training them systematically. While some societies concentrated on teaching, the CIM's published figures demonstrate its success in winning and establishing believers in stable, proliferating congregations from the outset. Moreover, adaptation by the missionary to China and the Chinese, not Chinese Christians to foreign ways, was the other side of the same coin.

First steps at Ningbo

It became more and more apparent . . . that any who might be brought to Christ would need the constant care and teaching of older and more experienced Christians. [Here he stressed fundamental principles:] *How* could this be done? As we foreigners could not then reside in the interior, it seemed desirable at first, to labour (at Ningbo) until a native church was formed; to spare no pains in thoroughly instructing the converts in the Word of God; to pray that evangelistic and pastoral gifts might be developed among them; and then to encourage them to locate themselves in the interior, visiting them frequently, and aiding them in their work in every possible way (HTCOC Book 5, p 351).

1867

May 7 saw the first baptisms at Hangzhou of four men and two women, including Dengmiao the printer and Ling Zhumou, an assistant cook. On June 2 three more men were baptised, none of them employees of the Mission. They had nothing else to gain from association with the foreigners. On July 21 two of Jennie's women and another man brought the number to twelve. Six or eight more were preparing to follow their example. Moreover, each of the baptised ones was 'showing concern to spread the Gospel'. The time had come to bring them together in the form of a local church, independent of the missionaries (HTCOC Book 4, p 312).

Wang Lae-djün had arrived and on July 16 was appointed pastor of the church of eighteen (of whom fourteen were men), with fifteen more applicants for baptism including six women. Mr Tsiu was named church-evangelist, three others as elders and two on account of their testifying were recognised as 'exhorters'. This, after nine months since reaching China – evangelism consolidated by the organisation of a self-governing church, as a stride towards wider evangelism. Jennie wrote,

> Everything will not be so immediately dependent on Mr Taylor . . . (The) organization and responsibility thrown upon the (Chinese) will be for good . . . We want to see large flourishing churches in this city and . . . (Chinese Christians) to go and proclaim the truth with power . . . in other parts (HTCOC Book 4, p 337). [And Hudson Taylor continued:]
> We wish to see Christian (Chinese) – true Christians, but withal true *Chinese* in every sense of the word. We wish to see churches and Christian Chinese presided over by pastors and officers of their own countrymen, worshipping the true God in the land of their fathers, in the costume of their fathers, in their own tongue wherein they were born, and in edifices of a thoroughly Chinese style of architecture.
> It is enough that the disciple be as his master (Jesus Christ) . . .
> If we really desire to see the Chinese such as we have described, let us as far as possible set before them a correct example: let us in everything unsinful become Chinese, that by all things we may save some. Let us adopt their costume, acquire their language, study to imitate their habits, and approximate to their diet as far as health and constitution will allow. Let us live in their houses, making no unnecessary alterations in external appearance, and only so far modifying internal arrangements as attention to health and efficiency for work absolutely require (HTCOC Book 4, pp 354–6).

1870

When James Meadows wanted to return to Ningbo he had to be told that the Bridge Street church had been successfully indigenous for too long already to be set back by the re-appointment of a foreigner. Hudson Taylor replied to him,

> It would throw matters back considerably now for any foreigner to be resident in Ningbo. The Church are beginning . . . to grasp the idea that they should not always be dependent on foreign teaching. And much of McCarthy's labour in this direction might be thrown away (HTCOC Book 5, p 279).

A discussion at the Fuzhou Missionary Conference in 1870 on how to establish Chinese churches on a self-supporting basis had been followed by an appeal from Sia Sek-ong of the Methodist Episcopal Church, to his fellow-ministers,

> The trouble is with us. We are afraid to trust God in this matter. But why should we fear? . . . (God) knows where our support is to come from; can we not trust Him? . . . Will He not feed us who go forth to preach His Gospel, and to suffer for Him? Don't trouble yourselves so much about the people; don't be always looking back to see where your supplies are to come from . . . If we were to give as much for Christ as the heathen give to the devil, we would soon be able to support our own pastors. We pay less money as Christians than the heathen do. We must give money to support the Gospel, and give liberally, or the church can never be established here. . . . Henceforth let everyone say – 'The Saviour is my Saviour, the Gospel is my Gospel, the Church is my Church, the preachers are my preachers', and let us never cease our efforts until the Church of God is firmly established in China (HTCOC Book 5, p 337).

Progress 1871–72

The Mission's work continued to look up. The New Lane church at Hangzhou had fifteen candidates for baptism, about to swell the church membership to sixty-seven. Wang Lae-djün, declining any salary from Mission sources, and trusting God to meet his needs, had opened four country outposts with regular services, and was supervising seven full-time evangelists and colporteurs. He had been up the Qiantang river to Lanxi preaching the gospel in an area where new churches were to result as this evangelism progressed – and on beyond Lanxi to Qü Xian. John McCarthy's continuous training classes were preparing more to join them either locally or far afield as missionaries to other cities. The future pastor Ren was among them (HTCOC Book 5, p 293).

In November 1871 the *Monthly Gleaner* carried important notes from McCarthy as 'a member of the China *Inland* Mission', here abridged. His concept was that of the Pauline 'tent-maker', widely adopted in years to come.

How is the Gospel to spread in China? . . . While by no means undervaluing itinerant labours . . . in *addition* there must be *lengthened* residence of the preacher among the masses. . . . Of course not *foreign* labour . . . there must of necessity be a large influx of the (Chinese) element. . . . That houses should be rented . . . is *not* necessary; nay more, not *desirable*. . . . The *Foreigner's* (house and) chapel are looked upon by the Christians as the Foreigner's. Thus the spirit of self-support which we hope to see grow and mature, is almost strangled at its very birth. . . . The *spirit* of the Gospel would certainly lead men to self-support, and thankful effort for Him who has done so much for them. . . . Is it not *unfair* to expect them to be bound to our arrangements for them? . . . A Chinese tradesman finds no difficulty in getting lodgings in any place he comes to. . . . Where God has blessed their labours it would not be difficult to arrange for the baptism of converts. . . . It may be asked, where are they to meet? . . . Why not in the house of one of their number? . . . If, however, the number increased (they would) get their own meeting-room or chapel . . . the point being that the room and all its surroundings would grow out of the felt need on the part of the *native* (Christian). . . . Such converts would be more likely to stand, and in their turn advance the cause of the Redeemer.

(Lo) Ah-ts'ih (was) for a year or two engaged in evangelistic work in the interior, far away from (Hangzhou), and his whole soul was stirred with a deep sense of his countrymen's need, and of the wide opening for (the) Gospel. . . . When in (Hangzhou) he called the Christians together and [quoting McCarthy] 'explained his plan for the formation of a native missionary society; namely that each (church) member should give something each month . . . and select some man or men to be their representative, supported by them. This money, he said, should not be used for any purpose but the spread of the Gospel; *not* for the poor (or) a fund from which they could borrow money. . . . Wang Lae-djün then told them how glad he was to hear of (it). . . . The popular belief that they got so much a month for being Christians would be effectually refuted, if it were known that, instead . . . they themselves *gave out* money for the spread of the Gospel. . . . They collected more than sufficient for one man's support for a month and . . . intend to send to the other stations of our mission . . . inviting (the Christians) either to co-operate, or else to act in the same way independently'. . . .

When we remember how recently the work at (Hangzhou) was commenced, and how poor the native Christians are in this world's goods, we . . . thank God and take courage (HTCOC Book 5, pp 333–5).

1873–75

'If our native helpers improve as they are doing, we shall soon *need* very few foreign helpers for our older work. If we have a few men of the right stamp, we shall soon see more than one unoccupied province invaded' (HTCOC Book 5, p 362).

Hudson Taylor also had the good of Hangzhou in mind. He planned to go there himself but to be busy with administrative work while delegating much of McCarthy's work to Chinese. They would have him and Wang Lae-djün, their pastor, to consult while they found their feet. Complete devolution to the church would follow naturally. Already Wang Lae-djün 'really looks to God for his sustenance'.

> If we can remain in China for a time [he explained] the Mission may be put on an entirely new footing, I think. I am striving to make the work more and more *native* and *interior*, so as to be workable with as few foreign helpers as possible.
>
> [And to his mother a week later] I am aiming at such organization of our forces, as will make us able to do more work with fewer foreign missionaries. I think I may *eventually* attain to one superintendent and two assistant foreign missionaries in a province, with qualified (Chinese) helpers in each important city, and colporteurs in the less important places. *I hope* I may be able ere the year closes to commence a college for the more thorough training of our native helpers. Long desired, there is more *probability* of our attaining this than heretofore.
>
> [In June he added] Pioneers are trying in several parts of (Anhui) to establish themselves. . . . The path of patient perseverance in well-doing, of voluntary taking up of the Cross, of forbearance under annoyance, and even persecution, without attempted retaliation is a difficult one; none perfectly pursue it; those whose work involves much of it need our special prayers.
>
> [And in July, 1873, in a statement of classic significance in the strategy of mission,] The work . . . is steadily growing and spreading – especially in that most important department, *native* help. The helpers themselves need much help, much care and instruction; but they are growing more and *more efficient* as well as more numerous; and the future hope of China doubtless lies in *them*. I look on all us foreign missionaries as platform work round a rising building; the sooner it can be dispensed with the better; or rather, the sooner it can be transferred to other places, to serve the same temporary purpose, the better for the work sufficiently forward to dispense with it, and the better for the places yet to be evangelized (HTCOC Book 5, p 373).
>
> There is nothing more evident than that the evangelization of China must be mainly effected by Christian (Chinese); and that (they) can only *effectively* work in or near their own native districts.

Elsewhere they were handicapped. They could learn a different dialect, but the tendency was for them to be treated as strangers, whereas a native of the same province was more likely to be welcomed without question (HTCOC Book 5, p 434).

Consolidation of the gains already made was no less Mission policy than breaking new ground. 'The evangelization of China must be mainly effected by Christian (Chinese)', so constant teaching and training of them in the course of field work would be continued. The deliberate transfer of foreign missionaries from established churches would encourage congregations to conduct their own affairs. To demonstrate their progress, from time to time he published translations of sermons preached by men who had so recently been unenlightened pagans. Their grasp of truth and ability to expound it were apparent. Work built muscle, and learning in action was the best kind of school for Chinese and missionaries alike. Both were to advance together. The foreigners were to be the catalysts and examples, the scaffold, not the main frame of the Church. His aim was that they should be far outnumbered by Chinese working Christians. Some with families would have to be salaried or as colleagues have their expenses paid, but a greater and greater proportion would earn their own living or be supported by growing congregations. Mission statistics might well not include such men and women. But 'the conversion, instruction and qualifying of evangelists was a slow process.' Two guiding principles needed to be kept in mind. The older work needed time to develop, but to limit a mission to this was to run into soft sand. The sooner work began in every province the better, for great distances and marked dialect and cultural differences meant that each needed its unique methods.

Twenty-eight churches with more than a score of 'outstations' had already been formed under the leadership of seven ordained Chinese pastors, with thirty-three evangelists, twenty-seven colporteurs, six Scripture-readers or 'Bible-women' and two schoolmasters. 'Upwards of fifty' places were occupied by resident Chinese and foreign church workers, and this consolidating work was itself expanding.

> We may, therefore, anticipate the necessity of a somewhat prolonged residence in our districts, for the purpose of instructing in the word of God those who may be converted . . . Those who will be the Chinese workers of the future first need to be . . . given time to show what gifts they possess.

His logic was convincing and satisfied his friends. Expansion and consolidation were to proceed hand in hand, the one nourishing the other (HTCOC Book 6, pp 37–9).

Misconceptions of the aims and methods of the CIM led him also to reiterate year by year the core of his 'Plan of Operation'. Like the apostles, missionaries (Chinese and foreign together) would travel in small teams to strategic centres, stay there or return again for long enough to establish 'a work of God' and, trusting its continuation to the keeping of God, would move on to new regions. 'The necessity of a somewhat prolonged residence . . . for the purpose of instructing in the Word of God those who may be converted' was *as much part of the plan as the itineration*.

The emphasis on an indigenous Chinese Church, in *China's Millions* of 1875–76 and again after the Shanghai conference in 1877, reflected the importance Hudson Taylor attached to the establishment of self-governing, self-supporting churches. 'We propose to itinerate constantly *at first*, and consequently to carry on localised work *only for a time* [the emphasis is his] – till native churches can be left to the ministrations of native labourers', with the help of visiting foreign teachers as long as it was needed and welcomed. Any perpetuation of Western denominational differences would be accidental, as individual missionaries left the mark of personal conviction on their teaching (HTCOC Book 6, p 163).

In his preface to the 1878 bound volume of *China's Millions*, after dealing with the great famine and iniquitous opium trade, he enlarged on the importance of Chinese missionaries.

> No greater blessing can be desired for China than that there may be raised up . . . a large number of men qualified to do the work of evangelists and pastors . . . The sooner a few converts can be gathered in each of the interior provinces, the sooner may we hope to have men in training for Christian work in widely distant parts of the empire (HTCOC Book 6, p 209).

'In all matters connected with Church or Refuges, Mr Hoste and I have united in prayer and consultation . . . We mutually help one another, without any distinction of native or foreigner, because the Lord has made us one' (Hsi Shengmo, 1896).

How Kenneth Latourette would have enjoyed these documents if he had lived to see them.

1879

Meanwhile progress was being made in another direction. John Nevius, a good friend since 1855, came to see Hudson Taylor and discussed with him the 'indigenous principles' he was developing in his Shandong work, later to be applied so successfully in Korea (Book 6, p 203).

After twenty years – 1885–86

In mid-December Hudson Taylor was back at Hangzhou to visit Jinhua with Wang Lae-djün. The Taylors' action in leaving Hangzhou in 1868 to pioneer Yangzhou and the Yangzi valley had been fully vindicated. An indigenous church movement had grown up without dependence on foreign oversight. Lae-djün's pastoral oversight extended a hundred and fifty miles and more, over several churches with their own pastors. The country churches were going through severe harassment and Hudson Taylor's presence was timely. While he was at New Lane (Xinkailong), two persecuted Christians were brought to him (*see* Book 6, p 394).

1887

> In brief, my experience has been this: Chinese Christian men in their leisure time did a useful work as evangelists which God blessed. Then, funds were supplied for their maintenance, in the hope that by giving the whole of their lives to evangelistic work they would be much more used of God. The amount supplied to the native helpers was, in most cases, less than that which they had procured by their own exertions, and not more. But although many of them were not personally injured in spirit by being supported, yet their influence was so diminished that the fruit of their labour was less after their whole time was devoted to it than it had been before, when they were working for their own maintenance; and this because of the prejudice created against them, by

the fact that they were supported by foreign funds; and were considered by the natives around them, though most unjustly, as *rice Christians*. In our own work, while we have still such supported agents, we are discouraging this kind of thing, and, as much as possible, substituting unpaid voluntary labour for a paid native agency. In proportion how wonderfully the Holy Spirit teaches some among each little company of converted heathen and qualifies them to be teachers. Dr Nevius has found it possible to collect from a wide area a number of such teachers, and to give them from time to time a month's Scriptural instruction and training, sending them back again to work on their farms or at their trades, and to communicate that which they have learned to their little flocks around them. Dr Nevius's work is extensive. I believe he has sixty or seventy little churches or gatherings of Christians, and he and only two paid native helpers superintend the whole work. Might not this line of things be greatly extended? (From a letter by Hudson Taylor to *The Christian*, April 21, 1887.)

ASSOCIATE MISSIONS OF THE CIM
1884–1952

May 1884	The (Quaker) Friends Foreign Mission
August 1884	(Methodist) Bible Christian Mission
1890 reorganised 1897	German China Alliance
1895	St Chrischona Pilgrim Mission

These relinquished or modified their associate status while continuing to work in China.

In 1950 a total of 394 members of associate missions (263 women, 131 men) were named in the CIM Directory.

> Alliance China Mission: German, Swiss, Czech
> Danish Missionary Union
> Finnish Free Missionary Society

1889	Free Church of Finland Mission
1911	Friedenshort Deaconess Mission
1908	German Women's Bible Union
1908	German Women's Missionary Union
1906	Liebenzell Mission (integral since 1897)
1900	Norwegian Alliance Mission (TEAM)
1889	Norwegian Mission in China
1890	The Evangelical Alliance Mission (Scandinavian: TEAM)
1892	Swedish Alliance Mission (Scandinavian China Alliance: Chicago)
1890	Swedish Holiness Union
	Swedish Mission in China
	Yunnan Mission (German, Czech, Polish)

Of the full members of the CIM remaining after the Second World War and civil war in China, many were also from Scandinavia, Switzerland, Holland, and one from Estonia.

A CHRONOLOGY OF THE BOXER CRISIS
1898–1901

In this Appendix place names appear in capitals, martyrs in bold and survivors in italic type.

'Herod killed James . . . and seized Peter . . . [but God] brought Peter out' (Acts 12)

1898–99

Nov 4, 1898	**Wm S Fleming**, CIM; Pan Shoushan, killed by sword, GUIZHOU
May 26, 1899	Boxer Society formed, Shandong
June 14–25	Kienning, Fujian, riots; missionaries escape
Nov 1899	Ci Xi's edict: resist foreign aggression; Boxers dominate Shandong, enter Zhili
Dec 30, 1899	**S M Brooks**, SPG, Shandong, killed by sword, beheaded

1900

Jan 11	Ci Xi's edict supports Boxers
April 20	Yü Xian, governor, arr Taiyuan, trains Boxers
May 12–14	**61 RCs** massacred, ZHILI
May 14	**Elder Si**, HONGTONG, sword thrust, dies Oct 1901
May 17	GONGCUN, Zhili, Prot. **pastor** and **Christians** massacred
May 23	*Mother, wife of Hsi Shengmo* beaten, plundered, Shanxi
May 17–28	**Wm Cooper** at Shanxi conferences
May 29	30 railway **engineers** fight, 6 die from Baoding, Zhili, to Tianjin
May 31	Allied reinforcements arr Peking

JUNE 1900

June 1	**C Robinson**, SPG, YONGQING, Zhili, killed
June 2	**H V Norman**, SPG, YONGQING, killed
June 4	**Wm Cooper** dep Lu'an to Baoding
June 5	*Eva French* party to Jiexiu for safety
June 6	LU'AN riot; 5 **Christians** killed *A E Glover*, **wife**, *2 children*, and *C Gates* attacked
June 7	Ci Xi's edict justifies Boxers

June 8	TONG XIAN **Christians** massacred; Peking foreigners congregate for defence; cable US President, 'outlook hopeless'
June 9	*Tong Xian missionaries* to Peking; *Glovers* dep Lu'an for Tianjin
c 9	*(Fei Qihao* report) 100 + **Christians** massacred at YÜCI, Shanxi
June 10	*5 Am Board* dep Zhangjiakou to cross Gobi to Kiakhta
June 11	PEKING Jap **Chancellor** killed
June 13	PEKING massacre, 100s of **Christians**; Boxers burning, looting. *Glovers* arr Shunde c/o *Griffiths, Brown*; rioted
June 14	Boxers arr DATONG, N Shanxi; **McKees, I'Anson's, Aspden, M E Smith** cornered, doomed
June 14	PEKING RC Beitang siege begins
June 15	**Wm Cooper** arr BAODING c/o **Bagnall family**
June 19	**Dr Millar Wilson** dep Linfen
June 19, 20	**Swedish Holiness Union** (CIM) dep HENYUAN, YINGZHOU, ZUOYÜN to SOPING; **Christians** massacred
June 20	PEKING German **envoy** killed; legation siege begins; **Francis James** killed; massacre of **Christians**
June 21, 25	*Shandong missionaries* escape to coast; Christians persecuted
June 23	Tianjin settlement siege lifted
June 23	*Am Board 5* (June 10) joined by *17 C&MA, 4 Swedes,* cross Gobi
June 23–25	Manchuria foreigners escape
JUNE 24	EDICT TO KILL all foreigners; Prince Chuang supervises massacre of 100s of **Christians**; edict to kill changed to PROTECT by Yuan Zhang, Xü Jincheng
June 24	**Lt Watts-Jones** wrecked, killed
June 25	Gov Yü Xian unleashes Boxers
June 26	**Millar Wilson** arr TAIYUAN; Zhang Zhitong promises to protect foreigners in Yangzi valley provinces
June 26	*A R Saunders* family, *A Jenkins*, *E Guthrie* rioted at Pingyao
June 27	*Saunders* party dep Pingyao, to Taiyuan, Lucheng, arr July 5 TAIYUAN, hospital destroyed, **E A Coombs** killed; 6 flee to BMS
June 27	Jiexiu riot, *Eva French* party escape 28th to Linfen
June 28–29	BAODING, Pastor **Meng Jixian** killed; XINZHOU BMS 8 cornered
June 28	*Jonathan Goforth, Canadians* dep Anyang, Henan; YINGZHOU **Christians** burnt alive

June 29	SOPING massacre of **10 Swedish**, **4 C&MA**; *Wang Lanbu* escapes SHOUYANG **Pigott family**, **Robinson**, **Atwater girls**, **Duval** flee to hills
June 30	XIAOYI, **Whitchurch**, **Searell** killed Shunde riot, *Griffiths*, *Brown* escape BAODING North, **5 Am Presbys** killed, Mukden church, mission burnt

JULY 1900

July 1	BAODING South **Am Board 3** killed; CIM **Bagnall**, **wife**, **children**, and **Wm Cooper** all beheaded
July 2	new edict: expel foreigners, persecute Christians; *Eva French party* join *Dreyers*, *Lutleys* at Linfen
July 2	**Pigott party** return to Shouyang. Huolu, Zhili, *CHS Green family*, *J Gregg* hear of massacres, riots
July 2–3	Yüncheng, S Shanxi, *Swedish Mission* given safe passes; leave funds with 'CCH' undercover; dep Shanxi
July 3	*Glovers* arr Lu'an from Shunde; MUKDEN **RCs** massacred; *O'Neill*, Irish Presby, dep Fakumen with Russians
July 3	Huolu riot, *Greens*, *Gregg* to hills; Imperial Govt appeals to foreign government for help!
July 4	*Goforth Canadians* and *engineers* through Xiangcheng, Henan
July 4	Xin'an *3 Swedish ladies* dep to Anhui
July 4	QÜWU, Shanxi, 2 parties, **Duncan Kay family**; *Graham McKie*, *Way*, *Chapman* separately to hills
July 4	**Barratt**, **Woodroffe** to hills; *Gracies*, *Macfarlane* dep Xiangcheng; *C H Bird* stays; **Alfred**, *Olivia Ogren* hear of Xiaoyi murders
June 4	Yong Lu refuses artillery to Tong Fuxiang
July 5	*Saunders* party arr Lucheng
July 6	*Dr Hewett*, Yüwu to Lucheng, back; *Saunders*, *Jennings*, *Guthrie* join *E J Cooper*, **wife**, **Huston**, **Rice** party of 14 dep Lucheng, attacked
July 7	Lucheng, Lu'an riots; *Glover* family *C Gates* dep LU'AN
July 7	Henan riots: Sheqidian, *W Guinness party*, Sihua, *C M Lack* escapes; Nanyang, *Goforth party* attacked
July 8	First Shanghai–London crisis cables; *Glovers-Gates* destitute on hilltop; *A Argento* escapes from Guangzhou, Henan; *Gracies*, *Macfarlane* rescued
July 8, 9	*Greens*, *Gregg* from temple to cave, *Argento* left for dead, Guangzhou
July 9	Sheqidian attack, *Guinness party* hide; arr Hankou 30 days later

July 9	TAIYUAN MASSACRE: **35 Protestant British**, **12 RC, about 30 Chinese** all beheaded
July 9	*Dreyer*, *Lutley*, *French* parties told to dep Linfen, insist on safe passes
July 9	Li Hongzhang reappointed viceroy of Zhili, orders protect foreigners
July 10	Zhoujiakou riot; police chief protects 9 CIM homeless
July 11	*C H Bird* dep Xiangcheng; *Glover*, *Gates* to die, pray for rain
July 12	DATONG CIM massacre: **McKee**, **I'Anson**, **Aspden**, **M E Smith**. **Nathan sisters**, **Heaysman** escape from DANING to hills
July 13	*Saunders*, *Cooper parties* flogged, **Rice** killed. **Huston** terribly injured. Ogrens flee Yongning to Shaanxi
July 14	*Saunders*, *Cooper* parties dep Changzhi (Tsechou). *Dreyer*, *Lutley*, *French* parties dep Linfen; forced through hostile Henan
July 15	False news of Peking legation massacre; Blagoveshchensk, Manchuria, massacre by Russians
July 15–17	HEJIN **McConnell**, **Young** party killed
July 16	*Saunders*, *Cooper party* enter Henan
July 19	*Greens*, *Gregg* to isolated farm
July 21	QÜ XIAN, Zhejiang, massacre of **Thompsons**, **Desmond**, **Manchester**, **Sherwood**, **magistrate's family**
July 21	XI XIAN, Shanxi, **Peats**, **Hurn**, **Dobson** to hill caves
July 22	CHANGSHAN, Zhejiang, **Wards**, **Thirgood** escape to Qü Xian, killed. *Saunders*, *Cooper party* arr Zhangzhou; rabid mandarin
July 24	*Argento* destitute meets Godsend, Lo
circa July 25	*Griffiths*, *Brown* protected at Zhengding RC cathedral by brigadier
July 27	Kaiser's Attila speech
July 28	Yuan Zhang, Xü Jincheng (June 24) beheaded
July 30	*Saunders*, *Cooper party* join *Glover*, *Gates* at Xinyang, S Henan; some near death. *Am Board*, *C&MA Gobi party* arr URGA
July 31	*Argento* and Lo arr Hankou; TAIGU, Shanxi, **Oberlin 6 and 8** Chinese beheaded

AUGUST 1900

Aug 3	**Mary Lutley** dies at Zhengzhou; *Saunders*, *Coopers*, *Glovers*, *Gates* dep Xinyang; **Jessie Saunders** dies
Aug 4	**Huston**, **Gates** manhandled by soldiers. Allied relief force starts to Peking
Aug 5, 6	Battles at Beicang, Yangcun

Aug 5	*Dr Hewett* to police cell
Aug 6/8	**Mrs E J Cooper** dies at Yingshan from injuries, 100 miles from Hankou
Aug 9	XINZHOU **BMS 8** massacred
Aug 9, 10	*Greens, Gregg* in farm cave, found, *Green* shot, all captured, taken to Huolu
Aug 11	**Mary Huston** dies
Aug 12	**Flora Glover** as if dying; LMS Christians' welcome
Aug 13	DANING, Shanxi, **Nathan sisters**, **Heaysman**, **Christians** killed. *Am Board, C&MA party* arr Kiakhta. *Greens, Gregg* in Baoding prison
Aug 14	PEKING SIEGE lifted; *Saunders, Cooper, Glover* party arr Hankou; **Brainerd Cooper** dies; *Greens, Gregg* by boat past Anxin
Aug 15	Imperial court flee to Kalgan, Xi'an; FENYANG **Oberlin 4**, **Atwater family**, **CIM Lundgrens**, **Eldred** killed; *Fei Qihao* escapes to Tianjin
Aug 16	Peking RC Beitang siege lifted
Aug 17	*Hewett* sentenced, imprisoned until November
Aug 18	**Glover baby** born; *Hedley Glover* dying, recovers
Aug 20	**Edith Lutley** dies
Aug 20, 21	Yü Xian's successor orders stop killing
Aug 21	*Pastor Zhang and son* of Daning saved by order to stop killing
Aug 21–24	**C&MA** desert fugitives killed
Aug 22	'CCH' reports on Shanxi killings
Aug 23–24	*J Gregg's* 'little tuft of paper'
Aug 24	Li Hongzhang, Prince Qing appointed plenipotentiaries and
Aug 25	issue orders to stop killings
Aug 28	**Glover baby** dies; *Dreyer, Lutley, French party* arr Hankou
Aug 28	**A & O Ogren** reunited
Aug 30	**Peats, Hurn, Dobson** killed

SEPTEMBER 1900

Sep 1	**Scandinavian Alliance** (Chicago) 4 killed in Ordos desert
Sep 3	*Greens, Gregg* danger from Boxers
Sep 5	*Greens, Gregg* by boat to Baoding prison; 8th to *yamen*, 6 weeks
Sep 8, 11, 16	Punitive expeditions by allies
Sep 15	**Duncan Kay family** and **Christians** killed near QÜWU
Sep 18	Germans demand punishments before negotiations
Sep 19	*Wang Lanbu* arr Beijing from Soping. 'CCH' reports **Barratt**, **Woodroffe** dead from privations

Sep 20	Li Hongzhang arr Tianjin, assumes viceroyalty Oct 1
Sep 24	Russians begin complete occupation of Manchuria
Sep 24–Oct 22	News of allies in control reaches Shanxi Christians

OCTOBER 1900

	J Walter Lowrie returns to Baoding, saves hundreds from allies' revenge
Oct 5	**Alfred**, *Olivia Ogren* dep Daning, wait 1 week while Ci Xi and court pass
Oct 10	**Vera Green** dies, *C H S Green* has typhoid; Dr *Hewett* freed, to Hankou
Oct 13	French occupy Baoding
Oct 14	Ogrens arr Linfen
Oct 15	**Alfred Ogren** dies
Oct 16	*Greens*, *Gregg* to French camp
Oct 17	Germans set up allied HQ in Imperial palace; *Griffiths*, *Brown* dep Zhengding to Baoding
Oct 19	British force arr Baoding, visit *Greens*, *Gregg*
Oct 20	*Greens*, *Gregg* to field hospital
Oct 22	*Greens*, *Gregg*, *Griffiths*, *Brown* c/o army doctors by boat to Tianjin, arr 27th, Green delirious
Oct 24	*Olivia Ogren*, *McKie*, *Chapman*, *Way* together at Linfen
Oct 25	**Flora Glover** dies at Shanghai
Oct 29	*Green* conscious; gunshot pellets removed at Shanghai

NOVEMBER 1900

Nov 5	Guilty Baoding mandarins executed
Nov 6	Dr *Hewett* arr Hankou
Nov 13	Allied punitive expedition to Zhangjiakou (Kalgan)
Nov 26	Telegram: *McKie*, *Chapman*, *Way*, *O Ogren*, *child* safe

DECEMBER 1900

Dec 6	Ogren baby born

JANUARY 1901

Jan 6	*Ogren*, *McKie party* dep Linfen with big escort

FEBRUARY 1901

Feb 16	*Ogren*, *McKie party* arr Hankou; 28th Shanghai
Feb 22	Yü Xian executed at Lanzhou. *Dr E H Edwards* investigation team exhume BAODING martyrs' remains

MARCH 1901

Mar 23, 24	Baoding funeral and memorial services
Mar 27	**J Stonehouse**, LMS, shot by ex-Boxer outlaws

THE MARTYRS OF 1900

MARTYRED MISSIONARIES
OF THE CHINA INLAND MISSION

Associates

	Date of Decease.		Date of Decease.
N Carleson		O A L Larsson	
Miss J Engvall		Miss J Lundell	
Miss M Hedlund	June 28, 1900	S A Persson	June 28, 1900
Miss A Johansson		Mrs Persson	
G E Karlberg		E Pettersson	

Members

Emily E B Whit-church	June 30, 1900	Elizabeth Burton	July 16, 1900
Edith E Searell	Do.	John Young	Do.
William Cooper	July 1, 1900	Alice Young	Do.
Benjamin Bagnall	Do.	David Baird Thomp-son	July 21, 1900
Emily Bagnall	Do.	Agnes Thompson	Do.
William Millar Wilson, MB., CM	July 9, 1900	Josephine Desmond	Do.
		Emma Ann Thir-good	July 22, 1900
Christine Wilson	Do.	G Frederick Ward	Do.
Jane Stevens	Do.	Etta Ward	Do.
Mildred Clarke	Do.	Edith Sherwood	July 24, 1900
Stewart McKee	July 12, 1900	Etta Manchester	Do.
Kate McKee	Do.	David Barratt	(?)
Charles S I'Anson	Do.	Alfred Woodroffe	(?)
Florence I'Anson	Do.	Margaret Cooper (Mrs E J)	Aug 6, 1900
Maria Aspden	Do.	Mary E Huston	Aug 11, 1900
Margaret E Smith	Do.	Francis Edith Nathan	Aug 13, 1900
Hattie Rice	July 13, 1900		
George McConnell	July 16, 1900	May Rose Nathan	Do.
Isabella McCon-nell	Do.	Eliza Mary Heays-man	Do.
Annie King	Do.		

Anton P Lundgren	Aug 15, 1900	Emma Georgiana	
Elsa Lundgren	Do.	Hurn	Aug 30, 1900
Annie Eldred	Do.	Duncan Kay	Sept 15, 1900
William Graham		Caroline Kay	Do.
Peat	Aug 30, 1900	P A Ogren	Oct 15, 1900
Helen Peat	Do.	Flora Constance	
Edith Dobson	Do.	Glover	Oct 25, 1900

Children

	Date of Decease.		Date of Decease.
Gladys Bagnall	July 1, 1900	Herbert Ward	July 22, 1900
Alexander Wilson	July 9, 1900	Isabel Saunders	July 27, 1900
Baby McKee	July 12, 1900	Jessie Saunders	Aug 3, 1900
Dora I'Anson	Do.	Mary Lutley	Do.
Arthur I'Anson	Do.	Brainerd Cooper	Aug 17, 1900
Eva I'Anson	Do.	Edith Lutley	Aug 20, 1900
Alice McKee	July 13, 1900	Faith Glover	Aug 28, 1900
Kenneth McCon-		Margretta Peat	Aug 30, 1900
nell	July 16, 1900	Mary Peat	Do.
Edwin Thompson	July 21, 1900	Jenny Kay	Sept 15, 1900
Sidney Thompson	Do.	Vera Green	Oct 10, 1900

Associates	Members	Children	Total
10	48	21	79

MARTYRED MISSIONARIES
OF OTHER PROTESTANT MISSIONARY SOCIETIES

Society for Propagation of the Gospel

Rev S M Brooks

Rev H V Norman   Rev C Robinson

English Baptist Missionary Society

Rev S W Ennals   Miss B C Renaut
Rev and Mrs Herbert Dixon   Rev and Mrs W A M'Currach
Rev and Mrs F S Whitehouse   Rev and Mrs T J Underwood
Rev and Mrs G B Farthing   Miss Stewart
  with three children

The Sheo Yang Mission

Mr and Mrs T W Pigott   Dr and Mrs A E Lovitt
  and son, Wellesley   and one child

Mr and Mrs Stokes
Mr John Robinson

Mr and Mrs Simpson
Miss Duval
Miss Coombs

Unconnected

Mr A Hoddle

The British and Foreign Bible Society

Rev and Mrs W T Beynon, with three children

The Swedish Mongolian Mission

Mr and Mrs Helleberg
and one child

Mr Wahlstedt

The Christian and Missionary Alliance

Mr and Mrs Emil Olssen
and three children
Mr and Mrs W Noren
and two children
Mr and Mrs O Bingmark
and two children
Mr and Mrs C Blomberg
and one child
Miss E Erickson
Mr and Mrs O Forsberg
and one child

Mr and Mrs C L Lundberg
and two children
Mr and Mrs E Anderson
and three children
Mr and Mrs M Nyström
and one child
Miss A Gustafson
Miss C Hall
Mr A E Palm
Miss K Örn (*unconnected*)

The Scandinavian Alliance Mongolian Mission

Mr D Sternberg
Miss H Lund

Mr C Suber
Miss Clara Anderson
Miss Hilda Anderson

American Board Mission

Rev and Mrs E R Atwater
and four children
Rev and Mrs C W Price
and one child
Miss Bird
Miss Partridge

Rev and Mrs D H Clapp
Rev F W Davis
Rev H T Pitkin
Rev G L Williams
Miss A A Gould
Miss M S Morrill

American Presbyterian Mission

Rev. and Mrs F E S Simcox   Dr and Mrs C V R Hodge
and three children   Dr G Y Taylor

ANALYSIS AND SUMMARY

	Adults	Children	Total
Society			
China Inland Mission	58	21	79
Christian and Missionary Alliance	21	15	36
American Board of Commissioners for Foreign Missions	13	5	18
English Baptist Mission	13	3	16
Sheo Yang Mission	11	2	13
American Presbyterian Mission (North)	5	3	8
Scandinavian Alliance Mongolian Mission	5	—	5
Swedish Mongolian Mission	3	1	4
Society for the Propagation of the Gospel	3	—	3
British and Foreign Bible Society	2	3	5
Independent (Mr Hoddle)	1	—	1
	135	53	188
Province			
Shan-si and over the Mongolian Border	113	46	159
Chïh-li	13	4	17
Cheh-kiang	8	3	11
Shan-tung	1	—	1
	135	53	188
Nationality			
British	71	29	100
Swedish	40	16	56
United States of America	24	8	32
	135	53	188

THE ILL-OMENED *GENGZI* YEAR 1900

Since BC 2697 the Chinese system of 60-year cycles had been observed, each year known by one of twelve titles. A *gengzi nian* or year of the character 'geng' (*see* C H Fenn's *Five Thousand Dictionary* pp xviii—xxix *The Sexagenary Cycle* 1804–1983 AD) occurring at sixty-year intervals, fell in 1840, 1900 and 1960. A year of twelve lunar months containing 354 or 355 days, with the resulting discrepancy from the solar calendar, needed the insertion of an intercalary month in seven of every nineteen years, characterised by the sun entering the fifteenth step of a sign of the zodiac. The system current in 1900 was further complicated by the need for the summer and winter solstices and spring and autumn equinoxes to fall within predetermined months: Summer in 5th, Winter in 11th, Spring in 2nd, Autumn in 8th month. The intercalary month of the *gengzi* year 1900 was the 8th lunar month, an occurrence last found in 1680. To the superstitious, such a concatenation of factors spelled disaster. (See C H Fenn's *Five Thousand Dictionary*; and Morse, H B: *International Relations of the Chinese Empire*, Vol 3 p 183.)

鳳 shu²	Rat	甲 1804 1864 子 1924	丙 1816 1876 子 1936	戊 1828 1888 子 1948	庚 1840 1900 子 1960	壬 1852 1912 子 1972
牛 niu²	Ox	乙 1805 1865 丑 1925	丁 1817 1877 丑 1937	己 1829 1889 丑 1949	辛 1841 1901 丑 1961	癸 1853 1913 丑 1973
虎 hu²	Tiger	丙 1806 1866 寅 1926	戊 1818 1878 寅 1938	庚 1830 1890 寅 1950	壬 1842 1902 寅 1962	甲 1854 1914 寅 1974
兔 t'u⁴	Hare	丁 1807 1867 卯 1927	己 1819 1879 卯 1939	辛 1831 1891 卯 1951	癸 1843 1903 卯 1963	乙 1855 1915 卯 1975
龍 lung²	Dragon	戊 1808 1868 辰 1928	庚 1820 1880 辰 1940	壬 1832 1892 辰 1952	甲 1844 1904 辰 1964	丙 1856 1916 辰 1976
蛇 she²	Snake	己 1809 1869 巳 1929	辛 1821 1881 巳 1941	癸 1833 1893 巳 1953	乙 1845 1905 巳 1965	丁 1857 1917 巳 1977
馬 ma²	Horse	庚 1810 1870 午 1930	壬 1822 1882 午 1942	甲 1834 1894 午 1954	丙 1846 1906 午 1966	戊 1858 1918 午 1978
羊 yang²	Sheep	辛 1811 1871 未 1931	癸 1823 1883 未 1943	乙 1835 1895 未 1955	丁 1847 1907 未 1967	己 1859 1919 未 1979
猴 hou²	Monkey	壬 1812 1872 申 1932	甲 1824 1884 申 1944	丙 1836 1896 申 1956	戊 1848 1908 申 1968	庚 1860 1920 申 1980
雞 chi¹	Fowl	癸 1813 1873 酉 1933	乙 1825 1885 酉 1945	丁 1837 1897 酉 1957	己 1849 1909 酉 1969	辛 1861 1921 酉 1981
狗 kou⁴	Dog	甲 1814 1874 戌 1934	丙 1826 1886 戌 1946	戊 1838 1898 戌 1958	庚 1850 1910 戌 1970	壬 1862 1922 戌 1982
豬 chu¹	Pig	乙 1815 1875 亥 1935	丁 1827 1887 亥 1947	己 1839 1899 亥 1959	辛 1851 1911 亥 1971	癸 1863 1923 亥 1983

NOTES

Page Note

Prologue
34   1   Stott: OMFA 5431a, 5412f, T, V; Stott, G: *Twenty-six Years in China*, Apl 23, 1889; *China's Millions* 1889 p 77
34   2   King: OMFA N14b.33, 37, 40–1, 46; 5412E, 5433
35   3   T James: OMFA 6114 April 29, 1887; 6211, Hunan or Sichuan
37   4   Benj B: Broomhall, M: *Heirs Together* p 97; OMFA 5445d; he had been Secretary of the Anti-Slavery Association, was on the Committee of the Society for the Suppression of the Opium Trade, and a supporter of the campaigns against vice and other moral evils in Britain.
37   5   Veterans: Council: OMFA 5445d; 6111; J 251. Meadows: Feb 5, 1887. Those over 20 years in CIM were Meadows, Stevenson, Williamson, Rudland, Mary (Bowyer) Baller, Louise (Desgraz) Tomalin, John McCarthy, the Cardwells and Charles Judds.
37   6   Strong words: OMFA 5431a (letters not preserved); 6111 Feb 12; 6211

Chapter 1
39   1   Engagements: OMFA 6224. In J 215 Stevenson was mistaken; BB made all the arrangements and held the fort while JHT travelled. JWS was in China.
40   2   Sharp: OMFA 6111 Mar 24
41   3   JWS: OMFA 6114, 6211; *China's Millions* 1884 p 69
41   4   Studd: *China's Millions* 1884 p 69
42   5   Nevius principles: OMFA I 319; *The Christian* Apl 21, 1887
42   6   Consolidate: Latourette, K S: *A History of Christian Missions in China* p 386
42   7   Hundred: Broomhall, M: *The Jubilee Story of the China Inland Mission* p 173; *China's Millions* 1887 pp 88, 92
43   8   Shanghai: OMFA 6114, 6211, 6212
43   9   Security: London Council Minutes, Sep 29, Oct 11, 1887
44   10   Newington Green: payment completed Oct 4, 1887; adjoining house bought for £1,000, Feb 19, 1889. For the Monte Cristo property behind Inglesby House £8,550 was asked on May 13, 1890; negotiations continued into Aug 1891; building in preparation, Oct 1893, completed 1894.
44   11   Newington Green: *China's Millions* 1888 p 94
46   12   Tibet: Morse, H B: *International Relations of the Chinese Empire*, Vol 2 p 372

46	13	Lanzhou: *China's Millions* 1887 p 156
47	14	Arthington: 1823–1900; Neill, S C: *Concise Dictionary of the Christian World Mission* p 35; OMFA 6211, 6113xi; *China's Millions* 1896 p 38, Jas. Gilmour.
47	15	Lansdell: OMFA 6226, July 8, 1887. Central Asian Scriptures: *see* Broomhall, M: *The Chinese Empire* pp 410–18
47	16	Lansdell-Parker: OMFA 6212 July 22, Oct 27; 6231 Oct 27; 6311xxiv Dec 24, 1887; *China's Millions* 1889 pp 87–96; K 412; Broomhall, M: *Chinese Empire* p 296, G Hunter named Lansdell with Parker in Xinjiang 1888.
48	17	Travellers: Hopkirk, P: *Foreign Devils on the Silk Road* (OUP 1984); *Trespassers on the Roof of the World*; *China's Millions* 1889 pp 87–96
48	18	Younghusband, Capt F E: *The Heart of a Continent*, 1896 pp 70–05
49	19	'Trio': Eva and Francesca French and Mildred Cable dep Shanxi to Xinjiang 1923; dep Xinjiang 1938
50	20	*Book of Arrangements*: OMFA 6114, 6211 June 3, 1887; 6212
50	21	Tankerville: OMFA 6232
51	22	Wilmot Brooke: *see* at length, Stock, E: *The History of the Church Missionary Society* Vol 3 pp 362–3 and Index; OMFA 61130
51	23	Handbill: OMFA 6111 July 12, 13, 1887
52	24	Berger: OMFA 6113z; *China's Millions* 1887 pp 92, 99
52	25	Hundred: OMFA 6212 Oct 14, 1887; 6223q,v
52	26	Shanxi: OMFA 6212 Oct
53	27	Colville: OMFA 6231 Oct 30, Dec 12
54	28	Forman-Wilder: OMFA 6231; 6113F,Q,xv
54	29	Speer: Robert E (1867–1947); graduate, Princeton 1889, later Secretary, Board of Foreign Mission of Presby. Church, USA. Robert Parmelee Wilder (1863–1936); graduate, Princeton 1886; travelling secretary, Student Volunteer Movement, N American universities, British Isles, Continent of Europe and, 1892–1900, India. Neill, S C: *Concise Dictionary*.
55	30	Frost: Taylor, Dr and Mrs Howard: *By Faith: Henry W Frost and the China Inland Mission*.
56	31	Frost-JHT: *China's Millions* 1932 pp 89–90; Taylor, Dr and Mrs Howard: *By Faith* pp 49ff; OMFA 6225; *China's Millions* 1893 pp 45–6, 59–61, 73–5
56	32	Holmgren: OMFA 7113a,d.e.f; N13b.31; Mildmay: Pyrland Road or conference centre.
57	33	Swedish: OMFA 7133e,i,j
58	34	Benj B: OMFA 6211 June 17, 1887; 6225j; 6212 Dec 22, 1887
58	35	Conferences: Liverpool 1860; London 1888; New York 1900; Edinburgh 1910; Neill, S C: *Concise Dictionary*.
58	36	Stevenson: *China's Millions* 1887 p 73, letter to CIM
60	37	Studd: *China's Millions* 1887 p 73; 1892 p 90; OMFA 6212
60	38	Maria: *China's Millions* 1887 p 79. Annie Royle Taylor: *China's Millions* 1887 p 156
60	39	Tibet: *China's Millions* 1887 p 156
61	40	'NOW': *China's Millions* 1888 p 95
61	41	Griffith John: Latourette, K S: *Christian Missions* p 364
62	42	Advancing: OMFA 6213

Chapter 2

63	1	Pilkington: Stock, E: *The History of the CMS* Vol 3 pp 361–4; *China's Millions* 1889 p 87; 1890 p 101
64	2	Barclay: OMFA 6227a
64	3	Hundred: OMFA 6222, Engagement Calendar
65	4	Cassels: Broomhall, M: *W W Cassels* pp 143–8
65	5	Horsburgh: Stock, E: *History of the CMS* 3.433, 577; Horsburgh, J H: *Do Not Say* p 36
65	6	Hsi: Taylor, Mrs H: Pastor Hsi: *Confucian Scholar and Christian* pp 213–24; *China's Millions* 1888 p 44
66	7	Opium: wars 1840, 1858–60; Thompson, R Wardlaw: *Griffith John* p 287; HTCOC Book 2 pp 383, 422; Book 3 p 139; *China's Millions* 1877 pp 112, 147–8; *Chinese Recorder* 1876 p 422; Stock, E: *History of the CMS* 3.233–4
68	8	Opium: examples in *China's Millions* 1875 pp 77, 82, 105; 1877 pp 39, 105; 1878 p 77; 1879 pp 35, 75, 94; 1880 pp 95, 100, 104; 1881 pp 6, 38–9, 62, 85, 90–1; 1882 pp 38, 49, 53, 57–8, 119–25, 148; 1883 pp 6–7, 45, 118, 148 (*see* Indices)
68	9	*China's Millions* 1882 p 39; extracts, 119–25. British Library ref: 8425–c75
68	10	*Chinese Recorder* 1881 p 418
69	11	R N Cust: Stock, E: *History of CMS* 3.348, 688; *Church Missionary Intelligencer* Dec 1884 p 279
70	12	Birdwood: Stock, E: *History of CMS* 3.233–4
70	13	Broomhall, B: editor *National Righteousness* Vol 1 Nos 1–13; Vol 2 No 26; *The Truth about Opium Smoking:* Broomhall, M: *Heirs Together* pp 95–114
70	14	*China's Millions* 1885 pp 63, 85, 89, 102–3 (see Note 8 above), by a duty of 90 taels = £30 per chest free from inter-provincial *likin* tariff.
71	15	*National Righteousness* Aug 1911, Vol 2 No 26
71	16	Covell, R: *W A P Martin* p 62; Martin to American Board, May 22, 1856, and Nov 16, 1859
72	17	*National Righteousness* Vol 1 No 1, Dec 1888 p 8
73	18	R N Cust: Stock, E: *History of CMS* 3.649
74	19	J L Maxwell: *National Righteousness* Dec 1888 Vol 1 pp 2–5
74	20	Christian Union: a list of 'well-known names' followed: Dr Baedeker, Dr Barnardo, Andrew Bonar, George Cadbury, Rev C C Fenn (Gen Sec of CMS), Eugene Stock, Grattan Guinness, Evan Hopkins, Maj-Gen Hoste, Donald Matheson (one-time director of Jardine Matheson), Handley Moule, C H Spurgeon, and a sprinkling of titled supporters.
77	21	North America: Taylor, Dr and Mrs Howard: *By Faith: Henry W Frost and the CIM* p 76; *Hudson Taylor* Vol 2 p 439; Broomhall, M: *The Jubilee Story of the China Inland Mission* p 184; *China's Millions* 1893 p 46
78	22	Student movements: Johnson, D: *Contending for the Faith* pp 32–65; Moule, H C G: *Charles Simeon*, 1892 and IVF 1948 seq.
78	23	Northfield: Pollock, J: *Moody without Sankey* p 186ff
80	24	SVM: Taylor, Dr and Mrs Howard: *Hudson Taylor and the China Inland Mission* (Vol 2) p 442 footnote; Broomhall, B: *The*

Evangelization of the World; Johnson, D: *Contending for the Faith* pp 61–2

80	25	Volunteers: Neill, S C: *Concise Dictionary of the Christian World Mission* pp 570–1
80	26	Taylor, Dr and Mrs Howard: *By Faith: Henry W Frost* pp 76–108; *China's Millions* 1888 p 151; 1889 p 113; 1893 pp 45–6; 59–61, 73–5; 1930 passim; Michell, D: 'One Hundred Years of the CIM–OMF in North America, 1888–1988' (D Missiology thesis).
81	27	JHT expositions: *China's Millions* 1932 Centenary Vol, No 5; Taylor, Dr and Mrs Howard: *By Faith: Henry W Frost* p 78
82	28	Zwemer: OMFA 6321j
83	29	Frost and Moody: Taylor, Dr and Mrs Howard: *By Faith: Henry W Frost* p 79; OMFA 6322b,c
84	30	Candidates and costs: *China's Millions* 1893 p 46; OMFA 6311j,k; J 233b
84	31	Taylor, Dr and Mrs Howard: *By Faith: Henry W Frost* p 85; *China's Millions* 1893 p 46; OMFA 6311j,k
85	32	Selection: *China's Millions* 1888 p 151; 1889 p 112; Broomhall, M: *Jubilee Story* p 185; OMFA 6311k; J 412; Taylor, Dr and Mrs Howard: *Hudson Taylor* Vol 2 p 449
86	33	Lammermuir: *China's Millions* 1889 p 112; 1893 p 46; Broomhall, M: *Jubilee Story* p 185; OMFA 6322b,c; J 231
86	34	JHT in N.Am: OMFA 6311n; 6312 Aug 3; J 313
87	35	Canada: OMFA 6311o, 6321b,g,k; Broomhall, M: *Jubilee Story* p 186; Taylor, Dr and Mrs Howard: *By Faith: Henry W Frost* pp 95–6
88	36	Chicago: OMFA 6311q,T,S; Taylor, Dr and Mrs Howard: *By Faith: Henry W Frost* pp 93–4
88	37	Candidates: OMFA 6311n,s,u
89	38	Trains: OMFA 6331. Two versions demonstrate unreliability of faulty memories: 1. *Henry W Frost* pp 89–90: Northfield Aug 9 – Attica Sept 18; Clifton Springs Aug 11–13; Rochester Sept 15. 2. Howard Taylors: Vol 2(1918) pp 451–2 use the recollections of Christina K Cameron of St Louis (6321w), a child at the time but told of the train incident by the Rev Dr Brookes, convener of the Niagara Conference. Either he or she seems to have mistaken the facts and expressed the principle as 'My Father manages the trains.' Henry Frost's eyewitness account by J S Helmer (6331) reads more convincingly and was used in the Howard Taylors' 1938 biography of Henry Frost.
89	39	Last days: *China's Millions* 1888 p 152; 1889 p 113; 1893 p 59; OMFA 6321n,u; 6322a,b,c; 6331; 6411c–w; 6412, 6413, 6414, J 231, J 234
91	40	Fourteen: OMFA 6322
91	41	Council: OMFA 6331.210–12; *China's Millions* 1893 p 60
92	42	Magazine: OMFA 6331.213–15
92	43	Voyages: OMFA 6311c,w; 6413

Chapter 3

93	1	Norris: *China's Millions* 1889 pp 3–4
95	2	Dorward: *China's Millions* 1889 pp 4, 5, 117; Broomhall, M: *Pioneer Work in Hunan* pp 62–73; OMFA 6412 Dec 12

96	3	Administration: OMFA 6322b; 6422 Feb 1; 6423 Jan 29
97	4	Troubles: OMFA 6412, 6422, J 313
97	5	Shanghai house: corner of Peking and Jiangxi Roads
97	6	Maggie McKee: *China's Millions* 1889 p 33; OMFA 6422
97	7	Henan: *China's Millions* 1889 p 22 (Oct 21, 1888); OMFA 6413
98	8	Floods: *China's Millions* 1889 pp 25, 29, 33, 57–8, 70; OMFA 6412 Nov 28; 6414; 6422
98	9	C L Williams: distinguish from L C Williams, married Marcus Wood
98	10	'Crucifixion': OMFA 6422 Feb 1, 1889. 'It *is* crucifixion, this constant separation,' was how he had put it in 1885.
98	11	Editor: *China's Millions* 1888 Nov pp 139–41; OMFA 6312 Nov 17; 6411i,j
99	12	Duckling: OMFA J 323–4
100	13	N Am 'question': OMFA 6411c,d,f,h,k,l; J313, J322; 6414; 6422 Feb 22, Mar 1
101	14	Satan: OMFA 6422 Feb 8, Mar 8, 15
102	15	N Am separate: OMFA 6333 p 254
103	16	JHT: OMFA J 322e; 6422 Mar 27, April 5
103	17	Wusong plans: OMFA 6425, £5000
103	18	JHT: Samson: OMFA 7122 May 3
104	19	Theodore Howard: OMFA 7123 May 7, 16, 19, 20
105	20	'Stone rolled away': OMFA 6225j; 7122 May 29, 31; 7123
108	21	'Old Buddha': Haldane, C: *The Last Great Empress of China* p 118
108	22	Emperor: Little, Alicia Bewicke: *Li Hung-chang* p 169, *passim*
108	23	Temple of Heaven: Little, A B: *Li Hong-chang* pp 169, 177; not the open marble altar of sacrifice used for emperor's annual act of atonement.
109	24	Yangzi riots: Fairbank, J K: *The Cambridge History of China*, OUP, Vol 10 p 573
110	25	JHT: N. America: *China's Millions* 1889 p 143; OMFA 7124b,g
110·	26	Council for N Am: Broomhall, M: *The Jubilee Story of the China Inland Mission* p 188 (list).
111	27	Frost's faith: Taylor, Dr and Mrs Howard: *By Faith: Henry W Frost* Chapters 16, 17; *China's Millions* 1893 p 73
111	28	Niagara conference: *China's Millions* 1893 p 45; OMFA J 412, K 412; 7121g,j
112	29	Funds: OMFA 7121k; 7124g
112	30	Fifty million: OMFA 7121e
113	31	Howard Taylor: OMFA 7132; J 425
113	32	Berger: London Council Minutes, April 1, 1890; OMFA 7121k; 7123 June 5, 1889; J 425.5
114	33	JHT advice: OMFA 7132 Sept 12, 24; Oct 4
114	34	'Ladies Council': London Council Minutes, June 1889; OMFA 7132
115	35	Cummings-JHT: OMFA 7135d
115	36	Cost of furloughs: OMFA 7135A
117	37	'To Every Creature': *China's Millions* Feb 1890; Fairbank, J K: *Cambridge History* Vol 10 pp 555–7
118	38	Associate Missions: Grist, W A: *Samuel Pollard*. Bible Christian Mission: 1907, Bible Christian Society joined New Connexion and

Methodist Free Churches to form United Methodist Church. Pollard, S: *Tight Corners* p 18

119 39 Minority races: Baber, Nicoll journeys, *see* HTCOC Book 6 Index. 1888 Anshun occupied by Thomas Windsor and James Adam.

120 40 Pollard and Nosu: Grist, W A: *Samuel Pollard* pp 167–78

121 41 Students Foreign Missionary Union: Johnson, D: *Contending for the Faith* p 61. F Howard Taylor: Doctor of Medicine, London University; Member of the Royal College of Physicians; Fellow of the Royal College of Surgeons of England

122 42 JHT, humility: *China's Millions* 1890 p 2; 1895 pp 116–17; Broomhall, M: *Jubilee Story* pp 194, 357–8; OMFA J 425; 7133b, 7134, 8336a

122 43 Queen Sophia, Stockholm: OMFA J 411, J 42.14; 7134 Nov 23, 26, 1889; 8336a–c

123 44 Norway: the initiative of all JHT travels, America, Australasia came from the countries visited, except Basel (Basle), Switzerland, accidental. Broomhall, M: *Jubilee Story* p 361 (1889 given in error); *China's Millions* 1890 p 2; of HTCOC 6.349; Torjesen, Edvard P: *Fredrik Franson: A Model for Worldwide Evangelism.*

123 45 Norwegian Mission in China, Oslo: known first as Norwegian China Committee, then as Christiania Committee for the Norwegian Mission in China. 'The Christian Committee of the Norwegian Mission in China' (as it was called) which had invited him to Norway, had like its Swedish counterpart come into being in 1887.

124 46 Franson: Torjesen, E P: *Fredrik Franson* pp 49, 65–86; *China's Millions* 1891 p 54; London Council Minutes, June 2, 24, 1890

124 47 Swedish Holiness Union: Broomhall, M: *Jubilee Story* p 359

125 48 TEAM: Torjesen, E P: *Fredrik Franson passim.*

125 49 Liebenzell: OMFA 8334; Taylor, Dr and Mrs Howard: *Hudson Taylor* Vol 2 pp 519, 561 footnotes; Broomhall, M: *Jubilee Story* pp 362–3

125 50 Pilgrim Mission: HTCOC 3.393–4; Broomhall, M: *Jubilee Story* p 364

126 51 St Chrischona, Basel: HTCOC 3.393; OMFA 8335, 8421; Broomhall, M: *Jubilee Story* p 361

Chapter 4

129 1 Xinjiang pioneers: Broomhall, M: *The Jubilee Story of the China Inland Mission* p 288–90. Evangeline (Eva) French (1869–1960), Francesca French (1873–1960) and Mildred Cable (1877–1952). In China 'Eva' was the 'Trio's' leader. But Mildred Cable had gifts useful for public relations in the West, so they called her 'our star' and let her take the limelight as author and speaker (close friends of my family in China and Dorset).

130 2 Persistence: *China's Millions* 1890 pp 29, 150–1; OMFA 7142, J 425

130 3 Annie R Taylor: OMFA 7132

131 4 Guidance: OMFA 7124b, 7142

131 5 Shanxi: OMFA 7132, 7142 Feb 14, 1890

132 6 The P and P and Arrangements had been referred to London and Mission members for discussion before being promulgated. The

London Council mistakenly thought it a *fait accompli* and were indignant, while JHT assumed they understood. Incorporation: A 'Memorandum of Association of the China Inland Mission Corporation' acting as Trustee for CIM property, gave temporary cover until formal incorporation could be completed on Nov 25, 1890. But before he left home on March 17 he signed and sealed (on the 14th) a printed copy of a Deed of Constitution or description of the CIM comprising a minimal statement of faith and particulars of councils in Britain, China and North America with himself as 'Director in Chief' (OMFA 7142 Feb 3, 1890). C T Fishe became financial secretary to a finance committee; Marcus Wood was brought home from China to run a men's training home in Inglesby House; Henrietta Soltau opened a women's training home in Pyrland Road; Barton, the Harley House tutor, became assistant to Benjamin B, relieving him of much pressure; Robert Scott (of Marshall, Morgan and Scott) accepted the task of Treasurer; and Jenny Taylor continued as sub-editor of *China's Millions*. Because of the cramped quarters at Pyrland Rd, Benjamin proposed extending the property on Newington Green and erecting an adequate office and Mission Home building. It was completed in 1894 and occupied in 1895.

133	7	Discord: OMFA J 425
135	8	Separation: OMFA 7143, 7244 Apr 10, 14, 1890
135	9	1000: OMFA 7224 May 1
136	10	Melbourne: OMFA 7231a,b; 7224 May 1
136	11	Wusong Rd: Broomhall, M: *Jubilee Story* pp 196–8; OMFA 7224, K 112; Shanghai premises: Nov 1873–Sept 1876 Broadway; 1876–78 nil; April 1878–80 Suchow Creek until demolished; 1880–84 Seward Rd; 1885–90 Yuanmingyuan Buildings; Feb 1890–1930 Wusong Rd; 1930–42, 1945–51 Sinza Rd.
136	12	Opium: *National Righteousness*; OMFA K 212; *China's Millions* 1892 re April 10, 1890
137	13	Protestant staff in China, 1890: 1295 men and women from 520 organised Chinese churches of which 94 were entirely self-supporting and 22 partially so. Missionaries: 589 men, 390 wives, 316 single women. Chinese: 209 ordained, 1,260 not ordained; 180 women. 61 hospitals treating 1/3 of 1 million patients each year; among them the Schofield Memorial Hospital and Chapel at Taiyuan, begun in 1887. *China's Millions* 1890.51
137	14	1000: OMFA J 112; 7142 Jan 17, 1890
138	15	Third General Missionary Conference: *Records of the General Conference of Protestant Missionaries in China 1890, Shanghai*, 1891; *China's Millions* 1890 pp 108–11; *Report of the Missionary Conference, Shanghai, 1890*; 'Ancestors' pp 57–9, 61–5; *Items of Interest*,'S F Whitehouse: an informal record of the General Missionary conference and subsequent CIM conference, May 26–28, 1890 (published by CIM).
138	16	Policy: Latourette, K S: *A History of Christian Missions in China* p 414; *China's Millions* 1890 pp 108–11
139	17	Ancestors: *Christian Alternatives to Ancestor Practices*; editor Bong Rin Ro, 1985, Asia Theological Association, 1985, considers a

resurgence of unbiblical compromise and a sincere search for cultural observances honouring ancestors without contravening Biblical principles. This debate is complicated by mistaken understanding of the evangelical position and by unfactual statements on the history of the Shanghai conferences of 1877 and 1890, particularly about Hudson Taylor. He drew the limelight upon himself by *asking* for a standing vote but did not in fact play a leading role in the arguments. Phrases like 'as decreed by Hudson Taylor' are very wide of the mark. cf George Minamiki S J, Loyola Univ. Press, 1985: *The Chinese Rites Controversy from its beginning to Modern Times.*

140	18	Martin: Covell, R: *W A P Martin* pp 249–50
142	19	Martin: Latourette, K S: *Christian Missions* p 414; *Conference Report* p 65; Whitehouse, S F: *Items of Interest* p 22
142	20	Tablets: eg *China's Millions* 1882 p 110
143	21	*Christian Alternatives* (Ed. Bong Rin Ro); *Chinese Recorder* 1901 pp 253–5; 1902 pp 117–19, 201 Martin; 253–5 Price; 258–70; 1903 p 199 Walker; 1904 pp 237–45; 301–8 Martin; 419–21 Wolfe; 1907 p 504 T Richard *Conversion by the Million* 1911 pp 408–11 Wei.
143	22	Whitehouse, S F: *Items of Interest* pp 15, 21; *China's Millions* 1890 pp 109, 124 (photograph); OMFA 7143, 7224, 7222b; K 112, 113
143	23	Smallpox: OMFA 7224 May 13, 1890
144	24	CIM expansions: Fairbank, J K: *Cambridge History of China*, Vol 10 p 555; OMFA K 113
145	25	Committees: Whitehouse, S F: *Items of Interest*
145	26	Administration: OMFA 7228, 7143; K 113
146	27	Offices: OMFA 7143, 7228 June 6, K 113
146	28	Henry Reed: HTCOC 1.292; OMFA 7231a
147	29	Reed sisters: Guinness, H W: *Journey among Students* pp 17–18
147	30	Australian Council: OMFA 7224, 7231a Feb 23, 1890; 7231b May 19
148	31	JHT's children: OMFA 7232
149	32	Separation: OMFA 7232 July 24, 30
149	33	Drummond: OMFA 723*ly*,K; 7232
149	34	Australia: OMFA 7231X; Broomhall, M: *Jubilee Story* p 199
151	35	Circumstance: OMFA 7231E,J; 7232 Sept 19, 1890; 7233; *China's Millions* p 3
151	36	First Australians: Loane, Marcus: *The Story of the China Inland Mission in Australia and New Zealand* pp 151–70, all members and particulars tabulated; *China's Millions* 1891 p 14
152	37	Darwin: OMFA 7231 0
152	38	Council: OMFA 7232; 7351d; K 311

Chapter 5

153	1	Swedish: Latourette, K S: *A History of Christian Missions in China* pp 392–3; Broomhall, M: *The Chinese Empire* p 221; *The Jubilee Story of the China Inland Mission* pp 357–9
154	2	Flood: *China's Millions* 1891 pp 63–4; Taylor, Dr and Mrs Howard: *Hudson Taylor and the China Inland Mission*, Vol 2 pp 499–502
154	3	Franson letter: *China's Millions* 1891 pp 81–2
154	4	Franson: OMFA M 321; 7143
155	5	Swedes: OMFA K 212, 213

155	6	Pressures: OMFA 7441 Mar 24, 1893; Latourette, K S: *Christian Missions* p 392 – Continental Missions resulting from Hudson Taylor's influence listed.
156	7	Happer: OMFA 7234 July 2, 3
156	8	Baptist: HTCOC 3.251 and Appendix 2 p 477 here shown to be mistaken; should read: 'His membership of the Westbourne Grove Baptist Chapel and brief links with the Baptist Missionary Society reflect the personal choice of a most open-minded man.'
157	9	Slanders: OMFA 7321b, Nov 27, 1890; Feb 23, 1891; K 113
157	10	Th. Howard, Sharp: OMFA 7331 April 7; 7321b,d,e,f
158	11	Council: OMFA 732li, Aug 28, 1891
158	12	Minute: OMFA; K 113, 213
159	13	Criticisms: *Chinese Recorder* Dec 1890; Jan 1891
160	14	Accuser: OMFA 7311 A, C; 7351l
160	15	Vaccination: *Chinese Recorder* Jan 1891; OMFA 7312, K 11.10
160	16	Deaths: On Saturday 26, 1892, in a Shanghai prayer meeting, Hudson Taylor prayed with unusual urgency and concern for D L Moody. It proved to be the day his ship the *Spree* came close to sinking in the Atlantic. OMFA 7311c; 7352; *China's Millions* 1890 pp 146, 159; 1891 p 77; Pollock, J: *Moody without Sankey* pp 241–3
161	17	Trials: *China's Millions* 1892 pp 1, 2
161	18	Huc: HTCOC 1.296–7; Neill, S C: *Concise Dictionary of the Christian World Mission* p 261: Evariste Régis Huc; Lhasa 184–6; Huc's *Travels in Tartary, Tibet and China*.
162	19	Annie R Taylor: OMFA 5433, 7132, 7143; Hopkirk, P: *Trespassers on the Roof of the World*, 1982
162	20	Polhill, Arthur and Cecil: 'Two Etonians' (unpublished) pp 109–28
164	21	A W Douthwaite, Sept 25, 1893; unpublished MS by his great-niece Mrs W P K Findlay. (In my own experience in China and Mindoro, Philippines, 1947–64, the same held true.)
164	22	Ethnic Tibet: modern Chinese maps carry the political boundary between Sichuan and Xizang (Tibet proper) far to the west of the ethnic dividing line, but add to Qinghai at Gansu's expense. Xikang (Sikang) is no longer recognised, and the whole drainage area of the Yalong River is now in Sichuan. The new border follows the Jinsha Jiang, 'the River of Golden Sand', which is the upper stretch of the Yangzi River.
164	23	Wang Cuan-yi: also called Wang Zongyi (Wang Ts'uan-i and Wang Tsung-i); Polhill-Turner, 'Two Etonians' pp 139–49
165	24	Songpan: Polhill-Turner: 'Two Etonians' pp 146–9; *China's Millions* 1892 pp 163–5; 1895 p 78; 1898 p 5
165	25	Wang and Zhang: *China's Millions* 1893 pp 105–7; 1894 pp 75–7, 80; J G Cormack, CIM; Knipe and another, CMS holding fort until Cecil Polhill returned.
165	26	Annie R Taylor: Hopkirk, P: *Trespassers* pp 92–8; *China's Millions* 1893 pp 103–4, 160
166	27	Annie R Taylor and Pontso: OMFA 7441, 7442; *China's Millions* 1893 p 112; 1894 pp 46–8; OMFA 8224a
167	28	North American funds : OMFA 7331; K 212, 213
167	29	Hunan: OMFA 7331d; K 212

168	30	Riot rumour: *China's Millions* 1891 pp 113, 156; 1896 p 84; OMFA 7331d, 7352e
169	31	Yangzi riots: Fairbank, J K: *Cambridge History of China* Vol 10 p 573
169	32	Hard for persecutors: OMFA 7331d
170	33	Disturbances: *China's Millions* 1891 pp 100, 141–2; OMFA 7331d, 7351k,m; 7352e,i; K 212
170	34	Wenzhou: OMFA 7311C, also Nov 26, 1892
170	35	Zhou Han pamphlets: Broomhall, M: *Jubilee Story* p 230; *The Chinese Empire* p 175; *China's Millions* 1893 pp 23, 39
171	36	Riots: *China's Millions* 1893 p 105; OMFA 7441, 7442
171	37	Songbu murders: *China's Millions* 1893 p 148; OMFA 7442
173	38	London Council: Minutes Mar 7, 1889; OMFA 7141a,b,f,m; 7228 May 31, 1890
174	39	Final headship: OMFA 7331d May 30, 1891; K 214
175	40	JHT-Th. Howard: OMFA 7311A,B
175	41	Reasons: OMFA 7311D; 7411a
175	42	Controversy: OMFA 5431c; 6114, 6227, 6412 Dec 28, 1888; 7122, 7124b, 7132, 7141, 7227, 7228, 7311, 7321, 7331, 7341, 7342, 7343, 7352, 7361, 7362, 7363, 7411, 7412, 7414, 7442
176	43	Ultimatum: London Council Minutes, Oct 20, letter Oct 22, 1891; OMFA 7342a–e
177	44	JHT to Council: OMFA 7352i Dec 5, 1891; 7342d
178	45	Conversions: OMFA 7352j; 7363
178	46	China Council: *China's Millions* 1892 p 96; OMFA 7361, 7363
179	47	JHT in UK: OMFA 7412l,o,q,r,w; K 313
180	48	Difficulty: OMFA 7412A,B,C
180	49	'Breakup': OMFA 7412J,M,O,R
181	50	Partnership: OMFA 7412Q,R,S; 7441
181	51	Sloan, Frost: OMFA 7412W; Codes: 7352o, 7437, 7411d
182	52	Amy Carmichael, Eva French: OMFA 7437; July 4, 1893
183	53	Councils advisory: OMFA 7141b; 7441
184	54	Frost to Hoste: OMFA 7442D
184	55	'Unanimity of decision': a twentieth-century term not found in the archives; OMFA 7311B; 7411a,b
185	56	Newington Green: OMFA 7422; London Council Minutes, Oct 31, 1893
186	57	Newington Green: OMFA 7437, 7441, 7442. Oct 4, 1887, payment for Inglesby House completed; Feb 19, 1889, house adjoining Inglesby purchased for £1000; June 14, 1889, discussion on buying a strip of land adjoining Inglesby House; June 21, 1889, and Dec 3, 1889, purchase of 'Monte Cristo' property again discussed; April 1, 1890, first mention of building; May 13, 1890, £8550 asked for Monte Cristo property; Feb 17, 1891, Monte Cristo auction on 27th; Aug 4, 1891, Monte Cristo negotiations continued; Oct 31, 1892, decision to proceed; Dec 1893 foundations in; Mar 8, 1894, Newington Green building occupied.

Chapter 6

187	1	Opium: *National Righteousness* Vol 1 No 7, 1891
188	2	Parliament: Stock, E: *The History of the Church Missionary Society*

Vol 3 p 575; *National Righteousness* Vol 1 No 7, April 1891 pp 1–48;
Resolution: 'That this House is of opinion that the system by which
the Indian opium revenue is raised is morally indefensible, and would
urge upon the Indian Government that they should cease to grant
licenses for the cultivation of the poppy and sale of opium in British
India, except to supply the legitimate demand for medical purposes,
and they should at the same time take measures to arrest the transit
of Malwa opium through British territory.'

188	3	Committee of Urgency: *National Righteousness*, Vol 1 No 13, Sept 1893 p 13
188	4	Opium: *China's Millions* 1890 pp 86–8, 125; 1892 pp 41–2
188	5	Prime Minister: Gladstone PM 1868–74, 1880–85, 1886, 1892–94, d 1898. Salisbury PM 1885–86, 1886–92, 1895–1902
189	6	'Missions 'doomed': OMFA K 316; *National Righteousness* 1899
190	7	Gladstone: *National Righteousness* No 10 Feb 1893 pp 3–5; No 11 April 1893; Parliamentary blue book Feb 9, 1892, C.6562; Stock, E: *History of CMS* 3.506
191	8	Opium: *China's Millions* 1894 pp 102–4, 106
191	9	Royal Commission: Stock, E: *History of CMS* 3.575–6; *China's Millions* 1894 p 106 verbatim; 1899 p 21
192	10	CIM: *China's Millions* 1893 p 115; 1894 pp 91–2; Broomhall, M: *Faith and Facts* pp 75–7
193	11	Ageing: OMFA 7412E; 7421b
194	12	Wusong Rd: *China's Millions* 1893 p 9; OMFA K 13.11, 7433, 7434C, 7441, 7442D
194	13	Rijnhardt: OMFA 7412o,p, F,G,L,W; 7442, 7443e–h; 8113. Has been called Dr Petrus Rijnhardt in error.
195	14	SVMU: Neill, S C *et al: Concise Dictionary of Christian World Mission* p 571
195	15	CIM Trust: OMFA 7442B Feb 14, 1894; 7443
196	16	Scandinavians: OMFA 8111a
196	17	Nevius: HTCOC 3.370, 412–3; Smith, A H: *The Uplift of China* p 183; Nevius, Helen: *John Livingston Nevius passim.*
198	18	Korea: Neill, S C *et al: Concise Dictionary* pp 326, 437; Neill, S C: *A History of Christian Missions* pp 343–4; Latourette, K S: *A History of the Expansion of Christianity* Vol 6 pp 308, 425
198	19	Nevius, Douthwaite: unpublished MS by Mrs W P K Findlay quoting Mrs Douthwaite (Connie Groves) October 22, 1893; Latourette, K S: *History of Christian Missions* pp 367, 427, 430
199	20	Scandinavians: OMFA 7441, Mar 24, 1893; 7442; 8113 Apr 27, 1894; May 11, 1894; *China's Millions* 1893 p 83; Latourette, K S: *History of Christian Missions* p 399
200	21	CIM pool funds: OMFA 7442, Nov 10, Dec 9, 12, 1893
200	22	Wm Cooper: OMFA 7441, Mar 31, May 22, 1893; 8116d, May 22, 1893; 7442, Nov 17, 1893; 8116d, May 22, 1894
201	23	Mandarins, consuls: OMFA 7441, Mar 24, 1893; 8111a, Apr 24, 1894
201	24	Shaanxi journey: OMFA 8113, May 11, 1894
203	25	Botham: OMFA 7351 Aug 25, 1891
204	26	Li Hongzhang: Three-eyed peacock feather first given to Li after Nianfei campaign, HTCOC 4.384–5

204 27 Shaanxi-Shanxi: OMFA 8112, May; 8 Book 2,3; *China's Millions* 1894 pp 118–9, 134–6, 148–9, 155; 1895 pp 2–3, 16–18, 33–4

206 28 Rules: OMFA 8115a, Sept 1894; 8112, July 16, 1894; 'the sabbath is made for man, not man for the sabbath.'

207 29 'Shanxi spirit': Neill, S C: *History of Christian Missions* pp 358–9 re India; Latourette, K S : *History of Christian Missions* p 619; *Chinese Recorder* 1901 p 124

208 30 Chinese dress: OMFA 8112 Aug 24, 1894; 8113

209 31 Shanxi alone: OMFA 7442D; 8114 Oct 5, 15, 1894; N17 pp 22–8

209 32 Danger: OMFA 10.351; 8114, 8115

210 33 Studd, S P Smith: OMFA 8114 Oct 18, 1894

211 34 War: Morse, Hosea Ballou: *The International Relations of the Chinese Empire* Vol 3 pp 27–39

212 35 Old Buddha: *China's Millions* 1897 pp 23, 38; 1895 p 22; Haldane, Charlotte: *The Last Great Empress of China* p 127

212 36 Li Hongzhang: Later it was claimed that if he had not been removed from Zhili the Boxer rising would not have taken place.

215 37 Taiwan: Morse, H B: *International Relations* 3.49,50 footnote, 56; Little, Alicia Bewicke: *Li Hung-chang passim*.

216 38 Douthwaite, Yantai: *China's Millions* 1895 p 65; Judd, F H: *The Chefusian*, 1987; Mrs W P K Findlay MS; *China's Millions* pp 152–3; 1897 pp 73, 102–4; OMFA 8213 Aug 15, 1895

216 39 Zhou Han: Morse, H B: *International Relations* 3.54; U S Foreign Relations 1895 pp 87–98; *North China Herald* Oct 11, Nov 8, Dec 6, 1895

Chapter 7

220 1 Sun Yatsen: Morse, Hosea Ballou: *International Relations of the Chinese Empire* 3.129–32 citing Cantlie, J: *Sun Yatsen* p 63 seq.

220 2 Kang Yuwei: Morse, H B: *International Relations* 3.131 seq; *North China Herald*, Dec 6, 1895. *Xiucai*, Bachelor; *Qüren*, Master; *Jinshi*, Doctor; *Hanlin*, Academician – the former two by provincial examination, the latter two at Peking.

220 3 Zhang Zhitong: Morse, H B: *International Relations* 3.129. Zhang Zhitong (Chang Chih-t'ung) = Governor of Shanxi, 1882–84; viceroy of Guangxi-Guangdong, 1884–90; viceroy of Hunan-Hubei, 1890–1909 with interlude at Nanjing.

220 4 Memorials: Little, Alicia Bewicke: *Li Hung-chang* p 247

221 5 Rebellion?: OMFA 8223, Aug 30, 1895; 8213 June 1895

221 6 Convulsions: Smith, A H: *The Uplift of China* p 166; Little, A B: *Li Hung-chang* p 12; *China's Millions* 1896 p 1

222 7 Xining; Wenzhou: *China's Millions* 1895 p 103; 1896 pp 25, 98; OMFA 8213

222 8 Sichuan: *China's Millions* 1895 p 53; OMFA 8223, May 30, June 4, 1895

225 9 Leshan (Jiading): OMFA 8212, June 12; 8223, June 5

225 10 Chengdu: Stock, E: *History of the Church Missionary Society* 3.581; OMFA 8212, July 23

225 11 Qionglai: OMFA 8223, July 6, 1895

226   12   Langzhong: *China's Millions* 1895 pp 93, 134; 1896 p 14; OMFA
                 8212, 8213
226   13   JHT-Ririe: OMFA 8223 Oct 1895
227   14   Indemnities: OMFA 8212 Aug 19, 28, 1895
228   15   JHT re government intervention: OMFA 8221c Nov 17, 1895
228   16   Langzhong: Broomhall, M: *W W Cassels* p 177; OMFA 8212 Aug 4
228   17   Viceroy: *China's Millions* 1895 p 159; Little, A B: *Li Hung-chang*
                 pp 159, 201, 252; Stock, E: *History of the CMS* 3.582
228   18   Vale: *China's Millions* 1896 p 48
229   19   Kucheng: Stock, E: *History of the CMS* 3.582–7
230   20   Codrington: MacGillivray, D: *A Century of Protestant Missions in
                 China* p 54; both breasts severed.
230   21   Cassels: *China's Millions* 1895 pp 129, 131, 159
230   22   Saunders: *China's Millions* 1896 p 6
231   23   Fujian Church: MacGillivray, D: *A Century of Protestant Missions* pp
                 51–4
231   24   Unsafe: Smith, A H: *The Uplift of China* p 165
231   25   Xining siege: *China's Millions* 1895 p 144; 1896 pp 9, 65–6; 1898
                 pp 124, 145; 1897 p 89; 1899 pp 110–11; 1900 p 40; OMFA K 424,
                 8 Book 5; 8233
233   26   Mesny: personal communications: P D Coates, one-time HBM
                 Consular Service, China; Dr G A Curwen, School of Oriental and
                 African Studies, Lond. Univ.; Hon. Librarian-Archivist, Société
                 Jersiaise, Jersey.
236   27   General Sun: OMFA 8233; friend of Douthwaite.
237   28   Tibetan Pioneer Mission: OMFA 8114, 8213, 8224a–f
238   29   Xining: *China's Millions* 1896 pp 35, 75; OMFA 8232 Jan 18, 1896
239   30   Tibetan Mission Band: OMFA 8231, 8232 Mar 1896; 8234; Polhill:
                 'Two Etonians' pp 151 seq.
239   31   H N Lachlan: OMFA 8231 Apr 1896; 8233
239   32   Tibet: Hopkirk, P: *Trespassers on the Roof of the World* pp 104,
                 137–48
241   33   Rijnhardt, Shelton: Latourette, K S: *A History of Christian Missions
                 in China* pp 579–80
241   34   H R Davies: Polhill: 'Two Etonians' p 158
241   35   Younghusband: Hopkirk, P: *Trespassers* pp 159–92

Chapter 8
242   1   Chefoo: OMFA 8213; London Council Minutes, Sept 17, 1895
242   2   *After Thirty Years*: OMFA 8 Book 1; 8221c, 8213
244   3   'My head': of Robert Morrison, HTCOC 1.218; OMFA 8232
244   4   Rebellion: *China's Millions* 1895 p 145; OMFA 8223
244   5   Chefoo: OMFA 8212 Aug 13, 28, 31, Nov 9
245   6   Cholera: OMFA 8221c, 8236; *China's Millions* 1895 pp 130, 150, 173;
                 1896 pp 1, 2, 7; Wenzhou cholera: *China's Millions* 1895 p 173; 1896
                 p 7; OMFA 8221c June 16, 1905; 8213 Oct 17
245   7   Shouyang: OMFA 8231, 8232, 8235
245   8   Authority: OMFA 8235 Jan 1896
245   9   Unite: OMFA 8231, 8233 Oct 1898
246   10   Lucy Guinness: 1900 married H K W Kumm of North Africa

Mission, co-founder of Sudan United Mission; OMFA 8312, 8323

246   11   Ernest Taylor: *China's Millions* 1897 p 1
247   12   Hoste: Thompson, P: *D E Hoste: A Prince with God* pp 82–3;
             OMFA 8111b, 8233
247   13   Shipwrecks: *China's Millions* 1898 pp 8, 15; OMFA 8312, 8324
247   14   Associate: OMFA 7435, 8312, 8313, 8331, 8334, 8336; *China's
             Millions* 1896 p 134
248   15   Directors: OMFA 8312 Oct 1
248   16   1000: *China's Millions* 1890 p 111; 1895 pp 134, 157–8
249   17   Christianity in China: Latourette, K S: *History of Christian Missions*
             pp 370, 567ff
249   18   Cassels: Broomhall, M: *W W Cassels* pp 146–7, 177; OMFA 8212,
             8213, 8222, J 313
250   19   CMS: OMFA 8213, 8222; Stock, E: *History of CMS*, Dr A C
             Lankester: 3.476; Herbert Lankester, 3.310, 661, physician to CMS,
             p 695, 705
250   20   Sichuan: Broomhall, M: *The Chinese Empire* p 224
250   21   Hunan: Broomhall, M: *Pioneer Work in Hunan* pp 72–80; *China's
             Millions* 1891 p 91; 1892 p 158; 1898 p 104, 106
250   22   Geo. Hunter (Hunan): *China's Millions* 1898 p 43; 1899 pp 53, 101–2;
             OMFA 8411 Feb 1887
252   23   Geo. Hunter, death: *China's Millions* 1898 pp 104, 106; 1900
             pp 18–28, 87–8; OMFA 9221
252   24   Changsha: *China's Millions* 1898 p 26
252   25   Jakobsen: OMFA 7441 Feb 3, 1893; L 12.13; *China's Millions*
             1897 pp 55, 74, 96, 98–9, 104–6, 114–16; 1898 p 99; 1899 pp 53,
             101–2, 150
253   26   Jakobsen-Cheng: OMFA 8515a–d (7441)
254   27   F A Keller: OMFA 8421; *China's Millions* 1897 pp 5, 7; Broomhall,
             M: *Pioneer Work in Hunan* pp 82–3
254   28   Training: *China's Millions* 1897 Dec; 1898 pp 69 editorial, 102–3
254   29   Reinforcements: 1894, 71 added; 1895, 71; 1896, 79
255   30   Gregg: father of Dr Gregg of Manchuria.
255   31   J T Morton: OMFA 8221c June 1895, 8321, 8412; McKay, M J:
             thesis, Aberdeen, (unpublished) 1981 p 240 seq.
255   32   R Arthington: OMFA 8221c Sept 24, 1895
256   33   J T Morton: OMFA 8312 Aug 11, 1896
257   34   JHT: OMFA 8312 Aug 11, Oct 13; 8422 June 11; 8414. 'Mumps':
             recurrent episodes with toothache, with frequent visits to dentist in
             1896–97 suggest dental abscess.
257   35   J T Morton: OMFA 8321 Mar 12, 1897; particulars requested by
             donors to guide contributions were supplied (unsolicited): £10,000.
             OMFA 8321, 8412, 8422 Sept 2, 16
258   36   J T Morton: OMFA 8412, J W Stevenson notes; Broomhall, M: *J W
             Stevenson* p 72; *China's Millions* 1898 p 24
259   37   J T Morton legacy: OMFA 8522 Jan 29, 1898; L 213, 122, 128;
             London Council Minutes, Sept 20, 1898; *China's Millions* 1907
             editorial notes. An annual income of £12,500 from J T Morton came
             to China at least until 1907, and in 1912 £14,000 of it were received
             for missionaries' needs, with 6,000 taels 'for permanent school

buildings'. £2,000: This may have been the bequest later referred to as the 'Joy' legacy.

260   38   'Forward': OMFA 8322 May, June 5, 1896; *China's Millions* 1898 pp 151, 156

260   39   Volcano: *China's Millions* 1897 p 96

261   40   Switzerland: *China's Millions* 1897 p 119; OMFA 8414, 8422

262   41   To New York: *China's Millions* 1898 pp 9, 53, 99; OMFA 8413, 8423

262   42   Rapids: *China's Millions* 1898 p 53 Reuter cable; first to reach Chongqing, Mar 8, 1898

262   43   Li Hongzhang: Little, A B: *Li Hung-chang* p 266; Haldane, C: The *Last Great Empress of China* p 124

263   44   Shandong: Morse, H B: *The International Relations of the Chinese Empire*, Chronology; Latourette, K S: *History of Christian Missions* p 489

264   45   Memorial: *China's Millions* 1896 p 145. From time to time in the archives reference is made to a quotation alleged to be from Napoleon Bonaparte: 'China? There lies a sleeping giant. Let him sleep, for when he wakes he will move the world.' Used by John R Mott in addressing invited guests in London 1902, and quoted in his report of his world tour as gen. sec. of the World's Christian Students' Federation: *Strategic Points in the World's Conquest*. And by B Broomhall as the title to an article in *China's Millions* April 1902 anticipating the effect of Chinese evangelists worldwide. Cited in full by Robt Payne in *Mao Tse-tung* p 275, 1950 edn, Abelard-Schuman Ltd, but omitted from 1961 edn. (cf Ch 17 n38)

Chapter 9

265   1   Reform: Morse, H B: *The International Relations of the Chinese Empire* 3.128; Kang Yuwei: Fairbank, J K: *Cambridge History of China*, Vol 10 p 586

265   2   Foreigners: Neill, S C: *A History of Christian Missions* p 339; Morse, H B: *International Relations* 3.132–3

266   3   Li Hongzhang: Morse, H B: *International Relations* 3.134

266   4   J K Mackenzie's *History*: Fairbank, J K: *Cambridge History of China* pp 581, 587

266   5   'Learn': Morse, H B: *International Relations* 3.128–37

267   6   Richard, Allen, Reid: Fairbank, J K: *Cambridge History of China* Vol 10 pp 559, 581–2, 587; *Chinese Recorder* 1888 pp 358–64, 397–402, 465–72. Gilbert Reid 1857–1927. Soothill, W E: *Timothy Richard of China* p 183

267   7   Western ways: Woodcock, G: *The British in the Far East* p 183; Covell, R: *W A P Martin* pp 220–1; *China's Millions* 1898 p 26

269   8   Coverts: Fairbank, J K: *Cambridge History of China* Vol 10 pp 567–73 quoting Cohen pp 568, 572

269   9   Yü Manzi: OMFA 8512, 8522 Nov 7; *China's Millions* 1899 pp 12, 30, 97; Beresford, Lord Charles: *The Break-up of China* pp 140–2

270   10   Hundred days: Morse, H B: *International Relations* 3.153, 155 Oct 24, 1898, 157

270   11   Martin, T Richard: Fairbank, J K: *Cambridge History of China* Vol 10 p 587; Soothill, W E: *Timothy Richard* p 238; Covell, R: *W A P*

Martin p 185. Mandarin buttons: HTCOC 4 Appendix 5, p 415; Morse, H B: *International Relations* 3.87, Mines and Railways assent; Yong Lu to prepare naval academy and training ships.

271   12   *Fengshui*: see Glossary; HTCOC 4 Appendix 8 p 423

271   13   Yü Manzi: Morse, H B: *International Relations* 3.151; Latourette, K S: *History of Christian Missions in China* p 498; Broomhall, M: *The Chinese Empire* p 233; Sir C Macdonald to Lord Salisbury, Parliamentary Papers No 1, 1899

271   14   Franciscan: Latourette, K S: *History of Christian Missions* p 498

271   15   Riots: *China's Millions* 1898 pp 117, 136–7, 150–1, 155–6; OMFA 8522, May 16, 1898; 8521 July 1, 1898

272   16   G King: *China's Millions* 1898 pp 117, 151

273   17   Xinjiang: OMFA 8523, 9111

274   18   'Joshua': OMFA 8116c, 8231, 8522, 9114, L 2117, circular letter; L 21.11, L 222

274   19   'Special support': OMFA 8116 May 11, 1894

275   20   'Special support': OMFA 8116, 8231, 8522, L 2117, L 21.11, L 222, 'though a mistake was unwittingly made (when special support was welcomed, its recognition demands its correction: China Council, July 1898) It is therefore concluded . . . that from 30th June, 1899, the system be discontinued (whereby) sums of money become the definite salary [donations] towards the support and share of expense of a missionary (will be pooled in the General Fund and distributed) on a uniform scale . . .'

275   21   Unity, not uniformity: OMFA 851.12, 8522 Oct 10

275   22   Sharp: OMFA 8513

277   23   Emperor's Bible: Haldane, C: *The Last Great Empress of China* p 131

277   24   Zhang Zhitong: Morse, H B: *International Relations* 3.135, 137, 140–7

277   25   Foreign Office: Parliamentary Papers China No 1 1899 p 240, Sept 8, 1898

279   26   Ci Xi: Morse, H B: *International Relations* 3.141–7; Haldane, C: *Last Great Empress* p 136

279   27   Guang Xü: *North China Herald* Oct 10, 1898; Little, A B: *Li Hung-chang* p 283; Soothill, W E: *Timothy Richard* pp 238–9; Morse, H B: *International Relations* 3.145 fn.

279   28   Kang Yuwei: Morse, H B: *International Relations* 3.146, Consul Brennan, Shanghai, met Kang at Wusong and had him transferred to P&O ss *Ballarat*.

280   29   Coup: Morse, H B: *International Relations* 3.143; *North China Herald* Oct 10, 1898; Haldane, C: *Last Great Empress* pp 145–7

281   30   Tong's cavalry: Broomhall, M: *Martyred Missionaries of the China Inland Mission* p 4 footnote (1st edition p 6); Morse, H B: *International Relations* 3.150

281   31   Murder: F O Parl. Papers, China No 1, 1899, p 336; April 15–Dec 26, 1898; Latourette, K S: *History of Christian Missions* p 501

282   32   Tong's cavalry: Little, A B: *Li Hung-chang* pp 289–90

282   33   Rifts: Morse, H B: *International Relations* 3.xxxv.87

282   34   Isabella Bird (Bishop): *The Yangtze Valley and Beyond* (1899) last of

series: Pacific Islands, (1875); Rocky Mts (1879); Haokkaido, Japan (1880); Malaya (1883); Persia (1891); Ladakh (1894); Korea (1898); *China's Millions* 1897 pp 90, 92; 1899 p 46

283   35   Beauchamp: *China's Millions* 1899 p 46
284   36   Methodist: see Wm Fuller, HTCOC 3, Index
284   37   Germany: Latourette, K S: *History of Christian Missions* pp 490–501
284   38   'Secular missionaries': Fairbank, J K: *Cambridge History of China* Vol 10 pp 543–4, 574–81
285   39   Catholic status: Latourette, K S: *History of Christian Missions* p 500 footnote
287   40   Fleming: OMFA 8512, 8522, 9112a; *China's Millions* 1899 pp 6, 22, 121; Broomhall, M: *The Chinese Empire* p 267

Chapter 10

291   1   Hart-Morse: Morse, H B: *The International Relations of the Chinese Empire* 3.157; *North China Herald* June 6, 1900
292   2   Child-stealers: *China's Millions* 1899 p 65 seq.
292   3   Fujian (Kienning): Latourette, K S: *A History of Christian Missions in China* p 501; Grist, W A: *Samuel Pollard*
292   4   Chaling: Broomhall, M: *Pioneer Work in Hunan* pp 83–8; *China's Millions* 1899 p 107; OMFA L 21.13
293   5   Hunan: Broomhall, M: *The Chinese Empire* pp 183–4
293   6   Yü Manzi: OMFA 9112a; *China's Millions* 1899 pp 12, 30, 97; *North China Herald* 1899, May 13, June 17, Aug 28, Sept 4, Oct 9, 23, Dec 4: Morse, H B: *International Relations* 3.169, clashes in many provinces.
295   7   Boxers: An imperial edict approved, transparently: 'When peaceful and law-abiding people practice their mechanical skill for the self-preservation of themselves – this is in accordance with the public spirited principle (enjoined by Mencius) of keeping mutual watch and giving mutual help.' Morse, H B: *International Relations* 3.175 seq; Fairbank, J K: *Cambridge History of China* Vol 10 p 573
296   8   Ci Xi: Haldane, C: *The Last Great Empress of China* pp 178–80; Fairbank, J K: *Cambridge History of China* Vol 10 p 573; Hubbard, G E: Royal Institute of International Affairs, Chambers Encycl. Vol 3 pp 474–6
296   9   S M Brooks: *North China Herald*, Mar 21, 1900
297   10   JHT: OMFA 8517, 8522, 8523, 9113d
297   11   Hoste: OMFA 8514b, 8521, 8522, 8523, 10.351
298   12   Henrietta Soltau: OMFA 8522, Oct 17, 1898
298   13   Chongqing conference: OMFA 8517, 8523, 9111, 9112a; *China's Millions* 1899 pp 71, 80, 120; *Chinese Recorder* 1899 pp 157–60; Latourette, K S: *History of Christian Missions* p 496
299   14   JHT ill: OMFA 9111a, 9112a
299   15   Cooper: OMFA 8522 Nov 3, 1898
300   16   Th. Howard: OMFA 9112b, Jan 11, Sept 8, 1899
301   17   Keller: OMFA 9112a, L 21.13
301.   18   Berger: M J McKay thesis, Aberdeen, (unpublished): W T Berger's financial contributions to CIM totalled approx. £18,000; *China's Millions* 1899 pp 18–20, 47

302	19	Toronto: OMFA 9114, 9212; Taylor, Dr and Mrs Howard: *By Faith: H W Frost and the China Inland Mission* pp 238–41
302	20	JHT before 1900: OMFA 9112, Sept 11, 1899
304	21	Deaths: Pollock, J: *Moody without Sankey* p 270; *China's Millions* p 87; OMFA 9221
304	22	Chinese Church: OMFA 9112, L 222; *China's Millions* 1899 pp 108, 185
305	23	Frost, on martyrs: *China's Millions* 1898 pp 156–7
305	24	Miscalculation: Morse, H B: *International Relations* 3.177–91; Broomhall, M: *Jubilee Story of the China Inland Mission* pp 242–6; Haldane, C: *Last Great Empress* pp 176–85; Little, A B: *Li Hung-chang* pp 291–306; Forsyth, R C: *The China Martyrs of 1900* passim
306	25	Guang Xü: Little, A B: *Li Hung-chang* p 296: eyewitness account by Chinese eunuch; *North China Herald*, Mar 14, 1900
307	26	Yü Xian: F O Parl. Papers China No 3, 1900, Mar 29 p 12; Latourette, K S: *History of Christian Missions*, pp 501–26; *History of the Expansion of Christianity*, Vol 6 p 291
307	27	Prince Tuan: *North China Herald*, April 11, 18, 1900
307	28	Li Hongzhang: Broomhall, M: *Jubilee Story* p 245
308	29	Blood bath imminent: *North China Herald* May 8, 16, 1900
308	30	Warnings: Little, A B: *Li Hung-chang* pp 304–6
310	31	Volcano: OMFA 9112a; L 222
310	32	Australia: OMFA L 226, 9112a, 9121, 10.351; Loane, Marcus: *The China Inland Mission in Australia and New Zealand passim.*
312	33	No light: OMFA 9211b, 10.351; 9115 Jan 30, 1900; Morse, H B: *International Relations* 3.178
312	34	Stevenson-Cooper: OMFA N17.1900 p 2; 9215a
314	35	New York: OMFA 9212, 9213 D M Stearns, Aug 6, 1905; Taylor, Dr and Mrs Howard: *By Faith: Henry W Frost* pp 242–3
315	36	Ecumenical Conference: *China's Millions* 1900 p 115
315	37	Polygamy: OMFA N17.1900 p 9, F Howard Taylor report.
316	38	JHT breakdown: OMFA N17.1900 p 10; 9212 July 6
317	39	Boxer rising: This is only a summary. Research is needed into the archives of each society in China at the time, and the many publications on the subject. Most narratives relate to localities with little attention to chronology. This one attempts to keep the perspective of chronology, at the cost of interrupted narratives.
317	40	Discrepancies: eg see Forsyth, R: *China Martyrs of 1900* pp 202–18 and *Chinese Recorder* 1900 pp 458–63

Chapter 11

318	1	Jenny: both spellings common; JHT using this more often in later years.
318	2	Miscalculation: Broomhall, M: *Martyred Missionaries of the China Inland Mission*, Preface
320	3	Causes: Broomhall, M: *Martyred Missionaries* pp 2, 3–10
320	4	Kongcun: Morse, H B: *The International Relations of the Chinese Empire* 3.191

321 5   Boxers: Forsyth, R C: *The China Martyrs of 1900 passim*; Broomhall, M: *Martyred Missionaries* p 19

322 6   Hongtong; Lu'an: Broomhall, M: *Martyred Missionaries* pp 77, 103

322 7   Engineers: Little, A B: *Li Hung-chang* p 306; Haldane, C: *The Last Great Empress of China* p 185; Morse, H B: *International Relations* 3.199

323 8   Norman, Robinson: Forsyth, R C: *China Martyrs* pp 13–18

323 9   Glover: *A Thousand Miles of Miracle in China passim*

323 10 Mayhem: Morse, H B: *International Relations* Vol 3 *passim, see* pp 231, 233 fn; Haldane, C: *Last Great Empress*; Broomhall, M: *Martyred Missionaries*; Little, A B: *Li Hung-chang*.

324 11 Sugiyama: Haldane, C: *Last Great Empress* p 187; Haldane says killed June 12; Forsyth and Broomhall, 11th.

324 12 Peking: Morse, H B: *International Relations* 3.205 seq (Ch 8); Haldane, C: *Last Great Empress* pp 188–9; Forsyth, R C: *China Martyrs* p 101; Broomhall, M: *Martyred Missionaries* p 260

326 13 Peking: Morse, H B: *International Relations* 3.280; *Chinese Recorder* 1900 p 475; Latourette, K S: *A History of Christian Missions in China* p 508; *A History of the Expansion of Christianity* Vol 6 pp 291–2

326 14 Morrison; Shiba: Broomhall, M: *Martyred Missionaries* pp 259–60

327 15 Ci Xi, Tuan: Haldane, C: *Last Great Empress* p 190

327 16 Datong: Broomhall, M: *Martyred Missionaries* pp 144, 297; *Last Letters and Further Records of Martyred Missionaries of the China Inland Mission* pp 51–61; Forsyth, R C: *China Martyrs* p 77

328 17 Manchuria: *Chinese Recorder* 1901 p 423; Forsyth, R C: *China Martyrs* p 298

328 18 Soping: Broomhall, M: *Martyred Missionaries* p 144; Forsyth, R C: *China Martyrs* p 79

328 19 Ketteler: Forsyth, R C: *China Martyrs* p 102; Haldane, C: *Last Great Empress* p 194; Morse, H B: *International Relations* 3.247

329 20 Wang Mingdao: *A Stone Made Smooth* p 2, *see* Personalia.

329 21 Legations: Morse, H B: *International Relations* 3.225; F D Gamewell, E G Tewkesbury; Francis James; Forsyth, R C: *China Martyrs* p 475

330 22 Rewards: Morse, H B: *International Relations* 3.238–9; Jingshan's Diary.

330 23 Hart: Morse, H B: *International Relations* 3.263

330 24 Slay!: Morse, H B: *International Relations* 3.236–8; Jingshan's Diary p 287; Broomhall, M: *Martyred Missionaries* p 9; Smith, A H: *China in Convulsion*, Vol 2 p 294

331 25 Heroes: Yuan Zhang, Xü Jingcheng (Yuan Chang, Hsü Ching Ch'eng); Morse, H B: *International Relations* 3.238

332 26 Tuan Fang: Broomhall, M: *Martyred Missionaries* pp 286–7; Forsyth, R C: *China Martyrs* p 489

332 27 Viceroys: F O Parliamentary Papers, China No 3, 1900, p 67: Admiral Bruce to Admiralty; Morse, H B: *International Relations* 3.227–8, 231–2

333 28 Pact: *North China Herald*, July 11, 1900; Morse, H B: *International Relations* 3.232; Consul Warren to Lord Salisbury, June 29, 1900, Parl Papers, China No 3, 1900, p 85

334	29	Great flight: Morse, H B: *International Relations* 3.265, 268; Little, A B: *Li Hung-chang* p 308; Alicia Bewicke Little, herself a refugee from Chongqing.
334	30	Hanlin: *Chinese Recorder* 1900 pp 512–5
334	31	Wei Xian: Forsyth, R C: *China Martyrs* pp 250–70
335	32	Manchuria: Forsyth, R C: *China Martyrs* pp 299–302
335	33	Gobi: Forsyth, R C: *China Martyrs* pp 85–7; Broomhall, M: *Martyred Missionaries* p 144; *Chinese Recorder* 1900 p 528; Latourette, K S: *History of the Expansion of Christianity* p 339. Swedes not identified; possibly C&MA, making their party seventeen; Mr and Mrs C Blomberg, Mr and Mrs O Forsberg and child, of C&MA, died with Swedish Holiness Union ten.
336	34	Soping: named in Forsyth, R C: *China Martyrs* p 79–80; Broomhall, M: *Martyred Missionaries* pp 144–9: Mr and Mrs S A Persson, Miss J Lundell, E Pettersson, N Carleson, O A L Larsson, S McKee, Miss M Aspden, Mr and Mrs C S I'Anson, Miss M E Smith.
336	35	Watts-Jones: Morse, H B: *International Relations* 3.242, citing 'North China Herald, July 25, 1900 and private notes'.
337	36	Recantation: Forsyth, R C: *China Martyrs* pp 346–82
337	37	Chinese martyrs: Forsyth, R C: *China Martyrs* pp 346–82
337	38	Wilson, Saunders: Broomhall, M: *Martyred Missionaries* pp 67–76, 107–8, 126, 130; Forsyth, R C: *China Martyrs* pp 116–17
338	39	Taiyuan: Broomhall, M: *Martyred Missionaries* pp 69–70, 114–15, 126, 140; Forsyth, R C: *China Martyrs* pp 33–4, 117, 430
338	40	Women: Broomhall, M: *Martyred Missionaries* p 101: Eva French, Johnson, Gauntlett, Higgs, Rasmussen, Eldred; *China's Millions* 1900 p 74
340	41	Ci Xi, Henan: Broomhall, M: *Martyred Missionaries* p 147
341	42	Henan Canadians: *Chinese Recorder* 1900 pp 458–63; Forsyth, R C: *China Martyrs* pp 202–18; Broomhall, M: *Martyred Missionaries* p 147
341	43	Canadians: another, Griffiths, mentioned later; *Chinese Recorder* 1900 pp 458–63 by yet another, T Craigie Hood; no list complete.
341	44	Shouyang: Forsyth R C: *China Martyrs* pp 34–7, 428–9
342	45	Xinzhou: Forsyth, R C: *China Martyrs* p 43–64, 443–51; Broomhall, M: *Martyred Missionaries* p 145
343	46	Xinzhou: Forsyth, R C: *China Martyrs* p 45, July 25; Chinese Christians: pp 368–73
343	47	Lists: Broomhall, M: *Martyred Missionaries* pp 110, 103–25
344	48	Xiaoyi: Broomhall, M: *Martyred Missionaries* pp 24, 26, 29, 109, 268, 293, 295; *Last Letters* pp 30, 34, 37, 66; Forsyth, R C: *China Martyrs* pp 65–8
346	49	Baoding: *Chinese Recorder* 1901 pp 264–6; Forsyth, R C: *China Martyrs* pp 25–6 (19–29), 412–24
346	50	Meng Jixian: *Chinese Recorder* 1901 p 265; Latourette, K S: *History of the Expansion of Christianity* p 338; Presbyterians: Forsyth R C: *China Martyrs* pp 23–4
348	51	Wm Cooper: Broomhall, M: *Martyred Missionaries* pp 57, 77, 103, 112, 154–7, 293; *Last Letters* pp 28, 98; Forsyth, R C: *China Martyrs* pp 25–6; Latourette, K S: *History of Christian Missions* pp 777–9

348 52 Feng Yüxiang: Latourette, K S: *History of Christian Missions* pp 777–9; Broomhall, M: *Marshal Feng: A Good Soldier of Christ Jesus* pp 5–12

350 53 Ci Xi: Morse, H B: *International Relations* 3.248; Broomhall, M: *Martyred Missionaries* p 299

351 54 Ci Xi's perfidy: Morse, H B: *International Relations* 3.246–7 citing Jingshan's diary, July 4, pp 284–8; July 7 p 288

351 55 Mukden: *Chinese Recorder* 1901 pp 423–35, general review; Morse, H B: *International Relations* 3.242; Forsyth, R C: *China Martyrs* pp 273–310, 489; Latourette, K S: *History of Christian Missions* p 511; *History of the Expansion of Christianity* pp 292, 339

352 56 Huolu: Green, C H S: *In Deaths Oft passim*; Broomhall, M: *Martyred Missionaries* pp 161–7. So recent were these events, that many of the individuals involved were personally known to large numbers of people still living.

Chapter 12

355 1 Telegrams: Broomhall, M: *Martyred Missionaries of the China Inland Mission* pp 293–7

356 2 Hewett: Broomhall, M: *Last Letters and Further Records of Martyred Missionaries of the China Inland Mission* pp 89–93

358 3 Barratt, Woodroffe: Broomhall, M: *Martyred Missionaries* pp 25, 54, 116, 268, 297

358 4 'CCH': Broomhall, M: (Chang Chih-heng) *Martyred Missionaries* pp 11–12, 262–3, 268–72; Swedish Mission pp 17, 22–4, 230–5, 245, 263, 305

361 5 Hills: Broomhall, M: *Martyred Missionaries, passim*, p 265; *Last Letters* pp 27, 84, 86, 88; Forsyth, R C: *China Martyrs* pp 134–47

361 6 M E Chapman: Loane, Marcus: *The Story of the China Inland Mission in Australia and New Zealand* p 28

362 7 D Kay: Broomhall, M: *Martyred Missionaries* pp 110–12, 262–3; Forsyth, R C: *China Martyrs* p 75

362 8 A R Saunders: *The Times*, Sept 19, 1900; *A God of Deliverances, passim*; Broomhall, M: *Martyred Missionaries* pp 66–78, 82, 100, 115, 294; *Last Letters* p 89; Forsyth, R C: *China Martyrs* pp 116–26

364 9 M Huston, H Rice: Broomhall, M: *Martyred Missionaries* pp 73–5

364 10 A E Glover, C Gates: Glover, A E: *A Thousand Miles of Miracle in China*, 1904, abridged 1957, *passim* (outstanding among all missionary literature); Broomhall, M: *Martyred Missionaries* pp 25, 64, 66, 75, 77–8, 81–8, 89–101, 293–4, 297; Forsyth, R C: *China Martyrs* pp 127–33

370 11 Hankou: Wuhan of today is the conurbation of Hankou, Wuchang and Hanyang. By 1900 Hankou was the commercial, consular and missionary centre (the name most used in literature of the period). Wuchang was a Chinese city, seat of mandarins; Hanyang, industrial. Retaining Hankou here avoids an anachronism.

371 12 Whitfield Guinness: Broomhall, M: *Martyred Missionaries* pp 205–17, 254, 293–4; Forsyth, R C: *China Martyrs* pp 219–27

372 13 C M Lack: Broomhall, M: *Martyred Missionaries* pp 205, 233–4

372	14	A Argento: Broomhall, M: *Martyred Missionaries* pp 236–43, 276; Forsyth, R C: *China Martyrs* pp 238–49
374	15	C H Bird: with A Gracie family, John Macfarlane (also as MacFarlane, McFarlane, M'Farlane): Loane, Marcus: *Story of the CIM in Australia and New Zealand, passim*; Broomhall, M: *Martyred Missionaries* pp 205, 217–9, 245, 273
374	16	C H Bird: Broomhall, M: *Martyred Missionaries* pp 205, 231, 295; escape pp 244–50; Forsyth, R C: *China Martyrs* pp 228–37
376	17	Henan: Mr and Mrs Shearer, two children; Mr and Mrs Biggs; Robert Powell, Charles M Lack; Misses Kidman, E L Randall, Taylor, Bevin: Broomhall, M: *Martyred Missionaries* pp 205, 225–9, 287
377	18	Taiyuan: Broomhall, M: *Martyred Missionaries* pp 69, 107, 111, 114–6, 127, 140 list, 163, 261, 264, 266–7; Forsyth, R C: *China Martyrs* p 40 list. BMS: G B Farthing, Mrs Farthing, 3 children; Miss E M Stewart; S F Whitehouse, Mrs Whitehouse; Shouyang: T W Pigott, Mrs Pigott née Kemp, child; Miss Duval, J Robinson, Ernestine and Mary Atwater, children, ABCFM; Taiyuan: Dr A E Lovitt, Mrs Lovitt, child; G W Stokes, Mrs Stokes; J Simpson, Mrs Simpson; Miss A E Coombs; independent, A Hoddle; CIM: Dr W Millar Wilson, Mrs Millar Wilson, child; Mrs J Stevens, M Clarke; B&FBS: W F Beynon, Mrs Beynon, 3 children. Previously CIM: Pigotts, Beynons, Hoddle, Simpsons, Stokes.
377	19	Edict: *Chinese Recorder* 1901 pp 132–7; Broomhall, M: *Martyred Missionaries* p 155; murders: p 265; Forsyth, R C: *China Martyrs* p 32
379	20	Bureau wait: Forsyth, R C: *China Martyrs* pp 34, 37–40; *Chinese Recorder* 1901 p 210; Broomhall, M: *Last Letters* pp 21–24; Latourette, K S: *History of Christian Missions* p 510
381	21	Bishop Fogolla: Latourette, K S: *History of Christian Missions* p 510, from R C sources: 'Yü Xian himself dealt the aged Fogolla the first blow' – whether the facial wound or decapitation, not clarified.
381	22	Yong Zheng's report: recorded by J A Creasey Smith; *Chinese Recorder* 1901 pp 210–11; Morse, H B: *International Relations of the Chinese Empire* 3.241
381	23	Yü Xian's rewards: Forsyth, R C: *China Martyrs* pp 40–1
382	24	Jingshan diary: Morse, H B: *International Relations* 3.241 citing Jingshan's diary July 16 p 292. Woman referred to was a CIM missionary, unnamed.
382	25	'CCH': Broomhall, M: *Martyred Missionaries* pp 264–9. August 22 CCH added, 'Some say forty-two foreigners (and) one hundred (Chinese Christians)'. Hearsay, dates unspecified, perhaps not only Taiyuan. Yong Zheng more precise.
382	26	Foreign child: Broomhall, M: *Martyred Missionaries* p 266 re CCH.
382	27	Yong Zheng: *Chinese Recorder* 1901 pp 211, 134 (132–7)
383	28	Chinese martyrs: Broomhall, M: *Martyred Missionaries* pp 264–6; *Last Letters* pp 27, 84, 86, 88; Forsyth, R C: *China Martyrs, passim*, pp 135, 346–82
384	29	Glover, Gates: Glover, A E: *A Thousand Miles of Miracle* (1957 edn) pp 123–4

385 30 Glover, A E: *A Thousand Miles of Miracle* (1904 edn) pp 251–3; (1957) pp 144–5

385 31 Glover A E: *A Thousand Miles of Miracle* (1904) pp 335, 355, (1957) pp 145–51; Broomhall, M: *Martyred Missionaries* pp 97–9

386 32 Datong: Broomhall, M: *Last Letters* pp 27, 51–3, 56–7, (51–61); *Martyred Missionaries* p 144; Forsyth, R C: *China Martyrs* pp 77–8; Morse, H B: *International Relations* 3.242; Latourette, K S: *History of Christian Missions* p 514; *China's Millions* 1902 pp 32–3

387 33 Daning, Hejin: Broomhall, M: *Martyred Missionaries* pp 25, 47, 113–14; *Last Letters* pp 34–42, 47; *see* HTCOC 6.407–8, Pastor Qü or Zhang Zhiben.

388 34 McConnell, Young, King, Burton, Nathan: Broomhall, M: *Martyred Missionaries* pp 30, 113, 265, 309; *Last Letters* pp 43–8; Forsyth, R C: *China Martyrs* p 74. Report by Miss E G Ulff, Shaanxi, from Chinese sources. Nathan sisters, Heaysman: *Last Letters* pp 34–8.

389 35 Linfen: Broomhall, M: *Martyred Missionaries* pp 67, 103–31, 294

390 36 Linfen: A Lutley, Mrs Lutley, 2 children; F C H Dreyer, Mrs Dreyer; Misses E Gauntlett, A F Hoskyn, A Hoskyn, E French, E Higgs, E C Johnson, R Palmer, K Rasmussen (fourteen); Broomhall, M: *Martyred Missionaries* pp 66–7 lists, 117–22, 125, 272, 288

392 37 Qü Xian: Broomhall, M: *Martyred Missionaries* pp 183–97, 276–7; *Last Letters* pp 9, 10, 21–3; Forsyth, R C: *China Martyrs* pp 90–7; Latourette, K S: *History of Christian Missions* pp 512, 516

393 38 Manchester, Sherwood: accounts differ in details; I judge this sequence to be correct.

394 39 Yüshan: HTCOC 5.337; 6.347, 395–8; Molly Robertson who typed these seven volumes is Kate Lachlan's granddaughter.

Chapter 13

395 1 Miracles: Broomhall, M: *Martyred Missionaries of the China Inland Mission* pp 77–126

395 2 Glover, A E: *A Thousand Miles of Miracle in China* (1904) using 20th edition (1944) pp 268–313 and (abridged 1959) pp 152–69

396 3 Glover, A E: *A Thousand Miles* (1944) pp 311–14

397 4 Glover, A E: *A Thousand Miles* (1944) pp 326–32; Broomhall, M: *Martyred Missionaries* p 100

397 5 Saunders, A R: Broomhall, M: *Martyred Missionaries* pp 74–6

399 6 Glover, A E: *A Thousand Miles* (1944) pp 333–40. With medical knowledge they would probably have said 'purulent' or 'suppurating' instead of 'gangrenous'.

402 7 Gobi party: Forsyth, R C: *The China Martyrs of 1900* pp 88–9

403 8 Xi Xian six: Broomhall, M: *Last Letters and Further Records of Martyred Missionaries of the China Inland Mission* pp 29–33; Forsyth, R C: *China Martyrs* pp 76–7

403 9 Oberlin: Forsyth, R C: *China Martyrs* pp 68–9, 453–6

404 10 Fei Qihao: Forsyth, R C: *China Martyrs* pp 41, 383–98

405 11 Kong Xiangxi: Forsyth, R C: *China Martyrs* p 386; Latourette, K S: *A History of the Expansion of Christianity*, Vol 6 p 339

405 12 Tianjin: Morse, H B: *International Relations of the Chinese Empire* 3.230 seq., Chronology.

406	13	Tianjin: Morse, H B: *International Relations* 3.245; Decennial Reports 2.521; F O Parliamentary Papers, China No 3, 1900, p 101. Bullion: Tokyo Press, August 3, 1900; Savage-Landor: China and the Allies 1.201; Smith, A H: *China in Convulsion* 2.583
406	14	Truces: First on June 25 (day after edict to kill); second, July 18–28; third, August 3–4
407	15	Yuan Zhang, Xü Jingcheng: Morse, H B: *International Relations* 3.254; Broomhall, M: *Martyred Missionaries* p 9
407	16	Yong Lu: Morse, H B: *International Relations* 3.233 from Hart, R: *These from the Land of Sinim* p 39
407	17	Troops: Morse, H B: *International Relations* 3.265
408	18	Conger: Morse, H B: *International Relations* 3.253, 257, citing Jingshan diary p 295
409	19	Shanghai: *Chinese Recorder* Aug 1900 pp 434, 512–5; 1901 W A P Martin pp 83, 206–7. Beijing: Morse, H B: *International Relations* 3.275–87
410	20	Siege lifted: Morse, H B: *International Relations* 3.275–87 citing J H Macoun, Imperial Customs Service; Psalm 124; *Chinese Recorder* 1901 p 838
411	21	Siege: *Chinese Recorder* 1901 pp 83–8
412	22	Orgy: Morse, H B: *International Relations* 3.284; Jingshan diary Aug 15 p 302; Putnam Weale: *Indiscreet Letters* pp 227–301; Latourette, K S: *History of Christian Missions* p 506. Japanese: Morse, H B: *International Relations* 3.285, R Hart to E B Drew Aug 18, 1900
413	23	Russia: Morse, H B: *International Relations* 3.306; F O Parl Papers China No 1, 1901 p 128
414	24	J W Lowrie: Latourette, K S: *History of Christian Missions* p 520
414	25	Ci Xi, Yü Xian: Haldane, C: *The Last Great Empress of China* pp 216, 222. Death of Yü Xian, eyewitness account; *China's Millions* 1902 p 67
415	26	Plenipotentiaries: Forsyth, R C: *China Martyrs* p 382
416	27	'CCH': Broomhall, M: *Martyred Missionaries* p 267
416	28	Xinzhou: *Chinese Recorder* 1901 pp 134–6; Forsyth, R C: *China Martyrs* pp 43–6, 49–64, 443–51
416	29	Guihuacheng: Forsyth, R C: *China Martyrs* pp 82–4; Emil Olson (Superintendent), Mrs Olson, 3 children; Mr and Mrs C Noven, 2 children; Mr and Mrs E Anderson, 2 children; Mr and Mrs O Bingmark, 2 children; Mr and Mrs M Nystrom, 1 child; Mr and Mrs C L Lundberg, 2 children; Misses K Hall, K Orn, A Gustasson, E Erickson, A E Palm (12 couples, 12 children, 5 single ladies).
416	30	Mongolia: Forsyth, R C: *China Martyrs* pp 80–1: D W Stenberg, C J Suber, N J Friedstrom, Misses Clara Anderson, Hilda Anderson, Hannah Lund
417	31	Catholics: Latourette, K S: *History of Christian Missions* p 511
417	32	Dreyer party: Broomhall, M: *Martyred Missionaries* p 122; *Chinese Recorder* 1900 pp 484–7, G Parker report.
417	33	Green, Gregg: Green, C H S: *In Deaths Oft* (publ. 1901) 1936 edn. pp 25–41; Broomhall, M: *Martyred Missionaries* pp 167–9, 173, 300; Forsyth, R C: *China Martyrs* pp 43–6
421	34	Green, C H: *In Deaths Oft* (1936 edn) pp 42–61

426 35 Fei Qihao: Forsyth, R C: *China Martyrs* pp 383–98
427 36 Rag: Forsyth, R C: *China Martyrs* p 390 footnote says 'written in blood': almost certainly a gloss, for until the last moment they thought they were being escorted to safety.
427 37 Allies' outrages: Forsyth, R C: *China Martyrs* p 392
428 38 Greens, Gregg, 'little bird': Aug 9 captured; Aug 10 dep from Huolu to Zhengding; Aug 12 at Ding Xian; Aug 13 arr. Baoding; Aug 14 by boat past Anxin; Aug 15 in reed beds, captured; Aug 16–18 on show at Anxin; c Aug 23–4 'tuft of paper'; Sept 3 hostile Boxers arr Anxin; Sept 4 hidden in storeroom; Sept 5 told of consul demand for their protection; Sept 5 dep Anxin; Sept 7 arr Baoding; c Sept 14 Greens' telegram to John Stevenson; c Sept 28 letter from consul and note from J W Lowrie; five to six weeks at Baoding as hostages till Oct 14; Oct 10 Vera died; C H S Green ill; Oct 8 French expedition dep Tianjin; Oct 13 French enter Baoding; Oct 16 Greens to French camp; Oct 18 international column arr Baoding; Oct 19 Gen Gaselee visits Greens at *yamen*; Oct 20 to British military hospital; Oct 21 Griffiths and Brown arr Baoding; Oct 27 all arr Tianjin; Nov 1 Vera buried at Tianjin; early Dec to Shanghai; Jan 5 1901 dep Shanghai to UK.
428 39 Fei Qihao: Forsyth, R C: *China Martyrs* p 41. Wang Lanbu: Broomhall, M: *Martyred Missionaries* pp 145–7
431 40 Ogren: Broomhall, M: *Last Letters* pp 65–83
434 41 Olivia Ogren: Broomhall, M: *Last Letters* pp 65–83
437 42 'CCH': Broomhall, M: *Martyred Missionaries* p 268

Chapter 14
441 1 Hoste: OMFA 9215a; 9319 Nov 8, 1900: *Monthly Notes* Apr 1; 9325
442 2 Switzerland: sequence of residences: OMFA N18.1900; L 21
442 3 J W Stevenson: OMFA 9212; L 234
443 4 Travel: *China's Millions* 1900 pp 122–3; OMFA 9319
444 5 Refugees: OMFA 9214a,b
446 6 JHT: OMFA 9214a,b
447 7 J W Stevenson: OMFA 9214a
448 8 Successor: OMFA 9215b
449 9 JHT: OMFA 9214c
450 10 Hoste: OMFA 9215b
452 11 J W Stevenson – JHT: OMFA 9311
452 12 Sloan, Frost: *China's Millions* 1901 p 100. W B Sloan, autumn 1900; H W Frost, winter 1900; both in China until April 22, 1901, sailed for Europe, shipwrecked.
452 13 A Orr Ewing: OMFA 9315 Mar 13, 1901; 9319 Mar 26
453 14 Sichuan: Soothill, W E: *Timothy Richard of China* pp 251–2
454 15 Hoste: churches: *Chinese Recorder* 1900, *passim*; *China's Millions* 1901 p 163; OMFA L 21.12
454 16 Nevius; Korea: *Chinese Recorder* 1900 p 384
454 17 Shanghai conference: *Chinese Recorder* 1900 pp 529–30
455 18 Shanxi news: *China's Millions* Oct 1900 pp 151–5
457 19 Superstition: Smith, A H: *The Uplift of China* p 187
458 20 A R Saunders: 'not death': *China's Millions* 1901 p 41

459	21	Ci Xi: Morse, H B: *International Relations of the Chinese Empire* 3.308, 320
459	22	Ci Xi: Morse, H B: *International Relations* 3.308, 320
460	23	Li Hongzhang: Morse, H B: *International Relations* 3.339, 343–4
461	24	Taels: Morse, H B: *International Relations* 3.352, tables of international equivalents.
461	25	Reparations: Taylor, F H: *These Forty Years* p 433, quoting *North China Herald*; Broomhall, M: *Last Letters and Further Records of Martyred Missionaries of the China Inland Mission* p 13; Latourette, K S: *History of Christian Missions in China* pp 521–5; *History of the Expansion of Christianity* p 260
461–2	26,27	Degradation: Morse, H B: *International Relations* 3.359, 262
462	28	Finland: *Chinese Recorder* 1901 p 382–3
463	29	Reparations: Broomhall, M: *Last Letters* p 13; *China's Millions* 1902 p 38
463	30	Protestant indemnities: Taylor, F H: *These Forty Years* pp 392–3
464	31	Shanghai conference: *Chinese Recorder* 1900 pp 529–30
464	32	'Blood money': *Chinese Recorder* 1900 pp 537–50, 617–9; Latourette, K S: *History of Christian Missions* p 818
464	33	Missions indemnities: Morse, H B: *International Relations* 3.314 footnote; General Chaffee to Minister Conger, Oct 1900
464	34	Latourette, K S: *History of Christian Missions* p 523
464	35	Indemnities: *Chinese Recorder* 1923 pp 257 seq.
465	36	Baoding: *China's Millions* 1902 pp 38, 65
465–6	37,38	Baoding: Forsyth, R C: *China Martyrs* pp 26–29; Broomhall, M: *Last Letters* pp 98–100
466	39	Ceng Chunxüan: son of viceroy of Yunnan, Guizhou 1875 (HTCOC 5.431; 6. *passim*); Li Hongzhang: Soothill, W E: *Timothy Richard*, Index, pp 168, 188, 225; Zhou Fu: *Chinese Recorder* 1901 p 312
466	40	Investigations: Broomhall, M: *Last Letters* p 100
467	41	CIM indemnities? OMFA 9221, 9316, 9319
467	42	J L Krapf: Stock, E: *History of the Church Missionary Society* 1.462
468	43	Reoccupation: OMFA 932; N18 Nov 22, 1900; Broomhall, M: *Last Letters* p 104
469	44	No claims: OMFA 9311, L 243; Broomhall, M: *Jubilee Story of the China Inland Mission* p 257
470	45	JHT; 'Dissociate': OMFA 9313
471	46	Investigators: OMFA 9321 pp 91–9, 114 July 22; L 242, 245 July 12 to JHT.
471	47	Mandarins: *China's Millions* 1901 pp 143–4, 164
473	48	Persecuted: *China's Millions* 1901 pp 145–6; OMFA 9322
474	49	Elder Xü Puyüan: OMFA 932 pp 97–9 July 12; 9322 Oct 26; L 245 Hoste July 22
476	50	Taiyuan: personal communication, BCB to AJB; Broomhall, M: *Last Letters* p 14
476–7	51,52	Daotai: Hoste, OMFA 932; L 245
478	53	Investigators: Taylor, F H: *These Forty Years* p 425; OMFA 932 pp 116, 118; *China's Millions* 1902 p 53 A Orr Ewing, colourful account
478	54	Reoccupied: OMFA 9323, 9412

478	55	Women to Shanxi: Taylor, F H: *These Forty Years* pp 4, 7–8; cf. *Chinese Recorder* 1901 p 147; *China's Millions* 1902 p 169; Indigenous: OMFA 9322 Oct 26
479	56	Shanxi University: Soothill, W E: *Timothy Richard* pp 253 seq.
481	57	Gov Ceng's proclamation: *China's Millions* 1902 pp 33, 36; Broomhall, M: *Jubilee Story* pp 258–9; *Last Letters* p 14
481	58	'Blood of martyrs': *Chinese Recorder* 1901 p 441
482	59	Pigott: Broomhall, M: *Last Letters* pp 15–16

Chapter 15

483	1	Ci Xi: Little, A B: *Li Hung-chang* p 317 seq.; Fleming, P: *The Siege of Peking*; Haldane, C: *The Last Great Empress of China* p 229
483	2	Guang Xü: Little, A B: *Li Hung-chang* p 321
483	3	Li Hongzhang: Little, A B: *Li Hung-chang* p 329; Haldane, C: *The Last Great Empress* p 231; 223; Soothill, W E: *Timothy Richard* p 272
484	4	Sir Robert Hart: Morse, H B: *International Relations of the Chinese Empire* 3.362, 470, Appendix E
485	5	Manchus: Haldane, C: *Last Great Empress* p 220; *China's Millions* 1902 p 153; Yong Lu, 1903 p 64; Yü Xian, 1902 p 67
485	6	Ci Xi's return: Little, A B: *Li Hung-chang* pp 318, 331; Haldane, C: *Last Great Empress* pp 231–5, 240
486	7	Reform: Hsü, Immanuel C Y: *The Rise of Modern China* (OUP) p 499 seq.
488	8	Japan: Morse, H B: *International Relations* 3.434, 436; *Chinese Recorder* 1901 p 356
488	9	Bruce, Lowis: *China's Millions* 1902 Oct p 131, 138, 141; 1903 pp 93b, 106; 1904 p 136
488	10	Church welcomes: *Chinese Recorder* 1901 p 572; 1902 p 100, 147, 180; 1905 p 171
489	11	R Powell, H Taylor: OMFA 9412; HTCOC 6.53–5, 63, 84
489	12	Hunan: *Chinese Recorder* 1901 p 314; Thompson, R Wardlaw: *Griffith John: The Story of Fifty Years in China, passim.*
489	13	Reaction: *China's Millions* 1902 p 166; 1903 p 93
490	14	JHT; photography: OMFA N18. p 5 footnote: box and half-plate stand cameras, Zeiss lens, darkroom, enlarging equipment; Taylor, Dr and Mrs Howard: *Hudson Taylor* Vol 2 Ch 40
490	15	Joseph Faulding: William in early Vols.
491	16	Stroke? OMFA 9313 Aug 17; 9314, 9316; N18.1901 p 7, 8
491	17	S P Smith: OMFA 9421 Oct 19, 1901; N18.1901 p 19
492	18	JHT, retires: OMFA 9411; N18.1902 p 20
492	19	Hoste: Thompson, P: *D E Hoste: A Prince with God* pp 96–102; OMFA 9413, June 25, 1902; *China's Millions* 1903 monthly covers: May, JHT: General Director, DEH: Acting GD; June, JHT: Consulting Director, DEH: General Director: July–Aug JHT: Founder and Consulting Director, DEH: General Director; *China's Millions* 1903 p 87
493	20	Chefoo deaths: OMFA 9423
494	21	Coillard: OMFA 9423 Aug 14; Francis Coillard died May 29, 1904
495	22	Frost, S P Smith: OMFA 9313 Oct 3, 1901; 9314 Oct, 1901; 9318, 9413 July 19, Sept, Oct; 9421 S P Smith papers 1901; 9422 D E Hoste

		1912 on disruptive effect of such debates; London Council Minutes, especially Oct, Dec 1902; OMFA L 244, N18.1901 p 19; N18.1902 p 14; N18.1902 Aug 8, pp 24–6; N18.1902 Dec 27
496	23	Walter B Sloan: *China's Millions* 1903 p 36, Assistant Home Director, by Theodore Howard's appointment.
496	24	JHT swansong: OMFA 9511a,b; N18.1903 pp 30–3
497	25	Sister Eva von Thiele-Winkler
497	26	Frost, S P Smith: China Council Minutes, April 1, 1903: OMFA N18.1903 p 11 (10–15), 20; 9414 Sept 1902
498	27	W E Geil re CIM: OMFA N18.1903 pp 9–10
499	28	Shanxi Christians: OMFA N18.1903 pp 12, 96–111
499	29	Neo-Boxers: Sichuan and S Henan
499	30	Gov.Ceng, Chengdu: *China's Millions* 1903 pp 22, 93b, 154, 157; 1904 p 7
502	31	Bibles: Wm Moseley had published in 1798 his *Memoir on the Importance and Practicability of Translating and Printing the Holy Scriptures in the Chinese Language*. Six years to the day later, on March 7, 1804, the Bible Society had been formed and turned its attention to doing what Dr Moseley urged. On Sept 19, 1853, the Bible Society resolved to print one million copies of the Chinese New Testament – the day young Hudson Taylor sailed from home for the first time.
502	32	Lausanne: Oct 19, 1903 – March 14, 1904
502	33	Jenny Taylor: *China's Millions* 1904 p 122; 1903 pp 117–22; Rev. 21: 18,21; Bunyan's *Pilgrim's Progress*
503	34	JHT to Changsha: *China's Millions* 1905 p 94
504	35	Chinese dress: London Council Minutes Nov 24, 1904 p 236, Feb 5, 1907 and June 18, 1907 pp 112, 115
505	36	Three veterans: OMFA N18.1905 gives May 29, but Taylor, Dr and Mrs Howard 2.608 says April 29. They met in Hankou on both days, photographs taken both times. *China's Millions* 1905 p 103; p 395 says May 24 in error.
505	37	Covell, R: *W A P Martin* p 188
508	38	JHT's last day: *China's Millions* 1905 pp 94, 119–29
510	39	Chariots: *Chinese Recorder* 1905 p 373; OMFA N18.1905 p 19
510	40	Gravestone: 'Sacred to the Memory of the Rev J Hudson Taylor, the revered Founder of the China Inland Mission, born May 21, 1832, died June 3, 1905. "A MAN IN CHRIST" 2 Cor. XII.2' and 'This Monument is Erected by the Missionaries of the China Inland Mission as a Mark of their Heartfelt Esteem and Love.' (Quoted from 'I know a man in Christ Jesus who . . . was caught up to the third heaven . . . caught up to Paradise.')
511	41	Tributes: *Chinese Recorder* 1905 pp 379–86, 387–95, 423; Martin, W A P: *A Cycle of Cathay* p 24; *China's Millions* 1905 pp 105, 106, 110, 131–4; OMFA N18.1905 p 17
515	42	W B Sloan, Elder Cumming: *China's Millions* 1905 pp 114–15. J W Stevenson: *China's Millions* 1905 pp 118–19, 131–4
516	43	A H Smith: *Chinese Recorder* 1907 p 419; *China's Millions* 1905 pp 131–4
517	44	JHT meditation: OMFA H 517

Chapter 16

518   1   Ci Xi's treasure: Haldane, C: *The Last Great Empress of China* p 238;
          Morse, H B: *International Relations of the Chinese Empire* 3.442
          footnote; *North China Herald* April 17, 1909, citing Chinese press.

519   2   Opium: Morse, H B: *International Relations* 3. 437–9; Broomhall, M:
          Heirs Together pp 134–5

520   3   Manchus: Morse, H B: *International Relations* 3.446

520   4   Monarchy: Morse, H B: *International Relations* 3.440–2; Hsü
          Immanuel C Y: *The Rise of Modern China*, (OUP), pp 504–10

522   5   'China Centenary Missionary Conference Records'

523   6   'Christian Church in China': Latourette, K S: *A History of Christian
          Missions in China* pp 665–70

523   7   Secular: Fairbank, J K: *Cambridge History of China* (CUP) Vol 10
          pp 559, 589; medical, pp 574–6

523   8   'Christianise': *Chinese Recorder* 1901 pp 124–5; Latourette, K S:
          History of Christian Missions p 619

525   9   Progress: Fairbank, J K: *Cambridge History of China* Vol 10
          pp 581–9

526   10 'Rope of sand': Stock, E: *The History of the Church Missionary
          Society* 2,652; *China's Millions* May 1932, Centenary Number, p 93

527   11 CIM members: Broomhall, M: *The Jubilee Story of the China Inland
          Mission*, Appendix 3, tables; Shanghai Resolution: *Jubilee Story*
          p 269

529   12 Social service: Broomhall, M: *Present Day Conditions in China*
          pp 35–41

529   13 Medical: Latourette, K S: *History of Christian Missions* pp 268–9,
          452–60; *Chinese Recorder* 1875 p 342; 1878 p 115; 1882 p 308

530   14 Li Hongzhang, F H Taylor: Broomhall, M: *Jubilee Story* p 298

531   15 Der Ling: Haldane, C: *Last Great Empress* pp 113, 243, 280 seq.;
          Morse, H B: *International Relations* 3.441; *The Times* Nov 15, 1908

533   16 Ci Xi: Hsü, Immanuel C Y: *The Rise of Modern China* pp 539–48

534   17 Yuan Shikai: Morse, H B: *International Relations* 3.442

534   18 Prince Qing: *The Times*, May 17, 1911

535   19 Xi'an, revolution: Beckman, E R: *The Massacre at Sianfu, passim*,
          pp 79, 100. C T Wang: (Wang Chang-tsuen, Wang Zhang-cun).
          Scandinavian Alliance Mission of North America. Martyrs: Mrs
          Beckman, W T Vatne, Hilda Nelson (aet 15), Selma Beckman (13),
          Ruth Beckman (8), Oscar Bergstrom (13), Hulda Bergstrom (12),
          George Ahlstrand (10). C T Wang became Foreign Minister.

535   20 Republic: Hsü, Immanuel C Y: *The Rise of Modern China, passim*;
          Morse, H B: *International Relations* Vol 3, *passim*; *Chinese Recorder*,
          1896–1912, *passim*; *China's Millions*, 1896–1912, *passim*.

Chapter 17

538   1   Chief sources: Hsü, Immanuel C Y: *The Rise of Modern China*;
          Chinese Recorder, 'The Month' series; Latourette, K S: *A History of
          Christian Missions in China*; Broomhall, M: *The Jubilee Story of the
          China Inland Mission*; Neill, S C: *A History of Christian Missions*.

538   2   Ideals: Latourette, K S: *History of Christian Missions* p 609; *China
          Mission Year Book* 1913, p 95

539	3	Day of Prayer: *North China Herald*, May 3, 1913; Latourette, K S: *History of Christian Missions* p 612; Broomhall, M: *Jubilee Story* p 325
540	4	Warlords: Hsü, Immanuel C Y: *The Rise of Modern China* p 374; Broomhall, M: *Jubilee Story* p 324
542	5	Yüan Shikai: Hsü, Immanuel C Y: *The Rise of Modern China* pp 575–83; *Chinese Recorder* 1908–13, The Month series.
542	6	Chief sources: Latourette, K S: *History of Christian Missions* pp 527–823; Broomhall, M: *Jubilee Story* pp 322–7; Lyall, L T: *A Passion for the Impossible* pp 81–7
542	7	Christian colleges: Neill, S C: *History of Christian Missions* p 338
543	8	Primary aim: *Chinese Recorder* 1912 p 543–6
543	9	'Biola': Bible Institute of Los Angeles
544	10	A R Saunders: Broomhall, M: *Jubilee Story* p 324
544	11	Warlords: Lyall, L T: *A Passion for the Impossible* pp 85–95; Hsü Immanuel C Y: *The Rise of Modern China* pp 584–8; Latourette, K S: *History of Christian Missions* pp 687–704
545	12	Feng Yüxiang: Broomhall, M: *Marshal Feng: A Good Soldier of Christ Jesus* (1924)
546	13	Hazards: Latourette, K S: *History of Christian Missions* p 818
546	14	Church (CCC): Neill, S C: *History of Christian Missions* p 551
548	15	Latourette, K S: *A History of the Expansion of Christianity*, Vol 6 p 329; Houghton, F: *The Two Hundred*, Appendices; two hundred named.
549	16	Mao: Hsü, Immanuel C Y: *The Rise of Modern China* pp 666–74
551	17	Long March: Bosshardt, R A: *The Restraining Hand*; Lyall, L T: *A Passion for the Impossible*, pp 109–11
553	18	Stam: Taylor, Mrs Howard: *The Triumph of John and Betty Stam* pp 102–14; *China's Millions* 1934–35, *passim*.
554	19	Alfred Bosshardt: still living (in his 90s) as we go to press.
554	20	Trio: *see* Bibliography: Cable and French; Platt, W J: *China's Millions*, *passim*; firsthand, as friends of author's family.
555	21	George Hunter: distinguish from George Hunter of Hunan.
555	22	Muslim uprising: Cable, M and French, F: *The Gobi Desert* pp 232–57
558	23	Beauchamp: as one of the doctors, I (AJB) was Sir Montagu's driver-attendant.
559	24	Henry Pu Yi: Haldane, C: *The Last Great Empress of China* pp 274–5
560	25	Leading Christians: Lyall, L T: *John Sung Three of China's Mighty Men* (Yang Shao-tang; Nee Tuo-sheng; Wang Ming-dao); 'T'uo' is a watchman's rattle.
561	26	J R Adam: Clarke, S R: *Among the Tribes of South-west China* (315 pages); Broomhall, M: *Jubilee Story* pp 274–89; *China's Millions*, *passim*.
562	27	Lisu: Taylor, Mrs Howard: *Behind the Ranges: J O Fraser*; Crossman, E: *Mountain Rain: A New Biography of James O Fraser*; Lyall, L T: *A Passion for the Impossible* p 133; *China's Millions*, *passim*.

562   28   Gates: Psalm 107.16; Lyall, L T: *A Passion for the Impossible* pp 132 seq.; *God Reigns in China* p 125 seq.

564   29   Exodus: Neill, S C: *History of Christian Missions* p 467; Lyall, L T: *God Reigns in China* p 127

564   30   Sinza Rd: (*see* Ch 4 note 11, p 148); Thompson, P: *China: The Reluctant Exodus* pp 55–72, 103

568   31   Red Guards: Lyall, L T: *God Reigns in China* pp 140–7, 162–5

569   32   Church: *see* Bibliography: Adeney, D A: *China: Christian Students Face the Revolution*, *passim*; *China: The Church's Long March*, *passim*.

570   33   Persecution: Lyall, L T: *New Spring in China*, pp 168–9

570   34   Persecution: Lyall, L T: *God Reigns in China* p 148

573   35   Chao, Jonathan: *China's Religious Policy: An Analysis*, Chinese Church Research Center, Hong Kong, 1979

573,   36   China Christian Council: Keston College: *Religion in the Communist*
575   *World*, Autumn 1984: Religious Policy in China and its implementation in the light of Document No 19 (Peter Morrison). Y T Wu: Neill, S C: *Colonialism and Christian Missions* p 162, 'A few like Y T Wu were already enthusiastic Marxists.'

574   37   *Tian Feng*, Sept 5, 1954; *Documents of the Three Self Movement*, National Council of the Churches of Christ, USA, 1963, pp 85–95; *Report of the Centenary Conference on the Protestant Missions of the World*, Ed. James Johnston, Conf. Secy., Vol 1 pp 172–7

575   38   Napoleon: original not traced; John R Mott to guests, 1902, Report of world tour as Gen. Sec. of World's Christian Students' Federation, 'When China is moved it will change the face of the globe' (*see* Ch 8 note 45).

577   39   'Masquerading': D Randall, USA, in *Church World News*, Dec 9, 1983; cf. Wuhan Theol. Seminary lecture notes, 1986. Coal: *see* remarks by von Richtofen and China's Marquis Zeng, HTCOC 6 pp 86, 134.

579   40   *China Inland Mission Private Telegraph Code*: Methodist Publishing House, Shanghai, 1907; Tientsin Press, 1929; cf. Marconi's Wireless Telegraph Code: compiled by S F Cuthbertson.

PERSONALIA

Chinese, Manchu

'CCH' (Chang Chih-heng, Zhang Zhiheng): trusted undercover cell leader during Boxer crisis; supplied and assisted persecuted Christians, missionaries.

CHENG CHUNXÜAN (Ts'eng Ch'un-hsüan): governor of Shanxi after Yü Xian (qv); viceroy of Sichuan 1902; of Canton, Guangdong-Guangxi 1903; made pro-missions proclamations.

CHIANG KAI-SHEK (Jiang Jiaishi) (1887–1975): chief Chinese leader 1925–49; president 1928–31, 1943–49, Republic of China, Taiwan, 1950–75; 1926 Northern Expedition; 1930 baptised, married Soong Meiling; 1936 arrested by 'Young Marshal' Zhang Xüeliang (qv).

CHUANG, Prince: bloodthirsty Manchu appointed 1900 by Ci Xi (qv) to command Boxers with Kangyi (qv); decapitated hundreds of Christians and friends of foreigners; himself executed on Ci Xi's orders.

CI XI (1835–1908): Yehonala (Yehe Nara), (Ts'u Hsi); Manchu concubine Yi, mother of Tong Zhi emperor (qv); Empress Dowager, co-regent with Ci An; 1860–1908 supreme power in China, 22 Sept 1898 imprisoned emp. Guang Xü (qv) till death 1908; d 15 Nov 1908, day after Guang Xü.

FEI QIHAO: Christian educated by Am Board, Tong Xian, colleague of Oberlin teams, Taigu, Fenyang, Shanxi; survived massacre, escaped to Tianjin with first news; probable source of C H S Green's (qv) 'little tuft of paper'; friend of Kong Xiangxi (qv).

FENG YÜXIANG: b circa 1880; soldier influenced by courage of Mary Morrill (qv) on way to execution; 1913 converted through John R Mott; baptised in Am Episc Church; 1923 promoted field marshal; 23 Oct 1924 occupied Beijing, invited Sun Yatsen (qv) to assume presidency. Second to Chiang Kaishek, Nanjong, 1928.

GIH, Andrew: Post Office official fired by Paget Wilkes' preaching; formed Bethel Worldwide Evangelistic Band; joined by John Sung (qv).

GUANG XÜ (Kuang Hsü) emperor: 1875, 4-year-old puppet of Ci Xi (qv); son of Prince Chun, 7th son of Dao Guang emperor; 1889 assumed power; 1898 imprisoned after *coup d'état* by Ci Xi, d. 14 Nov 1908, day before Ci Xi, poisoned?

HSI SHENGMO (Xi Liaozhi) (1830–96): Shanxi classical scholar, opium addict, converted 1879 through David Hill (qv); 1886 ordained as leading pastor, south Shanxi; established scores of opium refuges, Shanxi, Shaanxi, Henan, Zhili; secured influential foothold in anti-Christian Xi'an, Shaanxi; had D E Hoste (qv) as colleague 1886–96; d. 19 Feb 1896.

JIANG QING: actress wife of Mao Zedong (qv), later estranged; radical, one of the 'Gang of Four', arrested 26 Oct 1976.

JINGSHAN: Manchu diarist, source of inside information on Boxer rising.

KANG YI: Manchu nobleman, 'Lord High Extortioner' in Ci Xi's (qv) administration; with Prince Chuang (qv) i/c Boxers; died during flight to Xi'an.

KANG YUWEI: 'Erasmus of the Reform Movement', author of *The Reform of
Japan*, *The Reform of Russia*; tutor to Guang Xü emp; fugitive with price on his
head till 1912; favoured constitutional monarchy.

KONG, Prince: son of Dao Guang emperor; brother of Xian Feng emperor and
Prince Qün; survived Jehol plot; 1860 negotiated treaty with Allies at Peking; rank
equivalent to Prime Minister; his own son rejected by Ci Xi and Prince Qün's made
emperor; repeatedly degraded by Ci Xi; died 1898, 'a national calamity'.

KONG XIANGXI (K'ung Hsiang-hsi): descendant of Confucius; Oberlin College
friend of Fei Qihao (qv); became a leading figure in Nationalist govt.

LIANG QICHAO (Liang Ch'i-ch'ao): reformer in exile with Sun Yatsen (qv) in
Japan since 'Hundred Days of Reform'.

LI HANZHANG (Li Hanchang): brother of Li Hongzhang (qv); viceroy of Hubei,
Hunan.

LI HONGZHANG (Li Hung-chang) (1823–1901): holder of the highest academic
degrees, highest honours after defeat of Taiping rebels; enlightened liberal but
failed in modernisation of China; 1895 forced to cede Taiwan to Japan; the Grand
Old Man of China, leading statesman until death, 7 Nov 1901.

LI LIANYING: Chief Eunuch; unscrupulous tool of Ci Xi (qv).

LIU KUNYI: viceroy of Nanjing (Jiangxi, Jiangsu, Anhui); with Zhang Zhitong
(qv) defied Ci Xi's (qv) edicts to kill foreigners; preserved peace in Yangzi valley
provinces, protected foreigners.

MAO ZEDONG (Mao Tse-tung) (1893–1976): founding member of CCP (1921);
with Sun Yatsen (qv) and Chiang Kaishek (qv) but separated 1926; formed soviet
in Jiangxi 1931–34; led Long March 1935–36; inaugurated People's Republic of
China 1949; chairman until 1959; CCP chairman until death; launched Cultural
Revolution 1966; d. 9 Sept 1976 aged 83.

MENG JIXIAN (Meng Chi-hsien): Boxer martyr; first pastor of Am Board
congregation, Baoding, Zhili; tortured, beheaded 28 June 1900.

NI TUOSHENG (Ni T'uo-sheng): name means a watchman's warning (*tuo* =
rattle), hence 'Watchman Nee'; b. 4 Nov 1903; 1928 originated church movement
known as 'Little Flock'; prolific author; 1952 arrested, released April 1972;
d. 1 June, 1972.

PAN SHOUSHAN: He (Black) Miao evangelist, martyred with Wm S Fleming,
CIM, Panghai, Guizhou, 4 Nov 1898.

PU JÜN: Manchu noble, son of Prince Tuan (qv); made Heir Apparent by Ci Xi (qv)
on forced abdication of Guang Xü (qv) emp; fled with Court from Beijing on
15 Aug 1900; a ne'er-do-well; deposed, banished Nov 1901.

PU LUN: Manchu noble elevated to Heir Apparent replacing Pu Jün (qv); deposed
by Ci Xi (qv) in favour of Pu Yi (qv) just before death of Guang Xü emp (qv) and
Ci Xi.

PU YI, HENRY (1906–67): last of Manchu Qing dynasty; named Heir Apparent
aged 2 by Ci Xi (qv) circa 10 Nov 1908; grandson of Yong Lu (qv), son of Prince
Qün (qv); known as Xüan Tong emp; 'abdicated' 12 Feb 1912; abortive restoration 1–12 July 1917; puppet emp 'Kang De' (1934–5) of Japanese 'Manchuguo';
taken by Russians to Moscow for indoctrination, 're-educated' by CCP.

QING, Prince: Manchu, adversary of Yong Lu (qv); backed Boxers with 50,000
men; plenipotentiary with Li Hongzhang (qv) after Boxer rising; senior statesman
of Grand Council after death of Ci Xi's (qv) best men, Prince Kong (qv), Li

Hongzhang, Yong Lu; weak, vacillating; briefly first premier, May 1911, Republic of China.

QÜ (Ch'ü): scholar of Daning, Shanxi, became Christian with Zhang Zhiben (qv) through studying Mark's Gospel; three times publicly flogged; pastor; survived Boxer rising; with Elder Xü (qv) negotiated with governor Ceng (qv) rehabilitation of persecuted Christians.

QÜN, Prince (Ch'ün): Guang Xü emperor's brother; married Yong Lu's (qv) daughter; 4 Sept 1901 conveyed China's regrets to Potsdam for murder of German envoy Baron von Ketteler (qv); regent of his son Pu Yi (qv); d. 1891.

REN CHENGYÜAN (also Ren Ziqing): b. 18 Feb 1852, ordained 24 June 1877, d. 11 Feb 1929; descended from a Tang dynasty marquess; son-in-law of Wang Lae-djün (qv) co-pastor with him at Hangzhou, Zhejiang; testified to JHT's constant insistence on indigenous church principles (see Bibliography).

SANG Sifu: CIM Linfen, Shanxi, courier; heroic leading voluntary escort-attendant to Dreyer (qv) refugee party, 14 July–28 Aug 1900.

SHAO MIANZI: Yangzhou, Jiangsu, schoolgirl; 25 Feb 1880 married G Parker; pioneer in Gansu, Xinjiang, Henan; finally doyen of CIM after husband died 17 Aug 1931.

SHEN DENHE: Chinese Foreign Office *daotai*, trained at Cambridge, appointed to agree reparations for Shanxi foreigners, Christians, mission premises.

SI, Elder: of Hongtong, Shanxi; brother-in-law of Hsi Shengmo (qv); died 2 July 1902 from sword thrust 14 May 1900; with Qü and Xü (qv) and D E Hoste (qv) negotiator for church reparations.

SOONG family: father a Methodist minister; daughter Qingling (b. 1890) m. Sun Yatsen (qv), Meiling (b. 1898) m. Chiang Kaishek (qv); son, T V Soong, financier.

SU, Prince: agreed that 2000 Christian fugitives occupy his palace adjoining foreign legations, Peking; palace defended, protected, by Japanese marines, Col Shiba.

SUNG, John (Song Shangjie, Sung Shang-chieh) (1901–1944): of Fujian, Ph D, Ohio, joined Andrew Gih (qv), Bethel Band, 1928–34; independent missioner to all China, S E Asia.

SUN YATSEN (Sun Zhongshan) (1866–1925): Chinese statesman; 1891 first medical graduate, Hong Kong; 1905 founded China Revolutionary League, in Europe, Japan; 1911–12 founder and first president Republic of China; m. descendant of Paul Xü (SOONG QINGLING, dep. chairman Nat. People's Congress till d. 1981). Dec 29, 1911 elected provisional president, Republic of China; 1914 organised Chinese Revolutionary Party to resist Yüan Shikai; 1924 invited by Feng Yüxiang and associates to Peking to re-establish the republic; died of cancer, March 12, 1925; 1929 buried in mausoleum at Nanjing.

TONG FUXIANG: Muslim general i/c 15,000 Gansu Muslim cavalry; rallied to Ci Xi (qv) Beijing 1900; supported Boxers, commanded forces against legations; escorted exiled Court to Zhangjiakou (Kalgan), Xi'an; 'too powerful to punish'.

TONG ZHI, emperor: only son of Ci Xi (qv); 1861 acceded to throne aged five; rejected Ci Xi's choice of consort, chose Alude (qv); died of smallpox 3 Jan 1875 having reinstated Ci An (qv) and Ci Xi as regents; Ci Xi believed guilty of ordering his infection.

TUAN FANG: Manchu acting-governor, Shaanxi; without knowing of viceroys' support defied edicts to kill, saved lives of hundreds of foreigners, Christians; became a viceroy, supported reform, 1911 revolution.

TUAN QIRUI (T'uan Ch'i-jui): premier under Pres. Li Yüanhong, 1916; on his own responsibility declared war on Germany, 14 May 1917; dismissed; after abortive restoration of Pu Yi emp. (qv) July 1–12, 1917, premier again; negotiated Japanese loan for WWI war effort and used it against Sun Yatsen (qv) and Constitution Protection Movement.

TUAN, Prince: Manchu 'evil genius', ruthless ally of Ci Xi (qv); provided 8,000 men to reinforce Boxers; 10 June 1900 Pres. of Zongli Yamen; forged an ultimatum 'by foreign envoys', swayed Ci Xi to attack; Tuan offered 500 taels per dead foreigner; escaped from Beijing with Court; 25 Sept 1900 sent for trial.

WANG CUANYI (Wang Ts'uan-i or Tsung-i): Christian ex-soldier, evangelist with Cecil Polhill; volunteered to be flogged instead of Polhills; East Sichuan evangelist.

WANG LAE-DJÜN: Ningbo Mission convert; with JHT in London 1860–64, taught systematically, always practised indigenous church principles; pastor, Hangzhou, Zhejiang, until death, Sept 1901; daughter m. Ren Chengyüan (qv).

WANG LANBU: doorkeeper for Swedish Mission, Soping, Shanxi; survived massacre, June 24 1900; took news to Tianjin, arr. Oct 19.

WANG MINGDAO: 'man of iron', son of Dr Wang Dehao who took his own life during Peking siege; born in Prince Su's (qv) palace, 25 July 1900; school name, Wang Yong-sheng; a preacher from age 22; edited *Spiritual Food Quarterly*; 1950 attacked by TSPM leaders; arrested midnight 7 Aug 1954, wife also, imprisoned; 1970 labour camp, Datong, Shanxi; released May 1979; still living, Shanghai.

WENG TONGHO: Imperial Grand Tutor to Guang Xü emp; 1889 commended Kang Yuwei (qv), reformer, so degraded by Ci Xi (qv).

WU DINGFANG: Chinese ambassador to Washington; conveyed Major E H Conger's coded report of impending massacre, Peking; key to rescue.

XI (*see* Hsi).

XÜ JINGCHENG: with Yüan Zhang (qv) government minister; altered Ci Xi's (qv) edict telegrams from 'kill' to 'protect'; savagely executed.

XÜ PUYÜAN: leading Shanxi church elder, survived Boxer rising with Qü (qv) and Si (qv); met D E Hoste (qv) investigators; negotiated with Gov Ceng (qv) reparations for Christian Boxer victims, property.

YANG CUNLING: (Yang Ts'un-ling) ex-soldier; evangelist; 1877 with J McCarthy (qv) in Yichang riot; on foot Yichang to Bhamo and back; strong bond with JHT.

YANG SHAOTANG: son of one of the first Christians at Qüwu, Shanxi; born during persecutions of 1900; became Qüwu pastor; 1934 formed Ling Gong Tuan (Spiritual Action Team); 1948 China Bible Seminary, Shanghai.

YAN XISHAN (Yen Hsi-shan): 'model governor' of Shanxi after 1911–12 revolution; resisted Yuan Shikai's (qv) attempt to seize power, be emperor.

YONG LU: Manchu imperial bannerman related to Ci Xi (qv); counsellor to Tong Zhi emperor; 1875 protected Ci Xi in her coup; loyal even when disgraced; became Viceroy of Zhili, Senior Guardian of the Throne, but supported Ci Xi's (qv) coup 22 Sept 1898 deposing Guang Xü (qv); resisted 1900 attempts to exterminate foreigners; wisest statesman after Li Hongzhang (qv); d. 11 April 1903.

YONG ZHENG: trustworthy Christian eyewitness, reported on N Shanxi Boxer events.

YÜAN SHIKAI: Chinese Resident, Seoul, 1894; governor of Shandong after Yü Xian (qv) viceroy of Zhili after Li Hongzhang (qv); negotiated abdication of last emperor, Pu Yi (qv), 1911–12; tried to seize power; president of new republic 10 March 1912; schemed to become emperor 1915; d. 6 June 1916.

YÜAN ZHANG: with Xü Jingcheng (qv) heroically changed 'kill' edict telegrams to 'protect'; executed.

YÜ MANZI: anti-Catholic, anti-foreign, Sichuan outlaw, 1896–98.

YÜ XIAN: Gov. of Shandong, encouraged Boxers' murder of foreigners; deposed but appointed Gov. of Shanxi; recruited Boxers; 'Butcher of Shanxi', executed hundreds; himself executed on Ci Xi's orders.

ZENG, Marquis: son of viceroy Zeng Guofan; 1879 ambassador to France, Russia, Britain; 1880 negotiated favourable treaty with Russia over Ili after Chonghou (qv) debacle; author *The Sleep and the Awakening*.

ZHANG XÜELIANG (Chang Hsüeh-liang): son of Zhang Zuolin (qv); 'Young Marshal', arrested Chiang Kaishek (qv) Xi'an, 1936, precipitating joint action against Japan, expansion of Communism.

ZHANG ZHIBEN (Chang Chihpen): 1885–86 leading Buddhist priest; converted with Qü (qv) through reading Mark's Gospel; beaten unconscious by magistrate; church leader, Daning, Shanxi; survived Boxer rising; pastor.

ZHANG ZHITONG (Chang Chih-t'ung): viceroy of Hunan, Hubei (Wuchang); of Jiangxi, Jiangsu, Anhui (Nanjing); scholar, author, *Learn*; with other Yangzi valley and south and west China viceroys resisted Ci Xi's (qv) edicts, protected foreigners; reformer; co-plenipotentiary with Li Hongzhang (qv), Prince Qing (qv).

ZHANG Zuolin (Chang Tso-lin): northern warlord, father of 'Young Marshal' Zhang Xüeliang (qv); with Wu Peifu last of old power-seeking veterans; subdued by Chiang Kaishek, 1928, Northern Expedition.

ZHOU ENLAI (Chou En-lai) (1898–1976): with Mao and Chiang Kaishek joined Sun Yatsen's Nationalists, Canton, (Guomindang); joined Mao in breakaway 1926 during Northern Expedition; 1936 with Zhang Xüeliang (qv) nogotiated terms of Chiang Kaishek's release; foreign minister of People's Republic 1949–58; premier 1949–76.

ZHOU FU (Chou Fu): Provincial treasurer, Sichuan, persuaded viceroy Gui Zhen to suppress edicts to kill; *daotai* of Zhili; old friend of T Richard (qv); governor of Shandong; viceroy of Jiangxi, Jiangsu, Anhui (Nanjing); of Guangdong, Guangxi (Canton); supported T Richard's appointment to negotiate Shanxi reparations; 'of all Chinese officials he was the most lovable,' (T Richard).

ZHU DE (Chu Teh) (1886–1976): 1928 joined Mao in Jiangxi soviet; commander-in-chief, Red Army 1931, on Long March, 1935–36, to Yan'an, Shaanxi; leading politician, statesman of PRC (1959–76).

ZUO ZONGTANG (Tsuo Tsung-t'ang): one of China's greatest generals; quelled Muslim north-western rebellion; 1875 sowed and reaped harvest for troops, Hami; reached Kashgar 1876; quelled Yakub Beg (qv) forces; viceroy of Gansu-Shaanxi; and later of Nanjing.

PERSONALIA

Non-Chinese

(*see also* Personalia, HTCOC Books 1–6)

ADAM, James R: CIM arr. China 1887, settled Anshun, Guizhou, 1888; 1889 began work among Miao minority people; baptisms 1898; 1903 met Gobu (Kopu) Miao, began Gobu church; killed by lightning in own home.

ALLEN, Young J; Am. Meth, Episc. (South); 1860 Shanghai; edited reform publications read by Chinese from peasants to emperor; 1868–74 *Church News*, *Globe News*, *Review of the Times*; 1882 founded Anglo-Chinese College, Shanghai; 1887 Member, Socy. for the Diffusion of Christian and General Knowledge among the Chinese; consulted by reformers.

ANDREW, George; CIM, dep. UK 5 Jan 1881; Guizhou (Supt.), Yunnan; 17 Oct 1883 m. J Findlay, 1895–97 as supt. walked 2432 miles in Yunnan, Guizhou, Sichuan; 1898 Guizhou supt. leader.

ARTHINGTON, Robert (1823–1900); wealthy Quaker, lived frugally supporting missions; 'Arthington's millions' through Arthington Trust, half to BMS, two-fifths to LMS, £2000 to Free Church of Scotland Missionary Society, £100 to Müller's orphanage, sums to other institutions (incl. CIM) (ref. LMS archives).

ASPDEN, Maria: CIM, arr. China 6 Feb 1892 martyred at Datong, N Shanxi, 12 July 1900.

ATWATER, Ernest R: Oberlin College: wife d. 1896; m. Eliz. Graham 1898; daughters Ernestine and Mary killed at Taiyuan 9 July 1900; Celia, Bertha and one unborn all killed at Fenyang, 15 Aug 1900.

BABER, Edward Colborne (1843–90); 1872 vice-consul, Taiwan; 1876 interpreter to Hon W G Grosvenor expedition; 1877 Commercial Resident, Chongqing; explorer; consul; Chinese Secretary of Legation, Peking; 1883 Medal of RGS; 1885–86 Consul-General, Korea; Resident, Bhamo; 16 June 1890 died at Bhamo. (*see* Bibliography.)

BAGNALL, Benjamin; B&FBS, arr. China 1873; Taiyuan; 1886, joined CIM; Supt. Shanxi, Zhili; 1894, Baoding, Zhili; 1 July 1900 killed by Boxers with wife and child.

BALLER, Fredk. William (1852–1922); linguist, Sinologue; b. 21 Nov 1852; one of H Grattan Guinness' first Institute students; CIM, dep. UK 3 Sept 1873 with C H Judd, M Hy Taylor, M Bowyer (*see* HTCOC 4 Personalia); arr. Shanghai 5 Nov 1873; m. M Bowyer 17 Sept 1874; Supt. Anhui, Jiangsu: Hubei, Henan; pioneer traveller; famine relief: 1876 with G King to Shaanxi; 1878 with Mrs Hudson

Taylor, Misses Horne, Crickmay to Shanxi; 1880 took party through Hunan to Guiyang: 1885, secretary, first China Council; 1887 began literary work, *Mandarin Primer* (used by consular service), 1900 *Analytical Chinese-English Dictionary*; translator, member Union Mandarin Bible Revision Committee, NT 1907, OT 1907–18 Peking; 1915 Life Governor of B&FBS; Vice-President Nat. B S of Scotland; Life Member Am. B S; author in Chinese of 18 books; pamphlets, millions in circulation; April 1922 Life of JHT in Chinese; widowed 1909; 23 Jan 1912 m. H B Fleming; 1919 first furlough, after 21 years; d. 12 Aug 1922.

BARCLAY, Florence; dtr of Robt Barclay, Reigate; CIM dep. UK 13 Dec 1880; 24 May 1892 m. M. Beauchamp (qv); d. 2 May 1955.

BARNARDO, Thomas John (4 July 1845–19 Sept. 1905); 1862 converted; 1866 met JHT in Dublin; April 1866 to London; 1866–9 CIM candidate; 1872 CIM Referee, while developing orphan work.

BEAUCHAMP, Rev Sir Montagu Harry, Proctor-, Bart.; (1860–1939); b. 19 April 1860, son of Sir Thomas (qv); Repton, Trinity Coll., Camb.; CIM dep UK 5 Feb 1885, 'Camb. Seven'; pioneer, Shanxi, Sichuan; travelled extensively with JHT; 24 May 1892 m. F Barclay (qv); World War I Hon. Chaplain to Forces, Egypt, Greece, Murmansk; 1915 inherited baronetcy; 26 Oct 1939 d. at Langzhong, Sichuan.

BERGER, William Thomas (c 1812–99); director Samuel Berger & Co, Patent Starch manufacturer, St Leonard St, Bromley-by-Bow; CES supporter; early donor to JHT; 1865 co-founder and UK director, CIM; generous life-time donor; home at Hackney village, then Saint Hill, East Grinstead, devoted to CIM; last years in Cannes, d. 9 Jan 1899.

BEYNON, W T and wife: CIM 1885; Shanxi; 1895 B&FBS; 9 July 1900 killed by Boxers.

BIRD, C Howard: CIM dep. UK 9 Oct 1896; Xiangcheng, Henan; 11 July 1900 escaped, robbed, destitute, via Taihe, Anhui to Zhenjiang.

BIRD, Rowena: Oberlin College, Am Board; b. 31 July 1865; dep. to China Sept 1890; Taigu, Shanxi; 31 July 1900 killed by Boxers.

BISHOP, Isabella Bird: (1831–1904) independent traveller, author (*see* Bibliography); 1881 m. Dr John Bishop who d.1886; 1896 c/o JHT, CIM, Shanghai, Sichuan, Tibetan marches; donated hospital premises, Langzhong.

BONAR, Andrew (1810–92): Scottish Free Church divine; author; friend of Wm Burns (qv) and JHT.

BORDEN, William Whiting: b. 1 Nov 1887; descended from Normans 1066 and Col Wm Whiting, Yarmouth, UK, founder of Hartford, Conn. USA; 1905–09 Yale Univ; 1909–12 Princeton Seminary; spring 1910 CIM delegate to Edinburgh Conference; autumn CIM N Am Council declared his goal, Muslims of N W China; Dec 1912 dep. USA to Cairo for Arabic studies; d. April 1913, meningitis, aged 25; legacies, CIM $250,000; $100,000, $50,000, $25,000 to churches, Theol. Insts, missions; CIM residuary legatee; Borden Memorial Hospital, Lanzhou, Gansu.

BOSSHARDT, Rudolf Alfred: CIM; hero, with Arnolis Hayman, of Communist 'Long March', 1935–36, still living, 1989, aged 96.

BOTHAM, Thomas Earlum S; CIM dep. UK 26 Aug 1885; pioneer in Shaanxi; Supt. Shaanxi, Gansu; China Council; 1889 m. Ella A Barclay; d. 22 Oct 1898.

BROOKE, Graham Wilmot; CMS 3 Dec 1889; pioneer leader in W Africa and Sudan; d. 5 March 1891.

BROOKS, S M: SPG, first martyr of Boxers, Shandong, 29 Dec 1900, aged 24.

BROOMHALL, A Gertrude; eldest dtr of Benjamin (qv) and Amelia HT (qv); b. 18 June 1861; CIM dep. UK 24 Sept 1884; Shanxi; 7 Sept 1894 m. D E Hoste (qv); 3 sons; d. 12 April 1944.

BROOMHALL, Benjamin (1829–1911) b. 15 Aug 1829; m. 10 Feb 1859 Amelia Hudson Taylor (qv), 4 sons 6 dtrs; Sec. Anti-Slavery Assn; 1875 CIM, Pyrland Rd; 1878–95 Gen. Sec. CIM, London; 1888 Sec. Christian Union for the Severance of. the British Empire with the Opium Traffic; editor, *National Righteousness*; 3 sons, 2 dtrs in China; d. 29 May 1911.

BROOMHALL, Albert Hudson (1862–1934) eldest son of Benjamin (qv); b. 31 Aug 1862; CIM dep. UK 24 Sept 1884; Shanxi; m. 14 May 1890 Alice Amelia Miles; treasurer CIM, Shanghai; d. 18 Aug 1934.

BROOMHALL, Marshall, 2nd son of Benjamin (qv), MA Cantab.; author (*see* Bibliog.); CIM dep. UK Oct 1890; editor, Lond., d. 24 Oct 1937.

BROUMTON, James F; brother of Eliz. Judd; one of the Eighteen, dep. UK 21 Oct 1875; pioneer Guizhou; m. 1881 Mrs Wm McCarthy (qv); 1886–1905, treasurer CIM Shanghai.

BURDON, John Shaw (1826–1907); CMS 1853, Shanghai; pioneer evangelist; 1857 m. Burella Dyer, sister of Maria Taylor (qv); 1862 Peking; 1874 3rd Bishop of Victoria, Hong Kong; Bible translator (*see* Blodget); Jan 1897 resigned bishopric, to Pakhoi aged 71; dep. China 1907.

BURNS, William Chalmers (1815–68); first English Presby. to China; 1847 Hong Kong; Amoy; 1855 Shanghai; 1856 Swatow; 1863 Peking; 1867 Niuchuang (now Yingkou), d. Niuchuang; translated *Pilgrim's Progress*; close friend of JHT.

BURTON, Eliz: CIM, to China Sept 1898; Hejin, Shanxi with McConnells (qv), A King; 12 July 1900 left hiding, killed beside Yellow R 16 July 1900.

CABLE, A Mildred (1877–1952): CIM 1901, Huozhou, Shanxi, with E and F French (qv) youngest of 'The Trio'; qualified chemist; Shanxi 1901–23; 1923–36 Gansu, Xinjiang, Gobi Desert; author, public speaker, B&FBS (*see* Bibliography).

CAMERON, James (1845–91): CIM, one of the Eighteen; dep. UK 4 Aug 1875; pioneer traveller until end of 1881; 1884 supt. Shandong, later Sichuan; 1884 MD (USA); m. Mrs Randall; 1886 China Council; d. 14 Aug 1891.

CARDWELL, J E; CIM, 1867 Hangzhou; 1868 Taizhou, Zheijiang; Dec 30, 1869 Jiujiang, pioneered Jiangxi; Shanghai business manager.

CARMICHAEL, Amy Beatrice (Wilson) (1868–1951); first Keswick missionary, 1892; Japan, Ceylon, S India; founded Dohnavur Fellowship; author, crippled by arthritis from 1930s; lifelong friend of JHT, CIM.

CASSELS, William Wharton (1858–1925) b. 11 March 1858; Repton; 1877–80 St John's College, Cambridge; Ridley Hall; ordained 1882; 'Cambridge Seven', CIM dep. UK 5 Feb 1885; 1885–86 Shanxi; 1886 Supt. China Council; Sichuan; 4 Oct 1887 m. M L Legge; 18 Oct 1895 consecrated Bishop in W China; d. 7 Nov 1925, typhus (wife d. 15 Nov).

CLAPP, Dwight H: b. 1 Nov 1841; Oberlin College; m. 1884 Mary Jane b. 1845; Am Board to Taigu, Shanxi; killed 31 July 1900.

CLARKE, Mildred: CIM, Linfen, Shanxi; to Taiuan June 1900; killed 9 July 1900.

CLARKE, George W; CIM, one of the Eighteen, dep. UK 4 Aug 1875; Dali, Yunnan; m. F Rossier 15 Sep 1870; (d. 7 Oct 1883); 1886 Guihuacheng; Supt. N Shanxi, Zhili; China Council; m. A Lancaster, April 1886, (d. 8 Aug 1892); m. R Gardiner 12 Oct 1893.

CLARKE, Samuel R; CIM dep. UK 2 May 1878; Chengdu, Sichuan; m. A L Fausset (qv); 1889 Guiyang; 1892 to Guizhou minority races.

CLINTON, T A P: CIM, first to obtain deeds to property in Hunan, Changde Sept 1897; occupied.

COOMBS, Edith A: b. 1862; BA (Oxon); CIM; Shouyang Mission Hospital, Taiyuan (Schofield Memorial); 27 June 1900 riot, tried to save Chinese child; stoned, killed.

COOPER, E J: CIM 1888, 'architect' of CIM buildings, Shanghai, Hankou, Chefoo schools, sanatorium, with JHT; m. 1891 Margaret; Lucheng, Shanxi; 6 July 1900 dep; after great suffering arr. Hankou 14 Aug; Margaret d. injuries Aug 6, son Brainerd d. Aug 14; author of lucid reports.

COOPER, William; YMCA secretary, Gourock; CIM dep. UK 24 Nov 1880; Anqing Training Inst; Supt. Anhui; China Council 1885; completed Maria (Dyer) Taylor's Romanised NT, published by BFBS 1888; m. 1887; Asst. China Director; Travelling Director; d. 1 July 1900, killed by Boxers, Baoding, Zhili.

COULTHARD, J J; CIM dep. UK 7 March 1879; personal secretary to JHT; Supt. Henan, 1888 m. Maria Hudson Taylor (qv); China Council.

CRANSTON, David; Shanghai merchant, Shanghai & Putong Foundry & Engineering Co.; Feb 1874 victim in Shanghai riot; friend of CIM; directed CIM HQ building developments.

DAVIES, Major H R; prospected proposed Burma–Yunnan railway; travelled widely, Dali, Batang etc.; met C Pohill at Kangding.

DEAN, William (1806–77) Am. Baptist; 1834, 1864 Bangkok; 1845 Hong Kong.

DESGRAZ, Louise, Swiss governess to Wm Collingwood family, as a daughter; 1866 CIM, *Lammermuir*, Hangzhou; 1865 Yangzhou, riot; 1878 m. E Tomalin.

DESMOND, Josephine, RC, Irish American; b. 1867; to Moody, Northfield, BTI Chicago; CIM 1898; Xiaoshan, Qü Xian, Zhejiang; killed 21 July 1900.

DICK, Henry; CIM dep UK 29 Aug 1883; 1884 joined A C Dorward, Hunan pioneer; daring visit to Changsha.

DIXON, Herbert: BMS 1881, 21 years; 5 years Congo; m. 1884; Taiyuan, Shanxi 1885; Xinzhou; 29 June 1900 heard of Coombs murder (qv); 8 BMS fled to hills; captured 25 July; killed 9 Aug 1900.

DOBSON, Edith: CIM nurse, 1894; Chefoo with Dr Douthwaite (qv), Red Cross Hospital, Sino-Jap war 1894–95; to Xi Xian, Shanxi, with Peat family and A Hurn (qv) 21 July 1900 to hill caves; 30 Aug 1900 killed near Qüwu.

DORWARD, Adam C; Scottish manufacturer; Harley House under H Grattan Guinness, CIM dep. UK 2 May 1878; entered Hunan 18 Oct 1880; Supt. Hunan, Guangxi; China Council; d. 2 Oct 1888.

DOUTHWAITE, Arthur Wm.; Harley House 1874; CIM dep. UK 26 Feb 1874; Zhejiang; 6 Feb 1875 m. E Doig; Qü Xian; 1882 Yantai; 1883–84 first Prot. missionary to tour Korea, distributed Scripture; 15 Oct 1890 m. Groves; MD (USA) 1894 Order of Double Dragon for service in Sino-Jap war; d. 5 Oct 1899.

DREYER, F C H: CIM 1895; Qüwu, Linfen; 14 July 1900, Lutley (qv) ill, so Dreyer i/c party of 14 dep. midnight, through hostile Henan; 28 Aug arr. Hankou; author, report on Shanxi events.

DUVAL, Mary: aged 42 offered to CMS; 1899 with Pigotts (qv) to Shouyang, Shanxi, to teach Pigott, Atwater children; killed 9 July 1900, Taiyuan.

DYER, Samuel Sr (1804–43); Cambridge law student; 1827 LMS, m. Maria Tarn, daughter of LMS director; 1827 Penang; 1829–35 Malacca, 1835–43 Singapore; d. Macao.; father of Maria, m. JHT.

DYER, Samuel Jr; b. 18 Jan 1833, son of Samuel Sr.; brother of Maria Taylor (qv); 1877 agent of B&FBS, Shanghai, after Alex. Wylie (qv); d. 1898.

DYMOND, Francis (Frank) John: Bible Christian Mission, dep. UK 27 Jan 1887, with S Pollard (qv); arr. Shanghai, CIM associates, 14 March; 1888 Yunnan; daughter Roxie m. J O Fraser (qv).

EASTON, George F; printer; CIM, one of the Eighteen, dep. UK 21 Oct 1875; 29 Dec 1876–77 pioneer Xi'an, Shaanxi; Jan 1877 Lanzhou; with G Parker; Aug 1881 m. Caroline Gardner; 1885 Supt. Gansu, Shaanxi; China Council.

EDKINS, Joseph, (1832–1905); LMS evangelist, linguist, translator, philologist, expert in Chinese religions; 1860 visited Suzhou Taiping rulers; 1862 Nanjing; 1848–60 Shanghai; 1860–61 first to Shandong, Yantai; 1862 Tianjin, Peking; 57 years in China, 30 in Peking; 1880 retired from LMS, attached to Imperial Maritime Customs; author 1853 *Grammar Shanghai dialect*; 1857 *Mandarin Grammar*; 1859 *The Religious Condition of the Chinese*; 1878 *Religion in China*; 1880 *Chinese Buddhism*; 1875 DD (Edin.); 1877 second wife died; *aet.* 80 survived typhoid; *aet.* 81 still writing, d. Easter Sunday.

EDWARDS, Dr Ebenezer Henry; CIM dep. UK 20 Aug 1882; Taiyuan, Shanxi; 1896 CIM Taiyuan work transferred to Shouyang Mission; m. Florence Kemp, sister of Jessie Pigott (qv); 1900 in UK; with J W Lowrie (qv) found Baoding martyrs' remains; BMS; with Moir Duncan, Creasey Smith (qv) and CIM team to Taiyuan 1901, to negotiate reparations; 1910 Order of the Double Dragon.

ELDRED, Annie: b. 22 Dec 1871; CIM dep. UK Sept 1898, Linfen, Hongtong, Shanxi; 1900 from Jiexiu with A P Lundgrens (qv) to Fenyang c/o Oberlin ABCFM; killed 15 Aug 1900.

ENNALS, Sydney W: b. 1 Nov 1872; BMS dep. UK 11 Sept 1899; Shanxi, Xinzhou; killed 9 Aug 1900.

FARTHING, George Bryant: b. 19 Dec 1859; BMS, dep. UK 12 Sept 1886; m. 23 Apr 1889, Catherine Wright; Taiyuan, Shanxi; 9 July 1900, first Taiyuan martyr beheaded, with wife, children Ruth (10), Guy (8), Eliz (3).

FERGUSON, Henry S: USA; 15 Feb 1895 arr. China with F C H Dreyer (qv); Taihe, Anhui; 1932 flood relief in Jiangxi; prisoner of Bolsheviks, executed.

FISHE, Charles Thomas; son of Col. Fishe, Dublin; influenced by H G Guinness (qv), JHT; 1867 asst. to W T Berger (qv); 1868 CIM, Yangzhou; 1871 China Secy; m. Nellie Faulding; Financial Secretary CIM London; London Council; 1889 to China (in clipper *Lammermuir*); 17 years, administrator; China Council.

FLEMING, William Small: aged 17 to sea 6–7 years; worked his passage Australia to Shanghai 1895; Guizhou He Miao minority people; killed 4 Nov 1898 with He Miao evangelist Pan Shoushan (qv) near Panghai.

FOLKE, Erik: first individual associate of CIM; Swedish Mission in China formed to support him; initiated S Shanxi-Henan field; supt; 1900 led team to safety at Hankou.

FORD, Henry T: CIM dep. UK 28 Oct 1892; Taikang, Henan; dep. 11 July 1900 safely to Zhenjiang.

FORMAN, John N; Princeton Univ; Trav. Secy. Student Volunteer Movement, USA; 1887 to Britain, travelled with JHT, Scotland, Ireland, England.

FORSYTH, Robt. Coventry: BMS, Shandong; author *The China Martyrs of 1900*.

FOSTER, Arnold; LMS; 1871 Hankou; 1887–89 Secy. China Famine Relief Committee, London; d. 1919.

FRANSON, Fredrik (1852–1908): Swedish evangelist, long resident USA; studied D L Moody's methods (qv); strongly influenced by JHT (qv) *To Every Creature*; sent many missionaries to China, India; influenced formation of several European associate missions of CIM.

FRASER, James O: CIM, graduate engineer, musician; apostle to minority peoples of W Yunnan; 1918, 60,000 church members of strong indigenous church; CIM superintendent, China Council; d. malignant malaria, 25 Sept 1938.

FRENCH, Evangeline (1871–1961); CIM dep. UK 1 Sep 95; Huzhou, Shanxi; leader of 'the Trio' with Francesca French and Mildred Cable (qv); 1923 to Xinjiang till 1936; d. 1961 aged 90.

FRENCH, Francesca (1873–1961); CIM Shanxi (*see* Evangeline); d. 3 weeks after Eva.; co-author with M Cable (qv).

FROST, Henry Weston (1858–??); 1876–79 Princeton; civil engineer; 1885 read *China's Spiritual Need and Claims* and *A Cambridge Band*; influenced by J Goforth; 1887 London, met JHT; 1888 JHT to N. Am.; HWF secy., 1889 secy, treasurer, N. Am. Council; 1893 Home Director.

GATES, Caroline: CIM, dep. UK 10 Mar 1887; Fancheng, Hubei; 1896 Lu'an, Shanxi; intrepid companion of Glover family, *1000 Miles of Miracle*, escape from Boxers.

GLADSTONE, Wm Ewart (1809–98); 1832 MP; Liberal PM 1868–74, 1880–85; 1892–94.

GLOVER, Archibald E: MA (Oxon.); curate to Preb. Webb-Peploe; CIM 1897; Lu'an, Shanxi with S P Smith (qv); 1900 escaped with family and C Gates (qv); author, *1000 Miles of Miracle*; wife d. 25 Oct 1900.

GOFORTH, Jonathan (1859–1936); Canadian Presby Church; applied to join CIM 1885, 1888, 1911; advised to stay with own Church; 1888 arr. China; pioneer in Henan; Changde 1895; 1908 led great revival, Manchuria; 1900 escaped with family and party, Anyang (Changde) Henan to Hankou.

GOODRICH, Chauncey; American Board; Zhangjiakou (Kalgan); m. May 30, 1878, widowed Sep 3; Bible translator, Union Version with Mateer and Baller (qv); 1872 hymnbook with Blodget.

GOUGH, Frederick Foster, DD; CMS 1849–61 Ningbo; Mary, first wife, d. 1861; 1862–69 London, Ningbo vernacular romanised NT revision with JHT; 1866 m. Mary Jones (qv); 1869 Ningbo; founded Camb. Univ. Prayer Union; Bible translator-reviser; 34 years in CMS, Zhejiang.

GOULD, Annie Allender: b. 18 Nov 1867; Am Board 1893; Baoding, Zhili; killed 1 July 1900.

GREEN, C H S: arr. China 1891; to Zhili, Huolu; 1900 escaped Boxers with wife, children Vera, John and J Gregg (qv); Vera died, buried at Tianjin; author *In Deaths Oft*; returned to Huolu Nov 1903.

GREGG, Jessie G: CIM, arr. 1895; Huolu, Zhili; 1900 escaped with C H S Green (qv) family; returned 1903.

GUINNESS, Dr Harry; eldest son of H Grattan Guinness (qv); principal, Harley College.; m. Annie dtr of Henry Reed, Tasmania.

GUINNESS, Henry Grattan DD, FRAS (1835–1910); 1855 left New Coll. Lond. to become great evangelist of Evangelical Awakening; 1859 Ulster revival, drew thousands; 1865 offered to CIM, JHT advised continue UK; became JHT's friend; 1872 CIM Referee; 1873 founded East London Miss. Training Institute (Harley College); trained 1,330 for 40 societies of 30 denominations; 1877 Livingstone Inland Mission; 1888 Congo-Balolo Mission; 1898 initiated RBMU; NAM founded on his advice; greatly influenced Barnardo, John R Mott; author, astronomy, eschatology; 7 children, grandchildren in Christian ministry.

GUINNESS, Mary Geraldine (1862–1949) b. 25 Dec 1862; CIM dep. UK 26 Jan

1888; 24 April 1894 m. F Howard Taylor (qv); author (see Bibliog); d. 6 June 1949; biography, *Her Web of Time* by Joy Guinness CIM 1949.

GUINNESS, G Whitfield; son of H Grattan G (qv); BA, MB, B Ch; CIM 1897; Henan; 1900 led colleagues to safety at Hankou; Kaifeng Hospital; d. typhus.

HAIG, Maj. Gen. F T; active Christian in Indian army; 1881 served in CMS Godavari Mission; CMS committee; Eastern surveys; friend of CIM.

HANNINGTON, Bishop James; Oxford; 1882 CMS dep. UK; 1884 first bishop, Eastern Equatorial Africa; 29 Oct 1885 murdered on Mwanga's orders; death roused 'the whole Church'; *Memoirs* inspired thousands; Hannington Hall, Oxford, counterpart of Henry Martyn Hall, Cambridge.

HAPPER, Andrew P, DD; Am. Presby.; 1844–46 Macao (debarred from Canton); 1847 Canton; 1887 first president Canton Christian Coll. d. 1897.

HART, Sir Robert (1835–1911); b. 20 Feb 1835; 1854 consular interpreter, Ningbo; 1857 Canton; Nov. 1862 Inspector-General, Chinese Imperial Maritime Customs; 1865 Peking; 1864 3rd class mandarin; 1869 2nd class; 1881 1st class; 1885 Peacock's Feather; 1889 1st class of 1st Order for 3 generations; 1901 Junior Guardian of the Heir Apparent; 1911 posthumous Senior Guardian; CMG, 1882 KCMG, 1889 GCMG; 1st Baronet 1893; 1885 succeeded Sir Harry Parkes as Br. Minister, Peking; resigned to resume IG: 1900 40-year diary and house burned by Boxers; 1 May 1906 resigned, but Emeritus IG until death.

HEAYSMAN, Mary: b. 29 July 1874; CIM dep. UK 1897; Daning, Shanxi with F E, M R Nathan; Boxer rising, 1900, July 12 fled to hills, Aug 13 killed.

HEDIN, Sven; Swedish archaeologist, explorer; studied under von Richtofen; 1894 aged 28, Tashkent to Kashgar; 1895 crossed Taklamahan Desert; 1899–1902 explored Tarim Basin.

HILL, David (1840–96); 1865 WMMS. Hankou (independent means); 1878–80 with J J Turner (qv) CIM, to Shanxi famine relief; 1879 means of conversion of 'Pastor Hsi' (qv); Wuxüe; founded houses for aged, blind, orphans; fought opium trade; started a hospital; 1890 co-chairman with J L Nevius General Missionary Conference, Shanghai; d. 1896 aged 56, typhus from famine relief.

HILL, Richard Harris, FRIBA; civil engineer, evangelist; helped build Mildmay Miss. Hosp., CIM Newington Green; m. Agnes, daughter of Henry W Soltau (qv); 1872 Hon. Sec. London CIM.

HODDLE, Alexander: Canada 10 years; YMCA local sec. UK; CIM 1889; Huolu, Baoding, Zhili; Taiyuan, Shanxi, in Shouyang Mission, then independent; 9 July 1900 killed by Boxers.

HODGE, C van R: MD Pennsylvania; Am Presby Mission, Baoding, Zhili; killed 30 June 1900.

HOLMGREN, Josef: Swedish pastor, Örebro; Sept 1883 met JHT in London; 1887 translated *China's Spiritual Need & Claims*; pastor Stockholm, formed committee of Swedish Mission in China to support Erik Folke (qv).

HOPKINS, Evan H (1837–1919) 1874 met American Pearsall Smith, 'Higher Christian Life' conference, Oxford; 1875 with Canon Battersby, G R Thornton, H W Webb-Peploe at Keswick for embryo Keswick Convention meetings: 1883 Cambridge convention on Keswick lines; 1884 published *Law of Liberty in the Spiritual Life*; 1886 joined by Handley Moule (qv).

HORSBURGH, J Heywood: CMS, contemporary of Graham Brooke (qv), G L Pilkington (qv), Barclay Buxton; 1883 to Zhejiang; 1890 wrote *Do Not Say*, great effect; 1891 led team to W Sichuan; 1895 at Chengdu calm humour quelled riot; retired.

HOSTE, Dixon Edward (1861–1946) b. 23 July 1861, son of Major-Gen. D E Hoste, RA; Clifton College and Royal Military Academy, Woolwich; 1882 Lieut. R.A.; 1882, converted at D L Moody meetings; 23 July 1883, approached JHT; met Council Feb 1884, accepted 7 Oct 1884; 'Camb. Seven', dep. UK 5 Feb 1885; Shanxi 1885–96 colleague of Hsi Shengmo (qv); 1896 sick leave Australia; Supt. Henan; China Council; 1900 assistant to J W Stevenson; Jan 1901 Acting GD; Nov 1902 General Director; 7 Sep 1894 m. Amelia Gertrude Broomhall (qv); three sons; d. 11 May 1946; succeeded by G Gibb after 33 years GD.

HOUGHTON, Frank; b. 4 April 1894, CIM dep. UK 10 Nov 1920; Sichuan; 1923 m. Dorothy Cassels, dtr of WWC; 1926–36 editorial secretary, London; 25 Jan 1937 consecrated bishop, East Sichuan; 21 Oct 1940 General Director after G Gibb; 1951–72 Consulting Director; d. 25 Jan 1972. Author.

HOWARD, Theodore; son of Robert, nephew of J E Howard (qv), 1872 CIM Lond. Council; Director, Howard Brothers, quinologists, manufacturing chemists; 1875 Council Chairman; 1879 first Home Director CIM UK.

HUC, Abbé Everiste Régis, travelled with Gabet 1844–46, Mongolia, Tibet; 1846 in Lhasa, deported; 1857 author, *Christianity in China, Tartary and Thibet*; d. 1860.

HUNTER, George: CIM Hunan; Scot. Presby.; 1889 headmaster Chefoo schools; 1895 Yichang, base for Hunan; d. 1900.

HUNTER, George W (1861–1946): Scotsman; 1889 CIM Gansu, Xinjiang 1905, itinerating from Lanzhou; 1906 Urumqi as base; 1907 to Kashgar; 1914 P Mather as colleague; Cable-French 'Trio' occasionally; prisoner of NKVD during Soviet occupation, tortured, expelled, d. 20 Dec 1946.

HURN, Georgiana: b. 6 July 1868; CIM, dep. UK 3 Jan 1898; 21 July 1900 hid in hills with Peat family (qv) and E Dobson (qv); killed 30 Aug 1900.

HUSTON, Mary E: b. 1866 Pennsylvania; CIM, 1895 to China; 6 July 1900 dep. Lucheng, Shanxi, with E J Cooper family (qv), Hattie Rice (qv), and A R Saunders party (qv); 13 July 1900 savagely wounded, H Rice killed; MEH d. 11 Aug 1900.

I'ANSON, Chas: Harley College; CIM dep. UK 3 Nov 1887; wife Florence, children Arthur, Eva, Dora, all killed by Boxers 12 July 1900, Datong, Shanxi.

JAMES, Francis Huberty, b. June 1851; CIM, one of the Eighteen, dep. UK 1876; 1877–79 Shanxi famine relief; Sep 1878 m. Marie S Huberty, Belgian; 1881 to UK; 1883 BMS, Shandong, Qingzhou, Jinan; 1890 paper on Chinese secret sects, Shanghai General Conference; 1892 resigned from BMS; Europe and USA, 1895 Lowell lectureship, Boston, following Prof Henry Drummond; 1897 Imperial Arsenal, Shanghai; 1898 Imperial Univ., Peking; 1900 with Dr Morrison rescued 2000 Chinese Christians, protected by Br. legation forces; 20 June 1900 killed.

JAMES, Thomas; CIM dep. UK 15 Jan 1885; April 1885 Hunan with Dorward (qv) and Dick (qv); Sichuan; m. F (Stroud) Riley (qv).

JOHN, Griffith (1831–1912); LMS; 1855 Shanghai; pioneer evangelist; 1861 Hankou; 1863 Wuchang; 1867 Hanyang; 1888 declined chairmanship, Congregational Union of Eng. and Wales; 1889 Hon. DD (Edin.); Sep 24, 1905 jubilee in China; April 1906 retired ill; author, many publications in Chinese; translator, NT into 'easy Wenli', and OT (part) into colloquial Mandarin, commissioned by B&FBS and NBSS.

JUDD, Charles H Sr (1842–1919); 1867 CIM through influence of T J Barnardo; 1868 Yangzhou; 1869 Zhenjiang; 1872–3 UK; 1874 Wuchang, with JHT; 1875 with 'Yao' (qv) and 'Zhang' (qv) rented house at Yueyang (Yochow), Hunan, forced out; 1877 with J F Broumton via Hunan to Guiyang, Guizhou; via Chongqing to Wuchang; 1879 built at Yantai before school and sanatorium.

KAY, Duncan: CIM dep UK 8 Oct 1884; Anhui; 1889 Qüwu, Shanxi; energetic evangelist, beloved by Chinese; 4 July 1900 fled to hills with wife, child; killed 15 Sept 1900.

KERR, Dr John G, MD; Am. Presby Mission (North); 1854 Canton; trained 200 Chinese medical students; translated many medical books; performed 480,000 surgical operations; founded the Asylum for the Insane; d. Canton 1901.

KING, Annie: b. 16 Mar 1870; CIM dep. UK 22 Sept 1898; Hejin, Shanxi; killed 16 July 1900.

KING, George; CIM dep. UK 15 May 1875, aged 18; one of the Eighteen, arr. Shanghai July 14 after shipwreck; pioneer, Shaanxi, Gansu, Henan; m. (1) E Snow (d. Hanzhong 10 May 1881); (2) Harriet Black; qualified physician; resigned, 1902 Peking Syndicate.

KING, Dr George Edwin: son of G King (qv) b. 20 Nov 1887 on Han R; excelled at school; Edinburgh Med Missionary Socy; Edin. Univ. graduated 1909 first class w. distinctions; CIM dep. UK 22 Nov 1910; Kaifeng with G W Guinness (qv), S H Kerr; March 1912 Linfen (Pingyang) Shanxi at Millar Wilson Memorial Hosp.; Feb 1914 arr. Lanzhou, Gansu with P Mather (qv) en route Urumqi; m. 6 Feb 1915; had Dr Gao Jincheng as colleague, R C Parry; 1927 general evacuation by foreigners during nationalist movement; 5 June 1927 drowned in Yellow R.

KRAPF, Johann Ludwig (1810–81), German; linguist; 1836 CMS to Ethiopia; 1844 Mombasa; 1849 first Westerner to see Mt Kenya; 1853 broken health, Europe; author.

LACHLAN, H N, barrister; CIM dep. UK 29 Nov 1888 aged 31; Guizhou, Yunnan, Chongqing; Principal, Anqing Training Inst. after Baller (qv); 29 Oct 1892 m. Katherine Mackintosh (qv); dtr H Evelyn m. D de B Robertson, CIM architect; d. 18 April 1896.

LANKESTER, Dr Herbert; consultant physician, 1892 CMS Medical Board, Hon Sec; physician to all CMS members, 55 medical staff, 30 mission hospitals overseas.

LANSDELL, Dr Henry, DD, FRGS, traveller in Bokhara, Samarkand; attempts on Tibet supported by Am. Bible Socy. and JHT, with G Parker (qv) foiled; may have reached Xinjiang, colportage with Parker.

LATOURETTE, Kenneth Scott; late Willis James and Sterling Prof. of Missions and Oriental History, Yale Univ.; author, *see* bibliography.

LEGGE, James, DD, LLD (1815–97); LMS; 1835 MA (Aberdeen), Congregational; 1839–43 Anglo-Chinese College, Malacca; 1843–70 Anglo-Chinese College, Hong Kong; 1861–86 translator, Chinese classics; 1875 Fellow, Corpus Christi, Oxford; 1877–97, first Prof. of Chinese, Oxford Univ.

LITTLE, Alicia Bewicke; author, *Li Hung-chang, His Life and Times*, 1903; wife of Archibald Little, British consul, Legation official, Peking.

LORD, Edward Clifford, DD (1817–87); ABMU; 1847 first Am. Baptist to Ningbo; 1853 NT Baptist version, with Dean and Goddard; 1863 independent Am. Bapt. Mission, Ningbo; 1887 still there; appointed US consul by Abraham Lincoln; JHT's friend; d. with wife, of cholera, 17 Sept 1887.

LOVITT, Arnold E: b. 4 Feb 1869; London Hosp., Mildmay Mission Hosp; Shouyang Mission, 1897 Taiyuan, Shanxi, Schofield Memorial Hosp; killed 9 July 1900.

LOWRIE, J Walter: Am Presby Mission, Baoding, Zhili; absent when Boxers struck; interpreter to allied force; saved 100s of Chinese from vengeance; with Dr E H Edwards (qv) found remains of Am Board, CIM and Chinese martyrs; arranged official burial and memorial honours.

LUNDGREN, A P: b. Denmark 1870; to N. Am. 1887; dep. USA 1891 Scand. China Alliance; 1898 full member CIM, Pingyao and Jiexiu, Shanxi; with Oberlin Am. Board, Fenyang, killed by Boxers 15 Aug 1900.

MACKENZIE, Dr John Kenneth; LMS 1875, Hankou, Tianjin; saved life of viceroy Li Hongzhang's wife; 1880 built hospital, trained doctors, sponsored by Li; 1882 to UK; d. 1888. Author, *A History of the Nineteenth Century*, translated by T Richard sold 1 million.

MACKINTOSH, Katherine B; CIM dep. UK 22 Oct 1884; one of the Seventy; Guangxin R pioneer, Yüshan; 29 Oct 1892 m. H N Lachlan (qv); mother of HB (Anuei) Lachlan who m. D de B Robertson, CIM architect.

MANCHESTER, M Etta: b. 11 Nov 1871: dep. US 12 Aug 1895; 1897 Qü Xian, Zhejiang; killed 24 July 1900.

MARGARY, Augustus Raymond; b. 1845; HBM consul Yantai; 1874 as interpreter to Col. Browne's Burma-Yunnan expedition, dep. Shanghai 22 Aug 1874, via Hunan, arr. Bhamo 17 Jan 1875; murdered Feb 21 at Manyün.

MARTIN, William Alexander Parson, DD, LL D (1827–1916); Am. Presby. Mission; educationalist; 1850–60 Ningbo; 1858 with S Wells Williams (qv) interpreter, Am. treaty; 1862 Peking; 1869 president, Tongwen Imperial College; 57 years in China; book on Christian evidences had huge circulation, China, Japan.

MARTYN, Henry (1781–1812); Fellow of St John's Coll, Cambridge; inspired by Chas. Simeon; ordained 1805; chaplain, East India Co, Calcutta, translated Urdu NT; worked on Persian, Arabic NTs; d. 10 Oct 1812 in Asia Minor.

MATEER, Calvin Wilson, DD (1836–1908) Am. Presby; 1862 Dengzhou, later Yantai, Shandong; founded Shandong Christian Univ.; author *Mandarin Lessons*; opposed Nevius' methods; chairman, translation committee, Union Mandarin Verson of Bible with Baller, Blodget, Nevius *et al.*

MATHER, Percy Cunningham: b. 9 Dec 1882; applied to CIM Mar 10, 1908; CIM dep. UK 10 Sept 1910; 1911 Anhui, 1914 to Xinjiang; 5 June 1914 joined G Hunter (qv); 1928 to Kashgar; 1932 six of 'Two Hundred' arr. Urumqi; Muslim rebellion, Mather d. typhus, 24 May 1933; Dr Emil Fishbacher 27 May (*see* Bibliography).

MATHESON, Donald; merchant partner, Jardine, Matheson; 1837 converted at Hong Kong; 1849 resigned over opium traffic; active in Presby. Missions; 1892 chairman, Soc. for the Suppression of the Opium Trade.

MATHIESON, James E; noted evangelist; director, Mildmay Conference Centre; with Grattan Guinness, Reginald Radcliffe promoted missions.

MAXWELL, James Laidlow, MD (b. 1836); English Presby. Mission; 1863 Amoy; 1865 Taiwan pioneer, Tainan, Dagao; 1871 invalided to UK, 8 years on his back; publ. vernacular NT; 1883 Taiwan again; 1885 founded Medical Missionary Association (London), Secy; 1888 co-founder with B Broomhall (qv), 'Christian Union for the Severance of the Connection of the British Empire with the Opium Traffic'.

McCARTHY, Frank, John's eldest; CIM dep. UK 31 Dec 1886; 1 March 1887 Chefoo School staff under H L Norris (qv), promoted morale, discipline; 20 Oct 1893 m. E Webb; March 1895–1930, Principal, 'did more than any for the schools.'

McCARTHY, John; Dublin, member H G Guinness (qv) training class; Feb 1866 influenced by JHT; 1866 CIM; 1867 Hangzhou; 1877 Jan–Aug Hankou to Bhamo,

Burma on foot; 1886–91 Supt. Jiangxi, Jiangsu (Guangxin R and Yangzhou language school); influential speaker UK, USA.

McCONNELL, George: N Ireland, Dundee; CIM dep. UK Jan 1890; Hejin, Shanxi; m. Bella Dec 1894, son Kenneth; all killed by Boxers 16 July 1900.

McCURRACH, Wm Adam: b. Aberdeen 30 Mar 1869; BMS, dep. UK autumn 1896; wife Clara; to Xinzhou, Shanxi; 29 June 1900 cornered by Boxers; 9 Aug 1900, 8 BMS killed.

McKEE, Stewart and Kate: CIM, 10 years Datong, Shanxi; 24 June 1900 attacked by Boxers, wounded, fled to yamen; 27 June son born; 12 July killed; child Alice hid, killed 13 July.

MEADOWS, James J (1835–1914); JHT's first recruit to Ningbo Mission, 1862, and CIM; wife Martha d. Ningbo 1863; 1866 m. Eliz. Rose (qv); 1868 began pioneering; 1869 Anqing; 1874 Shaoxing, 40 years; 1882 Supt. Zhejiang; China Council; 52 years' service.

MESNY, William (1842–1919) Jersey, Channel Is.; arr. China 1860; officer in Chinese army suppressed Miao rebellion; high rank in command Guiyang arsenal; with Gill (qv) travelled Chengdu, Batang, Dali, Bhamo; 1896 equiv. Brevet-Lt. Gen. under Zuo Zongtang in campaign to suppress Yakub Beg (qv), Kashgar.

MOODY, Dwight Lyman (1837–99); 19th century's greatest evangelist; 1873–75 first Br. mission; 1882 Cambridge Univ. mission stimulated 'Cambridge Seven'; 1886 first Northfield student conference gave impetus to Student Volunteer Movement.

MORRILL, Mary S: b. 24 Mar 1864; Am. Board, Baoding, Zhili; killed 1 July 1900; her calmness before execution impressed Feng Yüxiang (qv), future army marshal.

MORSE, Hosea Ballou; Imperial Chinese Customs, Taiwan; commissioner Hankou; historian, author (see Bibliog).

MOTT, John Raleigh (1865–1955): b. Iowa, USA; with 100 others signed first Student Volunteer Movement declaration, after being 'won for the cause of Christ at Cornell University by J E Kynaston Studd'; and influenced by Robert Wilder (qv), 1883; 1895 launched World Student Christian Federation; Hon Sec, later chairman; 1910 chairman, Edinburgh World Missionary Conference; widely travelled.

MOULE, Handley Carr Glyn (1841–1920); 1880–99 Principal, Ridley Hall, Camb; Bishop of Durham 1901–20; author; Keswick Council.

MUIRHEAD, William, DD (1822–1900); LMS; evangelist, renowned preacher, translator, like a son to W H Medhurst; 'a gigantic worker'; 1846–90 (53 years) at Shanghai; 1848 victim of 'Qingpu (Tsingpu) Outrage', Shanghai; 1877–79 organised famine relief funds; warm friend of JHT, CIM; 'passionately fond of children'. (Chinese Recorder 1900 Vol 31 pp 384, 625; 1902 Vol 32 pp 1, 42.)

MÜLLER, George (1805–98); German-born; converted aged 25 through LMS speaker; trained in London for mission to Jews; 1830 Teignmouth, pastor; m. sister of A N Groves; 1832 read biography of A H Francke; 1832 with Craik to Bristol; 1834 founded Scriptural Knowledge Institution for Home and Abroad; 1835 founded Orphan Homes, Bristol, on Francke's principle of trusting God to provide; 2000 children; 1872 CIM Referee, visited China; d. 10 March 1898.

NATHAN, Frances Edith and May Rose: CIM; F E dep. UK Sept 1894, M R dep. Jan 1899; Daning, Shanxi; 12 July 1900 fled to hills with M Heaysman (qv); killed 13 Aug 1900 by Boxers.

NEILL, Stephen C; b. 31 Dec 1899; Dean Close; 1924 Fellow of Trinity College

Cambridge, 1924 India; Bishop of Tinnevelly (120,000 Anglicans), member Joint Committee, result Church of S. India; 1944 invalided Europe; author; 1962 Prof. of Missions and Ecumenical Theology, Univ. of Hamburg; Ridley Hall, Oxford (*see* Bibliography).

NEVIUS, John Livingston (1832–93); Am. Presby. Mission; 1854 Ningbo; 1859 Hangzhou; 1860 Japan; 1861 Shandong (Shantung); 1864 UK, USA; 1867 DD; 1869 Shandong, Denglai; Bible translator, author; 1890 Moderator; co-chairman, Shanghai Miss. Conf.; 1886–87 exponent of 'indigenous church' policy, Korea 1890.

NORMAN, Henry V: SPG; arr. Yantai 1891; ordained 1892; 1897 with Chas. Robinson (qv) to Yongqing, Zhili; 1 June 1900 escaped from Boxers, killed June 2.

NORRIS, Herbert L; CIM dep. UK 28 Jan 1885; headmaster Chefoo School; d. rabies 27 Sept 1888.

OGREN, P Alfred, wife Olivia, son Samuel; Alfred b. 1874, Jonkoping, Sweden; full members of CIM; 1893 Shanxi; 1899 Yongning; 1900 after terrible suffering Alfred d. 15 Oct; baby born Dec 6; Olivia, Samuel, baby arr. Hankou 16 Feb 1901.

ORR EWING, Archibald; b. 1 Aug 1857; 4th of 7 brothers, heirs to uncle's fortune, nearly £500,000; litigation settled by law lords July 1885; 1880–81 toured China coast; 1882 Moody Mission in Glasgow, dedication to Christ; invited J McCarthy; 6 April 1884 committed to China, 1885 with W B Sloan at Keswick commitment confirmed; CIM dep. UK 21 April 1886; 17 July 1886 officially joined CIM after Shanxi conference; 4 years Shanxi; walked 50 miles daily on trek; 6 May 1890 m. Mary Scott (of Morgan and Scott); 1891 Supt. Jiangxi 20 years; donor of Wusong Rd HQ and Chefoo schools.

PARKER, George; CIM, one of the Eighteen, dep. UK 5 April 1876; Nov 8 with Easton (qv) dep. Wuhan to Shaanxi, Gansu; Dec 20–24 Xi'an; 20 Jan 1877 Lanzhou; 1878 forced out of Xi'an; worked Han R by boat; 1879 Chongqing, engaged to Shao Mianzi (qv); Sept–Oct, Gansu with Easton; 25 Feb 1880 m. Shao Mianzi; to Hanzhong and Gansu; 1882 Tibet border; 1887–89 Xinjiang with Lansdell (qv); 1905 G Hunter of Urumqi reported evidence of Parker-Lansdell colportage found; d. 1931 doyen of CIM.

PARTRIDGE, Mary L: b. New York 27 Mar 1865; Oberlin College, Am Board; arr. China Oct 1893; Taigu, Shanxi; killed 31 July 1900.

PEARSE, Edward S; CIM, one of the Eighteen dep. UK 26 Jan 1876, m. 18 Dec 1877 L E Goodman; 1879 Anhui pioneer; ubiquitous, 1886–87 Shaanxi, Sichuan; supt. Guangxin R region.

PEAT, Wm Graham: CIM, dep. UK 1 Dec 1887, one of the Hundred; Pingyao, Shanxi; Mar 1891 m. Helen Mackenzie; Xi Xian; 21 July 1900 fled to hill caves with children Margretta, Mary, and Edith Dobson (qv) and 'Georgie' Hurn (qv); all killed 30 August.

PENNEFATHER, Wm (1816–73): vicar, Christ Church, Barnet; hymn writer, friend of JHT; 1864 St Jude's, Mildmay, N London; director Mildmay Conf. Centre and hospital; deaconess and missionary training school; 1872 CIM referee.

PIERSON, A T, DD; New York evangelist, Bible teacher; friend of JHT; 1886 with Moody held student conference for SVM (newly founded); 1888 at Centenary Conf. of Prot. Missions, Lond.; 1896 chief speaker, SVMU Liverpool Conference; editor *The Missionary Review of the World*; leading delegate, speaker, international conferences; shared platform at JHT's last public address, Boston, USA, 1900.

PIGOTT, Thomas Wellesley: b. 6 Aug 1847; Trinity Coll. Dublin; CIM, dep. UK 9 Mar 1879; pioneer with Jas Cameron (qv) in Manchuria, Shanxi; 1881 Taiyuan; 1883 m. Jessie Kemp, sister of Florence Edwards (qv); contributed to Wusong Rd HQ, Newington Green HQ, Schofield Memorial Hospital (destroyed 27 June 1900); 1893 formed Shouyang Mission; 29 June–2 July, 1900 in hiding with wife, son Wellesley, M Duval (qv), J Robinson (qv), Atwater girls; in chains to Taiyuan; all killed 9 July 1900. His sister wrote, 'Jesus, I am resting, resting' (hymn).

PILKINGTON, George Lawrence: b. 1864; converted through CICCU; 1887–88 offered to CIM; persuaded by his father to delay two years; 1889 to CMS; Master of Pembroke said: 'There is a Hannington or a Gordon in him'; to Uganda; shot 11 Dec 1897 aged 33, in mutiny.

PITKIN, Horace Tracy: b. Philadelphia 28 Oct 1869; graduate, Yale 1892; Union Seminary 1896; m. Oct 1896; to China Am Board Nov 1896; wife and son Horace to USA 1900; HTP killed by Boxers 1 July 1900.

POLHILL-TURNER, Arthur Twistleton; 3rd son, Capt. F C Polhill, 6th Dragoon Guards; MP, JP, High Sheriff, Bedfordshire; 'Camb. Seven'; CIM dep. UK 5 Feb 1885; Hanzhong; Bazhong, Sichuan; ordained Anglican; 1892 furlough, first trav. sec. SVMU, UK.

POLHILL-TURNER, Cecil Henry; 2nd son Capt. F C Polhill (see above); Eton and Jesus Coll. Cambridge; 2nd Lieut., Bedfordshire Yeomanry, 1880; Dragoon Guards, 1881; Lieut. 1884; 'Cambridge Seven', dep UK 5 Feb 1885; Hanzhong, Xining, Gansu; Songpan, Sichuan, rioted, flogged; Darjeeling, leader, Tibetan Mission Band, to Kangding, Sichuan. Retired, Howbury Hall, Bedford.

POLLARD, Samuel: b. 20 April 1864, Methodist, Bible Christian Church, Cornwall; 1885 with F J Dymond offered, 27 Jan 1887 dep. UK, first associate mission of CIM; shipwrecked in Yangzi gorges; Chaotong, Yunnan, 1888; 1905 to minority peoples; devised Pollard script for Miao; d. 15 Sept 1915.

RADCLIFFE, Reginald; leading UK evangelist; 1860 initiated theatre services, Lond; the first in Victoria Theatre, Lambeth, denounced as travesty of religious worship, even illegal; 24 Feb 1860 defended in House of Lords 3-hour speech by Lord Shaftesbury describing the poor and common folk who flocked to hear Radcliffe; leading part in evangelical revival following 1858 US revival; devoted last active years to advocating worldwide evangelism, 'Consecration and the Evangelisation of the World ought to go together'; 1886–87 secured use of Keswick Convention tents for missionary use, JHT as speaker, 1887; travelled and preached in USA and Canada with JHT, 1888.

RADSTOCK, Lord; Hon Granville Augustus Wm Waldegrave, (1833–1913); 3rd Baron; converted at Crimean War; raised, commanded W. Middlesex Rifles for 6 years; evangelical Anglican evangelist in aristocratic Russian, E. European society; closely associated with Brethren; friend of JHT and CIM; 1872 CIM Referee.

RENAUT, Bessie Campbell: b. 1871; BMS, Xinzhou, Shanxi, with Dixons (qv); killed 9 Aug 1900.

RICE, Hattie Jane: b. USA 1858, 1888 heard JHT at Northfield, offered, sailed 1892; Lucheng, Shanxi with M Huston (qv), E J Coopers (qv); 6 July 1900 Saunders (qv), Cooper party dep. Lucheng, July 13 all flogged, HJR killed.

RICHARD, Timothy (1845–1919); converted in Evang. Awakening 1859–60, Wales; offered services to JHT, referred to BMS; 1870 Shandong; 1875 sole survivor of twelve; 1876–79 Shandong, Shanxi famine relief; educationalist, views changed, left BMS, founded Univ. of Shanxi, Taiyuan (8 years), 1891 Soc. for

Diffusion of Chr. & Gen. Knowledge; 1906 Christian Literature Soc.; his policies to Christianise China akin to the techniques of Ricci (qv); adviser to emperor, Chinese govt. and Kang Yuwei; translated *History of the Nineteenth Century* (1 mill. copies); 1885 proposed a Christian college in every prov. capital; 1901 with Boxer indemnity funds founded Taiyuan Univ. College; received two of the highest honours of the empire.

RICHTOFEN, Baron Ferdinand von (1833–1905); geologist, geographer, explorer; 1860, first East Asian expedition; 1875 Prof. of Geology, Bonn; 1882 Leipsig; 1886 Berlin; author, *China*, 5 vols and atlas; 1872 dep. Chengdu to reach Dali, Kunming via Xichang (Ningyuan); forced back by troops on Da Xiang Ling; showed Jianchang valley to be Marco Polo's 'Caindu'.

RIDLEY, H French: CIM, dep. UK 2 Oct 1890; 1892 Guihuacheng; Xining, Gansu; 1895 Muslim rebellion, Xining siege till April 1896; Ridleys (untrained) did relief, medical work throughout, till Jan 1897.

RILEY, J H; dep. UK 2 May 1878; Sichuan pioneer, Chongqing, Chengdu; urged by G Nicoll to take gospel to Nosu, Daliangshan; Oct 1882 m. (1) J Kidd d. 1886; (2) F Stroud on own deathbed, d. 19 April 1886.

RIRIE, Benjamin: CIM, 1887 arr. China; 1889 Leshan, Sichuan; 1895 Sichuan riots; model evangelistic missionary.

ROBINSON, Charles: SPG; 1897 to Yongqing, Zhili; 1 June 1900 killed by Boxers.

ROBINSON, John: b. 1 Sept 1875; BA Lond. Univ. 1896; YMCA sec; became Baptist; with T W Pigott (qv) to Taiyuan, Shanxi; Shouyang; 29 June–2 July, 1900 hiding in hills; in chains to Taiyuan, killed July 9

SCHOFIELD, Robert Harold Ainsworth; b. 18 Jan 1851; 1869 grad. London Univ; 1870 Oxford; 1877 MA, BM Oxon.; May 1878 FRCS Eng.; dep UK 7 April; 1880 with wife; Taiyuan, Shanxi; d. typhus 1 Aug 1881.

SEARELL, Edith: New Zealand; 1895 to China; musician, linguist, taught at Chefoo schools; May 1896 to Taiyuan, Shanxi; Xiaoyi with Emily Whitchurch (qv); 30 June 1900 killed together.

SHARP, William; solicitor; 1883 CIM London Council, active member; patron, secretary, Tibetan Pioneer Mission.

SIMCOX, F E S: b. USA 30 Apr 1867; 1893 grad. Western Theol. Seminary; m. June; dep. US Sept 1893; children Paul (5) Francis (2) Margaret; Am Presby, Baoding, Zhili; all killed 30 June 1900.

SIMEON, Chas: b. 24 Sept 1795; Kings Coll, Camb.; Fellow; ordained 1782–83; vicar Holy Trinity Church, Camb. 1782–1836 (54 years); d. 13 Nov 1836; had profound influence on Henry Martyn (qv) among many.

SIMPSON, James: Aberdeen YMCA, wife YWCA; CIM, dep. UK 15 Dec 1887; Taiyuan, Shanxi; joined Shouyang Mission; 27 June 1900 rioted out of Schofield Memorial Hosp; 9 July 1900 killed.

SLOAN, Walter B; company secretary, Keswick Convention speaker; CIM dep. UK Sep 1891; became Gen. Secy. CIM UK after B. Broomhall.; 11 Nov 1902 Asst Home Director.

SMITH, Margaret Eliz.: b. Canada 1858; CIM dep. 1896; Datong, Shanxi; killed 12 July 1900 with McKee family (qv).

SMITH, Stanley Peregrine; b. 19 March 1861; youngest son of Henry Smith, FRCS; Repton and Trinity Coll., Cambridge; 1882 BA; influenced by Granville Waldegrave (qv); capt. of Trinity boats, stroke of Camb. Univ. eight 1881; 'about the end of 1883' in touch with JHT; 1 April 1884 accepted by CIM Council; 5 Feb 1885 'Camb. Seven' dep. UK; 1885 Shanxi; 1889 opened Lu'an, Lucheng; 1902

Jincheng (Tsechou); m. (1) Sophie Reuter (Norwegian) who d. 7 Mar 1891; (2) Feb 1893 Anna M Lang.

SOLTAU, George; son of Henry W; Lamb and Flag Mission and schools, London; 1872 on first CIM London Council; Tasmania; Australian Council.

SOLTAU, Henrietta E; daughter of H W Soltau (*see* Book 6, p 502); 1873 London, asst. to Emily Blatchley; Tottenham home for children of missionaries; later, CIM Women's Training Home and Ladies' Council.

SOOTHILL, Prof. W E; United Meth. Free Church; 1888 translated Gospels, Acts into Wenzhou dialect, publ. 1894; 1901 NT completed, printed by CIM press; educator, author, biographer of T Richard; Analects of Confucius in English; elected President, projected Wuhan Christian University; Prof. of Chinese, Oxford Univ. following Legge (qv) 1897.

SOUTHEY, John and wife: CIM dep. Australia Mar 1891; Feb 1896 invalided to New Zealand; Dec 1896 to Melbourne, training new missionaries; 1898 Austr. Council; 1908 Home Director; 5 Jan 1900 with JHT, JET to NZ; 1914 home in NZ till d. 6 Jan 1922.

SPEER, Robert E (1867–1947); son of lawyer, member of Congress; 1889 graduated, Princeton; Student Volunteer Movement; 1886 travelling secy; Board of Foreign Missions, Presby. Church of USA, senior Secy till 1937; Moderator; author.

SPURGEON, Charles Haddon (1834–92); renowned Baptist preacher, Metropolitan Tabernacle; lifelong friend of JHT.

STAM, John, Betty (née Eliz. Alden Scott), both Moody Bible Inst.; m. 25 Oct 1932; Priscilla born Sept 1934; captured by Communists at Jingde (Tsingteh) 6 Dec 1934; killed Dec 7.

STEVENS, Jane: CIM dep. UK Sept 1885; Shanxi, Huo Xian (Hochow) with Mildred Clarke (qv); 9 July 1900 killed at Taiyuan.

STEVENSON, John Whiteford (1844–1918); son of laird of Thriepwood, Renfrewshire; m. Anne Jolly; with G Stott (qv) first of CIM after Crombie; Oct. 1856 dep. UK; 1866–74 Ningbo, Shaoxing; 1875–80 Burma; 1880 with H Soltau, Jr. (qv) crossed China W. to E., Bhamo-Chongqing-Wuchang then Shanghai; 1,900 miles, 86 days; 1885–1916 deputy director, CIM.

STEWART, Ellen Mary: b. 11 May 1871; 1894 governess to E H Edwards (qv) children, BMS, Taiyuan, Shanxi; killed 9 July 1900.

STEWART, Robt W: graduate, Dublin; reading for Bar when converted through Evan Hopkins (qv); ordained 1876; CMS, Fuzhou 1878; 1 Aug 1895 killed with 7 other colleagues and own children, Kuchang.

STOCK, Eugene (1836–1928); CMS UK staff; editor Dec. 21, 1875–Dec 11, 1906; historian, author *This History of the Church Miss. Soc.*, Vols I–III; warm friend of CIM; d. 7 Sep 1928 aged 92.

STOKES, George W: b. Dover 1863; printer; Harley House; CIM dep. UK 1892; Shunde, Zhili; Taiyuan, Shanxi; 1897 m. Margaret Whittaker, Shouyang Mission, nurse; both killed 9 July 1900.

STUDD, Charles Thomas; 3rd son of Edward Studd, Tedworth House, Andover; b. 2 Dec 1860; Eton and Trinity Coll., Cambridge; 1884 BA; cricket 'blue' 4 years, captain 1883; CIM dep. UK 5 Feb 1885; Hanzhong, Shaanxi; Shanxi; Jan 1888 m. Priscilla Livingstone Stewart (arr. Shanghai 1887); Lu'an, Shanxi; sick leave, resigned; 1900–06, India; founded Heart of Africa Mission; d. 16 July 1931.

STUDD, George; 2nd son, Eton and Cambridge, cricketer, captain 1882; Nov 1883 seriously ill; 1887 visited Shanghai, Shanxi; pastor, Los Angeles, USA.

STUDD, Sir John Edward Kynaston, Bart.; eldest son; Eton and Cambridge cricketer, captain 1884; 1885 m. Hilda Beauchamp; twice Lord Mayor of London, 1st baronet.

TAYLOR, Annie Royle; dtr of well-to-do Cheshire businessman; aged 28 sold valuables, took basic medical course as lady probationer, London Hospital; CIM dep. UK 24 Sept 1884 aiming for Tibet; Taozhou, Gansu-Qinghai border nr. Kumbum; 2 Sept 1892 dep. Taozhou; 3 Jan 1893 100 miles from Lhasa; expelled; 1893 to Darjeeling, India–Tibet border. Tibetan Pioneer Mission.

TAYLOR, Ernest Hamilton 6th son of JHT, by JET, b. 7 Jan 1875; accountant, m. E Gauntlett; dep. UK after 1900 Boxer rising, volunteered (with C H Judd) for Shanxi; 9 July 1901 arr. Taiyuan with D E Hoste, A Orr Ewing (first anniversary of massacres).

TAYLOR, Frederick Howard (1862–1946); b. 25 Nov 1862, 2nd son of JHT, by M J Dyer; present at Yangzhou riot; qualified MB, BS, 1888 MD Lond; 1889 MRCP; FRCS Edin.; initiated Student Foreign Missionary Union (later combined with SVMU); 1888 toured US, Canada with JHT; 23 Jan 1890 dep. UK Henan, peripatetic medical; 24 April 1894 m. M Geraldine Guinness; Supt. Henan; travelled frequently with JHT; JHT's biographers; d. 15 Aug 1946.

TAYLOR, George Yardley: b. USA 18 May 1862; 1885 MD Univ. of Pennsylvania; 1888 Am Presby Mission, Beijing, Baoding; killed 30 June 1900.

TAYLOR, Herbert Hudson; eldest son of JHT and Maria; b. London 3 April 1861; CIM dep. UK Jan 1881; 24 Nov 1886 m. Jeanie Gray (CIM 1884); Jiangxi, Henan; 1886 travelled with JHT, Shanxi and Shaanxi; father of James Hudson Taylor II; d. 6 June 1950; grandfather of James Hudson Taylor III, General Director 1980–

TAYLOR, James (1807–81); father of JHT; chemist; founded, managed Barnsley Permanent Building Society 1855–75; retired Dec 1875.

TAYLOR, James Hudson (21 May 1832–3 June 1905); 1853 dep. UK; 1 Mar 1854 arr. Shanghai; 20 Jan 1858 m. Maria Jane Dyer; 1857 with J Jones (qv) began Ningbo Mission; June 1865 founded China Inland Mission; 28 Nov 1871 m. Jane E Faulding; 3 June 1905 d. Changsha, Hunan.

TAYLOR, Jane (Jennie) Elizabeth (née Faulding) b. 7 Oct 1843; 1865 assistant to JHT and Maria, London; 1866 CIM; *Lammermuir*; Hangzhou; m. JHT 28 Nov 1871; 1877–78 took Anna Crickmay (qv) and Celia Horne (qv) to Shanxi famine relief, Taiyuan; first women deep into interior; d. 30 July 1904.

TAYLOR, Maria Hudson, daughter of JHT and Maria; b. Hangzhou, Feb 3, 1867; 1884 CIM to China aet. 17; m. J J Coulthard (qv) d. Sept 28, 1897.

TAYLOR, Maria Jane, née Dyer (1837–70); daughter of Samuel Dyer (qv); wife of JHT; mother of Grace, Herbert Hudson, Frederick Howard, Samuel, Jane, Maria, Charles, Noel; d. Zhenjiang, July 23, 1870.

TAYLOR, M Henry; CIM dep. UK 3 Sept 1873; first CIM pioneer Henan; met strong opposition, heartbroken; to Zhejiang; 1878 Henan famine relief rejected by mandarins; resigned.

TERTULLIAN: c160–c220 AD; theologian of Carthage; his *Apology* before pagan judges, re 'blood of the martyrs'.

THIRGOOD, Emma Ann: CIM dep. UK 28 Nov 1889; to Changshan, Zhejiang with G F Wards (qv); killed at Qü Xian 22 July 1900.

THOMPSON, David Baird: CIM dep. UK 1880; 1885 m. Agnes Dowman; Qü Xian, Zhejiang; both killed 21 July 1900.

TURNER, Joshua J; CIM, one of the Eighteen, dep. UK Nov 1875; Oct 1876 to Jan

1877 Shanxi; famine relief, typhoid, Taiyuan; 1 Feb 1881 m. A Crickmay; in UK 1900; BMS to Taiyuan.

WARD, George Fredk: CIM dep. UK 1893; 1895 itinerating; 1897 m. Etta L Fuller, b. 1866, dep. USA 1894; Changshan, Zhejiang; 22 July 1900 escaped to Qü Xian, killed.

WHITCHURCH, Emily: of Downton, Salisbury; 1883 heard JHT; CIM 27 Feb 1884, dep. UK as one of 'Seventy'; taught at Chefoo; 1887 to Xiaoyi, Shanxi; 30 June 1900 killed by Boxers.

WHITEHOUSE, Silvester Frank: b. 14 Aug 1867; CIM dep. UK 5 Oct 1888 with JHT as private secretary; 1892 Harley House; B&FBS 3 years colportage; 1893 m. Legerton, CIM Chefoo; Spurgeon's College; July 1899 BMS; Taiyuan, Shanxi; 9 July 1900 both killed.

WILDER, Robert Parmelee (1863–1938); son of India missionary; 1886 grad. Princeton; initiated SVM; 1886 promoted SVM at Moody's student conference; 1888 travelled for SVM to colleges, univs; 1889 to UK univs, after J N Forman (qv); Gen. Sec. SVM; 1891–92 UK, SVMU; 1902 India, students; thereafter evangelist to students in UK, Europe. (1891–92 at Med. Miss. Ass. c/o Dr J L Maxwell, negotiated union of (FHT's) Students' Foreign Miss. Union with SVM, completed April 2–9, 1892, with A T Polhill as trav. sec.)

WILLIAMS, E O; Trinity Coll Oxford; vicar, St Stephen's, Leeds; CIM dep. UK 13 Dec 1888; East Sichuan; d. July 1899, typhoid.

WILLIAMS, Sir George (1821–95) of Hitchcock, Williams & Co, London; 1844 founded YMCA for employees; friend of CIM, of Lord Shaftesbury (first YMCA President); chairman, CIM meetings; 1894 YMCA Jubilee, knighted.

WILLIAMS, Samuel Wells DD (1812–84); Am. Board, printer, scholar; 1833 Canton; 1847 author *The Middle Kingdom*; 1851 succeeded E C Bridgman (qv) as editor, *Chinese Repository*; 1856 interpreter and Secy. to US minister, Peking; 9 times chargé d'affaires to 1876; 1884 *Syllabic Dicty. of Chinese Language*, 12,527 characters; prof. of Chinese, Yale Univ. 8 years.

WILLIAMSON, Alexander, LL D (1829–90); Falkirk, Scotland, b. Dec 5, 1829, eldest of seven sons; Glasgow Univ.; 1858–63 LMS invalided UK; 1863 National Bible Soc. of Scotland, Shandong, Yantai; 1864–69 travelled extensively distributing Scripture, Peking, Mongolia, Manchuria; Aug 1869 brother, James Williamson, LMS, murdered near Tianjin; 1869 UK; 1871 LL D Glasgow, 1871–80, 1881–83 Yantai, NBSS and United Presby. Soc. of Scotland; 1883–85 Scotland ill, founded Book & Tract Socy. for China, later (1887) Socy. for Diffusion of Christian and General Knowledge among the Chinese (Christian Lit. Soc.); 1886 Shanghai, wife d.; 1890 d. Yantai. Author, *Natural Theology*, and others. 'Very tall, striking in appearance; intellectually also among the giants.'

WILSON, Dr Wm; Oxford; nephew of Eliz. Wilson (qv); CIM dep. UK 20 Aug 1882; pioneer, rejected at Xi'an, welcomed at Hanzhong, Shaanxi, m. Caroline Sarah Goodman; used science museum to befriend literati.

WOLFE, John R; 1862 CMS, Fuzhou; 'missionary par excellence of Fukien'; 1864 began indigenous expansion of church by deploying catechists and visiting them; 1873–75 alone, missionary colleagues all ill or dead; church members, adherents, doubled 800 to 1656 under persecution; 4450 in 1882; 1884 and 1886 visited Korea; 1884 Fujian Christians to Korea learned language, withdrew after two years; 1899 JRW still active in Fujian.

WYLIE, Alexander (1815–87); LMS; 1847 Shanghai, printer, Delegates' version of Bible; 1863 Bible Soc. (B&FBS); one of the greatest Sinologues; completed distribution of the million NTs provided 1855 by Bible Soc. special fund; 1877 retired with failing eyesight; succeeded by Maria Taylor's brother Samuel Dyer, Jr (qv).

YAKUB BEG; Muslim conqueror, 1864 captured Kashgar, Yarkand; appointed ruler by Emir of Bokhara; added Urumqi, Turfan to his kingdom; 1872 independence recognised by Russia, GB, Turkey; honoured with title only used by caliphs of Baghdad; great Muslim revival predicted, with conquest of China; but 1876 Urumqi fell to Zuo Zongtang (Tso Tsung-t'ang) (qv); May 1877 Yakub Beg died suddenly; Dec 1877 Kashgar taken, kingdom ended.

YATES, Mathew T (1819–88); Am. S. Baptist; 1847 Shanghai; Sinologue, learned contributor to *Chinese Recorder*; Am. vice-consul; translator, Shanghai vernacular NT; leading proponent of orthodox views on Ancestor Worship at Gen. Miss. Conf, May 1877.

YOUNG, John: Glasgow BTI; 1894 CIM, dep. UK 1 Oct 1896; to Ji Xian (Chichou) Shanxi; 1 April 1899 m. Sarah Alice Troyer, b. USA 1871; CIM, Jan 1896 dep. to China; 16 July 1900 both killed with McConnells.

YOUNGHUSBAND, Lt. Col. Sir Francis Edward; 1887 (Lieut.) across China and Turkestan by Mongolian route; 1889 wished to attempt Lhasa, politically untimely; 1902 Russian intentions re Tibet prompted Brit. armed expedition, 1000 troops, 10,000 coolies, 7000 mules entered Tibet 12 Dec 1903; 1904 led troops into Lhasa; 23 Sept 1904 dep. Lhasa; 1919–22 Pres. R G Soc.; 1936 founded World Congress of Faiths.; as Pres. R G Soc supported, honoured 'Trio' (*see* Cable, French).

ZWEMER, Samuel Marinus (1867–1952): b. Michigan, USA; Reformed Church; July 1888 asked JHT how to join CIM; 1890 accompanied Thomas Valpy French, CMS Bp of Lahore (1825–90) to Muscat, Arabia; arr. Feb 8; May 14 French died; Zwemer lived 60 more years; 1890 to Basrah, Bahrein; m. CMS Australian; 1911 editor, *The Muslim World*; 1912 Cairo for Arabic Christian literature; 1917 to China, promoting mission to Muslims; 1929–37 Prof. of Christian Missions and History of Religions, Princeton Seminary; author of 37 books; co-author 12 more.

SELECTED BIBLIOGRAPHY

(See also HTCOC BOOKS 1–6 Bibliographies)

ADENEY, David H: *China: Christian Students Face the Revolution*; S U Book Centre, Singapore 1973
    China: The Church's Long March; Regal Books, and OMF Publishers, Singapore 1985

AITKEN, J T, Fuller, H W C, and Johnson, D, *The Influence of Christians in Medicine*, Christian Medical Fellowship, London 1984

ATLAS of China, *Zhonghua Renmin Gongheguo Fen Sheng Dituji*, Ditu Chubanshe, Beijing (Chinese People's Republic Provincial Atlas)

BABER, E Colborne, *Supplementary Papers of the Royal Geographical Society*, 'Travels and Researches in Western China'; John Murray, London, 1882; Journal of the RGS, 1884, Vol XLIX, pp 421 *seq*

BARBER, W T A, *David Hill, Missionary and Saint*, Charles H Kelley, London 1903

BARRETT, David B: *see International Bulletin of Missionary Research*

BECKMAN, E R: *The Massacre at Sianfu*; (personal) 1913

BERESFORD, Lord Charles: *The Break-up of China*

BISHOP, Isabella Bird: *The Yangtze Valley and Beyond*; John Murray 1899 (Virago Press Ltd 1985)

BOSSHARDT, R A: *The Restraining Hand: Captivity for Christ in China*; Hodder & Stoughton 1936

BONG RIN RO: (Editor) *Christian Alternatives to Ancestor Practice*, Asian Theological Association 1985

BOTHAM, Mrs Mark: *Two Pioneers: Thomas and Mark Botham*; CIM/RTS 1924

BROOMHALL, Benjamin, *The Evangelisation of the World; A Missionary Band; A Record of Consecration and an Appeal*, China Inland Mission, 1886–'87–'89
    National Righteousness (Editor); periodical of The Christian Union for the Severance of the Connection of the British Empire from the Opium Traffic, 1888–1911
    The Truth About Opium Smoking (?) Hodder & Stoughton, 1882

BROOMHALL, Marshall, *Archibald Orr Ewing, That Faithful and Wise Steward*, China Inland Mission, 1930

The Chinese Empire, A General and Missionary Survey,
Marshall, Morgan & Scott, and China Inland Mission 1907   BL 4767.eeee.4
   *Faith and Facts, as Illustrated in the History of the China
Inland Mission*, China Inland Mission 1909
   F W Baller, A Master of the Pencil, CIM 1923
   *Heirs Together of the Grace of Life; Benjamin Broomhall and
Amelia Hudson Broomhall*, Morgan & Scott, and CIM 1918
   Hudson Taylor's Legacy, Hodder & Stoughton 1931   BL 10823.a.16
   In Memoriam: Rev J Hudson Taylor; CIM/Morgan & Scott
1905
   Islam in China, Marshall, Morgan & Scott, and CIM 1910
   The Jubilee Story of the China Inland Mission, Morgan &
Scott, and CIM, 1915   BL 4763.g.4
   John W Stevenson, One of Christ's Stalwarts, Morgan &
Scott, and CIM, 1919   BL 4956.aa.33
   *Last Letters and Further Records of Martyred Missionaries of
the China Inland Mission*, Morgan & Scott, and CIM 1901
   Marshal Feng: A Good Soldier of Christ Jesus; CIM/RTS
1923
   *Martyred Missionaries of the China Inland Mission, with a
Record of the Perils and Sufferings of Some who Escaped*,
Morgan & Scott, and CIM 1901
   Our Seal: The Witness of the CIM to the Faithfulness of God;
CIM/RTS 1933
   *Pioneer Work in Hunan by Adam Dorward and Other
Missionaries of the China Inland Mission*, Morgan & Scott, and
CIM 1906
   W W Cassels, First Bishop in Western China, CIM 1926
BROOMHALL, Marshall and F A KELLER: *Concerning
Hunan and Changsha*; CIM 1910
BROWNE, Stanley G et al: *Heralds of Health: The Saga of
Christian Medical Initiatives*; Christian Medical Fellowship 1985
CABLE, Mildred and FRENCH, Francesca: *The Gobi Desert*;
Hodder & Stoughton 1943 (ten reprints, and Landsborough
Publications Ltd 1958 pocketbook)
   Through Jade Gate and Central Asia; Constable 1927
   Something Happened: Hodder & Stoughton 1933
   A Desert Journal, Letters from Central Asia; Constable 1934
(with Evangeline French)
   The Making of a Pioneer: Percy Mather of Central Asia;
Hodder & Stoughton 1934
   George Hunter: Apostle of Turkestan; CIM 1948
   Wall of Spears; Lutterworth Press 1951
CHEFOO MAGAZINE, THE: Organ of the Chefoo Schools
Association; Vol 1 No 1 Christmas 1908; Vol 81 No 2 Christmas
1988
CHINA'S MILLIONS, Magazine of the China Inland Mission
1875–1951
CHINESE RECORDER AND MISSIONARY JOURNAL: Vols
1–3, 5–12 May 1868–May 71, editor Justus Doolittle; Vol 5

bi-monthly Jan–Dec 1874 (after 2-year interlude) – Vol 72, 1941

CLARKE, Samuel R: *Among the Tribes of South-West China*; CIM/Morgan & Scott 1905

COATES, P D: *The China Consuls: British Consular Officers in China 1843–1943*; OUP (Hong Kong) 1988 — ISBN 0-19-584078-X

CORDIER, Henri, *The Life of Alexander Wylie*, 1887 — BL 10803.cc.4/6

COVELL, Ralph R, *Confucius, The Buddha and Christ, a History of the Gospel in Chinese*, Orbis Books 1986 (USA)
    W A P Martin, Pioneer of Progress in China, Wm B Eerdmans Publishing Company 1978
    Days of Blessing in Inland China, being an Account of Meetings held in the Province of Shansi (compiled), Morgan & Scott 1887

CROSSMAN, Eileen: *Mountain Rain: A New Biography of James O Fraser*; OMF Books 1982

EDGAR, J Huston: *The Marches of the Mantze*; CIM 1908

FAIRBANK, John King: *The Cambridge History of China*, Vol 10; OUP
    Trade and Diplomacy on the China Coast, 2 vols 1953 Edn. Cambridge, Massachusetts — BL Ac.2692.10

FOREIGN OFFICE LIBRARY, Public Records Office, *A Century of Diplomatic Blue Books*, China FO/17

FORSYTH, R C, *The China Martyrs of 1900*, Religious Tract Society 1904

GLOVER, A E: *A Thousand Miles of Miracle in China*; CIM 1904, 20th edn 1944; abridged by L T Lyall 1957, reprinted 1962, 1965, 1971

GOFORTH, Rosalind, *Goforth of China*, Marshall, Morgan & Scott 1937

GREEN, C H S: *In Deaths Oft*; CIM 1901, reprinted 1912, 1923, 1936 (27,000 copies)

GRIST, W A, *Samuel Pollard, Pioneer Missionary in China*, Cassell & Co, Ltd (undated)

GRUBB, Norman P, *C T Studd, Cricketer and Pioneer*, Religious Tract Society 1933

GUINNESS, Joy, *Mrs Howard Taylor: Her Web of Time*, CIM 1949

GUINNESS, M Geraldine, *The Story of the China Inland Mission*, 2 vols, Morgan & Scott, London 1893

HALDANE, Charlotte, *The Last Great Empress of China*, Constable 1965

HART, Sir Robert, *These from the Land of Sinim* — BL 8022.cc.48/01 and 0817.d.10

HOPKIRK, Peter, *Foreign Devils on the Silk Road; the Search for the Lost Cities and Treasures of Chinese Central Asia*, Oxford University Press 1984
    Trespassers on the Roof of the World; the Race for Lhasa, John Murray 1982

HOSIE, Alexander, *Three Years in Western China; A Narrative of Three Journeys*, George Philip & Son, London 1890

HOUGHTON, Frank: *George King: Medical Evangelist*; CIM 1930
    The Two Hundred: CIM 1932

HOUGHTON, Stanley et al: *Chefoo*; CIM 1931

HSÜ, Immanuel C Y: *The Rise of Modern China* (2nd Edn) OUP 1975

INTERNATIONAL BULLETIN OF MISSIONARY RESEARCH: Annual Statistical Table on Global Mission: 1987 (David B Barrett)

JOHNSON, Douglas, *Contending for the Faith; a History of the Evangelical Movement in the Universities and Colleges*, Inter-Varsity Press 1979

JOHNSTON, James: *Report of the Centenary Conference on Protestant Missions*, London 1888   BL 4766.ee.13

JUDD, Fredk H: *A History of the China Inland Mission School at Chefoo, China (1880–1942)*; The Chefoo Magazine Vol 79 No 2 December 1986 pp 3–39

KUHN, Isobel: *Green Leaf in Drought: The Story of the Escape of the Last CIM Missionaries from Communist China* (Rupert Clarke, Arthur Mathews) CIM-OMF 1954

LATOURETTE, Kenneth Scott, *A History of Christian Missions in China*, SPCK 1929   BL 4763.g.4
    A History of the Expansion of Christianity 1800–1914, Eyre and Spottiswoode   BL 4533.ff.22
    These Sought a Country: Tipple Lectures, 1950 edn, Harper & Brothers   BL 4807.e.25

LITTLE, Mrs Archibald, (Alicia Bewicke) *Li Hung-chang, His Life and Times*, Cassell & Co Ltd 1903

LOANE, Marcus, *The Story of the China Inland Mission in Australia and New Zealand*, CIM Overseas Missionary Fellowship 1965

LYALL, Leslie T: *John Sung, A Flame for God*; CIM 1954
    Come Wind, Come Weather; Hodder & Stoughton 1961
    A Passion for the Impossible; Hodder & Stoughton 1965;
    OMF Books 1976
    Red Sky at Night; Hodder & Stoughton 1969
    Three of China's Mighty Men; OMF Books 1973
    New Spring in China; Hodder & Stoughton 1979
    God Reigns in China; Hodder & Stoughton 1985

MacGILLIVRAY, Donald, *A Century of Protestant Missions in China* (Centennial Conference Historical Volume) Shanghai 1907   BL 4764.ff.11

McCARTHY, John, 'Across China from Chinkiang to Bhamo', *Proceedings of the Royal Geographical Society*, Vol 1 Aug 1879, No 8, pp 127, 489 *seq*

MARTIN, W A P, *A Cycle of Cathay*, 1896   BL 010056.g.7

MINAMIKI, George: *The China Rites Controversy from its Beginning to Modern Times*; Loyola Univ. Press 1985

MORSE, Hosea Ballou, *The International Relations of the Chinese Empire* vols 1–3, 1910   BL 2386.c.17

MOULE, Handley C G: *Charles Simeon*; 1892, first IVF Edn 1948

NEILL, Stephen C, *A History of Christian Missions* (Pelican History of the Church) Penguin Books 1964; *Colonialism and Christian Missions*, Lutterworth Press: Foundations of Christian Mission 1966

NEILL, S C *et al*, *Concise Dictionary of Christian World Mission*, United Society for Christian Literature, London 1971

NEVIUS, Helen S C, *The Life of John Livingston Nevius*, Revell 1895   BL 4985.eee.5

NEVIUS, John L: *Methods of Mission Work*; CIM 1898 reprint from Am Presby Mission

NORTH CHINA DAILY NEWS (newspaper)   British Library, Colindale

NORTH CHINA HERALD (newspaper)   British Library, Colindale

OVERSEAS MISSIONARY FELLOWSHIP ARCHIVES (OMFA)

PARLIAMENTARY PAPERS: Foreign Office Blue Books, Official Publications Office

POLLOCK, John C, *The Cambridge Seven, A Call to Christian Service*, Inter-Varsity Fellowship 1955; Centenary Edition, Marshalls 1985
Moody without Sankey, A New Biographical Portrait, Hodder & Stoughton 1963

POTT, F L Hawks, *A Short History of Shanghai*, Kelly & Walsh 1928   010056.aaa.46

RATTENBURY, Harold B, *David Hill, Friend of China*, Epworth Press 1949

REAVELY, Wm *Reminiscences of the late Adam C. Dorward, Missionary to China* (publ. 1904)

REN Cheng-Yüan: *Autobiography, A Tamarisk Garden Blessed with Rain*; CIM/RTS 1930

ROYAL GEOGRAPHICAL SOCIETY, *Journal* IV, p 713 'The South China Borderlands', Colquhoun; Vol XLIX, pp 421 *seq*, Baber; Vol XLVIII pp 57 *seq*, Gill; *Magazine* iii pp 493, 564; *Proceedings* X.485 'A Journey across Central Asia', Younghusband; *Supplementary Papers* Vol I, Part I, Baber: 'Travels and Researches in Western China'

SMITH, Arthur H, *The Uplift of China*, The Young People's Missionary Movement of America 1909

SOOTHILL, Wm E, *Timothy Richard of China*, Seeley, Service & Co, Ltd, London 1924

STOCK, Eugene, *The History of the Church Missionary Society*, Vols I–III 1899–1916   BL 4765.cc.28

STOTT, Grace: *Twenty Six Years of Missionary Work in China*; Hodder & Stoughton 1897

TAYLOR, Dr & Mrs Howard, *Hudson Taylor in Early Years: The Growth of a Soul*, CIM and RTS, 1911
Hudson Taylor and the China Inland Mission: The Growth of a Work of God, CIM and RTS, 1918

Hudson Taylor's Spiritual Secret, CIM, 1932
By Faith; Henry W Frost and the China Inland Mission, CIM 1938
TAYLOR, Mrs Howard (M Geraldine Guinness), *The Story of the China Inland Mission*, 2 vols, 1892, Morgan & Scott
Behind the Ranges: A Biography of J O Fraser, CIM
Borden of Yale; CIM 1926, revised by D Bentley-Taylor 1952
Pastor Hsi: One of China's Scholars (2 vols), CIM
Pastor Hsi, Confucian Scholar and Christian, CIM 1900, 23rd edn 1962
The Triumph of John and Betty Stam; CIM 1935
TAYLOR, F Howard: *These Forty Years, A Short History of the China Inland Mission*; CIM/Pepper Publ Co, Philadelphia 1903
TAYLOR, J Hudson, *China: Its Spiritual Need and Claims*, 1st–6th edns 1865 et seq, CIM
China's Spiritual Need and Claims, 7th edn. 1887, CIM 8th edn. 1890, CIM
Brief Account of the Progress of the China Inland Mission, May 1866 to May 1868, J Nisbet & Co 1868
A Retrospect, 1875, CIM
After Thirty Years, 1895, Morgan & Scott and CIM
Occasional Paper Vols 1–6, Jas Nisbet & Co
Summary of the Operations of the China Inland Mission, 1865–1872, J Nisbet & Co 1872
THOMPSON, Phyllis: *China: The Reluctant Exodus*; Hodder & Stoughton/OMF 1979
D E Hoste, 'A Prince with God', CIM 1947
Proving God: Financial Experiences of the China Inland Mission; CIM 1956
THOMPSON, R Wardlaw: *Griffith John, The Story of Fifty Years in China*, Religious Tract Society 1907
TORJESEN, E P: *Fredrik Franson: A Model for Worldwide Evangelism*; publ. William Carey Library 1983
WILLIAMS, Fredk Wells, *The Life and Letters of Samuel Wells Williams, LLD, Missionary, Diplomatist, Sinologue*, G P Putman & Sons, New York and London 1889
WILLIAMS, Samuel Wells, *The Middle Kingdom*, 1847
WONG MING-DAO: *A Stone Made Smooth*; Mayflower Christian Books 1981
WOODCOCK, George, *The British in the Far East*, Weidenfeld & Nicolson 1969 (A Social History of the British Overseas)
YOUNGHUSBAND, Capt Francis, *The Heart of a Continent*, abridged as *Among the Celestials*, John Murray, London 1898; *Proceedings of the RGS*, X.485 'Journey across Central Asia'
YULE, Sir Henry, *The Book of Ser Marco Polo the Venetian*, 1878, 2 vols
*Introductory essay to Gill, Wm, *River of Golden Sand*, 95 pp.

A SHORT SEQUENCE INDEX
TO THE BOXER NARRATIVES
(*see* Appendix 6, p 615, and main Index)

INDEX

(page numbers mostly follow chronological sequence)